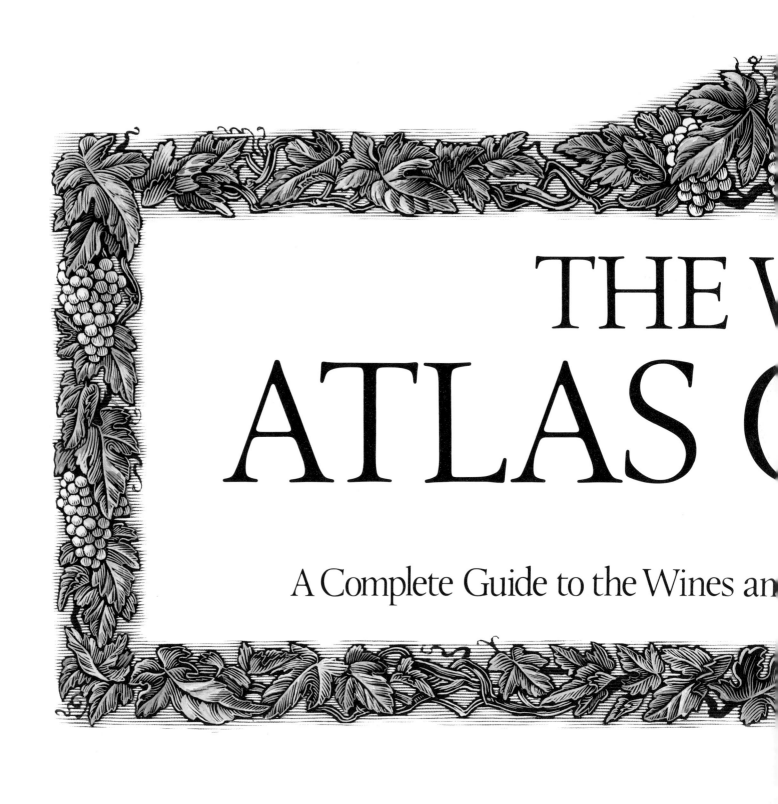

THE WORLD ATLAS OF WINE

A Complete Guide to the Wines an

WORLD OF WINE

Spirits of the World/Hugh Johnson

SIMON AND SCHUSTER
NEW YORK

Editor Dian Taylor
Senior Designer Paul Drayson
Cartographic Editor Anita Wagner
Editorial Assistants Alison Hancock, Liz Parks
Associate Designers Eljay Crompton, Lynn Hector
Cartographic Assistants Jean Gordon,
Catherine Palmer
Proofreader and Indexer Kathie Gill
Gazetteer Tom Blott
Production Philip Collyer

Senior Executive Editor Chris Foulkes
Senior Executive Art Editor Roger Walton
Cartographic Consultant Harold Fullard

Revisions and new cartography for the
1985 edition Thames Cartographic Services
Original Cartography Clyde Surveys Limited

Published by Simon and Schuster
A Division of Simon & Schuster, Inc.
Simon & Schuster Building
Rockefeller Center
1230 Avenue of the Americas
New York, New York 10020

SIMON AND SCHUSTER and colophon are
registered trademarks of Simon & Schuster, Inc.
Published in Great Britain
by Mitchell Beazley Publishers
First published 1971
Revised 1977
Enlarged and completely revised 1985
Edited and designed by Mitchell Beazley International
Limited, Artist's House, 14–15 Manette Street,
London WIV 5LB

Filmset by Vantage Photosetting Co. Ltd, Eastleigh
and London
Colour reproduction by Gilchrist Brothers Limited,
Leeds
Printed in West Germany by Mohndruck GmbH,
Gütersloh

2 3 4 5 6 7 8 9 10

ISBN: 0-671-50893-8

Contents

1 Introduction

2 Choosing and Serving Wine

3 France

How the maps work
The maps in this Atlas vary considerably in scale, the level of detail depending on the complexity of the area mapped. There is a scale bar with each map. Contour intervals vary from map to map and are shown in each map key. Roman type on the maps generally indicates names and places connected with wine; other information is in italics.

Each map page has a grid with letters down the side and numbers across the bottom. To locate a place, château, winery, etc., look up the name in the Gazetteer (pages 310–320) which gives the page number followed by the grid reference.

Every effort has been made to make the maps in this Atlas as complete and up to date as possible. In order that future editions may be kept up to this standard, the publishers will be very grateful for any information about changes of boundaries or names which should be recorded.

A detail from 'Wine-tasting in London docks' by George Cruikshank, 1821

Office international
de la vigne et du vin

Institution intergouvernementale créée pae l'arrangement
international du 29 Novembre 1924
(SIRET 784 354 615 00014 - APE 9321)

La parution, en 1971, de l'Atlas mondial du vin fut saluée par l'Institut National des Appellations d'Origine des Vins et Eaux-de-vie comme un événement dans la littérature viticole, une appréciation que je partage entièrement. En réalisant cette oeuvre, Monsieur Hugh Johnson a mis à la disposition des spécialistes et praticiens de la vigne et du vin ainsi qu'aux amis et amateurs de cette noble boisson un ouvrage qui contient une multitude de renseignements sur les vins d'appellation notamment. Le succès a été remarquable puisque l'Atlas mondial a été traduit dans une douzaine de langues et que six années plus tard déjà, une deuxième édition devait paraître. Cette troisième édition, revue et amplifiée, semble donc assurée du même accueil enthousiaste que les précédentes.

Si l'Atlas mondial a largement contribué à mieux faire connaître et apprécier les vins de qualité, il rejoint aussi, dans une large mesure, les buts de l'Office International de la Vigne et du Vin. En tant qu'institution intergouvernementale regroupant 33 pays adhérents, l'OIV étudie l'ensemble des problèmes de la viticulture, de l'oenologie et de l'économie viti-vinicole mondiales afin de formuler aux Etats membres des recommandations susceptibles d'assurer la protection des appellations d'origine des vins et de garantir l'authenticité de ces produits. En tant que président de l'OIV, je me fais un plaisir de féliciter l'auteur et les éditeurs de cette oeuvre unique dans le monde viti-vinicole et de présenter un Atlas qui a été remis à jour tant pour ce qui touche la production et la préparation des vins de qualité que leur classification.

Dans la nouvelle présentation, l'auteur a tenu compte des nombreux changements enregistrés au cours des dernières années et l'ouvrage offre toujours plus de détails et un plus grand nombre d'illustrations en couleurs. Depuis sa première parution, des changements significatifs sont survenus dans le monde viticole; certains pays ont vu s'élargir leurs régions de production et de nouvelles appellations de vins de qualité ont fait leur apparition sur le marché mondial. D'autre part, nous assistons à un accroissement marqué du volume de la production vinicole et les faits démontrent clairement que la viticulture de demain ne pourra trouver son équilibre qu'à la condition que tout soit mis en oeuvre pour améliorer la qualité.

Cet ouvrage trouvera certainement sa place dans les bibliothèques de tous les spécialistes et amateurs de vins de qualité.

B. Neuhaus, président de l'OIV

Introduction

This Atlas was conceived as a way of making the happily absorbing study of wine easier, clearer and more precise. To anyone who hopes to distinguish and remember among the bewildering thousands of the world's wines, maps are the logical, the vital, ally. With a map distinctions and relationships become clear, names are no longer isolated but part of a picture, tastes begin to form a pattern more memorable than individual impressions.

So it seemed to me, 15 years ago, in compiling and writing the first edition. Its success, and that of the second, published in 1977, has confirmed my view. So has the industry with which law-givers around the world have recently set about mapping their respective winegrowing regions. This third edition reflects this industry, portraying the world of wine as it is now, and setting the scene for the further changes which will doubtless continue far into the future.

It is exactly 50 years since France set the example when she instituted the Institut National des Appellations d'Origine. The new appellations were beautifully mapped by Louis Larmat in the 1940s. Larmat's maps were the only detailed wine maps of any country until the first edition of this Atlas appeared in 1971. Since that date, country after country and region after region has defined or redefined its vineyards on the map.

Italy started in the 1960s, Spain in 1970, Germany in 1971, Austria and South Africa in 1972. More recently Greece, Yugoslavia, New Zealand, Argentina, Chile, Bulgaria and, since 1980, the United States have plotted, or started plotting, appellations, under whatever name or guise. The maps in this Atlas were originally based largely on informal sources, on usage rather than statute. Every year has brought more precise data, more appellations with the force of law, and more refinements of existing appellation systems – all grist to the mapmaker's mill. This third edition incorporates a greater body of detail than has ever been available before.

Not even France, so rigorously mapped already, has stayed as immutable as we generally suppose. The most highly developed system of appellations in the world, that of Burgundy's Côte d'Or, has been completely revised over the last decade by the 'engineers' of the Institut National des Appellations d'Origine. The boundaries of all the Grands Crus, Premiers Crus and 'village' wines have been officially debated, defined and entered on the statute book for the first time. It is thanks to the gracious collaboration of the Beaune publisher M. Jacques Michot, M. Pierre Poupon and M. Silvain Pitiot, his cartographer, that this edition incorporates their masterwork – Burgundy in sharper focus than ever before.

To provide a sharper focus for Bordeaux, and in particular the Médoc, perhaps today the world's single most important source of fine red wine, I approached the Union des Grands Crus de Bordeaux. With their generous cooperation the cartographer M. Patrick Niquin was engaged to survey the present planting of the Médoc and to plot for the first time the exact extent of the land owned by châteaux with the right to call themselves 'crus classés'. In this edition we have also added innumerable smaller properties to the maps of Bordeaux and surveyed the 'Bas' Médoc, increasingly important for good-value claret, for the first time.

This is the second aspect of this new edition that makes it a very different creature from the old. Not only are existing maps revised, but a total of 50 completely new maps record the coming-of-age of new, or newly important, wine areas all over the world. Italy has added some 70 new Denominazioni di Origine since 1977. All these are recorded (in colour for the first time, which makes them much clearer). At the same time six Italian regions not mapped before in full topographical detail have been given this revealing treatment.

Perhaps the most historic innovation of this Atlas is the first-time plotting of the new 'viticultural areas' of California and the Pacific Northwest. I have to thank Bob Thompson of St. Helena, my long-time friend and collaborator, for the original research that was necessary to add this crucial new dimension to the maps of the West – which in this edition are five more in number, recording the planting of thousands of new acres and the building of more than 200 new wineries.

The same principles have been applied throughout the world in which we buy our wine – in the measure of detail appropriate to their quality and the availability of their produce. The emphasis of this Atlas continues to be on the consumer's point of view. My priorities are those of a wine lover of the Western world, unattached to any particular country or region except by the appeal of its produce.

There can be no question of finding one style or one set of criteria to apply to every map. For the very fact that is most enthralling about wine is that no two regions have the same standards, or place emphasis on the same things. In Burgundy there is the most complex grading of fields ever attempted: each field, and even parts of fields, being classified in a hierarchy that is cut-and-dried. In parts of Bordeaux there is a formal grading of properties; not directly related to the land but to the estates on it. In Germany there is no land classification at all, but an ingenious hierarchy of ripeness. In Champagne whole villages are classed, in Jerez soils of certain kinds, in Italy some traditonal wine zones, but not others.

Behind all this tangle of nomenclature and classification lies the physical fact of the hills and valleys where the vine grows. In each case I have tried to make it plain, so far as I have been able to discover, not only which corner of the countryside gives the best wine, but why; what happy accident of nature has led (in many cases) to the development of a classic taste which has become familiar – at least by name – to half the world.

If the maps succeed in portraying wine country clearly and appealingly, as I believe they do, it is largely due to the care and vision of Harold Fullard, the cartographer who designed the first edition, and to the skilled hands at Thames Cartographic Services, who have laboured lovingly on the equally demanding task of extending and elaborating them.

There are reproductions of paintings; music has scores; poems are printed; architecture can be drawn – but wine is a fleeting moment. One cannot write about wine, and stumble among the borrowed words and phrases which have to serve to describe it, without wanting to put a glass in the reader's hand and say, 'Taste this'. For it is not every Nuits-St-Georges that answers the glowing terms of a general description – the corner shops of the world are awash with wine that bears little relation to the true character of the land.

This is the object of giving the most direct form of reference available: the labels of more than 1,000 producers whose wines and spirits truly represent the subject matter of the Atlas. Among the many thousands who qualify in every way to be included, the choice of which to use is almost impossible. As it stands it is partly personal, as anything to do with taste must be, and partly arbitrary, as the limitations of space ruthlessly cut out firm favourites.

No book like this could be attempted without the generous help of authorities in all the countries it deals with. Their enthusiasm and painstaking care have made it possible. On page 304 there is a list of government and local offices, and some of the hundreds of others, growers, merchants and scholars, who have so kindly helped, and to whom I owe the great volume of information embodied both in the maps and the text. The facts are theirs; unless I quote a source, on the other hand, I must be held responsible for the opinions.

Apart from those named above and those whose help is acknowledged on page 304, I want here to record my special thanks to those who have seen front-line action in getting this third edition ready for the press. Jack Briggs and the staff at Thames Cartographic Services produced masterpieces of the most demanding form of draughtsmanship. Anita Wagner, in charge of map research, briefing and checking, was indefatigably calm and cheerful among 10,000 clamouring details. Di Taylor, as editor, performed the task of coordinating and making sense of every aspect of the book with true Australian grit and good humour. Roger Walton and Paul Drayson meticulously refreshed and renewed the design. Alison Hancock was a most willing and able researcher and assistant. Chris Foulkes, in overall charge, kept his head despite us all, and flung himself into wherever the fray was thickest.

To all of them, and to my secretary, Valerie Dobson, I publicly acknowledge that the author of such a book as this gets far more than his proper share of the credit.

Right: the cellar of the 12th-century Cistercian abbey of Eberbach in the Rheingau has sheltered the wines of the Steinberg for 700 years. Today it is also the headquarters of the German Wine Academy.

8

The World of Wine

The world has some 25 million acres – 10 million hectares – of vineyards. They produce an annual crop of more than 40,000 million bottles of wine; enough, if there are 4,000 million people on earth, to give us ten bottles a year each. (A 'bottle', for statistical purposes, is assumed to contain the traditional 750ml – 0.75 litres – of wine.)

Yet wine, food and comforter as it is, is very far from being a universal phenomenon. It is part of a cultural and agricultural pattern that is peculiar to the temperate zones of the earth where Mediterranean, or 'Western', man has flourished. Winegrowing and wine drinking are attached at the roots to the most widespread and longest-lived civilization the earth has known. But they have never yet successfully or significantly colonized other cultures.

The map shows the distribution of vineyards, of wine production and of wine drinking around the world. Many Eastern countries have considerable vineyards but produce no wine, or very little; table-grape acreage is included in the figures. France and Italy remain far and away the biggest producers (with the USSR now in third place) – but no longer the biggest consumers by their traditional massive margin. In the 15 years from 1968 to 1983 the French average consumption fell from 150 bottles per head a year to 112 – and it continues to fall. Italian wine drinking is dwindling at a similar rate. The countries that are increasing their consumption (although not at a rate anything like fast enough to absorb the surplus) are those where wine is considered a luxury rather than a staple beverage: the USA, Britain, Australia, Germany, the Netherlands and Scandinavia.

In the 1960s and 1970s the world's vineyard acreage was increasing fast, with the USSR and other communist-bloc countries, Argentina and the United States leading the way. Now it is stabilizing, with the likelihood that it will begin to diminish as two perceptible trends continue. One is greater productivity from a smaller acreage with more efficient farming. The second, which really points the way to the future, is the increased emphasis on quality at the expense of quantity. The French are drinking less but spending more. The new recruits in North America, northern Europe, Australasia are being trained to demand well-made wine.

Alas, for the poor traditional wine farmer the 'wine lake' will not go away. From time immemorial there has been a glut of third-rate wine on earth. Never before, until the present age of scientific advance and technological control, has there been enough good wine, as there is now, to go round.

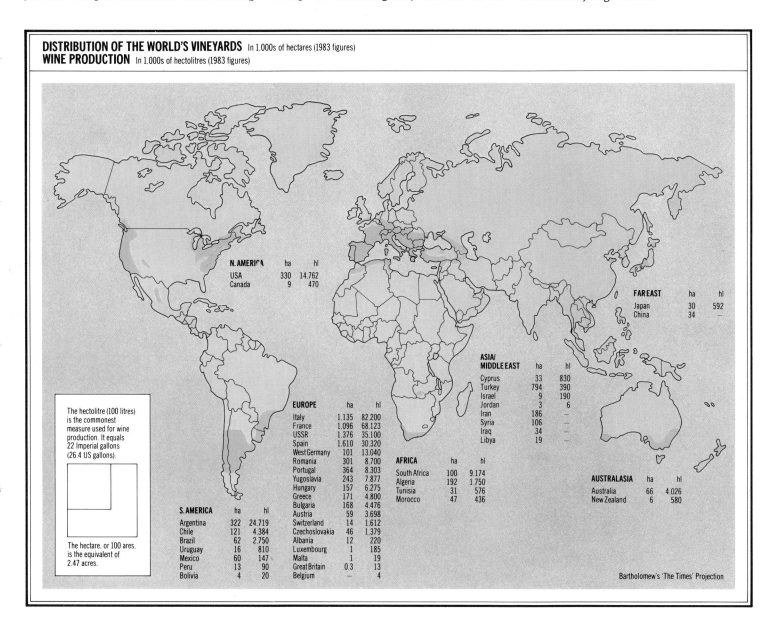

DISTRIBUTION OF THE WORLD'S VINEYARDS In 1,000s of hectares (1983 figures)
WINE PRODUCTION In 1,000s of hectolitres (1983 figures)

The hectolitre (100 litres) is the commonest measure used for wine production. It equals 22 Imperial gallons (26.4 US gallons).

The hectare, or 100 ares, is the equivalent of 2.47 acres.

N. AMERICA	ha	hl
USA	330	14.762
Canada	9	470

FAR EAST	ha	hl
Japan	30	592
China	34	—

ASIA/ MIDDLE EAST	ha	hl
Cyprus	33	830
Turkey	794	390
Israel	9	190
Jordan	3	6
Iran	186	—
Syria	106	—
Iraq	34	—
Libya	19	—

EUROPE	ha	hl
Italy	1.135	82.200
France	1.096	68.123
USSR	1.376	35.100
Spain	1.610	30.320
West Germany	101	13.040
Romania	301	8.700
Portugal	364	8.303
Yugoslavia	243	7.877
Hungary	157	6.275
Greece	171	4.800
Bulgaria	168	4.476
Austria	59	3.698
Switzerland	14	1.612
Czechoslovakia	46	1.379
Albania	12	220
Luxembourg	1	185
Malta	1	19
Great Britain	0.3	13
Belgium	—	4

AFRICA	ha	hl
South Africa	100	9.174
Algeria	192	1.750
Tunisia	31	576
Morocco	47	436

AUSTRALASIA	ha	hl
Australia	66	4.026
New Zealand	6	580

S. AMERICA	ha	hl
Argentina	322	24.719
Chile	121	4.384
Brazil	62	2.750
Uruguay	16	810
Mexico	60	147
Peru	13	90
Bolivia	4	20

Bartholomew's 'The Times' Projection

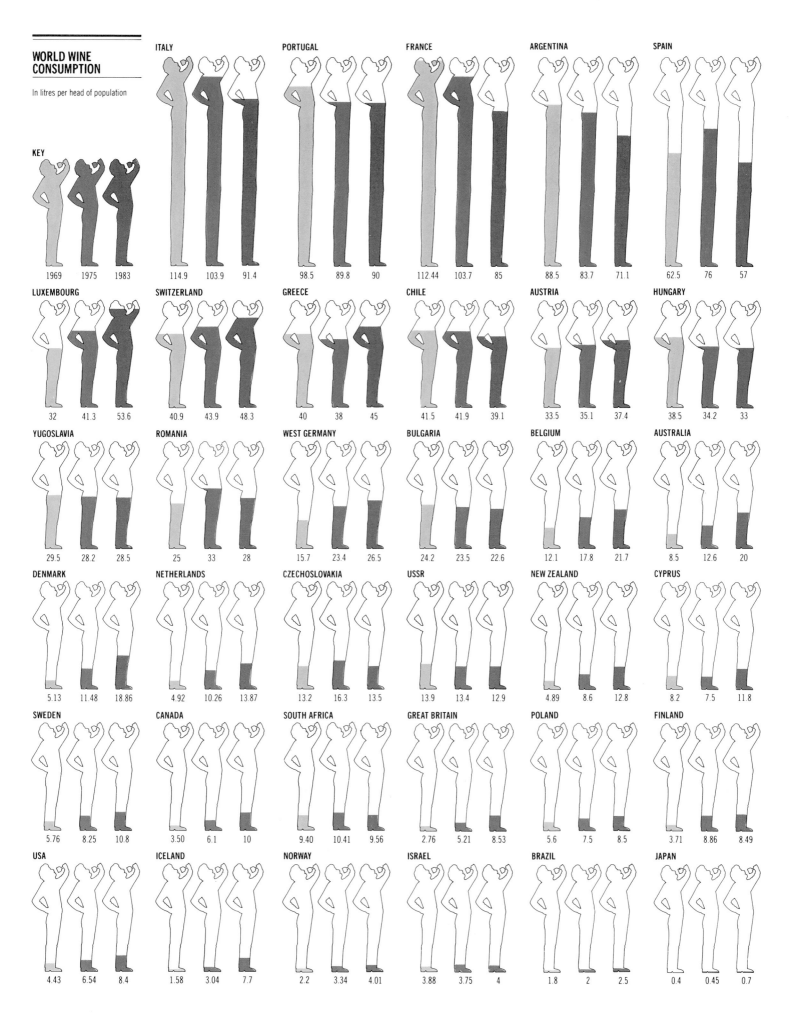

WORLD WINE CONSUMPTION

In litres per head of population

KEY

| 1969 | 1975 | 1983 |

ITALY
114.9   103.9   91.4

PORTUGAL
98.5   89.8   90

FRANCE
112.44   103.7   85

ARGENTINA
88.5   83.7   71.1

SPAIN
62.5   76   57

LUXEMBOURG
32   41.3   53.6

SWITZERLAND
40.9   43.9   48.3

GREECE
40   38   45

CHILE
41.5   41.9   39.1

AUSTRIA
33.5   35.1   37.4

HUNGARY
38.5   34.2   33

YUGOSLAVIA
29.5   28.2   28.5

ROMANIA
25   33   28

WEST GERMANY
15.7   23.4   26.5

BULGARIA
24.2   23.5   22.6

BELGIUM
12.1   17.8   21.7

AUSTRALIA
8.5   12.6   20

DENMARK
5.13   11.48   18.86

NETHERLANDS
4.92   10.26   13.87

CZECHOSLOVAKIA
13.2   16.3   13.5

USSR
13.9   13.4   12.9

NEW ZEALAND
4.89   8.6   12.8

CYPRUS
8.2   7.5   11.8

SWEDEN
5.76   8.25   10.8

CANADA
3.50   6.1   10

SOUTH AFRICA
9.40   10.41   9.56

GREAT BRITAIN
2.76   5.21   8.53

POLAND
5.6   7.5   8.5

FINLAND
3.71   8.86   8.49

USA
4.43   6.54   8.4

ICELAND
1.58   3.04   7.7

NORWAY
2.2   3.34   4.01

ISRAEL
3.88   3.75   4

BRAZIL
1.8   2   2.5

JAPAN
0.4   0.45   0.7

The Ancient World

The history of wine runs back before our knowledge. It emerges with civilization itself from the East. The evidence from tablets and papyri and tombs can – and does – fill volumes. Man as we know him, working and worrying man, comes on the scene with the support of a jug of wine.

Historical evidence gets closer to our experience with the expansion of the Greek Empire, starting a thousand years before Christ. It was then that wine first met the countries it was to make its real home: Italy and France. The Greeks called Italy the Land of Vines, just as the Vikings called America Vinland from the profusion of its native vines 2,000 years later. It seems probable that North Africa, Andalusia, Provence, Sicily, the Italian mainland and perhaps the Black Sea had their first vineyards in the time of the Greek Empire.

The wines of Greece herself, no great matter today, were lavishly praised and generously documented by her poets. There was even a fashionable after-dinner game in Athens which consisted of throwing the last few mouthfuls of wine in your cup into the air, to hit a delicately balanced dish on a pole. Smart young things took coaching in the finer points of 'kottabos'. But such treatment of the wine, and the knowledge that jugs of hot water for diluting it were on every table, makes it seem improbable that the wine was very good. What would have been nectar to Homer, or even to Jove, would probably seem to us like an oversweet vin rosé,

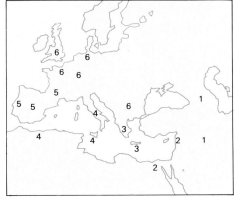

Above right: this Egyptian painting of treaders under an arbour of vines comes from the tomb of Nakht, a Theban official who died in the 15th century BC.
Below: feast scenes are one of the favourite motifs of Greek vase-painting. On a wine vase of about 480 BC (in the British Museum) the left-hand guest is playing the fashionable after-dinner game of kottabós, which consisted of throwing the last of the wine in the cup at a special mark, a dish balanced on a pole.

possibly with a flavour of muscat, possibly tasting of resin, and possibly concentrated by cooking, and needing dilution before drinking.

So much was written about wine and wine-making in ancient Rome that it is possible to make a rough map (right) of the wines of the early Roman Empire. The greatest writers, even Virgil, wrote instructions to wine-growers. One sentence of his – 'Vines love an open hill' – might be called the best single piece of advice which can be given to a winegrower.

There has been much speculation about the quality of Roman wine. It apparently had extraordinary powers of keeping, which in itself suggests that it was good. The great vintages were discussed and even drunk for longer than seems possible; the famous Opimian – from the year of the consulship of Opimius, 121 BC – was being drunk even when it was 125 years old.

Certainly the Romans had all that is necessary for ageing wine. They were not limited to earthenware amphoras like the Greeks – although they used them. They had barrels just like modern barrels and bottles not unlike modern bottles. It is reasonable to suppose that most Italians of 2,000 years ago drank wine very like their descendants today; young, rather roughly made, sharp or strong according to the summer weather. The Roman method of cultivation of the vine on trees, in the festoons which became the friezes on classical buildings, is still practised, particularly in the south of Italy and northern Portugal.

Left: the early movements of the vine. Starting in Caucasia or Mesopotamia 1 in perhaps 6000 BC it was cultivated in Egypt and Phoenicia 2 in about 3000 BC. By 2000 BC it was in Greece 3 and by 1000 BC it was in Italy, Sicily and North Africa 4. In the next 500 years it reached at least Spain, Portugal and the south of France 5 and probably southern Russia as well. Finally (see map on opposite page) it spread with the Romans into northern Europe 6, getting as far as Britain.

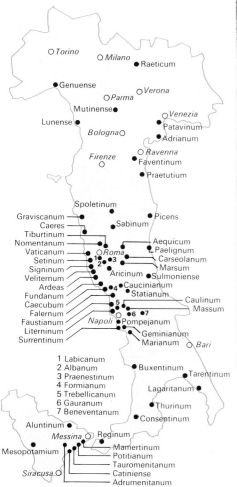

Torino ○
Milano ○
Raeticum ●
Genuense ●
Parma ○
Verona ○
Mutinense ●
Lunense ●
Bologna ○
Venezia ○
Patavinum ●
Adrianum ●
Firenze ○
Ravenna ○
Faventinum ●
Praetutium ●
Spoletinum ●
Graviscanum
Caeres
Tiburtinum
Nomentanum
Vaticanum
Setinum
Signinum
Veliternum
Ardeas
Fundanum
Caecubum
Falernum
Faustianum
Literninum
Surrentinum
Sabinum
Picens ●
Aequicum
Paelignum
Carseolanum
Marsum
Sulmoniense
Caucinianum
Statianum
Caulinum
Massum
Roma ○
Aricinum
Napoli ○
Pompejanum
Geminianum
Marianum
Bari ○

1 Labicanum
2 Albanum
3 Praenestinum
4 Formianum
5 Trebellicanum
6 Gauranum
7 Beneventanum

Buxentinum ●
Tarentinum ●
Lagaritanum
Thurinum ●
Consentinum ●
Aluntinum ●
Messina ○
Reginum
Mamertinum
Potitianum
Tauromenitanum
Catiniense
Adrumenitanum
Mesopotamium ●
Siracusa ○

Above left: the wines the Romans drank; a reconstruction of winegrowing Italy in AD 100. Names of modern cities are given in italics; wine names in Roman type.
Above: the Romans interpreted the graceful Greek wine god Dionysus as a more fleshly creature; in a mosaic from Pompeii, now in the Museo Nazionale, Naples, he rides his traditional mount, a lion, but boozes from a monstrous pot.

But the move of most consequence for history that the Romans made with their vines was to take them to Gaul. By the time they withdrew from what is now France in the fifth century they had laid the foundations for almost all the greatest vineyards of the modern world.

Starting in Provence, which had had vineyards already for centuries, they moved up the Rhône valley, and across (or by sea?) to Bordeaux in the time of Caesar. All the early developments were in the river valleys, the natural lines of communication, which the Romans cleared of forest and cultivated. Besides, boats were the best way of moving anything so heavy as wine. Bordeaux, Burgundy, Trier probably all started as merchant-centres for imported wine, then planted their own vines and surpassed the imported product.

By the second century there were vines in Burgundy; by the third on the Loire; and by the fourth at Paris (not such a good idea), in Champagne, and on the Moselle and the Rhine. Languedoc and the Auvergne also had vineyards. It seems that Alsace is the only major French wine region not to have Roman origins at least in part. It had to wait until about the ninth century.

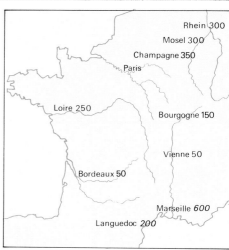

Rhein 300
Mosel 300
Champagne 350
Paris
Loire 250
Bourgogne 150
Vienne 50
Bordeaux 50
Marseille 600
Languedoc 200

Left: barrels were used by the Romans. This one was found being used as the lining of a well at Silchester in southern England, and is now in Reading Museum.

Above: the vineyards of France and Germany at the fall of the Roman Empire. The dates of their founding are mainly conjectural. Vineyards in the Languedoc and Marseille (BC dates in italics) were founded by the Greeks; the rest by the Romans in the heyday of Roman Gaul. The history of all these vineyards has been continuous; Alsace – which does not appear here – was probably founded in about AD 800.

The Middle Ages

Above: wine had an important place in medieval life as part of both Jewish and Christian observance. This picture of a Jewish Passover is from an early 14th-century haggadah from northern Spain or Provence.

Below: in the Bayeux tapestry, Bishop Odo blesses wine before the invasion of England.

ut of the Dark Ages which followed the fall of the Roman Empire we emerge into the illumination of the medieval period, to see in its lovely painted pages an entirely familiar scene; one which was not to change in its essentials until this century. The Church had been the repository of the skills of civilization in the Dark Ages. As expansionist monasteries cleared hillsides and walled around fields of cuttings, as dying winegrowers bequeathed it their land, the Church came to be identified with wine – not only as the Blood of Christ, but as luxury and comfort in this world. For centuries it owned many of the greatest vineyards of Europe. Within this stable framework, in which tools and terms and techniques seemed to stand still, the styles of wine familiar to us now slowly came into being.

The illuminated capital at the top of this page is from a northern French manuscript of about 1320.

14

Far left: tying up the vines.
Left: picking the grapes.
The crisp and expressive little woodcuts which illustrated the 1493 Speyer edition of Piero Crescentio's *Opus Ruralium Commodorum* have been reprinted constantly ever since.

Below: in 1497 the Royal Exchequer of England laid down that eight gallons make one Winchester bushel; and 'too pottelys maketh one gallon'. The Winchester bushel is still a legal measure in the USA.

Left: a late 15th-century tapestry in the Musée de Cluny in Paris shows the court happily obstructing the vintagers on the banks of the Loire.
Right: English wine measures of 1497 included a hogshead (63 gallons), a pipe (two hogsheads) and a tonne (two pipes). The size of ships was measured by the number of tonnes they could carry.

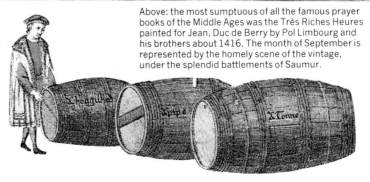

Above: the most sumptuous of all the famous prayer books of the Middle Ages was the Très Riches Heures painted for Jean, Duc de Berry by Pol Limbourg and his brothers about 1416. The month of September is represented by the homely scene of the vintage, under the splendid battlements of Saumur.

The Evolution of Modern Wine

It is possible to piece together, from the first enthusiastic mentions of particular growths in the 17th century, the rise of reputations and the evolution of our modern wines. For none of the familiar types sprang fully grown from the head of Bacchus. Nor is their evolution complete today: change continues. Burgundy, within the last 20 years, has seen a swing to much lighter wines, paler, with less depth of flavour and less able to mature – and the start of a swing back to the old style of dark and deep.

It is hard to have confidence in the descriptions of wine which survive from before about 1700. With the exception of Shakespeare's graphic tasting notes: 'a marvellous searching wine, and it perfumes the blood ere one can say "What's this?"', they tend to refer to royal recommendations or miraculous cures rather than to taste and characteristics.

Burgundy comes into focus in the 18th century: white wines 'spirity, faintly bubbly, fine and clear as spring water'; 'delicate pink wine' from Savigny. Nuits is 'wine to keep for the following year', in contrast to all the others, which were wines to drink as soon as the winter weather had cleared them. There was no call for strong, firm burgundy to lay down. Nobody knew what marvellous searching stuff it could be. Among the *vins de primeur* the first choice was Volnay.

But by the early 19th century there had been a complete revolution. Suddenly the vin rosés went out of fashion; the demand was for long-fermented, dark-coloured wine. In the Côte de Beaune, whose wines are naturally light, prices dropped. Demand moved to the Côte de Nuits, whose wines are naturally *vins de garde* – wines to keep and mature.

The explanation of the change was the discovery of the effect on wine of storing it in bottles. Since Roman times it had spent all its life in a barrel. If bottles were used they were

Left: Phillipe Mercier's *'Le Jeune Dégustateur'*, painted in London in the 1740s, is one of the first illustrations of a corkscrew.
Right: Bordeaux's wine production in relation to wars, diseases, pests, slumps and the weather, first plotted (to 1975) by Philippe Roudie of Bordeaux University. Two great chemical aids, sulphur (against oidium mould) and Bordeaux mixture (copper sulphate and lime) against mildew had immediate effect. The dip in vineyard area around 1980 can be traced to the replanting of white-wine vineyards with more profitable red.

simply carafes for serving at table. But late in the 17th century someone discovered the cork. Bit by bit it became clear that wine kept in a tightly corked bottle lasted much longer than wine kept in a barrel, which was likely to go off at any time after the barrel was broached. It also aged in a different way, acquiring what is known as a 'bouquet'.

The wine that benefited most from this treatment was the fiery port the English had started to drink in the late 17th century. They had doubts about it at first, but as the century, and their bottles, grew older, their opinion of it rose sharply. The trend is graphically illustrated by the way the port bottle changed shape from a carafe within a hundred years. The old model would not lie down, so its cork dried out. The slimmer bottle is easy to 'bin' horizontally in heaps. Before long the benefits of bottle-age

were beginning to change the style of all the best wines of Europe.

In 1866 A. Jullien published the figures for the alcoholic strengths of recent vintages. By today's standards the burgundies are formidable: Corton 1858, 15.6%; Montrachet 1858, 14.3%; Clos de Bèze 1858, 14.3%; Volnay 1859, 14.9%; Richebourg 1859, 14.3%. In contrast the wines of Bordeaux in the same two years ranged from 11.3% (St-Emilion Supérieur) to 8.9% (Château Lafite).

The low natural strength of the Bordeaux wines explains what seems today a curious habit of the old wine trade. Up to the mid-century the Bordeaux wines for England – which was most of the best of them – were subjected to what was known as *le travail à l'anglaise*. The recipe called for 30 litres of Spanish wine (Alicante or Benicarlo), 2 litres of

Below: the evolution of the port bottle in the century from 1708 when it was a carafe to 1812 when it had reached its modern proportions is a vivid record of the emergence of vintage wine. As it was discovered that bottled and corked wine improved immeasurably with keeping, bottles began to be designed to be 'laid down' on their sides. This collection of bottles is at Berry Bros & Rudd, the London wine merchants.

1708   1719   1739   1741   1753

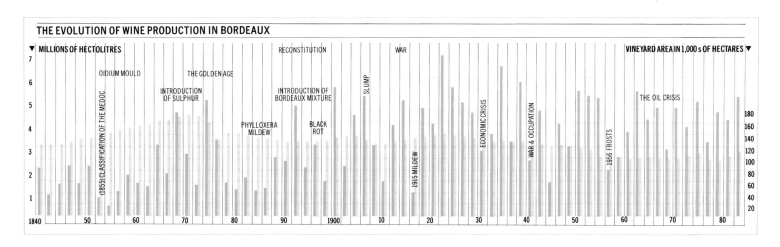

THE EVOLUTION OF WINE PRODUCTION IN BORDEAUX

▼ MILLIONS OF HECTOLITRES   VINEYARD AREA IN 1,000 s OF HECTARES ▼

Labels on chart: OIDIUM MOULD · (1855) CLASSIFICATION OF THE MEDOC · INTRODUCTION OF SULPHUR · THE GOLDEN AGE · RECONSTITUTION · WAR · SLUMP · PHYLLOXERA MILDEW · INTRODUCTION OF BORDEAUX MIXTURE · BLACK ROT · 1915 MILDEW · ECONOMIC CRISIS · WAR & OCCUPATION · 1956 FROSTS · THE OIL CRISIS

Time axis: 1840 · 50 · 60 · 70 · 80 · 90 · 1900 · 10 · 20 · 30 · 40 · 50 · 60 · 70 · 80

unfermented white must and a bottle of brandy to each barrel of claret. The summer after the vintage the wine was set to ferment again with these additives, then treated as other wines and kept several years in wood before shipping. The result was strong wine with a good flavour, but 'heady and not suitable for all stomachs'. It fetched more than natural wine.

Today's preoccupation with authenticity, even at the expense of quality, makes these practices seem abusive. But it is rather as though someone revealed as a shocking instance of fraud the fact that brandy is added to port. We like Douro wine with brandy in it; our ancestors liked Lafite with Alicante in it.

German wines of the last century would be scarcely more familiar to us. It is doubtful whether any of today's pale, rather sweet, intensely perfumed wines were made. Grapes picked earlier gave more acid wine, which needed longer to mature in cask. People liked the flavour of oak – or even the flavour of

oxidation from too much contact with the air. 'Old brown hock' was a recommendation, whereas today it would be as rude a remark as you could write on a tasting card.

Champagne too was fuller in colour and flavour – although otherwise very like it is today. Port and sherry had both been perfected. There was much more strong sweet wine from the Mediterranean to be seen: Malaga and Marsala were in their heydays. Madeira, Constantia and Tokay were all as highly regarded as the Trockenbeerenausleses of modern Germany.

The wine trade was booming. In the wine-growing countries an unhealthy amount of the economy rested on wine: in Italy in 1880 it was calculated that no less than 80% of the population more or less relied on wine for a living. This was the world phylloxera struck like a plague. The methods of this little bug are described on page 18. At the time, when he had succeeded in destroying or causing the

pulling up of almost every vine in Europe, it seemed like the end of the world of wine.

The last 90 years have seen wine's Industrial Revolution. More particularly in the last 25 years, the scientific background to winemaking has become so much clearer that many things which were thought impossible before have become easy. The modern winemaker is embarrassed by the number of options open to him. At the same time have come temptations to lower the standards of the best, to make more wine at the expense of quality.

Today's great danger is the insidious trend towards making neutral, safe wine, without character, to please every taste. Winegrowers are anxious for a new market, and technology has shown them how to control what they make. It is essential for wine drinkers to demand unblended, individual wines with all their local character intact. It is up to us to see that the most enthralling thing about wine – its endless variety – survives.

1780   1793   1807   1812

Right: it is interesting to compare A. Jullien's classification in 1866 of the great wines of the world with the wines of today. His list in *Topographie de Tous les Vignobles Connus* (in its original spelling) ran:

Red
A Châteaux Margaux, Laffitte, Latour, Haut-Brion, Rauzan, Lascombes, Léoville, Larose-Balguerie, Gorce (Cantenac), Branne-Mouton, Pichon-Longueville
B Romanée-Conti, Chambertin, Richebourg, Clos Vougeot, Romanée-St-Vivant, La Tâche, Clos St-Georges, Le Corton, Clos de Prémeaux, Musigny, Clos de Tart, Bonnes-Mares, Clos de la Roche, Les Véroilles, Clos Morjot, Clos St-Jean, La Perrière
C (Hermitage) Méal, Gréfieux, Beaume,

Raucoule, Muret, Guoignière, Les Bessas, Les Burges, Les Lauds
D High Douro

White
1 Sillery, Ay Mareuil, Dizy, Hautvillers, Pierry, Le Clozet
2 Mont Rachet
3 First-growths of Barsac, Preignac, Sauternes, Bommes; dry

wine of Villenave-d'Ornon
4 Château Grillet
5 Hermitage Blanc
6 Schloss Johannisberg, Rüdesheim, Steinberg, Graffenberg, Hochheim, Kiedrich
7 Liebfraumilch
8 Leist, Stein
9 Sherry from the white soil, Paxarete
10 Sercial [Madeira]

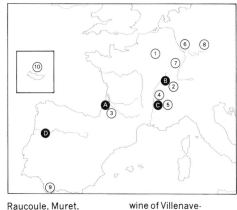

The Vine

As early as the beginning of April in northern Europe (or September in the southern hemisphere) the gnarled wood of the vine sports tender shoots.

Within ten days of budding the stalk, leaves and tendrils are all obvious – and also vulnerable to nights of frost, which can come in late May.

In late May or early June the vine forms its flower buds, looking like tiny bunches of grapes in the place where the grapes will eventually be.

Early in June comes the vital flowering, which must go on for 10–14 days for good grapes to form. Heavy rain now is fatal to the vintage.

If the flowers escape rain and frost, their place is taken by baby grapes in June. In August the grapes 'set': turn colour from green to red or translucent yellow; at

this point the ripening process begins. From flowering to harvest in September or October is about 100 days (see the chart on page 26).

Wine is the juice of grapes. Every drop of wine is rain recovered from the ground by the mechanism of the grape-bearing plant, the vine. For the first four or five years of its life the vine is too busy creating a root system and building a strong woody stalk to bear a crop of grapes. Thereafter, left to nature, it would rampage away, bearing fruit but spending much more of its energy on making new shoots and putting out long wandering branches of leafy wood, until it covered as much as an acre (half a hectare) of ground, with new root systems forming wherever the branches lay along the ground.

This natural form, known as *provignage*, was used as a vineyard in ancient times. To prevent the grapes rotting or the mice getting them, since they lay on the ground, little props were pushed under the stems to support each bunch. If the vine grew near trees, it used its tendrils to climb them to dizzy heights. The Romans planted elms specially for the purpose.

In modern vineyards, however, the vine is not allowed to waste its precious sap on making long branches. Better-quality grapes grow on a vine that is regularly cut back almost to its main stem. The annual pruning is done in mid-winter, when the vine is empty of sap.

Vines, like most other plants, will reproduce from seed. Sowing grape pips would be much the easiest and cheapest way of getting new vines. But like many highly bred plants its seeds rarely turn out like their parents. Pips are used for experimenting with new crosses between different varieties. For planting a new vineyard, though, every vine has to be a cutting – either planted to take root on its own or grafted to a rooted cutting of another species.

Great care is taken to see that the parent vine is healthy before cuttings are taken. The little 'slips' are put in sand in a nursery for a season until they form roots. They then go out into rows, in traditional vineyards 3 feet (a metre) apart but often today one and a half, two or even three metres apart. Oddly enough experiments have found that the total yield of the vineyard in wine remains the same with half as many vines exploiting the same volume of soil.

Pests which threaten the vine include, top left, the grub of the cochylis moth, seen here eating the flower buds; top right, the tiny red spider, which sucks the sap from the undersides of leaves; lower left, mildew, which attacks anything green. Mildewed grapes never ripen properly and have a peculiar taste. Lower right: oidium, or powdery mildew, is often more serious; its attack on Madeira in 1852, just before phylloxera hit the island, began the decline in Madeira's fortunes. It rots the stalks, shrivels the leaves and splits the grapes, ruining the wine and finally killing the vine.

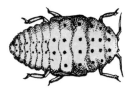

Left and below: the vine's deadliest enemy, *Phylloxera vastatrix*, in its root-eating form and its flying form. Below right: larvae and eggs. A century ago this American bug almost destroyed the vineyards of Europe.
Right: every European vine is now grafted on to American roots, which resist attack. There used to be fierce debate as to whether European wine has suffered, but few now remember pre-phylloxera wine.

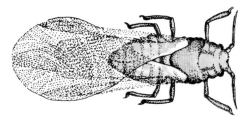

As a vine grows older its roots penetrate deeper into the earth. While it is young and they are near the surface they are quickly affected by drought or floods or the spreading of manure (which put on the land too liberally can affect the taste of the wine); the vine has little stability; its wine will never be first-class. But if the soil near the surface does not provide enough food it will send its roots down and down (see right).

Unfortunately, being a pampered plant, the vine is subject to all manner of diseases. Some varieties fall sick of one particular disease (e.g. oidium or mildew) so readily that they are gradually being abandoned. The best combine reasonable hardiness with fine fruit (although rarely with a very generous yield).

One insect pest is disastrous: the phylloxera, which lives on the roots of the vine and kills it. In the 1870s it almost destroyed the entire European vineyard, until it was discovered that the roots of the native American vine (phylloxera came from America) are immune. Virtually every vine in Europe had to be pulled up and replaced with a European cutting grafted on to a rooted cutting from an American vine.

Red spiders, the grubs of the cochylis and eudemis moths, various sorts of beetles, bugs and mites all feed on the upper works of the vine. Most of them, however, are taken care of by the various sprays to which the vine is subjected summer-long. In California the worst scourge is known as Pierce's disease.

Various moulds attack the vine as well. Oidium and mildew are the two worst in Europe; white, black and grey rot are among the others. All have to be prevented or at least treated by regular sprayings with a copper sulphate solution and sulphur powder for as long as the vine has leaves and green wood which they can attack.

Below: the map plots the progress through France of phylloxera, starting in the *département* of Gard in the south in 1864 and not finishing its destruction for 30 years. France regained her production by 1920, but never her pre-phylloxera vineyard area.

☐ by 1869		☐ 1880–89	
☐ 1870–79		☐ after 1889	

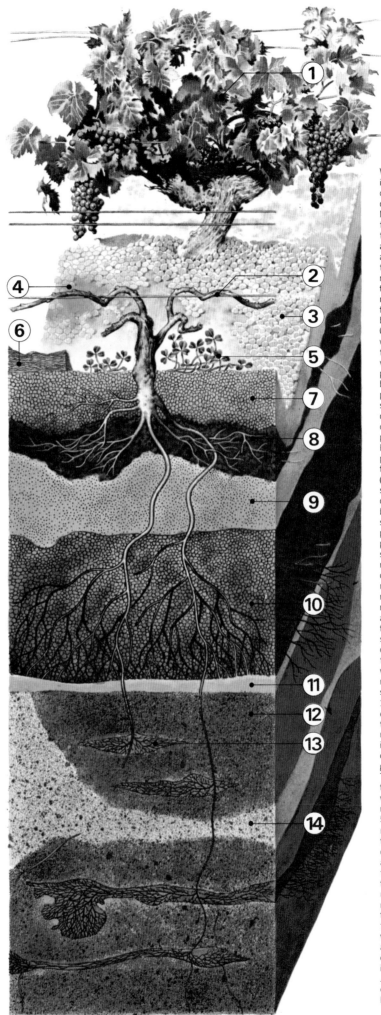

Wine has its origin as water in the soil. This cross-section of the vineyard of a riverside château in St-Julien in the Médoc shows how a vine finds enough moisture and food in poor soil by exploiting a deep and wide area. Gravel and sand are here plus factors for quality. They make the ground permeable to a great depth, let the rain run through, and encourage the vine to go deep. In the background a 50-year-old Cabernet vine **1**, trained on wires, bears fruit. In the foreground a 20-year-old vine **2** is in its winter state; pruned and with the earth banked up around it for protection. Pebbles **3** on the surface are stained with copper sulphate **4**. Clover **5** or other crops are often ploughed in as fertilizer. Pressed skins **6** (marc – see page 30) are also spread on the ground. The top 12 inches (30cm) of soil **7** is pebbly and sandy with few roots. Then comes a layer of marl **8** brought from elsewhere and spread by hand years ago, possibly when the vines were planted. Roots and rootlets spread horizontally in it. The next layer **9** is sandy but compacted hard and has nothing to offer. There are no feeding rootlets but only main roots descending to another thicker layer **10** like the surface, gravelly and sandy, but slightly richer in organic matter (possibly from manuring years ago) where roots abound. These roots are again brought up short by a compacted layer **11** of sand at 4 feet (just over a metre) deep. Below this different colours of sand, rusty **12** and yellow **14**, lie in clearly defined layers, with odd horizontal patches of grey sand **13** among them. The grey is evidently where the water drains; it is filled with rootlets, which are nowhere else in the area. A 50-year-old vine still has roots an inch (25–30mm) thick here, going down to deeper layers of grey sand and gravel. Roots can only find so much of the minerals they seek in a form they can use (i.e. in solution). The more grapes a vine bears, therefore, the less of these flavouring elements there will be per grape; the argument for restricting the crop to achieve maximum intensity of flavour. In St-Julien one vine produces enough juice for only half a bottle of wine.

Based on investigations by Gérard Seguin published in his *Etude de Quelques Profils de Sols du Vignoble Bordelais* (Bordeaux 1965).

The Modern Vineyard

The last few years have seen the study of viticulture, the science of growing grapes for wine, advance by leaps and bounds. Until recently planting was mainly a question of replacing old vineyards in the same fashion as before. Although the amount of wine was growing, the world's vineyard area was contracting: healthier plants and more fertilizers accounted for the bigger yield.

But in the last 15 years the demand for more good wine has started a planting boom, and at the same time set winegrowers to questioning traditional forms of vineyard. The questions they ask are not just 'what vines?', but 'on what roots?', 'how far apart?', 'trained high or low?', 'up the slope or across it?'. New vineyards (and there are a lot in this Atlas) embody the latest thinking about what makes grapes ripen in good health.

One of the most radical studies of the subject has been going on for some years at the viticultural research station at Geisenheim in the Rheingau. The result of one of their earlier surveys of their own region appears on page 143. Since then more detailed and elaborate research has continued. A paper by the late Dr G. Horney of the Agrarian Meteorological Department of the German weather service at Geisenheim sums up part of the findings.

Dr Horney began by asking basic questions about the vine. What sort of plant is it in nature, and what are its needs? He described it as a climber of lowland woods in the Mediterranean region. As such it needs a great deal of light (its reason for climbing), a warm climate, plenty of water (it is confined in nature to low land with a relatively high water table) and relatively humid air.

The immediately interesting thing is that the last two points clash with the classic formula for successful winegrowing: Virgil's 'vines love an open hill'. High-quality wine seems to come from dry (certainly well-drained) ground where humidity is relatively low.

Dr Horney examined each point as it applies to the Rheingau, starting with sunlight. Rheingau vines can be proved to receive as much sunlight as they can assimilate, even in a cloudy year. Therefore the importance of sunshine is a question of heat, not light.

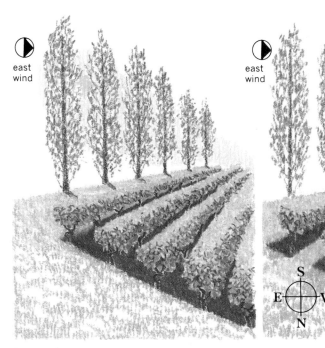

The two illustrations above show an ideal vineyard in the Rheingau (see the text on this and the opposite page) in early morning (above left) and at noon (above right) at the end of September – the crucial ripening season. It lies on a western slope, with a windbreak to the east to prevent the prevailing summer wind

blowing a warm microclimate out from between the rows. The rows run north–south for the same reason (see diagrams below). In the morning mist envelops the vines – the low sun with long shadows does little good – but at noon when the mist clears and the sun is warmest it floods the vines with warmth and light.

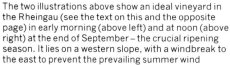

The direction of vinerows affects the time of day when the sun reaches and warms the ground. In the vineyard, left, the rows run north–south. At noon in September the maximum heat of the sun falls on the soil and vine leaves; the grapes are shaded. The soil will retain heat all afternoon. In the vineyard, right, with east–west rows the 'hedges' are fully in the sun at noon but the ground is in shade and stays several degrees cooler all day. The grapes will not be so ripe.

Vines can be trained to any shape or size. Different methods have evolved for different soils and climates, ranging from isolated low bushes where water is scarce to tree-high climbers where it is land that is in limited supply. The sequence of vines on the right shows some of the principal variations.

A Mosel vine after pruning. Two vigorous young canes are tied down to form a 'goblet' supported by an individual stake. New growth breaks from the topmost buds.

A traditional system on the scattered plots and terraces of the northern Rhône. New growth from a low base is tied to light stakes known as 'échallas'.

The principal system of Bordeaux and Burgundy is to train the vine on two wires; the lower for the main fruiting cane, the upper for young shoots and luxuriant foliage.

The high-wire system was developed in Austria by Lenz Moser. It encourages a big leafy canopy over the grapes; good in hot sunshine and easily cultivated by tractor.

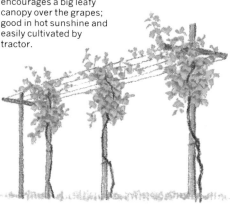

The temperature is all-important. The flowering of the vine starts in the spring as soon as the air starts to warm the ground. In autumn the reverse moment triggers the colouring of the leaves. Growth and every other function of the plant is linked to ground temperatures above 10°C (50°F). Assimilation and transpiration (the process of drawing up moisture and nourishment from the ground and 'breathing' through the leaves) proceeds more efficiently with rising temperatures up to a certain point. But at 28°C (82°F) evaporation overtakes assimilation: the vine demands more of its roots than they can draw from the ground – even damp ground. The growth (and ripening) process slows and stops. There is therefore an optimum temperature for vines – in the region of 25–28°C. Anything higher than this reduces their efficiency.

Turning to ground moisture, Dr Horney described the very deep roots vines can make as evidence that the plant must have extensive water supplies and will go to any length to get them. If there is water near the surface a vine roots shallowly; nor does flooding, at least for a while, harm it. Drought, on the other hand, stops the ripening process as the leaves flag. For this reason the autumnal dews and mists after a hot summer are vital; the vine can absorb enough water through the leaves to keep the foliage healthy.

As to humidity, the vine is apparently happiest with a relative humidity of 60–80% or even more. At such humidity, however, fungus diseases become a serious problem. The optimum for the crop is much lower.

As far as the Rheingau is concerned all the above conditions for success are met with the exception of temperature: it rarely reaches 25–28°C – or indeed above 20°C – in the Rheingau for very long. Therefore the ability of particular sites to heat up and stay warm must be a crucial factor for quality. 'Local climates' in vineyards are created above all by shelter from the wind: the vines sheltering each other, or a hedge or a hill sheltering the vineyard. For vines in the cool north mutual shelter is therefore vital. In the south, of course, where it is often *too* hot, the determining factor is the water supply: hence the widely

Below: pergolas are widely used in northern Italy, and in Portugal for vinho verde. They give cool ripening conditions by shading the ground but make machine cultivation difficult. In Japan they help to prevent rot by encouraging air circulation.

spaced bushes in Mediterranean vineyards. They also survive the summer winds better.

Dr Horney concluded by discussing how a northern vineyard can be given the best chance of being warmer than the prevailing temperatures. The first rule is to plant the rows across the direction of the prevailing wind in the warmest weather – in the Rheingau, the east wind. Rows planted north–south will avoid having their precious microclimate blown away. Another point in their favour is that the ground in the north–south alleys is warmed by the midday sun, whereas the lower leaves and grapes are shaded from it by the upper foliage: the ideal arrangement.

Best of all is a western slope, where not only is the east wind excluded but the afternoon sun of autumn can have most effect. For Dr Horney pointed out that it is precisely in the still, sunny, autumn weather which can do most good that morning mists are most common. An eastern slope can miss the best part of the day for ripening.

These conclusions, in favour of close rows of vines running north–south, preferably on western slopes and sheltered by windbreaks, are of course only a recipe for the Rheingau and similar vineyards. The ecological factors, on the other hand, are the same in different combinations for every vineyard. All calculations begin with the essential needs and nature of the vine.

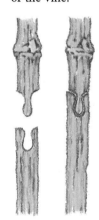

A new development in grafting technique. A simple stamping machine cuts a mortice and tenon in the rootstock and the scion of the variety to be grown. The two lock together and form a new plant almost immediately. Compare the old method on page 18 which involved knife-work and binding-up.

A FOOTNOTE ON COSTS

Good wine can only be made by limiting the crop of each vine (the object of pruning), and great wine by limiting it severely.

The grower, unfortunately, must make his choice before he discovers whether nature (by frost or hail or drought) will do it for him.

The economic implications (i.e. why fine wine is much more expensive to produce) are clearly displayed in a set of figures calculated in 1985 by Peter Sichel of the famous Bordeaux shippers Sichel & Co. The table below shows the costs of producing 'great' wine in quantities of 27 hecto-litres/hectare (290 US gallons/acre), 'good' wine at 45 hectolitres/hectare (486 US gallons/acre) and wine at 63 hectolitres/hectare (680 US gallons/acre). 'Great' wine costs more not only because of lower production but also because it must be stored in expensive new oak barrels, with consequent high loss by evaporation. 'Good' wine is matured in used barrels and plain wine in vats.

The question is whether the public will pay the higher basic costs (plus finance charges and overheads) for better, because more concen-trated, wine. The answer seems to be that a polarization tends to develop, with the readiest sale being for the cheapest and the most expen-sive – which sells because it has blue-chip invest-ment value. In terms of true value (that is, flavour) for money the best buy is really the good wine in the middle, which is made with almost as much care as the most expensive but does not fetch a premium for glamour. The prices below show only production costs. Amortization of land values, costs of bottling, etc., are not included.

	'great' 27 hl/ha	'good' 45 hl/ha	'ordinary' 63 hl/ha
Viticultural costs per hectolitre	Frs 1,815	Frs 1,088	Frs 778
Cost of storage per hectolitre	266	55	12
Quantity loss from evaporation, racking, fining (20% in cask, 7% in vat)	363	218	54
Labour costs, racking and fining	26	26	6
Cost per hectolitre	2,470	1,387	850

1 Franc = US $0.11 = £0.08 (April 1985)

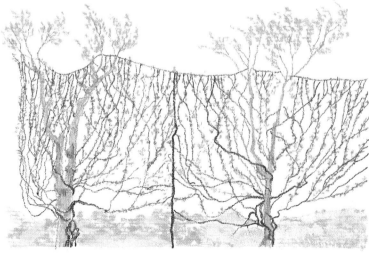

Left: vines have been grown up trees in Italy since earliest times. The Romans planted elms specially for the purpose. Standing a vineyard on end releases the ground for other crops – but never makes good wine, since hard pruning is impossible.

21

The Choice of a Grape:1

The wine vine is only one species of one genus of a vast family of plants, which ranges from a huge decorative Japanese climber to the familiar Virginia creeper.

The species is *Vitis vinifera*. Its varieties can be numbered in thousands – as many as 5,000 are named. Those that concern a wine lover, however, are probably not many more than about 50, of which we show 25 on these and the next pages, and in addition a few varieties from two or three other species of *Vitis* that are native to North America, and a handful of hybrids between these and *V. vinifera*.

All over the Old World of winegrowing, the natural selection of the variety that does best, and gives the best quality combined with reasonable quantity and a reasonable resistance to disease, has taken place gradually over centuries. In many places (the port country, for example, Chianti, Bordeaux, Châteauneuf-du-Pape) no one variety provides exactly what is needed: the tradition is either to grow a number together, or to grow them separately and blend the resulting wines.

It is not the traditional practice in the main wine districts of Europe even to mention the kind of grape that goes into a wine. For one thing, the choice is so old it can be assumed. For another, modern laws normally make the traditional variety a condition of using the traditional wine name. White burgundy, for example, to be called white burgundy must be made entirely of Chardonnay grapes.

Thus there are very many important grapes few people have ever heard of: the Palomino and the Pedro Ximénez of sherry; the Tintas of port; the Furmint of Tokay; the Syrah of the Rhône or the brilliant white Viognier; the splendid Nebbiolo of northern Italy; the Schiava of the Adige and the Sangiovese of Chianti; the Melon of Muscadet; the Folle Blanche and Ugni Blanc of Cognac; the Chasselas of Switzerland; the Malbec and Petit Verdot of Bordeaux; the Tempranillo of Rioja; the Savagnin of the Jura; the Arinto and Alvarinho of Portugal.

On the other hand, there are some, like the Sercial and Verdelho of Madeira, the Barbera of Piemonte or the Gewürztraminer of Alsace, that have become the names of their wines.

Ampelography – the study of grapes – is one of the most delicate and difficult studies connected with wine. Experts often disagree about the identities of grapes: their relationships remain far beyond lay comment. There are traditions that certain well-known grapes are 'really' something else. Several grapes in Portugal and Spain, for example, are said to be German Riesling, possibly brought by pilgrims to the shrine of Santiago. The Alvarinho of the Minho, Sercial of Madeira and Pedro Ximénez of Andalucia all make this claim.

In the New World the choice of grapes is not a question of tradition but of judgment: a balance of quality, quantity, hardiness and fashion. Today most of the best wines of the New World use a grape name to identify themselves. The immediate result may be over-simplistic: 100% one-variety wines are not necessarily better. Every vineyard presents its own opportunity – and challenge.

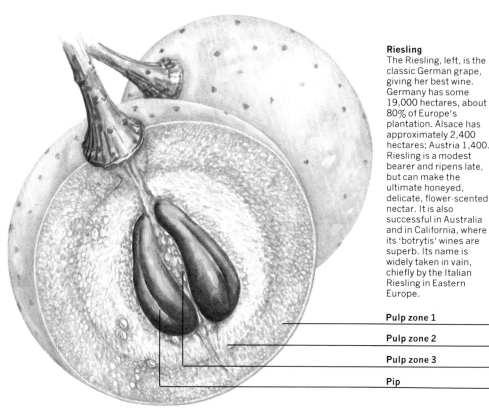

Riesling
The Riesling, left, is the classic German grape, giving her best wine. Germany has some 19,000 hectares, about 80% of Europe's plantation. Alsace has approximately 2,400 hectares; Austria 1,400. Riesling is a modest bearer and ripens late, but can make the ultimate honeyed, delicate, flower-scented nectar. It is also successful in Australia and in California, where its 'botrytis' wines are superb. Its name is widely taken in vain, chiefly by the Italian Riesling in Eastern Europe.

Pulp zone 1

Pulp zone 2

Pulp zone 3

Pip

Above: an enlargement of a Riesling grape one month before the vintage. It is still green, and about half its final size. Ripening, it grows translucent gold with distinctive dark speckles on the skin (see the photograph of ripe Riesling on page 117).

The stalk is normally torn off before the grapes are pressed in modern winemaking. Formerly they were left on, but they made the wine watery and could make it bitter. In red wine they also absorbed valuable colouring matter.

The pulp divides naturally into three zones. Zone 2 gives up its juice in the press first, before the two zones in contact with pips and skin. The first juice from the press has long been held to make the best wine; perhaps for this reason.

The pips should come through the press unscathed. If they are crushed they make the wine bitter. The skin is removed from the juice as quickly as possible for white wine; for red wine it is left in until the juice has taken its colour.

The distribution of ten important grape varieties in France

Red
- Cabernet Sauvignon
- Carignan
- Gamay
- Grenache
- Pinot Noir

White
- Chardonnay
- Sauvignon Blanc
- Chenin Blanc
- Riesling
- Ugni Blanc

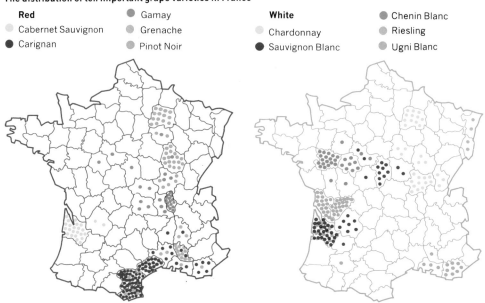

Gamay
Only makes first-class wine on the granite hills of Beaujolais, with their sandy soil. In the rest of Burgundy it is an inferior variety, although adequate in certain other parts of France (the Loire, Ardèche), in Switzerland and (alias Napa Gamay) in California. At its best Gamay produces wine that is incomparably light, fruity and gulpable, pale red, or, exceptionally, a dark wine ageing well for six or seven years.

Chardonnay
The grape of white burgundy (Chablis, Montrachet, Meursault, Pouilly-Fuissé) and Champagne. It gives firm, full, strong wine with scent and character, on chalky soils becoming almost luscious without being sweet. Ages well. Very successful in coastal California, parts of Australia, New Zealand, Bulgaria and, recently, Italy and Spain.

Muscat
Easy to recognize by its taste and smell, like a hothouse table grape's. Can be black or white. It spread from the Aegean with civilization, to the Crimea, Sicily, Italy and southern Spain. All muscat wine, except in Alsace, Bulgaria and a little from Australia, is sweet – often intensely sweet. The best in France comes from Beaumes de Venise near Avignon. Muscat wines or muscatels are made all over the world. They once included South Africa's Constantia. Australia's 'Liqueur Muscats' are its modern equivalent.

Sémillon
This grape has the great gift, shared with the Riesling, of rotting nobly. Under certain conditions of warmth and humidity a normally undesirable fungus softens the skin and lets the juice evaporate, concentrating the sugar and flavouring elements and producing luscious, creamy wine. The great golden wines of Sauternes are made like this, with a proportion of Sauvignon, not so subject to '*Pourriture noble*'. In Australia Sémillon makes wines which, although labelled anything from Riesling to Chablis, can be extremely good.

Cabernet Sauvignon
Small, tough-skinned grape that gives the distinction to the red wines of Bordeaux, although always blended with Merlot and sometimes Malbec. The best Médoc vineyards have up to 80% Cabernet, but in St-Emilion and Pomerol the Cabernet Franc is used. Cabernet Sauvignon is widely planted in Australia, where its best wine needs long ageing, in South Africa and in California, where it has scored its greatest successes outside France. All Cabernet wines gain by age in bottle as well as wood.

Sauvignon Blanc
The chief white Bordeaux grape, used with Sémillon and a little Muscadelle to make dry Graves and sweet Sauternes. Makes interesting, clean, lighter wine on its own elsewhere: at Pouilly and Sancerre on the upper Loire and throughout Touraine; in the Dordogne, near Chablis; in northeast Italy, in Chile and in the coastal valleys of California, where its wine can be dry, gold and of considerable character.

Chenin Blanc
The white grape of Anjou and Touraine on the Loire gives nervy, intense wine, honey-like when very ripe but always with high acidity, so it ages well. Its finest wines are Vouvray, Coteaux du Layon, Savennières; at Vouvray and Saumur it also makes sparkling wine. Often called Pineau de la Loire. A form called Steen is South Africa's favourite white grape. Chenin can also be admirable in California.

Pinot Noir
The single red grape of the Côte d'Or in Burgundy (Chambertin, Romanée, Corton, Beaune), i.e. the world's best red-wine grape, in the right place. In Champagne it is pressed before fermentation to make white wine, which becomes the greater part of the best champagnes. At its best the scent, flavour, body, texture of its wine are all profound pleasures. It makes light wines in Germany and Eastern Europe, where it goes by various names, and increasingly interesting wines in California and Australia.

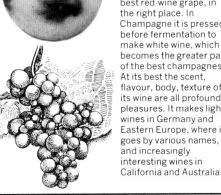

Grenache
A sweet grape making strong wine with character but not much colour, used in a blend to make Châteauneuf-du-Pape and on its own to make Tavel, the best rosé of the Rhône. Known as Garnacha in Rioja, where it is the most important red variety. Used for dessert wines at Banyuls near the Franco-Spanish frontier. In Australia and California it makes pleasant rosés, which often bear its name.

The Choice of a Grape: 2

The wine world has become steadily more grape-variety-conscious over the last two decades. Probably the first reason was that the New World started giving 'varietal' names pride of place on its best wines. Equally important were the successful breeding of new varieties and selections of exceptional 'clones' of old ones in research establishments around the world, but especially at Geisenheim in Germany and Davis in California.

A pioneering and most helpful discussion of the variety of grapes was published in 1965 by Doctors Amerine and Singleton in *Wine – An Introduction for Americans*. They divided wine-grape varieties into four categories. The largest (in volume grown) is of grapes that give no special flavour or character to their wine. By and large these are the grapes of the Mediterranean basin: the Carignan of the south of France is a good example; it is widely planted under local names in both Italy and Spain, but is nowhere outstanding. The wine of these grapes is not necessarily bad; it simply has no distinctive taste. For certain purposes (making sherry, for example) this can be an advantage. The Swiss say each Chasselas (a non-Mediterranean example) is a 'picture postcard' of where it is grown – being so neutral in itself. On the other hand the movement to improve Midi wine consists largely of replacing Carignan and the like with grapes of character.

Grapes with distinctive flavour (whose homes, on the whole, are the cooler vineyards of northern Europe) include all those whose names appear on 'varietal' labels, from Cabernet Sauvignon to Riesling. It may well be that the long process of selection for harder conditions has improved flavour as well as performance.

The degree of flavour depends more than anything on the quantity the vine is allowed to carry. Other things being equal five tons of grapes from one acre contain as much flavour as ten tons in half as much fruit. There is little doubt that the surprising concentration and lasting power of very old wine is at least partly due to much smaller crops.

Muscat-flavoured grapes are given a category of their own, so different is the muscat taste.

The fourth category is American: the wild vines of north America and their descendants, all of which are more or less 'foxy' in taste (see pages 242–243).

Grape breeders are constantly trying to find new varieties to improve on the old. The main centres of interest are hybrids between European and American vines, efforts in Germany to improve on the classic but difficult Riesling, and crosses in California designed to make good table wine in very hot conditions.

The original object of crossing American vines with French was to achieve a plant with built-in resistance to phylloxera (which American vines have) but with European-tasting grapes. These French-American hybrids, first developed in France by such breeders as Seyve-Villard, Baco and Seibel, are scorned in their native land, referred to as PDs (*producteurs directs*, since they are not grafted)

and banned from all Appellation Contrôlée areas – although still widely grown outside them. They have been welcomed, however, in many other countries for their hardiness and apparent potential for good, if not fine, wine. They are most used in the eastern States and Canada, and in England.

German breeders have been at work on the Riesling for a century. Müller-Thurgau made the first famous cross between the light-cropping, late-ripening Riesling and the early and prolific Silvaner. Today there is a growing catalogue of crosses of crosses, often between two or more selected clones of Riesling – even red Rieslings have been produced.

Some of the best of these are the Reichensteiner (which has French blood also), the Ehrenfelser (another Riesling × Silvaner; an improvement on Müller-Thurgau), Kerner (Riesling × the pale red Trollinger, giving fragrant and tasty wine), Bacchus and Optima (both Riesling × Silvaner × Müller-Thurgau; Optima being the better).

Meanwhile at Davis Dr Harold Olmo was developing several important new vines. His Emerald Riesling and Ruby Cabernet were

introduced in 1948 to give good balancing acidity in the hot San Joaquin valley. His later successful crosses used Cabernet Sauvignon × Carignan (the same as Ruby Cabernet) as a base and crossed it with Grenache ('Carnelian' and 'Centurion') or Merlot ('Carmine'). The first two make huge quantities: 11 or 12 tons to the acre. Carnelian is light wine; Centurion very heavy. Carmine is said to give wine like Cabernet Sauvignon, only twice as much of it.

It is easy to forget that a variety like the Pinot Noir, which has been in cultivation for centuries, has already naturally divided into many different 'clones'; some with more vigour, some ripening earlier; some with more flavour and aroma. When a winegrower goes to a nurseryman, therefore, for new plants, a good deal of the quality of his eventual wine is decided by the particular Pinot he chooses.

Today there is more emphasis than ever on the health of vines, although government programmes to stamp out viruses by heat treatment meet with mixed reactions. Some growers see virus stress as a quality factor. They also like the red leaves that viruses bring in the autumn.

MEASUREMENTS OF SUGAR-CONTENT

SPECIFIC GRAVITY	1.060	1.065	1.070	1.075	1.080	1.085	1.090	1.095	1.100	1.105	1.110	1.115	1.120	1.125
°OECHSLE	60	65	70	75	80	85	90	95	100	105	110	115	120	125
BAUMÉ	8.2	8.8	9.4	10.1	10.7	11.3	11.9	12.5	13.1	13.7	14.3	14.9	15.5	16.0
BRIX	14.7	15.8	17.0	18.1	19.3	20.4	21.5	22.5	23.7	24.8	25.8	26.9	28.0	29.0
% POTENTIAL ALCOHOL V/V	7.5	8.1	8.8	9.4	10.0	10.6	11.3	11.9	12.5	13.1	13.8	14.4	15.0	15.6

Each country has its own system for measuring the sugar content or ripeness of grapes, known as the 'must weight'. This chart relates the three principal ones: German (°Oechsle),

French (Baumé) and American (Brix) to each other, to specific gravity and to the potential alcohol by volume (v/v) of the resulting wine if all the sugar is fermented out.

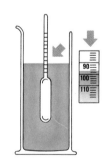

The grape's content of sugar and 'extract' measured by a hydrometer, left, is the first decisive factor for wine quality. A hydrometer is a float calibrated to show the specific gravity of a sugar and water solution at a certain temperature. (On page 161 a Rheinhessen grower is shown measuring the sugar content of his must with a hydrometer.)

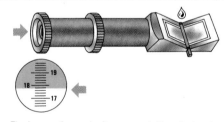

The ripeness of grapes is often measured with a refractometer. Light passing through a drop of juice held between two prisms bends at a different angle according to its sugar content. A scale, read through the eyepiece, gives the % of sugar in the juice.

WATER			70 - 85 %
EXTRACT		15 - 30 %	
CARBOHYDRATES		12 - 27 %	
PECTINS	0.01 - 0.10 %		
PENTOSANS	0.01 - 0.05 %		
INOSITAL	0.02 - 0.08 %		
ACIDS, TOTAL	0.3 - 1.5 %		
MALIC	0.1 - 0.8 %		
TARTARIC	0.2 - 1.0 %		
CITRIC	0.01 - 0.05 %		
TANNIN	0.0 - 0.2 %		
NITROGEN	0.01 - 0.20 %		
ASH	0.2 - 0.6 %		

This chart (adapted from 'Table Wines' by Amerine and Jocelyn) shows the proportions of different constituents of grape juice and the possible variations among more or less ripe grapes. Sugar and acid are the most important to a winemaker, but 'extract' —

other soluble solids — is also vital: the more the better. An ideal sugar/acid balance, according to a German rule of thumb, is 1 gram per 1,000 of acidity for each 10° Oechsle, e.g. sweet Ausleses at 90° would need 0.9 % acidity for perfect balance.

Silvaner (or Sylvaner) Germany's third grape after Müller-Thurgau and Riesling. Ripens early with big crops but only slight flavour, lacking Riesling's acidity. At its best in the dry Steinwein of Franken, when it can be superb. Also grown in Alsace, northern Italy and central Europe.

Sangiovese (or Sangioveto) is the principal red grape of Tuscany, and hence of Chianti. Only a moderate producer, rather late to ripen and without deep colour, but with good acid balance and pleasant flavour. One strain, the Brunello, is used alone to make the legendary Brunello di Montalcino, which ages, it seems, almost for ever.

Müller-Thurgau The historic forerunner of many crosses of Riesling with other grapes (here the Silvaner) and still one of the best German varieties. Now the chief grape in Rheinhessen, the Rheinpfalz, the Nahe, Baden and Franken. Its plentiful wine is highly aromatic, rather soft for lack of acid, never of Riesling standard, at its best when sweet.

Syrah (or Sérine) is the best red grape of the Rhône, making dark, tannic, long-lived Hermitage. As Shiraz it succeeds admirably in Australia, which has the largest planting – 21,000 acres (8,400 hectares) – and uses it for both table and dessert wines, blended or alone. Some of California's Petite Syrah may be the same, in which case it should have a great future.

Pinot Blanc A near relation to Chardonnay, grown with it in Burgundy and Champagne, but making wine with less character. Also much grown in N. Italy (where it makes the best dry sparkling wine), Alsace and central Europe. Its cousin Pinot Gris (Tokay in Alsace, Ruländer in Germany) has more personality, giving low-acid, blunt but pungent wine.

Merlot The noble cousin of the Cabernet grown in St-Emilion and Pomerol, ripening earlier than the Cabernet and giving softer, fleshier wine, which matures sooner. Used in the Médoc in a blend (up to 75%) with Cabernet and other grapes. Makes excellent wine in northeast Italy and good light wine in Italian Switzerland. Also good in cooler California regions.

Gewürztraminer is the spicy speciality of Alsace (where it occupies 20% of the vineyard). The most pungent wine grape, with rather small crops ripening early in the season. Called Savagnin in the Jura and used for *Vin Jaune*. Germany has a little, central Europe more. Can be excellent in California, Australia and New Zealand.

Palomino (or Listan) the great sherry grape, gives big quantities of rather neutral wine with low acidity which oxidizes easily. Widely grown in Australia, South Africa (where it is called White French) and California for sherry making, as well as Jerez (where it occupies 90% of the vineyard).

Folle Blanche A workhorse grape, once the third most widely grown white in France (after Sémillon and Ugni Blanc) but now in decline. Its aliases include Gros Plant (in Brittany) and Picpoul (in Armagnac and the Midi). Historically the great grape of Cognac, having ideal high acidity and little flavour, but now supplanted by Ugni Blanc. Promising in California.

Zinfandel Excellent red-wine grape peculiar to California, although it may be the same as the Primitivo of Puglia. Makes good lively fruity wine for drinking young, and can make top-quality, highly concentrated wine for long ageing, which at 50 years can taste like great Bordeaux. Likes a dry climate and gives best quality in cool areas (not the Central valley).

Welschriesling (or Wälsch-riesling, or Italian Riesling). The 'Riesling' of Austria, Yugoslavia, northern Italy and central Europe, giving good standard wine but never approaching real Riesling in quality. An early ripener and moderate cropper. The curious name 'Welsch' means 'foreign'. Since 1981, EEC law has banned the name 'Riesling', unqualified, for its wine.

Carignan By far the most common grape in France, where there are 511,000 acres (207,000 hectares), largely in the Midi. Makes huge quantities of harmless but dull red wine, low in acidity, extract and tannin, but useful for blending. Rots easily in wet weather, but much planted in Algeria, Spain and California. 'Ruby Cabernet' is a Carignan × Cabernet cross.

Kerner One of the new generation of German grapes produced by the Wine School at Geisenheim, a cross between Riesling and red Trollinger. Makes spicy, very fruity wine with good acidity, a bit blatant beside Riesling but a healthy reliable vine, increasingly used in Rheinhessen to make more exciting wine than the usual Müller-Thurgau.

Seyval Blanc (alias Seyve-Villard 5/276). One of the most successful of hybrids between French and American vines made by French breeder Seyve-Villard. The vine is very hardy and the wine attractively fruity, without a 'foxy' flavour. Banned from French Appellation areas, but winning converts to hybrids both in the eastern States and England.

Catawba Perhaps the most famous native American wine-grape, a chance cross of *Vitis labrusca*, which gives abundance of fruity, although strongly 'foxy', white or pale red wine. The mainstay of the mid-19th-century Ohio industry, whose Sparkling Catawba was world famous. Still popular in New York for sparkling wine; only the infamous Concord is more widely planted.

Wine and the Weather

The weather is the great variable in wine-growing. Every other major influence is more or less constant and known in advance. But in the end it is the weather that makes or breaks a vintage, so it receives constant study.

The vine is dormant from November to March in the northern hemisphere. Only an abnormally deep frost can harm it then. From the time it buds to the vintage in September or October, however, every drop of rain, hour of sunshine and degree of heat has its eventual effect on the quality and character of the crop.

The fine wines of northern Europe are those most affected by irregular weather. In the south and in the New World, vintages tend to be much more consistent. On these pages we look at some of the factors affecting France.

The chart at the bottom of this page shows the chief events in a vine's life cycle over 15 years in Bordeaux. There is a 38-day maximum variation in the starting and finishing of this cycle, and infinite variations in between, as the weather hurries it on or holds it back.

On the opposite page are isopleth graphs showing the average rainfall, temperature and sunshine for four wine regions of France. They prove nothing; but they provide a fascinating field of speculation into just what weather in what moment in a vine's cycle will result in a good or great vintage.

Hail and frost are the two most serious sudden weather hazards for winegrowers. Dramatic methods are used to combat them. Right: giant flame throwers heat the air on a frosty night in May (the tender new shoots of the vines can be seen). Below: an Australian grower prepares to fire a rocket into hail-bearing clouds to bring the hail down away from his vines.

A thorough study of this question in Burgundy was done by Rolande Gadille in her great book *Le Vignoble de la Côte Bourguignonne*, to which this atlas owes a considerable debt. The two lower graphs opposite show her plotting of the difference in reality over 17 years between good vintages, mediocre and the average; just where the weather changed to the benefit or detriment of the wine.

Frost in late spring and hail at any time are the grower's nightmares. Hail tends to be localized; one reason why growers like to have little holdings scattered all over the parish. A bad storm can not only wreck a vintage, but bruise the wood so as to affect next year's wine.

The determining factor for the quality of a northern vintage (in Burgundy, for instance, or Bordeaux) is the ripeness of the grapes. As a grape ripens its acidity decreases and its sugar increases. The primitive way of judging when to pick was to crush grapes in your hands; if they were sticky it was time. In the past the danger of a change in the weather (September rain bringing mildew) made growers often pick too soon, whereas today with chemicals and knowledge the vintage gets later and later.

It almost goes without saying that dry years are normally best. But the exact balance of importance between rain, sun, temperature and humidity has never been determined. What gives character to each individual vintage is the interaction between them: bright sunlight causing early ripening; overcast skies slowing growth but sometimes enriching the grapes with minerals which give the wine long life and complexity; high temperatures reducing acidity.

Even given exactly the same ripeness at picking, grapes reflect the year they have been through: scorching by sun or wind; too much vegetation (leaves and stems) or too little; mould resulting from damp ground or bruises

Left: the annual cycle of a Bordeaux Cabernet vine over 15 years. In late March or early April the buds break; between late May and mid-June the vines flower; between mid-July and mid-August the grapes 'set' – change from green to red. 100 days after flowering the grapes should be ripe. But the chart shows how widely the dates can vary. The three best vintages (1970, 75, 82) were all picked early, but the (very good) 78 was late from flowering to picking. From such different growth patterns Bordeaux vintages acquire their fascinating variations of style: no two are ever quite the same.

	BUD-BREAK		FLOWERING		GRAPES SET		VINTAGE	
	MARCH	APRIL	MAY	JUNE	JULY	AUGUST	SEPTEMBER	OCTOBER
WEEK: 1 2 3 4	1 2 3 4	1 2 3 4	1 2 3 4	1 2 3 4	1 2 3 4	1 2 3 4	1 2 3 4	1 2 3 4
1970		●		●		●	●	
1971		▼		▼		▼		▼
1972	▼			▼		▼		▼
1973		▼		▼		▼	▼	
1974		▼		▼	▼		▼	
1975		●		●		●	●	
1976		▼	▼		▼		▼	
1977	▼			▼		▼		▼
1978		●		●		●		●
1979		▼		●		●		●
1980		▼		▼			▼	▼
1981		●		●		●	●	
1982		●	●			●	●	
1983		●		●			●	●
1984		▼		▼		▼	▼	

● OUTSTANDINGLY GOOD VINTAGES

from hail. No two years are ever the same.

A grower can give a fair guess at vintage time at what the quality of his wine will be, weighing its ripeness against past experience. But there is always a good chance that weather factors he is unaware of have played a part. Two or three times in ten the spring after the vintage will bring him a surprise.

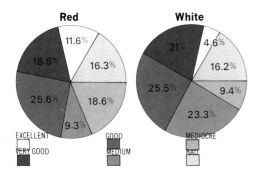

Red
- 11.6%
- 16.3%
- 18.6%
- 25.6%
- 9.3%
- 18.6%

EXCELLENT
VERY GOOD
GOOD
MEDIUM

White
- 4.6%
- 16.2%
- 9.4%
- 23.3%
- 25.5%
- 21%

MEDIOCRE
BAD

Above: white burgundy seems less affected by weather than red. Out of 43 vintages the white wines were outstandingly good or bad in only half; the reds divided almost equally into outstandingly good, bad or medium.

Below: the temperature and sunshine month by month in Burgundy are shown in relation to good, average and bad vintages. The important differences seem to be in midsummer temperature and spring sunshine. Bad vintages suffer cold at flowering time and never catch up.

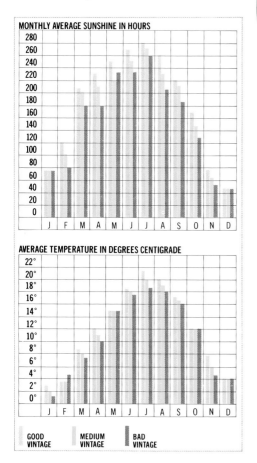

MONTHLY AVERAGE SUNSHINE IN HOURS

J F M A M J J A S O N D

AVERAGE TEMPERATURE IN DEGREES CENTIGRADE

J F M A M J J A S O N D

GOOD VINTAGE
MEDIUM VINTAGE
BAD VINTAGE

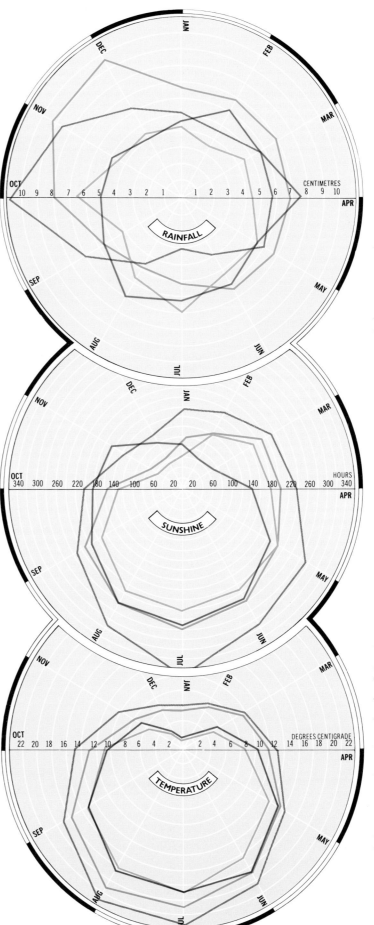

RAINFALL
SUNSHINE
TEMPERATURE

- CHAMPAGNE
- BORDEAUX
- MONTPELLIER
- BURGUNDY

Left: isopleth graphs show the year's weather as a continuous process in the four French wine regions marked on the map above.

Rainfall (top graph): sunshine and temperature come to a peak everywhere in midsummer; rainfall is more unpredictable. Bordeaux has a very wet winter, a comparatively rainy spring (flowering is in late May), but a long dry summer, growing wetter again, unfortunately for the vintage, in late September. Burgundy is dry in spring, wetter in summer but as dry as Bordeaux in early September. Champagne is wet in July but dry at vintage time.

Sunshine (left): all the regions get their maximum sunshine in July: the south by far the most all the year round. Bordeaux and Burgundy have curiously similar summer patterns from May to August, then Bordeaux has a distinctly sunnier end of season. Champagne has a good May, useful for the flowering of the vines.

Temperature (left): latitude is the chief factor. Only in June is Burgundy as warm as Bordeaux. By September it is getting cool in Champagne; by November both Burgundy and Champagne are really cold. Bordeaux stays almost as mild as the south all the winter. Regional temperature averages are the least accurate for any particular vineyard, since local altitude and exposure make wide variations, known as microclimates.

A Winemaker's Calendar

There is a job indoors in the cellar, and a job outdoors in the vines, for every day of a winemaker's year. Every district has different methods, and a different timetable, besides modern innovations. But this is the life of a typical traditional vigneron, somewhere in the heart of France . . .

JANUARY

Pruning Traditionally pruning started on St Vincent's Day, January 22nd. Nowadays it starts in December. If there is no snow the ground is often frozen. Vines will survive temperatures down to about −18°C (−0.4°F).

Barrels of new wine must be kept full to the top and their bungs wiped every other day with a solution of sulphur dioxide. In fine, dry weather, bottling of older wine can be done. Labelling and packing in boxes ready for shipment to customers.

FEBRUARY

Finish pruning and take cuttings for grafting. Make grafts onto rootstock and put them in sand indoors. Prepare machines for the outdoor work of the new season. Order copper sulphate for spraying.

Racking In fine weather with a new moon and a north wind (i.e. when there is high atmospheric pressure), start 'racking' the new wine into clean barrels to clear it. 'Assemble' the new wine in a vat to equalize the casks.

MARCH

Ploughing About mid-month the vine begins to emerge from dormancy; sap begins to rise; brown sheaths on buds fall off. Finish pruning. First working of the soil, deeply, to aerate it and uncover the bases of the vines.

Finish first racking before the end of the month. Some mysterious sympathy between vine and wine is supposed to start the second fermentation when the sap rises. Keep the casks topped up. Finish bottling.

JULY

Spray vines regularly with Bordeaux mixture. Third cultivation of the soil against weeds. Trim long shoots so that vines spend their energy on making fruit.

No shipping in hot weather. All efforts to keep cellar cool. In heatwaves, when close weather makes it necessary to shut doors at night, burn a sulphur candle. Vine growth slows down; bottling can start again when you have a spare moment.

AUGUST

Keep vineyards weeded and the vines trimmed. Black grapes turn colour. General upkeep and preparation of gear which will be needed for the vintage.

Inspect and clean vats and casks to be used for the vintage. Vine growth (and fermentation) starts again about mid-month so bottling must stop. Low-strength wine (being less stable) can turn in warm weather, so it must be carefully watched.

SEPTEMBER

Vintage Keep small boys and birds out of the vineyard. Keep vines trimmed, pray for sunshine. About the third week the grapes are ripe; the vintage begins. Activate your family.

Before the vintage scour out the cuvier where the wine will be made. Put anti-rust varnish on all metal parts of presses, etc. Fill fermenting vats with water to swell the wood and make them perfectly tight.

APRIL

Finish ploughing Clear up vineyard, burning any remaining prunings and replacing any rotten stakes. Plant one-year-old cuttings from the nursery. Pray for late vegetation, as frosts are frequent and hail (the grower's nightmare) possible.

Topping up must still go on. There must never be any ullage (empty space) in the cask. Five percent of the wine evaporates through the wooden sides of the barrel every year ('the angels' share').

MAY

Frost danger at its height. On clear nights stoves may be needed among the vines, which means sitting up to fuel them. Second working of the soil to kill weeds. Spray against oidium and mildew. Every ten days remove any suckers to encourage the sap to rise in the vines.

Send off orders to customers. Towards the end of May, just before vines flower, begin the second racking off the lees into clean barrels.

JUNE

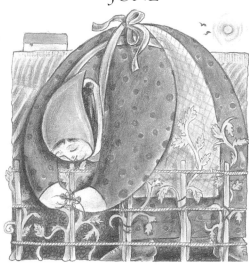

The vines flower at the beginning of June when the temperature reaches 18–20°C (65–68°F). Weather is critical: the warmer and calmer the better. After flowering, thin the shoots, tying the best ones to the wires. Spray for oidium with powdered sulphur.

Finish second racking of new wine and rack all old wines in the cellar. Evaporation is naturally accelerated by the warm weather; check all the casks for any weeping from between the staves.

OCTOBER

The vintage continues (see pages 34–35) for perhaps two weeks. When it is over, spread manure (pressed grape skins are good) and fertilizer on the vineyard. Deep-plough the land for new plantations.

New wine is fermenting. Year-old wine should be given a final racking, the barrels bunged tightly and rolled a quarter-turn so the bung is at the side. Move barrels to the second-year cellar to make room for the new wine.

NOVEMBER

Cut off long vine shoots and collect them for fuel. Finish manuring. Plough the vineyard to move soil over the bases of the vines to protect them from frost.

Bottling Rack and 'fine' (filter by pouring in whisked egg white which sinks to the bottom) wine to be bottled. In rich and ripe vintages rack new wine now; in poor ones leave it on the lees another month.

DECEMBER

If soil has been washed down slopes by rain it must be carried back up and redistributed. Pruning the vines can start before Christmas, on about December 15th.

Casks must be topped up frequently. More bottling of older wine can be done. Start tasting the new wine with old friends.

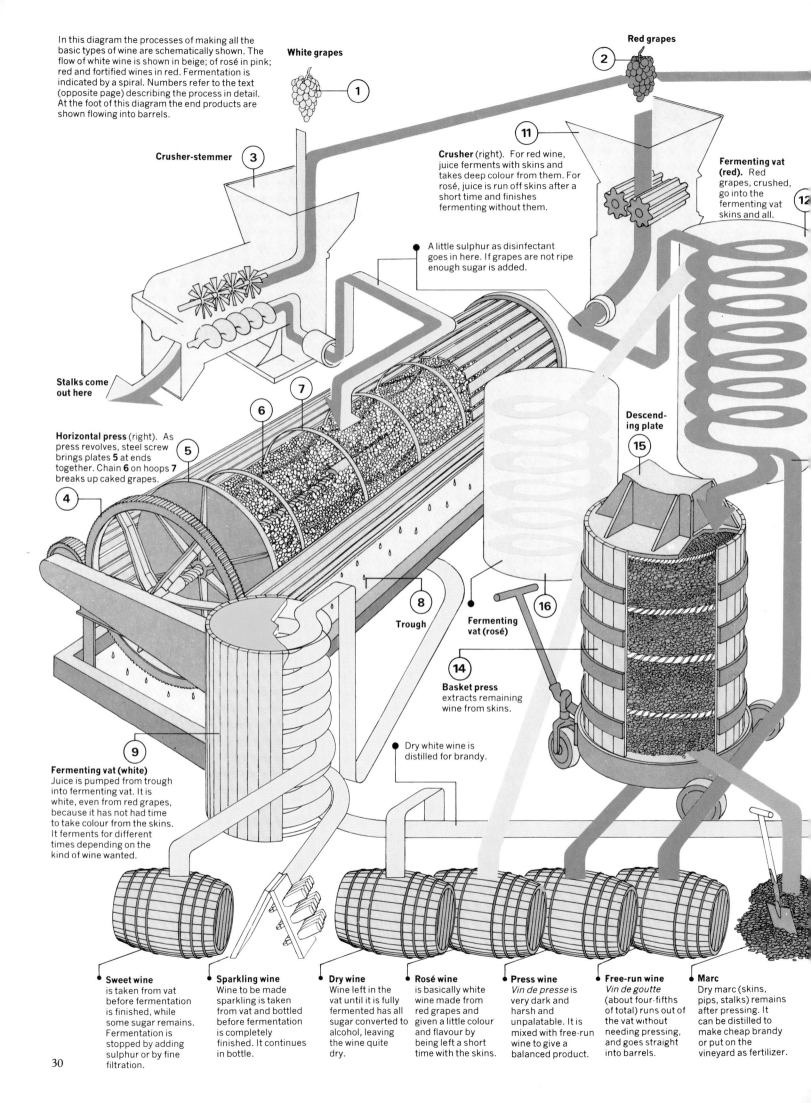

In this diagram the processes of making all the basic types of wine are schematically shown. The flow of white wine is shown in beige; of rosé in pink; red and fortified wines in red. Fermentation is indicated by a spiral. Numbers refer to the text (opposite page) describing the process in detail. At the foot of this diagram the end products are shown flowing into barrels.

White grapes ①

Red grapes ②

Crusher-stemmer ③

⑪ **Crusher** (right). For red wine, juice ferments with skins and takes deep colour from them. For rosé, juice is run off skins after a short time and finishes fermenting without them.

Fermenting vat (red). Red grapes, crushed, go into the fermenting vat skins and all.

⑫

A little sulphur as disinfectant goes in here. If grapes are not ripe enough sugar is added.

Stalks come out here

Horizontal press (right). As press revolves, steel screw brings plates **5** at ends together. Chain **6** on hoops **7** breaks up caked grapes.

④ ⑤ ⑥ ⑦

Descending plate ⑮

⑧ **Trough**

Fermenting vat (rosé) ⑯

⑭ **Basket press** extracts remaining wine from skins.

⑨

Fermenting vat (white)
Juice is pumped from trough into fermenting vat. It is white, even from red grapes, because it has not had time to take colour from the skins. It ferments for different times depending on the kind of wine wanted.

Dry white wine is distilled for brandy.

Sweet wine is taken from vat before fermentation is finished, while some sugar remains. Fermentation is stopped by adding sulphur or by fine filtration.

Sparkling wine Wine to be made sparkling is taken from vat and bottled before fermentation is completely finished. It continues in bottle.

Dry wine Wine left in the vat until it is fully fermented has all sugar converted to alcohol, leaving the wine quite dry.

Rosé wine is basically white wine made from red grapes and given a little colour and flavour by being left a short time with the skins.

Press wine *Vin de presse* is very dark and harsh and unpalatable. It is mixed with free-run wine to give a balanced product.

Free-run wine *Vin de goutte* (about four-fifths of total) runs out of the vat without needing pressing, and goes straight into barrels.

Marc Dry marc (skins, pips, stalks) remains after pressing. It can be distilled to make cheap brandy or put on the vineyard as fertilizer.

30

How Wine is Made

17 **Treading trough.**
Grapes for port are trodden to extract colour from skins.

18

Fermenting vat (port). Juice ferments until half its sugar is alcohol.

Free-run wine comes out without pressing.

Brandy is added to stun the yeast and stop fermentation.

10

Brandy
The product of distilling (see pages 288–289) wine is brandy. If grape skins (marc) are distilled the product is called marc.

Port
and most fortified wines and 'vins doux naturels' have their fermentation arrested with alcohol. They need ageing to 'marry' their different elements.

Above: a jar used for fermenting experimental lots of wine at Germany's Geisenheim Institute is closed with a bung containing an air-lock. Carbon dioxide bubbles out; air cannot get in.

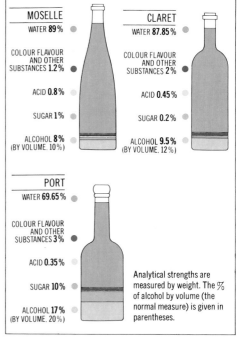

MOSELLE		CLARET	
WATER **89%**		WATER **87.85%**	
COLOUR FLAVOUR AND OTHER SUBSTANCES **1.2%**		COLOUR FLAVOUR AND OTHER SUBSTANCES **2%**	
ACID **0.8%**		ACID **0.45%**	
SUGAR **1%**		SUGAR **0.2%**	
ALCOHOL **8%** (BY VOLUME. 10%)		ALCOHOL **9.5%** (BY VOLUME. 12%)	

PORT	
WATER **69.65%**	
COLOUR FLAVOUR AND OTHER SUBSTANCES **3%**	
ACID **0.35%**	
SUGAR **10%**	
ALCOHOL **17%** (BY VOLUME. 20%)	

Analytical strengths are measured by weight. The % of alcohol by volume (the normal measure) is given in parentheses.

Above: the proportions of constituents in wines of three different types. The Moselle is an almost-dry white wine; a little sugar has been kept in it, probably by filtering the yeast out. The claret is a totally natural red wine. The brandy added to the port has increased its strength to 17°.

All that is needed to turn grape juice into wine is the simple, entirely natural process of fermentation. Fermentation is the chemical change of sugar into alcohol and carbon dioxide gas brought about by yeasts – micro-organisms which live (among other places) on grape skins. They need only to have the grape skin broken to go to work on the sugar which comprises about 30% of the pulp. And in an instant there is wine.

Under normal conditions the yeast will go on working until all the sugar in the grapes is converted into alcohol, or until the alcohol level in the wine reaches about 15% of the volume – on the rare occasions when the grapes are so sweet that this happens naturally, the yeast is overcome and fermentation stops.

Left to nature, therefore, almost all wine would be dry.

But it is possible to stop the fermentation before all the sugar is used up; either by adding alcohol to raise the level up to 15%, or by adding sulphur – both these anaesthetize the yeast – or by filtering the wine through a very fine filter to take the yeast out. These are the methods that are used to make sweet wine.

One wine differs from another first and foremost because of differences in the raw material, the grapes. But various ways of arranging the fermentation can produce all the other differences: between red, white, rosé, sweet, dry or sparkling. The diagram opposite shows how, starting with one basic material – red or white grapes – six quite distinct kinds of wine can be made.

White
Either white **1** or red **2** grapes are fed into a crusher-stemmer (or *égrappoir*) **3** which tears off the stalks and pumps the broken grapes into a horizontal press **4**. The press revolves as the steel screw brings the plates **5** at the ends together. Chains **6** and hoops **7** break up the caked grapes. The skins (marc) are left behind as the must (fresh juice) falls into a trough **8** from which it is pumped into a fermenting vat **9** after which several courses are open to it. It may be made into sweet wine by having its fermentation stopped while it still contains sugar, or bottled before fermentation is finished, to make sparkling wine.

Or it may be fermented until all its sugar is used up, to make dry wine. And finally, the dry wine may be distilled **10** to make brandy.

Red
Red grapes **2** are fed through a crusher **11** (or often a crusher-stemmer) and pumped into a vat **12** where they ferment with their skins. Traditionally the stalks go in too but they are usually removed today. The wine gradually draws out the colour and tannin from the skin. Fermentation is allowed to go on until all sugar is gone (up to 14 days). Then the tap is opened and the 'free-run' wine **13** is run off. For lighter, quicker-maturing wine the modern practice is to take the wine off the

skins after a few days to finish fermenting separately. The skins are pressed in a hydraulic basket press **14** by a descending plate **15** which forces the juice out through slatted sides. Layers of matting help juice run out. This press wine (*vin de presse*), deeply coloured and tannic, is usually mixed with the free-run wine. The 'marc' left in the press is used as fertilizer or distilled to make cheap brandy.

Rosé
Red grapes **2** are fed through a crusher **11** and straight into a vat **12** complete with their skins to begin fermentation. The juice for rosé wine takes a light pink colour from the skins but almost

immediately it is run off into another vat **16** to ferment without them. Normally it is allowed to finish fermentation naturally, and is thus completely dry.

Port
(the process is similar for other fortified wines) Red grapes **2** are put in a stone trough **17** and continuously trodden with bare feet for 12 hours to make the juice take the colour of the skins. The juice is run into a vat **18** to ferment until half its sugar is converted to alcohol, when it is mixed with brandy from the still **10** to raise the alcohol level to above 15%. This stuns the yeast and stops fermentation, so the wine is both strong and sweet.

31

The Art of the Winemaker

The previous two pages showed the simple steps that are common to all winemaking. Twenty-five years ago there was not much else to be done: you made your wine, more or less carefully and skilfully with better or worse grapes, and then waited to see how it would turn out.

The best wines of the classic French and German regions are still, on the whole, made in the same spirit. One of the reasons for the emergence of these very regions is that natural conditions (autumn and winter temperatures, for example) provide natural controls. The winemaker in such cases sees himself more as midwife than creator.

What has changed radically is the making of wine in warmer regions, where however good the grapes it was rarely possible in the past to make outstanding wine. Italy, the south of France, California, Australia, much of Spain, South Africa, Chile and Argentina are all examples.

With modern knowledge the winemaker no longer merely watches – he controls. Technology supplies him with a vast range of alternatives. And as he controls, so at every stage of the process he must decide.

His decisions start with the fruit in the vineyard. When to pick it. Hazards of weather apart, as it ripens its balance of sugar, acids, extracts and water alters daily. *Force majeure* may make him take grapes when he can get them, but a winemaker in full control can take his idea of the wine he wants to make into the vineyard with him, analyse the grapes as they hang on the vine and calculate how the wine will be if he picks today – or tomorrow.

Having chosen his moment, even his time of day to pick (early morning picking in hot weather gets the grapes into the vat cooler, which can make a difference to freshness and aroma), the winemaker will inspect the grapes as they come in. If he finds many of them underripe, overripe or rotten he must decide whether to include them or throw them out (an expensive decision). Whichever he decides will affect the character of the wine.

For white wine he may believe in separating the juice from the skins immediately; or he may think it is better to let them separate gently and naturally; or he may want to leave them in contact for a while.

In the first case he can press the grapes straight away (with or without their stalks; the stalks make pressing easier but can give the wine a stalky flavour) and then use a centrifuge, which separates the clear liquid from the remaining suspended solids instantly, expensively, and some say too violently. Another alternative is to dispense with the press and use a 'drag-screen', which pulls the crushed grapes over a mesh, letting the liquid drop through.

In the second case he can again crush the grapes but not press them, leave them in a vat with a draining vent at the bottom while the liquid runs out naturally, then press the remaining solids. Some think this 'free-run' wine is always better. Certainly it is lighter, more limpid, quicker-maturing. But it lacks the tannin that gives pressed wine a more stable structure, more resistance to oxidation and a

Above: control panels now allow one man to operate a whole winery at vintage time simply by pressing buttons. This is the degree of change that has overtaken the wine industry in the last 20–30 years.

Right: the photograph of naked men breaking up the 'cap' of skins in a fermenting vat (from the Musée des Arts et Traditions Populaires) was taken in Burgundy as recently as the 1950s.

longer life . . . hence more opportunity to grow complex and interesting as it matures.

The third method is traditional in hot areas where the grapes lack acid: by macerating in the juice (even in some places briefly fermenting in the juice) the skins give tannin and aroma to wine that would otherwise be too soft and oxidize too easily. This treatment gives certain Italian wines – Frascati, for example – their peculiar grape-skin character.

The next stage is fermentation. Traditionally, for certain strong, high-flavoured wines (white burgundy, for example) this is done in small oak barrels, which give a noticeable taste of oak to the wine. Modern practice is almost always to ferment in concrete, stainless steel or glass- or tile-lined vats. The first decision here is what yeast to use. 'New World' wineries almost always prevent any 'wild' yeasts on the

grapes from starting the fermentation (a strong dose of sulphur dioxide, wine's all-purpose antiseptic, does this). Instead they choose a pure yeast culture. The vineyards of Europe, by contrast, generally have a sufficient natural population of benevolent yeasts to start the fermentation without help.

The second decision is the temperature of the fermentation. In a warm climate, without control, fermenting wine will get hotter and hotter until the yeasts can no longer multiply and the fermentation 'sticks' – which can easily lead to vinegar. Modern practice is to ferment white wine very cool (at about 15.5°C, or 60°F). Cold fermentation takes a long time – four to six weeks and even more. Some winemakers take it faster and warmer, others even slower.

If the winemaker wants a very delicate, grapey wine he will take every precaution to

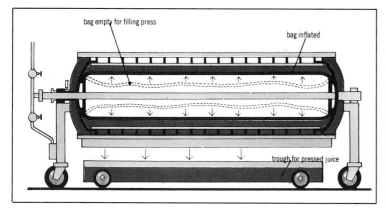

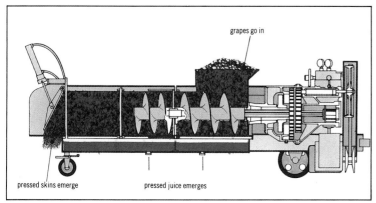

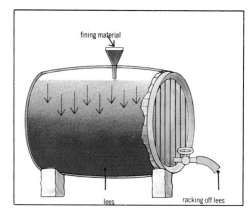

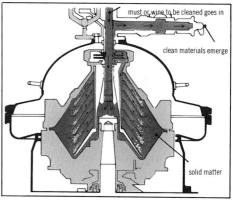

Left and below left: how the grapes are pressed affects both the quality and quantity of the wine. The air-bag press, in which a huge balloon is inflated, squeezing the grapes against the slatted sides of a cylinder, is gentle but slow. The quality is high, but each batch must be filled and emptied by hand. The continuous press is faster but can be brutal, grinding skins and crushing pips, unless it is run slowly and at low pressure.

Above right and right: good wine 'falls bright' (i.e. clarifies itself) naturally. The traditional way of giving it a final polish is by 'fining' and 'racking'. Fining consists of pouring beaten egg whites, ox blood or isinglass into the barrel; as it sinks it carries all suspended solids with it. The clear wine is then 'racked' off the residue at the bottom. The centrifuge, right, is a modern method of separating solids.

keep oxygen away from it at every stage. For example, he will fill a tank with carbon dioxide gas before he pumps the wine in and keep a 'blanket' of the gas in the space at the head of the vat all the time. This has the added advantage of preventing the natural carbon dioxide, dissolved in the wine after fermentation, from escaping into the air. A little carbon dioxide gives white wine a pleasant freshness, a faint prickle on the tongue, especially valuable when it is low in acid.

It is common practice today to adjust the acidity in warm areas by adding either tartaric acid before fermentation or citric acid after. It would be nice if it were not necessary, but since both these acids are natural components of wine no one can object to their being boosted. Sugar, after all, is often added in France.

As soon as fermentation is finished the wine must be syphoned ('racked') off the lees, the dead yeast cells and other solids at the bottom of the container. There is a natural tendency in most wines to start fermenting again soon after. This 'secondary' or 'malolactic' fermentation is, in fact, the action of bacteria which feed on the malic (apple) acid and convert it to lactic (milk) acid, which is less sharp to taste. In cool areas with acid wines, malolactic fermentation is a boon: it softens the sharpness of the wine, and also contributes in ways which are not fully understood to its general complexity and distinction. Low-acid, hot-country wines, however, need to keep all the acidity they have, and the winemaker must decide whether he wants secondary fermentation or not. If not, he can stop it by keeping the

sulphur dioxide level in the wine high (it constantly drops as the SO_2 combines with other elements and needs replenishing) and by frequent racking (or rapid sterile bottling).

Does the winemaker want a freshly grapey, pale wine? He must keep it protected from air until it is bottled. Does the wine have the strength and potential to mature into something rich and deep? He has a choice of containers to keep it in, allowing just enough interaction with the air for it to mature. California winemakers have recently made remarkable discoveries about the different ways different oak barrels act on wine. They have tried oak of various French forests, traditionally used in Bordeaux and Burgundy, as well as Balkan and American white oak. Each has a subtly different effect on the taste and texture of the wine. This is another decision the winemaker can take.

I have not mentioned the choice of whether the white wine is to be dry or sweet. If sweet wine is wanted, there is a choice of ways of stopping the fermentation from using up all the sugar. There is also the alternative, commonly used in Germany, of adding sweet unfermented grape juice to a dry wine.

Nor have I discussed the similar range of alternatives in making red wine – of which perhaps the most crucial is the length of the fermentation of juice and skins together. The modern tendency is to try to get as much colour from the skins as possible with as little tannin. Tannin is the awkward element, the natural preservative which tastes hard and harsh itself but without which no red wine can keep long

enough to mature. In the last decade or so very short fermentations have been in vogue. Winemakers have felt that the public does not understand the hard taste of new red wine and has no patience to keep it for maturing. But they are beginning to realize that there is no shortcut: two or three days may be long enough to give a fine red tint to the juice (there is even a 'heat treatment' practised to extract the colour quickly), but ten days' slow fermenting at about 24°C (about 75°F) is what is needed for deep colour and long-lasting, satisfying wine.

One interesting alternative method of fermenting red wine has long been practised in Beaujolais and is gaining ground elsewhere, particularly in the south of France. It is to put the whole bunches of grapes, uncrushed, stalks and all, into a closed vat full of carbon dioxide. A different sort of fermentation starts inside the grapes, extracting the skin colour internally and eventually bursting the berry. This carbonic maceration makes well-coloured, very aromatic, soft-flavoured wine, but with limited possibilities for maturing.

Even when the wine is ready for bottling there are decisions to make. The safe course to ensure shining and brilliant wine is to strain it through a fine filter. But filters remove flavour as well as specks and motes. Ideal wine eventually 'falls bright' in the barrel without special treatment, or by simple 'fining' with beaten egg whites. At this stage, as at every other, the less the wine can be manipulated the better. The ultimate art of the oenologist is to know when to do nothing.

Anatomy of a Château

Compared with modern industrial wine-making, the routine at a Bordeaux château, reasonably typical of the whole of France, seems as natural and uncomplicated as any traditional harvest scene. The grapes are simply picked, destalked, crushed; the rest is nature . . . but nature kept under careful watch, with discreet adjustments where necessary.

Château Lynch-Bages at Pauillac in the Médoc is typical of the long-established *cru classé* which retains its traditional equipment while using the prosperity of recent years to update its winemaking methods, mainly in terms of convenience, hygiene and precise control.

Stainless-steel vats (much easier to clean, and to cool, than oak) are installed to take over from what is rapidly becoming a museum piece in the Médoc: the old-world oak *cuvier*, or vat room.

The time-honoured technique is simple: the wine is made in oak vats in the *cuvier*. It ferments for about ten days before it is run off the skins and the skins are pressed. If the weather is too hot and the fermentation generates too much heat, it must be cooled by hosing down the *cuves* with water, or even (in emergencies) throwing blocks of ice in them. One of the major advantages of steel vats is that they conduct heat perfectly: a stream of cold water down the sides is highly effective.

From the *cuvier* the wine is pumped into another vat, formerly cement, now stainless steel, for two weeks before it is *débourbé* – pumped off its heaviest sediment into another tank. In this it spends the winter, going through its gentle secondary or malolactic fermentation which rids it of malic acid, making it less harsh. Traditionally, secondary fermentation does not start until March, when the sap rises in the vines, but modern practice brings it forward. In February the wine is pumped into *barriques* (hogsheads) in the first-year *chai*.

It stays here for a year, being constantly topped up and occasionally 'racked' into a fresh barrel; in some years going on fermenting slightly through the summer.

In the following year it is moved into the second-year *chai*, where it is bunged tight and left to mature until, after two years, it is ready for bottling. Today all bottling is done at the château with a permanent bottling line. But the bottle cellar has an important role as well: no good red Bordeaux is ready to drink before it has been in bottle at least two years.

Château Lynch-Bages, classified as a fifth-growth in 1855, has long been considered as better than its rank, making some of the most full-flavoured and vigorous wine of Pauillac. The house, built in 1830, is modest compared with some more voguish mansions, but its *cuvier* and *chais* are on the grand scale necessary for 170 acres (70 hectares) of vines. Wine from its younger vines is sold under a 'second label': Château Haut-Bages-Averous.

Pickers **1** use secateurs; they are often students and earn 120 francs a day plus keep for about two weeks of very hard work. The grapes are collected from them in tubs on a horse-cart or tractor-trailer.

The old system was to hoist the heavy tubs of grapes up to a floor that was level with the tops of the fermenting vats **2**. They were dumped into a trolley on rails, then wheeled to the vat to be filled.

From the trolley they were loaded into a turbine-like *fouloir-égrappoir* **3** to be crushed and stripped of their stalks, then tipped or pumped into the vat. The fermenting vat is filled four-fifths full to allow room for seething movement.

Remontage **4**. Every morning and evening the fermenting wine is pumped up and sprayed over the floating 'cap' of skins. In fine years it is pumped via an open tub for aeration.

When fermentation is complete the 'free-run' wine is drained from the tank. The residue of skins is pumped into a container on rails **5** and wheeled to a hydraulic press.

The hydraulic press **6** will press the skins to extract the remaining one-fifth of the wine after the rest has been run off (see pages 30–31). A little of the deeply coloured *vin de presse* is mixed with the rest.

Stainless-steel *cuves* **7** hold the new wine over the winter while it undergoes secondary (malolactic) fermentation and rids itself of heavy sediment.

The first-year *chai* **8**. New wine is pumped into oak hogsheads and stoppered with loose glass bungs. At some châteaux wine goes straight into barrels; here it waits until the following February.

The second-year *chai* **9**. *Barriques* (which hold 24 dozen bottles) are moved here after a year to make room for the next vintage.

All bottling is done in this bottling room **10** using modern equipment.

The office and tasting room **11**. Its walls are lined with plans showing every barrel and every vine. Here at vintage time the *maître de chai* measures the basics (sugar content, acidity) of the new vintage, and *courtiers* (brokers) arrive to form their first impressions of its quality and quantity.

After bottling, wine at a château of this quality is immediately labelled and packed in wooden boxes of 12 bottles, six magnums or smaller numbers of bigger bottles **12**.
About half the wine is usually sold in a first 'tranche' in the spring after the harvest. By the time it is bottled most has been sold and will be delivered to the buyer without delay.

Barns **13** hold the château's agricultural equipment, including the high tractors that straddle the vine rows.

The vineyard **14**, 70% Cabernet Sauvignon, 15% Merlot, with lesser amounts of Cabernet Franc, Malbec and Petit Verdot, spreads around the château in a solid block on a relatively high plateau of very gravelly clay soil.

The bottle cellar **15** under the house has examples of the château's and its neighbours' wines going back 50 years.

Anatomy of a Winery

Most modern wine is made in what amounts to a wine factory: in western Europe most commonly a cooperative owned by the farmers (and their bank); in eastern Europe by the State; in the New World more often by a public or private company.

The term winery is not particularly appealing, and indeed the biggest wineries resemble oil refineries more than part of an essentially agricultural operation. Even in the New World, though, some wineries have a history as long as most Bordeaux châteaux.

The fairly typical mid-sized California winery here is based on Simi, a century-old foundation near Healdsburg in Sonoma, but keeping little from the past except its splendid great stone and redwood barn beside the railroad track that used to bear away its produce. Its cavernous ground floor still contains tall redwood vats, useful short-term containers but now largely superseded by stainless steel. Two immensely strong floors above them support the barrels for fermenting and maturing the best qualities of wine.

All the new buildings are designed on the dominant principle of a modern winery: flexibility. It must be able to handle different grapes from different sources and turn them into different kinds of wine. In contrast to the château on the preceding pages, which follows a single-minded course year after year, a winery may make a dozen different wines, reproducing the conditions (in European terms) of Bordeaux, Burgundy, Alsace, the Rhine and perhaps Spain or Portugal or Italy under one roof. Most wineries keep their options as open as possible to adapt to the market. The best (Simi among them) limit themselves today to half a dozen wines or less. Specialization is on the increase.

Efficiency in a winery includes having the longest possible winemaking season, using its presses and fermenting vats continually from the arrival of 'precocious' grapes in early autumn to the latest ripeners, after the first frosts. Ideally its sources of grapes, therefore, include farmers growing many different kinds, or with widely different ripening conditions. At least one new winery saves fermenting capacity by chilling the whole crop and fermenting it in batches all the year round.

1 Grapes are delivered from local vineyards by tractor and 'gondola', or distant ones by trucks hauling 25 tons. They are tipped into a pit and carried by Archimedean screw **2** to the de-stemmer and crusher **3**.

The crushed white grapes are pumped into 'de-juicing' or draining tanks **4** to separate the best-quality 'free-run' juice. Crushed red grapes are pumped straight to fermentation tanks **5**.

The white solids (skins, or 'pomace') from the draining tank are pressed within a few hours of picking **6**. Reds ferment, are then drained of 'free-run' wine, then their pomace is pressed in horizontal presses **7** and the dry pomace blown by compressed air to a waiting truck **8**.

Redwood 'uprights' are the traditional California holding tanks **9**. The wood has no effect on the taste of the wine.

S BIESTY

High-quality reds and certain white wines are given from a few months' to two years' ageing in French or American oak barrels **10** depending on the degree and type of oak fragrance desired in the wine. The barrels are stacked with space between them for ease of access.

In the tasting room and laboratory **11** the winemaker keeps a constant check on the progress of each of many lots of wine, including detailed chemical analysis.

The bottling line **12** can handle up to 55 bottles a minute. Bottles arrive already in cartons, are taken out, filled and put back, then stacked on palettes ready for dispatch.

The filter area **13**. Most wine is fine-filtered before bottling. A little unfiltered wine is sometimes kept for wine lovers who value flavour more than perfect clarity.

Barrels are filled, emptied and cleaned in this roofed-over yard **14**.

The winery needs substantial storage **15** for bottled and packed wine, normally giving it at least several months' bottle-age before releasing it.

Beside the maintenance building **16** is the weighbridge **17** for checking in the arriving grapes on their trucks.

Reception and tasting rooms **18** occupy this building. Visitors are encouraged to tour the winery and taste. Most wineries sell direct to private buyers as well as wholesale. Appearances are important.

19 Most wineries own at least some vines, but for many they produce a small proportion of the grapes they use. The rest are bought from specialist farmers. Mechanical harvesting is becoming standard practice in much of California.

A laboratory and computer room **20** control the condition and whereabouts of hundreds of different batches of wine from fermentation to bottling and dispatch. Record keeping is a vast but essential task.

Stainless-steel tanks **21** can be used for both fermentation and storage, which increases the winery's capacity. The Simi winery stores one million gallons, yet is still among the smaller ones. A vast variety of tank sizes gives flexibility for handling big or small lots of wine.

Many modern wineries dispense with roofs and build stainless-steel tanks for fermentation and storage in the open air. Their great bulk and a jacket of circulating cooling fluid keep them at the ideal temperature in any weather.

Wine and Time

Louis Pasteur, born at Dôle in the Jura in 1822, was the first scientist to turn his mind to wine. He discovered that yeast causes fermentation, as well as other facts of enormous importance to winemakers.

In these hand-coloured illustrations from his *Etudes sur le Vin*, Pasteur recorded the effect of time and oxygen on red and white wine.

Far left: Pasteur found that red wine without air did not change colour. Left: with air it faded.

Left: white wine without air was unchanged. Right: with air it grew brown.

Some wines are ready to drink as soon as they are made. Others improve immeasurably by being kept for even as much as 50 years. As a general rule these *vins de garde* are the better. But why? And why is it that such a mystique attaches to an old bottle of wine?

Most white wines, rosé wines and such light reds as Beaujolais and Valpolicella are at their best young. The pleasure in them is a matter of grapiness and freshness. We want them to be close to fresh fruit; direct in scent and flavour.

The great white wines and most of the best reds, however, are grown to be as full of their own particular character as possible. There resides in them when young an unresolved complex of principles: of acids and sugars, minerals and pigments, esters and aldehydes and tannins. Good wines have more of these things than ordinary wines, and great wines more than good wines. Which is why, in the end, they have more flavour. But it takes time for these elements to resolve themselves into a harmonious whole and for the distinct scent of maturity, called (by analogy with flowers) the bouquet, to form. Time, and oxygen.

It was not until Louis Pasteur was asked by Napoleon III in 1863 to find out why so much wine went bad on its way to the consumer, to the great harm of French trade, that the role of oxygen was discovered. Pasteur established that too much contact with the air allows the growth of vinegar bacteria. On the other hand he found that it was very slight amounts of oxygen that makes wine mature; that the oxygen's action is not 'brusque' but gradual, and that there is enough of it dissolved in a bottle of wine to account for an ageing process lasting for years. He showed, by sealing wine in test tubes, alternately full and half-full, that oxygen in the air of the half-full tube caused the same deposit in a few weeks as is found in very old bottles, and that it affected colour in exactly the same way as extreme old age.

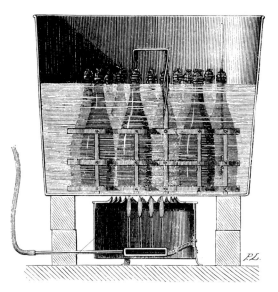

Above: Pasteur's original diagram of his method of 'pasteurizing' wine by heating it in hot water.
Right: a Roman bottle of wine, now in Speyer museum. Air is kept from the wine by a layer of oil on top.

In fact he immensely speeded up the process that happens in a bottle: the oxygen in the wine acts on its constituents to mature them, but beyond the period of maturity it continues to act; from then on the wine deteriorates.

Pasteur found that even wine that is carefully kept from the air has opportunities to absorb oxygen: when it is being racked from one barrel to another; even through the staves of the barrel (so that their thickness, whether or not they are encrusted with tartrate crystals, the capacity of the barrel, whether it stood in a draught, all become relevant). He told the story of a painted cask at the Clos de Vougeot whose wine always tasted a year or two younger than wine from the others that were unpainted.

If wine in barrels is more subject to the action of oxygen it also has the wood itself as an agent for change. It picks up certain characteristics – extra tannin, and vanillin, which gives a vanilla flavour, particularly to spirits – from the oak. Oxygen and oak together age wine far faster than it will age in bottle.

Left too long in a barrel a light wine fades rapidly: its colour goes, its fruitiness disappears, it starts to taste dry, flat and insipid. The same wine bottled after a year or less will keep the colour, the fruit and the acidity, and last (and perhaps improve) for several more years.

The question on every wine lover's lips is: 'when will this wine be at its best?'

For most everyday-quality wines the answer is the simplest possible: now. If freshness and fruitiness is the charm of the wine there is no object in keeping it – except to find out what takes the place of the freshness when it goes.

It would be a logical and desirable development to abandon the traditional cork for this class of wine and use screwstoppers, which suggest that there is nothing to wait for: the product is ready to be consumed. The air of permanence about a cork can be misleading. Since there is a world shortage of good

cork, it should be kept for wines that need it.

There is no English equivalent to the French term *vins de garde* for wines that need 'laying down' to achieve their full potential. We know which they are by experience, tradition – and price: high price takes into account a long potential life span in which the asset can increase in value.

We know which they are – but not how long to keep them. Convention can only give the vaguest guidance: '. . . at its best between five and fifteen years'. For awkward as it is, every wine and every vintage has its own time scale. The same red burgundy of 1982 and 1983 will be at its best three years after the vintage (the '82) or (the '83) at perhaps thirteen.

The deciding factors are ripeness and concentration. Can they not be measured? They can, of course; yet even such measurement is no clear guide to the future. A *vin de garde* goes through a number of stages in its maturation.

The duration of each stage is one of the most unpredictable things about wine.

A graph to express the improvement of flavour may climb steeply at first, then flatten out, climb and flatten out again . . . it may even dip at certain points over a number of years.

The graph for another vintage of the same wine may climb very slowly, may take eight or nine years to reach a plateau, then hold a level or only edge imperceptibly upwards for another ten years. Even at 20 years the future is not certain. There are wines that keep an equilibrium for decades, and others that grow sharp or dry and dismal, losing their vitality and the sweet taste of fruit without warning after a long plateau of excellence.

The vintage charts on pages 53–56 offer a degree of guidance as to how long the wines of recent vintages may benefit from keeping. With true *vins de garde* the verdict is never in until the last bottle has been opened.

The Price of Wine

When the brokers of Bordeaux set out to establish the famous 1855 classification of the Médoc they took as their guide the prices fetched by the different châteaux over the previous hundred or so years. They were safe in assuming that something for which the world is consistently prepared to pay more for so long must be better.

Things are more confused today. The 'great' wines are bought more for their reputations than for their quality. Their high price, in fact, has become the reason for buying them.

The advertising of brands similarly distorts prices: so much is for the wine in the bottle, so much for the feeling of confidence because it has been on television.

Recently the cost of the non-wine elements attaching themselves to a bottle (that is the bottle itself, the cork, label, handling and shipping, not to mention financing) have risen much faster than the price of the almost insignificant commodity inside. When taxes are taken into account a tiny proportion of the

cost (to the consumer) of a bottle of ordinary wine is for the actual wine – a prima facie case for buying better wine.

Information about the price of wine is scattered in relevant places throughout the Atlas. On this page are some examples of the way in which wine prices have fluctuated over recent years.

The graphs plot the retail prices of ten representative wines over the last 15 years at one of the world's most famous wine retailers – Berry Bros & Rudd of St James's Street, London. Customs duties, the only factor that would make them different from prices in comparable shops anywhere in the world, have been subtracted. The wines chosen are of currently mature vintages for the year in question. Although inflation is the keynote, one can see in them the influence of fashion and the quality of vintages. Most revealing of all is to compare them with the British retail prices index, the last graph. It can be seen that in relation to most other goods the prices of

several wines have actually come down considerably in the last few years.

First-growths of Bordeaux, and the leading white burgundies (the figures are for Corton-Charlemagne) lead the field. The price of the second-growth Bordeaux has ridden up on the coat-tails of the first-growths. Looking at figures compiled for previous editions of this Atlas, second-growths climbed only slowly until 1973, while the first-growths leapt ahead in the investment craze of the early 1970s. Recently, vintage port has put on a spurt, and red burgundy, although not as expensive as the top whites, has increased at a faster rate.

The champagne price (for a non-vintage famous brand) reflects in its fluctuations the varying harvests, and the swings in the world's economic mood, of the past few years.

There are a very few German wines whose graphs would be more like that of Lafite. But who would have suspected the steadiness of price of good everyday German wine? Or, indeed, of Scotch whisky?

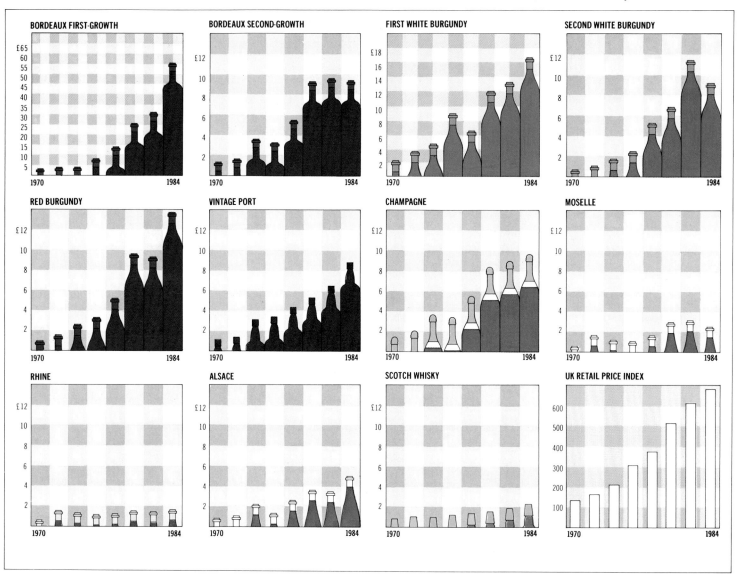

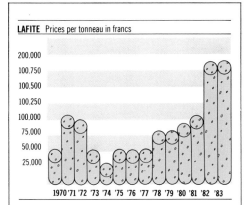

LAFITE Prices per tonneau in francs

200.000
100.750
100.500
100.250
100.000
75.000
50.000
25.000

1970 '71 '72 '73 '74 '75 '76 '77 '78 '79 '80 '81 '82 '83

The graphs above and below vividly illustrate the boom in Bordeaux prices in the early 1970s, the reaction that followed, and the recovery prompted by the run of good vintages in the early 1980s.

Above are prices at the château (given in francs per tonneau, although all serious claret is now sold in bottle) for the first-growth Château Lafite. Below are the prices for a first-class Cru Bourgeois (Château d'Angludet). Through the 1960s, until 1968, both prices had held remarkably steady, with the Cru Bourgeois at around a quarter of the first-growth price. Then the failure of the 1968s and the small size of the 1969 vintage coincided with growing American demand. In 1970, the economics of scarcity took over. The price of Lafite doubled in a year between the 1970 and 1971 vintages. D'Angludet kept pace, doubling although at a much lower level.

The boom reached a peak with the small 1971 vintage, and the plentiful 1972, poor though it was. Then in 1973 came war in the Middle East. Suddenly everyone wondered who was going to drink all this expensive wine. The bubble burst, with the big vintages of 1973 and 1974 helping to force prices down. It was not until 1981 that Lafite again commanded its 1971 price. The fame of the 1982 and 1983 vintages drove prices up once more.

In contrast, the Cru Bourgeois price rose and dipped less dizzily. The ratio between its price and that of the first-growth, back to about 1:4 in the mid-1970s, has opened up again.

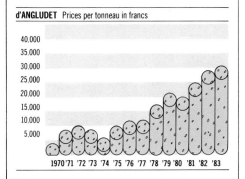

d'ANGLUDET Prices per tonneau in francs

40.000
35.000
30.000
25.000
20.000
15.000
10.000
5.000

1970 '71 '72 '73 '74 '75 '76 '77 '78 '79 '80 '81 '82 '83

Auction prices give the clearest idea of the relative values put on wine on the open market. In 1966 Christie's, the London fine-art auction house, restarted the practice of auctioning wine (which they originally began in the 18th century). The tables show the movements of the prices of fine claret and vintage port over the years 1971–84. The claret prices represent the figures achieved by a dozen of the top châteaux, including all the first-growths, from the 13 most successful post-World War II vintages. The port prices are similarly based on the prices reached by wines from nine leading shippers

The tables clearly show the dramatic leap in the 'silly' season of 1972–73, when wine suddenly became a fashionable commodity for investment (there was even talk of 'holding portfolios' of wine; a perversion that was then mercifully shortlived but which emerged again in 1984 and 1985). A flood of wine from overstocked speculators brought prices down to their 1972 levels in 1974. Since then, prices have risen steadily to, in the case of the claret index, more than ten times their 1971 level.

The rise in prices has been matched by a rise in the level of activity. More and more wine is being sold at auction, often with the wine itself lying overseas when sold. In addition, important cellars of old wines are sent to London for sale from all over the world. Since the majority of buyers are overseas as well, London has a unique situation in the world of wine as the place where values are established.

Claret and vintage port are always the most popular wines at auction for at least two reasons. First because they mature more slowly than any other wines, and therefore have a longer life in which they can safely be bought and sold. Secondly because they are clearly identifiable and easily understood: almost, in fact, a negotiable currency. There is only one Château Latour 1961 or Croft 1963. In contrast there are a dozen different growers of Chambertin and no accepted touchstone for distinguishing between them. Moreover, modern burgundy cannot be relied on to keep for long in bottle.

One might hazard that German wines (except the very finest and rarest) suffer from similar disadvantages. Certainly their average lot values (not shown) follow the same pattern as burgundy rather than claret. Their bottle-life is considered – often wrongly – to be short, and the sheer complications of their naming system deters the majority of potential bidders. Beerenausleses fetch high prices, but the price gap between these and Ausleses is exaggerated. There are no greater German wines than the finest Ausleses – only sweeter ones.

Burgundy and Germany are therefore two of the areas to explore for bargains.

Others are white Bordeaux, old champagne, and the infrequently seen lots of non-French wines (with the exception of Tokay Essence, which always fetch fantastic prices). Sauternes (Château d'Yquem apart) is consistently undervalued for one of the world's great wines. It can still sometimes be bought for less than many banal commercial productions.

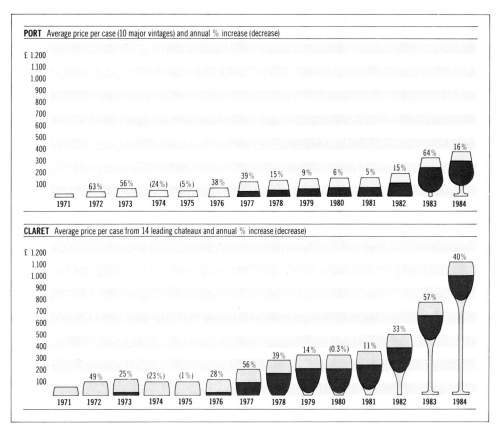

PORT Average price per case (10 major vintages) and annual % increase (decrease)

£ 1.200
1.100
1.000
900
800
700
600
500
400
300
200
100

1971 | 1972 63% | 1973 56% | 1974 (24%) | 1975 (5%) | 1976 38% | 1977 39% | 1978 15% | 1979 9% | 1980 6% | 1981 5% | 1982 15% | 1983 64% | 1984 16%

CLARET Average price per case from 14 leading chateaux and annual % increase (decrease)

£ 1.200
1.100
1.000
900
800
700
600
500
400
300
200
100

1971 | 1972 49% | 1973 25% | 1974 (23%) | 1975 (1%) | 1976 28% | 1977 56% | 1978 39% | 1979 14% | 1980 (0.3%) | 1981 11% | 1982 33% | 1983 57% | 1984 40%

The Literature of Wine

Books on wine and winegrowing have been appearing since Roman times. A gentleman farmer in the days of the Empire would have had wine books in his library by several of the greatest writers, including Virgil, Horace, Cato, Varro and Martial.

The first known farming manual was written by Mago of Carthage (in modern Tunisia) at the end of the 4th century BC. Columella, who was born in Cadiz in the sherry country, wrote his classic *De Re Rustica* in about AD 65. Both these books treated winegrowing as an important part of general agriculture, and showed that long study had already been given to factors governing the quality of wine, as well as the economics of vine husbandry . . . largely in those days a matter of how hard you could drive your slaves.

Since the 18th century a great library of technical works has accumulated. In France, particularly, some of them are treated with reverence as classics, so that modern writers still quote what Lavalle, Rodier, Roupnel, Guyot had to say about the character of a certain wine.

Some of these books have as much value today as they ever did. The place of others has been taken by fresh works. The list that follows is a personal selection of current books, along with a few irreplaceable classics.

GENERAL
Maynard A. Amerine and Vernon L. Singleton
Wine, An Introduction for Americans (Berkeley & Los Angeles, 1965, 1977)
Maynard A. Amerine and M. A. Joslyn
Table Wines – the Technology of their Production (Berkeley & Los Angeles, 1970)
J. M. Broadbent
Wine Tasting (London, 1968)
The Great Vintage Wine Book (London, 1980)
J. Gabler
Wine into Words (Baltimore, 1984) (the only up-to-date bibliography)
Edward Hyams
Dionysus, A Social History of the Wine Vine (London, 1965)
Hugh Johnson's
Wine Companion (Modern Encyclopedia of Wine) (London/New York, 1983)
A. Jullien
Topographie de Tous les Vignobles Connus (Paris, 1866)
Alexis Lichine
Encyclopaedia of Wines and Spirits (London, 1967, 1975 ....)
Lenz Moser
Un Nouveau Vignoble (Translated from the German, Cadillac-sur-Garonne, 1960)
Louis Pasteur
Etudes sur le Vin (Paris, 1866)
J. Ribéreau-Gayon and Emile Peynaud
Traité d'Oenologie (Paris, 1960)
George Saintsbury
Notes on a Cellarbook (London, 1920)
Frank Schoonmaker
Encyclopaedia of Wine (London, 1967, '83)
André Simon's
Wines of the World (2nd edition, S. Sutcliffe, London, 1981)
Philip M. Wagner
Grapes into Wine (New York, 1974)

Albert J. Winkler
General Viticulture (Berkeley, 1962)
William Younger
Gods, Men & Wine (London, 1966)

FRANCE
John Arlott and Christopher Fielden
Burgundy: Vines & Wines (London, 1976)
Pierre Bréjoux
Les Vins de la Loire (Paris, 1956)
Les Vins de Bourgogne (Paris, 1967)
Cocks et Féret
Bordeaux et ses Vins (Bordeaux, 1982: 13th edition)
Paul de Cassagnac
French Wines (Translated by Guy Knowles, London, 1930)
R. Dion
Histoire de la Vigne et du Vin en France (Paris, 1959)
Hubrecht Duijker
The Great Wine Châteaux of Bordeaux (London, 1983)
Patrick Forbes
Champagne (London, 1969)
Rolande Gadille
Le Vignoble de la Côte Bourguignonne (Paris, 1967)
R. George
The Wines of Chablis (London, 1984)
B. Ginestet
Le Grand Bernard des Vins de France (Volumes on Margaux, St. Julien, Pomerol, Bourg . . .; Paris, 1984 ....)
A. Hanson
The Wines of Burgundy (London, 1982)
Louis Larmat
Les Vins des Côtes du Rhône (Paris, 1943)
Les Vins de Bordeaux (1944)
Les Vins de Champagne (1944)
Les Vins des Coteaux de la Loire: Touraine et Centre (1946)
Le Cognac (1947)
Les Vins de Bourgogne (1953)
A. Lichine's
Guide to the Wines and Vineyards of France (New York, revised 1984)
J. Livingstone-Learmonth and M. Master
The Wines of the Rhône (London, 1983)
J. Long
The Century Companion to Cognac and other Brandies (London, 1983)
Edmund Penning-Rowsell
The Wines of Bordeaux (London, 1969, '85)
D. Peppercorn
The Wines of Bordeaux (London, 1982)
Pierre Poupon and Pierre Forgeot
Les Vins de Bourgogne (Paris, 1969, 1980....)
P. Vandyke Price
The Penguin Book of Wines (London, 1965, 1984)
Camille Rodier
Le Vin de Bourgogne (Dijon, 1948)
Gérard Seguin
Les Sols des Vignobles du Haut-Médoc (Bordeaux, 1970)
S. Spurrier
French Country Wines (London, 1984)

GERMANY
Hans Ambrosi
Wo Grosse Weine Wachsen (Munich, 1973)
Deutsche Weinatlas (Bielefeld, 1973)

Becker and Ambrosi
Vinothek der Deutschen Weinberg-Lagen (11 Vols, Stuttgart, 1979)
H. Becker, H. Zakosek and others
Die Standortkartierung der Hessischen Weinbaugebiete (Wiesbaden, 1967)
I. Jamieson
Pocket Guide to German Wine (London, 1984)
Frank Schoonmaker
The Wines of Germany (London, 1978, 1983)

AUSTRALIA
Len Evans
Australia and New Zealand – The Complete Book of Wine (Sydney, 1973; revised 1984)
J. Halliday
The Wines of South Australia, Victoria, New South Wales (Queensland, 1980)
André L. Simon
The Wines, Vineyards and Vignerons of Australia (Melbourne, 1966)

CENTRAL EUROPE
R. E. H. Gunyon
The Wines of Central and South-East Europe (London, 1971)
Z. Hálász
The Book of Hungarian Wines (Budapest, 1981)

ITALY
B. Anderson
Vino (Boston, 1980)
V. Hazan
Italian Wine (New York, 1982)

SCOTLAND
D. Cooper
The Century Companion to Whiskies (London, 1978, 1983)

SOUTH AFRICA
J. Kench, P. Hands, D. Hughes
Complete Book of South African Wine (Cape Town, 1984)
K. W. V. (ed)
Wines of Origin (Paarl, 1974)

SPAIN & PORTUGAL
Sarah Bradford
The Englishman's Wine (Port) (London, 1969)
N. Cossart
Madeira, The Island Vineyard (London, 1984)
J. Jeffs
The Wines of Sherry (3rd edition, London, 1982)
J. Read
The Wines of Spain (London, 1982)
Rioja (London, 1984)
The Wines of Portugal (London, 1982)

USA
Leon Adams
The Wines of America (Boston, 1973; revised 1984)
Bob Thompson and Hugh Johnson
The California Wine Book (New York, 1976)
University of California
Book of California Wine (San Francisco/London, 1984)

CANADA
J. Schreiner
The World of Canadian Wine (Vancouver, Toronto, 1984)

Choosing and Serving Wine

Tasting and Talking about Wine

Most good, even most great wine is wasted. It flows over tongues and down throats of people who are not attuned to it; not receptive to what it has to offer. They are preoccupied or deep in conversation; they have just drunk strong spirits which numb the sense of taste, or taken a mouthful of vinegary salad which overwhelms it; they have a cold; or they are simply unaware of where the difference between plain wine and great wine lies. Nothing the winemaker can do dispenses with the need for a sensitive and interested drinker.

If the sense of taste were located in the mouth (where our impulses tell us it is), anyone swallowing a mouthful of wine would get all the sensations it has to offer. But as this model of Bacchus shows, the nerves that receive anything more distinctive than the basic sensations of sweet, sour, salt and bitter are higher in the head and deeper in the brain.

In fact we smell tastes, rather than tasting them with our lips and tongues and palates. The real organ of discrimination is in the upper nasal cavity, where in normal breathing the air never goes. And the only sensations that can reach it are the vapours of volatile substances. To reach the brain the vapours of wine need to be inhaled (either through nose or mouth) into the upper part of the nasal cavity, where they are dissolved in moisture. From the moisture long, thin nerve processes (vacilli) take the sensations to the olfactory bulb, above the nasal cavity and right in the brain.

It is often remarked how smells stir memories more rapidly and vividly than other sensations. From the position of the olfactory bulb, nearest neighbour to the temporal lobe where memories are stored, it seems that smell, the most primitive of our senses, has a privileged position of instant access to the memory-bank. Experienced tasters often rely on the immediate reaction of their memory to the first sniff of a wine. If they cannot relate it straight away to wines they have tasted in the past they must fall back on their powers of analysis, located in the parietal lobe. In the frontal lobe their judgment of the wine is formed (to be stored in turn in the temporal lobe for future reference).

The range of reference available is the great difference between an experienced taster and a beginner. There is little meaning in an isolated sensation – although it may be very pleasant. Where the real pleasures of winetasting lie are in the cross-references, the stirring of memories, the comparisons between similar and yet subtly different products of the same or neighbouring ground.

Wines differ from one another in colour, texture, strength and 'body', as well as smell or 'taste'. A taster takes all these into account.

What is much harder than appreciating wine is communicating its sensations. There is no notation of taste, as there is of sound or colour; apart from the words sweet, salt, sour and bitter every word in the language of taste is borrowed from the other senses. And yet words, by giving an identity to sensations, help to clarify them. Some of the most helpful of the many words tasters use are listed opposite.

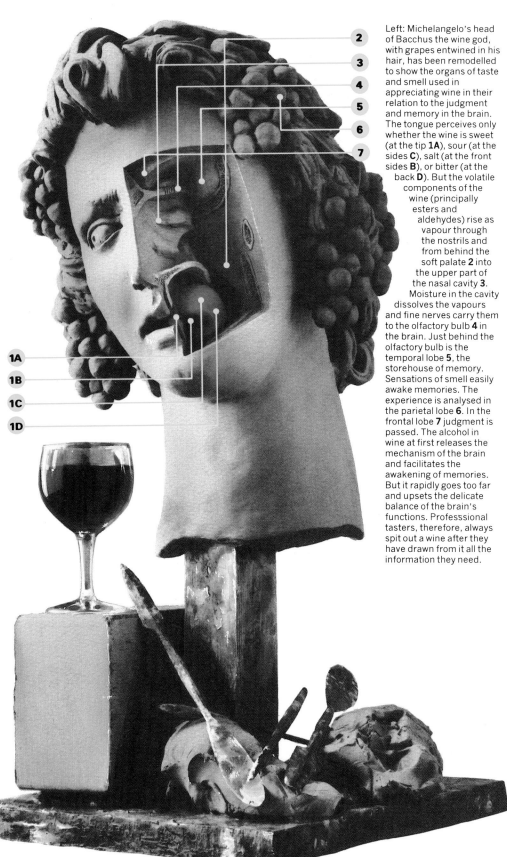

Left: Michelangelo's head of Bacchus the wine god, with grapes entwined in his hair, has been remodelled to show the organs of taste and smell used in appreciating wine in their relation to the judgment and memory in the brain. The tongue perceives only whether the wine is sweet (at the tip 1A), sour (at the sides C), salt (at the front sides B), or bitter (at the back D). But the volatile components of the wine (principally esters and aldehydes) rise as vapour through the nostrils and from behind the soft palate 2 into the upper part of the nasal cavity 3. Moisture in the cavity dissolves the vapours and fine nerves carry them to the olfactory bulb 4 in the brain. Just behind the olfactory bulb is the temporal lobe 5, the storehouse of memory. Sensations of smell easily awake memories. The experience is analysed in the parietal lobe 6. In the frontal lobe 7 judgment is passed. The alcohol in wine at first releases the mechanism of the brain and facilitates the awakening of memories. But it rapidly goes too far and upsets the delicate balance of the brain's functions. Professsional tasters, therefore, always spit out a wine after they have drawn from it all the information they need.

The colour of the wine at the rim of the glass, tipped against a white background, gives the taster his first information. Is it clear? Is it red-purplish (young) or turning to brick with age? Great wines have strikingly deep and fresh colour. Is white very light, touched with youthful green (chlorophyll), or turning to gold?

The wine's appearance

Blackish Young red, perhaps very tannic, will take a long time to mature
Brick-red Colour of mature claret
Brilliant Completely clear
Brown Except in sherry or madeira, brown wine is too old
Cloudy Something is wrong; all wine should be bright
Gris Very pale rosé, the speciality of some parts of France
Intense A useful but undefinable word for colour
Maderized Brown or going brown with the effect of oxygen and age
Pelure d'oignon Onion skin; the tawny-pink of Provençal rosés or the signs of browning in an ageing wine
Perlant 'Pearling' (or *pétillant*); wine with natural fine bubbles which stick to the glass
Purple A young colour; translucent in good Beaujolais, deep in red wine which will take time to mature
Rosé Pink; neither red nor white; a term of abuse for red wine
Ruby (of port in particular) The full red of young wine
Tawny (of port in particular) The faded amber of old wine

The smell of wine

Acetic Wine that is 'pricked' or gone irredeemably sour through contact with the air smells of acetic acid or vinegar
Aroma The simple grape-smell of young wine
Bouquet The complex smell arising with maturity in good wine
Complex Scents-within-scents; suggestions of many different analogies with fruits, flowers, etc
Corky The smell of the (very rare) bottle that has had a mouldy cork

Foxy The characteristic smell of the native American grape; not like foxes
Heady Attractively high in alcohol
Lively An indefinable good sign; a fresh, frank, good smell from wine that is young and will last
Musty Unpleasant smell, probably from a barrel with a rotten stave
Rancio The smell of oxidized fortified wine, the speciality of southwest France and Catalonia
Sappy Translation of the French 'sève'; the lively, forthright style of a fine young wine, especially burgundy
Sulphury The hot and nose-tickling smell often given by cheap white wine in which sulphur is used as a preservative. It will go off if the wine gets enough air
Yeasty The smell of yeast can be attractive in young wine, although it usually means it has been fermenting slightly in the bottle and is unstable

Describing wine
Many words are borrowed to describe the qualities of their originals: flavours that can be conveyed in no other way, appearing in wine in traces of the same chemical constituents as the fruit (or whatever) in question. Such are:
Apples Malic acid is common in good young wine. In Moselles it is very apparent

Almost everything about a wine is revealed by its scent. The taster inhales deeply. The first impression is the most telling. Is there any 'foreign' or 'wrong' smell? Does it smell of fresh grapes or have a complex 'bouquet' from age in barrel and bottle? Is the grape identifiable (as Riesling, Pinot, Cabernet)?

Blackcurrants Smell and flavour in many red wines
Earthy A virtue or fault depending on the context. A common quality of Italian wines
Flowery Used generally for an attractive and forthcoming scent
Grapey A great wine has more than grapiness, but a fresh-grape smell is always a good sign

Gunflint Scent of flint sparks in some white wine – e.g. Pouilly-Fumé
Honey Associated particularly with 'noble rot' in great sweet wines
Nuts Nuttiness is usually found in well-aged wines. It is very marked in good old sherry

The taste in the mouth confirms the information given by the nose. The taster takes a good mouthful, not a sip, and lets it reach every part of his mouth. The body, or wineyness, now makes its impact. Is it generous or meagre? Is it harsh with tannin as young reds should be? Is it soft and flat or well balanced with acidity?

Oak The character given to wine by the barrel. Important and attractive as it is, it should not be obvious enough to be identified as oak
Peaches Associated with a certain fruity acidity, e.g. in some Loire wines
Petroleum A smell found, often in association with lemons, in mature Rieslings
Raspberries A common flavour in very good red wine, particularly of Bordeaux and the Rhône valley
Smoke Smokiness is claimed for many white wines
Spice Very pronounced in Gewürztraminer
Stalks A green-wood smell which can arise in an under-ripe vintage
Truffles The most elusive of all scents, found by Burgundians in Burgundy, Barolans in Barolo, hermits in Hermitage
Vanilla Scent given to wine and (much more) brandy by a component of the oak of the cask
Violets A distinctive 'high-pitched' scent, especially in fine burgundy

The list could be much extended; many tasters play the free-association game and jot down 'rubber', 'pear-drops', 'wool', etc.

General terms of appreciation
Baked Flavour resulting from very hot sun on grapes
Big Strong, round, and satisfying
Body The 'volume' of a wine, partly due to alcoholic strength
Breed Balance of qualities in good

wine due to grapes, soil and skill
Clean Refreshing; free from defects
Coarse Tasting crudely made
Complete Balanced, satisfying
Distinctive Having its own character
Dry The opposite of sweet
Dumb Not offering its full quality (wine is too young or too cold)
Elegant As of a woman; indefinable
Fat As of a man, well fleshed. Not a desirable characteristic in itself
Fiery A good quality, in moderation
Finesse Literally, fine-ness
Finish Aftertaste; in great wine the exact flavour remains in the mouth for a considerable period after swallowing
Firm Young with a decisive style
Flat The opposite of firm
Fruity Ripe-tasting
Hard Tannin makes young reds hard
Long What the finish should be
Nervy Vigorous and fine; good in wine as in horses
Noble The ultimate combination of breed, body, maturity; use with care
Old By itself often means too old
Racy From French *race*, meaning breed; or vital and exciting
Rough Poor, cheap, badly made
Séché 'Dried up' – too-old red wine
Short What the finish should not be
Silky Accurate word for a certain texture (found in good Beaujolais)
Stiff Similar to dumb
Stuffing The body and character of certain red wines (Côte de Nuits, St-Emilion)
Supple Opposite of hard, but not pejorative as soft would be
Unresolved Not old enough for components to have harmonized
Vigorous Young and lively

Holding the wine in his mouth, the taster draws air between his lips. The warmth of his mouth helps to volatilize the wine; a more positive impression of the taste materializes at the very back of the mouth as vapours rise to the nasal cavity from behind. After swallowing (or spitting) is the flavour short-lived or lingering?

Taking Notes

From talking about wine to writing about it is but a step – which few wine drinkers ever take. Yet there is a strong case for keeping tasting notes in a more or less organized way. In the first place, having to commit something to paper makes you concentrate; the prime requirement for being able to taste wine properly at all. In the second it makes you analyse and pin labels on the sensations passing across your palate. In the third it is an aide-mémoire: when somebody asks you what a wine is like you can look it up and say something definite. In the fourth it allows you to extend comparisons between wines over time – either the same wine a year later, or different but related wines on different occasions.

In short, keeping tasting notes is like keeping a diary: obviously a good idea, but hard to get off the ground.

For this reason I asked Michael Broadbent, Director of the Wine Department of Christie's, London, whose book *Wine Tasting* is the standard work on the subject, to collaborate with me in compiling a suitable tasting card for keen amateurs to use.

There have been many studies (notably at the University of California) of what they call Sensory Methods of Evaluating Wine. Most depend on a scoring system of points (for clarity, colour, aroma and the rest) which lends a slightly inappropriate air of indoor games to what is really an analytical exercise.

The Broadbent-Johnson card, reproduced below, does encompass a way of scoring with points if this is what you want to do. It can be used perfectly well without them. On the other hand, scoring points does force you to make up your mind.

The notes at the bottom right of the card explain its use. The left-hand column divides each of the three basic aspects of wine (sight, smell and taste) into facets that can be isolated and examined. One of the listed descriptions of these facets in the first column should fit every wine.

The centre column is simply a list of suggested adjectives for what you may find in the glass before you. These are the words (see page 45) that are most often used in discussing wine. None of them may apply to any given wine – which is the purpose of the right-hand column: this is to record your own impressions, again analytically, by sight, smell and taste.

After the analysis, the judgment. The space for Overall Quality allows your general feelings of pleasure or dislike to override your objective assessment, as in the end it will, and should, do.

Left: a pre-auction tasting at Christie's Restell auction rooms, London. Concentration is difficult at crowded tastings: note-taking is essential.

Below: a consistent analytical approach is the best way to learn about, judge and remember wine. Scoring is not compulsory, but forces you to decide.

Name of Wine	Vintage
District/type	Date purchased
Merchant/bottler	Price

SIGHT · Score (maximum 3)		Comments
CLARITY cloudy, bitty, dull, clear, brilliant DEPTH OF COLOUR watery, pale, medium, deep, dark COLOUR (white wines) green tinge, pale yellow, yellow, gold, brown; (red wines) purple, purple/red, red, red/brown VISCOSITY slight sparkle, watery, normal, heavy, oily	starbright, tuilé, straw, amber, tawny, ruby, garnet, oeil de perdrix, hazy, opaque	
SMELL · Score (maximum 6)		
GENERAL APPEAL neutral, clean, attractive, outstanding, off (e.g. yeasty, acetic, oxidized, woody, etc.) FRUIT AROMA none, slight, positive, identifiable, e.g. Riesling BOUQUET none, pleasant, complex, powerful	cedarwood, corky, woody, dumb, flowery, smoky, honeyed, lemony, spicy, mouldy, peardrops, sulphury	
TASTE · Score (maximum 8)	appley, bitter, burning, blackcurrants, caramel, dumb, earthy, fat, flinty, green, heady, inky, flabby, mellow, metallic, mouldy, nutty, salty, sappy, silky, spicy, fleshy, woody, watery	HOW TO USE THIS CHART Wine appeals to three senses: sight, smell and taste. This card is a guide to analysing its appeal and an aide-mémoire on each wine you taste. Tick one word for each factor in the left-hand column and any of the descriptive terms that fit your impressions. Then award points according to the pleasure the wine gives you. Use the right-hand column for your comments.
SWEETNESS (white wines) bone-dry, dry, medium-dry, medium-sweet, very sweet TANNIN (red wines) astringent, hard, dry, soft ACIDITY flat, refreshing, marked, tart BODY very light and thin, light, medium, full-bodied, heavy LENGTH short, acceptable, extended, lingering BALANCE unbalanced, good, very well balanced, perfect		
OVERALL QUALITY · Score (maximum 3) Coarse, poor, acceptable, fine, outstanding	supple, finesse, breed, elegance, harmonious, rich, delicate	
SCORING · Total Score (out of 20)	DATE OF TASTING	

Compiled by Hugh Johnson and Michael Broadbent M.W. © 1975, 1985

Choosing Wine

The French have an inimitable way of expressing the character of a wine in terms of the perfect dish to accompany it; '. . . sur un foie gras' they say with relish: one immediately has a useful idea of the kind of wine and its appropriate place at table. With the thousands of wines in this Atlas such an approach is impossible. Here we put forward some suggestions for the choosing of wine by the sort of occasion when it will be drunk, with the object of guiding the reader who is looking for (for example) an after-dinner wine, a wine to order for everyday use or an attractive wine to take on a picnic, with the Atlas page where a major reference to the wine will be found.

Apéritifs
The ideal apéritif stimulates the appetite as well as the wits. It is brisk and dry, with either a sparkle or a tang. Cocktails leave the palate unable to appreciate good wine with the meal.
Sparkling wines Champagne, page *110*; Anjou-Saumer, *120*; Vouvray, *122*; St-Péray or Die, *124*; burgundy, *60*; Savoie, *133*; Limoux, *130*; Sekt, *141*; Asti Spumante, *184*; Neuchâtel, *168*; Spanish, *198*; California, *244*; New York, *264*; Australian, *266*.
Fortified wines Sherry, *200*; madeira, *218*; white port, *214*; Marsala, *197*; vermouth, *176*.
Natural wines Mâcon blanc, *75*; dry white Graves, *98*; Alsace Sylvaner or Riesling, *114*; Muscadet, *118*; Anjou, *120*; Sancerre or Pouilly, *123*; vin jaune or Apremont, *133*; Luxembourg Moselle, *148*; German Kabinett wines, *140*; Hungarian Riesling, *220*, *222*; Tokay Szamarodni, *221*; Yugoslav Riesling, *224*; Romanian Cotnari or Riesling, *226*; Bulgarian Riesling, *228*; vinho verde, *213*; Alella, *206*; Soave, *186*; California Johannisberg Riesling or Gewürztraminer, *244*.

Everyday wine
Wine for everyday, for meals in the kitchen, can be plain *vin ordinaire* – or something a little more interesting: the wine of a specific region.
Red Côteaux du Languedoc, *130*; Fronsac, *106*; Bourg, Blaye, *108*; Bordeaux Supérieur, *81*; Mâcon rouge, *75*; Côtes du Rhône, *124*; commune Bordeaux wines, *81*; Algerian, Tunisian, Moroccan, *234*; Corvo red, *202*; Sardinian, *197*; Klevner, *169*; Valdepeñas, *198*; Rioja Clarete, *204*; Dão Tinto, *213*; Portuguese branded wine, *210*; Argentine red, *282*; Gamza, *228*; Demestica, *236*; South African Hermitage, *280*; Kadarka, *220*; Australian Claret, *266*; Cyprus red, *238*; California Burgundy, *244*.
White Edelzwicker, *114*; Gros Plant du Pays Nantais, *118*; Entre-Deux-Mers, *81*; Hungarian or Yugoslav Riesling, *220* or *224*; Austrian Schluck, *175*; German Tafelwein, *140*; Bulgarian Chardonnay, *228*; Verdicchio, *190*; Lacrima Christi, *197*; Capri, *196*; 'Chablis' or many wineries' 'mountain white', *244*.

Alfresco wine
The wine for a picnic or a meal in the garden should be something lighter, better and with more character than your everyday wine.
Red Beaujolais-Villages, *76*; Chinon, Bourgueil, *121*; Cabernet d'Anjou, *120*; Bergerac,

109; local VDQS red, *136*; Chianti in *fiaschi*, *192*; Barbera or Dolcetto, *180*; Lago di Caldaro, *187*; Valpolicella, *186*; Valdepeñas, *198*; Zinfandel, *244*; Dôle, *170*.
Rosé Marsannay, *73*; Cabernet rosé d'Anjou, *120*; Provençal, *132*; Jura *vin gris*, *133*; Chiaretto del Garda, *184*; Ravello, *197*.
White Bourgogne Aligoté, *66*; Alsace Sylvaner or Traminer, *114*; Muscadet, *118*; dry Vouvray, *122*; vinho verde, *213*; Grüner Veltliner, *172*; Bernkasteler Riesling, *150*; Steinwein, *164*; California Riesling, *244*; Steen or Riesling, *278*; English white, *284*.

Family Meals
This big category includes the good but not the great wines of the world, perfect for leisurely but not grand meals. Sunday lunch with the family or entertaining friends. These wines have real character and quality; they are worth taking note of and discussing, without demanding attention and respect. For most formal occasions as well such wines as these are the perfect choice.
Red Côte d'Or commune wines and some Premier Crus of Santenay, Volnay, Pommard, Nuits, etc., *64*; Grand Cru Beaujolais, *76*; good Cru Bourgeois and lesser classed growths of the Médoc, *86–94*; similar wines from Graves, Pomerol and St-Emilion, *98*, *102*, *104*; Châteauneuf-du-Pape, *127*; Cahors, *134*; Chinon, Bourgueil, *121*; Bandol, *132*; Barolo, Barbaresco, *180*; Chianti Riserva, *192*; Alto Adige Cabernet, *186*; Lambrusco, *184*; Rioja Reserva, *204*; Colares, *211*; Dão Reserva, *213*; Australian Private Bin type clarets from Hunter, Coonawarra, etc., *266*; California Cabernet Sauvignon, *244*; Chilean Cabernet, *282*.
Rosé Tavel, *128*; Marsannay, *73*; Cabernet

Rosé d'Anjou, *120*; Chiaretto del Garda, *184*.
White Graves Crus Classés, *98*; Chablis Premier Cru, *78*; Côte de Beaune commune wines, *65*; estate-bottled Muscadet, *118*; Vouvray, *122*; Sancerre, Pouilly Fumé, *123*; Pouilly-Fuissé, *75*; Mâcon Viré, *75*; Côte Chalonnaise, *74*; Alsace Riesling, Traminer, *114*; Middle Mosel, *148*; Nahe, *152*; Rheingau, *152*; Rheinpfalz, *158*; Rheinhessen, *160*; Franconian and Baden Kabinett wines, *162*, *164*, and Spätleses of lighter vintages from these German areas; Soave, *186*; Frascati, *190*; Alvarinho, *213*; Fendant de Sion and Dorin of Vaud, *170*; Rheinriesling from Burgenland and Wachau, *172*, *175*; Balatoni Szürkebarát and Kéknyelü, *222*; California Chardonnay or Johannisberg Riesling, *244*; Barossa Riesling, *272*; California Chenin Blanc or Fumé Blanc, *260*; Australian Riesling or Semillon, *266*.

Great wines
The great wines should never be served except to wine lovers under ideal conditions – when there is time to appreciate their qualities, to compare them with lesser wines or their own peers, and when they can be partnered with well-chosen and well-prepared dishes. They should have the best glasses, and candlelight – a certain formality enhances their enjoyment. Uninhibited discussion of their qualities is essential – or they are wasted.
Red Grands Crus and outstanding Premiers Crus of the Côte d'Or, *64*; the best classed growths of the Médoc, *86–94*; Graves, *98*; Pomerol, *102*; St-Emilion, *104*; Côte Rôtie, *125*; Hermitage, *126*; top California Cabernets, *258*; Australian Shiraz or Cabernet, *266*.
White The Montrachets, *65*; outstanding Premier Cru Meursaults, *66*; Grand Cru Chablis, *78*; Corton-Charlemagne, *68*; exceptional Alsace Rieslings or Gewürztraminers, *116*; exceptional Vouvrays, *122*; Quarts de Chaume, Savennières, *120*; Château Grillet, *125*; Spätleses and Ausleses of the Saar, *144*; Ruwer, *146*; Middle Mosel, *148*; Nahe, *152*; Rheingau, *154*; Rheinpfalz, *158*; top California or Australian Chardonnays, *246*, *266*.

The end of the meal
Natural (or sparkling) sweet wines go admirably with a sweet course at the end of the meal – although there are certain dishes, particularly chocolate ones or those containing citrus fruits, that do not agree with them – or equally well as after-dinner drinks on their own. The strong dessert wines (port, madeira, Tokay and the rest) go well with cheese, apples (if they are good) or nuts, but less well with sweet dishes, except quite plain and cake-like ones.
Natural wines Sauternes, *100*; exceptional Vouvrays, *122*; Quarts de Chaume, etc., *120*; Monbazillac, *109*; Jurançon, *134*; German Ausleses, Beerenausleses, etc., *140*.
Sparkling wines Sweet champagne, *112*; Asti Spumante, *181*.
Dessert wines Port, *214*; Tokay, *221*; Malmsey or Bual madeira, *218*; cream sherry, *202*; Commandaria, *238*; vin santo, *176*; Marsala, *197*; Tarragona, *206*; Malaga, *198*; sweet muscat wines – Beaumes de Venise, *124*; Setúbal, *210*; Sicilian, *197*; Russian, *230*.

Looking after Wine

To buy good wine and not to look after it properly is like hanging a masterpiece in a dark corner, or not exercising a racehorse, or not polishing your Rolls-Royce. If good wine is worth paying extra for it is worth keeping, and above all serving, in good condition.

There is nothing mysterious or difficult about handling wine. But doing it well can add vastly to the pleasure of drinking it – and doing it badly can make the best bottle taste frankly ordinary.

Wine only asks for two things: to be kept lying quietly in a dark, cool place and to be served generously, not hurriedly, with plenty of time and room to breathe the air.

Storage is a problem to almost everyone. Cellars like the one opposite, the perfect place for keeping a collection of wine, are rarely built today. Most people have to make shift with a cupboard. But even a cupboard can have the simple requirements of darkness, freedom from vibration, and – if not the ideal coolness – at least an even temperature. Wine is not overfussy: anything from 7–21°C (45–70°F) will do. What matters more is that it stays the same. No wine will stand alternate boiling and freezing. In high temperatures it tends to age quicker – and there is the danger of it seeping around the cork – but if coolness is impracticable, steady warmth will do.

No special equipment is needed in cellar or cupboard. Bottles are always kept lying down to prevent the cork from drying and shrinking and letting in air. They can be stacked in a pile if they are all the same; but if they are all different it is better to keep them in a rack so that bottles can easily be taken from the bottom. Failing a wooden or metal rack, cardboard delivery boxes on their sides are satisfactory until they sag – which in a damp cellar does not take long.

Given the space, there is every argument for buying wine young, at its opening price, and

Finest Bordeaux served the English way: decanted into a claret jug over a candle flame – one of wine's best-established rites, but one that still arouses controversy.

'laying it down' in cellar or cupboard until it reaches perfect maturity. Wine merchants are not slow to point out that it may appreciate in monetary, as well as gastronomic, value out of all proportion to the outlay. While at the top end of the market with château- or domaine-bottled wines this can mean making a fortune, at the bottom it can mean that even cheap red wines become very pleasant after six months or a year longer in bottles than the shop gives them. (See also the charts on pages 53–56.)

It was Pasteur who discovered (see pages 38–39) the effects on wine of exposing it to the air. The same effects lie behind the custom of decanting, or pouring wine from its original bottle into another – more often a glass carafe – before serving it. Decanting is much discussed but little understood, largely because its effect on a given wine is unpredictable.

There is a mistaken idea that it is something you only do to ancient bottles with lots of sediment – a mere precautionary measure to get a clean glass of wine. In reality it is young wines that benefit most. The oxygen they contain has had little chance to take effect. But the air in the decanter works rapidly and effectively. In a matter of a few hours it can produce the full flowering of what was only in bud. This can mean literally twice as much of the scent and flavour that you paid for. Some strong young wines can benefit by even as much as 24 hours in a decanter. An hour makes all the difference to others. The more full-bodied the wine the longer it needs.

It is exceptions to this general rule that cause confusion. The French rarely decant at all. They miss a great deal.

The technique of decanting is illustrated below. The only essential equipment is a carafe and a corkscrew. But a basket is a good way of keeping the bottle in almost the same position as in the rack where it was lying, so that any sediment remains along the lower side. And a corkscrew that pulls against the rim of the bottle makes it easy to avoid jerking.

Cut the lead capsule and take it off completely. Take the cork out gently. Wipe the lip of the bottle. Hold the bottle (with or without the basket) in one hand and the decanter in the other, and pour steadily until you see the sediment (if any) moving into the shoulder of the bottle. Then stop. Having a flashlight behind or below the neck of the bottle makes it easier to see when the dregs start to move – although a candle is more in keeping with the pleasantly sensuous ritual.

A wine basket should not appear on the table. It is to hold the bottle steady for opening before decanting. A 'port-slide' (left) is an alternative.

A corkscrew with counter-revolving screws gives a strong and steady pull. Left: a modern alternative that draws the cork with a single screwing action.

A candle below the neck of the bottle makes it easier to see when the sediment in the wine comes to the neck: the time to stop pouring.

A small private wine cellar has a brick floor and brick 'bins' where the wine is laid, either on the floor or on a shelf. In the bins in this cellar, which can contain about 500 bottles, are, top row, left to right: white burgundies and German Ausleses laid down for maturing; bottles in racks (red, white and champagne) where they can easily be removed without disturbing others. These are ready for drinking. Then two more bins of red wines laid down for maturing, labels uppermost and capsules (with their names) facing out. Bottom row: claret stored in original cases from the château. Magnums of red burgundy and Bordeaux. Vintage port binned for long ageing. Red burgundy newly bought and not yet laid down. The table with candles and a funnel is for decanting.

Another technique to avoid disturbing the wine: a silver funnel with the bottom curved to make the wine run down the side of the decanter.

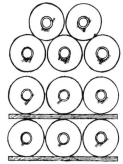

Left: professional cellarmen 'bin' bottles as much as 40 deep; by placing laths between rows they can take one bottle from the bottom of the pile. A simpler method (top) is to lay them directly on top of each other.

Right: racks are most convenient for small collections, whether kept in a cupboard or cellar.

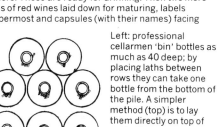

Right: a cellar book is a personal record of bottles (or cases) of wine bought, stored and eventually consumed. It has space for details about the wine – vintage, vineyard, source of supply – and the occasions when it is drunk. It is helpful to record the food, the company and, of course, the impression the wine makes.

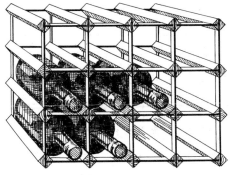

Serving Wine

The care we take in serving wine and the little customs and courtesies of the table cannot do much to change its virtues or vices. But they can add tenfold to its enjoyment. If there are different glasses, decanters, even rituals for different wines, it is not out of any physical necessity but as an expression of the varying sensuous pleasures they give. In helping to emphasize the different characters of wine – and reminding us of their origins – they add to the experience and make it memorable.

These pages show a number of the more practical, as well as pretty, forms of glass which have been evolved to put each kind of wine in its best light. What they have in common are the essentials of reasonably generous size (so that a good measure fills them only a half to two-thirds full), clear uncoloured glass so that the colour of the wine is undimmed, and a rim that cups in slightly towards the top, which makes it possible to swirl the wine in the glass to release its scent without spilling it. The exception in the last case is the champagne flute; but then champagne comes up to greet you – you don't need to swirl it.

The only cut glass in the picture is one for German wine. Some purists scorn all cut glass, but there is no doubt that the Treviris glass used on the Mosel reflects flashes of light into the pale green wine and gives it brilliance. Nor does it seem inappropriate to gaze at your hock through etched bunches of grapes – not, of course, in a clinical tasting room but out on the terrace where the wine is meant to be enjoyed.

It may seem too obvious to mention, but wineglasses should be clean, which means polished and untainted with smells of detergents or cupboards. Ideally they should be

1 A hand-made cognac glass in lead crystal from Sweden. Designed for cupping in the hand to warm the spirit; the vapour is caught and held in the bowl. Monster balloon glasses are never used by experts in Cognac.

2 A spirit decanter; a contemporary copy of an 18th-century Spanish travelling companion. There is no practical reason for using a decanter for spirits – they neither improve nor deteriorate for several weeks after opening the bottle. But as an elegant extra, decanting makes whisky, brandy, gin, rum or any spirit look its best.

3 Silver or gold labels for decanters are a practical old custom that is being revived. A London firm made the reproductions of famous examples used in the picture. They are suitable for any wine or spirit that is served or kept in a decanter.

4 A useful glass for port, sherry or madeira; not a classic design but well balanced and good for tasting.

5 The 18th-century equivalent of its neighbours: a cordial glass, satisfying to hold and excellent for port.

6 The sherry copita: one of the world's best-designed tasting glasses, funnelling the scent of the wine to the nostrils; also the perfect size for drinking sherry, filled two-thirds full.

7 Decanter for any wine: claret, sherry, port or madeira. For vintage port decanting is necessary, for the rest a luxury. This three-ring decanter of 1800 is from the classic period for English glass.

8 Many wine regions have their own style of wine glass, designed to show off the local wine. The vintners of Alsace use this original design for their fresh white wine. The long stem to hold prevents hands from warming the bowl. The clear glass allows the colour to be seen and the sloping sides concentrate the bouquet. The green stem reflects a pretty green gleam into the wine.

9 The traditional Rhine-wine or hock glass has a stout knobbed stem of brown glass, again to reflect the desired colour into the wine. Although today the fashion is for pale wine, its use continues.

10 The pretty engraved Trier or Treviris glass for Mosel. Even small cafés on the Mosel use this graceful glass to make their pale, delicate white wine catch the light and seem more inviting than ever.

rinsed with hot water and polished by hand. They are much easier to polish while they are still hot. No wisps of towel should stick to them. Cupboard smells usually come from keeping glasses upside down. On open shelves this may be necessary, but it is better to keep them right-way-up in a clean airy cupboard. Sniff them before putting them on the table.

Some of the attentions paid to wine are frivolous. Others (notably decanting, see page 48) can make all the difference between mere satisfaction and real delight.

Any good wine benefits by comparison with another. It is no affectation, but simply making the most of a good thing, to serve more than one wine at a meal. A young wine served first shows off the qualities of an older one; a white wine (usually) shows off a red one; a light wine a massive one; a dry wine a sweet one. But any of these combinations played the other way round would be disastrous for the second wine. In the same way a really good wine puts in the shade a lesser wine served after it, and the same thing happens to a dry white wine served after a red.

The question of how much to serve is more difficult. There are six good glasses of wine (which means big glasses filled half-full, not small ones filled to the brim) in a normal bottle. At a quick lunch one glass a person might be enough, whereas at a long dinner, five or six might not be too much. A total of half a bottle a person (perhaps one glass of white wine and two of red) is a reasonable average for most people and occasions – but the circumstances and mood of the meal, and above all how long it goes on, are the deciding factors. There is a golden rule for hosts: be generous but never pressing. And offer water, too.

11 Champagne or any white wine is at its best thoroughly cooled. The ideal way is in a deep ice bucket full of cold water, with ice cubes in the water. This more elegant but less conventional ice bucket is a Georgian tureen made by Matthew Boulton of Birmingham. Ideally it should be deeper. Most ice buckets are too shallow, so it is necessary to stand the bottle on its head in them for a few minutes to cool the top of the bottle as well as the bottom.

12 The most fashionable shape of champagne glass today, in hand-made Swedish crystal. Easier to polish inside than its neighbour.

13 The champagne 'flute': the traditional and most beautiful sparkling-wine glass. Slow to fill, as the bubbles rise like a rocket. 'Tulips' are also good for champagne; flat, shallow glasses are not.

14 A 'tulip' glass filled with red Bordeaux. One of the perfect all-purpose glasses – ideal for champagne or any white wine as well as for red. The in-turned rim helps to collect the scent.

15 This Georgian magnum decanter holds a double bottle. Apart from looking magnificent on the table in a decanter, many good red wines benefit from the air (see page 48).

16 A 17th-century Venetian wine glass, thin and fragile but a lovely adornment to any white wine or champagne.

17 A red-wine glass ideal for burgundy or Bordeaux, based on the classic Bordeaux model. Big enough to be filled only one-third full – the perfect amount for appreciating the wine. Hand-made lead crystal from Sweden.

18 It is customary (although not necessary) to serve white wine in slightly smaller glasses than red. This and its neighbour are part of a matching set, ideal for fine wines at a dinner party.

19 A Burgundian silver *tastevin*. Professional tasters in Burgundy keep one in their pockets. Its gleam through the wine in a dark cellar is a surer judge of colour and clarity than a glass would be, and it is unbreakable. This one is 100 years old.

20 Stands for decanters or bottles to prevent them from making rings on the table are known as 'coasters'. They used to be made of silver or gold, or wood, or papier mâché. Another adjunct to the serving of wine that is being revived.

51

Serving Wine: Temperature

Nothing makes more difference to the enjoyment of wine than its temperature. Stone-cold claret and lukewarm Rhine wines are abominations. And there are good reasons why this should be so.

Our sense of smell (and hence the greater part of our sense of taste) is only susceptible to vapours. Red wine has a higher molecular weight – and is thus less volatile – than white. The object of serving red wine at room temperature, or 'chambré', is to warm it to the point where its aromatic elements begin to vaporize – which is at a progressively higher temperature for more solid and substantial wines. A light Beaujolais can be treated as a white wine; even cold, its volatility is almost overwhelming. But a full-scale red wine needs the warmth of the room, of the cupped hand around the glass, and of the mouth itself to volatilize its complex constituents.

As an apparent exception to this rule the French tend to serve red burgundy cooler than red Bordeaux. Some grapes make wine that is inherently more volatile than others: Burgundy's Pinot Noir is one of the 'showy' grapes – the reason why young red burgundy is much more attractive than young Bordeaux.

Cold is also necessary to provide a sense of balance to the richness of very sweet wines, even if in doing so it masks some of their flavours. On the chart opposite, all the sweetest white wines are entered at the coldest point. It is a good idea to pour them very cold and let them warm up slightly while you sip them: the process seems to release all their aroma and bouquet. Extreme cold has also been used to make overaged white wine presentable.

The chart also sets out in some detail the wide range of temperatures that bring out the best in different wines. It is based on personal experience, often modified in discussions (not to mention arguments) with many wine lovers. Personal taste and habits vary widely from individual to individual; also from country to country. Americans tend to extremes of temperature, sometimes serving champagne, for example, so cold that it has no flavour, or taking 'room temperature' for red wine literally in a room at 24° or 26°C (75–80°F). The French, by contrast, can sometimes be accused of serving all wine at the same temperature. But it is worth remembering that when the term 'chambré' was invented the prevailing temperature in French dining-rooms was unlikely to have been above 15–16°C (60°F).

It is easier to serve white wine at the right temperature than red: a refrigerator can so simply make the necessary adjustments. The quickest way to cool a bottle is to put it in a bucket of ice and water (not ice alone). In a very warm room (and especially a hot garden) it is a good idea to keep the bottle in the bucket between pourings, even if it means pouring the wine a bit too cold; it warms up all too quickly in the glass. A useful tip for large quantities (several bottles in a big bucket) is to make a monster block of ice by putting a polythene bag of water in the deep-freeze: the bigger the block the slower it thaws. Tall German bottles should be put in the water upside-down for a few minutes first to cool the wine in the neck.

Persuading a red wine to reach the right temperature is harder. If it starts at cellar temperature it takes several hours in a normal room to raise it 10 or 12 degrees. The kitchen is the logical place – but many kitchens are well over 18°C (65°F), especially while dinner is cooking. At this sort of temperature any red wine is thrown out of balance; the alcohol starts to vaporize and produces a heady smell, which masks its character. The most practical way of warming red wine in a hurry is first to decant it, then to stand the decanter in water at about 21°C (70°F). It does no harm to heat the decanter (within reason) first.

Chart

CELLAR TEMPERATURE BANDS			
DOMESTIC FRIDGE TEMP.	▼ THE IDEAL CELLAR		ROOM TEMP. ►
SWEET WHITES	DRY WHITES	LIGHT REDS	FULL SCALE REDS

C° scale: 4 5 6 7 8 9 10 11 12 13 14 15 16 17 18
F° scale: 39 41 43 45 46 48 50 52 54 55 57 59 61 63 64

Wines (approximate serving temperature positions):

MUSCADET	VOUVRAY	GRAVES
CHABLIS	MACON	BEAUJOLAIS
CHINON	BEST WHITE BURGUNDIES	RED BURGUNDY
SAUTERNES	GEWURZTRAMINER	SANCERRE/POUILLY
COTES DU RHONE (RED)	TOP RED RHONE	
GROS PLANT	ALSACE RIESLING	MIDI REDS: CORBIERES. ETC.
VINTAGE PORT	MUSCATS	
TOKAY	FINO SHERRY	TAWNY PORT
CREAM SHERRY	ORDINARY RED BORDEAUX	
ALIGOTE	AMONTILLADO	MADEIRA
CAHORS	FINE RED BORDEAUX	
SYLVANER	VIN JAUNE	
SPARKLING WINE	NON-VINTAGE CHAMPAGNE	BEST CHAMPAGNE
TAFELWEIN	GOOD GERMAN WINES	BEST DRY GERMAN WINES
BEST SWEET GERMAN WINES	LIEBFRAUMILCH	
SPATLESES & AUSLESES	FRASCATI	VALPOLICELLA
CHIANTI RESERVAS	ORVIETO	FIASCO CHIANTI
RIOJA RESERVAS	SOAVE	SICILIAN REDS
PORTUGUESE REDS	SCHLUCK	VERDICCHIO
BADACSONYI WHITES	BULL'S BLOOD	BAROLO
VINHO VERDE	BARBERA	
FENDANT	VALDEPENAS	
DORIN	DOLE	
LAMBRUSCO	LIGHT ZINFANDELS	
RETSINA	YUGOSLAV RIESLING	CALIFORNIA 'BURGUNDY'
CHENIN BLANC	CALIFORNIA PINOT NOIR	
CHARDONNAY		
LIGHT MUSCATS	TOP CALIFORNIA CHARDONNAYS	BEST CALIFORNIA CABERNETS & ZINFANDELS
FUME BLANC	CALIFORNIA SAUVIGNON BLANC	
JOHANNISBERG RIESLING	OLD HUNTER VALLEY WHITES	
BAROSSA RIESLING	TOP AUSTRALIAN CLARETS	
VIN ROSE		

The chart above suggests ideal temperatures for serving a wide range of wines. 'Room temperature' is low by modern standards: all the better for fine wine.

Right: A bottle thermometer marked in degrees Centigrade which glow according to the temperature of the bottle, here the traditional shape used in Bordeaux, easily stacked for ageing. Left: a typical sherry bottle and the slope-shouldered Burgundy model; the 'flute' of Germany, brown for Rhine wine, green for Mosel (and Alsace); the sturdy champagne bottle, built for repeated handling and a pressure of five atmospheres; the Loire variant of the Burgundy shape and Chianti's litre *fiasco*.

Recent Vintages

Local weather conditions (and growers' reactions to them) vary so much that any vintage chart is only a broad generalization. Moreover, vintages vary not only in quality but in style; there are years of fruity tender wines and years of firm wines full of tannin and lasting-power: the latter ultimately make the best wine – for those with patience.

In these detailed charts the following information is given:

The size of the vintage where it varies much from the average. The greatest vintages are almost always small ones: the fewer grapes on the vine the more flavour is in each grape.

The general standard and particular style of the wine of each area for each year.

Dates when the wine will probably be at its best. The first date is for the lightest – which would normally be the cheapest – wine and the last for the best of the area and year. The last is impossible to calculate with precision, since the development of wine in bottle often produces surprises.

Other factors which affect ageing should also be taken into account. Half-bottles age quicker than bottles, and bottles than magnums. Warm cellars age wine faster than cold ones. Wine brought slowly to maturity in a magnum in a cold cellar is as good as it can be.

France

RED BURGUNDY

Côte d'Or Côte de Beaune reds generally mature sooner than the bigger wines of the Côte de Nuits. Earliest drinking dates are for lighter commune wines: Volnay, Beaune, etc. Latest for the biggest wines of Chambertin, Romanée, etc. Different growers make wines of different styles, for longer or shorter maturing, but even the best burgundies are much more attractive young than the equivalent red Bordeaux.

Year	Côte d'Or	When to drink
1986	Late sunshine after rain saved the day for perhaps half the crop: there will be fine wines (not very long keepers), but also poor ones.	'89–on
1985	An outstanding vintage made in a heatwave, hence liable to surprises as it matures. Many good wines are rich and intense, with great promise.	?'88–on
1984	Low in natural sugar but healthy and sound. Skilful winemaking should have made respectable or better wines, though probably not keepers.	Now–?'94
1983	Large crop complicated by rot (and hail in Chambolle and Vosne-Romanée) but overall strong in colour, flavours and tannin; the best since '78. For long keeping.	'88–?2000
1982	Larger vintage of agreeable, rather pale but round and full wines. Best in the Côte de Beaune. Perhaps one-third good enough for serious maturing.	Now–'90
1981	Hail damage in July reduced the crop. A hot August and September ripened it well but rain set in at vintage time. Turning out less well than the best of '80.	Now–'88
1980	A difficult wet year. Only very conscientious growers avoided rot. But the best wines have developed well.	Now–'88
1979	Big vintage, healthy and ripe but with rather low concentration and acidity. Most wines are soft and early-maturing. The best (especially in the Côte de Beaune) have developed well.	Now–'88
1978	An outstanding, very attractive and long-lasting vintage, saved by the exceptional autumn. Good wines to keep.	Now–'95
1977	Very wet summer, fine autumn. Overall light, many poor wines, a few good. Drink up.	Now
1976	Hot summer, excellent vintage. A classic; some wines will take 15 years to mature.	Now–'90
1975	Hot summer, small wet vintage. Rot was rife, particularly in the Côte de Beaune. Mostly very poor.	Avoid
1974	Another big wet vintage; mostly poor, even the best lean.	Now
1973	Again, vintage rain stretched the crop. Light wines, but many fruity and delicate. Now fading.	Now
1972	High acidity posed problems, but the wines are firm and full of character. Have aged well. Mostly fading now.	Soon
1971	Exceptional, splendid, powerful wines, fruity and well balanced. Small crop. Now nearly all mature.	Soon
1970	Attractive soft fruity wines, but few will develop much further and most are fading. Big crop.	Now
1969	A magnificent vintage with very few exceptions. Small crop. Most now ready, keep only the very best.	Now
1968	A disaster.	Never
1967	Not a good vintage but not a bad one either. The best have finesse, but most are now too old.	Now

Older fine vintages: '66, '62, '61, '59, '57, '55, '53, '52, '49, '47, '45.

Beaujolais Beaujolais is made in two ways: 'nouveau' or 'primeur' is for drinking immediately. Beaujolais-Villages and named Crus gain from one to five years in bottle. Exceptional Moulin-à-Vent vintages improve for as long as ten years.

	Beaujolais
1986	Not a classic.
1985	A classic vintage. The best will keep.
1984	Attractive wines for early use. Little to keep beyond two years.
1983	A splendid vintage, attractive as 'Nouveau' and fit to age up to 5 years.
1982	A big vintage, high in alcohol but short on fruit and charm. Drink up.

With very few exceptions (e.g. the best '76s) older Beaujolais is too old.

WHITE BURGUNDY

Côte de Beaune Well-made wines of good vintages with plenty of acidity as well as fruit will improve and gain depth and richness for some years – anything up to ten. Lesser wines from lighter years are ready for drinking after two or three years.

Year	Côte de Beaune whites	When to drink
1986	A good and plentiful vintage. Well-made wines have more acidity than '85 and will mature longer.	'89–on
1985	Very ripe grapes gave full-flavoured wines tending to low acidity, hence generally not for long life.	Now–'90
1984	Fresh and flowery wines. The best, with good acidity, should mature well.	Now–'92
1983	Very good vintage of powerful wines with great potential, likely to outlast the '82s.	Now–'95
1982	A good vintage for fat and tasty wines, tending to be low in acid but in some cases excellent.	Now–'89
1981	Crop reduced by hail but picked in perfect conditions. Much better than the red.	Now–'92
1980	Light, but some very harmonious small wines.	Now
1979	A big crop; quality good but not as high as quantity.	Now
1978	Excellent, the best of the decade.	Now–'90
1977	Pleasant light wines on the whole, some better than that.	Now
1976	Hot summer; very fine wines, some lacking acidity.	Now
1975	Hot summer, then vintage rain. Whites did much better than reds. Rot reduced quantity, but the grapes were ripe and the wine can be good.	Now
1974	Spring frosts reduced the crop. The hot summer made good wines, but they have aged disappointingly.	Now
1973	Very attractive, fruity, typical and plentiful, but not wines to keep any longer.	Drink soon
1972	Awkward wines to make with high acidity, even greenness, but plenty of character. The best have developed into classics.	Soon

The white wines of the Mâconnais (Pouilly-Fuissé, St-Véran, Mâcon-Villages) follow a similar pattern, but do not last as long. They are more appreciated for their freshness than their richness.

Chablis Grand Cru Chablis of vintages with both strength and acidity can age superbly for up to ten years. Premiers Crus proportionately less, but too many growers are stressing quantity, which results in wines that fade away without ever achieving the classic Chablis flavour. Only buy Petit Chablis of ripe years, and drink it young.

	Chablis	
1986	A welcome large crop of very good wines after two small ones.	Now–'91
1985	Crop reduced by winter damage, but high quality in a rather rich style.	Now–'90
1984	Another attractive vintage. Fresh bright wines.	Now–'89
1983	Excellent vintage. Plenty of typical firm Chablis, lovely Premiers Crus and superb Grands Crus to keep.	Now–'93
1982	Large quantities of ripe wines but low in acidity, good young drinking and good value.	Soon
1981	A small crop after hail and a cold flowering season means concentrated wine full of character and – rare in recent Chablis – fit to mature.	Now–'90
1980	Pleasant fragrant and fruity wine for drinking fairly young.	Now
1979	Too big a crop. Wines may be pleasant but cannot be truly first class.	Now
1978	Fine, firm, typical, developing beautifully.	Now–'88
1977	Good average in Grands and Premiers Crus, elsewhere badly frosted. Keeping well.	Now
1976	Heavy, soft wines, have not aged well.	Now
1975	Very good, most ready now.	Now
1974	A trifle sharp at first, but lively, attractive and typical.	Now

Older fine vintages: '71, '69, '67, '64, '61, '59, '57, '55, '53, '49.

Recent Vintages

RED BORDEAUX

For some wines bottle-age is optional; for these it is indispensable. Minor châteaux from light vintages need only two or three years, but even modest wines of great years can improve for fifteen years or so, and the great châteaux of these years need double that time.

Year	Médoc/red Graves	When to drink
1986	A monster vintage, again picked in hot sunny weather but on the heels of heavy rain. Concentration sometimes lacking, but many textbook wines.	'94–2005
1985	Big and excellent Médoc harvest in a heatwave; Graves crop reduced by spring frost. Splendid dark wines with good structure, potentially long-lived.	'92–2010
1984	A very difficult year with almost no Merlot, thus a tendency to hardness. Great skill needed to make balanced and typical wines. Graves and the northern Médoc (Pauillac, St-Estèphe) did best, Margaux least well.	Now–2000
1983	Third fine vintage in a row. Less of a blockbuster than '82; more variable, perhaps eventually no less satisfying.	Now–2010
1982	A large and early vintage. Deep colour, good tannin, low acid; in some cases the highest alcohol since '59. Hot fermentation caused some problems. The top wines are undoubtedly great; others may mature rather quickly.	Now–2010
1981	After three late harvests a normal one, fully ripe and healthy but picked in late September rain. Certainly good; in many cases very good, but some surprisingly light.	Now–2000
1980	Difficult and patchy; many good, wines for early drinking.	Now–'90
1979	Wet spring, moderate summer, fine autumn. A big crop, at least useful; at best very good.	Now–'95
1978	Excellent; deep-coloured and tannic; destined for long life.	Now–2000
1977	Very wet summer. Some very pleasant light wines.	Soon
1976	Excessively hot, dry summer, rain just before the vintage. Rather early-maturing, except for the best wines.	Now–?'95
1975	A splendid summer and very fine vintage, with deep colour, high sugar content and tannin. For long keeping.	Now to 2000 and on
1974	Oceans of disappointing light wines, though the best have good colour and have developed some character.	Now–'90
1973	Last-minute rain turned quality into quantity. A huge vintage, attractive young but lacking acidity and tannin.	Now
1972	High acidity from unripe grapes. Unripe wines, though the best may yet soften with age. Do not pay much for '72s.	Avoid
1971	Small crop. Less fruity than '70 and less consistent. Some top châteaux made very fine wine. Most are ready.	Soon
1970	Abundance *and* uniform quality. Big fruity wines with elegance and attractive suppleness. Although not tannic they are developing great distinction.	Now–late '90s
1969	Mean wines lacking fruit and colour.	Avoid
1968	This time a wet August was the culprit. Terrible.	Avoid
1967	Large; first judged to be light and for early drinking, has developed well in bottle and gained body and interest.	Now

Year	St-Emilion/Pomerol	When to drink
1986	In some parts, there was too much wine for concentrated quality, but many estates made close-to-perfect wine.	'94–2005
1985	A very good vintage, perhaps even better here than in the Médoc.	'92–2010
1984	The Merlot crop failed almost completely. Very little wine, and that disappointing.	Avoid
1983	Excellent, though technical problems will make it uneven.	Now–?2000
1982	Great concentration, colour depth and balance. A classic vintage to last out the century.	Now–1010
1981	Mostly picked before rain began; an excellent vintage – a great one in some cases.	Now–2000
1980	Merlot crop very low, quality very variable. Take great care.	Now–'87
1979	A good year for Merlot. Some very good wines, some even better than the preceding year.	Now–?'94
1978	Very good especially in Pomerol and neighbouring St-Emilion Crus, though some wines lack flesh.	Now–'95
1977	Terrible summer. Mediocre with few exceptions.	Avoid
1976	Very hot, dry summer and early vintage, but vintage rain made complications. Some excellent wines, if not very 'big'.	Now–'89
1975	Most St-Emilions good, the best superb. Frost in Pomerol reduced crops and made splendid concentrated wine.	Now–late '90s
1974	Vintage rain again. Mainly disappointing light wines.	Soon
1973	Good summer, big wet vintage. Pleasant; wines to drink young while the fruit is there.	Soon
1972	Poor summer but fine for the late vintage. Take care.	Now
1971	Small crop, fine wines with length and depth; many with more charm than Médocs.	Soon
1970	Glorious weather and beautiful wines with great fruit and strength throughout the district. Very big crop.	Now–'90s
1969	Fine summer, small wet vintage. At best agreeable.	Now
1968	A disaster. Endless rain.	Never
1967	On the whole better than Médoc and Graves.	Now

Older fine Bordeaux vintages: '66, '62, '61, '59, '55, '53, '52, '50, '49, '48, '47, '45.

SWEET WHITE WINES

Good vintages of Sauternes/Barsac and the luscious Chenin wines of Anjou (notably Coteaux du Layon) and Touraine (mostly Vouvray) are among the longest-lived white wines, improving for up to 25 years. Even moderate vintages are often worth keeping for the added depth of flavour that comes in bottle.

Year	Sauternes/Barsac
1986	Promising wines made.
1985	The hot autumn made very ripe strong wine, but only a minority benefitted from noble rot. The best will be in a very high category.
1984	Some good, though not grand, wines from determined growers who waited for late good weather.
1983	Too dry for much 'noble rot', but patient proprietors made good wines.
1982	Only Ch. Yquem had 'noble rot'; other châteaux had to settle for plain sweet wine – which can be delicious nonetheless.
1981	A good crop with plenty of 'noble rot', but a number of châteaux had trouble with volatile acidity. Some excellent wine, but be careful.
1980	Good conditions in November for a small crop with 'noble rot'. Gentle and enjoyable rather than impressive. Beginning to be ready.
1979	Light in alcohol but full of 'noble rot'. Many good wines to keep.
1978	Small crop. High alcohol but no 'noble rot'. Not for long keeping.
1977	Very small crop with no good sweet wines.
1976	Superb summer, damp autumn; excellent wines. Drink now–'95.
1975	Glorious October weather, rich wines. Drink now–'95.
1974	Rain ruined the crop.
1973	The same sad story.

Older fine vintages: '71, '70, '67, '62, '59, '53, '49, '45, '21.

Anjou/Touraine

1986	A wide range of qualities, mostly fair to good. Few fine sweet wines.
1985	A huge vintage of very high quality, some with noble rot; many moelleux wines for long maturing.
1984	One of the successes of the vintage: good sweet and dry wines.
1983	An excellent year. Both Vouvray and Layon made fine 'moelleux' wines.
1982	A very big early vintage with some 'noble rot' but also rain. Some good sweet wines and much ordinary.
1981	A small crop hampered by rain.
1980	Not a sweet-wine vintage.
1979	Big vintage, at least average quality. Keeping well.
1978	Small quantities of fine wine. Keeping well.
1977	Very limited crop; little sweet wine.
1976	A splendid year. Keeping well.
1975	Excellent, especially in Anjou.
1974	Some good wine, but a difficult cool vintage.

Older fine vintages: '73, '71, '64, '61, '59, '55, '49, '43, '34.

DRY WHITE WINES

White Graves and other dry white Bordeaux and Dordogne wines, the Sauvignon wines of the upper Loire (Sancerre/Pouilly Fumé) and Muscadet are all wines to drink young, though good white Graves can age well for up to ten years. Muscadet drinks best the year after the vintage, Sancerre/Pouilly Fumé up to three years later.

Bordeaux

1986	Excellent conditions for dry wines.
1985	Careful cool vinification was essential in a heatwave. Many wines are soft, but the best are big and age-worthy.
1984	Some text-book wines, fresh, fruity and charming for drinking in two or three years.
1983	An excellent year for balance and lively flavour. The best will keep.
1982	Cellars with cooling made excellent wines, in others fast fermentation was a problem. Few have enough acidity to keep.
1981	Deliciously round gentle wines – not for laying down.
1980	Problems with rot and unripeness. Needed sugar. But some successes.
1979	A difficult big vintage with low natural sugar. Some good delicate wines.
1978	Extremely good well-balanced wines. Developing well.

Sancerre/Pouilly Fumé

1986	Extremely fruity and crisp wines, fragrant and typical.
1985	After severe winter damage, a small but excellent harvest. The best wines are worth ageing.
1984	Good results. Some growers prefer '84 to '83.
1983	Finer quality and more character than '82.
1982	An all-round success, a big early and ripe vintage for drinking young.

Muscadet

1986	Excellent wines to last 2–3 years.
1985	Some untypically big and fruity wines; the best will mature well until 1990.
1984	A very good vintage with classic attributes.

Avoid older Muscadet.

Germany

RED RHÔNE

The classic wines of the Rhône valley include Côte Rôtie and Hermitage in the north, Châteauneuf-du-Pape in the south. Most Côte du Rhône-Villages are in the south.

Only the best wines are made for maturing, but those that do can achieve superlative flavour and bouquet. Châteauneuf-du-Pape is a particularly variable area: a few conservatives make wine to keep ten years; most only need four to five. Plain Côtes du Rhône matures in one to five years depending on the vintage and the maker.

Year	Northern (including Hermitage)
1986	A large vintage of similar quality to the last.
1985	Very ripe and strong wines tending to lack concentration. Hermitage best, but probably not for very long ageing.
1984	Very sound reds, for fairly early drinking. Attractive whites.
1983	A small crop of concentrated and tannic wines of fine quality, for a long life.
1982	Fine and balanced wines; much better than the south. Ready quite early.
1981	An average crop. The whites best.
1980	A reduced crop but quality at least good; some excellent.
1979	A very good vintage. Fine quality, if not as great as '78.
1978	A classic vintage, the best since '61. For long maturing.
1977	A poor light year.
1976	Excellent with big fruity wines, still needing time.
1975	Poor, as in Burgundy. Rain caused rot. Avoid.
1974	The best are light and fruity, for early drinking.
1973	Attractive, but not for keeping.
1972	Very good; now ready.
1971	Very good, with the strength and depth to last.
1970	Full, ripe and round. Now mature.
1969	Excellent, rich in alcohol, tannic and spicy, especially Côte Rôtie.
1968	Unremarkable.
1967	Full and heady, now mature.
1966	Rich and strong with a good bouquet. Most mature.

Year	Southern (including Châteauneuf-du-Pape and Côtes du Rhône)
1986	Quantity limited by drought: quality exceptional.
1985	Very large harvest, especially of Grenache, making very strong wines, but only the best will mature for long.
1984	The best wines may be the lively whites. The Grenache crop was poor, the reds rather edgy but aromatic. Top wines should age well.
1983	Reduced quantities of ripe, tasty wines; the best very good.
1982	A poor vintage: too much alcohol and too little colour and flavour.
1981	Drought resulted in a small crop of good wine; not exceptional.
1980	Abundance of good, relatively light, wines.
1979	A very useful big vintage. Good quality.
1978	A classic vintage, rich and strong. For long maturing.
1977	Ripe but needs drinking.
1976	Very good. Big wines to keep.
1975	Disappointing after high hopes in the summer. Avoid.
1974	Wide variation; the average is light. Some good Gigondas.

ALSACE
The ordinary cheaper wines need little or no ageing. Réserves and Grands Crus of good vintages gain interest and quality in bottle for five years or more.

1986	A very good vintage for well-balanced dry wines. *Vendanges tardives* fewer but excellent.
1985	Another splendid vintage, comparable to 1983 with many *vendanges tardives*.
1984	A very late but sound, typical and racy crop, particularly for Riesling.
1983	Superb, the best since 1976.
1982	A very big vintage of fine, some outstanding, wines.
1981	Highly satisfactory, plenty of good wine, though not for long keeping.
1979	Big, ripe vintage, successful for both Riesling and Gewürztraminer. Ready.
1978	Average or better. Some still need keeping.
1976	A stupendous vintage, many *vendanges tardives* (late pickings) to make Beerenauslese-type wine, which keeps excellently.

Older fine vintages: '70, '69, '67, '64, '61.

CHAMPAGNE

1986	A very large crop of mixed quality, unlikely to be outstanding.
1985	A large and excellent harvest, promising vintage wines.
1984	Average or below; unlikely to appear as a vintage.
1983	The record for quantity broken again. Decent quality.
1982	The biggest vintage ever (until the next). A godsend, since stocks were desperately low. Ideal non-vintage material, not for long life.
1981	A disastrously small crop, but of vintage quality.
1980	Tiny crop, good quality.
1979	Enormous harvest of remarkable quality.
1978	Very small vintage, some very good.
1977	Good non-vintage material.
1976	Drought caused difficulties. Good full-bodied vintage generally now ready.
1975	Very good despite late rain. Fine vintage wines which will keep.

Older champagne is a gamble, but can be one of life's great experiences. Only risk old vintages from top shippers. The following are relatively light; known for their finesse (and often keep better than heavier ones): '62, '53, '52, '43, '41. The '69, '66, '61 and '45 were bigger and heavier. The '45s have kept better than the '61s.

MOSEL/SAAR/RUWER

Mosels (including Saar and Ruwer wines) are so attractive young that their keeping qualities are not often enough explored, and wines older than seven years or so are unusual. But well-made wines of Kabinett class gain from two or three years in bottle, Spätleses by a little longer, and Ausleses and Beerenausleses by anything from 10 to 20 years, depending on the vintage. As a rule, in poor years the Saar and Ruwer fare worse than the Middle Mosel and make sharp, thin wines, but in the best years they can surpass the whole of Germany for elegance and 'breed'.

Year		When to drink
1986	A copious and useful Riesling vintage, with few stars but with good acidity, balance and length.	1988–94
1985	Winter damage, hail and drought all reduced the crop: autumn sunshine brought above-average ripeness. Riesling made racy typical wines, in the best sites three-quarters Kabinett and Spätlese which will mature well.	1988–2000
1984	Very late vintage with high acidity. Hardly any Kabinett or better wines, but QbAs should be firm and last well.	Now
1983	The best year since '76, nearly all Spätlese and Auslese – perhaps like '75 in style. Top wines are almost perfect.	Now–2000
1982	A very big crop of great promise was spoiled by harvest rain. Half in QbA, one-third Kabinett, only 10% Spätlese or better. The best sites made some fine wines.	Now
1981	The Middle Mosel had a bigger crop than 1980, spoilt only by heavy rain at harvest time. 30% of the wine is Kabinett and 20% Spätlese or better: a good result. The Saar and Ruwer had a very small crop of well-balanced wines.	Now–'89
1980	Miserably small crop. No late-picked, higher-grade wines, but standard ones are reasonably well balanced.	Now
1979	Severe winter damaged all but Riesling. Upper Mosel devastated. In Middle Mosel a good range of qualities, including fine Spätleses.	Now
1978	Small crop of only average quality; very few Kabinett or better wines, but well balanced.	Now
1977	A big crop of moderate quality, 75% of it 'Qualitätswein', only 10% in the top grades.	Soon
1976	Very good small vintage, with some superlative sweet wines and almost no dry. Keeping well.	Now–'90
1975	Very good; many Spätleses and Ausleses. Have matured faster than expected.	Soon

Older fine vintages: '71 '69, '67, '64, '59, '53, '49, '45.

RHINE/NAHE/PALATINATE (RHEINPFALZ)

Even the best wines can be drunk with pleasure after two or three years, but Kabinett, Spätlese and Auslese wines of good vintages gain enormously in character and complexity by keeping for longer. Rheingau wines tend to be longest-lived, often improving for ten years or more, but wines from the Nahe and the Palatinate can last nearly as long. Rheinhessen wines usually mature sooner, and dry Franconian wines are best at three or four years. The Riesling, predominant in the Rheingau, benefits most from hot summers; Palatinate wines can taste almost overripe.

1986	Plenty of well-balanced QbA Riesling which will mature well. Other grape varieties less successful.	1988–94
1985	Winter damage and drought led to a small crop (very small in Rheinpfalz). Many Kabinetts and Spätleses of good quality for the medium term.	1988–92
1984	A few Kabinett and very few Spätleses in Rheinhessen and Rheinpfalz. The vast majority decent QbA wine with some keeping potential.	Now–1992
1983	An enormous crop, and the best since '76, lacking only 'noble rot' to make it great. Many Spätleses, few Ausleses except in the Palatinate.	Now–2000
1982	The biggest harvest ever, but largely QbA quality because of heavy rain. Rheingau 25% Kabinett, Nahe 20% (and 10% Spätlese), Palatinate 10% (and 5% Spätlese). 'Useful' is the only word.	Now
1981	The Rheingau was unlucky, with scarcely any fine wines. The Nahe did better with 30% Kabinett or above; Rheinhessen was very satisfactory and the Rheinpfalz Rieslings have made exceptionally good Kabinetts and Spätleses.	Now
1980	Rheingau and Nahe suffered badly; small disappointing harvest. Rheinpfalz made more and better.	Now
1979	Severe winter damage in Rheinhessen but some good results in quality, especially from Riesling. About half 'Qualitätswein', half of better qualities. Keep only the best.	Now
1978	A disappointing year. Only 'table' or 'Qualitätswein' – very little better, except in Palatinate.	Soon
1977	Average quality in Palatinate, below in Rheingau.	Soon
1976	The richest vintage since 1921 in places. Very few dry wines.	Now–late '90s
1975	A very good Riesling year; a high percentage of Kabinetts and Spätleses. Many now already mature.	Soon

Older fine vintages: '71, '69, '67, '64, '59, '57, '53, '49, '45.
Franconia Generally follows Rhine vintages.

Recent Vintages

The detailed analysis which is given to the vintages of France and Germany is not so appropriate to the way the wines of the rest of the world are made and sold. Outstanding years are worth noting everywhere, and particularly in Italy and Austria, but the strict observance of vintage dates on labels is still only loosely practised in most of Portugal, Spain, Greece and the rest of wine-growing Europe, with the exceptions of vintage port and the fine wines of Rioja and Catalonia.

ITALY

Exceptional years in the last decade have been:				
Chianti Classico:	1975	1978	1982	1985
Piemonte (including Barolo):	1978	1982		1985

Very Good Years:				
Chianti Classico:	1970	1978	1983	1986
Piemonte (including Barolo):	1975	1979	1980	1986

1972 was poor, especially in Piemonte, where many Barolos were declassified into Nebbiolo. 1973 was large, but only average quality. 1974 was good, but nothing special. 1976 was wet, difficult and disappointing. 1977 was only average. 1979 was good in both regions, 1980 good in Piemonte but only adequate in Chianti. 1981 was hampered by rain in the north of Italy. Piemonte made some good wines. The centre and south of the country did very well. 1982 was excellent almost everywhere. 1983 was much more mixed; excellent for the whites of Friuli and the Northeast, very good in Piemonte and at least good in Tuscany: less satisfactory farther south. 1984 was disappointing in most regions.

AUSTRIA

1985 produced a good vintage. 1983 was an outstandingly ripe vintage. Some wines are low in acid but large amounts of Beerenauslese were produced, particularly in the Burgenland. 1984 made good wines for early drinking.

THE NEW WORLD: CALIFORNIA

In the New World vintages tend to be very much more regular than in Europe. It is not safe to assume, however, that every year has the same qualities. The following notes on recent vintages in California's Napa Valley indicate some of the climatic and other factors involved.

Year	The Napa Valley
1986	A very cool summer and a protracted vintage gave wine growers the opportunity to make very good wines of all sorts.
1985	Coolish ripening season. Good acidity should make elegant wines to last well.
1984	Spring was early and frost-free and flowering went well. July was very hot even in usually foggy areas. The vintage was very early and in places frantic, but very high quality was generally expected.
1983	A big crop was rained on at harvest time. Quality depends on the maker; whether he picked early or late, chose healthy grapes and rejected others, and resisted the temptation to blend watery batches. Plenty of 'noble rot'.
1982	Tropical storms bringing rain and hail in September damaged the prospects for a very good vintage. Rot (some 'noble') infected Riesling, Chenin Blanc and Zinfandel. Sauvignon Blanc, Chardonnay, some Pinot Noir and a good deal of Cabernet were successfully picked. Rather 'French-style' wines are the result. Sonoma and the Central Coast seem to have done best.
1981	A mild winter and frost-free spring, hot June and steady ripening weather brought an exceptionally early harvest. Extremely good whites include many late-harvest ones, but some too alcoholic. Reds will generally mature early.
1980	All-time record for quantity but awkward to handle, everything ripened at once. Sugar/acid balance was very good for growers who timed it right. Good reds and very good whites.
1979	Another record crop. Mild spring, fine summer, but hot September then cool October caused problems, especially with Cabernet Sauvignon. Uneven quality.
1978	Record crop. Wet winter, no spring frost, some early mildew, very warm autumn. Difficult conditions leading to wide variations in quality.
1977	Long drought ended at vintage time. Reduced quantity but surprising quality.
1976	Dry winter, hot flowering season and summer, extreme drought by autumn made a small crop, high in both sugar and acid. Reds variable; at best excellent, and some excellent whites.
1975	Wet spring, cool summer, late harvest into autumn rains. Good for whites and early ripening reds. Cabernet light and in some cases fine.
1974	Little frost, long cool summer, ideal ripening conditions. A big crop in perfect condition. Big-bodied healthy Cabernets; some considered great.
1973	Record vintage for quantity, quality overall fair to very good.

SPAIN: RIOJA

The best vintages in general of the last two decades have been 1964, '66, '68, '70, '74, '76, '78 '82 and '83. Degree of maturity (and indeed quality) depends entirely on the bodega. Some '76s are mature: some '64s will still improve. 1981 was a very good year in both Rioja and Penedes, where the whites were reported to be 'exceptional'. 1982 was a dry year with reduced crops, but the red wines look first-class. 1983 was good but sadly small. 1984 will probably produce some good wines, particularly in Rioja Alta. 1985 had drought problems, but Rioja reservas will be good. Vintage-time rain caused problems in 1986

PORT

Long ageing in bottle is part of the process of making vintage port. Each shipper each year decides whether his wine is worthy of early bottling and 'declaring' as 'vintage' port.

Year	Port
1986	Summer drought and a rainy start to the vintage. Quality probably average.
1985	A large and at first sight good-quality harvest.
1984	Very promising aromatic young wines. Too soon to say more.
1983	A very late harvest, but in the high Douro very good quality. Many shippers declared.
1982	Ideal conditions throughout the year. A small crop, likely to be an extremely good vintage.
1981	A difficult year with drought followed by rain at harvest. Not a vintage.
1980	A very hot dry summer, made powerful wine. Most shippers declared.
1979	Big crop of average quality.
1978	Small harvest after summer drought. Declared by eight shippers.
1977	30 shippers declared. An outstanding vintage with ten years to go.
1976	Very dry summer, wet autumn. Not declared.
1975	Declared by 24 shippers. Hot summer and autumn with just enough rain. An early-maturing vintage beginning to drink well.
1974	Cool year; late harvest; good but not vintage.
1973	Wet autumn; big watery crop. Not a vintage.
1972	Hot summer, wet vintage. Early pickers did well: only three shippers declared.
1971	Problems with rot. Not a vintage.
1970	Ideal weather. A very fine balanced vintage declared by 21 shippers.
1969	Not a vintage.
1968	Not a vintage.
1967	Good but delicate. Only declared by six shippers.
1966	A big and fruity vintage starting to drink well. 22 shippers declared.
1965	One shipper (Ferreira) declared.
1964	Not a vintage.
1963	The best of the sixties; one of the best this century. Classic, rich, strong but fruitier than '45. 23 shippers declared. Becoming excellent to drink.
1962	One shipper (Offley Forrester) declared.
1961	Not a vintage.
1960	Not heavy but reliable and now delicious. 26 shippers declared. Drink from now–1990s.
1959	Not a vintage.
1958	Declared by six shippers. Delicate, some elegant. Drink soon.

Earlier Vintages

1955	Big strapping wines, most now richly mature. 21 shippers declared.
1950	Like 1958. Drink soon.
1948	Lovely rich wine; now ready.
1947	Good, but mature now.
1945	A great classic; huge, dark and concentrated. Now reaching its best, but there is no hurry.

AUSTRALIA

1986	The third excellent vintage in a row. Very good Hunter whites, Victoria reds, and most wines in S. Australia.
1985	Very good, with finely balanced wines, the result of a cool season.
1984	Has been hailed as an Annus Mirabilis all over Australia. Both reds and whites should be exceptional.
1983	Drought and flood caused great problems, but a cool January gave well-balanced juice in most cases. Western Australia claims an outstanding vintage.

France

France

France has more than one million hectares of vineyards. Nurturing the vines is an unceasing task in all weathers. The cold-fingered January job of pruning is one of the most important. The quantity and quality of the next vintage depend on the pruner leaving precisely the right buds on each vine.

FINISTÈRE
o Brest

CÔTES-DU-
NORD
St-Brieuc o

o Quimper

MORBIHAN
Vannes o

ATL

Nan
Gros Pl

When the last raindrop has been counted, and no geological stone is left unturned, there will still remain the imponderable question of national character which makes France the undisputed mistress of the vine; the producer of infinitely more and more varied great wines than all the rest of the world.

France is not only sensuous and painstaking; France is methodical. She not only has good vineyards; she defines, classifies and controls them. The listing, in order, of the best sites has been going on for nearly 200 years. In the last 60 or so it has become more and more important, as the world's interest, not only in wine but also in consumer protection, has grown.

This atlas does not attempt to reproduce the boundaries set by law to every French wine region. It has the wine drinker rather than the lawyer in mind. There are three classes of wine with which we are concerned: Appellations Contrôlées, which are guarantees not only of origin but of a certain standard, administered by the Institut National des Appellations d'Origine. A second rank, for good wines of chiefly local interest, known as VDQS – Vin Délimité de Qualité Supérieure – is dwindling, as its members graduate to 'AC' status. But a third, Vins de Pays, introduced in 1973 to encourage local pride in what used to be the humblest grade, is a sector with a future.

— - — International boundary

— — — Département boundary

o   Chief town of département

•   Centre of VDQS area

Côte Roannaise   VDQS name – a guide to VDQS wines not n
elsewhere appears on pages 136–1

Appellation Contrôlée areas

Champagne (pages 110–111)
Loire Valley (pages 118–119)
Burgundy (page 61)
Savoie and Jura (page 133)
Rhône (pages 124 and 129)
Southwest (pages 134–135)
Cognac (page 291)
Bergerac (page 109)
Bordeaux (page 80)
Jurançon (pages 134–135)
Madiran and Armagnac (page 293)
Languedoc and Roussillon (pages 130–131)
Provence (page 132)
Alsace (page 115)
Other wine-producing areas

Proportional Circles

Area of vineyard per département in thousands of hectares   44

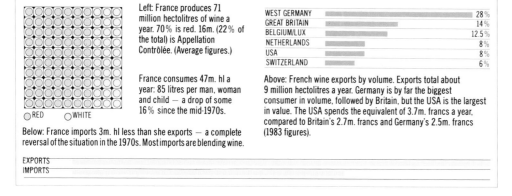

Left: France produces 71 million hectolitres of wine a year. 70% is red. 16m. (22% of the total) is Appellation Contrôlée. (Average figures.)

France consumes 47m. hl a year: 85 litres per man, woman and child – a drop of some 16% since the mid-1970s.

○ RED   ○ WHITE

WEST GERMANY	28%
GREAT BRITAIN	14%
BELGIUM/LUX	12.5%
NETHERLANDS	8%
USA	8%
SWITZERLAND	6%

Above: French wine exports by volume. Exports total about 9 million hectolitres a year. Germany is by far the biggest consumer in volume, followed by Britain, but the USA is the largest in value. The USA spends the equivalent of 3.7m. francs a year, compared to Britain's 2.7m. francs and Germany's 2.5m. francs (1983 figures).

Below: France imports 3m. hl less than she exports – a complete reversal of the situation in the 1970s. Most imports are blending wine.

EXPORTS
IMPORTS

Calais

PAS-DE-CALAIS

Lille

BELGIQUE

NORD

Arras

SOMME

Amiens

AISNE

Mézières

ARDENNES

LUXEMBOURG

DEUTSCHLAND

SEINE-MARITIME

OISE

Laon

Metz   *Vins de Moselle*

MOSELLE

BAS-

Le Havre

Rouen

Beauvais

Reims

MARNE

Châlons-sur-Marne

Bar-le-Duc

MEUSE

MEURTHE-

Toul   *Côtes de Toul*

Nancy

Strasbourg

RHIN

Caen

CALVADOS

EURE

Evreux

VAL-D'OISE

HAUTS-
DE-SEINE

SEINE-
ST-
DENIS

PARIS
ET MARNE

VAL-
DE-
MARNE

Melun

MARNE

19

ET-
MOSELLE

VOSGES

Épinal

Colmar

HAUT-
RHIN

ORME

Alençon

EURE-

Chartres

ESSONNE

SEINE

Troyes

AUBE

4

Aube

HAUTE-

Chaumont-
en-Bassigny

MARNE

Vésoul

Belfort

8

MAYENNE

Laval

le Mans

SARTHE

ET-LOIR

LOIRET

Orléans   *Vin de l'Orléanais*

Gien

Vins des Coteaux du Giennois

YONNE

Auxerre

Chablis

St-Bris-le-Vineux   *Sauvignon de St-Bris*

3

CÔTE-D'OR

Dijon

Doubs

Besançon

HAUTE-
SAÔNE

DOUBS

LOIR-ET-
CHER

Montoire-sur-le-Loir   *Coteaux du Vendômois*

Blois

Cour Cheverny   *Cheverny*

INDRE-
ET-
LOIRE

Angers   21   *nis*

aux d'Ancenis

MAINE-ET-
LOIRE

Tours   11

Valençay

12

Thouars   *Vin du Thouarsais*

INDRE

Châteauroux

CHER

Bourges

3

NIÈVRE

Nevers

1

Beaune

le Creusôt

SAÔNE-ET-LOIRE

11

Mâcon

JURA

Lons-le-
Saulnier

Genève

HAUTE-

SAVOIE

Annecy

DEUX-
SÈVRES

Niort

3

VIENNE

Poitiers

5

*Vins du
Haut-Poitou*

Châteaumeillant   *Châteaumeillant*

ALLIER

Moulins

St-Pourçain-
sur-Sioule   *St-Pourçain*

Bourg-en-Bresse

AIN

2

RHÔNE

Roanne   *Côte Roannaise*

Lyon

Rhône

Belley   *Vins du Bugey*

SAVOIE

Chambéry

3

Guéret

la Rochelle

CHARENTE-

Cognac

CHARENTE

MARITIME

Angoulême

52   45

18

CREUSE

2

HAUTE-
VIENNE

Limoges

PUY-DE-DÔME

Clermont-
Ferrand   *Côtes d'Auvergne*

Boën-sur-Lignon   *Côtes du Forez*

LOIRE

1

21

St-
Etienne

ISÈRE

Grenoble

ITALIA

CORRÈZE

Tulle

1

Périgueux

DORDOGNE

98

Aurillac

CANTAL

le Puy

HAUTE-LOIRE

1

Tournon

Valence

16

ARDÈCHE

Privas

18

DRÔME

HAUTES-ALPES

Gap

1

Bordeaux

GIRONDE

Libourne   *Dordogne*

Garonne

Entraygues   *Vins d'Entraygues et du Fel*

Estaing   *Vins d'Estaing*

Clairvaux   *Vins de Marcillac*   Rodez

LOT

Cahors

LOZÈRE

Mende

Saint-Remèze   *Côtes du Vivarais*

Tulette

VAUCLUSE

Avignon

Digne   2

ALPES DE
HAUTE-PROVENCE

ALPES-

MARITIMES

Nice

Marmande   *Côtes du Marmandais*

LOT-ET-
GARONNE

Buzet   *Côtes du Brulhois*
la Villedieu-du-Temple   *Vins de Lavilledieu*   Agen

9

Mont-de-Marsan

LANDES

Vins du Tursan   Geaune   *Côtes de St-Mont*

5

GERS

Auch

23

7

Montauban

TARN-ET-
GARONNE

AVEYRON

Gaillac   Albi

TARN

Tarn

16

St-Christol   *Coteaux de St-Christol*

Nîmes

GARD

Bellegarde   *Costières du Gard*   18

Pierrevert   *Coteaux de Pierrevert*

Tour d'Aigues   *Côtes du Luberon*

BOUCHES-
DU-
RHÔNE

les Baux   *Coteaux des Baux-en-Provence*

Coteaux Varois

45

Draguignan

Toulouse

HAUTE-
GARONNE

Pic-St-Loup

St-Saturnin
Montpeyroux   *St-Georges d'Orques*   St-Drézery

Vérargues   *Coteaux de Vérargues*

Cabrières   *Coteaux du Languedoc*   *Coteaux de la Méjanelle*

Marseille

VAR

Toulon

PYRÉNÉES

Pau

Tarbes

HAUTES-
PYRÉNÉES

Cabardès

Carcassonne   *Côtes de la Malepère*

Narbonne   *Quatourze, La Clape*

Lézignan-Corbières   *Corbières*   *Corbières Supérieures*

Pinet   *Picpoul de Pinet*

HÉRAULT

85

147

Montpellier

ATLANTIQUES

1

Foix

ARIÈGE

6

AUDE

Perpignan

110

55

PYRÉNÉES-
ORIENTALES

ESPAÑA

N

SUISSE

1:3,625,000

Km. 0   50   100   150 Km.
Miles 0   50   100 Miles

59

Burgundy

The very name of Burgundy has a ring of richness about it. Let Paris be France's head, Champagne her soul, there is no doubt about what Burgundy is: her stomach. It is a land of long meals, well supplied with the best materials (Charolais beef to the west, Bresse chickens to the east – and snails on the vines). It is the most famous of the ancient duchies of France. But even before Christianity came to France, it was famous for its wine.

Burgundy is not one big vineyard, but the name of a province which contains at least three of France's best. By far the richest and most important is the Côte d'Or, in the centre, composed of the Côte de Nuits and the Côte de Beaune. But Chablis and Beaujolais and the Mâconnais have old reputations which owe nothing to their elder brother's.

For all her ancient fame and riches, Burgundy still seems curiously simple and rustic. There is hardly a grand house from end to end of the Côte d'Or – none of the elegant country estates which stamp, say, the Médoc as a creation of leisure and wealth in the 18th and 19th centuries. Some of the few big holdings of land, those of the Church, were broken up by Napoleon. Now, in fact, it is one of the most

Above: Beaune is the wine capital of Burgundy; many would say of the world. The city's great landmark, the silvery roof of the medieval Hospices, gleams through the mist of an autumn evening.

○ RED ○ WHITE

Right: the whole of Burgundy produces four times as much red wine as white. The average total production of red wine is 1.6m. hectolitres.
Below: some 40% of Burgundy's wine is exported. Switzerland and the US taking almost half.

		BEAUJOLAIS	REST OF BURGUNDY
BELGIUM/LUX	8.5%		
CANADA	4%		
DENMARK	1.75%		
GREAT BRITAIN	14.5%		
ITALY	0.13%		
JAPAN	1.25%		
NETHERLANDS	6%		
SWEDEN	1%		
SWITZERLAND	24%		
USA	20%		
WEST GERMANY	12.5%		

fragmented of the important winegrowing districts of France.

The fragmentation of Burgundy is the cause of the one great drawback of its wine: its unpredictability. From the geographer's point of view the human factor is unmappable, and in Burgundy, more than in most places, it needs to be given the limelight. For even when you have pinned down a wine to one particular *climat* (field of vines) in one particular *finage* (village) in one particular year, it could still, in many cases, have been made by any one of six or seven men owning small parcels of the land, and reared in any one of six or seven cellars. 'Monopoles', or whole vineyards in the hands of one grower, are rare exceptions. Even the smallest grower has parcels of two or three vineyards. Bigger ones may own a total of 40 or 50 acres (16–20 hectares) spread in small lots in a score of vineyards from one end of the Côte to the other. The Clos de Vougeot has more than 60 growers in its 125 acres (50 hectares).

For this very reason the great majority of burgundy is bought in barrel from the grower when it is new by négociants (or shippers), who blend it with other wines from the same area to achieve marketable quantities of a standard wine. It is offered to the world not as the product of a specific grower, whose production of that particular wine may be only a cask or two, but as the wine of a given district (be it as specific as a vineyard or as vague as a village) *élevé* – literally, educated – by the shipper.

The reputations of these négociant-éleveurs (many of whom are also growers themselves) vary from being the touchstone of the finest burgundy to something rather more earthy.

What is certain is that all the very finest wine, and a growing proportion of the total, goes to market, as it does all over the world, with the most detailed possible description of its antecedents on its label . . . and these almost always include the name of the proprietor of the vineyard and the fact that he bottles the wine in his own cellars.

The map on this page shows the whole of winegrowing Burgundy, the relative sizes and positions of the big southern areas of Beaujolais and the Mâconnais, Chablis in the north, the tiny Côte Chalonnaise and the narrow strip of the Côte d'Or and its little-known hinterland, the Hautes Côtes de Beaune and the Hautes Côtes de Nuits. The key is an index to the detailed, large-scale maps of the areas which follow.

There are a hundred or so Appellations Contrôlées in Burgundy. Most of them refer to geographical areas and appear on the next 18 pages. Built into these geographical appellations is a classification by quality which is practically a work of art in itself. It is explained on page 64. However, the appellations Bourgogne, Bourgogne Aligoté (for white wine), Bourgogne Passe-Tout-Grains and Bourgogne Grand Ordinaire can be used for wine from the appropriate grapes coming from any part of Burgundy, including the less good vineyards within famous communes which have not the right to the commune name.

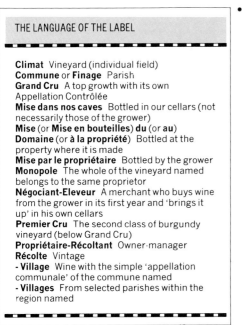

THE LANGUAGE OF THE LABEL

Climat Vineyard (individual field)
Commune or **Finage** Parish
Grand Cru A top growth with its own Appellation Contrôlée
Mise dans nos caves Bottled in our cellars (not necessarily those of the grower)
Mise (or **Mise en bouteilles**) **du** (or **au**)
Domaine (or **à la propriété**) Bottled at the property where it is made
Mise par le propriétaire Bottled by the grower
Monopole The whole of the vineyard named belongs to the same proprietor
Négociant-Eleveur A merchant who buys wine from the grower in its first year and 'brings it up' in his own cellars
Premier Cru The second class of burgundy vineyard (below Grand Cru)
Propriétaire-Récoltant Owner-manager
Récolte Vintage
- Village Wine with the simple 'appellation communale' of the commune named
- Villages From selected parishes within the region named

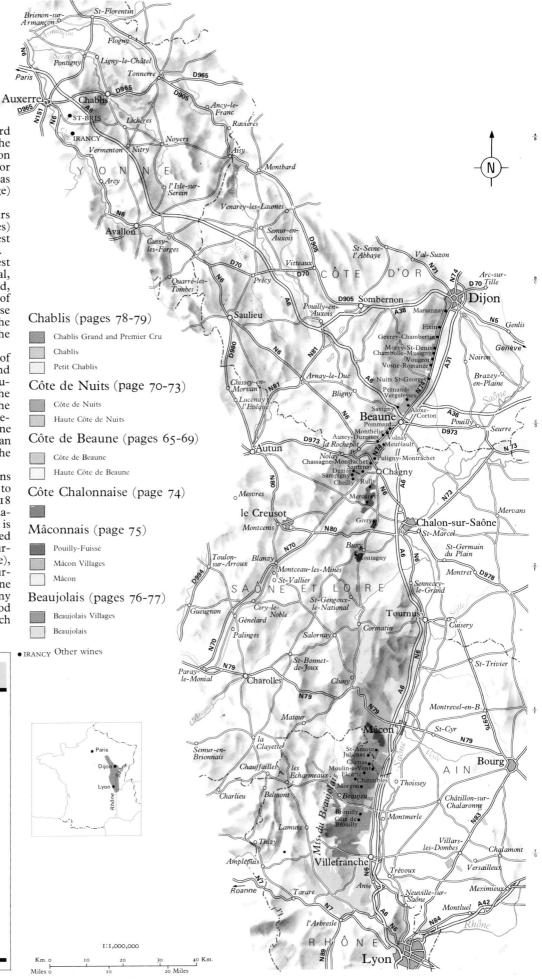

Chablis (pages 78-79)
Chablis Grand and Premier Cru
Chablis
Petit Chablis

Côte de Nuits (page 70-73)
Côte de Nuits
Haute Côte de Nuits

Côte de Beaune (pages 65-69)
Côte de Beaune
Haute Côte de Beaune

Côte Chalonnaise (page 74)

Mâconnais (page 75)
Pouilly-Fuissé
Mâcon Villages
Mâcon

Beaujolais (pages 76-77)
Beaujolais Villages
Beaujolais

• IRANCY Other wines

1:1,000,000

Km. 0   10   20   30   40 Km.
Miles 0   10   20 Miles

61

Burgundy: The Quality Factor

A Burgundian understandably feels a certain reverence towards the commonplace-looking ridge of the Côte d'Or, as towards an unknown god. One is bound to wonder at the fact that a few small parcels of land on this hill give superlative wine, each with its own positive personality, and that others do not. Surely one can discover the facts that distinguish one parcel from another – giving to some grapes more sugar, thicker skins, a pulp more rich in minerals.

One can. And one cannot. Soil and subsoil have been analysed time and again. Temperature and humidity and wind direction have been recorded; must has been examined under the microscope . . . yet the central mystery remains. One can only put down certain physical facts, and place beside them the reputations of the great wines. No one can prove how they are connected.

Burgundy is the northernmost area in the world which produces great red wine. Its climate pattern in summer is, in fact, curiously like that of Bordeaux – the continental influence making up to some extent for its

position farther north. Yet total failure of the vintage is a greater problem here. No overriding climatic consideration can explain the excellence of the wine – or even why a vineyard was established here in the first place. There are certain local or microclimatic advantages: the shelter provided by the hills from wet west winds; the slight elevation above the fogs of the plain; but nothing unique.

Looking further for reasons, one turns to the soil. Here there are more clues. The ridge of the Côte d'Or is the edge of a plateau built up of various sandy limestones. Erosion, by the action of ice in the last periglacial period 18,000 years ago and since then by weather and cultivation, has broken them down into soil. Rubble and soil fall down the slope, which benefits both the nourishment and the drainage of the vine lower down. The more the soil is cultivated the greater the mixture of varied soil types – helped also by the carting of good earth on to the better vineyards: in 1749 150 wagonloads of turf were spread on the vineyard of Romanée-Conti, and the same sort of earth-moving goes on today.

The Côte de Nuits is a sharper slope than the Côte de Beaune. Along its lower part, generally about a third of the way up the slope, runs a narrow outcrop of marlstone, making limy clay soil. Marl by itself would be too rich a soil for the highest-quality wine, but in combination with the silt and scree washed down from the hard limestone higher up it is perfect. Erosion continues the blend below the actual outcrop. Above the marl, the thin light limestone soil is generally too poor for vines.

In the Côte de Beaune the marly outcrop (Argovien) is wider and higher on the hill; instead of a narrow strip of vineyard under a beetling brow of limestone there is a broad and gentle slope vineyards can climb. The vines almost reach the scrubby peak in places.

On the dramatic isolated hill of Corton the soil formed from the marlstone is the best part of the vineyard, with only a little wood-covered cap of hard limestone above it.

In Meursault the limestone reappearing below the marl on the slope forms a second and lower shoulder to the hill, limy and very stony; excellent for white wine.

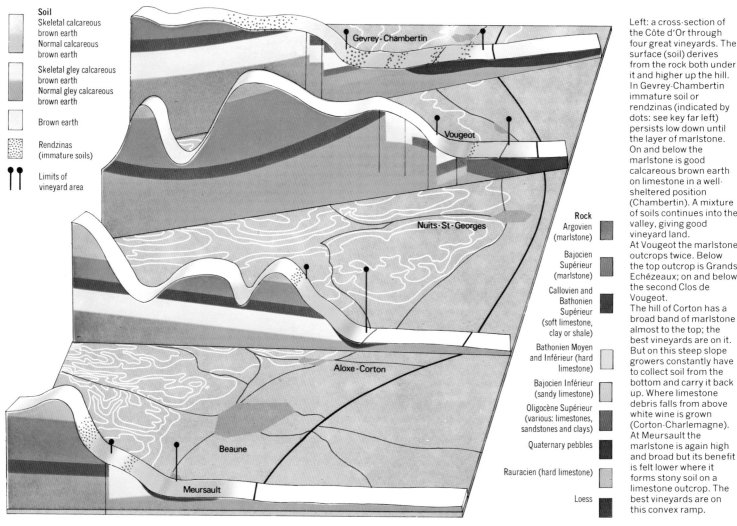

Soil

Skeletal calcareous brown earth
Normal calcareous brown earth

Skeletal gley calcareous brown earth
Normal gley calcareous brown earth

Brown earth

Rendzinas (immature soils)

Limits of vineyard area

Rock

Argovien (marlstone)

Bajocien Supérieur (marlstone)

Callovien and Bathonien Supérieur (soft limestone, clay or shale)

Bathonien Moyen and Inférieur (hard limestone)

Bajocien Inférieur (sandy limestone)

Oligocène Supérieur (various: limestones, sandstones and clays)

Quaternary pebbles

Rauracien (hard limestone)

Loess

Gevrey-Chambertin
Vougeot
Nuits-St-Georges
Aloxe-Corton
Beaune
Meursault

Left: a cross-section of the Côte d'Or through four great vineyards. The surface (soil) derives from the rock both under it and higher up the hill. In Gevrey-Chambertin immature soil or rendzinas (indicated by dots: see key far left) persists low down until the layer of marlstone. On and below the marlstone is good calcareous brown earth on limestone in a well-sheltered position (Chambertin). A mixture of soils continues into the valley, giving good vineyard land.
At Vougeot the marlstone outcrops twice. Below the top outcrop is Grands Echézeaux; on and below the second Clos de Vougeot.
The hill of Corton has a broad band of marlstone almost to the top; the best vineyards are on it. But on this steep slope growers constantly have to collect soil from the bottom and carry it back up. Where limestone debris falls from above white wine is grown (Corton-Charlemagne). At Meursault the marlstone is again high and broad but its benefit is felt lower where it forms stony soil on a limestone outcrop. The best vineyards are on this convex ramp.

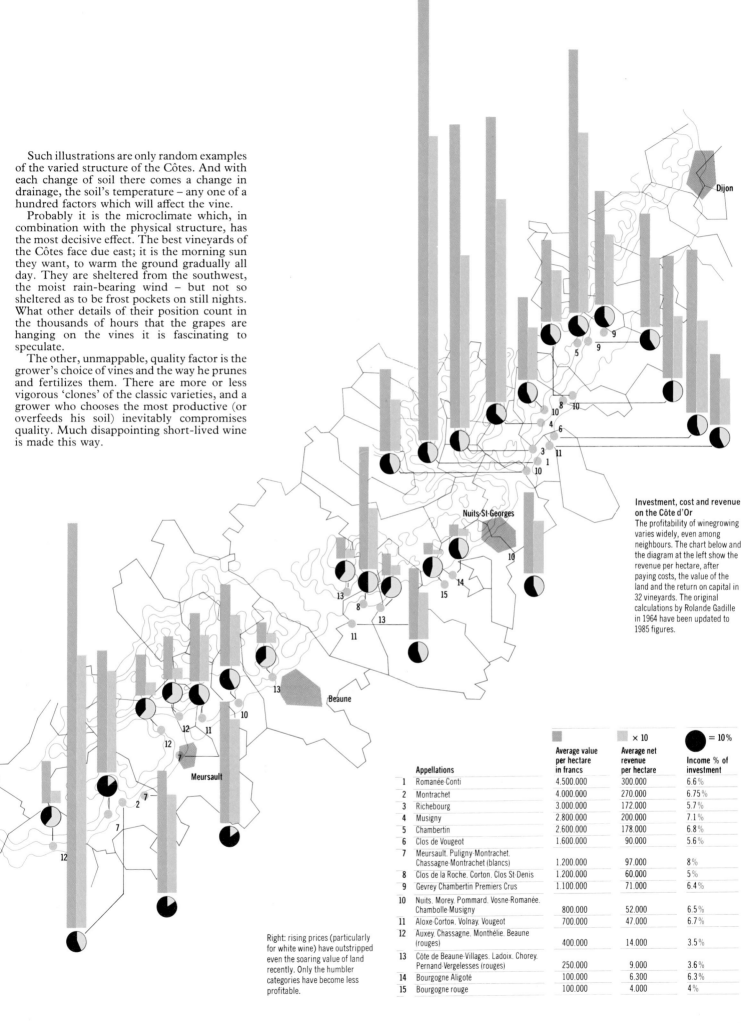

Such illustrations are only random examples of the varied structure of the Côtes. And with each change of soil there comes a change in drainage, the soil's temperature – any one of a hundred factors which will affect the vine.

Probably it is the microclimate which, in combination with the physical structure, has the most decisive effect. The best vineyards of the Côtes face due east; it is the morning sun they want, to warm the ground gradually all day. They are sheltered from the southwest, the moist rain-bearing wind – but not so sheltered as to be frost pockets on still nights. What other details of their position count in the thousands of hours that the grapes are hanging on the vines it is fascinating to speculate.

The other, unmappable, quality factor is the grower's choice of vines and the way he prunes and fertilizes them. There are more or less vigorous 'clones' of the classic varieties, and a grower who chooses the most productive (or overfeeds his soil) inevitably compromises quality. Much disappointing short-lived wine is made this way.

Dijon

Nuits-St-Georges

Beaune

Meursault

Investment, cost and revenue on the Côte d'Or
The profitability of winegrowing varies widely, even among neighbours. The chart below and the diagram at the left show the revenue per hectare, after paying costs, the value of the land and the return on capital in 32 vineyards. The original calculations by Rolande Gadille in 1964 have been updated to 1985 figures.

Right: rising prices (particularly for white wine) have outstripped even the soaring value of land recently. Only the humbler categories have become less profitable.

	Average value per hectare in francs	Average net revenue per hectare	Income % of investment
▪		▫ × 10	● = 10%
Appellations			
1 Romanée-Conti	4.500.000	300.000	6.6%
2 Montrachet	4.000.000	270.000	6.75%
3 Richebourg	3.000.000	172.000	5.7%
4 Musigny	2.800.000	200.000	7.1%
5 Chambertin	2.600.000	178.000	6.8%
6 Clos de Vougeot	1.600.000	90.000	5.6%
7 Meursault. Puligny-Montrachet. Chassagne-Montrachet (blancs)	1.200.000	97.000	8%
8 Clos de la Roche. Corton. Clos St-Denis	1.200.000	60.000	5%
9 Gevrey Chambertin Premiers Crus	1.100.000	71.000	6.4%
10 Nuits. Morey. Pommard. Vosne-Romanée. Chambolle-Musigny	800.000	52.000	6.5%
11 Aloxe-Corton. Volnay. Vougeot	700.000	47.000	6.7%
12 Auxey. Chassagne. Monthélie. Beaune (rouges)	400.000	14.000	3.5%
13 Côte de Beaune-Villages. Ladoix. Chorey. Pernand-Vergelesses (rouges)	250.000	9.000	3.6%
14 Bourgogne Aligoté	100.000	6.300	6.3%
15 Bourgogne rouge	100.000	4.000	4%

63

The Côte d'Or

The whole Côte d'Or – the Côte de Beaune and the Côte de Nuits, separated only by a few miles without vines – is an irregular escarpment some 30 miles (50 km) long. Its top is a wooded plateau. Its bottom is the beginning of the flat, plain-like valley of the River Saône. The width of the slope varies from a mile and a half to a few hundred yards – but all the good vineyards lie in this narrow strip.

The classification of the qualities of the land in this strip is the most elaborate on earth.

As it stands it is the work of the Institut National des Appellations d'Origine, based on classifications going back for more than 100 years but only finally perfected and mapped in 1984. It divides the vineyards into four classes, and lays down the law about the labelling of the wine accordingly. Grands Crus are the first class. There are 30 of them. Each has its own appellation. Grands Crus do not normally use the name of their commune on their labels. The single, simple vineyard name – Musigny, Corton, Montrachet or Chambertin – is the patent of Burgundy's highest nobility.

The next rank, Premiers Crus, use the name of their commune followed by the name of their vineyard (or, if the wine comes from more than one Premier Cru vineyard, the commune name followed by the words Premier Cru).

The third rank is known as Appellation Communale; that is, having the right to use the commune name. A vineyard name is permitted – although rarely used – if it is printed in letters much smaller than the name of the commune. A few such vineyards, often called Clos de . . . , although not officially Premiers Crus, are in the hands of a single good grower and can be considered in the same class.

Fourth, there are inferior vineyards, even within some famous communes, which have only the right to call their wine Bourgogne.

The system has only one drawback for the consumer. Elaborate as it seems, there remains a class of vineyards which it does not specifically recognize, but which do distinguish themselves in practice. For only in the Côte de Nuits and three communes of the Côte de Beaune are there any Grands Crus; all the rest of the finest vineyards are Premiers Crus, despite the fact that, particularly in such communes as Pommard and Volnay, some Premiers Crus consistently give better wine than the others.

Besides controlling the use of place names, INAO lays down the regulations which control quality, demanding that only the classic vines be used (Pinot Noir for red wine, Chardonnay for white); that only so much wine (from 40 hectolitres per hectare for the best, to 80 or so for more ordinary) be made; that it achieve a certain natural strength (from 12% alcohol for the best white and 11.5 for the best red down to 10% for the most ordinary red).

It remains up to the consumer to remember to make the distinction between the name of a vineyard and of a commune. Many villages (Vosne, Gevrey, Chassagne, etc.) have hyphenated their name to that of their best vineyard. The difference between a Chevalier-Montrachet (from one famous vineyard) and a Chassagne-Montrachet (from anywhere in a big commune) is not obvious; but it is vital.

Beaune has one of the world's most famous hospitals, built in the mid-15th century and still busily in practice. The Hospices was founded by Nicolas Rolin, Chancellor of the Duke of Burgundy, and his third wife, Guigone de Salins, in 1443, and endowed with vineyards in the surrounding country. Since then winegrowers have continued to bequeath their land to the hospital (or Hôtel-Dieu). The proceeds of the annual sale of its wine maintains it with all modern equipment, tending the sick of Beaune without charge. Above is a Victorian engraving of the founder and his wife. Top right is the splendid main courtyard. Right: the new wine in the cellars. The Hospices' vineyards are shown on the maps and their recent prices given on the following pages.

The wine merchants of Beaune

Beaune still keeps its town walls; their turrets are often used as cellars. Many of the best merchants of Burgundy work within the old city.

1 Pierre Ponnelle
2 Chanson Père & Fils
3 Bouchard Aîné & Fils
4 Patriarche Père & Fils
5 Caves de la Reine Pédauque
6 Calvet
7 Albert Morot
8 Jaffelin
9 Joseph Drouhin
10 Les Cordeliers
11 Léon Violland
12 Louis Latour
13 Remoissenet Père & Fils
14 Bouchard Père & Fils
15 Louis Jadot

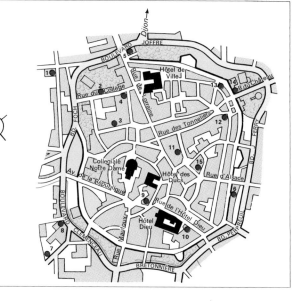

The Côte de Beaune: Santenay

The maps on this and the following eight pages represent the conclusion, in 1984, of the first complete official survey and classification of the vineyards of the Côte d'Or by the French Authorities, the INAO. They trace the vineyards of the Côte from south to north. The orientation of the maps has been turned through approximately 90 degrees so that what appears to be south is east-southeast.

The Côte de Beaune starts without a great explosion of famous names. It leads in gradually, from the villages of Sampigny, Dézize and Cheilly, with the one well-known cru of Les Maranges which they share (all beyond the limits of this map; see page 61), into the commune of Santenay. After the hamlet of Haut-Santenay and the little town (a spa, but not a very lively one) of Santenay, the Côte half-turns to take up its characteristic slope to the east.

This southern end of the Côte de Beaune is the most confused geologically and in many ways is untypical of the Côte as a whole. Complex faults in the structure of the hills make radical changes of soil and subsoil in Santenay. Part of the commune is analogous to parts of the Côte de Nuits, giving a deep red wine with a long life. Other parts give light wine more typical of the Côte de Beaune. Some of the highest vineyards have proved too stony to pay their way.

Les Gravières (the name draws attention to the stony ground, as the name Graves does in Bordeaux) and La Comme are the best *climats* of Santenay. As we move into Chassagne-Montrachet the quality of these excellent red-wine vineyards is confirmed. The name of Montrachet is so firmly associated with white wine that few people expect to find red here at all. But almost all the vineyards from the village of Chassagne south grow at least some red wine: Morgeot, La Boudriotte and (on page 66) Clos St-Jean are the most famous. Their wines are solid, long-lived and deep-coloured; among the strongest of the Côte de Beaune.

Indeed, no one really knows why white-winegrowing took over in this district. Thomas Jefferson reported that white-winegrowers here had to eat hard rye bread while red-wine men could afford it soft and white. Perhaps local growers were emulating the success of Le Montrachet (which had been famous for white wine since the 16th century). The Chardonnay is a more accommodating vine in stony soil – which it certainly finds in Meursault. Whatever the answer, Chassagne-Montrachet is known to the world chiefly for its dry but succulent, golden, flower-scented white wine.

The southern end of the Côte de Beaune is known principally for its substantial red wines. Maufoux is a distinguished négociant of Santenay; the remainder are some of the good growers whose vineyards appear on this map.

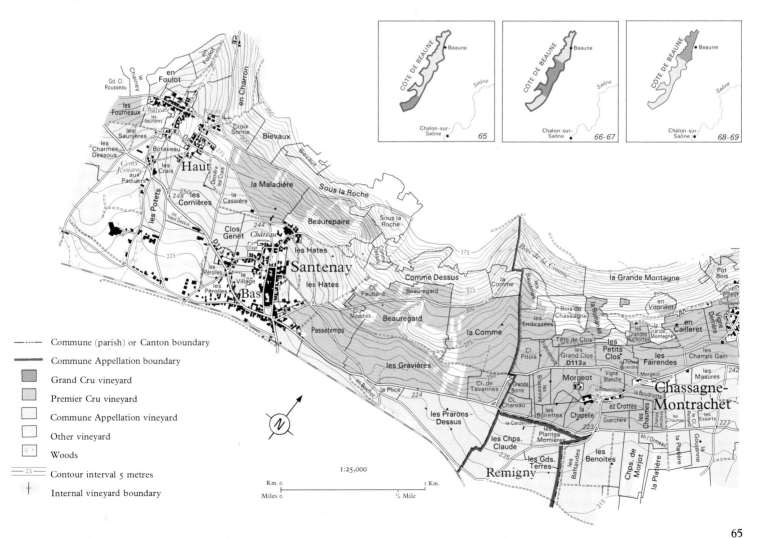

Commune (parish) or Canton boundary

Commune Appellation boundary

Grand Cru vineyard

Premier Cru vineyard

Commune Appellation vineyard

Other vineyard

Woods

Contour interval 5 metres

Internal vineyard boundary

1:25,000

Km. 0   1 Km.

Miles 0   ½ Mile

The Côte de Beaune: Meursault

A side valley in the hills just north of Chassagne, leading up to the hamlet of Gamay (which gave its name to the Beaujolais grape in the bad old days before the Pinot came into its own), divides the vineyards of the commune in two. South of it there is excellent white wine but the emphasis is on red. North, on the border of Puligny, there is the best white wine in Burgundy, if not the world.

The Grand Cru Montrachet earns its fame by an almost unbelievable concentration of the qualities of white burgundy. It has more scent, a brighter gold, a longer flavour, more succulence and yet more definition; everything about it is intensified – the mark of truly great wine. Perfect exposure to the east, yet an angle which means the sun is still flooding down the rows of vines at nine on a summer evening; a sudden streak of very limy soil, are factors in

Top: Volnay from the east.
Above left: Comte Lafon in his Meursault caves.
Centre: the Château de Meursault offers a self-guided tour and tasting in its splendid cellars.
Right: Le Montrachet at nine on a summer evening.

Average price a cask (228 litres) at the 1984 Hospices de Beaune auction			
Commune	**Vineyard**	**Cuvée**	**francs**
Auxey-Duresses	Duresses	Boillot	26,000
Monthélie	Duresses	Lebelin	19,200
Meursault	Charmes	de Bahèzre de Lanlay	42,500
Meursault	Charmes	Albert Grivault	50,000
Meursault	Genevrières	Baudot	50,000
Meursault	Genevrières	Philippe le Bon	50,000
Meursault	Poruzots	Goureau	32,500
Meursault	Poruzots	Jehan Humblot	33,000
Pommard	Epenots & Rugiens	Dames de la Charité	31,100
Volnay	Champans & Taille-Pieds	Blondeau	27,700
Volnay	Santenots	Gauvain	23,500
Volnay	Santenots	Jehan de Massol	24,400
Volnay	Village & Carelle	Général Muteau	30,800

The vineyards in which the Hospices de Beaune owns land are marked with a cross on this and the next map. Above and on page 69 are listed the 'cuvées', vineyards donated by the benefactors named, with the wines' prices in the 1984 sale, an indication of their relative reputations. The auction is held on the third Sunday in November.

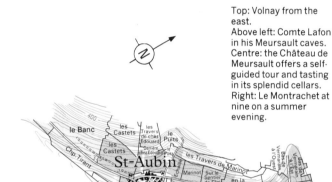

- - - - - Commune (parish) or Canton boundary

———— Commune Appellation boundary

Grand Cru vineyard

Premier Cru vineyard

Commune Appellation vineyard

Other vineyard

† Vineyard part-owned by the Hospices de Beaune

Woods

—25— Contour interval 5 metres

Internal vineyard boundary

1:25,000

Km. 0   1 Km.
Miles 0   ½ Mile

giving it an edge over its neighbours. For the other Grands Crus grouped about it come near but rarely excel it. Chevalier-Montrachet tends to be more delicate (coming from stonier ground; its best soil has been used for renewing Le Montrachet). Bâtard- lies on richer ground and often fails to achieve quite the same finesse. Les Criots and Bienvenues belong in the same class – and so very often do the Puligny Premiers Crus Les Pucelles and Le Cailleret.

There is a distinction between Puligny-Montrachet and Meursault, quite clear in the minds of people who know them well but almost impossible to define – and to account for. The vineyards of the one flow without a break into the other. In fact the hamlet of Blagny – which makes excellent wine high up on stony soil – is in both, with a classically complicated appellation: Premier Cru in Meursault, Blagny Premier Cru in Puligny-Montrachet, AC Blagny when (which is rare) the wine is red. White Blagny needs ageing.

Meursault is – to attempt the impossible – a slightly softer, less lively and fruity wine than Puligny-Montrachet. The words 'nutty' and 'mealy' are used of it, whereas Puligny is more a matter of peaches and apricots. On the whole there is less brilliant distinction (and no Grand Cru) but a very high and generally even standard over a large area, making it a reliable and relatively good-value wine to buy.

The big village lies across another dip in the hills where roads lead up to Auxey-Duresses and Monthélie, both sources of very good red and white wines which tend to be overlooked beside Beaune, Pommard and Volnay. The high Meursault *climats* Narvaux and Tillets, although not Premiers Crus, also make intense, age-worthy wines.

Meursault in turn flows into Volnay. A good deal of red wine is grown on this side of the commune, but called Volnay-Santenots rather than Meursault. White Volnay can similarly call itself Meursault.

Volnay and Meursault sometimes draw as near together as red and white wines well can without being rosé; both rather soft, delicate, the red rather pale yet with great personality and a long perfumed aftertaste. If Volnay makes the lightest wine of the Côte it can also be the most brilliant. Its lifespan is relatively short – perhaps ten years.

Caillerets is the great name in Volnay; Champans and Clos des Chênes are similar; the steep little Clos des Ducs is the best *climat* on the north side of the village.

Right: a handful of the dozens of famous growers of this part of the Côtes; Le Montrachet has five noted owners: Laguiche, Bouchard Père, Thénard, Calvet and the Domaine de la Romanée-Conti.

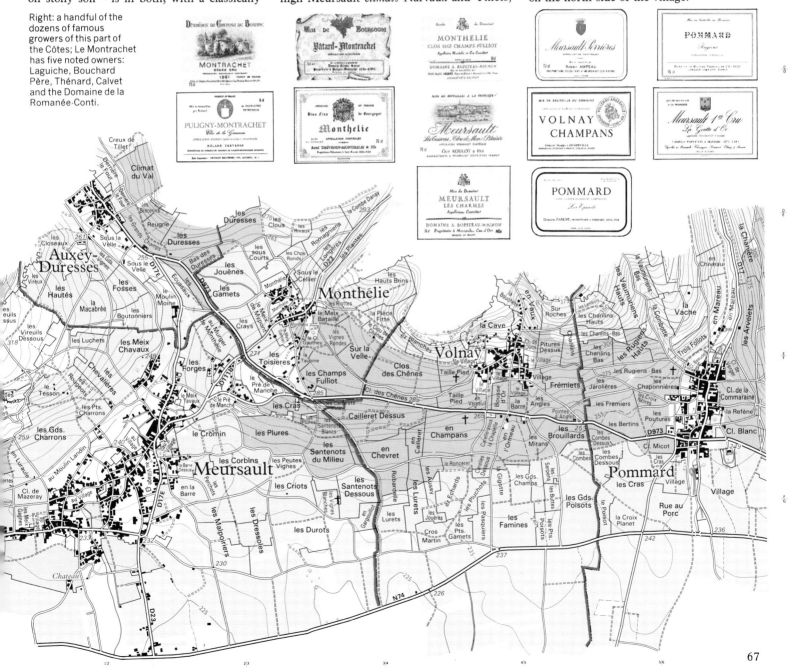

The Côte de Beaune: Beaune

Pommard (mapped on this and the previous page) is unaccountably the best-known commune of the whole Côte. Unaccountably, because the commune wine is not outstanding, and there is no single vineyard with a world-wide reputation. Most critics of burgundy find Pommard the slight levelling off between the high-points of Volnay and Beaune. But what should not be ignored is the individual growers. In Burgundy the grower counts as much as the vineyard; the saying goes 'there are no great wines; only great bottles of wine'.

Pommard's most prestigious vineyard is the lower part of Les Rugiens (map page 67) above the village. One of the best cuvées of the Hospices de Beaune, Dames de la Charité, is made from Rugiens and Epenots (combined). The Premier Cru Clos de la Commaraine and the wines of the growers Parent, Courcel, Armand, Gaunoux are among the great Pommards; medium-weight wines but needing ten years to develop the lovely savoury character of the best burgundy.

In the line of famous vineyards which occupy what the Burgundians call 'the kidney of the slope' above Beaune, a large proportion belongs to the city's négociants: Drouhin, Jadot, Bouchard Père et Fils, Chanson and Patriarche among them. The late Maurice Drouhin was one of the more recent of the centuries-old list of donors to the Hospices de Beaune. His firm's part of the Clos des Mouches is now famous; it makes a rare white Beaune there as well as a superb red one. A part of Grèves, belonging to Bouchard Père et Fils, is known as the Vigne de l'Enfant Jésus, and makes another marvellous wine. No Beaune is a Grand Cru; partly, it is said, because of the sustained high standard of so much land here. Beaune is usually gentle wine, lasting well but not demanding to be kept ten years or more, like a Romanée or a Chambertin.

After Beaune the road crosses a flat plain and the hills and vineyards retreat. Ahead looms the prow of Corton, the one isolated hill of the whole Côte d'Or, with a dark cap of woods. Corton breaks the spell which prevents the Côte de Beaune from having a red Grand Cru. Its massive smooth slide of hill, vineyard to the top, presents faces to east, south and west; all excellent. Indeed, it has not one but two Grand Cru appellations; for white wine and red, covering a large part of the hill. The white, Corton-Charlemagne, is grown on the upper slopes, where debris from the limestone top is washed down, whitening the brown marly soil.

The red, Le Corton, is grown in a broad band all round. The map names are misleading; they record the original sites of Corton and Corton-Charlemagne rather than the present appellations. The appellations cover a much wider area; the narrow strip labelled Corton is of little account, most red Corton comes from Renardes, Clos du Roi, Bressandes and the rest. Similarly the part marked Corton-Charlemagne grows both white wine (above) and red Corton (below). There is a slight Alice in Wonderland air about the legalities, but none whatsoever about the wine; both red and white are forceful, lingering, top-class burgundy.

The most celebrated grower of Corton is Louis Latour, whose fine presshouse, known as Château Grancey, stands in an old quarry in Les Perrières. Aloxe-Corton is the appellation of the lesser wines (red or white) grown below the hill, still often excellent.

If Savigny and Pernand are slightly in the background here it is only because the foreground is so imposing. The best growers of both make wines up to the highest Beaune standard; Savigny sometimes a marvel of finesse. Part of Pernand has the appellations Corton and Corton-Charlemagne.

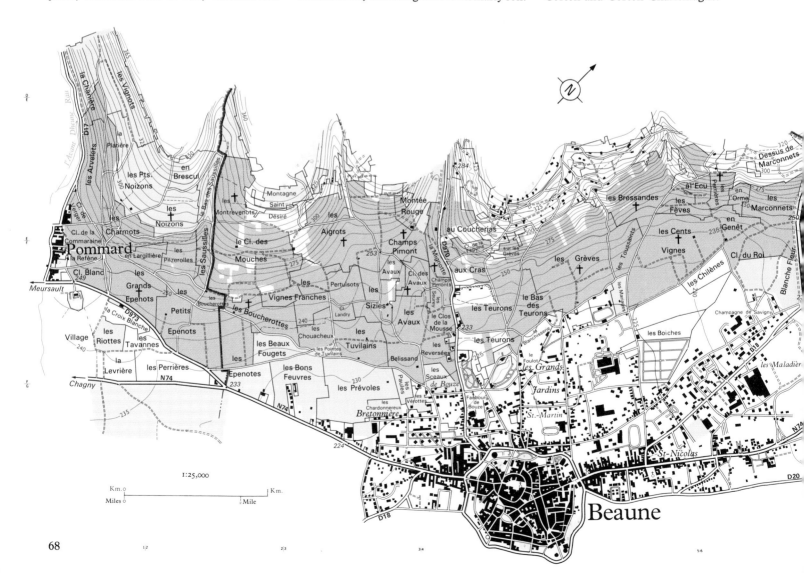

The hill of Corton from the southeast; left is the valley of Pernand-Vergelesses; centre right the village of Aloxe-Corton. High up under the woods Corton-Charlemagne is grown; lower on the right red Corton.

Average price a cask (228 litres) at the 1984 Hospices de Beaune auction

Commune	Vineyard	Cuvée	francs
Aloxe-Corton	Corton-Charlemagne (white)	François de Salins	105,000
Aloxe-Corton	Renardes & Bressandes	Charlotte Dumay	26,300
Aloxe-Corton	Bressandes & Clos du Roi	Docteur Peste	26,100
Beaune	vaux	Clos des Avaux	21,500
Beaune	Grèves & Aigrots	Bétault	19,300
Beaune	Bressandes & Mignotte	Brunet	20,325
Beaune	Bressandes & Mignotte	Dames Hospitalières	26,500
Beaune	Avaux, Boucherottes, Champs-Pimont & Grèves	Maurice Drouhin	19,300
Beaune	Cent-Vignes & Grèves	Nicolas Rolin	30,500
Beaune	Cent-Vignes & Montremenots	Rousseau-Deslandes	22,000
Beaune	Bressandes & Champs-Pimont	Guigogne de Salins	26,000
Pernand-Vergelesses	Basses Vergelesses	Rameau-Lamarosse	13,000
Savigny-les-Beaune	Vergelesses & Gravains	Fouquerend	19,000
Savigny-les-Beaune	Vergelesses & Gravains	Forneret	13,700
Savigny-les-Beaune	Marconnets	Arthur Girard	18,000

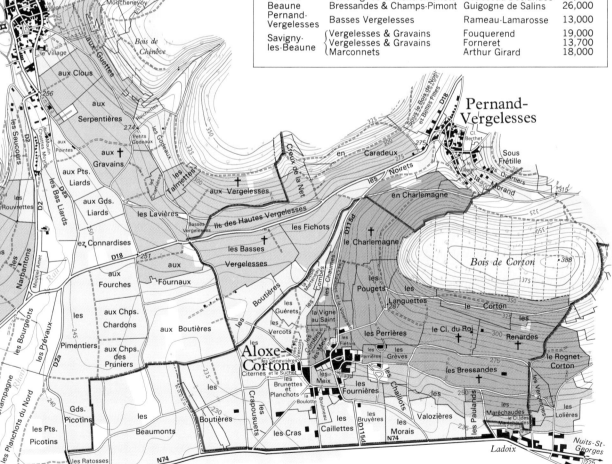

Right: the top label is a design adopted in 1969 by the Hospices de Beaune; among the others are some of Beaune's illustrious collection of merchant-growers.

Legend:

- —·—·— Commune (parish) or Canton boundary
- ——— Commune Appellation boundary
- Grand Cru vineyard
- Premier Cru vineyard
- Commune Appellation vineyard
- Other vineyard
- † Vineyard part-owned by the Hospices de Beaune
- Woods
- —300— Contour interval 5 metres
- Internal vineyard boundary

The Côte de Nuits: Nuits-St-Georges

The Confrérie des Chevaliers du Tastevin is Burgundy's wine fraternity and the most famous of its kind in the world. It was founded in 1933 and meets regularly for banquets with 600 guests, ceremonial (below) and songs from a choir of growers (left above), the Cadets de Bourgogne. Its headquarters is the old château in the Clos de Vougeot (bottom left); there are branches in many countries and members among wine men all over the world. The Confrérie's own label (detail above) may be used by wines which have been tasted and approved by a special committee.

More 'stuffing', longer life, deeper colour are the signs of a Côte de Nuits wine compared with a Volnay or Beaune. What little white is made shares the qualities of the red.

The line of Premiers Crus, wriggling its way along the hill, is threaded with clutches of Grands Crus. These are the wines that express with most intensity the inimitable sappy richness of the Pinot Noir. The line follows the outcrop of marlstone below the hard limestone hilltop, but it is where the soil has a mixture of silt and scree over the marl that the quality reaches peaks. Happily, this corresponds time and again with the best shelter and most sun.

The wines of Prémeaux go to market under the name Nuits-St-Georges. The quality is very high and consistent: they are big strong wines, almost approaching the style of Chambertin at their best. They age well, have a particularly marked scent, and deserve better than their reputation, which has suffered from 'la grande cuisine' of the blending vats. Les St-Georges is one of the best *climats* of the Côte; its neighbours Vaucrains, Cailles, Poirets and Pruliers are comparable.

Nuits is a one-restaurant town, unlike bustling Beaune, but it is the home of a number of négociants, some of whom make sparkling burgundy out of the year's unsuccessful wine.

Vosne-Romanée is a modest little village.

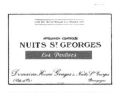

Left: Nuits-St-Georges has a Hospices like a smaller version of the Hospices de Beaune; Château Gris is not strictly a Grand Cru, as it says, but the excellent domaine of a shipper, Lupé-Cholet. Among the others are growers of some of the world's greatest red wines.

—·—·—·— Commune (parish) boundary

———— Commune Appellation boundary

Grand Cru vineyard

Premier Cru vineyard

Commune Appellation vineyard

Other vineyard

Woods

——250—— Contour interval 5 metres

Internal vineyard boundary

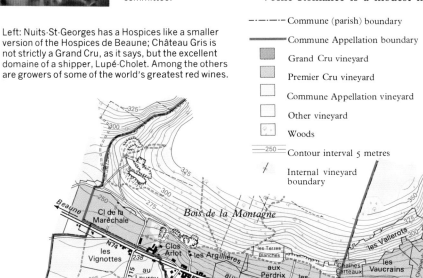

1:25,000

Km. 0 _____ 1 Km.

Miles 0 _____ ½ Mile

There is nothing to suggest that the world's most expensive wine lies beneath your feet. It stands below a long incline of reddish earth, looking up severely trimmed rows of vines, each ending with a stout post and a taut guy.

Nearest the village is Romanée-St-Vivant. The soil is deep, rich in clay and lime. Mid-slope is Romanée-Conti; poorer, shallower soil. Higher up, La Romanée tilts steeper; it seems drier and less clayey. On the right the big vineyard of Les Richebourgs curves around to face east-northeast. Up the left flank runs the narrow strip of La Grande Rue, and beside it the long slope of La Tâche. All are among the most highly prized of all burgundies. Romanée-Conti, La Tâche, Richebourgs and Romanée-St-Vivant are all owned or managed wholly or in part by the Domaine de la Romanée-Conti. For the finesse, the velvety warmth combined with a suggestion of spice and the almost oriental opulence of their wines the market will seemingly stand any price. Romanée-Conti is considered the most perfect, but the whole group has a family likeness.

Clearly one can look among their neighbours for wines of similar character at less stupendous prices. All the other named vineyards of Vosne-Romanée are superb. One of the textbooks on Burgundy remarks drily: 'There are no common wines in Vosne.'

The big 75-acre (30-hectare) *climat* of Echézeaux and the smaller Grands Echézeaux are really in the commune of Flagey, a village over the railway to the south, but they can use the name Vosne-Romanée for their wine if it does not reach the statutory standards for a Grand Cru. Some very fine growers have property here, and make beautiful, delicate, so-called 'lacy' wines. They are often a bargain – people say because the name looks hard to pronounce. Grands Echézeaux has perhaps more regularity, more of the lingering intensity which marks the very great burgundies; certainly higher prices.

One high stone wall surrounds the 125 acres (50 hectares) of the Clos de Vougeot; the sure sign of a monastic vineyard. Today it is so subdivided that it is anything but a reliable label on a bottle. But it is the *climat* as a whole which is a Grand Cru. The monks used to blend wine of top, middle and sometimes bottom to make what we must believe was one of the best burgundies of all . . . and one of the most consistent, since in dry years the wine from lower down would have an advantage, in wet years the top slopes. There are wines from near the top – La Perrière in particular (just outside the Clos) – that can be as great as Musigny. The name of the grower must be your guide.

Looking straight up the hill from the track above Romanée-St-Vivant; in the foreground Romanée-Conti with its stony red earth; beyond, La Romanée. This soil gives France's most perfumed, satiny, expensive wine.

The Côte de Nuits: Gevrey-Chambertin

Here, at the northern end of the Côte d'Or, the firmest, longest-lasting, eventually most velvety red burgundies are made. Nature here adds rich soil to the perfect combination of shelter and exposure which the hills provide. The narrow marlstone outcrop, lightly overlaid with silt and scree, follows the lower slopes. From it Chambertin and the Grands Crus of Morey and Chambolle draw their power. For these are wines of body and strength, unyielding when they are young, but eventually offering more complexity and depth of flavour than any others.

Musigny, the first of the Grands Crus, stands apart, obviously related to the top of the Clos de Vougeot. There is only just room for it under the barren limestone crest. The slope is steep enough to mean the vignerons must carry the brown limy clay, heavy with pebbles, back up the hill when it collects at the bottom. This and the permeable limestone subsoil allow excellent drainage. Conditions are right for a wine with plenty of 'stuffing'.

The glory of Musigny is that it adds to its undoubted power a lovely haunting delicacy of perfume; a uniquely sensuous savour. A great Musigny makes what is so well described as a 'peacock's tail' in your mouth, opening and becoming more complex and seductive as you swallow it. It is not so strong as Chambertin, not so spicy as Romanée-Conti – but he must have been a great respecter of women who called it 'feminine'. It needs 10 or 15 years' ageing. Les Bonnes-Mares is the other Grand Cru of Chambolle-Musigny. It starts as a slightly tougher wine than Musigny, and ages perhaps a little slower, but achieves a similar power and tenderness.

Les Amoureuses and Les Charmes – their beautiful names are perfectly expressive of their wine – are both among the best Premiers Crus of Burgundy. Any wine from Chambolle-Musigny, however, is likely to be very good.

The commune of Morey is overshadowed in renown by its five Grands Crus. Clos de la Roche, with little Clos St-Denis (which gave its name to the village), like Chambertin are wines of great staying power, strength and depth, fed by lime-rich soil. The Clos des Lambrays is a 'monopole' recently replanted and promoted to Grand Cru rank; a wine to wait for. Clos de Tart, the monopole of the house of Mommessin, is consistently fine, intense but not weighty.

Morey has more than 20 tiny Premiers Crus, few of whose names are well known. Indeed, its *village* wine is so good that the difference is often not important. The vineyards climb the hill, finding soil higher up than anywhere else in this area. The very high and stony Monts-Luisants is even used for white wine.

Gevrey-Chambertin has an amazing amount of good land. The ideal vineyard soil stretches farther out from the hill than elsewhere, so that even land beyond the main road has the appellation Gevrey-Chambertin, rather than plain Bourgogne. Its two greatest vineyards, Chambertin and Clos de Bèze, lie under the woods on a mere gentle slope. They were acknowledged Grands Crus at a time when the citizens of Gevrey were quarrelling with the worthies of Beaune who were handing out the honours. Otherwise it is probable that the constellation of vineyards – Mazis, Latricières and the rest – around them would have been Grands Crus in their own right as well. Instead they have an in-between status, with the right to add -Chambertin after their names, but not (like Clos de Bèze) before. The Premier Cru Combottes deserves the same rank. French wine law can be more subtle than theology.

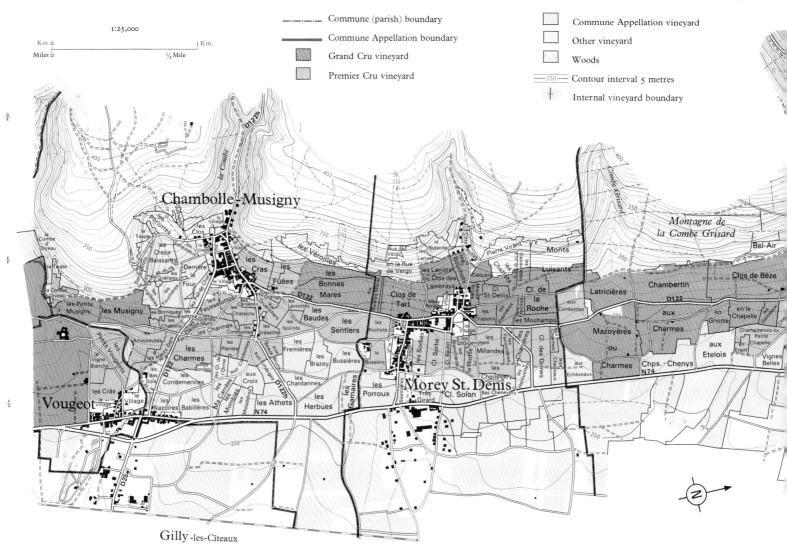

1:25,000

Km. 0   1 Km.

Miles 0   ½ Mile

—··—··— Commune (parish) boundary

—————— Commune Appellation boundary

Grand Cru vineyard

Premier Cru vineyard

Commune Appellation vineyard

Other vineyard

Woods

—250— Contour interval 5 metres

Internal vineyard boundary

The commune also has a higher slope with a superb southeast exposure. Its Premiers Crus, Cazetiers, Lavaut, Clos St-Jacques and Les Vérroilles, are arguably Grands Crus in everything but name.

There are more famous individual vineyards in this village than in any other in Burgundy. To many people the forceful red wine they make *is* burgundy. Hilaire Belloc told a story about his youth, and ended dreamily: 'I forget the name of the place; I forget the name of the girl; but the wine . . . was Chambertin.'

The slopes to the north used to be known as the Côte de Dijon, and until the last century were considered among the best. But their growers were tempted to use their rich land for bulk wine for the city and planted the 'disloyal plant', the Gamay. Brochon became known as a 'well of wine' from the quantities it made. Today it has no appellation of its own: its southern edge is included in Gevrey-Chambertin; the rest has only the right to the name Côte de Nuits-Villages.

Fixin, however, has a tradition of quality. The Premiers Crus Perrière, Hervelets and Clos du Chapitre are up to Gevrey standards – and notable value for money.

Aerial view looking north up the Côte de Nuits. Below is the Clos de Vougeot with its monastic 'château'; beyond lie Chambolle-Musigny (left), Morey-St-Denis (right) and in the distance Gevrey-Chambertin. Below: Gevrey-Chambertin is a big commune with more than 485 hectares of vines, nearly a fifth of which are Grands Crus. Many famous growers have holdings here. Others include Damoy, Ponsot, Rebourseau, Pernot, Roty, Camus.

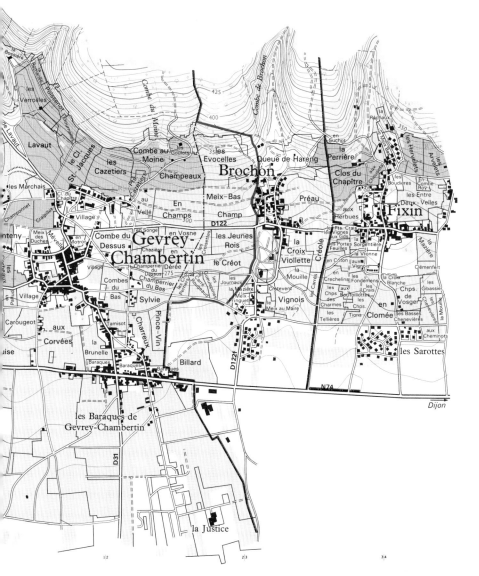

The Chalonnais

As demand and prices play leapfrog in the most famous wine areas of the world, the names of what used to be considered lesser regions inevitably come to the fore. The hills south of Chagny are in many ways a continuation of the Côte de Beaune, although the regular ridge is replaced here by a jumble of hillocks on which vineyards appear among orchards and crops. The 'Côte Chalonnaise' was named for its port of Chalon-sur-Saône to the east. Today most locals say the 'Région de Mercurey'.

The map shows the east-and-south-facing slopes of the Côte, with the four major communes which have appellations: Rully, Mercurey, Givry and Montagny, and some of their better-known vineyards.

Mercurey is much the biggest producer, and 90% of its wine is red; Pinot Noir at least on a par with a minor Côte de Beaune, firm and almost rough when young but ageing well, and steadily being improved by its growers as demand increases. Its neighbour Givry is almost equally dedicated to red, often more easy and accessible young than Mercurey.

Rully to the north makes red and white wines in equal proportions; the white (of Chardonnay and Pinot Blanc) brisk, high in acid, ideal material for sparkling Crémant de Bourgogne, and in good vintages much better than that: lively, long-lived white burgundy and exceptional value. Rully reds tend to leanness – but not without class.

Montagny to the south is the one all-white-wine appellation, and benefits from a unique rule that any wine over 11.5° natural alcohol can be labelled Premier Cru. Neighbouring Buxy is included. The whites here are more heavy and obvious than Rully: more in the style of Mâcon.

Meanwhile Bouzeron, at the top of the map, has recently been granted the only appellation for a single-village Aligoté white in Burgundy; a reward for perfectionist winemaking by, among others, the co-owner of the Domaine de la Romanée-Conti, a grower in the village.

The whole area, Bouzeron included, is a good source of plain Bourgogne Rouge which, at two or three years, can be marvellous drinking. But perhaps its most unexpected speciality is its sparkling Crémant; a revelation even to hardened champagne drinkers.

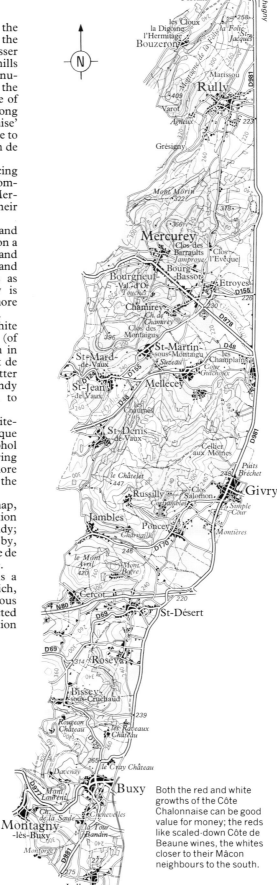

The singular profile of the Pouilly-Fuissé country. The rock of Solutré rears like a wave above the village. Prehistoric hunters used to drive their quarry over the edge: deer bones form a layer below the soil at the bottom of the hill.

1:100,000

Km. 0   1   2   3   4   5 Km.
Miles 0   1   2   3 Miles

----------- Canton boundary
- - - - - - Commune (parish) boundary
◻ Vineyards
◻ Woods
═══400═══ Contour interval 20 metres

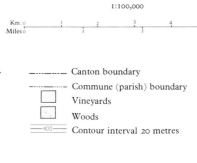

Both the red and white growths of the Côte Chalonnaise can be good value for money; the reds like scaled-down Côte de Beaune wines, the whites closer to their Mâcon neighbours to the south.

The Mâconnais

The town of Mâcon on the Saône, 35 miles (55 kilometres) south of Chalon, gives its name to a wide area which in general has neither the distinction of its neighbour to the north nor of Beaujolais to the south. Mâcon red is only just burgundian in character, the white definitely burgundy, but without frills.

On the Beaujolais border, however, there is a pocket of white winegrowing with distinction of a different order. The Pouilly-Fuissé district is a sudden tempest of wave-shaped limestone hills, rich in the alkaline clay the Chardonnay grape loves. The map shows how the four villages of Pouilly-Fuissé – Vergisson, Solutré-Pouilly, Fuissé and Chaintré – shelter on the lower slopes.

Good Pouilly-Fuissé is a pale, refreshing, often delicate wine for a Chardonnay, without the scent of a Meursault or the style of a Chablis Grand Cru, but in its gentle way exactly what one is looking for in white burgundy, and at its best a real personality.

Pouilly-Vinzelles and Pouilly-Loché are a shade lighter and less expressive. Much cheaper, though. A relatively new appellation, Saint Véran, applies to similar white wines from a handful of villages north and south of Pouilly-Fuissé. Mâcon-Prissé is similar.

In fact all over the Mâconnais the cooperatives are the dominant producers, and remarkably well run. That at Chaintré is the biggest producer of Pouilly-Fuissé. Others farther north (notably those at Viré, Lugny and Clessé) have wines of striking character to offer. Two estates at Viré, the Clos du Chapitre and the Château de Viré, are highly competent producers. Recently wine of brilliant quality has been made at Quintaine-Clessé by Jean Thevenet. The Mâconnais advances.

The way to buy white Mâcon is to look for the name of a particular village on the label. Failing '-Prissé' or '-Clessé', look for the suffix '-Villages'. Few modest wines anywhere are as reliably fresh and wholesome.

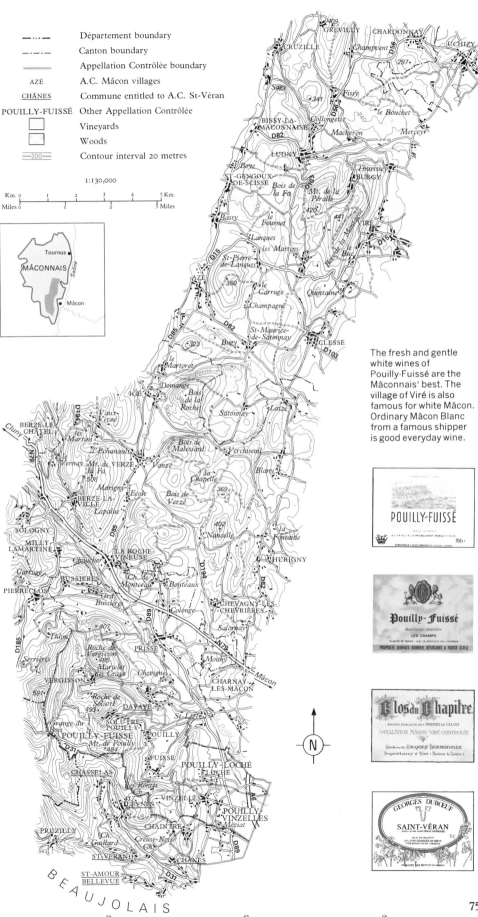

Département boundary
Canton boundary
Appellation Contrôlée boundary
AZÉ   A.C. Mâcon villages
CHÂNES   Commune entitled to A.C. St-Véran
POUILLY-FUISSÉ   Other Appellation Contrôlée
   Vineyards
   Woods
—200—   Contour interval 20 metres

1:130,000

Km. 0   1   2   3   4   5 Km.
Miles 0   1   2   3 Miles

The fresh and gentle white wines of Pouilly-Fuissé are the Mâconnais' best. The village of Viré is also famous for white Mâcon. Ordinary Mâcon Blanc from a famous shipper is good everyday wine.

75

Beaujolais

Above: the old winepress and the new in a Beaujolais *pressoir*. Many still use the old model.

Left: the lower hills sloping to south and east are almost unbroken vineyard. The Beaujolais mountains to the west, covered with pine and chestnut, rise to 3,000 feet (900 metres). Their few primitive villages were immortalized in the story of Clochemerle.

Right: the best Beaujolais is known by the name of its commune, and often of its vineyard or grower's property as well. The Hospices de Beaujeu is a local hospital owning vineyards.

Each November for a few weeks the new vintage of Beaujolais becomes the world's favourite drink: as though folk-memory were reviving the forgotten Bacchanalia of harvest time. Such rapid cash-flow is something all winemakers would like, yet only Beaujolais can generate. In one of the marriages of grape and ground the French regard as mystical, in Beaujolais the Gamay, growing in sandy clay over granite, gives uniquely fresh, vivid, light but fruity, fairly strong but infinitely swallowable wine.

The Beaujolais region covers a 45-mile (70-kilometre) long stretch of mainly granite hills south of Mâcon in south Burgundy. Most of its 60-odd villages remain obscure: the highest their wine can aspire to is the extra degree of alcohol to qualify as Beaujolais Supérieur. From this deep well a million hectolitres of wine a year are drawn – and rapidly drunk.

The northern part of the region, however, has different standards. A group of 35 villages on steep foothills leading up to the Beaujolais mountains are classified as Beaujolais-Villages. They are expected to give wine with a shade more strength, and with the extra strength an extra touch of character and style.

Nine of the villages use their own names and are expected to show distinct characteristics of their own. These are the Grands Crus. The group lies just south of the Mâconnais, adjacent to Pouilly-Fuissé. Part of the best Beaujolais cru of all, Moulin-à-Vent, is actually in the Mâconnais, although to simplify things it is all regarded as Beaujolais.

The Grands Crus villages lie on spurs, outlying knolls and on the Beaujolais mountains themselves. This is much more seriously hilly country than the Côte d'Or. The road climbs and twists and climbs until vines and farms are left behind, woods thicken and upland streams tumble by. Looking behind and below, the broad band of vineyards dwindles and an immense view of the plain of the Saône expands: in clear weather Mont Blanc hangs in the far distance to the east.

The country is owned mostly by small farmers who sell their wine through négociants but there are a few big estates. Their wine is the grandest of Beaujolais and is often bottled on the property; but this does not change its basic nature of being a delicious easy-going drink rather than a Grand Vin.

Lightest and most luscious of all is Fleurie, with its neighbour Chiroubles. Good young Fleurie seems to epitomize the Beaujolais style: the scent is strong, the wine fruity and silky, brilliantly translucent, a joy to swallow.

'Best' in the most serious sense is Moulin-à-Vent, which now includes some of Chénas and Romanèche-Thorins. In good years this wine has darker colour, more strength and initial toughness and improves with age: not the thing Beaujolais is known for nowadays. At ten years the best Moulin-à-Vent can have the bouquet of a great red burgundy.

Local experts will distinguish between all the other crus, telling you that Morgon lasts for longer, Juliénas has more substance and vigour, St-Amour is lighter, Brouilly is grapey and rich but Côte de Brouilly grapier and richer. It would be wrong to exaggerate the differences, however: what they have in common is more important, the beautiful inviting quality given by the Gamay.

This vine which is virtually outlawed from the Côte d'Or is in its element on the granite-derived soil of Beaujolais. Its plants are almost like people, leading independent lives: after ten years they are no longer trained, but merely tied up in summer with an osier to stand free. A Gamay vine will live as long as a man.

Beaujolais is traditionally made by carbonic maceration (see page 30). The low-key fermentation preserves the characteristic flavour of fruit. But the method is slow, and today's fashion for the *vin de l'année* calls for some drastic shortcuts to meet the mid-November deadline. The idea of the new wine is romantic, but Beaujolais Nouveau is never the best the country can produce. It is too often mere *vin rosé* with a purple tinge and a great surging sappy smell. The best Beaujolais has much more to it than this; but no wine of real quality was ever made overnight: it takes time, in bottle if not in barrel, to achieve the miracle.

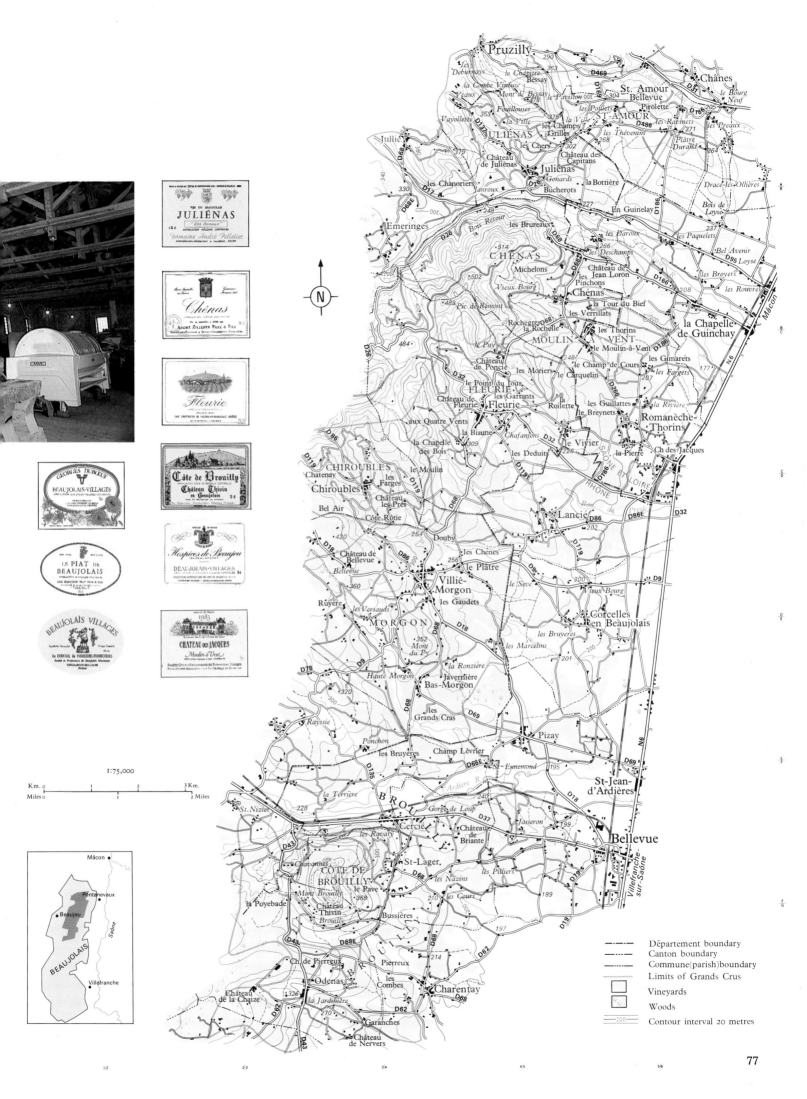

Chablis

Sleepy little Chablis on its reedy river in the valley does not look the part of the world's most famous wine town. There is not a hoarding, not an illumination, not a whisper of the fact that around the world, every day, as much wine is drunk under its name as it often produces in a whole harvest.

Thirty years ago it seemed possible that foreign imitations would indeed become its only memorial. In the 1950s devastating spring frosts and exhausted vineyards discouraged all but the toughest growers. The vineyard area stood at little more than 1,000 acres (400 hectares) – the rump of what was once the vast vineyard of the Yonne: Paris's principal supplier. It was Chablis' taste that saved it.

Chablis sends one rummaging for descriptive phrases even more desperately than most wines. There is something there one can so nearly put a finger on. It is hard but not harsh, reminds one of stones and minerals, but at the same time of green hay; actually, when it is young it looks green, which many wines are supposed to. Grand Cru Chablis tastes important, strong, almost immortal. And indeed it does last a remarkably long time; a strange and delicious sort of sour taste enters into it at ten years or so, and its golden-green eye flashes meaningfully.

Cool-climate vineyards need exceptional conditions to succeed. Chablis lies 100 miles (160 kilometres) north of Beaune – as near to Champagne, in fact, as to the rest of Burgundy. Geology is its secret: the outcrop of the rim of a great submerged basin of limestone. Its far rim, across the English Channel in Dorset, gives its name, Kimmeridge, to this unique pudding of prehistoric oyster-shells. Oysters and Chablis, it seems, have been related since creation.

The hardy Chardonnay (known here as the Beaunois – the vine from Beaune) is the only vine. Where the slopes of Kimmeridgian clay face the sun it ripens excellently. The classification of Chablis into four grades is one of the clearest demonstrations anywhere of the importance of southern slopes: Grand Cru wines always taste richer than the Premiers Crus, Premiers Crus than plain Chablis, and Chablis than Petit Chablis – an appellation that is slowly but surely fading away.

All the Grands Crus lie in a single block looking south and west over the village and the river. Each of the seven has its own style. Many regard Les Clos and Vaudésir as best of all. Certainly they tend to be the biggest in flavour. But more important is what all have in common: intense, highly charged flavour on the scale of the best whites of the Côte de Beaune – leading, with age, to noble complexity.

There used to be more Premiers Crus, but the names of the better known have recently been granted to their neighbours as well. Chief ones now are Monts de Milieu, Montée de Tonnerre, Fourchaume, Vaillons, Montmains, Mélinots, Côte de Léchet, Beauroy, Vaucoupin, Vosgros, Vaulorent and Les Fourneaux. A Premier Cru Chablis will be at least half a degree of alcohol weaker than a Grand Cru, and correspondingly less impressive and intense in scent and flavour. Nonetheless it will

be a very good wine indeed – all the better if it comes from one of the vineyards designated Premier Cru on the same (north) bank of the river as the Grands.

It is a sign of the expansion and growing competence of Chablis growers that a new Premier Cru, Vaudevey, has just been created: its first wines of the 1983 vintage. But this expansion has not been without controversy: the growers are split into two syndicates, one favouring more planting, the other fiercely resisting it.

The area of vines producing Chablis Premier Cru has increased by 50 percent in the last ten years. That for Chablis has almost doubled. In 1960 there was more Premier Cru than Chablis. Today there is twice as much Chablis as Premier Cru (and five times as much Premier Cru as Grand Cru).

Has the quality suffered? It remains, as it always will do, very uneven from year to year as

Above: in the cellars of a Chablis grower, a tasting glass of wine catches the light. The gold-green glint is characteristic.
Facing page: imitations of Chablis are so common that the labels of the real thing are strangely unfamiliar. Here are three of the Grands Crus, a Premier Cru from across the valley and two simple Chablis from good shippers.

well as variable (particularly in style) from grower to grower. Most growers today favour tank-fermented fresh wines with no barrels. A few traditionalists continue to show that oak has special properties to offer. But on balance Chablis is as good as ever – and maybe better.

Far more unpredictable is the quantity of each harvest – and hence its price. While prices seesaw precariously, the market remains uneasy. In truth, it shouldn't be. Grand Cru Chablis remains even now only about half the price of Corton-Charlemagne. Parity would be closer to justice.

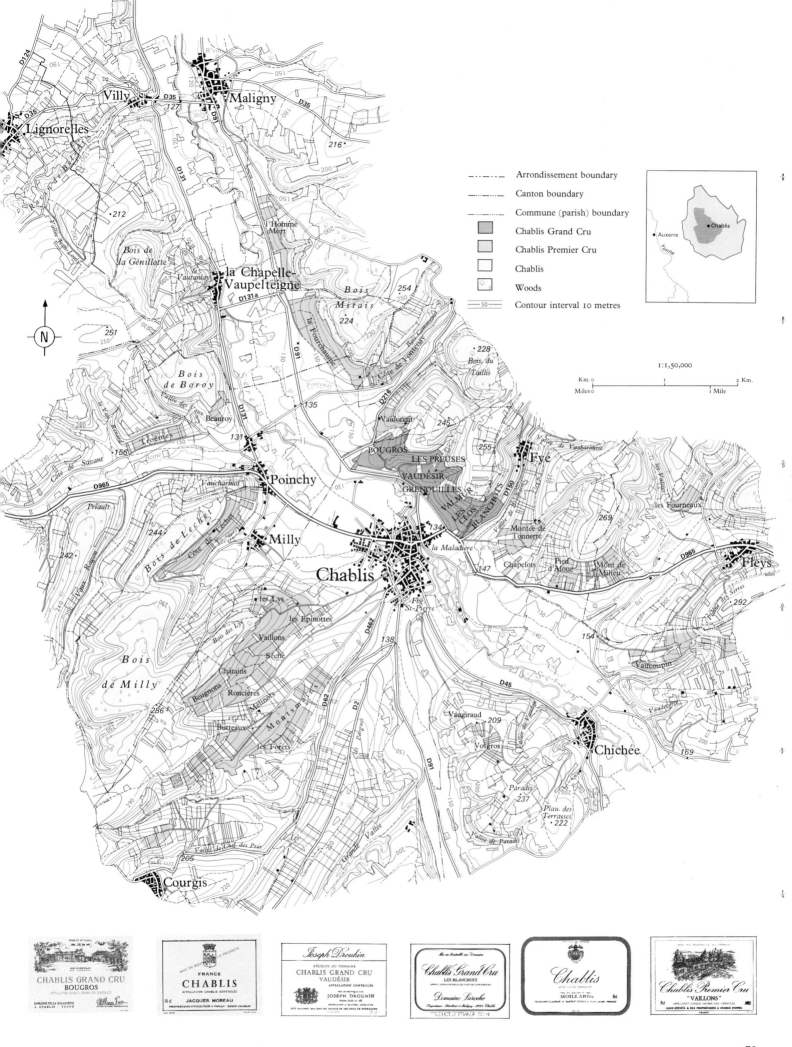

Bordeaux

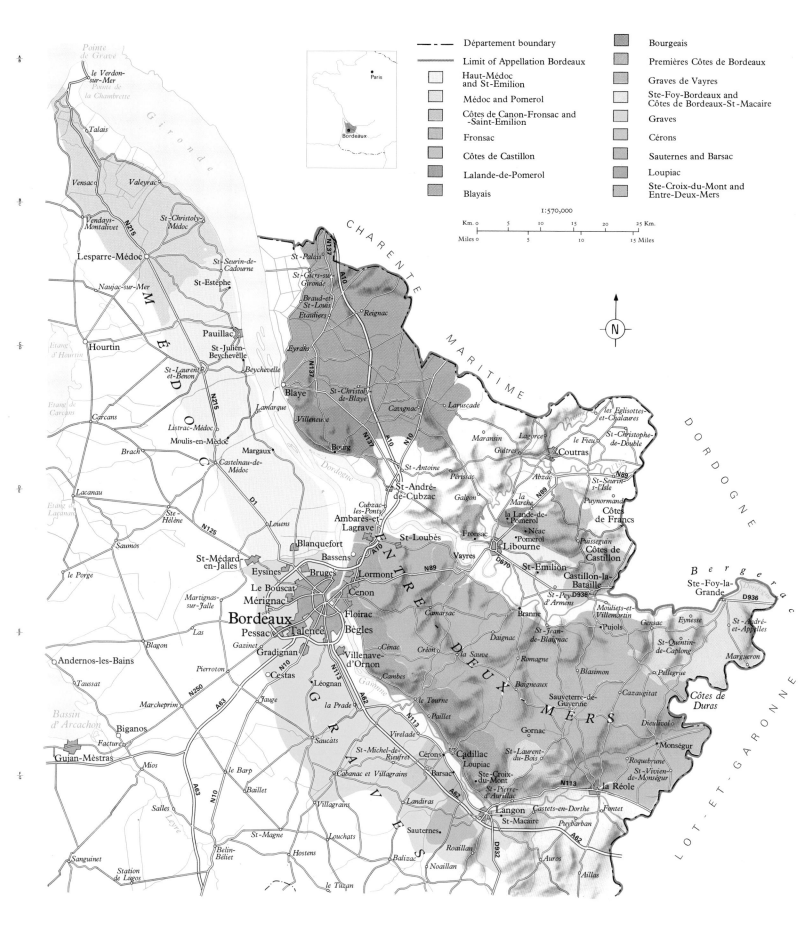

– · – · Département boundary	▨ Bourgeais
—— Limit of Appellation Bordeaux	▨ Premières Côtes de Bordeaux
▨ Haut-Médoc and St-Emilion	▨ Graves de Vayres
▨ Médoc and Pomerol	▨ Ste-Foy-Bordeaux and Côtes de Bordeaux-St-Macaire
▨ Côtes de Canon-Fronsac and -Saint-Emilion	▨ Graves
▨ Fronsac	▨ Cérons
▨ Côtes de Castillon	▨ Sauternes and Barsac
▨ Lalande-de-Pomerol	▨ Loupiac
▨ Blayais	▨ Ste-Croix-du-Mont and Entre-Deux-Mers

1:570,000

Km. 0   5   10   15   20   25 Km.
Miles 0   5   10   15 Miles

If the name of Burgundy suggests richness and plenty, Bordeaux has more than a hint of elegance about it. In place of the plump prelate who seems to symbolize Burgundy, Bordeaux calls to mind a distinguished figure in a frock-coat. Picture him tasting pale red wine from a crystal glass. He has one thumb tucked into his waistcoat, while through the open door beyond him there is a glimpse of a turreted house, insubstantial in the pearly seaside light. He enters his moderate enthusiasms in a leather pocket-book, observing the progress of beauty across his palate like moves in a game of chess.

Aspects of Bordeaux appeal to the aesthete, as Burgundy appeals to the sensualist. One is the nature of the wine: at its best indescribably delicate in nuance and complexity. Another is the sheer intellectual challenge of so many estates in so many regions and sub-regions that no one has mastered them all.

Bordeaux is the largest fine-wine district on earth. The whole Department of the Gironde is dedicated to winegrowing. All its wine is Bordeaux. Its production dwarfs that of Burgundy: 5.1 million hectolitres in 1983.

Red wines outnumber white by three to one. The great red-wine areas lie to the north: the Médoc; the country immediately south of the city of Bordeaux; the country along the north bank of the Dordogne and facing the Médoc across the Gironde. The country between the two rivers is called Entre-Deux-Mers. Most of its wine is white, except for a fringe of villages which make red wine as well, facing Bordeaux across the Garonne. Premières Côtes de Bordeaux is the name given to their wines. The bottom third of the map is almost all white-wine country.

But of the white wine of this large area a very small proportion is notably fine. Bordeaux's great glories are its range of good to superlative red wines, and the small production of very sweet golden wine of Sauternes.

Compared with Burgundy the system of appellations in Bordeaux is simple. The map opposite shows them all. Within them it is the wine estates or châteaux which look after their own identification problem. On the other hand there is a form of classification by quality built into the system in Burgundy which is missing in Bordeaux. In its place here there are a variety of local classifications, unfortunately without a common standard.

By far the most famous of these is the classification of the châteaux of the Médoc – and one or two others – which was finalized in 1855, based on the prices the wines had fetched over the previous hundred years or more. Its first, second, third, fourth and fifth 'growths', to which were added Crus Exceptionnels, Crus Bourgeois Supérieurs, Crus Bourgeois and later Crus Artisans and Crus Paysans, are the most ambitious grading of the products of the soil ever attempted.

The overriding importance of situation in deciding quality is proved by the accuracy of the old list today. Where present standards depart from it there is usually an explanation (an industrious proprietor in 1855, and a lazy one now). Even more to the point, in many

The city of Bordeaux glories in its grey stone architecture. Top: ships mount the Garonne to the old Pont de Pierre in the heart of the city. Left: 18th-century merchants' houses on the Quai des Chartrons. Right: the medieval town gate.

cases land has been added, or exchanged; the vineyard is not precisely the same.

In fact, more weight is placed today on the old classification than the system really justifies. The first-growths regularly fetch three times the price of the second-growths . . . without necessarily being much better. The relative qualities of different châteaux really need expressing in a more subtle way than by suggesting that one is always 'better' than another. The system adopted on the maps that follow is simply to distinguish between classed growths and Crus Bourgeois.

Château is the word for a wine estate in Bordeaux. Its overtones of castle or stately home are rarely justified. In most cases the biggest building at the château is the *chai* – the

long sheds, often half underground, where the wine is stored – attached to the *cuvier* where it is made. (A Bordeaux château and its working routine is anatomized on pages 34–35.)

The vineyards of the château sometimes surround it in a neat plot. More often they are scattered and intermingled with their neighbours. They can produce annually anything from ten to 1,000 barrels of wine, each holding 300 bottles. The best vineyards make a maximum of 4,000 litres from each hectare of vines, the less good ones rather more. A hectare can have anything from 6,500 to 10,000 vines.

The *maître de chai* is an important figure at the château. At little properties it is the owner himself, at big ones an old retainer. It is he who welcomes visitors, and lets them taste the new wine, cold and dark and unpalatable, from the casks in his care. Be knowing rather than enthusiastic; the wine will not be ready to drink for two years after it has been bottled at the very least – and maybe not for twenty.

Bordeaux: The Quality Factor

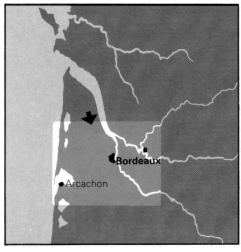

The advantages of the Bordeaux region for winegrowing can be listed quite simply. Its position near the sea and threaded with rivers gives it a moderate and stable climate. Forests on the ocean side protect it from strong salt winds and reduce the rainfall. The bedrock is well furnished with minerals, yet the topsoil in general is quite poor and often very deep.

The most earnest studies have been made to decide what it is that makes one piece of land superior to its neighbour. They all start by defining exactly the geological, pedological (i.e. soil) and climatological setup for a very fine vineyard . . . and then tend to find that exactly the same considerations seem to apply next door, where the wine is not and never has been half so good.

In Bordeaux, however, there are more variables to help explain the differences. Instead of one constant grape variety, like the Pinot Noir for all red wine on the Côte de Nuits, all Bordeaux is made from a mixture of three or four varieties, the proportions depending on the taste of the proprietor. To jump to the conclusion that, let us say, the soil of Château Lafite gives lighter wine than that of Château Latour would be rash, unless you have taken into account that Lafite grows a good deal of Merlot while Latour is nearly all Cabernet Sauvignon . . . and Merlot wine is lighter.

Another factor is the status of the vineyard. Success breeds success, meaning more money to spend on expensive care of the land – or on buying more. Differences that were originally marginal can thus increase over the years.

Furthermore the soil of the Médoc, to speak of only part of Bordeaux, is said to 'change at every step'. No one has ever been able to isolate the wine made from a vine on one patch and compare it with that from two steps away. So nobody really knows what vines, on what kind of soil, give what kind of wine – except in the

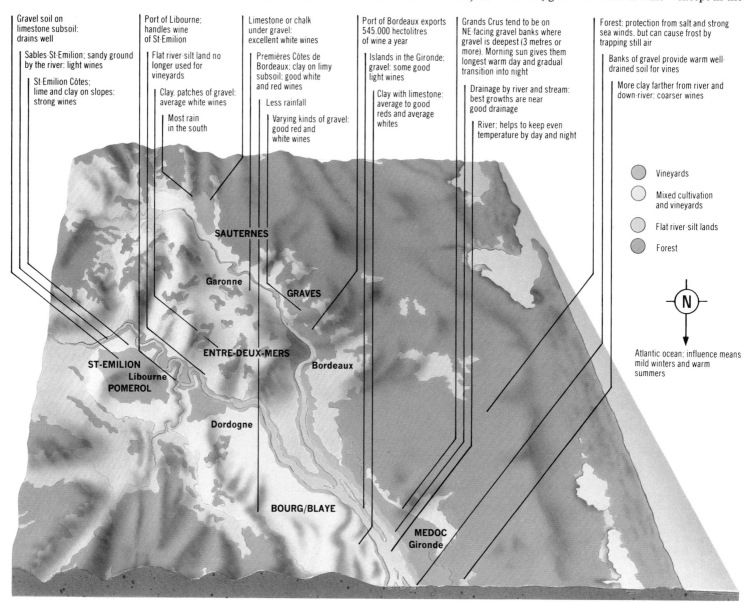

Gravel soil on limestone subsoil: drains well

Sables-St-Emilion; sandy ground by the river: light wines

St-Emilion Côtes; lime and clay on slopes: strong wines

Port of Libourne; handles wine of St-Emilion

Flat river-silt land no longer used for vineyards

Clay. patches of gravel: average white wines

Most rain in the south

Limestone or chalk under gravel: excellent white wines

Premières Côtes de Bordeaux; clay on limy subsoil: good white and red wines

Less rainfall

Varying kinds of gravel: good red and white wines

Port of Bordeaux exports 545.000 hectolitres of wine a year

Islands in the Gironde: gravel: some good light wines

Clay with limestone: average to good reds and average whites

Grands Crus tend to be on NE-facing gravel banks where gravel is deepest (3 metres or more). Morning sun gives them longest warm day and gradual transition into night

Drainage by river and stream: best growths are near good drainage

River: helps to keep even temperature by day and night

Forest: protection from salt and strong sea winds. but can cause frost by trapping still air

Banks of gravel provide warm well-drained soil for vines

More clay farther from river and down-river: coarser wines

SAUTERNES

Garonne

GRAVES

ENTRE-DEUX-MERS

Bordeaux

ST-EMILION
Libourne
POMEROL

Dordogne

BOURG/BLAYE

MEDOC
Gironde

Vineyards

Mixed cultivation and vineyards

Flat river-silt lands

Forest

N

Atlantic ocean; influence means mild winters and warm summers most general terms, and even then with many reservations.

You would not expect this to prevent the University of Bordeaux from going on trying, however. The theory that finds widest support is that (contrary to traditional belief) geology is scarcely a factor at all in deciding quality, at least in Bordeaux. A vine will find all the nourishment it needs almost anywhere; but the poorer the soil the deeper and wider the vine will root. Hence the mysterious fact that poor soil is often good for wine. Give a vine rich soil, or spread generous helpings of manure around it, and its roots will stay near the top. But plant it in stony ground, give it only the bare necessities, and it will plunge metres deep to see what it can find. For the deeper the roots go, the more constant is their environment, and the less they are subject to floods on the one hand, drought on the other, and fluctuations of food supply from manuring or lack of

manuring on the surface. Then there can be a lake around it, or total drought can parch and crack the ground, and the vine will feed normally. Provided only that the subsoil is well drained, so that the roots do not drown.

Enlarging on this idea, Dr Gérard Seguin of the University of Bordeaux has suggested that the nearer a vineyard is to an effective drain, the drier the subsoil will be and the deeper the roots will go; that the first-growths are vineyards nearest the drainage channels, the second-growths slightly farther from them, and so on. There has always been a saying that 'the vines should look at the river'. This theory explains it. It also explains why old vines give the best wine: their roots are deepest. The theory can be examined by studying the streams on the following maps in relation to the classed and other growths.

Hence, this theory continues, it is not the chemical composition of the soil but its

physical makeup that must be taken into account. Heavy clay or sand which drains badly is the worst for wine: gravel and larger stones are best. Add to this the way stones store heat on the surface, and prevent rapid evaporation of moisture from under them, and it is easy to see that they are the best guarantee of stable conditions of temperature and humidity that a vine can have.

In the Médoc it is the deep gravel beds of Margaux and St-Julien and Pauillac which drain best. As you go north the proportion of clay increases, so that in St-Estèphe drainage is much less effective. This does not mean that all Margaux wines are first-growths and all St-Estèphe fifth – although there are many more classed growths in Margaux – but it does account for higher acidity, more tannin, colour, and less scent in St-Estèphe wines. It is, after all, not only a question of quality but of the character of the wine.

Left: some of the factors affecting the varying qualities and character of Bordeaux wine are shown in this diagram of the river basin of the Gironde from the northwest. The Gironde is formed by the confluence of the rivers Dordogne (left) and the Garonne (right). Soil and subsoil have a bearing on the wine, but there is doubt about how important they are in determining its quality and character. Such factors as rainfall, and whether the sun reaches the vine in the morning or afternoon, and above all the rapid drainage of the ground may play just as large a part. The southern part of the area has most rainfall, the north the least. White wine is grown in the south, both red and white in the centre, and more red than white in the north. No positive link between the two facts can be proved, but it seems likely that the mists of the wetter area have been found helpful to white grapes over the years and have tended to cause rot in the red.

THE LANGUAGE OF THE LABEL

Négociant A shipping house which often buys wine from the château a few months old and keeps it (usually in Bordeaux) until it is ready to ship or bottle. Among the most famous négociants are Calvet, Eschenauer, Cordier, Moueix, Barton & Guestier, Ginestet, Sichel, Borie-Manoux, de Luze, Duclot

Château Estate

Récolte Vintage

Mis (or **Mise**) **en bouteille au château** Bottled at the property where it is made

Grand Vin Simply 'great wine', often to distinguish it from a 'second wine'

Cru Classé One of the first five official growths of the Médoc; also any classed growth of another district, however classified. The Médoc classifications are as follows – all go back to 1855

Premier Cru First-growth ⎫
Deuxième Cru Second-growth ⎪ rarely
Troisième Cru Third-growth ⎬ appear on
Quatrième Cru Fourth-growth ⎪ labels
Cinquième Cru Fifth-growth ⎭

Cru Exceptionnel In the Médoc, the second rank, below Cru Classé

Cru Bourgeois Supérieur The third rank

Cru Bourgeois The fourth rank – but often a very worthy wine – occasionally as good as most crus classés

Cru Artisan Rank below Cru Bourgeois

Cru Paysan Rank below Cru Artisan; these two terms are no longer used

Premier Grand Cru Classé The first rank of St-Emilion classed growths (1954 classification)

Grand Cru Classé The second rank of St-Emilion classed growths (1954 classification)

Supérieur (after the name of Graves or Bordeaux) indicates wine with 1° of alcohol above the minimum allowed

Haut A mere verbal gesture, except as part of the name of Haut-Médoc

Propriétaire Owner

Société Anonyme Limited company

Société Civile Private company

Héritiers The heirs of . . .

KEY ○ Red wine ○ White wine

Above: Bordeaux makes three times as much red wine as white, and accounts for 5.5% of all French wine production — almost twice as much as Burgundy.

Right and below: the average (1979-83) production of the major red and white wines of Bordeaux in 1,000 hectolitres.

BELGIUM/LUX.	18.2%
NETHERLANDS	14.4%
USA	13.3%
GREAT BRITAIN	13.0%
WEST GERMANY	11.5%
CANADA	5.8%
DENMARK	5.5%
SWITZERLAND	5.3%
SWEDEN	3.7%
JAPAN	2.3%
IRELAND	0.4%
ITALY	0.1%

Above: Bordeaux exports more than 1.2 million hectolitres a year. Belgium/Luxembourg has overtaken Germany as the largest single customer, taking 250,000 hectolitres — 18% of the total exports. In the mid-1970s Germany was buying 32%. The USA and Great Britain are Bordeaux's other biggest customers.

Red			White	
1 St-Estèphe	54		7 St-Emilion	246
2 Pauillac	36		8 Pomerol	30
3 St-Julien	35		9 Bourg & Blaye	248
4 Margaux	46		**White**	
5 All Haut-Médoc.			10 Graves	59
inc. the above	353		11 Barsac	14
6 Graves	83		12 Sauternes	29
			13 Entre-deux-Mers	119

KEY Red wine White wine

83

The Bas-Médoc

Geographically, the Médoc is a great tongue of land isolated from the body of Aquitaine by the broad brown estuary waters of the Gironde.

In common usage its name is given to more fine wine than any other name in the world: Margaux, St-Julien, Pauillac, St-Estèphe and their surrounding villages are all 'Médoc' in location and in style. But the appellation Médoc is both more limited and less prestigious. It is more clearly understood under its former name of Bas- (meaning lower-) Médoc. The term Bas was dropped for reasons of – shall we say? – delicacy. But the fact remains. The lower Médoc, the tip of the tongue, the farthest reaches of the region, has none of the high points, either physically or gastronomically, of the Haut-Médoc to its south.

The well-drained dunes of river gravel give way to lower and heavier land north of St-Estèphe, with St-Seurin, the last commune of the Haut-Médoc, riding a characteristic hump between areas of channelled marsh.

North and west of here is fertile, long-settled land, with the bustling market town of Lesparre as its capital since the days of English rule five centuries ago.

Until recently, vineyards took their place here with pasture and orchard and woodland. Now they have spread to cover almost all the higher ground where gravel can be found,

centring on the villages of St-Yzans, St-Christoly, Couquèques, By and Valeyrac along the banks of the Gironde, and covering much of the interior in St-Germain-d'Esteuil, Ordonnac, Blaignan and Bégadan.

There are no classed growths but an increasing number of worthy Crus Bourgeois. Fifteen years ago the names of only three or four were known to the wider world. Much replanting and upgrading has happened since, and the lower Médoc now has an important place as a supplier of sound solid reds. A few châteaux have built good reputations, using the expensive methods of the Haut-Médoc, and ageing their wines in new (or newish) barrels. The clearest way to see the difference between Médocs Haut and Bas is to compare one of the best of these wines with, say, a Cru Bourgeois from St-Estèphe or St-Julien. Young, there may be little to distinguish them: both are vigorous, tannic, dry and 'très Bordeaux'. At five years, though, the Haut-Médoc is finding that fine-etched personality, that clean transparency of flavour, that will go on developing. The Bas-Médoc has begun to soften, but remains a sturdy, rather rustic wine, often deep-coloured, satisfying and savoury rather than enlightening and inspiring. At ten years there has been more softening, but not the sort of opening-out of flavour that we find farther south.

The châteaux with most established reputations (and in some cases considerable output) begin with Loudenne, the Gilbey's stronghold at St-Yzans by the river, which also makes a good dry white wine. Most prestigious are Château Potensac (which also uses the names Gallais-Bellevue, Cru Lassalle and others), with the same perfectionist owners as Château Léoville-Las Cases in St-Julien, and the big new (since 1973) (Lafite)-Rothschild development of Château La Cardonne on the same slight plateau.

Châteaux Livran at St-Germain, Greyssac at St-Christoly and Laujac, west of Bégadan, all have well-established names, although today you can look for more modern-style wine, with more fruit and character, at Châteaux La Tour de By, La Clare, Monthil and Vieux-Château Landon in Bégadan, and Châteaux La Tour St-Bonnet and Les Ormes Sorbet in St-Christoly and Couquèques. The old embattled Château du Castera in St-Germain has also re-equipped with steel vats.

Bégadan is the most important commune of the area as a producer: its growers' cooperative uses the grapes from 1,400 acres (560 hectares) to make its very satisfactory wines under various labels. But the feeling of the area is still one of anticipation as more money is invested. The evidence is that in this reasonably priced area the rewards will increase.

Above: good value in sturdy red wine, full of flavour if not finesse, is rapidly making the most remote part of the Médoc better known.
Right: the architectural jewel of the lower Médoc is Château Loudenne, British-owned since the 1870s, dominating the Gironde from a gravel hill with vineyards sloping to the river.

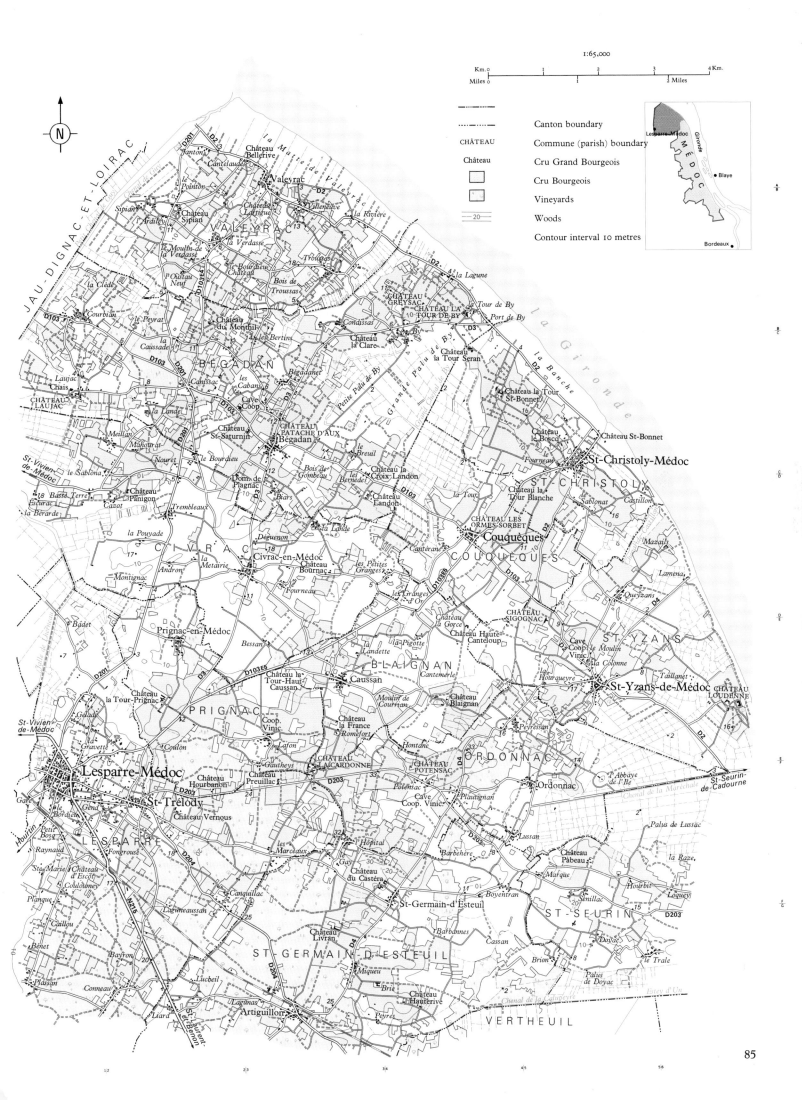

St-Estèphe

The gravel banks which give the Médoc and its wines their character and quality, stretching along the shore of the river Gironde, sheltered from the ocean to the west by forest, begin to peter out at St-Estèphe. It is the northernmost of the four famous communes which are the heart of the Médoc. A little *jalle* – the Médoc word for a stream – divides it from Pauillac, draining on the one hand the vineyards of Château Lafite, on the other three of the five classed growths of St-Estèphe: Châteaux Cos d'Estournel, Lafon-Rochet and Cos Labory.

There is a distinction between the soils of Pauillac and St-Estèphe: as the gravel washed down the Gironde diminishes there is a stronger mixture of clay found in it. Higher up, in Margaux, there is very little. In St-Estèphe it is heavier soil, which drains more slowly. The wines have more acidity, are fuller, more solid, often have less perfume but fairly fill your mouth with flavour. They are sturdy clarets which become with age gentle but still vigorous, unfaded.

Château Cos d'Estournel is the most spectacular of the classed growths. It is an eccentric Chinese-pagoda'd edifice, impressively crowning the steep slope up from the Pauillac boundary (with all too good a view of the Shell refinery below). Together with Château Montrose, overlooking the river, it makes the biggest and best of St-Estèphes; strong wines with a dark colour and a long life. 'Cos', as it is nearly always called, has been the leader in the commune in recent years, having a succulence and persistence of flavour (the result, perhaps, of a high proportion of Merlot in the vineyard) which is much more seductive than its rival second-growth, Montrose. Montrose is an excellent château to visit to get an idea of a prosperous estate in the old-fashioned style. Its rather dark *chai*, heavily beamed, and its magnificent oak fermenting vats have the same air of permanence as its dark, intense, deeply tannic wine. Classic Montrose vintages take 20 years to mature.

The other two classed growths near Cos, Châteaux Lafon-Rochet and Cos Labory, had not distinguished themselves in recent years until Lafon-Rochet was bought by M Tesseron, a Cognac merchant, when it gained the distinction of being the first new château to be built (or rebuilt) in Bordeaux in the 20th century. Its reputation is high today. Cos Labory is not so ambitious, content to be full of fruity flavour at a fairly young age. Calon-Ségur, north of the village and the northernmost classed growth of the Médoc, comes somewhere between Cos d'Estournel and Montrose in style: firm and long-lived but not overaggressive. Two hundred and fifty years ago the Marquis de Ségur, owner of both Lafite and Latour, reputedly said his heart was at Calon. It still is, on the label.

Above all, St-Estèphe is known for its Crus Bourgeois. There is an explosion of them on the plateau south and west of the village. Châteaux Phélan-Ségur and de Pez are both outstanding producers of very fine wine, year after year. In any new classification Château de Pez would find itself promoted to stand with

Above and right: the five Crus Classés of St-Estèphe, and Château de Pez, an example of the many Crus Bourgeois of outstanding quality.

Top: the view over St-Estèphe from a point above Château Lafite. The first buildings are Château Cos Labory. Just over the road lies the extravagant *chai* of Cos d'Estournel. In the distance across the Gironde estuary are the low hills of the Charente.
Above: a 100-year-old print from Château Loudenne shows hardly altered scenes of Médoc château life.

Cos, Calon and Montrose at the head of the commune. For reliability, style and substance combined (Pez is a vigorous, long-maturing wine), it cannot be faulted.

Among the many worthy burgesses of the commune, Château Meyney, like a huge and immaculate farmyard without a farmhouse, is biggest and best-distributed. Its situation by the river, neighbour to Montrose, might make one look for finer wine with more potential for

development. In practice it is sturdy and reliable without notable flair. More dashing wines, still in the hearty St-Estèphe style, are made at Château les Ormes de Pez by the owner of Château Lynch-Bages in Pauillac. Châteaux Tronquoy-Lalande, Beau-Site and Capbern Gasqueton (under several names) all deserve their good reputations. Château de Marbuzet is the name given to the second wine of Cos d'Estournel. Châteaux Haut-Marbuzet, Andron Blanquet, Houissant, Le Crock, Le Boscq and Canteloup continue the list of St-Estèphes that regularly give satisfaction, if not rapture. The growers' cooperative, the 'Marquis de St-Estèphe', is also an important source of typical wine.

To the north of St-Estèphe the gravel bank diminishes to a promontory sticking out of the *palus* – the flat river-silt land on which no wine of quality grows. On top of the promontory the little village of St-Seurin-de-Cadourne has a dozen Crus Bourgeois. The gentle Château Coufran, the more tannic Verdignan, the full-blooded Sociando-Mallet and the admirable Bel Orme Tronquoy de Lalande are the leaders here, along with a big cooperative whose wine is sold as 'Canterayne'.

Where St-Seurin ends is the end of the Haut-Médoc: any wine grown beyond that point is only entitled to the appellation Médoc, plain and simple (see pages 84–85). The beautiful Château Loudenne, for more than a century owned by the British firm of Gilbey, occupies its first gravel knoll.

The country behind St-Estèphe, farther from the river, has a scattering of Crus Bourgeois, few of them well known. Cissac and Vertheuil lie on stronger and less gravelly soil on the edge of the forest. Château Cissac is the outstanding growth: vigorous enough to be a Pauillac. At Cissac, Château du Breuil and the combined Châteaux Hanteillan and Larrivaux, and at Vertheuil the Châteaux Reysson, Le Bourdieu, Victoria and Le Meynieu are worth at least occasional investigation.

Pauillac

If one had to single out one commune of Bordeaux to head the list, there would be no argument. It would be Pauillac. Châteaux Lafite, Latour and Mouton Rothschild, three out of the first five of the Médoc and Graves, are its obvious claim. But many claret lovers would tell you that the wines of Pauillac have the quintessential flavour they look for in Bordeaux – a combination of fresh soft-fruit, oak, dryness, subtlety combined with substance, a touch of cigar-box, a suggestion of sweetness and, above all, vigour. Even the lesser growths approach their ideal claret.

At Pauillac the gravel *croupes* of the Médoc get as near as they ever do to being hills. The highest part, with Châteaux Mouton Rothschild and Pontet-Canet on its summit, reaches 100 feet (30 metres) – quite an achievement in this coastal area, where a mere swelling of the ground provides a lookout point.

The town of Pauillac is the biggest of the Médoc. Recently it has grown faster than ever before, as its long-established oil refinery has developed into an industrial monster in the heart of the world's most illustrious agricultural land. Its old quay has become a marina; a few restaurants have opened – yet it could still scarcely be called animated.

The vineyards of the châteaux of Pauillac are on the whole less subdivided than in most of the Médoc. Whereas in Margaux (for example) the châteaux are bunched together in the town, and their holdings in the surrounding

Below: loading Cabernet grapes at vintage in the vineyards of Château Latour. Château Pichon-Lalande dreams in the sunshine behind.

Left: Pauillac Crus Classés have a sober approach to labelling. The one tearaway is Mouton Rothschild, which commissions a different artist every year.

countryside are inextricably mixed up – a row here, a couple of rows there – in Pauillac whole slopes, mounds and plateaux belong to one proprietor. One would therefore expect greater variations between the wines.

The three great wines of Pauillac are all very much individuals. Lafite-Rothschild and Latour stand at opposite ends of the parish; the first almost in St-Estèphe, the second almost in St-Julien. Oddly enough, though, their characters tend the opposite way: Lafite more towards the smoothness and finesse of a St-Julien, Latour more towards the strength and firmness of a St-Estèphe.

Lafite, with 225 acres (90 hectares) one of the biggest vineyards in the Médoc, makes about 1,000 barrels of its fabulously expensive wine; a perfumed, polished, quintessentially gentlemanly production. Wine from its young vines is sold as Moulin des Carruades.

The firmer and more solid Latour does not ask quite such high prices, although there are few who would say it was worth less than Lafite. It has the great merit of evenness over uneven vintages and superb depth of flavour. Even the château's second wine, Les Forts de Latour, from separate parcels of land west of the main road (the D2), is considered and priced as a second Cru Classé.

Baron Philippe de Rothschild at Mouton makes a third kind of Pauillac: strong, dark, full of the savour of ripe blackcurrants. Given the ten or often even 20 years they need to mature (depending on the quality of the vintage), these wines reach into realms of perfection where they are rarely followed. But millionaires tend to be impatient: too much is drunk far too young.

The undoubted similarity in strength and staying power of Latour and Mouton can apparently be put down to the unusually high proportion of Cabernet vines in their vineyards: as high as 85% at Mouton.

No visitor to Pauillac should miss the beautiful little museum of works of art connected with wine – old glass, paintings, tapestries – as well as the very fine *chais*, which make Château Mouton Rothschild the showplace of the whole Médoc.

The two châteaux Pichon-Longueville – Baron and Lalande – face each other across the road south from Pauillac like mad old duchesses in party clothes. Lalande is the bigger half of what was one huge property – partly in St-Julien, mainly in Pauillac. Both are now in the top flight of second-growths; Lalande notably successful and fashionable.

The two best known of the remaining classified growths of Pauillac are Pontet-Canet, with the biggest production of any Cru Classé (as much as 1,500 barrels a year), and Lynch-Bages, whose rather full, heavy wine, with a most distinctive scented bouquet, is immensely popular in Britain.

Château Duhart-Milon belongs to the Rothschilds of Lafite, and Mouton Baronne Philippe to Mouton. Both clearly benefit from the wealth and technical knowledge of their proprietors and managers. The neighbouring classed-growth Clerc Milon also belongs to the (Mouton) Rothschild stable.

Km. 0   1 Km.

Mile 0   1 Mile

1:35,000

Châteaux Batailley and Haut-Batailley lie back in the fringe of the woods. (Haut-Batailley has the little Château La Couronne, classified below the Crus Classés as a Cru Exceptionnel, as neighbour and partner.) One does not expect quite the same finesse from them as from the great wines nearer the river, but both are consistently well made and good value. Haut-Batailley has the more finesse.

The two châteaux called Grand-Puy, Lacoste and Ducasse, both have high reputations, although the former is better known and has recently made some of Pauillac's most delicious wines. It is one fine continuous vineyard on high ground, surrounding its

château, while Ducasse is scattered in three separate parcels north and west of Pauillac, and its old château is now the Maison du Vin on the quay in the town itself.

Of the remaining classed growths, Croizet-Bages is probably the best. Haut-Bages Libéral, next door, has acquired new premises and a new lease of life lately. Pédesclaux and Lynch-Moussas (recently restored by the owners of Batailley) are smaller and – for the moment at least – less well-known châteaux.

Pauillac, having so many large estates, is not, like St-Estèphe, a warren of small-to-middling growers. Its one small Cru Exceptionnel, La Couronne, has already been mentioned. Of

the Crus Bourgeois, Fonbadet is perhaps best, Haut-Bages Monpelou is co-owned with Château Batailley, and Haut-Bages Averous is the second wine of Château Lynch-Bages. La Fleur Milon, Tour Pibran and Anseillan are all more or less familiar names. The local cooperative, under the name of La Rose Pauillac, also makes useful wine.

The map includes part of the next parish to the west, St-Sauveur. There are no wines of outstanding quality; the Crus Bourgeois marked, however, are respectable and useful. Châteaux Liversan (which includes Fonpiqueyre), Peyrabon and Ramage la Batisse are the best known.

St-Julien

Above: the sedate stone
country house of
Château Branaire-Ducru.

Left: barrels being filled
with new wine by hand
by Michel Rolland, the
maître de chai of
Château Léoville-Las
Cases.

No other commune in Bordeaux has so high a proportion of classed growths as St-Julien. It is a small commune, with the smallest production of the famous four of the Médoc, but almost all of it is superlative winegrowing land: typical dunes of gravel, not as deep as Pauillac (a cross-section of a St-Julien vine and its soil is on page 19), but very close to the river and consequently well drained.

There are few Crus Bourgeois, and those there are are very good indeed: one of them, Château Gloria, is easily on a par with the classed growths and sometimes makes a wine as good as any in the district.

If Pauillac makes the most striking and brilliant wine of the Médoc, and Margaux the most refined and exquisite, St-Julien forms the transition between the two. With one or two exceptions its châteaux make rather round and gentle wine – gentle, that is, when it is mature: it starts as tough and tannic in a good year as any.

The chief proponents of the typical smooth St-Julien style are Châteaux Gruaud-Larose and Talbot – both belonging to the négociant Cordier. There is drier, and usually more exciting, wine made at the Italianate mansion of Ducru-Beaucaillou, and sometimes more elegant wine (in keeping with a very beautiful Louis XV château) made at Beychevelle.

The principal glory of the commune is the vast estate of Léoville, once the biggest in the Médoc, now divided into three. It lies on the Pauillac boundary, and it would be a brave man who would say that he could distinguish a Léoville from a Longueville every time (although he certainly should be able to distinguish a Château Latour, which lies equally close).

Château Léoville-Las Cases has the biggest vineyards of the three, with more than 80 hectares (200-odd acres), and for some years has maintained a reputation as high as Château Pichon-Lalande in Pauillac for impeccable wine, although in a restrained, drier, more austere and 'classic' style; very much to the

St-Julien has many of the Médoc's most illustrious Crus Classés. Of the comparatively few but excellent Crus Bourgeois, Château Gloria is best known.

Map labels: PAUILLAC · Daubos · CHÂTEAU PICHON-LONGUEVILLE-BARON · CHÂTEAU PICHON-LONGUEVILLE-COMTESSE-DE-LALANDE · CHÂTEAU LATOUR · Ch. la Couronne · CHÂTEAU HAUT-BATAILLEY · Cach · Château La Rose-Trintaudon · Château Peymartin · Château la Bridane · CHÂTEAU LEOVILLE-LAS-CASES · St-Julien-Beychevelle · Château Capdelong · la Bergerie · CHÂTEAU LEOVILLE-POYFERRÉ · ST-JULIEN · Perganson · CHÂTEAU TALBOT · CHÂTEAU LANGOA-BARTON · CHÂTEAU LEOVILLE-BARTON · la Mouline · ST-LAURENT · Gare · le Long · le Bouscat · Château Barateau · Lesparre-Médoc · St-Laurent-et-Benon · Château du Glana · CHÂTEAU BELGRAVE · CHÂTEAU DUCRU-BEAUCAILLOU · Château Lalande-Borie · Château Gloria · Listrac · LA TOUR-CARNET CHÂTEAU · CHÂTEAU CAMENSAC · CHÂTEAU LAGRANGE · Château Terrey-Gros-Cailloux · Château Teynac · Château Moulin de la Rose · Beychevelle · CHÂTEAU BRANAIRE-DUCRU · Château Hortevie · CHÂTEAU SAINT-PIERRE · Lamothe · le Graveyron · CHÂTEAU GRUAUD-LAROSE · CHÂTEAU BEYCHEVELLE · le Vivey · le Bourdieu · le Marais de Beychevelle · Château Lanessan · le Cul du Bosc · Lamarque · CUSSAC

English taste. Léoville-Barton runs it close. It belongs, together with the neighbouring Langoa, to the old Irish family of Barton, who moved to Bordeaux as merchants in the 18th century.

Ronald Barton lives in the beautiful 18th-century Château Langoa, and makes his two wines side by side in the same *chai*. Langoa is usually reckoned the slightly lesser wine of the two, being fuller and more tannic, but both are among the finest clarets in a traditional manner. Such wines should be laid down for a good seven years even in lesser vintages; in great ones they will last for a generation or more.

Léoville-Poyferré one sees less. It sometimes seems to lack the roundness which makes St-Julien so pleasant to drink, although the first vintages of the '80s are splendid. Of course it is hard to know how much of such a characteristic is due to the techniques in use and how much to the soil and situation. A different balance of Cabernet and Merlot will produce different barrels from the same vineyard. On

the other hand, people who taste the wines of different grape varieties from one vineyard before they have been 'assembled' in one barrel have often said that even while they tasted of the different grapes, each had the characteristic style of the estate.

Château Beychevelle is even better known, its wine the height of elegance (sometimes rather plump elegance) rather than power. In 1983 it changed hands, after a slightly ragged recent record. Château Branaire-Ducru next door, although much less famous, could be said to sum up the appeal of St-Julien in its flavoury smoothness.

The group of classed growths that stand away from the river, on soil becoming slightly less outrageously stony, include the stablemates Gruaud-Larose and Talbot, which epitomize the tender, almost rich, easy-to-drink style of St-Julien. Both also make excellent second wines: respectively 'Sarget' and 'Connétable'. Château St-Pierre-Sevaistre, which separates them, was bought in 1983

by Henri Martin of Château Gloria, who should build on its already solid reputation.

Château du Glana, the large Cru Bourgeois next door, has not been as favoured recently as Hortevie, Moulin de la Rose, Terrey-Gros-Cailloux, and Lalande-Borie, a new creation of the owner of Ducru-Beaucaillou.

The last of the classed growths, Château Lagrange, used to be very highly regarded for its rich, substantial wine. A new (Japanese) régime since 1984 will undoubtedly bring it back into focus. It lies far back in the country, in the sleepy hinterland on the border of St-Laurent (whose appellation is Haut-Médoc) and in a group with three other classed growths, all in different stages of resurrection. La Tour Carnet is most advanced; recently very attractive. Camensac was replanted a few years later by the owner of the huge and popular Cru Bourgeois Larose-Trintaudon. Its wine is gaining substance and recognition. Château Belgrave is the latest to be restored. Its first '80s promise future satisfaction.

The Central Médoc

This is the bridge passage of the Médoc, the mezzo forte between the andante of St-Julien and the allegro of Margaux. Four villages pass without a single classed growth. Here the gravel dunes rise less proudly above the river. The commune of Cussac maintains some of the momentum of St-Julien with the outstanding Cru Bourgeois Château Lanessan, facing St-Julien across the canal that separates the parishes. Lanessan and its neighbour La Caronne Ste-Gemme (largely in neighbouring St-Laurent) are well-run properties whose owners can afford high standards.

Otherwise Cussac has little of the all-important gravel. Château Beaumont occupies its best outcrop, and has lately been re-equipped; Châteaux Tour du Haut-Moulin and Moulin Rouge do well with what they have in the narrow space between forest and river. The riverside here is worth a visit to see the handsome 17th-century battlements of the Fort-Médoc – an anti-English precaution now turned to peaceful uses. At Lamarque an earlier fortress, the splendid Château de Lamarque, has established a name for carefully made, satisfyingly full-bodied wine with the true stamp of the Médoc on it. Lamarque is the Médoc's link with Blaye on the other side of the Gironde: a regular car-ferry service runs from the pier.

The hand-operated press is obsolete, but an old photograph still perfectly catches the atmosphere of many small châteaux in this part of the Médoc.

A good deal of replanting has given the area a purposeful look which was lacking a few years ago. Château Malescasse now belongs to the Tesseron family of Pontet-Canet and Lafon-Rochet. And in the next commune south, Arcins, the big old properties of Château Barreyres and Château d'Arcins have been hugely replanted by the Castels, whose Castelvin is a staple of French diet. They, their well-managed neighbour Château d'Arnauld, and the cooperative 'Chevalier d'Ars' can hardly fail to make Arcins better known.

It is west of Arcins, though, that the gravel ridges rise and fan out inland, culminating at Grand Poujeaux (in the commune of Moulis) and at Listrac. These two communes are dignified with appellations of their own instead of the portmanteau 'Haut-Médoc'.

Quality rises with the gravel. Immediately over the parish boundary, Château Chasse-Spleen is one of the 'Exceptionnel' Bourgeois growths that can be considered as honorarily classified, almost as an honorary St-Julien, for its smoothness, its accessibility and yet its firm, oak-aged structure. Château Maucaillou can be almost as fine. And Grand Poujeaux is surrounded by a knot of excellent Crus Bourgeois with 'Poujeaux' in their names: Theil, Gressier, Dutruch, La Closerie and more, all reliable for stouthearted, long-lived red wines with the flavour that makes the Médoc unique.

Listrac has a higher plateau, chalk beneath its gravel and a name for tough, austere wines that need time. The name here is Fourcas: both

Châteaux that bear it, Hosten and Dupré, have long been outstanding. Much replanting and infilling has recently enlarged the vineyard considerably. Since 1973 Baron Edmond de Rothschild has created, with more than 200 acres (90 hectares plus), Château Clarke; the twin Châteaux Fonréaud and Lestage have 230 acres (92 hectares) between them; Château Mauvezin has planted 150 acres (60 hectares). The tendency in these redeveloped estates is to temper the Listrac austerity and make rounder wines, which can only help to make the appellation better known.

Beyond the Jalle de Tiquetorte, in the southeast corner of the area, we begin to enter the sphere of Margaux. The big Château Citran and the smaller Villegeorge (off the map; a Cru Exceptionnel to watch) lie in the commune of Avensan. Both are well known, and approach Margaux in style.

Soussans is among the communes whose Appellation Contrôlée is not merely Haut-Médoc but Margaux. Its Château La Tour de Mons might be called the Mouton of the Crus Bourgeois; a consistently excellent property. Château Paveil de Luze is also well known. Cocks and Féret's *Bordeaux et Ses Vins* says Soussans wines are '*promptement buvables*' – soon ready to drink. Soon in this context means at least four years.

Twenty or 30 Crus Bourgeois between St-Julien and Soussans, the beginning of Margaux, are well known for outstanding value in far-above-average claret.

Margaux and the Southern Médoc

By many accounts this, the southernmost stretch of the Haut-Médoc, makes the finest wine of all. Margaux has a tight concentration of classed growths, which continue into the hamlets of Issan, Cantenac and Labarde.

The map here shows a rather different picture from Pauillac or St-Julien. Instead of the châteaux being spread out evenly over the land, they are huddled together in the village. An examination of the almost unliftable volumes of commune maps in the Mairie shows a degree of intermingling of one estate with another which is far greater than in, say, Pauillac. One would therefore look to differences in technique and tradition more than changes of soil to try to explain the differences between one château and another.

In fact the soil of Margaux is the thinnest in the Médoc, with the highest proportion of rough gravel. It has the least to offer the vine in the way of nourishment but it drains well even in rainy years. The result is wines that start life comparatively 'supple', although in poor years they can turn out thin. In good and great years, however, all the stories about the virtues of gravel are justified: there is a delicacy about good Margaux, and a sweet haunting perfume, that makes it the most exquisite claret of all.

The wines of Château Margaux and Château Palmer next door are the ones that most often reach such heights. Château Margaux is not only a first-growth of the Médoc, it is the one that most looks the part: a pediment at the end of an avenue; the air of a mansion with *chais* to match. After over a decade in the doldrums, new owners began to make superlative wine here again in 1978. The third-growth Palmer, however, keeps up a formidable challenge.

Château Lascombes (which was restored to glory by Alexis Lichine, and now belongs to the English brewers Bass Charrington) also makes reliable and very attractive wine. Of the famous pair which used to be the big Rausan estate, as famous in the 18th century as Léoville was in St-Julien, Rausan-Ségla is today the more important as well as the bigger of the two – although neither has justified its official second-growth ranking for years.

There are several distinguished pairs of châteaux in Margaux. The two second-growths Brane-Cantenac and Durfort-Vivens are jointly owned (by the ubiquitous Lurton family), yet make distinctly different wine: the Brane smooth, the Durfort harder. The little third-growth Desmirail has recently been resurrected to join them as a third bowstring. Pouget is the brother of Boyd-Cantenac. Ferrière is made at Lascombes. Malescot St-Exupéry (often miraculously scented and one of the best of Margaux) was until recently linked with the heavier, more rustic Marquis d'Alesme-Becker.

Still in Margaux proper, Château Marquis de Terme, although rarely seen abroad, makes good, rather old-fashioned, wine, and Château d'Issan is perhaps the most beautiful house in the Médoc: a 17th-century fortified manor within the complete moat of an old *château-fort*. The admirable gentle slope of its vineyard to the road is one of the best situations in Margaux.

The Crus Bourgeois include a group on the theme of Labégorce; none is world famous but their names stick in the mind like a nursery rhyme. Of the three, Château Labégorce-Zédé is the best known. Soussans in the extreme north has the highly respected Château La Tour de Mons.

Our rather erratic path to and fro in Margaux becomes a little simpler as the châteaux thin out in Cantenac and farther south. Most of the land in the communes of Cantenac, Labarde and Arsac, as well as Soussans to the north, has been granted the appellation Margaux, making wines of very similar style and quality. If anything, Cantenac and hamlets farther south make more powerful but less fragrant wines.

In Cantenac itself, Alexis Lichine's own Château of Prieuré is deservedly famous for making some of Margaux's most consistently splendid claret. Château Kirwan was in eclipse, but has recently been restored and is beginning to shine.

Another recent tale of restoration and renewed quality has been the lonely Château du Tertre, isolated in Arsac. Recent vintages have been excellent.

Châteaux Cantenac-Brown and Boyd-Cantenac, which straddle the bigger and better-known Brane-Cantenac on the southern slope of Margaux's low dune of gravel, are both in capable hands. (The former belongs to the head of the famous négociant firm de Luze.) Both make the masculine style of Margaux.

There are three more big and famous classed growths before the vineyards come to an end: Giscours, whose half-timbered farm buildings in the graceless style of Deauville or Le Touquet face a most impressive sweep of vines and harbour dense, noble and concentrated wine; Cantemerle, a perfect Sleeping Beauty château, deep in a wood of huge trees and quiet pools; and the top-flight Château La Lagune, a neat 18th-century building just off the Bordeaux road (and the nearest classed growth of the Médoc to the city). They have in common a style that is bigger and more solid than a Margaux: Giscours usually firm and La Lagune rather soft, but both full of flavour; Cantemerle a powerful, long-lasting, deep-voiced wine, now made by the house of Cordier.

Dauzac, the fourth classed growth of this southern area, has recently raised its standards, although its nominally bourgeois neighbour Siran has long made better wine. Siran and Château d'Angludet, admirably situated on the banks of a stream, consistently make wine of classed-growth quality.

Below and right: a magnificent concentration of Crus Classés distinguishes Margaux and its area. They emphasize their prestige with more gilded labels than the rest of the Médoc.

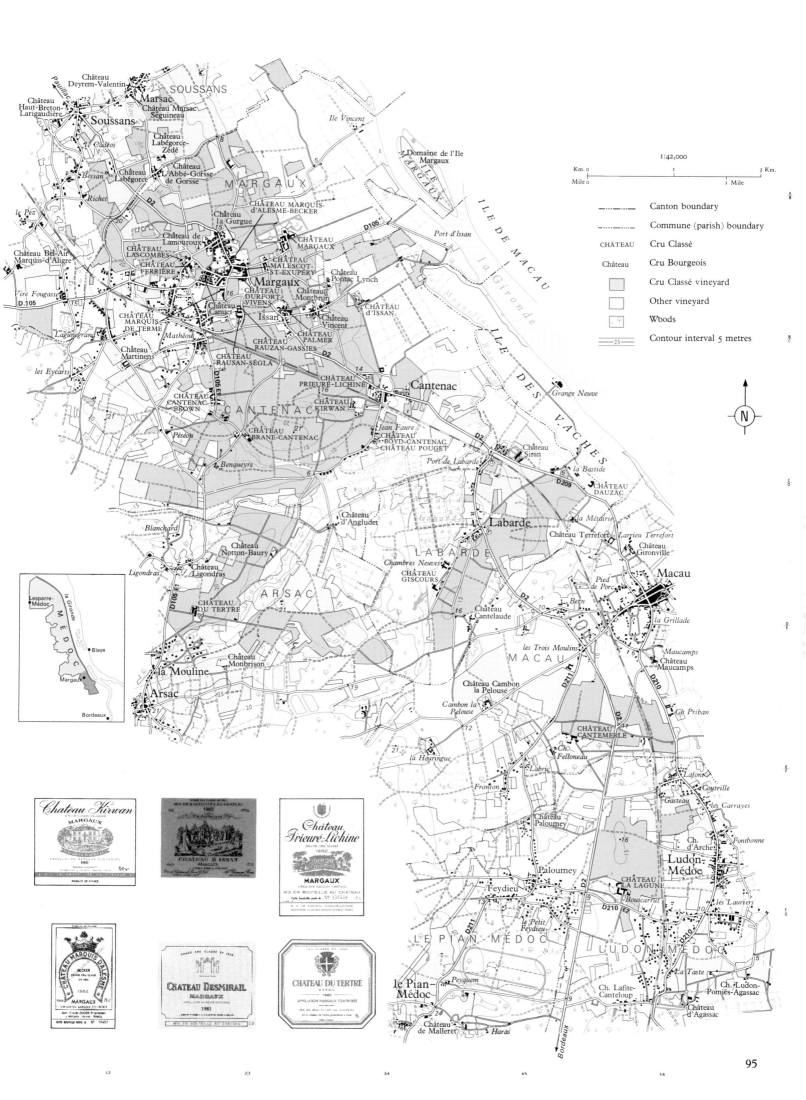

Graves and Entre-Deux-Mers

As little as five years ago there was no good reason for a detailed map of the southern half of the Bordeaux vineyard. All the interest lay to the north in the red-wine country of the Médoc and St-Emilion-Pomerol – except for the few classified Graves properties on the outskirts of the city (see pages 98 and 99), and the isolated concentration of Sauternes and Barsac (see pages 100 and 101).

There is very much more to the Graves region than the Haut-Graves, but it had not asserted itself, while the long lozenge of land between the rivers Garonne and Dordogne, Entre-Deux-Mers, was a generalized name for a harmless dry white. Few properties had established a name. The same was true of the hilly right bank of the Garonne opposite Graves from Langon through Cadillac and Langoiran right down to Bordeaux itself; the Premières Côtes de Bordeaux. The only names that made the knowing lick their lips were Ste-Croix-du-Mont and Loupiac. Occasional bottles of something remarkably like Sauternes kept their names alive.

Things have changed. The south end of the Graves has come to life. Langon is a regular resort of buyers looking for flavour and value. Old properties in the central Graves, notably in the once-famous parish of Portets, have new owners and new philosophies. The Premières Côtes are delivering better wine, abandoning a noncommittal style of not-quite-dry white in favour of clean, modern white wines and more red.

It is too much to claim that truly liquorous Ste-Croix-du-Mont has become a money-making proposition, as it once was, but Châteaux Loubens, de Tastes, Lousteau-Vieil and La Rame are making great efforts, and in neighbouring Loupiac the Châteaux de Loupiac, de Ricaud and du Cros are ready to run the risks inherent in making truly sweet, rather than semi-sweet, wine. Cérons, too, Barsac's northern neighbour in the Graves, a separate appellation long forgotten (it includes Illats and Podensac) has recently made some fine wine in a style midway between Graves and Barsac: softly rather than stickily sweet, with even a little finesse. The Châteaux de Cérons and de Calvimont are the leaders.

The ability of Graves soil to make red and white wine equally well is seen at Portets in the restored Château Rahoul, at Podensac in Château de Chantegrive, and in properties

dotted around Arbanats and Castres. It has also emerged in two noteworthy groups of small properties around Langon. One (including Châteaux Chicane, de Gaillat and others) is run by the Langon négociant Pierre Coste. He makes a singular style of fruity but slightly austere red. The other group centres around Château Magence at St-Pierre-de-Mons, which vies with its neighbours Châteaux Respide, Queyrats, Ludeman la Côte, Toumilon and others in making lively dry Sauvignon white and good sturdy red.

It is perhaps still too early to say which Premières Côtes properties will distinguish themselves. Their situation on the steep right bank of the river suggests, in places, the conditions that make such good wine at Fronsac and Bourg. Châteaux Fayau at Cadillac, Haut-Brignon at Cénac, Laurétan at Langoiran and above all Reynon at Béguey, for its remarkable Sauvignon from very old vines, have impressed me.

By far the biggest territory is Entre-Deux-Mers – a name that is synonymous with

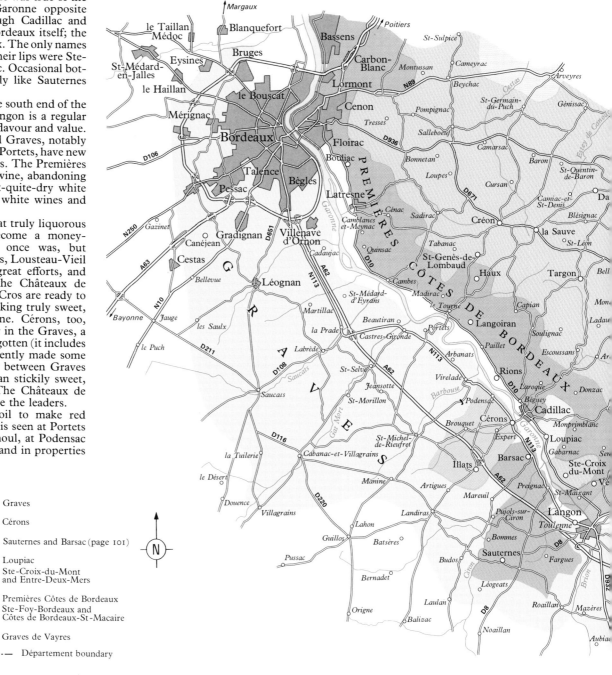

Graves

Cérons

Sauternes and Barsac (page 101)

Loupiac

Ste-Croix-du-Mont and Entre-Deux-Mers

Premières Côtes de Bordeaux

Ste-Foy-Bordeaux and Côtes de Bordeaux-St-Macaire

Graves de Vayres

—·—·— Département boundary

reputable if unglamorous dry whites, but now one of the principal sources of red Bordeaux or Bordeaux Supérieur as well. A number of substantial châteaux have changed the aspect of the region, especially of the parishes in the north along the Dordogne valley, from mixed farm and orchard to vinous monoculture. One of the best and almost certainly the biggest is Château Bonnet at Grézillac, with equally admirable modern white and red. La Gamage, a superior blend of cooperative wines named after the little river, is also rightly popular.

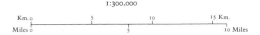

1:300,000

Km.0 .... 5 .... 10 .... 15 Km.
Miles 0 .... 5 .... 10 Miles

Above: the little Château du Pavillon near Cadillac is a typical Premières Côtes property, with the air of a villa and fruit trees among the vines.

Right: individual properties are starting to emerge in districts such as Loupiac, Ste-Croix-du-Mont and the southern Graves.

Graves

The wise heads of Bordeaux 'assemble' a first-growth. The late Jean Ribereau-Gayon and the celebrated Emile Peynaud make notes on the wines in every barrel of a vintage at Château Haut-Brion. Behind are stainless-steel vats. Haut-Brion was the first first-growth to install them in place of wood.

The change from the last section of the Médoc is obvious from the map. Here the city reaches out into the pine woods, which continue (as the Landes) from here to the Basque foothills of the Pyrenees. The vineyards are clearings, often isolated from one another in heavily forested country crossed by shallow river-valleys.

The district of Graves takes its name from its gravel-and-sand soil, which it came by in just the same way as the Médoc – the spoil of the Garonne from inland hills.

Graves wine was the first Bordeaux to be singled out for its quality: Bordeaux money was invested here, on the very fringes of the city, long before the opening up of the comparatively remote Médoc in the early 18th century. Château Haut-Brion, also known by the name of its owner as 'Pontac', was celebrated a hundred years before. Now the city has swallowed all the early vineyards in its path except the group on the deep gravel of Pessac: Haut-Brion and its neighbour and rival, La Mission Haut Brion, the little Les Carmes Haut Brion and, farther out of town, the ancient property of the Bishop of Bordeaux who became Pope Clement V, still known for its rich and silky red wine.

Châteaux Haut-Brion and La Mission (with its second wine La Tour Haut Brion and its splendid white vineyard, Laville Haut Brion) lie on opposite sides of the old Arcachon road through Pessac. Haut-Brion is every inch a First-Growth, a suave equilibrium of force and finesse. La Mission tastes denser, riper, more savage – and often just as splendid. In 1984

Haut-Brion bought its old rival – not to unite the vineyards but to continue the match. Few pairings show so vividly what the *terroir*, the uniqueness of each piece of ground, means on this Bordeaux soil.

The Graves region sweeps in a wide arc southeastwards, bordered by the river Garonne and enclosing Sauternes and Barsac in its perimeter. The whole appellation is shown in context on pages 80 and 96–97.

This map shows what has been termed 'Haut-Graves', on the analogy of the Haut-Médoc: the region where the longest-established properties occupy long-proved soil. Most of the wine is red, as in the Médoc. Haut-Graves differs in producing a very little white of sometimes superlative quality, in most cases from châteaux also classified for their red wine. A very simple 'yes or no' classification, last reviewed in 1959, includes 15 châteaux, six for both red and white and two for white wine only. Farther south white wine, of less remarkable quality, is in the majority – is, indeed, the standard Graves of commerce.

The commune of Léognan, well into the forest, is the hub of this region. Domaine de Chevalier is its outstanding property, despite its modest appearance. It resembles a small industrial building at the end of a flat field of vines surrounded by pine trees. Nonetheless it succeeds in making exceedingly fine red and white wine year after year. There is something almost Californian about the little winery with its two flavours . . . both of which turn out to be brilliant.

Château Haut-Bailly is the other leading classed growth of Léognan; it is unusual in these parts for making only red wine. Haut-Bailly has always been a respected name but its last few vintages have been particularly good.

Carbonnieux and Olivier are both big properties which have exported their wines, principally white, for many years. Châteaux de Fieuzal and Malartic-Lagravière are smaller but more distinguished, with a higher proportion of red grapes. The latter often makes one of the best white Graves. Château La Louvière is another big property with notable white wine, and a little red, although not among the classed growths. And oddly enough there is yet another Haut-Brion, Larrivet.

Three other communes, on the Bordeaux–Langon road to the east, have classed growths. In Villenave-d'Ornon there is Château Couhins, a white-wine château which also makes a vin rosé. Part of its vineyard is run separately as Château Cantebau-Couhins and makes a very good dry white wine. The small Châteaux Pontac Monplaisir and Baret are not classed. In Cadaujac there is the well-known Château Bouscaut, whose red wine is steady, if not thrilling. And finally in Martillac two classed growths, Smith Haut Lafitte and La Tour Martillac, make both red and white wine (their whites perhaps better) and an important Cru Bourgeois, Château La Garde, makes another good and full-bodied red.

Right: Crus Classés of Graves. Six are included in the classification for both red and white; two, Laville Haut Brion and Couhins, for white only; the rest for red.

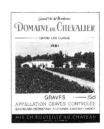

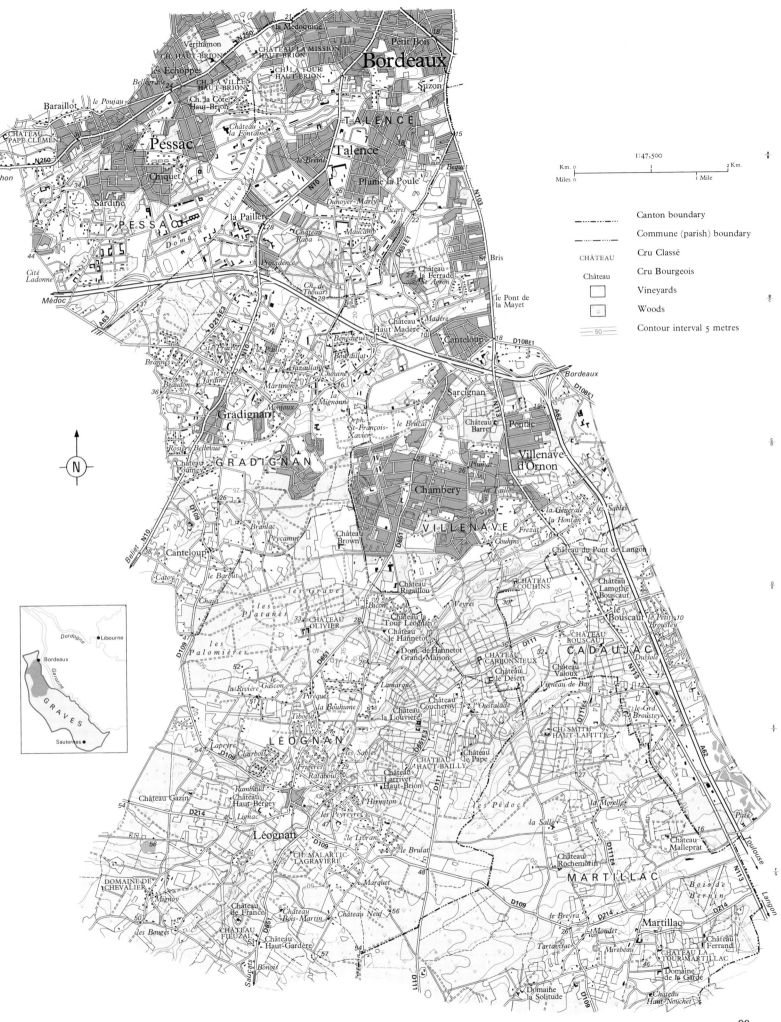

Sauternes and Barsac

All the other districts of Bordeaux mapped here make wines that can be compared with, and preferred to, one another. Sauternes is different. The famous white wine of Sauternes is a speciality which finds its only real rival not in France but in Germany. It depends on local conditions and a very unusual wine-making technique. In great years the results can be sublime: a very sweet, rich-textured, flower-scented, glittering golden liquid. In other years it can frankly fail to be Sauternes (properly so-called) at all.

Above all it is only a few châteaux of Sauternes – and in this we include Barsac – that make such wine. Ordinary Sauternes, whether called Haut or not makes no difference, is just sweet white wine. Very cold it makes a pleasant drink for serving before or after a meal.

The special technique which only the considerable châteaux can afford to employ is to pick over the vineyard as many as eight or nine times, starting in September and sometimes going on until November. This is to take full advantage of the peculiar form of mould (known as *Botrytis cinerea* to the scientist, or *pourriture noble* – 'noble rot' – to the poet) which forms on the grapes in a mild, misty autumn and reduces their skins to brown pulp.

Instead of affecting the blighted grapes with a flavour of rot, this botrytis engineers the escape of a proportion of the water in them, leaving the sugar and the flavouring elements in the juice more concentrated than ever. The result is wine with an intensity of taste and scent and a smooth, almost oil-like, texture which can be made no other way.

But it does mean picking the grapes as they shrivel, berry by berry – and the small proprietors of little-known châteaux have no alternative but to pick at once, and hope for as much botrytis as possible.

Production is very small, since evaporation is actually encouraged. From each one of its 250 acres (100 hectares) Château d'Yquem, the most famous of Sauternes, makes only about 9 hectolitres (about 1,200 bottles) of wine. A first-class Médoc vineyard would make three or four times as much.

The risk element is appalling, since bad weather in October can rob the grower of all chance of making sweet wine, and sometimes any wine at all. Costs are correspondingly high, and the low price of even the finest Sauternes (with the exception of Yquem) makes it one of the least profitable wines to the grower; to the drinker it is one of the great wine bargains.

Sauternes was the only area outside the Médoc to be classed in 1855. Château d'Yquem was made a First Great Growth – a rank created for it alone in all Bordeaux. Eleven châteaux were made first-growths and 12 more were made seconds. But the old ranks are out of date today. Dedication is what counts.

Five communes, including Sauternes itself, are entitled to use the name. Barsac, the biggest of them, has the alternative of calling its wine either Sauternes or Barsac, although its wine tends less to lusciousness, more to cleanness and finesse.

Sauternes labels match the glittering gold of the wine. A few châteaux make a strong dry wine as well as the famous sweet one, particularly in poor vintages.

Top: golden glasses of 12 vintages of Château Rieussec. Albert Vuillier, proprietor when this picture was taken, now manages the estate for the Rothschilds of Château Lafite.
Above: Château de Malle in its Italianate 17th-century gardens is the architectural masterpiece of the Sauternes country.

Styles of wine vary almost as much as standards. Château Suduiraut in Preignac (when on form) is lush and sumptuous; Château Rieussec (recently bought by the Rothschilds of Lafite) fine-drawn and elegant; Château Guiraud (newly restored) potentially a near-rival to Yquem. Haut-Peyraguey, Lafaurie-Peyraguey, Filhot, Gilette, the Château de Fargues and Château Raymond-Lafon are the present names to conjure with in Sauternes. In Barsac, Coutet, Climens, Nairac and all three châteaux with the prefix Doisy- lead the field.

The economics of Sauternes are always knife-edge. For decades it could not be produced profitably at all: poor vintages persisted; demand dwindled. Vineyards were pulled up, or planted with red grapes, or used to make dry white wine.

Happily today there is a revival. The late seventies saw a run of good vintages, new idealistic owners have appeared, and Sauternes is back in fashion. In France it is highly appreciated drunk with foie gras. The Anglo-Saxon world, with Germany and Scandinavia, drinks it as the perfect ending to a rich meal.

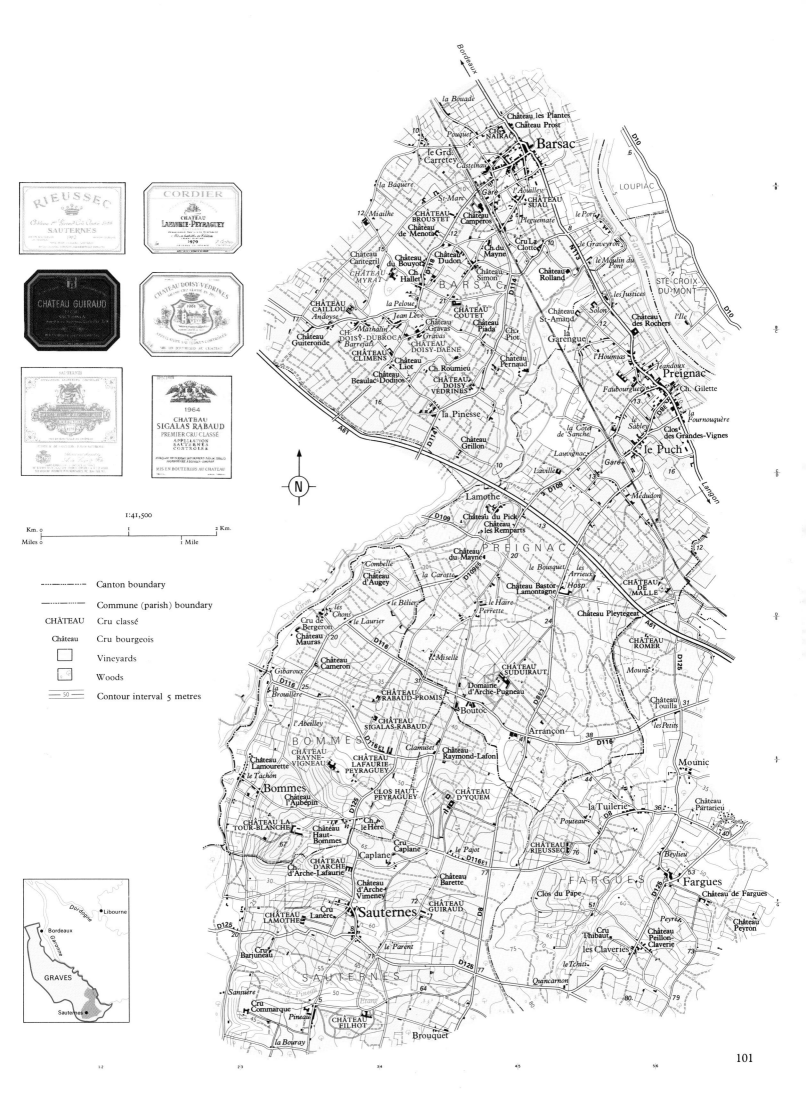

Pomerol

Above: crimson must from Merlot grapes – the variety which gives Pomerol its softness, fruitiness and strength.

The grapes are carried from the pickers to the *cuvier* in wooden tubs; each full tub makes a load for two men.

Left: Vieux Château Certan is one of Pomerol's best vineyards and also one of the few Pomerol châteaux that looks more imposing than the modest houses typical of the region. It makes on average about 75,000 bottles of wine a year, fetching a price similar to a very good classed growth of the Médoc.

It is surprising there should be a new star in such an ancient wine country as Bordeaux. You would think it had all been known for centuries. Yet although Romans had vineyards in Pomerol, a hundred years ago it was known only for 'good common wine'. Even 40 years ago it was not considered in the top flight. Yet today its best château fetches a higher price than the first-growths of the Médoc, and an astonishing number of properties, for such a small area, are generally agreed to be among the best in the whole of Bordeaux.

Pomerol is such a curious corner of the world that it is hard to get your bearings. It is a good 25 miles (40 kilometres) east of Bordeaux along the Dordogne, almost in the suburbs of the sleepy old port of Libourne.

There is no real village centre in Pomerol; every family there makes wine, and every house stands apart among its vines. The landscape is evenly dotted with modest houses – each rejoicing in the name of château. The church stands oddly isolated too, like yet another little wine estate. And that is Pomerol; there is nothing more to see.

Pomerol is another big gravel bank, or rather plateau, slightly rising and falling but remarkably flat overall. In the western part the soil tends to be sandy; to the east, where it meets St-Emilion, to be enriched with clay. It is entirely planted with vines, to the exclusion of all lesser plants. In the eastern part lie the best growths, so cheek by jowl with St-Emilion and under such similar conditions that it would be surprising to find any constant difference between them.

Nonetheless the consensus is that Pomerols are the gentlest, richest, most instantly appealing clarets. They have deep colour without the acidity and tannin that often goes with it, a comforting, ripe, almost creamy smell, and

sometimes great concentration of all their qualities: the striking essence of a great wine.

Pomerol is a democracy. It has no official classification, and indeed it would be very hard to devise one. There is no long tradition of steady selling to build on. Châteaux are small family affairs and subject to change as individuals come and go. Furthermore, a great number rank together as – to keep everyone happy – 'first-growths'.

The most potent influence in the district is the '*négoce*', the merchant-houses, of Libourne, led with authority and style by the family firm of Jean-Pierre Moueix. They either own or manage a high proportion of the finest properties. Meanwhile, a strong tradition of direct supply to customers in France flourishes. Many orders that go off by train are the odd case to some doctor or lawyer in Amiens or Clermont-Ferrand.

There is a good deal of agreement, however, about which are the outstanding vineyards of Pomerol. Pétrus is allowed by all to come first. Vieux Château Certan, next door, is perhaps runner-up. Then in a bunch come La Fleur-Pétrus, La Conseillante, Lafleur, L'Evangile, Trotanoy, Petit Village, Certan de May. It would be wrong to distinguish one group from another too clearly. Latour à Pomerol, L'Eglise-Clinet, Le Gay, Clos l'Eglise (how confusing the names are), La Croix de·Gay, Clos René, La Grave Trigant de Boisset, L'Enclos, each has extremely high standards. Châteaux Nenin and Gazin, although well known, and big in Pomerol terms (making about 10,000 cases a year each) are less exciting at present. But Châteaux de Sales, Rouget, Vraye Croix de Gay (hints of jealousy!), Lafleur-Gazin, La Pointe, Feytit-Clinet and Moulinet all make typical and desirable wines. On the map we distinguish the growths whose

wines usually fetch the highest prices today.

Before being overwhelmed by the complications of Pomerol (and St-Emilion, where the situation is similar), it is worth knowing that the average standard is very high here. The village has a name for reliability.

Another advantage that has certainly helped the popularity of this little region is the fact that its wines are ready remarkably soon for Bordeaux. The chief grape variety here is not the tough-skinned Cabernet Sauvignon, whose wine has to live through a tannic youth to give its ultimate finesse: in Pomerol and St-Emilion the Merlot, secondary in the Médoc, is the leading vine. Great growths have about 70 or 80% Merlot, with perhaps 20% of the local Cabernet cousin, the Bouchet. Merlot wine is softer than Cabernet, and ripens earlier. Helped by rather richer soil than in the Médoc and warmer ripening conditions, it gives the warmth and gentleness which characterize Pomerol. Even the best Pomerol has produced all its perfume and as much finesse as it will ever achieve in 12 or 15 years, and most are already attractive at five.

Canton boundary
Commune (parish) boundary
CHÂTEAU Leading châteaux
Château Other good châteaux
Vineyards
Woods
Contour interval 5 metres

LALANDE-DE-LIBOURNE

NÉAC

COMMUNE DE POMEROL

ST-EMILION

Libourne

Bel-Air
Château de Salès
le Petit Moulinet
Château Moulinet
Domaine de la Combe
Clos de la Combe
Château Patache
Marchesseau
le Moulin de Lavaud
le Grand Garrouil
la Patache
Château la Grave Trigant de Boisset
Château Rouget
le Moulin de Cazelis
Vieux Château Cloquet
Château Grand-Moulinet
Château Rêve d'Or
Château l'Enclos
le Grand Moulinet
Pont de Cloquet
CHÂTEAU LATOUR À POMEROL
CLOS L'ÉGLISE
Château Clinet
CHÂTEAU LE GAY
Pignon
CHÂTEAU la Croix-de-Gay
Domaine de l'Eglise
René
Ch. Clos-René
Château Bellevue
Château Bel-Air
Château Feytit-Clinet
Ch. Chêne Liège
CH. L'ÉGLISE-CLINET
Château la Cabanne
Ch. de la Nouvelle-Eglise
Château Vray-Croix-de-Gay
CHÂTEAU LAFLEUR
CHÂTEAU LAFLEUR-GAZIN
la Chichonne
Château Mazeyres
les Barrières
les Ormeaux
Château de Bourgueneuf
Château la Croix
Château de Grange-Neuve
Château Lagrange
CHÂTEAU PÉTRUS
CHÂTEAU LA FLEUR PÉTRUS
CHÂTEAU GAZIN
Château Cantereau
Tropchaud
Château Saint Pierre de-Pomerol
Certan Giraud
Château Franc-Maillet
Béquille
Château Bourgneuf-Vayron
CHÂTEAU TROTANOY
Château Gombaude-Guillot
CHÂTEAU LA-PROVIDENCE
Château Haut Maillet
Château Clos Mazeyres
Château la Violette
Château Certan-de-May
CHÂTEAU CLOS DU CLOCHER
VIEUX CHÂTEAU CERTAN
CHÂTEAU L'ÉVANGILE
Beauséjour
Bonalgue
Château Marzy
Château la Pointe
Château Grate-Cap
CHÂTEAU CROQUE MICHOTTE
la Gravette
CHÂTEAU NENIN
Catusseau
Ch. la Croix St Georges
CHÂTEAU PETIT VILLAGE
CHÂTEAU LA CONSEILLANTE
Château le Caillou
Château la Croix
Château Beauregard
CHÂTEAU LAFLEUR DU ROY
Château la Dominique
Château Plince
la Brandaude
Château la Croix-du-Casse
Château Ferrand
les Grands Sillons
Toulifaut
Château la Tour du Pin Figeac
CHÂTEAU CHEVAL BLANC
Château Tour Figeac
la Bordette
la Lambette
Château la Commanderie
Ch. la Croix Taillefer
Roiallednat
la Grange Neuve
Château Taillefer
Château du Tailhas

1:25,000
Km. 0   1 Km.
Miles 0   ½ Mile

Pomerol has no official
classification. These are
among the best growths,
but many of the other
'châteaux' make very
attractive reliable wine.

St-Emilion

The old town of St-Emilion is propped in the corner of an escarpment above the Dordogne. Behind it on the plateau vines flow steadily on into Pomerol. Beside it along the ridge they swoop down into the plain. It is the little rural gem of the Bordelais – inland and upland in spirit, Roman in origin, hollow with cellars and heady with wine.

Even the church at St-Emilion is a cellar: cut, like them all, out of solid limestone. The excellent restaurant in the town square is actually on the church roof, and you sit beside the belfry to eat your lampreys stewed in red wine à la Bordelaise.

St-Emilion makes rich red wine. Before many people can really come to terms with the dryness and delicacy of Médoc wine they love the solid tastiness of St-Emilion. The best of them in ripe and sunny seasons grow almost sweet as they mature.

The grapes of St-Emilion are the Merlot and the Cabernet Franc. On the whole their wines here take less long to reach perfection than Médoc wines, if a little longer than Pomerols: say four years for the wine of a poor vintage; eight and upwards for a good one. Yet they can live as long.

There are two distinct districts of St-Emilion, not counting the lesser vineyards of the river plain and the parishes to the east and northeast which are allowed to use the name (described and mapped on pages 106–107).

One group of the inner châteaux lies on the border of Pomerol, on the sandy and gravelly plateau. The most famous of this plateau, and the whole of St-Emilion, is Château Cheval Blanc, a trim cream-painted house in a grove of trees which is far from suggesting the splendid red wine, some of the world's most full-blooded, which its vines produce.

Of Cheval Blanc's neighbours, Château Figeac comes nearest to its level, but in a different style, from even more gravelly soil and with a proportion of Cabernet Sauvignon.

Châteaux La Tour Figeac, Corbin Michotte and La Dominique are also outstanding.

The other, larger group, the Côtes St-Emilion, occupies the escarpment around the town. At the abrupt edge of the plateau you can see that not very thick soil covers the soft but solid limestone in which the cellars are cut. At Château Ausone, the most famous château of the Côtes, you can walk into a cellar with vines, as it were, on the ground floor above you.

The Côtes wines may not be quite so fruity

Above: the Jurade de St-Emilion, the district's ancient association of winegrowers, processes in scarlet robes through the streets of the town.
Below: Château Ausone commands a view of the Côtes to the east and of the valley of the Dordogne.

as the 'Graves' wines from the plateau (the name Graves is confusingly applied to them because of their gravelly soil), but at their best they are some of the most perfumed and 'generous' wines of Bordeaux. They usually have 1% more alcohol than wine from the Médoc. Alkaline (i.e. chalky) soil aids ripening, hence strength; here it has the help of a full south-facing slope and in many places shelter from the west wind as well.

One other advantage the Côtes châteaux have over the Graves is their relative immunity to frost. Around Château Cheval Blanc a slight dip in the ground acts as a sump in which freezing air can collect on cloudless winter nights. On one dreadful night in February 1956 the temperature went down to −24°C. So many vines were killed that it took five or six years for production to pick up again.

Château Ausone is to the Côte what Cheval Blanc is to the Graves. Château Belair, in the same hands, is only a short step down. Châteaux Canon, Magdelaine, La Gaffelière, Pavie and Clos Fourtet would certainly be on a short shortlist of the top Côtes wines: but the comfort of St-Emilion to the ordinary wine lover is the number of other châteaux of moderate fame and extremely high standards providing utterly enjoyable but relatively accessible wine.

St-Emilion is not classified as the Médoc is. It merely divided its châteaux (in 1954) into Premiers Grands Crus, Grands Crus Classés and plain Grands Crus. There were 12 of the first, headed by Cheval Blanc and Ausone in a separate category of two, and 72 of the second. The plain Grands Crus run into hundreds. Since 1984 all châteaux have had to meet certain objective criteria, including tasting by jury, to claim 'Classé' status. In practice the list has changed little.

On the map the Grands Crus which normally fetch the highest prices are indicated in bigger type than the others.

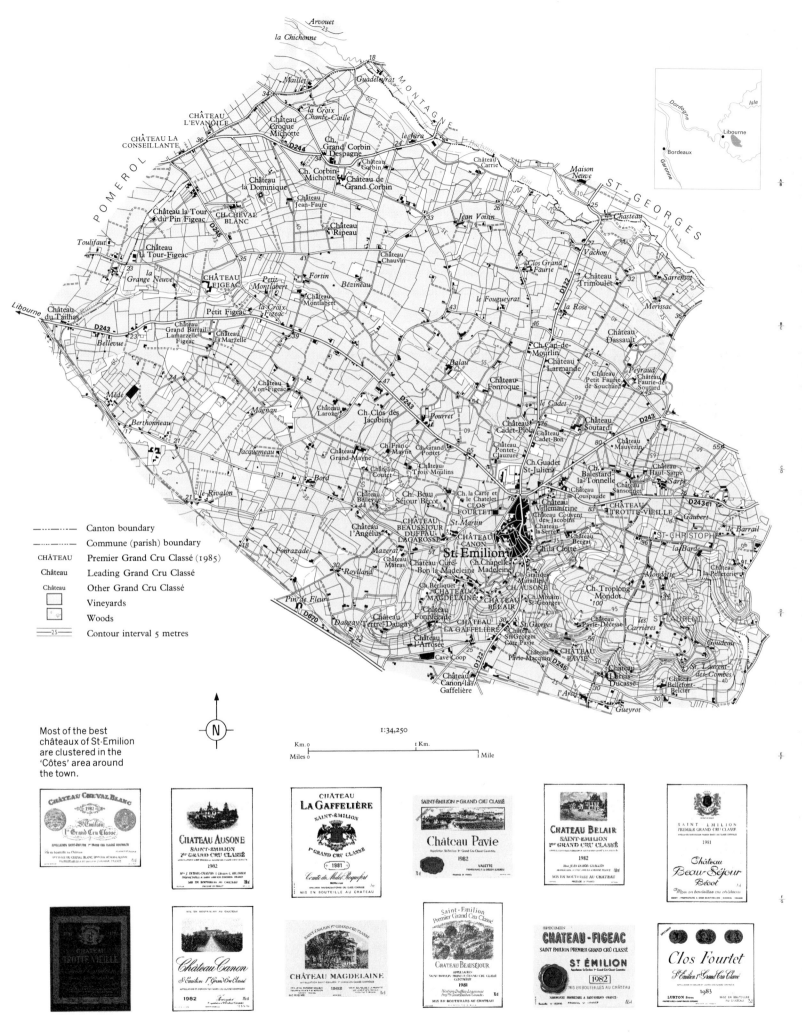

Most of the best
châteaux of St-Emilion
are clustered in the
'Côtes' area around
the town.

Canton boundary
Commune (parish) boundary
CHÂTEAU   Premier Grand Cru Classé (1985)
Château   Leading Grand Cru Classé
Château   Other Grand Cru Classé
          Vineyards
          Woods
—25—   Contour interval 5 metres

1:34,250

Km. 0   1 Km.
Miles 0   1 Mile

The Surroundings of St-Emilion and Pomerol

Château St-Georges
dominates the plateau of
St-Emilion from its hilltop
in the neighbouring
village of St-Georges. It
was built in 1774 by
Victor Louis, the
architect who designed
Bordeaux's theatre, the
finest in France.

Below: the reputation of
Fronsac steadily grows.
Its wines have the classic
attributes: deep colour,
attractive fruitiness and
long life.

The illustrious parishes of Pomerol and St-Emilion are the heart of a much larger and more diffuse wine district. St-Emilion's name is shared by seven small villages south and east, and a further five to the northeast can add the name of St-Emilion to their own. Pomerol adjoins the communes of Fronsac, Néac and Lalande.

With their mixture of vines and woods and pastures and their little hills and valleys, the villages east and north and west are more attractive than the monotonous vineyard of the plateau in the centre.

Even today they are still a little-known wine country. It is hard even to identify the modest châteaux. One wonders how their wine is distributed in a world which likes the re-assurance of a famous name. Yet a network of private contacts all over France is well satisfied with their sound and solid red wine, besides what reaches 'le grand négoce' one way or another.

The châteaux shown on this map are most of the bigger and better known of the hinterland. Fronsac, for example, has many small proper-ties; those on the map have more than local reputations. Fronsac has long been reputed the coming thing in Bordeaux. Its wines are splendidly fruity and full of character, yet such is competition among the smaller fry in the huge region that they are also still (quite) cheap. The wines of Canon-Fronsac, nearer the Dordogne, fetch a premium.

North of Pomerol, Néac shares the appella-tion of Lalande-de-Pomerol: both are like Pomerol, unpolished. Châteaux Tournefeuille and Siaurac provide polish, too.

The equivalent back-country châteaux north of St-Emilion are probably slightly less known, with the exception of the splendid St-Georges, which overlooks the whole district from its hill, and makes excellent wine.

The vine is still dominant in this pretty, hilly landscape, even if there are no names to conjure with among the châteaux. Montagne makes excellent 'satellite' St-Emilion. So do Lussac and Puisseguin, often making up in satisfying solidity what they lack in finesse. Still farther east the Côtes de Castillon and Francs keep up the family resemblance.

The cluster of villages east of St-Emilion, however, are a different matter. In St-Laurent, Château Larcis Ducasse is a Grand Cru and rated among the top 25 or so wines of St-Emilion. In the same commune Château Bellefont-Belcier is also well known. To the north in St-Christophe, Château Haut-Sarpe is another Grand Cru, and Château Fom-brauge has a high reputation. On the outcrop of the Côtes at St-Hippolyte, Châteaux de Ferrand and Capet-Guillier make good wine and just to the east in St-Etienne Château Puy-Blanquet has a distinguished name. These châteaux and several others command prices comparable to St-Emilion Grands Crus from the central area mapped on the previous page.

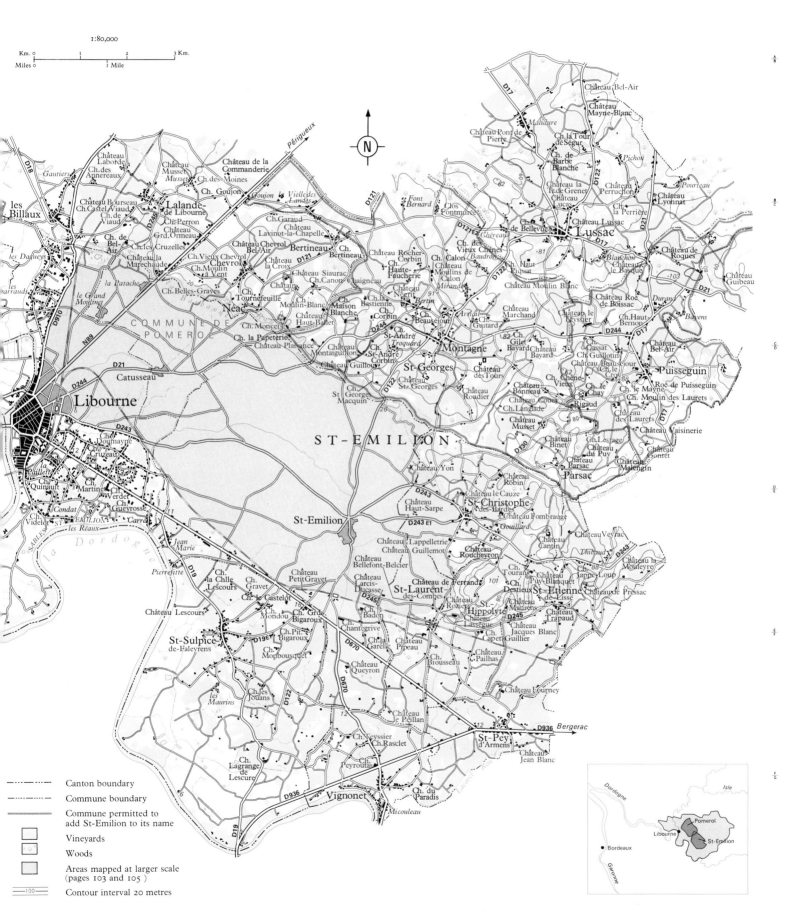

Bourg and Blaye

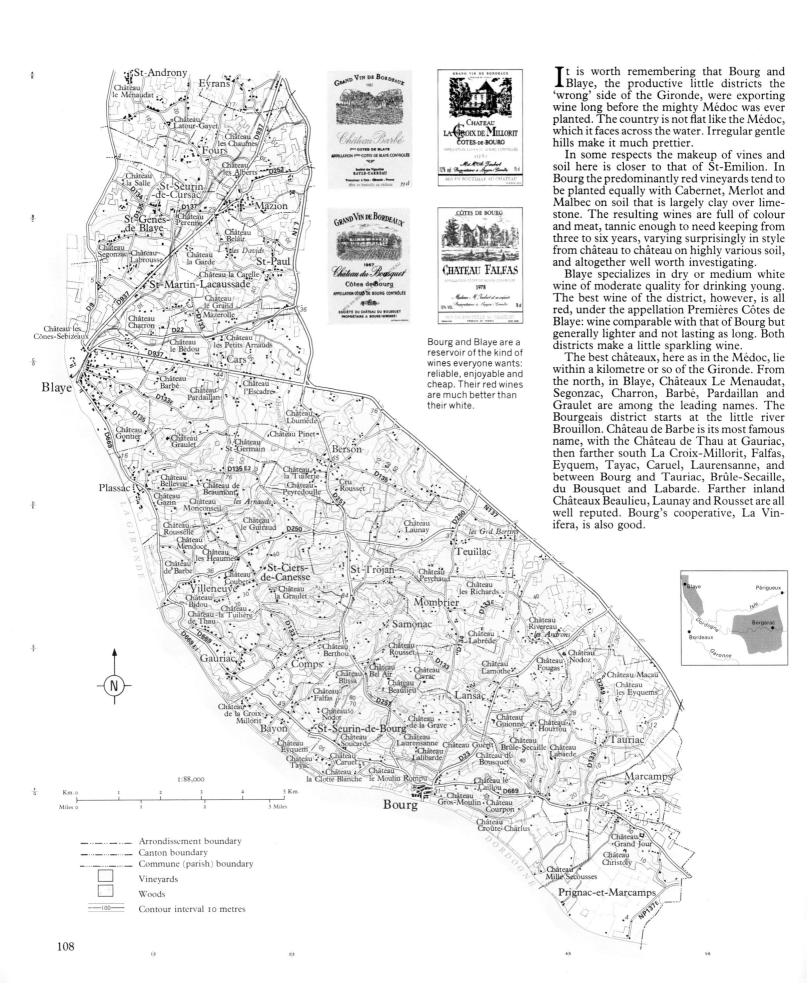

It is worth remembering that Bourg and Blaye, the productive little districts the 'wrong' side of the Gironde, were exporting wine long before the mighty Médoc was ever planted. The country is not flat like the Médoc, which it faces across the water. Irregular gentle hills make it much prettier.

In some respects the makeup of vines and soil here is closer to that of St-Emilion. In Bourg the predominantly red vineyards tend to be planted equally with Cabernet, Merlot and Malbec on soil that is largely clay over limestone. The resulting wines are full of colour and meat, tannic enough to need keeping from three to six years, varying surprisingly in style from château to château on highly various soil, and altogether well worth investigating.

Blaye specializes in dry or medium white wine of moderate quality for drinking young. The best wine of the district, however, is all red, under the appellation Premières Côtes de Blaye: wine comparable with that of Bourg but generally lighter and not lasting as long. Both districts make a little sparkling wine.

The best châteaux, here as in the Médoc, lie within a kilometre or so of the Gironde. From the north, in Blaye, Châteaux Le Menaudat, Segonzac, Charron, Barbé, Pardaillan and Graulet are among the leading names. The Bourgeais district starts at the little river Brouillon. Château de Barbe is its most famous name, with the Château de Thau at Gauriac, then farther south La Croix-Millorit, Falfas, Eyquem, Tayac, Caruel, Laurensanne, and between Bourg and Tauriac, Brûle-Secaille, du Bousquet and Labarde. Farther inland Châteaux Beaulieu, Launay and Rousset are all well reputed. Bourg's cooperative, La Vinifera, is also good.

Bourg and Blaye are a reservoir of the kind of wines everyone wants: reliable, enjoyable and cheap. Their red wines are much better than their white.

Bergerac

Bordeaux's beautiful hinterland, the Dordogne, leading back into the maze of succulent valleys cut in the stony upland of Périgord, makes simple country wine compared with Bordeaux. Yet Périgord's restaurants are famous, and their wine is the local wine. The driest (now often a Sauvignon Blanc) and the sweetest white wines of the area are good, and the red can be excellent lightweight claret. To the south, the Côtes de Duras makes similar wine.

Monbazillac is the best of the appellations within Bergerac. At one time it was a rival to Sauternes; old Château Monbazillac is supremely rich-textured, golden and intense. Now it is a cooperative and its wine, although good, is no longer made in the same laborious way. Pécharmant has the best red wine; Rosette and the Montravels better-than-average white.

Château Monbazillac, once a rival to the great Sauternes, is the star of Bergerac. The dry whites and everyday reds of Bergerac are first-rate 'country' wines. The Côtes de Duras, Bergerac's southern neighbour, makes similar red and white wines.

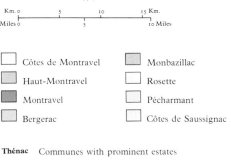

Above: the magnificent Château de Monbazillac dominates the Dordogne valley above Bergerac. Its liquorous golden wine (now made by the local cooperative) is the Sauternes of the region.

Left: the old fortress of Beynac broods over the timeless ritual of the vintage.

1:440,000

Km. 0   5   10   15 Km.

Miles 0   5   10 Miles

- Côtes de Montravel
- Haut-Montravel
- Montravel
- Bergerac
- Monbazillac
- Rosette
- Pécharmant
- Côtes de Saussignac

Thénac   Communes with prominent estates

—·—·—   Département boundary

For location map see opposite page

The Champagne Country

The crystal scintillation of a frosty morning at Cramant on the Côte des Blancs seems the image of the character of its wines. Cramant grows exclusively Chardonnay grapes to make champagne of the ultimate brilliance and finesse.

The name of champagne is limited not only to a defined area, like the appellations of Bordeaux, but to a process, through which every drop of wine must go before it can claim the name. A few countries outside Europe, indeed, use the name as though it only meant the process. But it is the special qualities of this northernmost of France's great wine regions that make champagne unique.

It would be claiming too much to say that all champagne is better than any other sparkling wine in the world. There are champagnes and champagnes. But good champagne has a combination of freshness, delicacy, richness and raciness, and a gently stimulating power, which no other wine has ever quite attained.

The region whose soil and climate have so much to offer is only 90 miles (145 km) northeast of Paris. It centres around a small range of hills rising from a plain of chalk and carved in two by the wanderings of the River Marne. Within this area the names of the villages do not directly concern the consumer as they do in, for example, Burgundy. For the essence of champagne is that it is a blended wine, known by the name of the maker, not the vineyard.

There are 66,640 acres (27,000 hectares) in Champagne, with 18,500 proprietors. Only 13% belongs to the famous firms who make and sell two-thirds of the wine. The country is owned not by great landowners but by thousands of local, often part-time, growers. There are 8,000 holdings of only an acre or less, and more than half of the 20,000 men who work in the vineyards own at least some vines.

What the map shows is the heart of the region, where the grapes which the best houses buy for their best champagne are grown. Outlying districts (the small map) are still legally Champagne; their wines are usually blended with those of the central zone. There are three distinct parts of the region shown here; some of the character of the wine of each is essential to the classic champagne blend.

The Montagne de Reims is planted with Pinot Noir vines, whose black grapes have to be pressed very rapidly to give white wine without a trace of colour. No one has quite explained how in this most northern vineyard a north slope, which some of the best of the Montagne is, can give good wine. The theory is that the air heats up on the plain below, and flows encouragingly up through the vines . . . Montagne wines contribute to the bouquet, the headiness and what the French call the 'carpentry' – the backbone of the blend.

The Vallée de la Marne, the next area, has south and southeast slopes which trap the sun and make these the fullest, roundest and ripest wines, with plenty of bouquet. These are largely black-grape vineyards as well; here the Pinot Meunier joins the Pinot Noir. Bouzy makes the small quantity of still red wine which the Champenois jealously keep for themselves. It can be like rather faint but exquisite burgundy.

The east-facing slope south of Epernay is the Côte des Blancs, planted with the white Chardonnay that gives freshness and finesse to the blend. Wine from here is frequently sold as Blanc de Blancs, without the traditional proportion of black-grape wine. It is a question of taste, but most experienced champagne lovers find Côte des Blancs wine on its own lacks the perfect balance – is too light. Nonetheless Cramant, Avize and Le Mesnil are three villages with long-respected names for their (unblended) wine; Cramant, confusingly, for its *crémant*, or half-sparkling, champagne.

Today, as much as a third of the crop is processed and sold by the growers themselves. Their market is mainly France. For the two-thirds that the famous 'Maisons' buy for their brands there is an unusual pricing system which expresses the quality of the different areas. At the start of the harvest, one price (per kilo of grapes) is decided on by a committee of growers and merchants. Growers in the best communes, or Grands Crus, are paid 100%, the full price. Premiers Crus receive between 90 and 99%, and so on down to 80% for some of the outlying areas.

On the maps the leading communes are shown in larger type. Most of the wine in all first-class brands comes from these villages.

Reims

Tinqueux

Treslon
Trainery
94
Bouleuse
Sarcy
Coulommes
la Montagne
St. Euphraise
et Clairizet
Aubilly
Bligny
Bouilly
Ville-Dommange
Sacy
Écueil
Chambrecy
135
Chaumuzy
244
267
Marfaux
Chamery
D26
Champlat et
Boujacourt
Bois de
Reims
Pourcy
268
VILLERS
ALLERAND
265
Jonquery
247
Courtagnon
182
Bois de la
Cohette
Bois de Courton
Cuchery
Belval
sous Châtillon
Nanteuil
la Fosse
Bois de
St. Quentin
263
Le Bois de Sermiers
Bois de
Nanteuil
Bois de Fleury
Cormoyeux
St. Imoges
Bois de Notre Dame
Bois de la
Rodemat
Bois du Roi
Fleury
la Rivière
Romery
Villers-
sous-Châtillon
FORÊT DE LA MONTAGNE DE REIMS
Reuil
154
HAUTVILLERS
Bois de
St. Marc
CHAMPILLON
Ventenil
CUMIÈRES
67
Damery
69
DIZY-
MAGENTA
MUTIGNY
Boursault
Mardeuil
N3
AY
Vauciennes
Épernay
CHOUILLY
PIERRY
242
106
Forêt D'Epernay
178
240
D11
Moussy
Vinay
88
Chavot
CUIS
Monthelon
Mancy
Butte
de Saran
CRAMANT
Morangis
AVIZÉ
Mostins
GRAUVES
B. d'Avize
OGER
Forêt d'Oger
239
Forêt du Mesnil
LE MESNIL-
SUR-OGER
229
245
Gionges
232
VERTUS
203
Bois de
Cormont
226

Janvry
Gueux
Ormes
Vrigny
Méry-
Prémecy
Pargny-
les-Reims
Jouy-
les-Reims
les Mesneux
Villers-
aux-Noeuds
Bezannes
Trois
Puits
Champfleury
Cité
Charbonneaux
Cormontreuil
Taissy
Mont de
la Cuche
SILLERY
PUISIEULX
MONTBRÉ
Mont Trouilly
RILLY-LA-
MONTAGNE
127
CHIGNY-
LES-ROSES
151
LUDES
276
BEAUMONT-
SUR-VESLE
Chemin de la Barbarie
128
D26
VERZENAY
MAILLY
VERZY
283
les Battis
D9
VILLERS-
MARMERY
279
FORÊT DE LA MONTAGNE DE REIMS
260
Ville-
en-Selve
208
Germaine
271
Mont Tournant
TRÉPAIL
Bois du Mont
St. Hubin
260
257
Bois des Dames
LOUVOIS
Bois du
Gouffre
TAUXIÈRES-
MUTRY
Fontaine
sur Ay
BOUZY
Mont Hurlet
234
Mt.
Ecueve
AMBONNAY
99
AVENAY
VAL D'OR
Mt
des Plantes
MAREUIL-SUR-AY
97
138
Mont Charlier
BISSEUIL
TOURS-
SUR-
MARNE
Condé-
sur-
Marne

Km. 0   1   2   3   4   5   6 Km.
Miles 0   1   2   3   4 Miles
1:157,000

Legend
- – ⋅ ⋅ – Département boundary
- – ⋅ – Arrondissement boundary
- – ⋅ ⋅ – Canton boundary
- **MAILLY** Commune (parish) with an average vineyard rating of 99% or more
- MONTBRÉ Commune (parish) with an average vineyard rating of 90-98%
- ☐ Vineyards
- ☐ Woods
- —200— Contour interval 20 metres

Soissons
Reims
Château-
Thierry
Épernay
Châlons-
sur-Marne
Paris
Marne
CHAMPAGNE
Troyes
Aube
Bar-sur-
Aube
Seine
Bar-sur-
Seine

The Champagne Towns

What happens in the towns of Champagne concerns us just as much as what happens in the country. The process of champagne making has only just begun when the grapes are picked and pressed. Without delay the opaque must is taken to the shipper's *'maison'* in Reims or Epernay or Ay. There it will spend at least the next two years.

It ferments busily at first, but as it slows down the doors are thrown open to let in the wintry air. In the cold (today, of course, controlled by air conditioning) the fermentation stops. The wine spends a chilly winter, still with the potential of more fermentation latent in it.

So it used to be shipped. England in the 17th century was an eager customer for barrels of this delicate, rather sharp wine. According to Patrick Forbes, the historian of champagne, the English bottled it on arrival; and found that they had created a sparkling wine.

Whether or not it was the English who did it first, early bottling is the vital stage in the historical process which changed the *vin du pays* of northern France into the prima donna of the world.

For the wine continued to ferment in the bottle and the gas given off by the fermentation dissolved in the wine. If the natural effect was given a little encouragement – a little more sugar, a little more yeast – what had been a slight, though very attractive, wine was found to improve immeasurably, gaining strength and character over a period of two years or more. Above all, the inexhaustible bubbles gave it a miraculous liveliness.

Dom Pérignon, cellarmaster of the Abbey of Hautvillers at the end of the 17th century, is credited (probably fancifully) with the next round of developments: the cork tied down with string, the stronger bottles (although still not strong enough; he lost half his wine through bottles bursting). Certainly he developed the art of blending wines from different parts of the district to achieve the best possible flavour.

The chief difference between the brands of champagne lies in this making of the *cuvée*, as the blending is called. All depends on the skill of the director tasting the raw young wines and peering into their future – and on how much his firm is prepared to spend on its raw materials, for the more top-quality wine that goes into the *cuvée* the better it will be. Each firm has a tradition of the kind of wine it makes; no difference should be noticeable in its nonvintage wine from year to year. One might instance Krug, Bollinger, Roederer, Clicquot, Pol Roger and Perrier Jouët as typical of the old style, making full-flavoured, mature-tasting champagne.

Another fashion today, started by Moët & Chandon with their 'Dom Pérignon', is to make a super-luxury wine, relegating (in theory) even the best vintages to second place. Dom Ruinart, Heidsieck Diamant Bleu, Roederer Cristal, Taittinger's Comtes de Champagne and Pol Roger's Sir Winston Churchill are all in this bracket.

The widow Clicquot made her contribution to champagne in the early years of the 19th century. She devised a method of removing the sediment which resulted from bottle fermentation without removing the bubbles at the same time. Briefly, what she invented was a desk of wood in which the mature bottles of wine could be stuck in holes upside down (*sur point*). Her cellarmen gave each bottle a gentle shake and twist (*remuage*) every day until all the sediment had dislodged from the glass and settled on the cork. Then they took out the cork with the bottle still upside down, let the eggcupful of wine containing the sediment escape (*dégorgement*), topped up the bottle with wine from another of the same and put in a new cork. To make disgorging easier today, the neck of the bottle containing the sediment is frozen first: a plug of murky ice shoots out when the bottle is opened, leaving perfectly clear wine behind.

The process which thousands of visitors go to Reims and Epernay to see remains essentially the same as ever. Not the least spectacular thing is the immense cellars where it is done. Some of them are Roman chalk pits under the city. One firm uses trains in its tunnels.

Every trace of sugar in champagne is used up when it is refermented in its bottle: it becomes totally dry – too dry for most tastes. A little wine-and-sugar is therefore added at *dégorgement*: less than 2% for wine labelled Brut; 1.5–2.5% for Extra Dry; 2–4% for Sec; 4–6% for Demi-Sec; more than 6% for Doux. The last two are properly dessert wines.

The full flavour of champagne is lost if it is served too cold. Ideally it should be thoroughly cool but not at all icy. Most important of all it should be mature. Very young champagne makes enemies. Time finds in it inimitable glorious flavours.

Left: the champagne caves of Reims were cut by the Romans as quarries. The Clicquot cellars have since been decorated with reliefs carved in the soft chalk walls, and filled with wine.
Top: central phase in the *méthode champenoise*. The redundant yeast is coaxed by a gentle daily shake and twist (*remuage*) to rest on the cork.
Above: the final act. The bottle is *dégorgé*, its gas blowing the congealed yeast out to leave behind brilliant clean champagne.

THE LANGUAGE OF THE LABEL

Vintage (e.g. 1976, 1979) The wine of one outstanding year
Non-vintage (without a date) A blend of the wines of several years
Cuvée Blend: all champagne is blended
Blanc de Blancs Made from the juice of white grapes only
Crémant Half-sparkling, or 'creaming'
Rosé Pink champagne made by blending in a little red wine
Réserve Any wine can be called Réserve
Reserved for England Implies that the wine is dry, since the English like dry champagne
Récemment dégorgé Recently disgorged (of wine laid down to mature upside down and disgorged when considered ready to drink)
Brut Bone-dry
Extra Sec (or **Extra Dry**) Dry
Sec Slightly sweet
Demi-Sec Sweet
Doux Very sweet
Magnum 2 bottles in one
Jeroboam 4 bottles in one
Rehoboam 6 bottles in one
Methuselah 8 bottles in one
Nebuchadnezzar 20 bottles in one

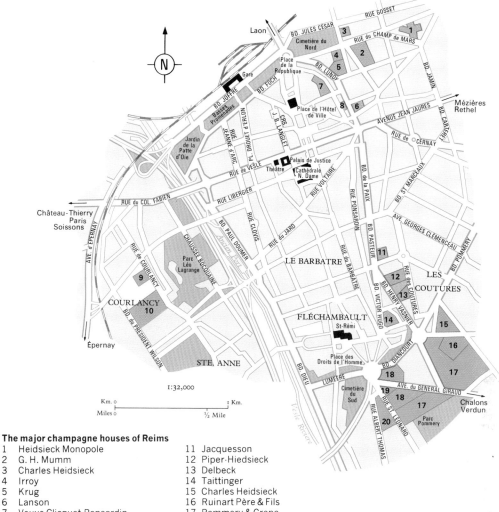

The major champagne houses of Reims

1	Heidsieck Monopole	11	Jacquesson
2	G. H. Mumm	12	Piper-Hiedsieck
3	Charles Heidsieck	13	Delbeck
4	Irroy	14	Taittinger
5	Krug	15	Charles Heidsieck
6	Lanson	16	Ruinart Père & Fils
7	Veuve Clicquot-Ponsardin	17	Pommery & Greno
8	Louis Roederer	18	Henriot
9	Massé	19	Abel Lepître
10	Lanson	20	Veuve Clicquot-Ponsardin

1:32,000

The major champagne houses of Epernay

1 Marne & Champagne
2 Moët & Chandon
3 Perrier-Jouët
4 de Venoge
5 Pol Roger
6 de Castellane
7 Mercier
8 Trouillard

1:18,500

Some of the most famous names of Champagne. The bottom left label is for a still white wine of the area, appellation Vin de Coteaux Champenois (not champagne). Bouzy is the rare still red.

Alsace

In Colmar, Alsace has one of the most complete and romantic medieval market towns of France. Among its treasures is the great masterpiece of Gothic art, Grünwald's altarpiece of the Crucifixion.

The wine of Alsace reflects the ambivalent situation of a border province. A traveller at the time of the French Revolution found it incredible that this land, so clearly intended by nature to be part of Germany, was actually annexed to France.

Today the Alsatians, although they still speak a sort of German, feel very differently. What has not changed is the physical barrier between them and the rest of France; for it is the Vosges, not the Rhine, which makes the great change in landscape, architecture, climate – and not least in wine.

Alsace makes Germanic wine in the French way. The tone is set by the climate, the soil and the choice of grape varieties: all comparable with the vineyards of slightly farther north, slightly farther down the Rhine valley, which are in Germany. What differs is the interpretation put on these things – because today German and Alsatian winegrowers hold opposite points of view of what they want their wine to do and be. In a nutshell, the Germans look for sweetness, the Alsatians for

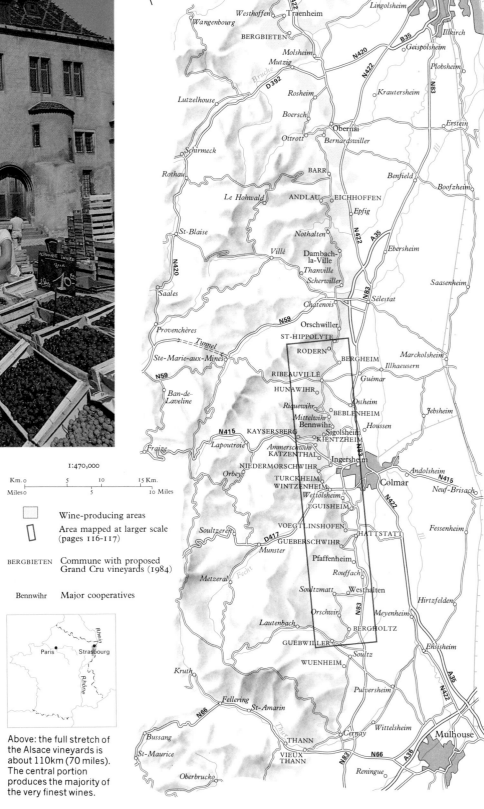

1:470,000

Km. 0   5   10   15 Km.
Miles 0   5   10 Miles

☐   Wine-producing areas

▯   Area mapped at larger scale (pages 116-117)

BERGBIETEN   Commune with proposed Grand Cru vineyards (1984)

Bennwihr   Major cooperatives

Above: the full stretch of the Alsace vineyards is about 110km (70 miles). The central portion produces the majority of the very finest wines.

Right: Alsace labels frequently feature the grape variety in type as big as the producer's name.

strength. German wine at its best is not for the table but for the drawing-room or the garden. Alsace wine is the great adjunct to one of France's most splendid cuisines. Alsace gives the flowery-scented grapes of Germany the body and authority of such table wines as white burgundy – proper accompaniments to strong and savoury food.

Instead of grape sugar lingering delicately in the wine, the grower likes a dry, firm, clean flavour. He ferments every ounce of the sugar which the long dry summers of Alsace give him, concentrating the essences of his highly perfumed German-style grapes into a sometimes astonishingly spicy fragrance.

The grapes that give their names and special qualities to the wines of Alsace are the Riesling of the Rhine – responsible here and in Germany for the best wine – the Sylvaner, Muscat, Pinots Blanc and Gris, the lesser Chasselas and Knipperlé, and the unique and fragrant Gewürztraminer.

The Gewürztraminer is the perfect introduction to Alsace. You would not think that so fruity a scent could come from any wine so clean and dry. Gewürz means spice in German; the spice is there all the way down, and stays on your palate for two or three minutes after you have swallowed.

To the initiated a wine with so marked a character becomes dull after a while. It has its place with some of the richest of the very rich Alsatian dishes: goose or pork. But Alsatians consider the Riesling their true Grand Vin. It offers something much more elusive: a balance of hard and gentle, flowery and strong, which leads you on and never surfeits.

These two, and two more less generally known, the Pinot Gris (traditionally, but no longer, called Tokay d'Alsace) and the Muscat, are classed as the Noble Wines of Alsace. Only these can be used to make Grand Cru wines under the new regulations.

Recently there has been renewed interest in the Pinot Gris, which makes the fullest-bodied but least perfumed wine of the region; it has obvious uses at table as an alternative to a 'big', and therefore more expensive, white burgundy. The Muscat surprises everyone who knows the wine the grape makes anywhere else in the world, which is almost always sweet. Here it keeps all its characteristic grapey scent but makes a dry wine as clean as a whistle, a very good apéritif.

Much more important is the Pinot Blanc, although its name is seldom seen on labels. It plays a large part in the better 'Edelzwicker' blends, and is often the base for the excellent sparkling 'Crémant d'Alsace' made by the champagne method, and a worthy rival to the Crémant of Burgundy and the Loire.

In a class above the common wines of the region, but not quite reckoned noble, comes the Sylvaner, the maid-of-all-work of the German vineyards. Alsace Sylvaner is light and sometimes nicely tart. Without the tartness it can be a little dull and coarse in flavour. It is often the first wine at an Alsatian dinner, to build up to the main wine, the Riesling.

The lesser grapes, the Chasselas and the Knipperlé (there are others, too), are not usually identified on the bottle – or indeed very often bottled at all. They are the open wines of cafés and restaurants. Very young, particularly in the summer after a good vintage, they are so good that visitors should not miss them by insisting on bottled wine. The term Edelzwicker ('noble mixture') is often applied to blends of more than one grape variety.

What all these wines have in common is the Alsatian style of winemaking, which is almost fanatically concerned with naturalness. To hear an Alsatian grower talking about German wines you would think they were all made by white-coated chemists on a laboratory bench. 'Once you let a chemist in your house he will make himself indispensable by frightening you with all the diseases your wine might catch', they say. They scorn refinements of fining, or anything that involves additions to the wine of any kind – except, alas, sugar: Alsace is not immune from the passion for adding sugar whether the wine needs it or not. Traditionalists (still in the majority) keep it undisturbed in huge wooden casks, racking and filtering as little as possible. They even take precautions to fill the bottle as full as possible and to use a specially long cork – all to protect the wine from the air. They achieve a remarkable balance of strength and freshness, fruit and acidity by their pains.

Nonetheless, when a really fine autumn comes on the heels of a good summer, and they find grapes ripening beautifully with no threat of bad weather, not even an Alsatian, dedicated as he is to clean, dry table wines, can resist doing as the Germans do and getting the last drop of sugar out of his vines.

These late pickings used to be labelled with the German words Auslese and Beerenauslese. Today the phrase Vendange Tardive (late vintage) is used. For the equivalent of a Beerenauslese, in which individual grapes are culled for their super-ripeness – sometimes with a degree of 'noble rot' – the term is 'Sélection des Grains Nobles'. Such wines can reach heights of lusciousness not far removed from the rarest and most expensive of all German wines. A late-picked Gewürztraminer or Muscat has perhaps the most exotic smell of any wine in the world, and can at the same time keep a remarkable cleanness and finesse of flavour. It is not necessarily very sweet: 'intense' is a better word.

A little red wine is made from the Pinot Noir, but it rarely gets a much deeper colour than a rosé and never a very marked or distinguished flavour. Rouge d'Alsace, and sometimes *vin gris*, or very pale pink wine, will be found in *brasseries* (the word for a restaurant serving Alsatian food, traditionally to go with beer) in Paris and elsewhere.

Alsace itself has two of the best restaurants in France: Gaertner's Aux Armes de France at Ammerschwihr and Haeberlin's Auberge de l'Ill at Illhaeusern. Foie gras frais (whole goose liver, as opposed to pâté de foie gras) is one of the dishes worth travelling for. In general, Alsace cooking demonstrates what a French artist can do with German ideas. Sauerkraut becomes choucroute, and suddenly delicious. Dishes which look as though they are going to be heavy turn out to be rich but light. Quiches and onion tart are almost miraculously edible. In Alsace no one looks beyond the range of white wines of the country to accompany this profusion of dishes.

The Heart of Alsace

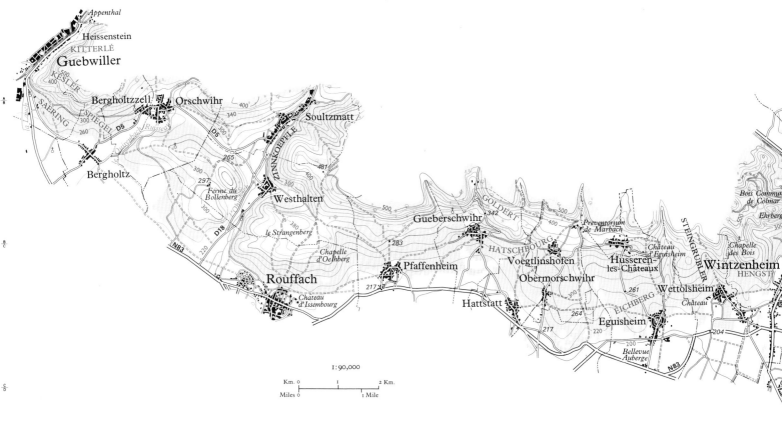

For location map see page 114

The map on these pages lays the heart of the Alsace vineyard on its side, making it directly comparable to the maps of the Côte d'Or of Burgundy. The north lies to the right. As in so many of the great wine regions of Europe, a range of east-facing foothills provides an ideal environment for the vine. Spurs and re-entrants offer extra shelter and a privileged sunwards tilt in places where the vines face southeast or south. Every nuance of the unfolding landscape is echoed in the alignment of the vine rows to catch every minute of sunlight.

And Alsace is sunny. The high Vosges to the west are the secret of these vineyards, which lie along their flank at an altitude of between 600 and 1,200 feet (180–360 metres), in a ribbon rarely more than one and a half kilometres wide.

The higher the mountains are, the drier the land they shelter from moist west winds. In the north where they are lower their influence is less marked; the wines of Bas-Rhin are often less richly ripe, although nonetheless fragrant and fine. ('Bas' has no connotation of being lower here – except in the sense of lower down the Rhine.) The map shows the central stretch of the Haut-Rhin vineyards, clustered north and south of the city of Colmar – where the mountains can keep the sky clear of clouds for weeks on end.

Alsace, like Champagne, is an exception to the usual French pattern of a complex structure of Appellations Contrôlées, pinning every wine down to the exact district of its birth. The trade is based on the activities of merchant houses, most of whom are also growers, but who can buy wine up and down the country for their branded blends. Instead of place names they market grape names. Alsace is the one part of France where you order 'a bottle of Riesling' or 'a bottle of Sylvaner', instead of specifying a vineyard, village or regional name.

—·—·—·—	Arrondissement boundary
—··—··—··—	Canton boundary
—···—···—···	Commune (parish) boundary
BRAND	Proposed Grand Cru vineyard (1984)
ZINNKOEPFLE	Other leading vineyard

▢	Vineyards
▢	Woods
—100—	Contour interval 20 metres

For location map see page 114

The Confrérie St-Etienne is Alsace's red-robed wine growers' and shippers' association.

Alsace vines are trained tall. On the wooded Vosges, Eguisheim's three ruined châteaux are a landmark.

The wines of the different merchants and growers, however, do tend to reflect the style and quality of the part of Alsace they come from. Barr, for example, is perhaps the best commune of the Bas-Rhin, in the north, but its wines have more acidity, are less substantial than those of Riquewihr. The region of Riquewihr, centrally placed with good south-facing slopes standing out from the Vosges, seems to have the ideal situation. At the far southern end of the region, at Guebwiller, the perfectly sheltered vineyards give distinctly softer and richer wine.

Up to 1975 the whole area had only one Appellation Contrôlée, local variations of sun and soil notwithstanding. In 1975 a new appellation, 'Alsace Grand Cru' was announced, to take effect (they said) in 1978. Ten years later we are still waiting. A preliminary list of more than 90 candidate sites has been whittled down to a (quasi-official) list of about 30. All these except five in the Bas-Rhin (at Andlau, Barr, Bergbieten and Eichoffen) and one celebrated hill, Rangen, at Thann, ten miles (16 kilometres) south of Guebwiller, appear on the map above. Those on the latest authorized list appear in red. But the names of several others are equally famous and well used: to omit the Kaefferkopf at Ammerschwihr would be absurd. It would be absurd, too, to leave out

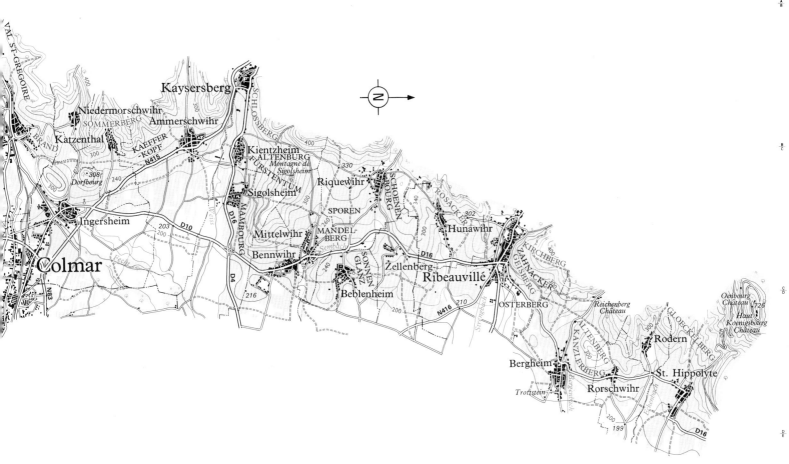

The finest of Alsace's many grapes, the Riesling of the Rhine is recognizably speckled when it is ripe.

The heart of Colmar, the wine capital of Alsace, is a typical superb survival from the 16th century.

Sporen at Riquewihr, often the very summit of Alsace winemaking. The names of these equally Grand but not so official Crus appear in black letters.

The principal reasons for delay in lawmaking are twofold. First, the wine trade is organized to sell brands and varieties, not vineyards. Its senior members point out that, outside of their own small domaines, they have no way to confirm exactly where each wagonload of grapes was picked. The premium on Grand Cru grapes would be a grievous temptation to a farmer who owned a little Grand Cru land and more land elsewhere.

Second, the decrees will stipulate which of

the noble wines each Grand Cru may grow. Some sites are best for Riesling, others for Gewürztraminer or Pinot Gris. It is uncomfortable for a grower to have the wrong variety in the ground.

It seems, for the moment, that the appellation is simply impracticable to operate. But this is not to deny the superiority of the wine of the best sites. Both independent growers and cooperatives are gradually associating certain grape varieties with the soils and slopes that suit them best. The Clos Ste-Hune of Trimbach, for example, is famous for its Riesling, Hugel's Sporen for its Gewürztraminer, Blanck's Schlossberg for its Riesling, Dopff & Irion's Clos des Amandiers for its Muscat, Zind-Humbrecht's Clos St-Urbain at Thann for its Riesling, Willm's Clos Gaensbronnel at Barr for Gewürztraminer.

But while the concept of the Clos, the little self-contained vineyard, appeals to some producers, others produce equally fine selections as 'Cuvées' of their best grapes. One is left wondering what would happen in Burgundy if tradition and authority (and the simplicity of only two grape varieties) had not imposed the familiar pattern of appellations.

A signposted Route des Vins takes visitors on a meandering course the whole length of the Alsace wine country. It calls on the way at some of the prettiest wine towns in the world.

The richest possible operatic Gothick is standard architecture here: overhanging gables and flowery courtyards and wellheads and cobbles and leaded lights and carved beams survive *en masse* in many of the villages. Riquewihr and Kaysersberg are the most beautiful. Colmar, the capital of Alsace wine, has a magnificent collection of timber-frame houses from the 15th century on.

Between them the high-trained vines block out the view along the narrow lanes, until you reach a ridge and suddenly see the gleaming green sea rolling against the mountains before and behind, disappearing in a haze in the distance.

The Loire Valley and Muscadet

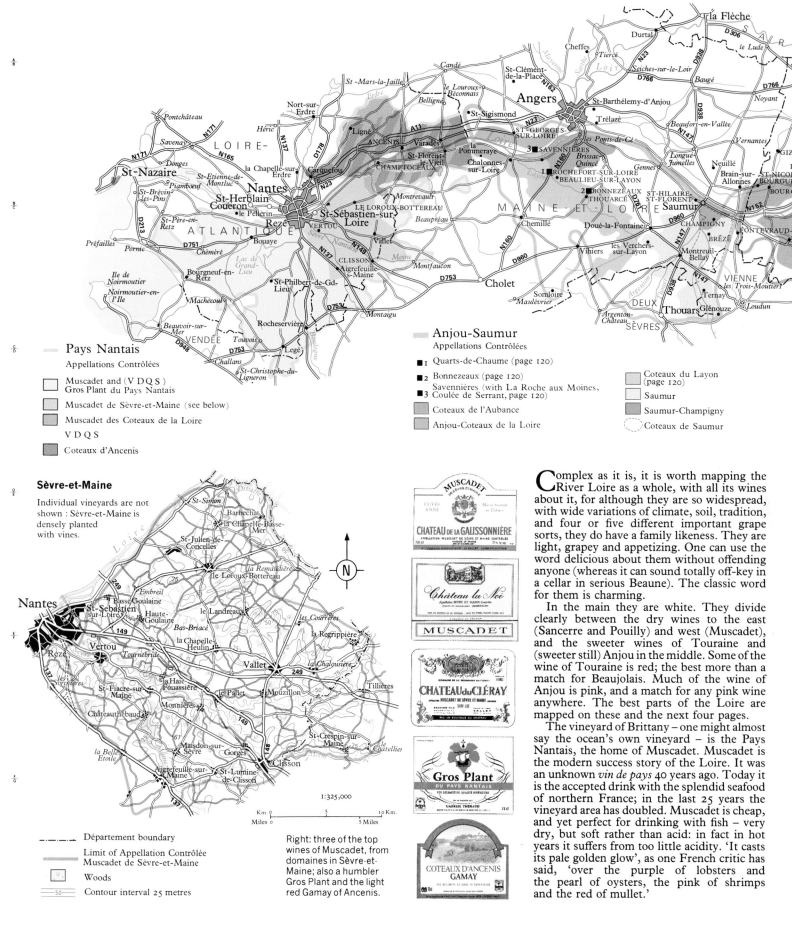

Pays Nantais

Appellations Contrôlées

- Muscadet and (V D Q S) Gros Plant du Pays Nantais
- Muscadet de Sèvre-et-Maine (see below)
- Muscadet des Coteaux de la Loire

V D Q S

- Coteaux d'Ancenis

Anjou-Saumur

Appellations Contrôlées

- ■1 Quarts-de-Chaume (page 120)
- ■2 Bonnezeaux (page 120)
- ■3 Savennières (with La Roche aux Moines, Coulée de Serrant, page 120)
- Coteaux de l'Aubance
- Anjou-Coteaux de la Loire
- Coteaux du Layon (page 120)
- Saumur
- Saumur-Champigny
- Coteaux de Saumur

Sèvre-et-Maine

Individual vineyards are not shown : Sèvre-et-Maine is densely planted with vines.

1:325,000

Km. 0   5   10 Km.
Miles 0   5 Miles

- - - - Département boundary
- Limit of Appellation Contrôlée Muscadet de Sèvre-et-Maine
- Woods
- 50 Contour interval 25 metres

Right: three of the top wines of Muscadet, from domaines in Sèvre-et-Maine; also a humbler Gros Plant and the light red Gamay of Ancenis.

Complex as it is, it is worth mapping the River Loire as a whole, with all its wines about it, for although they are so widespread, with wide variations of climate, soil, tradition, and four or five different important grape sorts, they do have a family likeness. They are light, grapey and appetizing. One can use the word delicious about them without offending anyone (whereas it can sound totally off-key in a cellar in serious Beaune). The classic word for them is charming.

In the main they are white. They divide clearly between the dry wines to the east (Sancerre and Pouilly) and west (Muscadet), and the sweeter wines of Touraine and (sweeter still) Anjou in the middle. Some of the wine of Touraine is red; the best more than a match for Beaujolais. Much of the wine of Anjou is pink, and a match for any pink wine anywhere. The best parts of the Loire are mapped on these and the next four pages.

The vineyard of Brittany – one might almost say the ocean's own vineyard – is the Pays Nantais, the home of Muscadet. Muscadet is the modern success story of the Loire. It was an unknown *vin de pays* 40 years ago. Today it is the accepted drink with the splendid seafood of northern France; in the last 25 years the vineyard area has doubled. Muscadet is cheap, and yet perfect for drinking with fish – very dry, but soft rather than acid: in fact in hot years it suffers from too little acidity. 'It casts its pale golden glow', as one French critic has said, 'over the purple of lobsters and the pearl of oysters, the pink of shrimps and the red of mullet.'

118

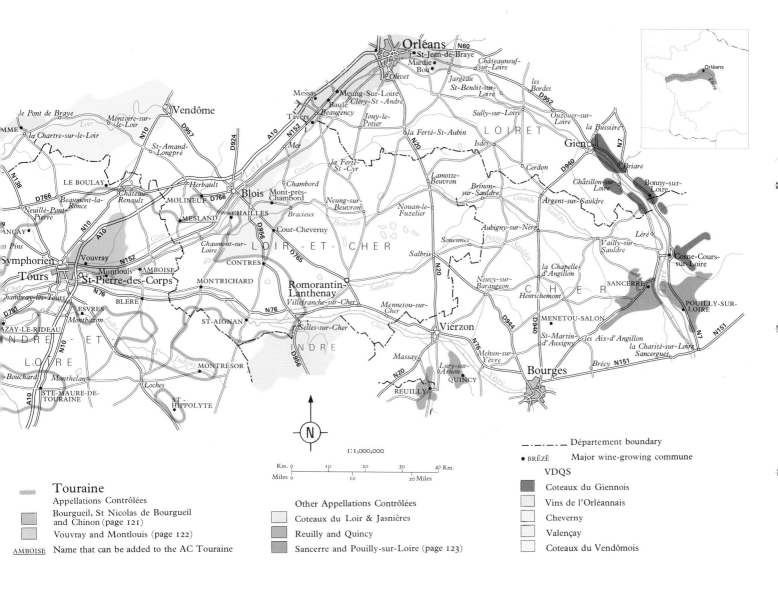

Touraine

Appellations Contrôlées

Bourgueil, St Nicolas de Bourgueil and Chinon (page 121)

Vouvray and Montlouis (page 122)

AMBOISE Name that can be added to the AC Touraine

Other Appellations Contrôlées

Coteaux du Loir & Jasnières

Reuilly and Quincy

Sancerre and Pouilly-sur-Loire (page 123)

1:1,000,000

Km. 0   10   20   30   40 Km.
Miles 0   10   20 Miles

N

—·—·— Département boundary

• BRÉZÉ Major wine-growing commune

VDQS

Coteaux du Giennois

Vins de l'Orléannais

Cheverny

Valençay

Coteaux du Vendômois

Muscadet is the name of the vine, not of a place. The region of Sèvre-et-Maine (page 118) is the heart of the vineyard, giving the softest wines; most scented, soonest ready. Within three months of the vintage they are sold 'sur lie' – straight from the barrel, unracked. The other important area, the Coteaux de la Loire, gives better wine in hot years, with more lasting properties. The second wine of the region, Gros Plant, is also good – a minor Muscadet with more acidity. Some minor red wine is made around Ancenis from Gamay grapes. Light and fruity Cabernet red is the speciality of Saumur-Champigny in Anjou, in

Above: the soft watery landscape of the Loire perfectly suggests the gentle spring-like quality of its wine. Here, near Saumur in Anjou, white, pink and red wines are all light and refreshing.

Right: sparkling Saumur, sweet Jasnières, Touraine both red and white and flinty Reuilly and Quincy are among the wide variety of Loire wines.

a region whose basic produce is white and medium-sweet (see next page).

The wines of the Upper Loire are really collectors' pieces today, with the exception of Pouilly and Sancerre (page 123). Quincy and Reuilly, and a remnant of vineyard at Menetou-Salon, make flinty, fruity white wine like light Sancerre and some pale Pinot Noir. The Coteaux du Giennois, downstream from Pouilly, has few growers left.

Orléans is best known for vinegar. Cheverny makes dry, often sharp white wine from a grape not found elsewhere, the Romorantin.

Elsewhere, across the breadth of Touraine, the broad appellation Touraine applies to generally rather thin Sauvignon whites and Gamay reds, with such local exceptions as Amboise, Azay-le-Rideau, Mesland and Valençay, which use Chenin Blanc and other grapes, while to the north the ACs Jasnières and Coteaux du Loir and the VDQS Coteaux du Vendômois make respectively Vouvray-style white, and light red of the local Pineau d'Aunis.

Irregular quality is the curse of winegrowing so far north. Many Loire growths vary so widely from one year to another that they seem hardly the same wine. A fine autumn makes it possible to gather grapes dried almost to raisins, but a wet one means a very acid product. Hence the importance of the sparkling-wine industry in Touraine and Anjou. The comparative failures of Vouvray or Saumur, fruity but acid, are ideal for transforming into sparkling Crémant de la Loire, using the champagne method.

Anjou

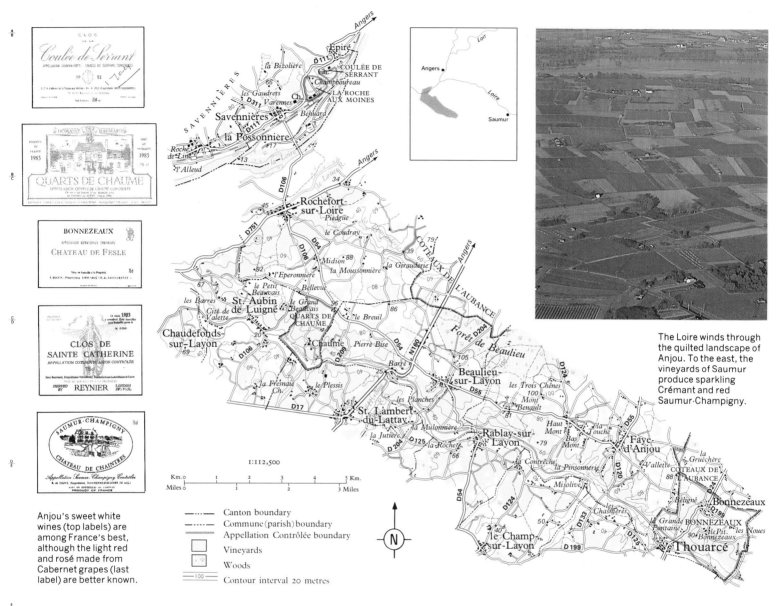

I:112,500

Km. 0   1   2   3   4   5 Km.
Miles 0   1   2   3 Miles

- - - - - Canton boundary
- - - - - Commune (parish) boundary
▨▨▨▨ Appellation Contrôlée boundary
▢ Vineyards
▢ Woods
—100— Contour interval 20 metres

The Loire winds through the quilted landscape of Anjou. To the east, the vineyards of Saumur produce sparkling Crémant and red Saumur-Champigny.

The white wines of Anjou and Touraine have this in common with those of Germany: the better they are the sweeter they are. At their very best they are dessert wines of velvet texture, smooth with glycerine, richly and yet freshly scented, tasting of grapes, peaches, apricots, hazelnuts, but with an underlying elusive flintiness which prevents them cloying. This is after a long warm autumn. Such wines go on improving for many years. But even in medium years they often have the balance of good German wines in which fruit and acid seem perfectly matched, making you want to sip and go on sipping.

The grape that gives us all this is the Chenin Blanc, called locally Pineau de la Loire. The area mapped on this page is where it reaches its ripest; several geographical circumstances combine to give it the dry open slopes, sheltered from north and east, which it needs. The River Layon, heading northwest to join the Loire, has cut a deep enough gully to provide perfectly exposed but sheltered corners of hill.

A large part of its course has the appellation Coteaux du Layon, providing sweet (or 'moëlleux') wines notably above the general Anjou standard. But Quarts de Chaume with only 120 acres (less than 50 hectares) and Bonnezeaux (about double) are outstanding enough to have appellations of their own, like Grands Crus in Burgundy. Beaulieu, Rablay, Rochefort, St-Aubin, Faye and Thouarcé are communes with particularly good wines.

The River Aubance, parallel with the Layon to the north, makes similar wines: both also grow the red Cabernet to make good light red wine, the famous delicate Cabernet Rosé d'Anjou and, paler still, vin gris, barely more than a blushing white.

Just south of Angers, and facing Rochefort, the north bank of the Loire has a series of small appellations which are locally important. Again it is the Chenin Blanc, although here – to confound all generalization – the wine at its best is dry. Savennières is the general appellation for this small region (which comes within the bigger one of the Coteaux de la Loire). Within Savennières there are two Grands Crus – La Roche aux Moines (about the same size as Quarts de Chaume) and the mere 12 acres (5 hectares) of La Coulée de Serrant.

La Coulée de Serrant epitomizes the exceptional situation which makes outstanding wine: it faces southwest in a side-valley even more sheltered than the main river bank. Its old stone presshouse has an ecclesiastical air. The view over the Loire with its wooded and flowery islands is like the background to one of the medieval tapestries of Angers.

Savennières wine has a honey-and-flowers smell which makes its dryness surprising at first. It is a 'big' wine which improves for two or three years in bottle. Salmon is said to be its perfect partner, but there is such pleasure in its lingering flavour that it is a pity not to drink it on its own before a meal.

Chinon and Bourgueil

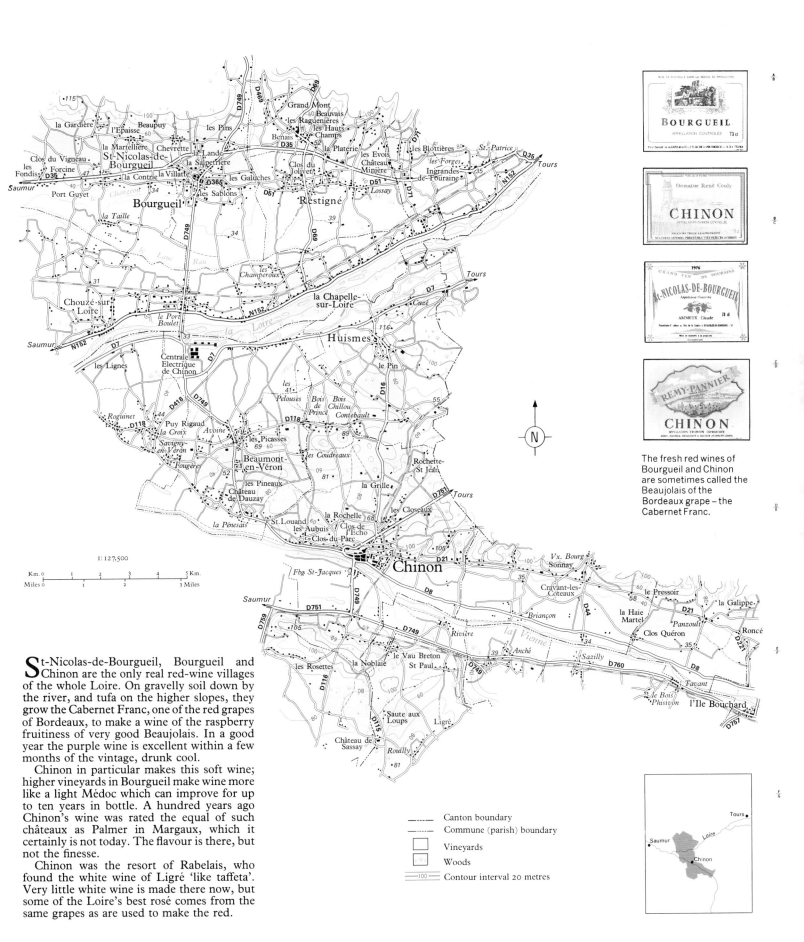

The fresh red wines of Bourgueil and Chinon are sometimes called the Beaujolais of the Bordeaux grape – the Cabernet Franc.

St-Nicolas-de-Bourgueil, Bourgueil and Chinon are the only real red-wine villages of the whole Loire. On gravelly soil down by the river, and tufa on the higher slopes, they grow the Cabernet Franc, one of the red grapes of Bordeaux, to make a wine of the raspberry fruitiness of very good Beaujolais. In a good year the purple wine is excellent within a few months of the vintage, drunk cool.

Chinon in particular makes this soft wine; higher vineyards in Bourgueil make wine more like a light Médoc which can improve for up to ten years in bottle. A hundred years ago Chinon's wine was rated the equal of such châteaux as Palmer in Margaux, which it certainly is not today. The flavour is there, but not the finesse.

Chinon was the resort of Rabelais, who found the white wine of Ligré 'like taffeta'. Very little white wine is made there now, but some of the Loire's best rosé comes from the same grapes as are used to make the red.

— — — —	Canton boundary
—·—·—	Commune (parish) boundary
☐	Vineyards
▨	Woods
—100—	Contour interval 20 metres

Vouvray

Km. 0   1   2   3 Km.
Miles 0   1   2 Miles

1:75,000

- - - - - - Canton boundary
· - · - · - Commune (parish) boundary
▢ Vineyards
▢ Woods
——100—— Contour interval 20 metres

Just as Savennières stands almost at the gates of Angers, Vouvray and Montlouis lie just outside Tours on the way to Amboise. Everything royal and romantic about France is summed up in this countryside of great châteaux and ancient towns along the gently flowing river.

Low hills of chalk flank the stream along the reach from Noizay to Rochecorbon. For centuries they have provided both cellars and dwellings in caves to the winegrowers of the district. The Chenin Blanc here, although often drier than in Anjou, at its best is honey-like and sweet. What distinguishes it more than anything, however, is its long life. For a comparatively light wine its longevity is astonishing. You may expect madeira to live for half a century, but in a pale, firm, rather delicate wine the ability to improve and go on improving for so long in bottle is very rare.

Most Vouvray today is handled by négociants, who blend the produce of one *clos* with another. The once-famous names of the individual sites are not often heard today. More important is the need to know whether any given bottle is dry, semi-sweet, sweet or for that matter *pétillant* or fully sparkling: Vouvray alters character radically from vintage to vintage, and its natural tendency to re-ferment in the bottle has led to an industry in converting less successful vintages into very good sparkling wine. Nonetheless growers do triumphantly bottle their best produce and keep it for a small band of connoisseurs. To them, names like Vallée Coquette are a rallying call.

Montlouis has very similar soil and conditions to Vouvray, without the perfect situation of the first rank of Vouvray's vineyards along the Loire. Montlouis tends to be slightly softer and more gently sweet, but it takes a native to tell the difference.

A dwindling number of small growers still make the great sweet wines of the Vouvray area. Much modern Vouvray is made sparkling, either sweet or dry, using the champagne method.

Pouilly and Sancerre

The wines of Pouilly and Sancerre on the upper Loire are perhaps the easiest to recognize in France. On these chalky hills, cut by the river, the Sauvignon grape gives a smell to the wine that is called gunflint; it is slightly smoky, slightly green, slightly spicy and appeals to most people intensely at first. Compared with the Chenin Blanc of the middle Loire, however, the Sauvignon lacks interest after a while. Sancerre and Pouilly Fumé have strong immediate appeal as good with food, particularly shellfish, but only exceptional vintages give wines of serious class. The same is true of Sancerre's Pinot Noir: a local passion.

Pouilly-sur-Loire is the town; its wine is only called Pouilly Fumé when made from the Sauvignon. Its second wine, from the Chasselas and often excellent in its own way, is called Pouilly-sur-Loire. Neither has anything to do with Pouilly-Fuissé, the white wine of Mâcon.

There is not much to choose between Pouilly Fumé and Sancerre. The best of each are on the same level; the Sancerre perhaps slightly riper-tasting. In bad vintages, however, they can be very acid; their smell has been compared to wet wool. A year or two in bottle brings out the qualities of a good one, but they are not wines to lay down, like Vouvrays.

There is a growing fashion for Sauvignon wine, and vineyard names are more and more in evidence. Les Monts Damnés in Chavignol and Clos du Chêne Marchand in Bué are the two best-known vineyards of Sancerre; the Château du Nozet and Château de Tracy the biggest and best-known estates in Pouilly.

The Loire meanders on a northwesterly route past the vineyards of Pouilly, on the right, towards the walled town of Sancerre on its abrupt hilltop in the distance. The Sancerre vineyards lie beyond, on a series of chalky ridges facing south and east.

Above: the best Sancerres come from Chavignol and Bué. Two big châteaux, du Nozet and de Tracy, dominate Pouilly. Only the best Pouillys are known as Fumé. The lesser (Chasselas) wines are called Pouilly-sur-Loire.

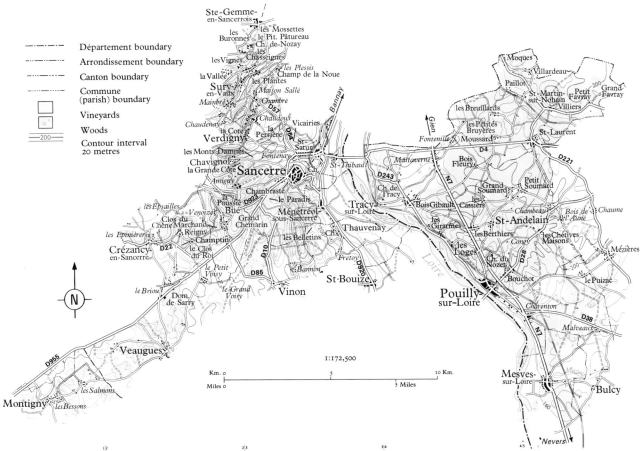

Département boundary
Arrondissement boundary
Canton boundary
Commune (parish) boundary
Vineyards
Woods
Contour interval 20 metres

1:172,500

Km. 0   5   10 Km.
Miles 0   5 Miles

The Rhône Valley

The valley of the Loire and the valley of the Rhône are two sides of the same coin. They contain respectively the best of northern and the best of southern French viticulture. Most Loire wine is white, most Rhône red. In each case there is a wide variety of styles of wine but a distinct family feeling.

Rhône red wines vary from the intensely concentrated and tannic, ruby-black or purple-black in youth, to some very wishy-washy productions. The best have depth, length and lingering harmony comparable to the greatest wines of Bordeaux. These are the limited output of the districts mapped in detail on the following pages. Everyday Côtes-du-Rhône is not the same sort of thing at all. The bulk comes from the wide southern area and needs choosing with great care. White wines are in the minority, tend to headiness but can be as notable as all but the best of the red.

In the course of the Rhône the country changes from oak forest, where the vine shares the fields with peach trees and nut trees, to the herbal scrub and olive groves of Provence. In the north the vine perches on terraced cliffs of crumbling granite wherever the best view of the sun can be found. In the south it lies baking in broad terraces of smooth round stones where the sun is everywhere.

Rhône wines are not as a rule made from one grape variety on its own, as burgundy is, but from a blend of anything from two to 13. It is common practice to add a little of a white variety to the very dark wine of the Syrah, the classic red-wine grape of Côte Rôtie and Hermitage. Châteauneuf-du-Pape, like Chianti, is made from a whole roll call of vines, including both red and white.

The vineyards around the Rhône fall naturally into two groups: northern and southern. The appellation Côtes du Rhône is a general one for the wine of 150-odd communes, red, white or rosé. Côtes du Rhône-Villages is applied only to 17 specific (and superior) communes in the southern part. Fifteen areas have their own separate appellations. All except Die are shown on the map.

On the following pages the best areas of the northern and southern Rhône are mapped in detail. Between them lie several others of strong local character, long traditions and rising reputations. North of Valence, Cornas is country cousin to the noble Hermitage, made of the same Syrah grapes: a dark red to reckon with. North of Tournon, St-Joseph has red to be favourably compared with Crozes-Hermitage, often having more 'grip', and excellent soft and subtle white. South of Cornas, St-Péray has an old name for its heavy-grade golden sparkling wine of the local Roussanne and Marsanne grapes (also made still), while on the river Drôme to the east totally different grapes (Clairette and Muscat) make another sparkler, Clairette de Die, in the very opposite mode: light and scented.

Meanwhile a new appellation, started in 1974 east of Montélimar, has added to the supply of good lively Côtes-du-Rhône style reds. The Coteaux du Tricastin uses the darkly tannic Syrah to give its round red wine a satisfying backbone of flavour.

Above: the mechanical grape-harvester is slowly becoming a familiar sight in France, in areas where vineyards are level enough and vine-rows wide enough. Here Clairette grapes are being shaken from the vines of the Drôme to make the sparkling Clairette de Die, one of the labels shown below.

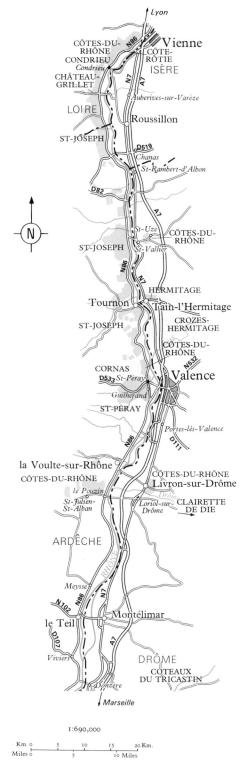

1:690,000

Km. 0   5   10   15   20 Km.
Miles 0   5   10 Miles

------ Département boundary

Appellation Contrôlée areas

For Southern Rhône map see page 129

Côte Rôtie and Condrieu

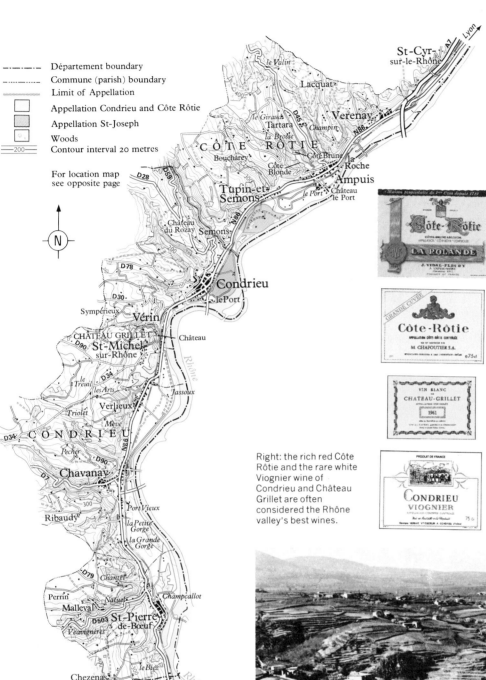

Côte Rôtie and Condrieu, in the northern group of vineyards around the Rhône, have nothing like the fame of Châteauneuf-du-Pape in the south. They are bound to remain collectors' wines because their vineyards are so tiny. But there is no doubt that Côte Rôtie is one of the best, if not the very best of the Rhône red wines. Those who have tasted Condrieu at the famous restaurant Pyramide at Vienne feel equally strongly about the white.

The right-hand bend of the river after Vienne provides a short stretch of very steep hill perfectly aligned for the sun. The soil varies even within the area of the vineyard, and there are three distinct appellations.

The northern part is called Côte Rôtie – literally 'roasted hill' – and is itself divided, although not legally, into Côte Brune and Côte Blonde: slopes with darker and lighter soil. The wines of the two are normally blended together. Côte Rôtie makes the Rhône's most complex and rewarding wine – not its strongest. With age it takes on an almost claret-like delicacy and an irresistible raspberry-like scent.

Condrieu is its white opposite number. A grape of strong character but unfortunately weak constitution, the Viognier, is the only one officially allowed within the area. It too makes a rather delicate wine for the Rhône: a dry wine with a haunting floral scent like a faint and disturbing echo from the Rhine and a very long, rather spicy aftertaste. Château Grillet is the inner sanctum of Condrieu. A perfect microclimate gives its wine an advantage that is reflected in its strength, quality and price.

Unlike most Rhône wines, the Viogniers are at their best when still young.

Right: the rich red Côte Rôtie and the rare white Viognier wine of Condrieu and Château Grillet are often considered the Rhône valley's best wines.

Right: Château Grillet lies below its amphitheatre of vineyard in a perfectly sheltered situation beside the Rhône. The 1.6-hectare (4-acre) estate is the smallest property with its own Appellation Contrôlée in France.

Hermitage

France's main north–south artery, the Rhône, and its accompanying roads and railway, snakes by under the stacked terraces of the hill of Hermitage, making the vineyard's magnificent stance looking south down the river familiar to millions.

The Romans grew wine here. Some say it was the first vineyard to be planted in the northward progression of the vine that led to Burgundy. A hundred years ago its 'mas' – the local name for the individual vineyards – were named beside Château Lafite and Romanée Conti as among the best red wines of the world. A. Jullien listed them in order of merit: Méal, Gréfieux, Beaume, Raucoule, Muret, Guoignière, Bessas, Burges and Lauds. Spellings have changed; the *mas* remain – but today few of their names are heard, and never in the same breath as Château Lafite.

The adjective 'manly' has stuck to Hermitage ever since it was first applied to it. It has almost the qualities of port without the added brandy. Like vintage port it throws a heavy sediment in the bottle (it needs decanting) and improves for many years until its scent and flavour are almost overwhelming.

Young Hermitage of a good vintage is as closed and tannic as any great red wine to taste, but nothing can restrain its abounding perfume and the fistfuls of fruit that seem crammed into the glass. As it ages the immediacy of its impact does not diminish, but its youthful assault gives way to the sheer splendour of its mature presence. You could not drink it and not be impressed.

Like most great wines it has its shadow. Crozes-Hermitage is to the Grand Cru what a village Gevrey-Chambertin is to Le Chambertin, or a Vosne-Romanée to Romanée-Conti. Crozes is the village at the back of the uprearing hill, and its appellation covers a very mixed bag of vineyards, both north and south of Tain and Hermitage itself. Only one Crozes wine, the Domaine de Thalabert of Paul Jaboulet, is regularly comparable to a Hermitage. Most are full and fruity without the classic bite and concentration. And some are very pallid.

Indeed some of the best Crozes-Hermitage is white, and the Hermitage hill is historically almost as famous for its white wine as its red.

'Raucoule' was named as the best white Hermitage by Jullien. Today Chante-Alouette is the best known. Besides being a *mas*, it is the trademark of the house of Chapoutier. The wine is golden, dry and full with a remarkably delicate and interesting flavour, and lasts, like the red Hermitage, for years.

Right: the river Rhône washes the foot of the hill of Hermitage, skirting the city of Tain. The old hermitage chapel still stands among the staked vines on top, in a patch giving some of the most potent wine.

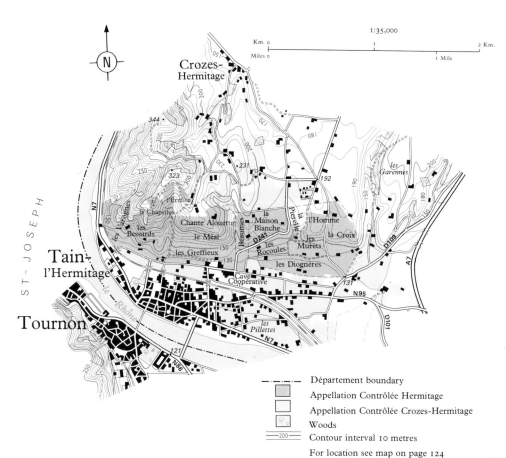

Département boundary
Appellation Contrôlée Hermitage
Appellation Contrôlée Crozes-Hermitage
Woods
Contour interval 10 metres
For location see map on page 124

Chante-Alouette is the best-known white Hermitage. Crozes-Hermitage is the appellation of the vineyards not on the Hermitage hill itself.

Châteauneuf-du-Pape

Châteauneuf-du-Pape lies in the centre of the biggest concentration of Rhône vineyards, on hills dominated by a ruined papal summer palace. Its vines are widely spaced; low bushes in a sea of smooth stones with no earth to be seen. The deep red wine of Châteauneuf has the distinction not only of having the highest minimum strength of any French wine (12.5% alcohol) but of being the first to be so regulated. Its most famous grower, the late Baron Le Roy, initiated here what has become the national system of Appellations Contrôlées. Part of his original proposal, made in 1923, was that suitable land for fine Châteauneuf vines (there are 13 varieties) should be identified by the conjunction of lavender and thyme growing there. In addition, grape sorts, pruning, quantity and strength were to be controlled.

The Baron's foresight has been rewarded by Châteauneuf-du-Pape emerging from obscurity to become one of the world's most famous wines.

Well over 45,000 hectolitres (a million gallons) of wine a year are made here, 97% of it red. Most of it is good average; made relatively light (although not in alcohol) by increasing the proportion of Grenache grapes so that it can be drunk after a mere year or two. A number of big estates, like Bordeaux châteaux, are the producers of the classic dark and deep Châteauneuf-du-Pape, each using its own cocktail of the 13 permitted varieties to make more or less spicy, more or less tannic or smooth, shorter- or longer-lived wine.

Modern winemaking methods have recently given new interest to what had become a somewhat disillusioned appellation. Today, such estates as the Domaine de Beaucastel, Châteaux Fortia and Rayas, Le Vieux Télégraphe and La Nerte have standards as high as the best in France.

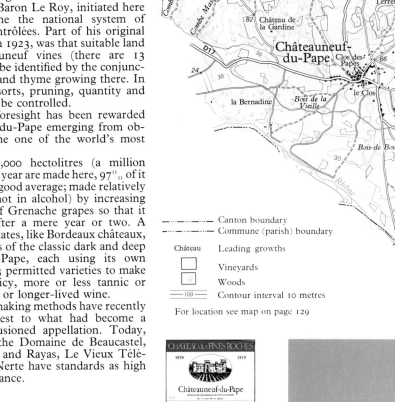

-·-·-·-·-	Canton boundary
-·-·-·-·-	Commune (parish) boundary
Château	Leading growths
☐	Vineyards
🌳	Woods
—100—	Contour interval 10 metres

For location see map on page 129

1:60,000

Km. 0   1   2   3 Km.
Miles 0   1   2 Miles

The soil of Châteauneuf-du-Pape is completely hidden by beach-like stones which retain the day's heat far into the night. The grapes ripen to very high sugar content. In the background stands the ruined summer palace of the Avignon popes.

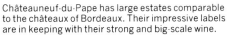

Châteauneuf-du-Pape has large estates comparable to the châteaux of Bordeaux. Their impressive labels are in keeping with their strong and big-scale wine.

The Southern Rhône

The funnel end of the Rhône valley, where it releases its traffic to the Mediterranean, has a place in every traveller's affections. History and natural history combine to make it one of the richest regions of France for interest of every kind. Who cannot picture the vast engineering of the Romans, lizards alert on its slumbering stones, patches of early vegetables screened around against the wind, the pines and almonds yielding to olive groves as you go south – and always, on hillside or plain, sand or chalk, the cross-stitch of vines?

The heart of the region, the vineyard that sums up all its qualities, is Châteauneuf-du-Pape. History does not make so much of its neighbours. The huge appellation Côtes du Rhône, most of it on this map (with a little to the north) covers nearly 83,000 acres (33,500 hectares) in more than 100 communes north of Avignon. They form a rough circle straddling the low hills where the valley begins to widen.

Its crop can be three times as much as that of Beaujolais, and not very much less than all of Bordeaux. Almost all is red, or rosé, soft, mildly fruity with a gentle warmth, much of it now made Beaujolais-style to accentuate its modest degree of flavour. It cannot compete with standard Bordeaux for freshness and sapidity. It is wine for the easily satisfied.

Immediately north of Châteauneuf-du-Pape, though, within a radius of 25 miles (40km), a group of communities had higher standards. In the 1950s four of them, Gigondas and Cairanne to the northeast, and Chusclan and Laudun on the west bank of the Rhône, were singled out by the authorities as superior, and directed to lower their productions and raise the strength and quality of their wines. Better prices proved them justified. In 1967 a new appellation contrôlée, Côtes du Rhône-Villages, was decreed for these four and a number of their neighbours, which has subsequently risen to 17 (printed in red roman type on the map). Gigondas has meanwhile raised its standards still further to become (in 1971) an appellation in its own right; a dark, deep red needing six or seven years' ageing, and a potential rival to Châteauneuf-du-Pape.

The Côtes-du-Rhône-Villages wines are all characters worthy of closer study. Cairanne and Vacqueyras are generally considered the best, and next in line to become appellations. They are both wines of firm 'structure', as the French say, that need at least four years' ageing. Some others, such as Sablet, Valréas, St-Gervais and Rochegude, tend to be milder and sooner ready to drink. Chusclan and Laudun specialize in vin rosé, as well as pleasant and fresh whites. But growers (and cooperatives) vary as much as Villages, particularly in the proportion of the tasty Syrah in relation to the merely strong Grenache in their wines, and it is better to taste before buying, looking for the flavour of concentrated, sometimes almost raisined, berries and currants that promises satisfaction.

The north of the -Villages area, Rousset- and St-Pantaléon-les-Vignes, used to sell its wine under the name Haut-Comtat, a name little seen today. Between here and the Rhône is the up-and-coming appellation Coteaux du

Tricastin, a parched, Mistral-swept landscape better known in the past for its truffles than its wine. Even the best Tricastin wines (Domaine de Grangeneuve is an example) need no more than two or three years' ageing.

East of the -Villages lies another area of recent development, the (1974) appellation Côtes du Ventoux. The tradition here is for light-coloured 'café' wines which are lively when young. The best-known *marque* is La Vieille Ferme. The *vin de pays* Coteaux des Baronnies to the north is not very different.

To their south the Montagne de Lubéron marks the northern boundary of Provence, with red wines comparable to the Côtes du Ventoux, surprisingly fresh whites and even a bargain sparkling wine from the *cave coopérative*.

The west bank of the Rhône has an even more varied range, starting in the north with the Coteaux d'Ardèche, only a *vin de pays* but a celebrated success recently with wines as different as Syrah and Cabernet made as straight 'varietals' in the New World manner. Gamay, Chardonnay and Merlot have all found niches here too. This is certainly a corner to watch.

To their south come the Côtes du Vivarais, like lightweight Côtes du Rhône, and to their south the two excellent Côtes du Rhône 'Villages' of Chusclan and Laudun, known as well for rosé (and white) wine as for red.

Rosé is the historic speciality of Lirac and Tavel, the southernmost of the true Rhône appellations. Tavel's potent dry rosé, orange tinted after a year or two, has its fervent admirers. Lirac, formerly also best known for rosé, inclines more today to full and fruity red.

Languedoc and Provence meet in the parched *causses* at Les Baux, whose famous restaurant serves the Provence-style local VDQS red and rosé. To the west Bellegarde has an appellation for its soft dry white – not a wine that 'travels' well. Costières du Gard is a big and busy VDQS for (principally) red and rosé Côtes-du-Rhône style, often made by the same producers as Bellegarde. Farther west come the isolated communes of the Coteaux du Languedoc which should not be overlooked.

Much the biggest producer of the region (indeed of the whole of France) is the extraordinary 4,200-acre (1,700-hectare) Domaine Viticole des Salins du Midi, whose 'Listel' wines are grown on the very beaches along the seashore. Listel has learnt to use the sand as what a gardener would call a neutral growing medium, applying all the water and fertilizer the vines need, excluding seawater with fresh-water dykes. Their wines are very clean, fruity, charming and well made: an extraordinary achievement. All in all, few maps contain so much variety as this, or so much promise.

Languedoc and Roussillon

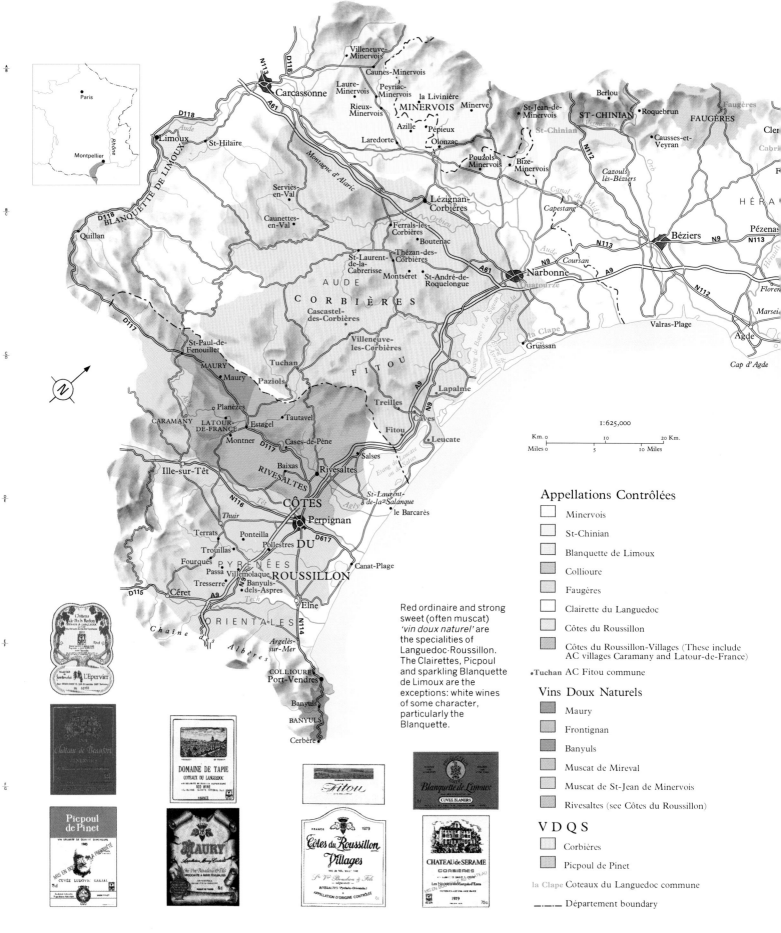

Red ordinaire and strong sweet (often muscat) *'vin doux naturel'* are the specialities of Languedoc-Roussillon. The Clairettes, Picpoul and sparkling Blanquette de Limoux are the exceptions: white wines of some character, particularly the Blanquette.

1:625,000

Km. 0   10   20 Km.

Miles 0   5   10 Miles

Appellations Contrôlées

Minervois

St-Chinian

Blanquette de Limoux

Collioure

Faugères

Clairette du Languedoc

Côtes du Roussillon

Côtes du Roussillon-Villages (These include AC villages Caramany and Latour-de-France)

•Tuchan AC Fitou commune

Vins Doux Naturels

Maury

Frontignan

Banyuls

Muscat de Mireval

Muscat de St-Jean de Minervois

Rivesaltes (see Côtes du Roussillon)

V D Q S

Corbières

Picpoul de Pinet

la Clape Coteaux du Languedoc commune

Département boundary

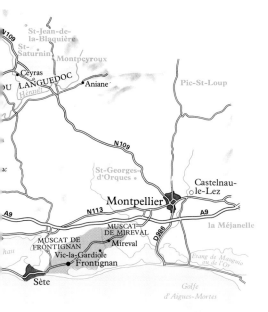

The walled city of Carcassonne dominates the valley of the Aude between Limoux and the Minervois. The medieval fantasy (largely rebuilt in the 19th century) marks the watershed between the realms of Atlantic and Mediterranean climates.

More than a third of all French wine is grown in the area covered by this map: the Midi. The *département* covering the eastern part, Hérault, has more vineyards than any other in France: more than 400,000 acres (160,000 hectares) compared with Bordeaux's 250,000 acres (100,000 hectares). This is the traditional territory of *vin ordinaire*: the *gros rouge* of the French workman's lunch, tea, and often breakfast too – plain red wine, and strong sweet Vins Doux Naturels.

The sheer quantity of nameless wine produced (and the strikes provoked by the recurring glut) has obscured the quality of the best wines of the south and the dedicated efforts which are making them better. Wine-growing here started with the Romans. (Narbonne was the first great city of Gaul.) The vine flourished where nothing else would in the stony hills, and its produce was good. It was not until phylloxera crushed the hill vignerons that the vine came down to the plain and the permanent crisis of overproduction began. There are still zones of admirable soil and climate dotted among the overfertile plains; in every case on high ground, where the soil is stony and well drained.

It is not easy to convince farmers that the way to prosperity is to grow less but better. The last few years, however, have seen real progress. *Gros rouge* is giving way to *vins de pays* (see pages 136–137), which abound here as nowhere else in France.

The staple vine of the south is the Carignan, a big producer of dull wine. The stress is on increasing the proportion of Syrah, Grenache, Mourvèdre – all Midi grapes of character – but even Cabernet Sauvignon is being planted in experiments. It does well in California: why not in the Midi?

In 1977 there were only two Appellation Contrôlée red wines in the whole of the Midi: Fitou and Collioure. Fitou is a group of nine communes in the Corbières making solid 12° wine with a certain potential for ageing; Collioure is a minuscule district almost on the Spanish border whose powerful red caught someone's eye. Today there are seven, encompassing most of the western hills of the region, and signs that more will soon follow.

The promotions to AC rank, going north from the Pyrenees, start with the Côtes du Roussillon for dark, warming, sometimes fairly fruity wines, largely of Carignan, from a wide area, and Côtes du Roussillon-Villages for bolder, more positive wines with a lower yield and higher alcohol from the valley of the Agly. Caramany and Latour-de-France are the best of these, with their own sub-appellations. Roussillon reds were celebrated in 18th-century England; investment in replanting and barrel-ageing is starting to show us why.

For the moment Fitou is still the only Appellation-rank Corbières. It is just a matter of time before the central and northern part of the region is promoted. From its arid limestone, good producers, particularly in the upper Orbieu valley, are making big and foursquare but highly drinkable wines, using Beaujolais-style vinification (carbonic maceration, see page 33) to extract the maximum flavour from the Carignan. As they plant more aromatic grapes their wine becomes even more attractive.

The red hills of the Minervois (AC since 1984) produce reds in a distinct style, at their best (particularly around La Livinière and Minerve) lively and firm, fresh and concentrated in the mouth. The firm of Chantovent is a major investor here, using the *vin de pays* name of Peyriac for much of its wine.

St-Chinian (AC since 1983) has the biggest production of the new appellations, and another style of wine, more 'open', rounder and perhaps potentially more subtle than its neighbours. It is the first of what may become a succession of Languedoc appellations in the Cévennes foothills going east. At present its neighbour Faugères, with sturdy, flavoury reds, is the end of the line, but the VDQS 'Coteaux du Languedoc' grouping seven other hill vineyards, quite distinct from the herd on the plains, also has potential. Experience will discover the outstanding sites, as it has at the Domaine de Daumas Gassac, at Aniane, north-west of Montpellier. This domaine, on a patch of volcanic debris, is making Cabernet Sauvignon of astonishing quality.

White wines are very much in a minority in the Midi. Most Midi whites, including the appellation Clairette du Languedoc, lack freshness or any flavour of fruit. The Clairette is a neutral grape: its soft, heavy and alcoholic wine is the traditional base for French vermouth. As table wine it leaves much to be desired, although conservative growers sometimes give it a bosomy southern lusciousness. The limestone massif of La Clape on the coast is noted for such wine (but better wine when it uses the golden Bourboulenc).

Picpoul de Pinet (the Picpoul is the acidic grape of Armagnac) has a certain notoriety and a VDQS label. Its 'Blanc de Blancs' is a lightweight for the Midi, but not otherwise distinguished. In Roussillon there is a tradition of picking underripe Maccabeo grapes to make a 'vin vert'. Portuguese vinho verde is much better.

All of which underlines the achievement of Limoux, in the hills to the west, in producing its highly palatable sparkling Blanquette. Altitude and Atlantic breezes provide part of the explanation. The local Mauzac grape (blended for flavour with a little Chardonnay) keeps sufficient fruity acidity to make an excellent base for the *méthode champenoise*. Blanquette de Limoux is certainly the best sparkling wine of the south of France.

The other face of the south is its dessert wines: its VDN or Vins Doux Naturels, produced by adding spirit to naturally sweet wine to arrest its fermentation – the same process as port, but with more wine and less spirit.

Roussillon is the headquarters of VDN-making, and Grand Roussillon the general appellation for its dessert and apéritif wines. The best areas, however, have their own restricted appellations: Banyuls and Banyuls Grand Cru on the rocky coastal hills just before the Spanish frontier; Rivesaltes and Maury inland. Most of these wines are made of Grenache and other non-aromatic grapes. Aged (in wood or 30-litre glass *bonbonnes*) they take on an oxidized flavour known by the Spanish term *rancio*.

Those (such as Muscat de Rivesaltes) that have the luscious muscat flavour say so. They include the rich brown wines of ancient fame from Frontignan, Mireval and Lunel in the coastal Hérault, and St-Jean-de-Minervois up in the hills: all good wines of their kind, alcoholic, velvety and aromatic.

Provence

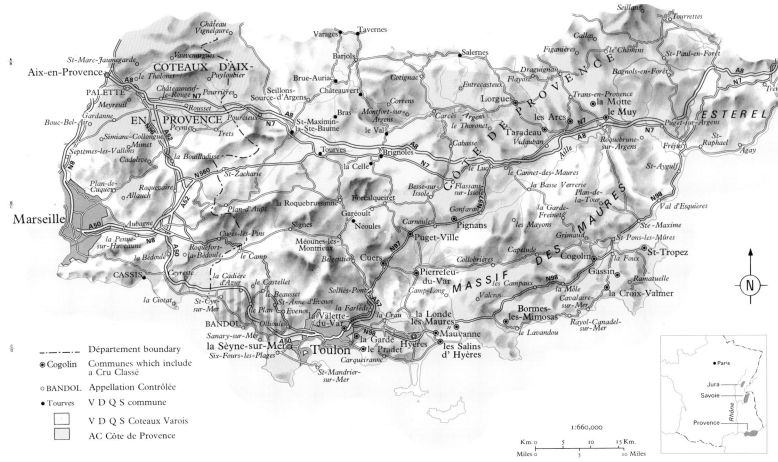

There used to be only four small areas of fully fledged Appellations Contrôlées along the Mediterranean coast east of the Rhône. The longest-established are Cassis (no relation to the blackcurrant syrup) for full-bodied and lively white, and Bandol for memorable, long-lived red based on an almost Syrah-like grape, the Mourvèdre. Palette near Aix was another tiny appellation for a patch of limestone soil exploited by one estate, Château Simone. Nice had its own high-priced reds, whites and rosés from tiny Bellet in the hills.

In 1977 the wider appellation Côtes de Provence was created for a far wider area, of great tourist fame but where fine wine was the exception. Overstrong rosé was the staple. Since then standards have generally improved – in some cases dramatically. There are 400 properties in the region now producing appellation wines, the majority still rosé, heady and orange-hued, or soft, rather pale reds of Grenache and Carignan, the minority experimenting with such nontraditional grapes as Syrah and even Cabernet to make some excellent wines with nerve and sinew. The term Cru Classé is allowed for the acknowledged best producers.

A description of Provence wines always mentions the sunbaked pines, thyme and rosemary and claims that the wine takes its character from them. It should add that rocky hills of limestone or shale, and in some cases a cool breeze off the sea, can give considerable distinction to certain crus.

Upgrading goes on. The old VDQS Coteaux d'Aix en Provence and Coteaux des Baux have recently become appellations. A new VDQS, Coteaux Varois, covers the heart of the inland Var. And farther north (off the map) the Coteaux de Pierrevert and Côtes de Luberon are making increasingly good wines, in a style not remote from the southern Rhône.

The vineyard soils of Provence vary from limestone for the Vaucluse in the north to red sandstone and slate in the Var towards the coast. A feature of the limestone country is the 'borie', an ancient design of shepherd's hut built of fieldstone laid with spaces to let the smoke out without letting the weather in.

Above: Bandol and Palette stand out, but several estates in the Côtes de Provence and Côteaux d'Aix-en-Provence ACs are aspiring to high standards. Bellet is a tiny AC above Nice.

Savoie and the Jura

Savoie

International boundary

Département boundary

Appellation Contrôlée

For location map see opposite page

1:1,000,000

Km. 0   10   20   30 Km.
Miles 0   10   20 Miles

The wine country of Savoie is diffuse and its produce little known. In many ways it epitomizes the 'little local wine' which travels only in legend: its cleanness and freshness are at one with the mountain air, the lakes and streams. Savoie wine is nearly all white – as water. There is a dry softness about it like ethereal Muscadet.

The sparkling version is better known than the still: it, too, has this pale, elusive quality. The best is drier and more delicate than any other sparkling wine – an intriguing alternative to champagne as an apéritif. The district of Seyssel in the Rhône valley is the specialist.

The appellation Vin de Savoie applies to white wines of a certain strength made of the predominant local grape, the Jacquère. Of these Ayse is the best-known commune for sparkling wine, Apremont, Abîmes and Chignin for still. A dwindling traditional white grape, the Altesse, carries the appellation Roussette de Savoie, best when qualified by such place-names as Monterminod, Frangy and (notably) Marestel.

Crépy is just across the border from Switzerland, its grape the Swiss Chasselas and its whole nature more Swiss than French.

Although Gamay and Pinot Noir fetch a higher price, the best Savoyard red grape is the Mondeuse (in Italy the Refosco): smooth, fruity and tannic at once – perfect skiing wine. Arbin, Montmélian and St-Jean-de-la-Porte are its best-known *crus*. Westwards, towards Lyon, the VDQS vineyards of Bugey, not in themselves remarkable, take a logical step towards the next region: the Beaujolais.

Most Savoie wine is white and very dry and light. Crépy and Seyssel are Appellations Contrôlées; Varichon & Clerc make excellent sparkling wine.

The Jura range (above) is wider than that of Savoie: yellow, red, white, 'grey' and 'mad' (*fou*) – sparkling wine.

A little enclave of vines scattered among woodland and meadow in what seem like France's remotest hills. . . . The Jura's production is a fraction of its old total; yet its wines are varied, good and wholly original. Its superior appellations, Arbois, Château-Chalon and l'Etoile, all count for something.

Jura wine is not only red, white and rosé, but yellow and grey. The best of it is 'yellow'; firm, strong white wine from the Savagnin (alias Traminer) which is kept for a minimum of six years in cask while it undergoes a transformation like that of sherry. The appellation Château-Chalon is limited to this odd but excellent wine, but good '*vin jaune*' is also made at l'Etoile and Arbois.

The 'grey' wine is simply very pale rosé, rather sharp and sometimes extremely appetizing. The best Jura vin rosé, from Arbois, by contrast is more like pale red wine, unusually silky. Some of the white is made from the Chardonnay and compares well with minor white burgundies – especially that from the appellation l'Etoile. The red is perhaps the least interesting, although it, too, can be soft, smooth and satisfying with the local game.

A small amount of excellent sparkling wine is made at Arbois (and a large amount of the widely advertised Vin Fou, an inferior substitute). One final speciality, liquorous *vin de paille*, made of loft-dried raisins, is almost extinct. Like genuine handmade Italian *vinsanto*, it is worth its very high price.

Jura

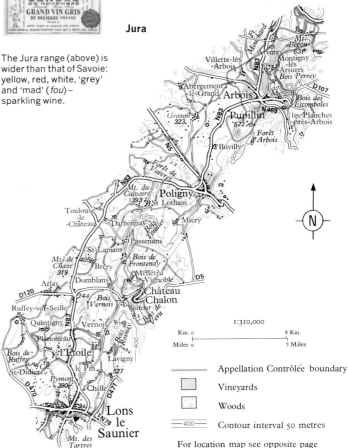

1:310,000

Km. 0   8 Km.
Miles 0   5 Miles

Appellation Contrôlée boundary

Vineyards

Woods

Contour interval 50 metres

For location map see opposite page

Wines of the Southwest

South of the great vineyard of Bordeaux, and west of the Midi, the vine flourishes in scattered areas of strong local traditions.

Cahors is the senior wine of this part of France, in reputation, though not in official recognition. It was only promoted to Appellation Contrôlée in 1971, although it had long been known as the 'First of the VDQS'. In Cahors they would tell you how, centuries ago, it was their wine, not meagre Médocs, that was most in demand among foreign buyers in the port of Bordeaux.

Cahors has recently come back strongly into favour, not as the 'black' wine of legend (and fact, a generation ago: its colour and tannin content well earned the epithet) but as a full-bodied, vigorous red with a definite bite in its youth, maturing fairly rapidly these days (four years is often enough) to a balance and complexity that would do credit to a St-Emilion.

The grape that Cahors uses, in large part, is the Malbec, which it calls the Auxerrois. Recent replanting has taken it from the alluvial gravel by the river up on to the rocky *causses*, where its wine is stronger, with more bite. Some of the best producers (who include Les Caves d'Olt) believe a blend of both is best. In fact, Cahors can be found in all shades and weights. Locally it is drunk rather cool.

The hills around the river Tarn just below Albi, and below the magnificent gorge the river makes in the Cévennes mountains, are still lovely country with beautiful towns and villages. Seventy-three of them are contained within the appellation Gaillac, which is thus a very general name for any wine, red, white or rosé, made from a mixture of a fairly wide choice of grapes, including local and both Bordeaux and Rhône reds, and the same white Mauzac that produces Blanquette de Limoux. Gaillac also has its Mousseux, traditionally made by the *méthode rurale*, the primitive forerunner of the champagne method. Better known, however, is its slightly fizzy dry white Perlé; an excellent summer drink. An inner-circle appellation, Premières Côtes de Gaillac,

defends what is left of the local tradition of sweet (in reality semi-sweet) whites. But today most Gaillac is frankly unpretentious cooperative-made wine that scarcely merits the dignity of an Appellation Contrôlée.

Just to the west between the Tarn and Garonne the Côtes du Frontonnais used to be simply the local wine of Toulouse. But enterprise has moved in here, led by the Château Bellevue-La-Forêt, to make of its native Négrette grapes, mixed with Cabernet, Syrah and Gamay, a notable red, limpid and fruity. Fronton and Villaudric are the leading communes.

North of Armagnac on the left bank of the Garonne lies the appellation Côtes de Buzet, whose production, from vineyards scattered over 27 communes of orchard and farm, is in the hands of one well-organized cooperative. Its top wine, Cuvée Napoleon, stands comparison with a Médoc or Graves of good quality. The VDQS Côtes du Marmandais, to the north, also has a very good cooperative (at Cocumont); so indeed does the AC Côtes de Duras, north again, whose largely Sauvignon white is comparable with Entre-Deux-Mers, although its red is more like that of its eastern neighbour, Bergerac.

The remaining wines on this map lie in the Basque province of Béarn, which has a general appellation to cover its red, white and rosé wines of a certain quality from vineyards outside its two best-known wine centres, Madiran and Jurançon.

The Madiran vineyards lie on the hills along the left bank of the river Adour, just south of the best section of Armagnac. A local red grape, the Tannat, is well named for the dark and tannic, rude but vigorous wines it makes. Twenty months is the minimum barrel-ageing period, and when the wines are bottled they are

still harsh. But after seven or eight years Madiran is admirable; full of flavour, fluid and lively. The Château d'Aydie is a good example.

Jurançon remains a name to conjure with, although few people have ever tasted the reason why. These steep Pyrenean foothills, with Pau as their market place, used to make France's best sweet wines, comparable to Sauternes or the rarities of the Loire.

Today production is a fraction of what it was, and the high risk of picking grapes as late as November, necessary for *vin liquoreux* has led most growers to make dry wine. The dry white still has richness of flavour allied to high acidity, but it is more of a historical curiosity than a gastronomic resource.

The tiny appellation of Irouléguy is the final Basque bastion, doggedly making rosé, red and white wines of the local grapes, the Tannat included. The rosé label carries what might well be a Basque rallying cry – Hotx Hotxa Edan. Alas, it only means 'Chill before serving'.

The ancient hillside ('coteaux') vineyards of the southwest produce all the good wine of the region. They suffered a terrible decline after phylloxera, but their reputation is growing again today.

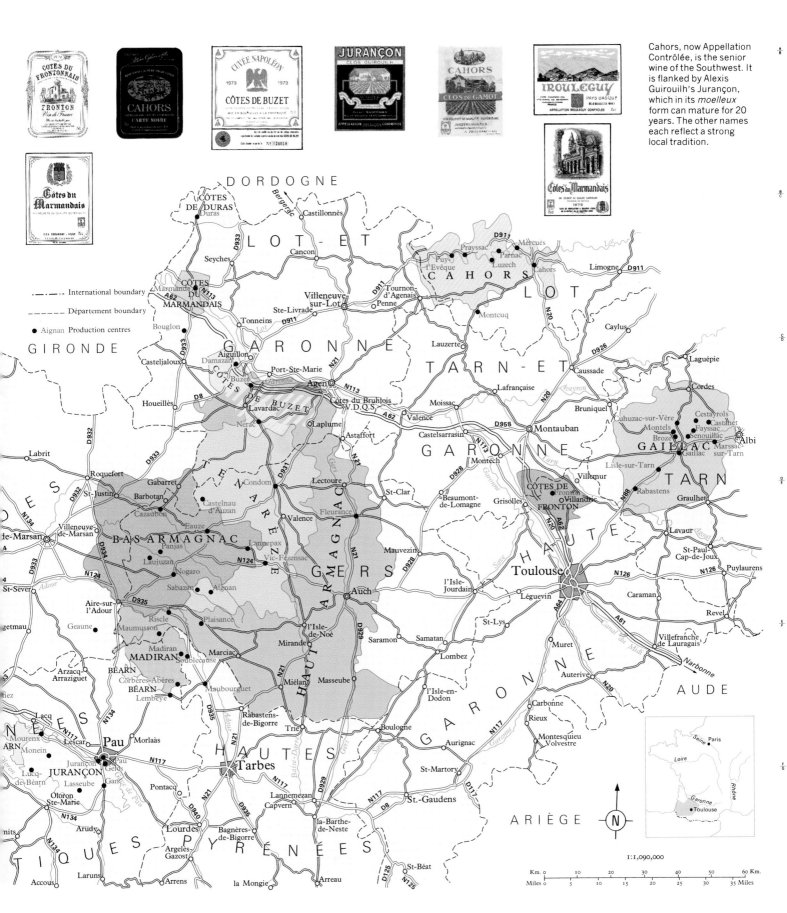

Cahors, now Appellation Contrôlée, is the senior wine of the Southwest. It is flanked by Alexis Guirouilh's Jurançon, which in its *moelleux* form can mature for 20 years. The other names each reflect a strong local tradition.

Vins de Pays

France has a way of producing, even in corners that have little contact with the outside world, wines that are better than any but the best from the rest of Europe. She is intensely aware of her 'little' wines, and through the corps of inspectors of her Institut National des Appellations d'Origine is constantly feeling their pulses, rather like a coach keeping an eye on the colts team.

The appellation system evolved by degrees in the 1920s and 30s. In 1949 it was followed by the creation of a second rank: Vins Délimités de Qualité Supérieure. VDQS wines have advanced steadily since their recognition. Many have already been promoted to AC. It is a fair bet that eventually almost all of them will.

Meanwhile there remained on the statute book an early version of the appellation laws known as *appellation simple*. Whereas AC regulations stipulate not only the area and the grape variety but maximum quantities, minimum strengths, methods of pruning and much else besides, AS wines needed only to be grown from tolerated grapes in recognized regions. An ordinary table wine could be labelled with a regional name but nobody paid much attention. No AS wine had enough of a reputation to command more than the basic commodity price.

The years 1973–79, however, saw a series of ordinances to give status and definition to the more identifiable of these 'table' wines, and at the same time the creation of a new authority, the Office National Interprofessionnel des Vins de Table, to look after them.

In the summer of 1976 a list of 75 Vins de Pays appeared – a list that reads like poetry to anyone with a feeling for the French countryside: Vals, Coteaux and Monts, Gorges and Pays, Marches and Vicomtes, Balmes and Fiefs. Who could resist Vallée du Paradis, Cucugnan, L'Ile de Beauté, Mont Bouquet?

The list in fact divides into three categories: local, commune or district names, names of *départements*, and names of regions as vast as the whole of the Loire valley.

It is frankly admitted that some of these names have more validity than others. Some, in fact, have scarcely been used. They are, on the other hand, a challenge and a rallying point for growers who want to build on their local traditions. It is probable that the best Vins de Pays will advance to VDQS and even AC rank in time.

The controls on Vins de Pays quality are most stringent for district names, least for regional names. But all include a maximum crop (of from 70 to 90 hectolitres per hectare) and minimum natural alcohol levels, and lay down appropriate upper and lower limits for acidity and other analysable components. The wines have to be approved by a tasting panel – which is not a requirement for, for example, German Tafelwein. And they have to be made from grape varieties specified as recommended area by area (or from the 'noble' varieties).

The list has grown since 1976 to no less than 92 'Vins de pays de zone' (or district), 45 departmental vins de pays, and three all-embracing regional names. The map shows the current situation.

Ardèche
1 Coteaux de l'Ardèche
Aude
2 Coteaux Cathares
3 Coteaux de la Cabrerisse
4 Coteaux de la Cité de Carcassonne
5 Coteaux de Miramont
6 Coteaux de Narbonne
7 Coteaux de Peyriac (also in Hérault)
8 Coteaux du Lézignanais
9 Coteaux du Littoral Audois
10 Coteaux du Termenès
11 Côtes de Lastours
12 Côtes de Pérignan
13 Côtes de Prouille
14 Cucugnan
15 Hauterive en Pays d'Aude (also includes 3, 20, 21)
16 Haute Vallée de l'Aude
17 Hauts de Badens
18 Val de Cesse
19 Val de Dagne
20 Val d'Orbieu
21 Vallée du Paradis
Aveyron
22 Gorges et Côtes de Millau
Bouches-du-Rhône
23 Petite Crau

Charente/Charente-Maritime
24 Charentais
Cher/Indre
25 Coteaux du Cher et de l'Arnon
Corsica
26 Ile de Beauté (not on map)
Drôme
27 Collines Rhodaniennes (also in Ardèche, Isère, Loire, Rhône)
28 Comté de Grignan
29 Coteaux des Baronnies

Gard
30 Coteaux Cevenols
31 Coteaux de Cèze
32 Coteaux du Pont du Gard
33 Coteaux du Salavès
34 Coteaux Flaviens
35 Côtes du Vidourle
36 Mont Bouquet
37 Sables du Golfe du Lion
38 Serre de Coiran
39 Uzège
40 Vaunage
41 Vistrenque

Gers
42 Côtes de Gascogne (includes 43 and 44)
43 Côtes de Montestruc
44 Côtes du Condomois (also in Lot-et-Garonne)
Hautes-Pyrénées
45 Bigorre

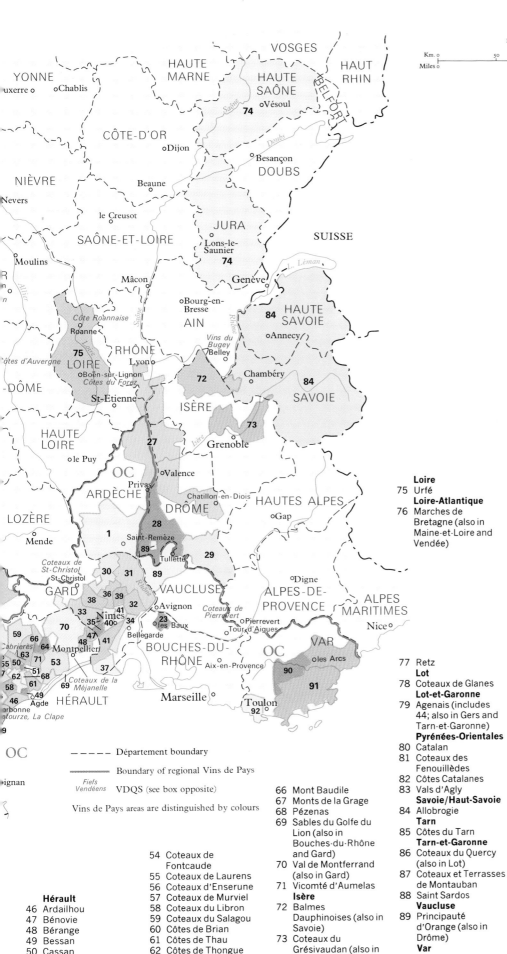

VDQS

France's VDQS wines (Vins Délimités de Qualité Supérieure) are marked on the general map of France on page 59, and some are also shown on larger-scale maps.

Those that do not appear in more detail elsewhere are shown on this map and listed below with their principal types of wine.

SAVOIE

Vins du Bugey: Roussette white, similar to Crépy, etc. Very light red, locally good. (Bugey plus a village name indicates slightly higher strength and, theoretically, quality.)

LOIRE VALLEY AND CENTRAL FRANCE

Châteaumeillant: grapey Gamay red, very pale *vin gris*.
Côte Roannaise: light red, of some character.
Côtes d'Auvergne: fresh Gamay red (Chanturgues) and rosé (Corent).
Côtes du Forez: Gamay red like light Beaujolais.
Fiefs Vendéens: white Muscadet alternatives, plus some red and rosé, from the Loire estuary.
St-Pourçain: attractive dry white; adequate red and rosé.
Vins du Thouarsais: sweetish white, light red and rosé.
Vins du Haut-Poitou: excellent dry whites, especially Sauvignon, plus Gamay rosé.

LANGUEDOC-ROUSSILLON AND PROVENCE

Cabardès: emerging rustic red and rosé.
Coteaux de Pierrevert: an expanding district; Provençal type wines.
Coteaux de St-Christol: light reds.
Coteaux de la Méjanelle: reds of some interest.
Côtes de la Malepère: above-average reds from Cabernets, Grenache and Syrah.
Quatourze: solid, full Midi reds.

SOUTHWEST

Côtes de St-Mont: reds based on Tannat, the Madiran grape.
Vins d'Entraygues et du Fel: very small area; light red and rosé, little white.
Vins d'Estaing: good reds and dry white.
Vins de Lavilledieu: also tiny; pleasant light red wine.
Vins de Marcillac: also tiny, similar wine.
Vins du Tursan: whites from a local grape plus reds of Tannat and Cabernet.

Three VDQS areas (both in Lorraine) appear only on the general map of France on page 59. These are:
Côtes de Toul and Vin de la Moselle: very pale *vin gris* and rather acid red. The grapes of this region used to be taken to Champagne, where they disappeared.
Sauvignon de St-Bris: small but prosperous neighbour to Chablis.

- - - - - - Département boundary

————— Boundary of regional Vins de Pays

Fiefs Vendéens VDQS (see box opposite)

Vins de Pays areas are distinguished by colours

Loire
75 Urfé
Loire-Atlantique
76 Marches de Bretagne (also in Maine-et-Loire and Vendée)

77 Retz
Lot
78 Coteaux de Glanes
Lot-et-Garonne
79 Agenais (includes 44; also in Gers and Tarn-et-Garonne)
Pyrénées-Orientales
80 Catalan
81 Coteaux des Fenouillèdes
82 Côtes Catalanes
83 Vals d'Agly
Savoie/Haut-Savoie
84 Allobrogie
Tarn
85 Côtes du Tarn
Tarn-et-Garonne
86 Coteaux du Quercy (also in Lot)
87 Coteaux et Terrasses de Montauban
88 Saint Sardos
Vaucluse
89 Principauté d'Orange (also in Drôme)
Var
90 Argens
91 Les Maures
92 Mont Caume

Hérault
46 Ardailhou
47 Bénovie
48 Bérange
49 Bessan
50 Cassan
51 Caux
52 Cessenon
53 Collines de La Moure
54 Coteaux de Fontcaude
55 Coteaux de Laurens
56 Coteaux d'Enserune
57 Coteaux de Murviel
58 Coteaux du Libron
59 Coteaux du Salagou
60 Côtes de Brian
61 Côtes de Thau
62 Côtes de Thongue
63 Côtes du Ceressou
64 Gorges de l'Hérault
65 Haute Vallée de l'Orb
66 Mont Baudile
67 Monts de la Grage
68 Pézenas
69 Sables du Golfe du Lion (also in Bouches-du-Rhône and Gard)
70 Val de Montferrand (also in Gard)
71 Vicomté d'Aumelas
Isère
72 Balmes Dauphinoises (also in Savoie)
73 Coteaux du Grésivaudan (also in Savoie)
Jura/Haut-Saône
74 Franche-Comté

Corsica

If Corsican wines were respected in Europe in the 18th and 19th centuries, the dreaded phylloxera completely obliterated their reputation. It has taken them nearly a century to struggle back into recognition. A residual traditional vineyard produced strong wines for local use, but nothing much happened in France's savagely beautiful island *département* until the 1960s, and the parting of France with her colony, Algeria – her chief source of high-strength blending wine.

Within 12 years Corsica's vineyard area quadrupled, almost entirely with bulk-producing vines planted on the eastern plains (in a region then notorious for its malarial mosquitoes). A certain amount of this hasty planting has since been pulled out again, but 90% of Corsican wine is still destined for blending, with a maximum ambition of becoming a vin de pays and carrying the island's seductive *nom de verre*, L'Ile de Beauté.

The remaining ten percent, however, is rediscovering its birthright in the hardy native varieties of grape and the rocky hillsides where they grow best. The classic Corsican red grape is the Sciacarello, grown principally on the west coast at Ajaccio, the capital, and in the Sartènais area around Propriano, to make highly drinkable red and rosé which remains lively despite its high alcohol content. The Niellucio, usually cited as the other original Corsican red grape, is in fact the Sangiovese of Chianti, which seems to be a relatively recent arrival on the island. Nonetheless it dominates the northern appellation of Patrimonio, the first full AC to be created in Corsica (in 1968) and still one of the best. Alone on the impressively craggy island it has chalky soil, which gives firm Rhônish reds, well-balanced whites and rich muscat Vin Doux Naturel of high quality. Sweet wines, of Muscat, Malvoisie or white Vermentino, are also the speciality of Cap Corse to the north. Certain good judges rate the Muscatellu of Rogliano, Cap Corse, as the finest of all French muscats, above Beaumes de Venise and Frontignan. Their appellation is Coteaux de Cap Corse. Vermentino also produces a much-appreciated dry white wine in the same area.

The AC Calvi in the northwest uses Sciacarello, Niellucio and Vermentino for heady table wines, while Figari and Porto Vecchio do the same in the southeast. The Figari vineyards surround Bonifacio, the ferry-port that links Corsica with Sardinia. It is thirsty-looking country with wines that could scarcely be called thirst-quenching. Porto Vecchio seems to have come further in producing wines, particularly whites, with a degree of modern fruity crispness.

In comparison with these concentrated wines of traditional character, the regular Vin de Corse, the general appellation used mainly around Aléria and Ghisonaccia on the east coast, is less likely to produce a memorable bottle.

In many ways Corsican wine can be compared with Provençal. The rosé in both cases is commonly the best. In both it tends to be overstrong. Both have found huge new markets waiting for their wines, eager to find in them the elusive smell of the hot herbs of the maquis.

Corsica's new vineyards in the east and south were planted by growers from Algeria in the 1960s. The old ones are starkly different: tight terraces on the rugged hills.

Patrimonio was Corsica's only Appellation Contrôlée wine until 1976. Its strong (12.5°) red, rosés and white are still among the island's best wines. Muscat can be outstanding.

PATRIMONIO Appellation Contrôlée

☐ Wine-producing area

1:1,585,000

Km. 0   10   20   30   40   50 Km.

Miles 0   10   20   30 Miles

Germany

Germany

Germany's best vineyards lie as far north as grapes can be persuaded to ripen. They lie on land unfit for normal agriculture: if they were not there, forest and bare mountain would take their place. All in all their chances of giving the world's best white wine look slim. And yet on occasion they do, and stamp it with a style that no one, anywhere, can imitate.

Their secret is the balance of sugar against acidity. Sugar without acid would be flat; acid without sugar would be sharp. In good years, when the equation works out right, the two are so finely counterpoised that they have the inevitability of great art. They provide a stage for a mingling of essences from the grape and the ground, an ensemble customarily described in the single word 'breed'. It is all the more apparent in German wines because they are low in alcohol; there is less body in the background; nuances of flavour are brilliantly distinct; more often than not there is a great canopy of bouquet.

The best such wines are so full of character and charm, and if the word does not sound too pedantic, interest, that they are best enjoyed, unlike French wines, alone rather than with food. A bottle of a Spätlese or Auslese from the Mosel or Rheingau is a complete experience from which food, however good it may be, can only detract.

Knowing how passionately wine lovers will follow his successes and failures, sensing vividly the drama in his battle to get the best from his grapes and from the ground he works, a German grower will treat his different barrels, from one year and one vineyard, as different wines. 'Best barrel' is not empty sales talk; cask numbers are matters for emotion. In France even Château d'Yquem 'equalizes' all the barrels of one year to make one standard wine – even if standard is hardly the word for it.

This is one side of the picture: the connoisseur's side. In Germany he is catered for as nowhere else in the world. On the other hand, the majority of German wine is blended if necessary, and gives uncomplicated pleasure.

Germany's vineyards lie along the river Rhine and its tributaries. They are scant in the extreme south and thickest near the French border in Rheinland-Pfalz. All the important areas are mapped on the following pages.

The German wine label, the most explicit on earth in the case of the higher qualities of wine, is explained in detail on page 166.

The Riesling (see page 22) is the great grape of Germany; virtually all the best German wines are made from it and it is planted to the exclusion of almost everything else in the best sites of Mosel, Saar, Ruwer, Rheingau, Nahe and Rheinpfalz (the Palatinate).

The price of quality, however, is limited quantity, and the dangers inherent in a grape that ripens late. For larger and less risky production, Germany has turned to the Müller-Thurgau, a supposed cross made a century ago between Riesling and Silvaner, formerly the most-planted grape, but now in retreat. Müller-Thurgau very rarely rises to heights of quality, except in late-harvested sweet wines. It lacks the lovely clean 'nerve', the backbone of fruity acidity (and the blossoming bouquet) of Germany's best wine. Nonetheless, today it covers 61,000 acres (24,000 hectares), while Riesling is only planted on three-quarters as much land. Middle-quality German wines that do not mention another grape on the label can be assumed to be made (at least mainly) from Müller-Thurgau.

Silvaner has fallen far behind, to some 22,000 acres (9,000 hectares). These include, however, the very best sites in Franken, where it makes better wine than Riesling, and some excellent ones in Rheinhessen and Baden. Silvaner is not undemanding, but it can be excellent.

New varieties (see page 24) have had a great vogue, and are still prominent in second-level areas, particularly in Rheinhessen and Rheinpfalz. Two factors have dampened some of the early enthusiasm for them: their sometimes strident, over-obvious flavours, and experience of very cold winters, when they have proved less hardy than the Riesling.

Pinot Noir (known as Spätburgunder – the late Burgundy) and the commoner Portugieser and, in Württemberg, Trollinger, are the main sources of red wine. Only the valley of the Ahr near Bonn specializes in red wine alone.

German wine laws do not classify vineyards as the French do. Any vineyard in Germany can, in theory, produce top-class wine. The law concerns itself instead with ripeness: Germany's only classification is by 'must weight', the measure of sugar in the grapes at harvest time. The system is explained on page 24.

Nobody truly pretends, however, that all German vineyards are equally well sited, with equally splendid soil. The Quality Factor maps on the next pages outline some of the physical considerations. The detailed maps that follow focus on those regions where millennia of experience have taught growers to plant the best varieties, and where premiums are paid for the names of specific sites. Once in a while a first-class wine will emerge from an unexpected quarter. But these are Germany's classic sites: her pride and innocent joy.

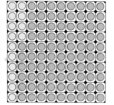
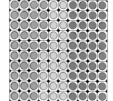

○ GERMANY ○ FRANCE
Germany's wine production averages 10 million hectolitres a year — only one-seventh that of France.

● GREAT BRITAIN ○ USA
Exports total more than 2m. hl a year and are rising. Great Britain taking 35 %, and the US, 25 %, are the biggest customers.

○ WHITE ○ RED
Almost 87 % of German wine is white. Red wine, mainly from the Ahr and Württemberg, is only produced for local consumption.

Germany consumed 16.4m. hl of wine in 1983: some 26.5 litres per head of population. Individual consumption is increasing, in contrast to France and Italy where it is decreasing.

The price for wine received by the grower varies from region to region, but the average in the large (and good) harvest of 1983 was DM 83 per 100 litres, down from DM 129 in 1982 and DM 176 in 1981.

Ten years ago Germany imported eight times as much as she exported. With recent sales successes the figure is now only four times as much.

EXPORTS
IMPORTS

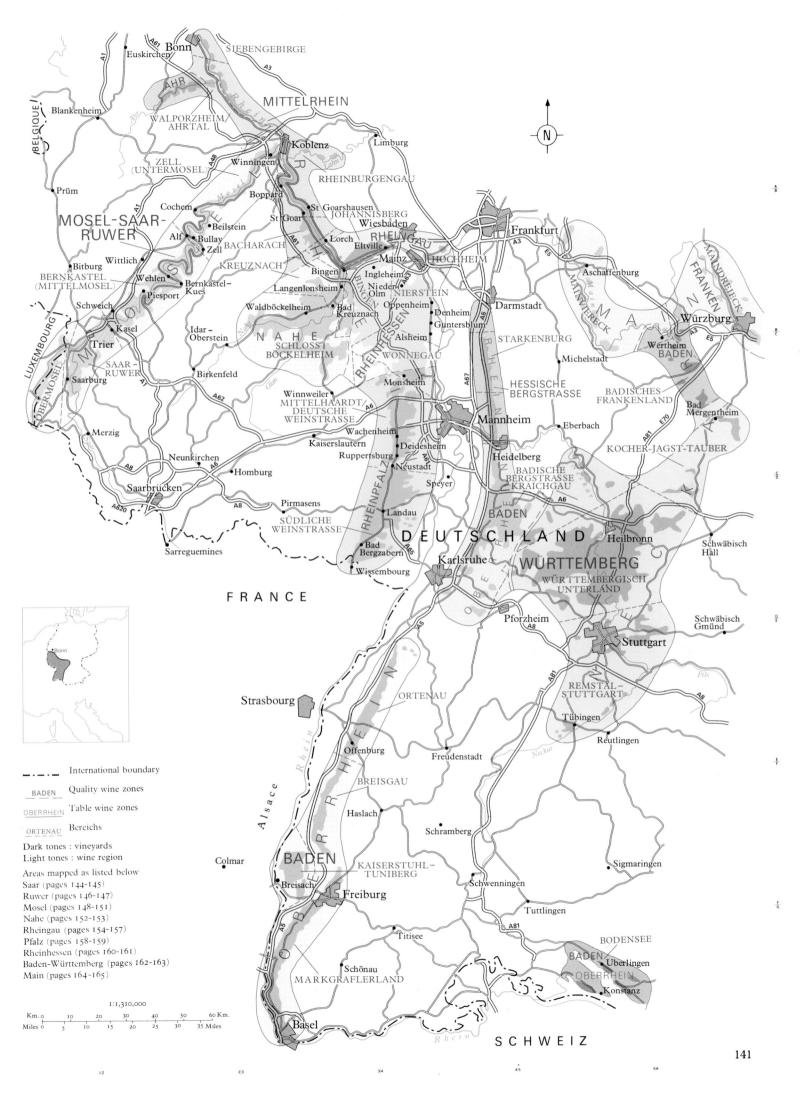

BELGIQUE

Euskirchen
Bonn
A61
A1
SIEBENGEBIRGE
A3
AHR
Blankenheim
WALPORZHEIM/
AHRTAL
MITTELRHEIN
Prüm
ZELL
(UNTERMOSEL)
Koblenz
Winningen
Limburg
A48
RHEINBURGENGAU
MOSEL-SAAR-
RUWER
Cochem
Boppard
St Goarshausen
JOHANNISBERG
Beilstein
St Goar
Wiesbaden
Frankfurt
Alf
Bullay
Lorch
RHEINGAU
Bitburg
Zell
BACHARACH
Eltville
A3
E5
Wittlich
KREUZNACH
Bingen
Mainz
HOCHHEIM
Aschaffenburg
Wehlen
Bernkastel-
Kues
Langenlonsheim
Ingleheim
Nieder-
Olm
NIERSTEIN
Darmstadt
Würzburg
BERNKASTEL
(MITTELMOSEL)
Piesport
Waldböckelheim
Bad
Kreuznach
Oppenheim
Denheim
STARKENBURG
Wertheim
BADEN
Schweich
Idar-
Oberstein
NAHE
RHEINHESSEN
Alsheim
Guntersblum
Michelstadt
BADISCHES
FRANKENLAND
LUXEMBOURG
Kasel
SCHLOSS
BÖCKELHEIM
WONNEGAU
HESSISCHE
BERGSTRASSE
Trier
Saarburg
Birkenfeld
Monsheim
Mannheim
Eberbach
Bad
Mergentheim
SAAR-
RUWER
A62
Winnweiler
MITTELHAARDT
DEUTSCHE
WEINSTRASSE
A6
Heidelberg
KOCHER-JAGST-TAUBER
Merzig
Wachenheim
Kaiserslautern
Deidesheim
BADISCHE
BERGSTRASSE
KRAICHGAU
Neunkirchen
A6
Homburg
Ruppertsburg
Neustadt
Speyer
Schwäbisch
Hall
Saarbrücken
RHEINPFALZ
Landau
BADEN
DEUTSCHLAND
Heilbronn
A8
Pirmasens
SÜDLICHE
WEINSTRASSE
A65
WÜRTTEMBERG
WÜRTTEMBERGISCH
UNTERLAND
Sarreguemines
Bad
Bergzabern
Karlsruhe
Pforzheim
Schwäbisch
Gmünd
Wissembourg
A5
A8
Stuttgart
FRANCE
REMSTAL-
STUTTGART
A81
Fils
Strasbourg
ORTENAU
Tübingen
Reutlingen
Offenburg
Freudenstadt
Neckar
BREISGAU
Haslach
Schramberg
Sigmaringen
Colmar
Schwenningen
BADEN
KAISERSTUHL-
TUNIBERG
Tuttlingen
A81
Breisach
Freiburg
Alsace
Titisee
BODENSEE
BADEN
Schönau
Überlingen
MARKGRÄFLERLAND
OBERRHEIN
Konstanz
Basel
Rhein
SCHWEIZ

International boundary

BADEN   Quality wine zones

OBERRHEIN Table wine zones

ORTENAU   Bereichs

Dark tones : vineyards

Light tones : wine region

Areas mapped as listed below
Saar (pages 144-145)
Ruwer (pages 146-147)
Mosel (pages 148-151)
Nahe (pages 152-153)
Rheingau (pages 154-157)
Pfalz (pages 158-159)
Rheinhessen (pages 160-161)
Baden-Württemberg (pages 162-163)
Main (pages 164-165)

1:1,310,000

Km. 0 10 20 30 40 50 60 Km.

Miles 0   5   10   15   20   25   30   35 Miles

141

Germany: The Quality Factor

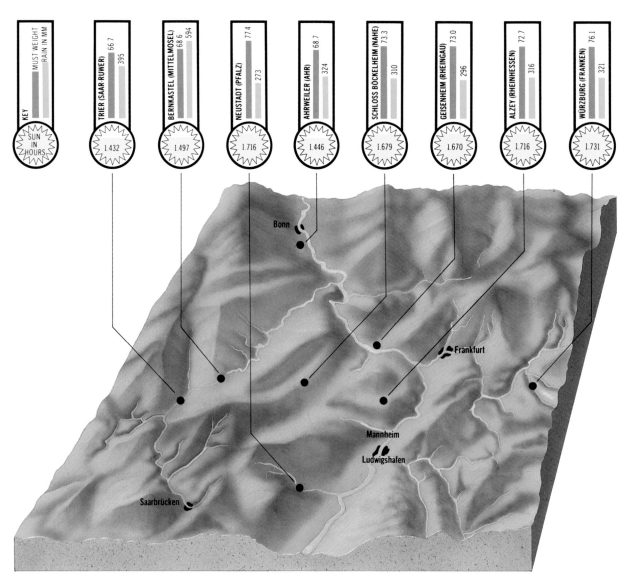

KEY — MUST WEIGHT / RAIN IN MM — SUN IN HOURS

Region	Must weight	Rain in mm	Sun in hours
TRIER (SAAR-RUWER)	66.7	395	1.432
BERNKASTEL (MITTELMOSEL)	68.6	594	1.497
NEUSTADT (PFALZ)	77.4	273	1.716
AHRWEILER (AHR)	68.7	324	1.446
SCHLOSS BÖCKELHEIM (NAHE)	73.3	310	1.679
GEISENHEIM (RHEINGAU)	73.0	296	1.670
ALZEY (RHEINHESSEN)	72.7	316	1.716
WÜRZBURG (FRANKEN)	76.1	321	1.731

Bonn — Frankfurt — Mannheim — Ludwigshafen — Saarbrücken

Left: the weather is the biggest single quality factor in Germany. This map shows the hours of sunshine and millimetres of rainfall from May to October, region by region, with the resulting ripeness of the grapes, averaged over ten years. Ripeness is measured by 'must weight': the higher the figure, the more sugar in the must.

Right: Germany's greatest wine area analysed: the Rheingau's soil, sunshine, frost and wind, all major factors affecting the quality of the wine, are recorded in these maps prepared by the Hessische Landesamt für Bodenforschung, Wiesbaden. They are reproduced with their kind permission. The significance of the maps is discussed below. The bottom map is the first attempt at classifying German winegrowing land, based on the findings in the maps above.

If in Burgundy the emphasis for the study of quality is on the soil and the microclimate, and in Bordeaux on the physical makeup of the soil affecting drainage, in Germany it centres on the weather. Every conceivable aspect of weather is examined for its possible effect on the specific gravity of the grape juice, or 'must weight': in other words, on the amount of sugar in the grapes.

The map above shows sunshine and rainfall in the growing season for the principal wine regions of Germany. On the page opposite are some of the findings of perhaps the most elaborate investigation ever mounted into wine quality. The government of Hesse has spent vast sums and many years studying the Rheingau – the state's best vineyard and probably the best in Germany.

They have recorded the soil (which changes abruptly and often) in great detail, and then the amounts of sunshine, wind, late frost (in May; which can interfere with flowering) and early frost (in September; which can kill the leaves and stop the grapes ripening: map not shown) that every spot of ground could expect. Finally, with a daring all too rare among scientists,

they plotted the area where the wine *should* be best (the last map).

Certain sites do emerge with a distinctive tint in almost every map. The Rüdesheimer Berg at the western end of the Rheingau is the only one that achieves 'excellent' in the aptitude test (map 5). But a consistent string of vineyards at a certain altitude is noticeable on each map. They happen to include most of the highest priced of the Rheingau. The Rüdesheimer Berg, Schloss Johannisberg, Schloss Vollrads, Steinberg, the southern slopes of Kiedrich and Rauenthal are among them. And curiously the most consistently noticeable down by the river is also a very expensive vineyard – Markobrunn, between Hattenheim and Erbach.

Much can be learned by comparing these maps with those on pages 154–157. But each region of Germany, of course, has its own peculiar interaction of soil and climate.

Since these maps were published, research has continued in even greater detail to define precise zones of soil and microclimate. The ideal vine and the ideal method of pruning, training and manuring is then recommended.

A definitive map of a small part of the Rheingau behind Mittelheim and Oestrich (including Schloss Vollrads) has been published, and the work continues. Some of the latest findings are explored in more detail on pages 20–21.

Rainfall is comparatively light in the Rheingau. Drainage is not a big quality factor – indeed there are places (Rüdesheim is one) that suffer from drought in dry years. Since winter rain sinks right in and summer showers run off quickly, the vines tend to root near the surface, and are thus particularly vulnerable to rain just before picking – water that the vine immediately pumps into the grapes. The must weight can easily be lowered by 10° by one downpour at the last moment. If frost and rain hold off long enough and Edelfäule (noble rot) takes a hold, the grapes go on sweetening until enormous must weights of as much as double the normal are recorded.

As a last resort, if the grapes do freeze on the vine, which is not uncommon, the grower can pick and press them frozen. The Eiswein (ice wine) he makes may not be as good as a Trockenbeerenauslese would have been. But there are worse risks in winegrowing.

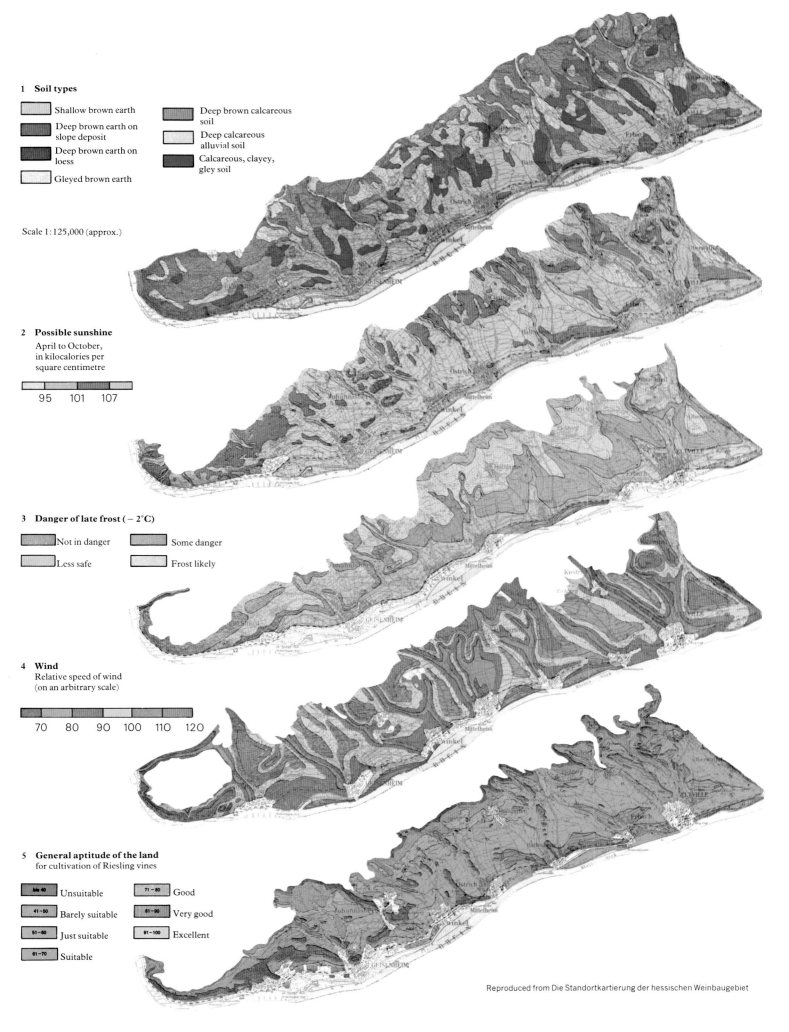

1 Soil types

- Shallow brown earth
- Deep brown earth on slope deposit
- Deep brown earth on loess
- Gleyed brown earth
- Deep brown calcareous soil
- Deep calcareous alluvial soil
- Calcareous, clayey, gley soil

Scale 1:125,000 (approx.)

2 Possible sunshine
April to October, in kilocalories per square centimetre

95   101   107

3 Danger of late frost (– 2°C)

- Not in danger
- Less safe
- Some danger
- Frost likely

4 Wind
Relative speed of wind (on an arbitrary scale)

70   80   90   100   110   120

5 General aptitude of the land
for cultivation of Riesling vines

- bis 40 — Unsuitable
- 41–50 — Barely suitable
- 51–60 — Just suitable
- 61–70 — Suitable
- 71–80 — Good
- 81–90 — Very good
- 91–100 — Excellent

Reproduced from Die Standortkartierung der hessischen Weinbaugebiet

143

The Saar

Below and right: more dignified than dashing, the labels of some of the most illustrious Saar estates. The label with the black eagle is that of the State Domain, founded in 1896 by the King of Prussia.

The dignified old manor house of Scharzhof stands at the foot of Wiltingen's Scharzhofberg. In its cellars lie some of the world's most exquisite steely-sweet Rieslings.

German wine with its problems and its triumphs is epitomized nowhere better than in the valley of the Mosel's tributary, the Saar. The battle for sugar in the grapes rages fiercest in this cold corner of the country. It is only won perhaps three or four years in ten. Yet those years give one of the world's superlative white wines; every mouthful a cause for rejoicing and wonder.

A mere 1,500 acres (600 hectares) of vines share the valley with orchard and pasture. It is calm open agricultural country; impossible to believe that only just upstream the blast furnaces of the industrial Saar are at work.

The map shows clearer than any other the way south slopes – here nearly all on banks of hill sidling up to the river – offer the wine-grower his chance of enough sunshine.

As in the best part of the Mosel, the soil is slate and the grape the Riesling. The qualities of Mosel wine: apple-like freshness and bite, a marvellous mingling of honey in the scent and steel in the finish, can find their apogee in Saar wine. If anything the emphasis here (again a question of weather) is more on the steel than the honey.

Unsuccessful vintages make wine so sharp that even the best growers can only sell their produce to the makers of sparkling Sekt, who are looking for something really acid to work on. But when the sun shines and the Riesling ripens and goes on ripening far into October, the great bosomy smell of flowers and honey which it generates would be too lush without the appley emphasis of acidity. Then the Saar comes into its own. It makes sweet wine which you can never tire of. The balance and depth make you sniff and sip and sniff again.

Some sites are better than others. Most are in the hands of rich and ancient estates which can afford to wait for good years and make the most of them. The labels of the principal ones – themselves austere compared with the flowery creations of some parts of Germany – are on these pages. One of the finest state domains operates here, with its headquarters in the nearby old Roman wine city of Trier. Its holdings in Ockfen (the Domäne house in the vines can be seen on the map) and in Serrig are celebrated. That at Serrig is unusual in having been created by the Prussian State from virgin woodland at the turn of the century: an optimistic move since Serrig has even more uncertain weather than the rest of the Saar. It takes a long golden autumn . . . but then it justifies everything.

The most famous estate of the Saar is that of Egon Müller, whose house appears on the map as Scharzhof at the foot of the Scharzhofberg in Wiltingen. Among the other owners of parts of the Scharzhofberg is the cathedral of Trier ('Hohe Domkirche'), which adds the word Dom before the names of its vineyards. Egon Müller also manages the Le Gallais estate, with the famous Braune Kupp vineyard at the other end of Wiltingen. Ayler Kupp and Herrenberger, Ockfener Bockstein and Herrenberg, Wawerner Ritterpfad and the Falkensteiner Hofberg above Niedermennig are all renowned . . . for their good vintages. The Grosslage name for the whole of the Saar is (Wiltinger) Scharzberg – unfortunately easy to confuse with the great Scharzhofberg.

Many of the vineyards of the Mosel, and particularly the Saar, belong to a group of religious and charitable bodies in Trier. The Friedrich-Wilhelm-Gymnasium (Karl Marx's old school); the Bischöfliches Konvikt (a Catholic boarding school); the Bischöfliches Priesterseminar (a college for priests); the Vereinigte Hospitien (an almshouse) and the cathedral are all important winegrowers. The two Bischöfliches and the cathedral operate their total of 260 acres (105 hectares) of vineyards, here and in the Middle Mosel, together as the Vereinigte Bischöfliches Weingut. In their broad, dark, damp cellars in the city, one has the feeling that wine is itself an act of charity rather than mere vulgar trade.

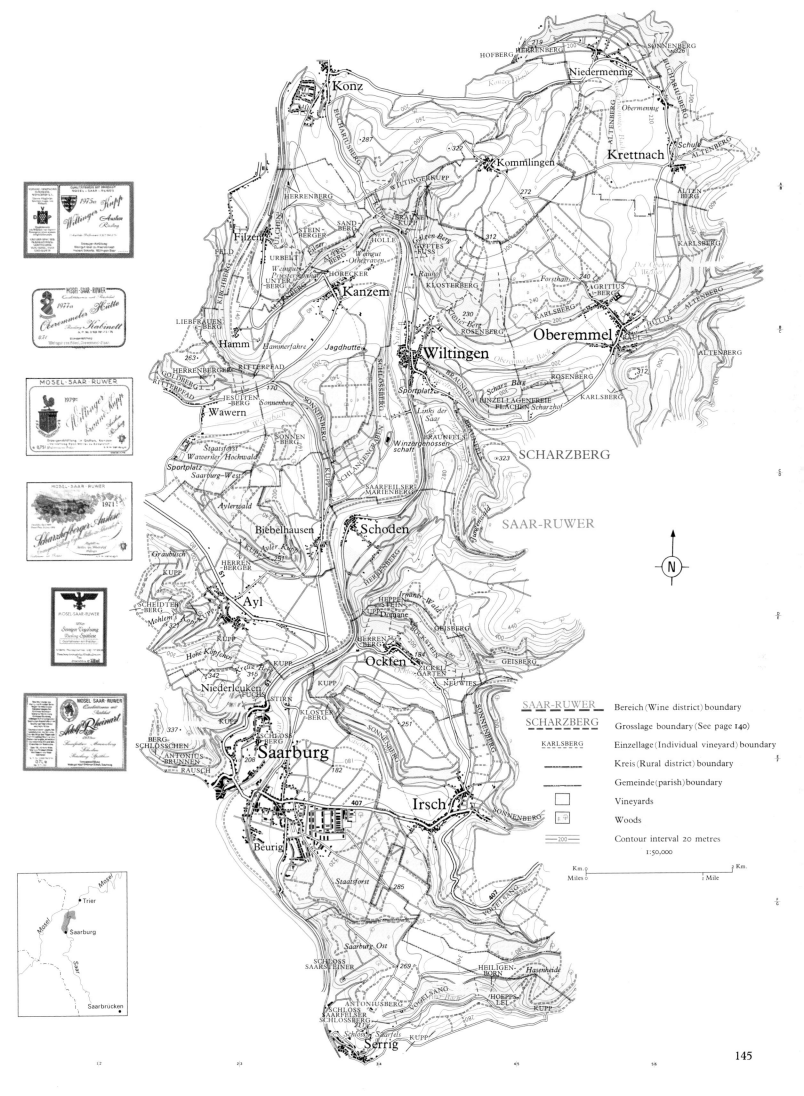

The Ruwer

The Ruwer is a mere stream. Its vineyards add up to about half those of one Côte d'Or commune. In many years its wine is unsatisfactory; faint and sharp. Yet like the Saar, when conditions are right it performs a miracle: its wines are Germany's most delicate; gentle yet infinitely fine and full of subtlety.

Waldrach, the first wine village, makes good light wine but rarely more. Kasel is more important. The von Kesselstatt estate and the Bischöfliches Weingut of Trier have holdings here. There are great Kaselers in hot years.

Mertesdorf and Eitelsbach could not be called famous names; but each has one supreme vineyard, wholly owned by one of the world's best winegrowers. Mertesdorf's Maximin Grünhaus stands obliquely to the left bank of the river, with the manor house, formerly monastic property, at its foot. The greater part of its hill of vines is called Herrenberg; the top part Abtsberg (for the abbot) and the less-well-sited part Bruderberg (for the brothers).

Across the stream Karthäuserhofberg echoes its situation, again with an old monastic building, now the manor house, below. The subdivisions of this hill are on the map.

The city of Trier lies 5 miles (8 kilometres) away up the Mosel. Included in the city limits is the isolated clearing of Avelsbach, belonging to the State Domain and Trier Cathedral, as well as the famous old Thiergarten. Avelsbach wine is like that of the Ruwer; perhaps even more perfumed and forthcoming.

Above: the beautiful old-fashioned label and (below) the manor of Maximin Grünhaus from its vineyard. In the background is Kasel and, beyond, Waldrach.

Above: the unusual label of Eitelsbacher
Karthäuserhofberg goes around the neck of the slim
green bottle; there is no normal rectangular label on
the body.

Right, above and below: estates on the Ruwer include
Trier Cathedral (top right), which shares the Avelsbach
vineyards with the State Domain. Avelsbach and
Eitelsbach are both officially parts of Trier.

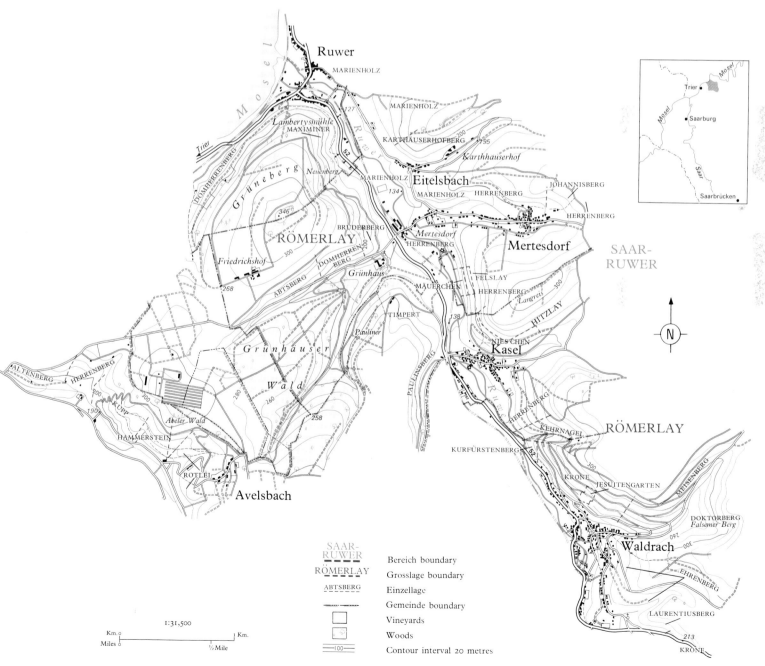

SAAR-
RUWER
RÖMERLAY
ABTSBERG

Bereich boundary
Grosslage boundary
Einzellage
Gemeinde boundary
Vineyards
Woods
Contour interval 20 metres

1:31,500

Km. 0 _____ 1 Km.
Miles 0 _____ ½ Mile

The Middle Mosel: Piesport

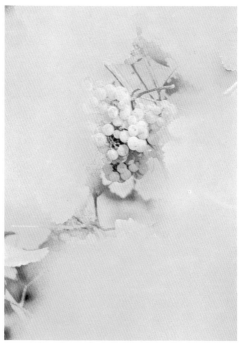

Far left and centre: dark grey slate and golden Riesling grapes are the elements which give Middle Mosel wine its quality. Each vine is staked independently on the vertiginous south-facing slopes above the river.

Left: Piesport is the hub of this upper stretch of the Middle Mosel, giving its famous name to a large proportion of the wine of the area. Growers with the confidence and pride to sell their produce under the names of less-renowned villages (such as Trittenheim, Leiwen or Neumagen) often offer more interesting wine at better value for money.

The river Mosel is acquainted with the reflections of vines all the way from its rising in the Vosges mountains to its union with the Rhine at Koblenz. Light wines of little consequence grow on the French Moselle; in Luxembourg considerable quantities are made, mainly of Rivaner and Elbling: light, often fizzy and very refreshing. But only in the central part of the German Mosel do the spectacular river walls of slate, rising sometimes to more than 700 feet (200 metres) above its course, provide the perfect conditions for the Riesling vine. It is in the central 40 miles (65 kilometres) of the river's snake-like meanderings – which only take it half that distance as the crow flies – that the Mosel's great wine is made.

The wines of the river vary along the banks even more than, say, the wines of Burgundy vary along the Côte d'Or. Given south, south-east or southwest exposure, the steeper the bank the better the wine. It is only because the thin soil here is pure slate, through which rain runs as if through a sieve, that any soil stays in place on near-precipices. The coincidence of quickly drying, stable soil in vineyards which are held up to the sun like toast to a fire is the Mosel's secret.

There is no formal agreement on what constitutes the Middle Mosel. In the maps on these pages we have extended it beyond the central and most famous villages to include several whose wine is often underrated.

The first that we come to is Klüsserath. The Bruderschaft vineyard is immediately typical of a fine Mosel site: a steep bank curving from south to southwest.

The long tongue of land which ends in Trittenheim is almost a cliff where the village of Leiwen jumps the river to claim part of the vineyard of Laurentiuslay, flattening to only a gentle slope before the bend. Down to here the Grosslage name is St Michael.

Trittenheim's best-exposed sites are Apotheke and Altärchen, over the bridge. These are the first vineyards of the Mosel that make wine of real breed. It is always delicate, but not faint. In such a year as 1983, when the wines of the Saar and Ruwer were Germany's best, Trittenheimers come into their own.

The town of Neumagen, a Roman landing place, keeps in its little leafy square a remarkable Roman carving of a Mosel wine ship, laden with barrels and weary galley slaves.

The wine of Dhron, its partner, is better known. Here the Mosel banks fall back as a gentle slope; it is the tributary River Dhron that has the steepest slopes and the best sites; above all Dhroner Hofberger.

Piesport has a standing far above its neighbours. It is the ideal site: a steep amphitheatre facing due south. The name of its Goldtröpf-chen, the slope above and around the village, is world-famous for round but gently honeyed wines, not with great power but with magic fragrance and breed. The vast plantation across the river known as Piesporter Trepp-chen is not in the same class.

Michelsberg is the Grosslage name for this part of the river, from Trittenheim to Min-heim. 'Piesporter Michelsberg', therefore, is not normally Piesporter at all.

Minheim, Wintrich and Kesten can all make fine wines. But there are no perfectly aligned slopes in this stretch, except for the beginning of the great ramp that rises to its full height opposite the village of Brauneberg. In Kesten it is called Paulinshofberg. In Brauneberg it is the Juffer, 100 years ago reckoned the greatest wine of the Mosel, perfectly satisfying the taste of the time for wine that was full-bodied and golden.

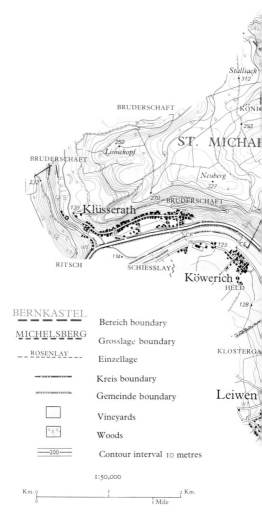

BERNKASTEL

MICHELSBERG

ROSENLAY

	Bereich boundary
	Grosslage boundary
	Einzellage
	Kreis boundary
	Gemeinde boundary
	Vineyards
	Woods
—200—	Contour interval 10 metres

1:50,000

Km. 0   1   2 Km.
0   1 Mile

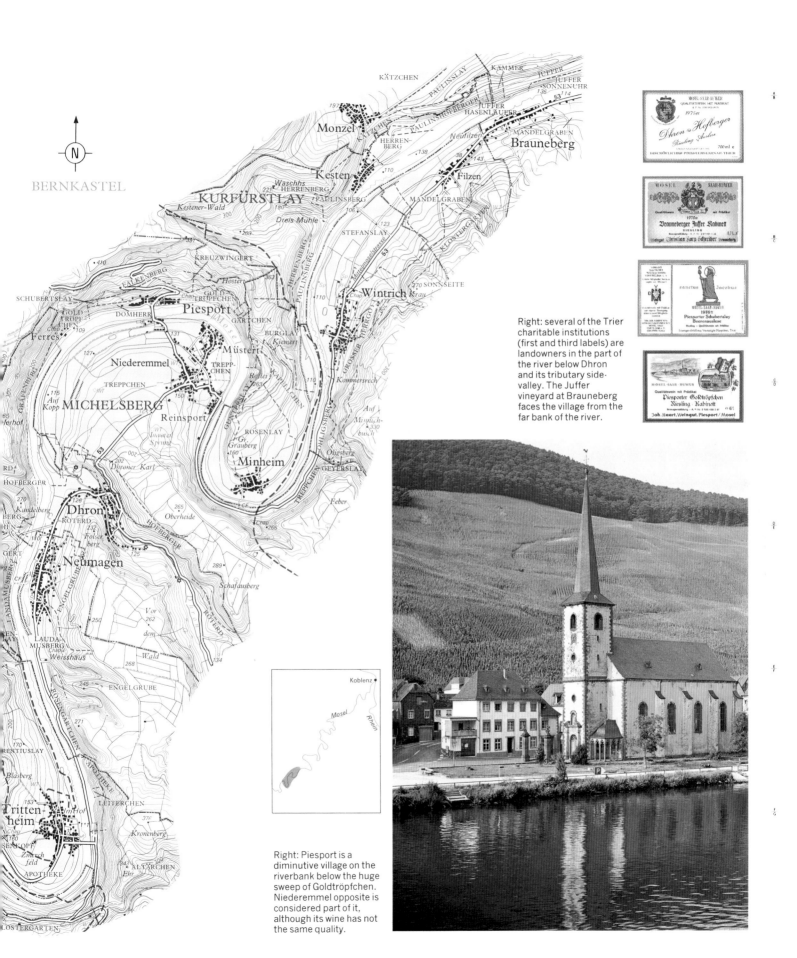

BERNKASTEL

KÄTZCHEN

PAULINSLAY

KAMMER

JUFFER
SONNENUHR

Monzel

Braaneberg

Kesten

Filzen

KURFÜRSTLAY

Kestener-Wald

Dreis Muhle

MANDELGRABEN

STEFANSLAY

KREUZWINGERT

Hostert

Wintrich

SONNSEITE

GOLD
TRÖPFCHEN

Piesport

GÄRTCHEN

SCHUBERTSLAY

DOMHERR

BURGLA

Ferres

GOLD
TRÖPFCHE

Müstert

Kiemert

Niederemmel

TREPP-
CHEN

Kommersrech

MICHELSBERG

Reinsport

ROSENLAY

Gr.
Grauberg

Auf
Minnich-
busch

Minheim

Oligsberg

GEYERSLAY

Feber

Dhron

Oberheide

Neumagen

Schafausberg

LAUDA-
MUSBERG

Weisshaus

ENGELGRUBE

Koblenz

Mosel

Rhein

Trittenheim

Kronenberg

ALTARCHEN

APOTHEKE

Right: several of the Trier
charitable institutions
(first and third labels) are
landowners in the part of
the river below Dhron
and its tributary side-
valley. The Juffer
vineyard at Brauneberg
faces the village from the
far bank of the river.

Right: Piesport is a
diminutive village on the
riverbank below the huge
sweep of Goldtröpfchen.
Niederemmel opposite is
considered part of it,
although its wine has not
the same quality.

The Middle Mosel: Bernkastel

The view from the bridge at Bernkastel is of a green wall of vines 700 feet (200 metres) high and 5 miles (8 km) long. Only perhaps the Douro in the whole gazetteer of rivers to which the vine is wedded has any comparable sight.

From Brauneberg to Bernkastel's suburb of Kues the hills are relatively gentle. The Kirchberg in Veldenz (the village is just off the map) is one of those marginal vineyards which, like the Trittenheimers, makes beautiful wine after a hot summer. Lieser is perhaps best known for the grim great mansion formerly owned by the von Schorlemer estate at the foot of the Rosenlay. Here again, hills at right angles to the river give good south slopes.

The Mosel's greatest vineyard starts abruptly, rising almost sheer above the gables of Bernkastel; dark slate frowning at slate. The butt of the hill, its one straight south elevation, is the Doctor – perhaps the most famous vineyard in Germany. From its flank the proudest names of the Mosel follow one another. Comparison of Bernkasteler with Graacher and Wehlener, often with wines from the same growers in each place, is a fascinating game. The trademark of Bernkastel is a touch of flint. Graachers are softer; Wehleners richer.

The least of these wines should be something of very obvious personality: almost water-white with a gleam of green and with 40 or 50 little bubbles in the bottom of the glass, smelling almost aggressively of grapes, filling and seeming to coat your mouth with sharpness, sweetness and scent. The greatest of them, long-lived, pale gold, piquant, profound as honey, frivolous as flowers, are wines that beg to be discussed in an evening garden in shameless comparisons with music and poetry.

Above: Bernkastel and the bridge to Kues seen from the Doctor vineyard high above. Imaginative tasters detect the smoke from Bernkastel's chimneys in the flavour of Doctor, often the most expensive Mosel.

Below: famous Bernkastel estates include two owners of the Doctor: Thanisch and Deinhard. In Wehlen and Graach the outstanding name is Prüm; four branches of the family are among the artists of German wine.

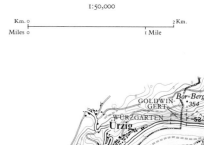

1:50,000

NACKTARSCH

KASTEL

SCHLOSSBERG
FALKLAY
EDELBERG
BURGLAY
MONTENEUBEL

Enkirch
STEFFENSBERG
STEFFENSBERG

LETTERLAY

KIRCHLAY

Kröv
Wolf

Kövenig

HERREN-
BERG

Staustufe
Enkirch

HUBERTUSLAY

KIRCHLAY

Corveyer
Werth

Kinheim

Heller Sass

Mosel-
flugplatz

Kaisergarten

Ev. Kinder-u
Jugehdheim

Mont
Royal

Das
Werth

Koppel-
berg

Rissbach

Mont Royal

Corveyer
Waldchen

Waldschenke

SCHWARZLAY

Königsberg

Schule

Traben-

Kräuterhaus

Starken-
burg

Trarbach
BURGBERG

Schloss-Berg

SCHLOSSBERG

KREUZBERG

Unheller
Kuppchen

KREUZBERG

Josephshöfer
Josephshof
DOMPROBST

Graach a.d.
Mosel
ABTSBERG
Graacher

Graacher
Schaferei

Schanzen

HIMMELREICH
ABTSBERG
Kaisergarten

Born-
miese
Bad

Schule

JOHANNIS-
BRUNNCHEN
Thanischwald

BADSTUBE

Bernkastel-Kues

GRABEN
DOCTOR
Bernkastel

Kues

SCHLOSSBERG

Jugend
herberge

Das
Werth
Zeltplatz

Schlossbrauerei
Waldschenke
Olymp

Heidesheim

STEPHANUS-
ROSENGÄRTCHEN
SCHLOSSBERG

BERNKASTEL — Bereich boundary
MÜNZLAY — Grosslage boundary
BURGLAY — Einzellage
— · — · — Regierungsbezirk boundary
— — — Kreis boundary
———— Gemeinde boundary
☐ Vineyards
▣ Woods
—100— Contour interval 20 metres

For this very reason the name of Bernkastel is used for very much more wine than her slopes can grow. The law allows it; Bereich Bernkastel is a possible name for any quality wine from the Middle Mosel. And Bernkastel has two Grosslage names: Badstube (exclusive to the five best sites) and Kurfürstlay, available to vineyards as far off as Brauneberg and Wintrich. The law works well only if you appreciate such niceties. Zeltingen brings the Great Wall to an end. It is the Mosel's biggest wine commune, and certainly among the best.

At Ürzig, across the river, reddish clay mixed with slate, in rocky pockets instead of a smooth bank, gives the wines of the Würzgarten ('spice garden') a different flavour, more penetrating and 'racy' than Zeltingers.

Erden at its best (especially Prälat) is in the same rank as Ürzig. Lösnich and Kinheim begin a decline. Kröv fills cafés with tourists giggling over the label of its Grosslage Nacktarsch, showing a boy with a bare bottom.

Traben-Trarbach is one community. Trarbach wines are well known. Enkirch should be better known than it is. In its ancient inn there is round, light, slightly spicy wine with all the delicate complexity the Middle Mosel is famous for.

The Middle Mosel ends here. Downstream towards Koblenz the vineyard continues among operatic villages, some with famous names and one or two with outstanding vineyards, but the whole loses its concert pitch. Zell is the best-known town for its (Grosslage) Schwarze Katz. Bullay has wine at least as good, and Neef (its best site the Frauenberg) rather better. Near Koblenz, little-known Winningen makes very good wine.

Below: old-fashioned hydraulic presses are used alongside modern ones by Deinhard's in their Kues cellars. The modern type contains a long balloon that squeezes the grapes against the sides as it inflates.

151

The Nahe

The superb Kupfergrube ('copper mine') vineyard of the State Domain at Schlossböckelheim overlooks the River Nahe on the site of what were copper workings until late in the 19th century. Its Rieslings are the most intense yet delicate of the whole valley.

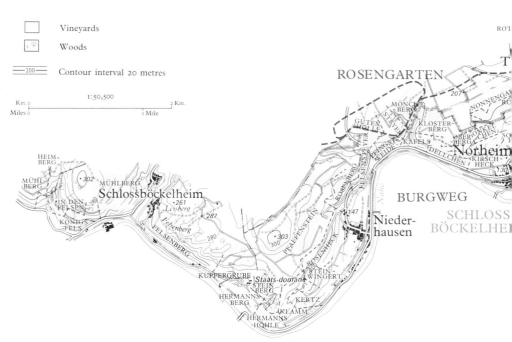

Vineyards

Woods

Contour interval 20 metres

1:50,500

The River Nahe, flowing north out of the Hunsrück hills to join the Rhine at Bingen, is surrounded by scattered outbreaks of winegrowing. But at one point a sandstone barrier impedes the river's flow, a range of hills rears up along the north bank; and suddenly there are all the makings of a great vineyard.

Its wine seems to capture all the qualities one loves best in German wine. It is very clean and grapey, with all the intensity of the Riesling, like a good Mosel or Saar wine. At the same time it has some of the full flavour that in the Rheingau makes one think of the alchemist's shop, as though rare minerals were dissolved in it, possibly gold itself. The word complexity, at a pinch, might do.

Bad Kreuznach is the wine capital of the Nahe. It is a pleasant spa, beneath hanging woods, with a casino and rows of strange brushwood erections like two-dimensional barns, down which salt water is poured to produce ozone for the benefit of convalescents.

Bad Kreuznach itself has a considerable

Bereich boundary

Grosslage boundary

Einzellage boundary

Kreis boundary

Gemeinde boundary

The small area of outstanding vineyards on the Nahe has only a few famous growers, but there are good cooperatives making good value wine under such names as Kreuznacher and Schlossböckelheimer.

proportion of the Nahe's best vineyards and the premises of most of the best growers. The Kahlenberg and Brückes sites, facing south over the town, often make exceptional wine. In addition it gives its name to the whole Bereich, or region, of the lower Nahe, down to the Rhine at Bingen. The upper Nahe is known as Bereich Schlossböckelheim, with the Grosslage names Burgweg and (for Bad Kreuznach) Kronenberg.

The fireworks really begin upstream at the Bad Münster bend. A red precipice, the Rotenfels, said to be the highest cliff in Europe north of the Alps, blocks the river's path. At the cliff-foot there is a bare 30 metres of fallen rubble, a short ramp of red earth. The vines are planted thick in the cramped space. They have ideal soil and a complete suntrap. This is the Traiser (formerly Rotenfelser) Bastei.

The degree of spice and fire in a Bastei of a good year is exceptional for such a northerly vineyard. It can remind one of great Palatinate wine, with some of the freshness and finesse of the Saar thrown in.

From this bend on upstream there is a succession of fine slopes, through the villages of Norheim and Niederhausen, to the Nahe's most illustrious vineyard of all: the Kupfergrube ('copper mine') on the eastern limit of the village of Schlossböckelheim.

The cellars where winemaking is brought to its highest peak here, if not in the whole of Germany, face the Kupfergrube from the last slope of Niederhausen. The Nahe State Domain has holdings in several Niederhausen vineyards, including the excellent Hermannshöhle and Hermannsberg, and has planted the Kupfergrube on the site of old copper diggings. Photographs still exist of the steep hill facing the cellars when it had no vines: it is easy to picture the director observing the daylong sun on the mine workings, and forming his plan.

Many find in this Domain everything they look for in white wine. The wines it makes are clean-tasting and fresh, fruity, racy and well balanced; very pale, with almost as much scent as a Bernkasteler and a long, lingering flavour in which sweetness and acidity are perfectly matched.

The State Domain also has vineyards on the lower Nahe, nearer to Bingen on the Rhine than Bad Kreuznach, in the parishes of Dorsheim and Münster-Sarmsheim in the Grosslage Schlosskapelle.

Here, as at Langenlonsheim, an east–west-running shoulder of hill presents a south slope of stony loam at right angles to the river. The best of the Riesling grown here, above all that from the Einzellage Münsterer Dautenpflänzer, has almost the beauty of the State Domain's upper Nahe wines, with more powerful and full-bodied flavours. The wines of these lower Nahe villages are less famous than the great Kreuznachers and Schlossböckelheimers, but stand equally far above the general level of the surrounding countryside, among the élite of all Germany's wines.

The Rheingau: Rüdesheim

The Rheingau is considered Germany's finest wine land, and the distinction of having owned the same Rheingau vineyard for as much as (in one case) 600 years is as great a patent of nobility as any in Europe. Among the big estates are the three shown here, and Prince Frederick of Prussia's at Erbach, Baron Langwerth von Simmern at Eltville, Count von Schönborn at Hattenheim, Baron Ritter zu Groenesteyn at Rüdesheim, the Landgraf of Hessen at Johannisberg and Prince Löwenstein in Hallgarten. The biggest estates outside this aristocratic circle are the 173-acre (70ha) von Mumm estate at Johannisberg, and the 136-acre (55ha) Wegeler property, which belongs

Above: the magnificent 12th-century Kloster Eberbach in Hattenheim is the symbolic headquarters of the German state domain, which has some 195ha in the Rheingau, including the great Steinberg, left.

to Deinhard's, the Koblenz shippers. Some Rheingau growers, particularly the three here, distinguish between their grades of wine with a complex code of labels, and as many as 12 different coloured lead capsules over the cork. These labels are for their higher-grade wines.

Schloss Vollrads, in the hills above Winkel, has been the home of the Counts Greiffenclau since the 14th century. Its 47 hectares produce some of Germany's most noble wines.

Schloss Johannisberg was granted to Prince Metternich by the Austrian Emperor in 1816. The present Fürst von Metternich consistently makes good wine from its 35 hectares.

The Rheingau is the climax of the wine-growing Rhine. For almost all its length the river flows steadily northwest, except for the point just below Mainz where the high forested Taunus mountains stand in its way. It turns southwest for only 20 miles (32 kilometres) until it reaches the Rüdesheimer Berg. There with a flurry of rocks and rapids it forces a passage northwards again. But the influence of its broad waters in that space gives Germany its most magnificent vineyard.

The best part of the Rheingau is mapped on the page opposite and the following two pages. Opposite is the downstream end, where the Rüdesheimer Berg Schlossberg drops almost sheer to the river. This is the only part of the Rheingau that is so steep. Most of it consists of stiff slopes but no more.

The Riesling is the grape of the Rheingau, as it is of the middle Mosel, but not of any except the best sites in the rest of the Rhine. The soil, described on page 142, is a great mixture but is nearer in type to the soil of Burgundy than of Germany's other Riesling areas. The climate is comparatively dry and sunny and the river's presence makes for equable temperatures, the mists which encourage the 'noble rot' as the grapes ripen and, they say, extra sunlight by reflection off its surface. The river is more than half a mile (800 metres) wide here, a throbbing highway for slow strings of barges.

The Rheingau style of wine, at its best, is the noblest in Germany. It unites the flowery scent of the Riesling with a greater and more golden depth of flavour than the Mosel. There is a strong sense of maturity about it; with maturity comes complexity and, in a strong character (the human parallel is irresistible), balance. Soft and charming are words you should never hear in the Rheingau.

The westernmost town which is mapped opposite is Assmannshausen, around the corner from the main Rheingau and an exception to all its rules, being famous only for its red wine. The grape is the Pinot Noir; its wine is very pale here and without the power it should have, but (among others) the state domain makes much-sought-after sweet pink wine by late-gathering the grapes. Dry red Assmannshauser is Germany's most famous red wine.

The Rüdesheimer Berg is distinguished from the rest of the parish by having the word Berg before each separate vineyard name. At their best (which is not always in the hottest years, since the drainage is too good at times) these are superlative wines, full of fruit and strength and yet delicate in nuance. In hotter years the vineyards behind the town come into their own.

Among the growers of the big parish is the wine school of Geisenheim, one of the most famous centres of wine learning in the world, which keeps, in the Fuchsberg, an experimental collection of vine varieties which may well revolutionize viticulture. Detailed soil and climate studies as well as new vine types developed here are of international importance (see pages 20–21).

The entire Rheingau, confusingly enough, was given the Bereich name of Johannisberg, its most famous single parish, in 1971.

Forschungsanstalt
Geisenheim am Rhein
RHEINGAU
1976er
Geisenheimer Fuchsberg
Riesling Spätlese
Qualitätswein mit Prädikat

RITTERHOFF VON RITTER ZU GROENESTEYN
1983er Spätlese
SCHLOSS GROENESTEYN
Rüdesheimer Berg Rottland Riesling
RHEINGAU 750 ml

RHEINGAU
19 79
RÜDESHEIMER BERG ROTTLAND
RIESLING SPÄTLESE

Left: growers in the big
commune of Rüdesheim
include, top, the famous
Geisenheim Research
Institute. The two lower
labels are from estates
on the Rüdesheimer
Berg.

Right: looking towards
the Rhine from the slope
of Schloss Johannisberg
in winter. There is a story
that Charlemagne
noticed the snow melted
first on this slope.

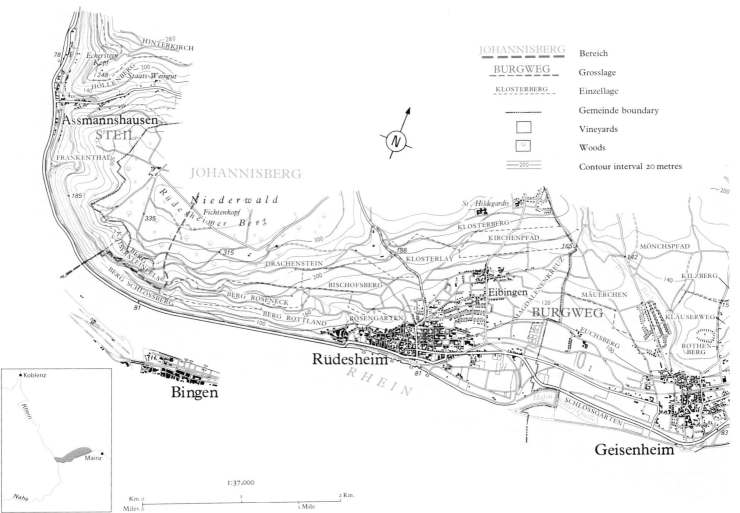

JOHANNISBERG	Bereich
BURGWEG	Grosslage
KLOSTERBERG	Einzellage
▬▬▬▬	Gemeinde boundary
☐	Vineyards
⌐	Woods
200	Contour interval 20 metres

1:37,000

Km. 0   1   2 Km.
Miles 0   1 Mile

The Rheingau: Eltville

Schloss Johannisberg, standing above a great apron of vines, dominates everything between Geisenheim and Winkel. The enormous prestige of its production, for which the winetaster's favourite term, 'elegant', might have been invented, tends to overshadow the excellent vineyards of the rest of Johannisberg.

Schloss Vollrads (see page 154) stands more than a mile (2 km) back from Winkel and leaves the name of the town off its labels – unfortunately for Winkel, whose name would otherwise be better known than it is. Even its second-best vineyard, Hasensprung (which means hare leap), is capable of producing superlative wine with the endless nuances that put the Rheingau in a class by itself.

Mittelheim has little identity as distinct from the more important Winkel and Oestrich. Its name does not appear on any wine of special note. There are those who say the same about

Oestrich. Oestrichers have been criticized for lack of 'breed'. But character and lusciousness they certainly have. Doosberg and Lenchen are not names to be dismissed.

In Hallgarten the Rheingau vineyards reach their highest point. Hendelberg is more than 1,000 feet (300 metres) above sea level. There is less mist and less frost up here. In the Würzgarten and Schönhell there is marly soil that gives strong wines of great lasting power and magnificent bouquet. No single vineyard makes the village name world famous – although the fact that a famous shipper has the same name makes it familiar.

The boundaries of Hattenheim stretch straight back into the hills to include the most illustrious of all the vineyards of the German state: the high ridge of the Steinberg, walled like the Clos de Vougeot with a Cistercian wall. Below in a wooded hollow stands the old

monastery which might fairly be called the headquarters of German wine, Kloster Eberbach (see page 154). The place, the astonishing wine and the implications of continuous industry and devotion to one idea of beauty going back 600 years makes any comment seem trivial. Today Kloster Eberbach is the base of the German Wine Academy, which runs courses open to all wine lovers.

Like Hallgarten, Hattenheim has marl in the soil. On its border with Erbach is the only vineyard that makes great wine right down by the river, in a situation which looks as though the drainage would be far from perfect. The vineyard is Marcobrunn, lying partly in Hattenheim but mainly in Erbach. Marcobrunner is very full flavoured, often rich, fruity and spicy. Its owners include Count Schönborn and Baron Langwerth von Simmern on the Hattenheim side, and the state domain and

Above: substantial private estates make the most celebrated Rheingau wine. Some of the growers' cooperatives, such as that at Erbach, also have excellent reputations. No outstanding wine is sold under any but a grower's label today.

JOHANNISBERG Bereich
GOTTESTHAL Grosslage
KLOSTERBERG Einzellage
—————— Gemeinde boundary

1:37,000

Km. 0   2 Km.
Miles 0   1 Mile

Prince Frederick of Prussia's estate in Erbach.

Again in Erbach the town's land goes back into the hills in a long narrow strip. These are good vineyards, but not the best. Steinmorgen, on the outskirts of the town, gives more powerful and memorable wine than Michelmark and Honigberg.

Kiedrich's beautiful Gothic church is the next landmark. The vineyards of the village make exceptionally well-balanced and delicately spicy wine. Dr Weil is the biggest Kiedrich-based grower. Gräfenberg is reckoned the best part of the vineyard, although Wasseros and Sandgrub are almost equally renowned.

Superlatives become tiring in an account of the Rheingau. Yet if the qualities of great white wine mean anything to you the peculiar sort of wine these growers make offers more to taste, consider and discuss than any other in the world. The wines that fetch the high prices, and by which the vineyards are ultimately judged, are always the late-picked, sweet and intense ones which demand to be drunk with conscious attention, and on their own rather than with food. There are better wines for any meal in other parts of Germany – and far better in Burgundy. The Rheingau's raison d'être is wine for wine's sake. And it does give rise to such scents and flavours that only superlatives will do.

Thus Rauenthal, the last of the hill villages and the farthest from the river, makes a different kind of superlative wine: the most expensive. Rauenthalers are the Germans' German wine. The Ausleses of the state domain and of two lordly growers, Baron Langwerth von Simmern and Count Schönborn, as well as those of smaller growers on the Rauenthaler Berg, are prized for the combination of power and delicacy in their flowery scent and in their spicy aftertaste.

Eltville makes bigger quantities of wine without the supreme cachet. It is the headquarters of the state domain (see page 154) as well as having the beautiful old mansions of the Eltz and von Simmern families, in a group of buildings of white plaster and rosy stone, draped with vines and roses, beside the river.

Without sharing the fame of their neighbours, the united Nieder- and Ober-Walluf and Martinsthal share much of their quality.

Some 15 miles (24 km) farther east, the Rheingau has an unexpected outpost: Hochheim. The Hochheim vineyards (which gave us the word hock) lie on gently sloping land just north of the River Main, isolated in country that has no other vines. Good Hochheimers add their own thrilling full-bodied earthiness to the other qualities of the Rheingau.

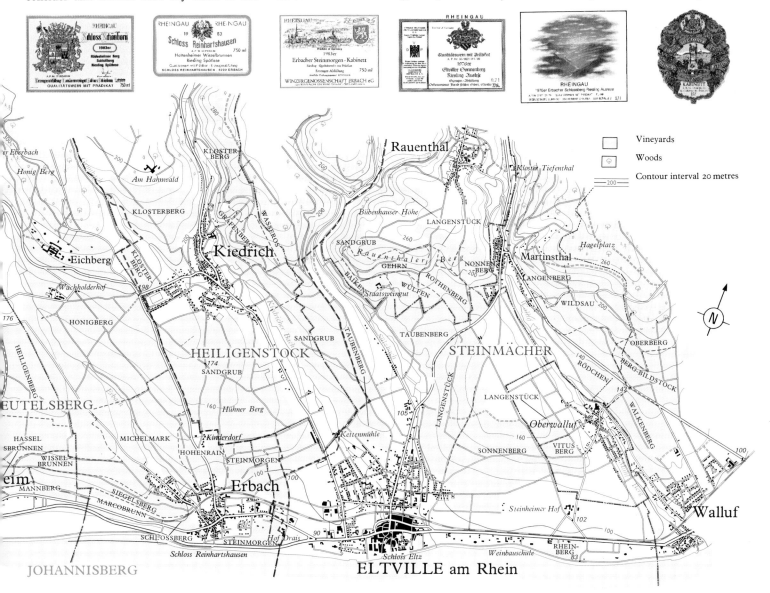

Vineyards

Woods

Contour interval 20 metres

157

The Rheinpfalz

Above: the first three labels – those of Bürklin-Wolf, von Bassermann-Jordan and von Buhl – are among the most famous designs in Germany, appearing on the cream of Palatinate wine. The remainder are also top Mittelhaardt growers; less familiar than the cooperatives of the Southern Palatinate, the Südliche Weinstrasse, which produces the bulk of the good-value wine of the huge area.

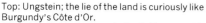

Top: Ungstein; the lie of the land is curiously like Burgundy's Côte d'Or.
Above left: Deidesheim; substantial houses with arches into courtyards are typical of the Mittelhaardt.
Above right: orchards surround winemaking villages along the route of the German Weinstrasse.

The Palatinate (German Pfalz) is Germany's biggest vineyard; a 50-mile (80km) stretch just north of Alsace, under the lee of the German continuation of the Vosges mountains – the Haardt.

Like Alsace, it is the sunniest and driest part of its country, and has the never-failing charm of half-timbered villages among orchards, seeming part of a better, sunlit, half-fairytale world. A labyrinthine road, the Deutsche Weinstrasse, like the Alsatian Route du Vin, starts at the gates of Germany (literally; there is a massive gateway called the Weintor on the border at Schweigen) and winds northwards through more vines and villages than you ever hope to see. A great part of the wine of the area (Südliche Weinstrasse is its Bereich name) is made by big and efficient cooperatives which have revolutionized casual old country methods and are making the district famous. Historically there is little Riesling here; the style

used to be sweetish and heavy. Refrigeration and replanting have made lighter, more fragrant and better-balanced wine available at very reasonable prices.

Most are sold under Grosslage names, since few Einzellagen here have reputations of their own. Among the most important are (Rhodter) Ordensgut, (Walsheimer) Bischofskreuz, (Bergzaberner) Kloster Liebfrauenberg and (Schweigener) Guttenberg.

North of Neustadt, however, you are in a different world. In the Mittelhaardt, the name of the short string of little townships mapped opposite, the wine suddenly achieves the unmistakable quality of 'breed'. Here Riesling jumps from 5% to 75% of the plantation.

It is the Einzellagen on the west, the hilly, side of the villages that attain summits of succulence. Almost all are contained in the Grosslage Mariengarten (whether Forster, Deidesheimer or Wachenheimer) but generally sold by the names of the 'Spitzenlagen' (top sites) of their parishes.

Ruppertsberg begins the Mittelhaardt in the south; its best sites (Spiess, Gaisböhl, Hoheburg, Reiterpfad, Nussbien) are all on moderate slopes, well exposed and largely

Riesling. It seems odd that they should share the Grosslage name of Hofstück with inferior vineyards on the plain to the east. At Deidesheim the hill slope sharpens where the Grosslage Mariengarten begins. Three famous producers dominate this, the kernel of the Rheinpfalz: Bürklin-Wolf, von Bassermann-Jordan and von Buhl.

In Deidesheim, generally reckoned the best village of the whole area, besides being one of the prettiest in Germany, von Bassermann-Jordan and von Buhl have their cellars. Hohenmorgen, Kieselberg, Kalkofen, Grainhübel and Paradiesgarten are the top Lagen.

Forst has a unique reputation, as the source of Germany's sweetest wine (not in mere sugar, but in style and character). A black basalt outcrop above the village provides dark soil, rich in potassium, which is not found elsewhere – although it is quarried and spread on other vineyards, notably in Deidesheim. Basalt here, as on Lake Balaton in Hungary, holds the heat and keeps the temperature up at night. Forst's one street is the main road. The Jesuitengarten, its most famous vineyard, and the equally fine Kirchenstück lie just behind the church. Freundstück (largely von Buhl's)

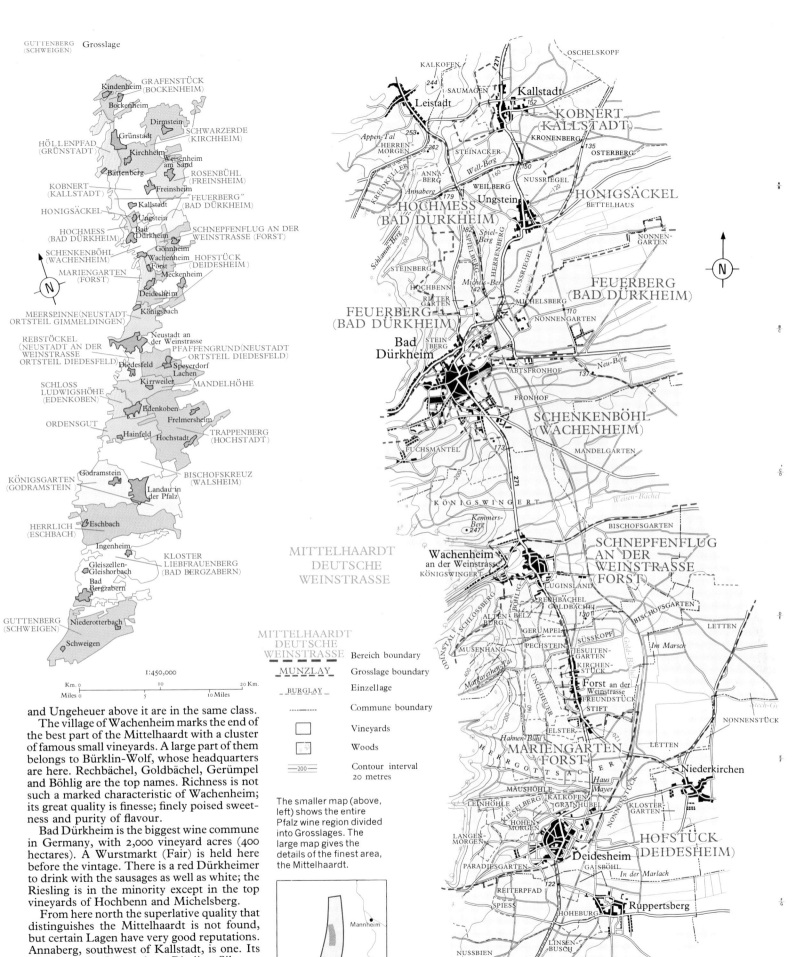

MITTELHAARDT
DEUTSCHE
WEINSTRASSE

Legend:

MITTELHAARDT DEUTSCHE WEINSTRASSE — Bereich boundary

MUNZLAY — Grosslage boundary

BURGLAY — Einzellage

------- Commune boundary

□ Vineyards

Woods

—200— Contour interval 20 metres

and Ungeheuer above it are in the same class.

The village of Wachenheim marks the end of the best part of the Mittelhaardt with a cluster of famous small vineyards. A large part of them belongs to Bürklin-Wolf, whose headquarters are here. Rechbächel, Goldbächel, Gerümpel and Böhlig are the top names. Richness is not such a marked characteristic of Wachenheim; its great quality is finesse; finely poised sweetness and purity of flavour.

Bad Dürkheim is the biggest wine commune in Germany, with 2,000 vineyard acres (400 hectares). A Wurstmarkt (Fair) is held here before the vintage. There is a red Dürkheimer to drink with the sausages as well as white; the Riesling is in the minority except in the top vineyards of Hochbenn and Michelsberg.

From here north the superlative quality that distinguishes the Mittelhaardt is not found, but certain Lagen have very good reputations. Annaberg, southwest of Kallstadt, is one. Its wine from the Scheurebe, a Riesling-Silvaner cross, is especially rich and distinctive. Honigsäckel and Saumagen are the Grosslage names for the best sites in, respectively, Ungstein and Kallstadt, the village that brings to a close this celebrated slope.

The smaller map (above, left) shows the entire Pfalz wine region divided into Grosslages. The large map gives the details of the finest area, the Mittelhaardt.

Rheinhessen

The Liebfrauenstift vineyard, origin of the name of Liebfraumilch (although long since divorced from it) lies around the Liebfrauenkirche in the city of Worms. Nylon netting protects the vines from birds.

Rheinhessen lies in the crook of the Rhine, hemmed in by the river on the east and north, the Nahe on the west, and the Rheinpfalz to the south. Its 150-odd villages, spaced out over an area 20 miles by 30 (30 by 50 kilometres), grow wine as part or all of their livelihood. It is dull, undulating, fertile country, without exceptional character except where the Rhine flows by.

The bulk of Rheinhessen wine, made from Müller-Thurgau or Silvaner grapes, is equally unexceptional; light, soft, usually sweetish, sometimes earthy, rarely vigorous enough to claim attention. It finds its outlet as Liebfraumilch, which is now legally defined as a Qualitätswein (QbA) from the Rheinhessen, Rheinpfalz, Nahe or Rheingau, made of Silvaner, Riesling or Müller-Thurgau grapes and 'with pleasant character'. You can expect any Liebfraumilch to be mild and semi-sweet. There are some good ones, but no wine of distinction is wasted on this kind of blend.

The map on the facing page shows the whole of the winegrowing Rheinhessen with its Grosslage divisions – the names most commonly seen (apart from Liebfraumilch, that is) on its wine, which very seldom assumes the distinction of an Einzellage name.

The vast majority of the growers, besides, have only a hectare or two of vines as part of a mixed-farming operation. It is the co-operatives, therefore, that make the wine.

Three Bereich names cover the whole region: Bingen the northwest, Nierstein the northeast, and Wonnegau the south, between the principal towns of Alzey and Worms.

The town of Bingen, facing Rüdesheim across the Rhine, has excellent vineyards on the steep slopes of its Scharlachberg. But by far the best and most important vineyards of Rheinhessen are concentrated in the short

Nierstein has as many as 300 sizeable wine estates. Those of Guntrum and Balbach (left, top and bottom) are among the biggest. Baron Heyl zu Herrnsheim is another excellent grower. The last label, right, is of the most important estate at Bingen to the west (see map on facing page).

stretch of the Rheinfront mapped on page 160.

The town of Nierstein has become, partly through its size and the number (about 300) of its growers, partly because its name was widely and shamelessly borrowed (usually with the site name Domthal attached) before the 1971 wine laws, but mainly because of its superb vineyards, as famous as Bernkastel. The two towns that flank it, Oppenheim and Nackenheim, have vineyards as good as most of the Nierstein, but none better than the sand-red roll of hill going north with the river at its foot. Hipping, Pettenthal and Rothenberg (which is in Nackenheim) and the small group of vineyards that share the Grosslage name Rehbach make wine as fragrant and full of character as the Rheingau, and thought by some to be a shade softer and more luxuriant.

Any true Niersteiner will use one of the Lage names on the map. The best will also specify that they are made from Riesling, although some interesting wines are being made from crosses such as Kerner.

There is no such wine as Niersteiner Domtal any longer. Niersteiner Gutes Domtal, on the other hand, is a Grosslage name available to 15 villages, but only to one part of Nierstein, and that the least distinguished.

Outside the area of this map the best villages are those just north and south: Bodenheim and Guntersblum and Alsheim.

Above: the best vineyards of Rheinhessen line the Rheinfront north and south of Nierstein on 300-foot (90-metre) hills. Most of the Riesling in Rheinhessen is grown here.

DOMBLICK **Grosslage**

1:417,500

Km. 0   10   20 Km.

Miles 0   5   10 Miles

Above: a Rheinhessen grower measures the sugar content of his must with a hydrometer. Fermentation in small barrels in a cool cellar is giving way to refrigerated vats in most districts.

Baden-Württemberg

You would expect the south of Germany, with its warmer climate, to be more of a wine region than parts farther north. A hundred years ago it was. But the peculiar combinations of soil, climate and social structure that make quality winemaking possible and worthwhile in apparently unlikely spots on the Mosel and Rhine have only a few parallels in the huge state of Baden-Württemberg. The best of its wine is excellent, but scattered here and there in penny numbers, much appreciated locally and rarely exported. So the outside world has tended to overlook a vast vineyard of great potential.

Until recently, that is. Nowhere in Germany has the rationalization and modernization of the wine industry gone further and faster. Baden's vineyards have doubled in size and quadrupled in production. Only the Rheinpfalz and Rheinhessen produce more. The locomotive of this great surge forward has been the cooperatives. Ninety percent of the crop is handled by more than 100 of these establishments, and more than half of all this wine is marketed by the mammoth ZBW, the Zentralkellerei Badischer Winzergenossenschaften, at Breisach, the frontier town on the Rhine between Freiburg and Alsace.

One way to define Baden's style is to say that it is the opposite of the Mosel. Ethereal floweriness is not so much the point as substantial wineyness. Alsace lies just across the Rhine. Baden is a trifle damper and cloudier than the vineyards over the Rhine, umbrella'd by the Vosges. Its vineyards skirt the Black Forest, where mist and rain form part of some of Germany's loveliest pictures. The bulk of Baden's vineyards lie in a narrow 80-mile (130km) strip between the forest and the Rhine valley; the best of them either on privileged southern slopes in the forest massif or on the volcanic outcrops that form two distinct islands of high ground in the Rhine valley: the Kaiserstuhl and Tuniberg.

No one grape variety is dominant. Müller-Thurgau forms one-third of the crop (the national average is closer to half). Spätburgunder (Pinot Noir) is the second variety, used for both lightweight reds and pale Weissherbst. Ruländer (alias Pinot Gris) is important for wines of high density and extract, Riesling for classically elegant and long-lived wines, Weissburgunder (Pinot Blanc) for smooth, soft wines, Gewürztraminer for spicy ones, Silvaner (on the Kaiserstuhl) for some wines almost as full of character as it makes in Franken. The highly aromatic new varieties are little used. Badeners regard wine primarily as accompaniment to food. Few German wines fill the role so well.

Kaiserstuhl and Tuniberg, united as one Bereich, furnish one-third of all Baden's wine. The landscape here has been remodelled on a massive scale to make modern vineyards out of old terraces and ledges. Red Spätburgunder is locally considered the best wine; Ruländer and Silvaner are sometimes splendid: stiff with flavour.

To the north, just south of the luxurious Black Forest spa of Baden-Baden, the Ortenau is a pocket of quality winegrowing with an

emphasis on red wine. The lordly estates at Durbach, those of the Margrave of Baden (Schloss Staufenberg), Baron von Neveu and Count Wolff Metternich make excellent Klingelberger (the local name for Riesling), Ruländer, Traminer and Spätburgunder. Much farther north the Kraichgau and Badischer Bergstrasse form one Bereich, disparate as they are, with their best wines, at least in a visitor's opinion, made from the minority grapes, Riesling and Ruländer, grown in the best sites.

Far to the south, in the Markgräflerland, the corner of Germany between Freiburg and Basel, the favourite grape is the Gutedel, the local name for the Chasselas of Switzerland. It makes very refreshing, if rather reticent, wine. Weissherbst is popular here, too. Perhaps the tastiest wine is from the Nobling, a cross between Gutedel and Silvaner.

The 'Seewein' (lake wine) of the southernmost area of all, around Meersburg on the Bodensee, is traditionally pink-tinted Weissherbst of Spätburgunder – almost a 'Blanc de Noir'. Müller-Thurgau is the principal white

grape. The Margrave of Baden has another splendid estate here, Schloss Salem – even if it has no Riesling to match up to his noble Durbacher wine.

Württemberg, extensive though its vineyards are, remains better known to the world at large for its motorcars (at Stuttgart) than its wine. The region grows more red (or Weissherbst) wine than white, largely of its own varieties, the Trollinger, Limberger and Schwarzriesling (or Pinot Meunier) as well as the universal Spätburgunder. The climate is not kind to winegrowers in Württemberg, so sites are chosen with care, lining the river Neckar and its tributaries. The Bereich to the north of the capital, the Württembergisch Unterland, has three-quarters of the region's vineyards.

Stuttgart and Heilbronn, in fact, almost bracket the whole industry. You must visit them to taste its products: pale pink Schillerwein, Muskateller, Müller-Thurgau, Silvaner . . . a wide selection. The Traminer is good, but the Riesling, as almost everywhere in Germany, stands in a class apart.

Left: the Black Forest is the heart of Baden, its dark ridges intruding in almost every vineyard view. The Bereich Ortenau has some of the most beautiful country, and some of the best of Baden's wine.

If 90% of Baden and Württemberg's huge harvest is handled by cooperative cellars, fine old estates are still scattered throughout the region. Lordly coats of arms distinguish such labels as the first here, from the Durbach estate of the Margrave of Baden.

International boundary
Land boundary
Grosslage
Bereich

STARKENBURG BREISGAU BODENSEE

WÜRTTEMBERGISCH UNTERLAND KAISERSTUHL-TUNIBERG

BADISCHE BERGSTRASSE KRAICHGAU MARK GRÄFLERLAND

ORTENAU REMSTAL·STUTTGART

1:160,000

Franken

Above: Franken (Franconia) is the one part of Germany that does not use the tall slim bottle. Its appetizing dry wines come in Bocksbeutels, a model protected by law for Franken.

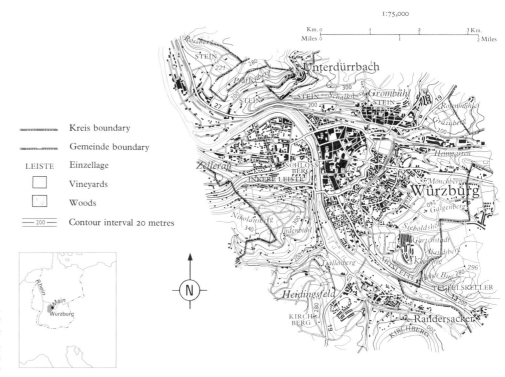

Franken is out of the mainstream of German wine both geographically and by its quite separate traditions. Politically it lies in the otherwise wineless former kingdom of Bavaria, which gives its State cellars a grandeur found nowhere else in Germany, and its consumers high expectations.

It makes the only German wine not to come in flute bottles; the only great wine made of the Silvaner instead of the Riesling. And in savour and strength it draws away from the delicate sweetness of most German and nearer to some French wines, making it one of the best of German wines to drink with food.

The name Steinwein is loosely used for all Franken wine. Stein is, in fact, the name of one of the two famous vineyards of the city of Würzburg on the Main, the capital of the district. The other is Leiste. Both distinguished themselves in the past by making wines that lasted incredibly long periods. A 16th-century Stein wine (of the great vintage of 1540) was still just drinkable only a decade ago, and the Pfalz Wine Museum at Speyer has bottles of early 17th-century Leisten with late 19th-century labels from the royal house of Bavaria.

Such wines were Beerenauslesen at least: immensely sweet. Franken makes few of such rarities today. The bulk of the wine in the pretty flask-shaped Bocksbeutel is full-bodied and dry by German standards, with something like the size and strength of white burgundy.

Franken takes the vine farther east and north than any other German region, into countryside whose climate is decidedly continental. In the Steigerwald, the easternmost of the three Franken Bereichs, the vine looks almost a stranger in a setting of arable fields with forests of magnificent oaks crowning its sudden hills. The doll's-house princedom of Castell is a sort of unofficial capital of this Bereich, producing, with Iphofen and Rödelsee, its finest wine.

This is the one part of Germany where the growing season is regularly too short for the Riesling to prosper. The traditional answer is

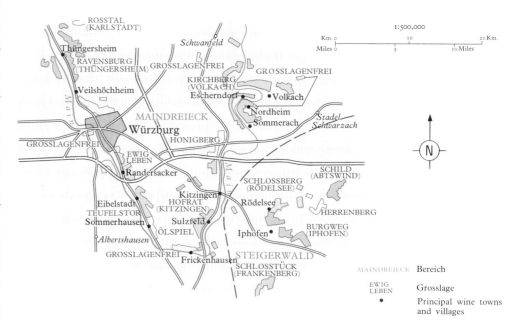

MAINDREIECK   Bereich

EWIG LEBEN   Grosslage

•   Principal wine towns and villages

the Silvaner. In Franken this normally second-division grape gains first-division status – not for pyrotechnics of fragrance but for a combination of the subtle and forceful that commands respect. Making allowance for the flavours of quite different grapes, Premier or even Grand Cru Chablis are comparable wines.

But even in Franken, unfortunately, Müller-Thurgau seems to offer a better return, at least on less-than-ideal sites. It has gained the upper hand in nearly half of the 10,000 acres (4,000 hectares) of vineyard in the region. (For comparison, the Nahe has about the same total acreage of vines, the Rheingau two-thirds as much and the Rheinpfalz five times.) A minority of Franken wines are made of the relatively new, super-aromatic varieties Bacchus and Kerner. The most promising innovation, though, is a late-ripening Riesling × Silvaner cross called Rieslaner.

The heart of winegrowing Franken is all included in the Bereich Maindreieck, following the fuddled three-cornered wandering of the Main from Escherndorf and Nordheim upstream of Würzburg, south to Frickenhausen, then north again through the capital to include all the next leg of the river and the outlying district around Hammelburg. What distinguishes all these scattered south-facing hillsites is the peculiar limestone known as Muschelkalk (whose origins are not so different from the Kimmeridgian clay of Chablis). The much smaller Bereich Steigerwald, to the east of the Main, has heavier (although still alkaline) clay soil. The third Bereich, farther downstream to the west, has lighter loam based on sandstone. This is the Mainviereck (see the map on page 141), of relatively small importance.

Where the legend 'Grosslagenfrei' appears on the map, it signifies that the wine villages are so scattered that they have not been grouped in Grosslagen. Their wines are sold under individual site names or the name of the Bereich. The majority of Franken wine, however, is made by cooperatives.

Würzburg is the essential visit: one of the great cities of the vine, with three magnificent estate cellars in its heart belonging respectively to the Bavarian State (the Staatliche Hofkellerei), a church charity (the Juliusspital) and a civic one (the Bürgerspital).

The Staatliche Hofkellerei lies under the gorgeous Residenz of the former prince-bishops, whose ceiling paintings by Tiepolo are reason enough to visit the city, even without the noble Marienburg Castle on its hill of vines, the great baroque river bridge or the bustling *Weinstuben* belonging to these ancient foundations, where all their wines can be enjoyed with suitably savoury food.

Wine has no more splendid home than the great baroque Residenz of the former prince-bishops of Würzburg, where the wines of the Bavarian State Domain mature in the vaults below halls and staircases decorated by the great Venetian painter Tiepolo (detail, top). Above: the ancient casks in the candlelit cellars include one that held the prince of all vintages, the wine of 1540.

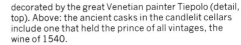

Left: Franken labels are frequently round, like the faces of their bottles. Top producers include two venerable charities, the Juliusspital and the Bürgerspital at Würzburg, and the Bavarian State Domain.

Germany: Wine Law and Labels

German wine laws do not classify vineyards as the French do. Any vineyard in Germany can in theory produce top-class wine. Instead, the law specifies exactly what degree of sugar the must (crushed grapes) should contain to qualify for each classification.

There are four basic grades of quality, each with its own set of rules. The highest grade, Qualitätswein mit Prädikat, is in turn subdivided into five categories directly related to the ripeness of the grapes.

The four grades are:

Deutscher Tafelwein Ordinary table wine, which need only attain 5% natural alcohol before sugaring and be made from approved grape varieties. It may use the name of a region or a village, but not a vineyard. It does not pass a test. If a grape variety (e.g. Riesling) is named on a label, a Tafelwein must contain 85% of wine made of that variety. Tafelwein without the 'Deutscher' contains wine from other European countries – usually Italy.

Landwein Must come solely from one of 15 designated Landwein regions, contain half a degree of natural alcohol more than Tafelwein, and not more than 18 grams per litre of residual sugar, which makes it relatively dry: at most a Halbtrocken (see glossary) in sweetness. It is, in short, intended to be a standard mealtime beverage of predictable character.

Qualitätswein bestimmter Anbaugebiete (QbA) Must come from a specified region (Gebiet), from certain grape varieties, attain a certain must weight (about 60°, which would give 7.5% natural alcohol – see page 24), and carry a test number (Amtliche Prüfungsnummer, or A.P. Nr. for short). It can carry a vineyard name if 85% of the grapes were grown there, a Grosslage name or a Bereich name (see page 140).

Qualitätswein mit Prädikat (QmP) The grade for the top wines which may not use sugar. Their natural must weight has to be 73° Oechsle (the equivalent of 9.5% alcohol) or more depending on the region; their grapes of a certain variety; they must come from a particular area (Bereich), be quality tested and carry their identifying test number.

Within the QmP grade, the traditional classification by sugar content of the top wines is given precise standards. They are:

Kabinett: minimum must weight of 73° (or more or less depending on the region)
Spätlese: minimum must weight 85°
Auslese: minimum must weight about 90°
Beerenauslese: minimum must weight about 120°
Trockenbeerenauslese: minimum must weight about 150°. (Weights vary by area and grape variety.)

In addition, **Eiswein** must be made of grapes that are frozen solid when picked (normally long after the rest of the harvest) and crushed while still frozen. The ice (which is pure water) is removed, leaving an intensely concentrated must of high sugar and acidity, but without the specific flavour of 'noble rot' normally associated with Beeren- and Trockenbeerenauslese. Eiswein is both very sweet and tart, and needs many years in bottle to arrive at what can be an exquisite harmony.

THE LANGUAGE OF THE LABEL

German wine labels give more precise information about the contents of the bottle than those of any other country – but in a language that takes some mastering. Below are examples of typical labels for the four basic quality categories of German wine, with a glossary of the words and phrases found on labels.

Deutscher Tafelwein

On this label: KellerPrinz is one of the brands of the wine merchants and growers Franz Reh & Sohn of Leiwen on the Mosel. The Bereich (district) of Bernkastel covers the whole of the Middle Mosel. As an alternative to a Bereich name a Tafelwein can claim a village name, but not a vineyard. Mosel (as opposed to Mosel-Saar-Ruwer on quality-wine labels) is the table-wine area. No other indications of quality or origin are allowed.

Qualitätswein bestimmter Anbaugebiete

On this label: Forschungsanstalt Geisenheim am Rhein is the Geisenheim Research Station, part of the School of Oenology, the headquarters of German viticulture. Rheingau is the name of the region (Gebiet). 1978er is the vintage. Fuchsberg is the Einzellage, or individual vineyard, in Geisenheim. Riesling is the grape. Erzeuger-Abfüllung = bottled by the grower. A.P. Nr. is the wine's test number (all Qualitätswein passes a tasting test). Institut für Kellerwirtschaft = School of Oenology (the official title of the overall organization of which the Forschungsanstalt – the Research Station – is a unit). QbA is the middle level of German wine, made with added sugar.

Preismünze

Strip-labels are used aslant the necks of German wines that have been awarded prizes in either state or federal competitions. Landesweinprämierung is the state competition. Bundesweinprämierung is for the whole of Germany, administered by the German Agricultural Society (DLG), and open to wines that have been successful in regional competitions. The prizes are awarded for a preordained number of points scored out of 20: 19.5 points gain a golden 'Grosser Preis'; 18.5 points gain a silver 'Silberner Preis'; 17.5 points gain a bronze 'Bronzener Preis'. In a typical year 2,000 or 3,000 prizes are issued.

Landwein

In 1982 Landwein, a category superior to Tafelwein with slightly higher and more specific standards, was introduced as an approximate equivalent to the French *vin de pays*. On this label: Gräflich von Hohenthal'sche is the producer. 1984er is the vintage. Nahegauer (from the Nahe) is the designated Landwein area. Müller-Thurgau is the grape. Halbtrocken = half-dry. Erzeugerabfüllung = bottled by the producer.

Qualitätswein mit Prädikat

QmP is the category that includes all the natural, unsugared, finest wines of Germany. On this label: Mosel-Saar-Ruwer is the region (Gebiet). 1981 is the vintage. A.P. Nr.: each Qualitätswein passes an analytical and tasting test and receives a number by which it can be identified. Ürzig is the village (the suffix -er is as in Londoner or New Yorker). Goldwingert is the Einzellage (vineyard). Riesling is the grape. Spätlese ('late-gathered') is the quality in terms of ripeness. Alleinbesitz indicates that the vineyard is owned exclusively by the estate. Nicolay'sche Weinguts-Verwaltung, C. H. Berres Erben is the estate. Erzeuger-Abfüllung = bottled by the grower.

Weisswein White wine
Rotwein Red wine
Weissherbst Pink wine from red grapes
Schillerwein Pink wine made from red and white grapes mixed
Perlwein Slightly sparkling (carbonated)
Schaumwein Sparkling wine
Sekt Sparkling, subject to quality controls
Halbtrocken 'Half-dry', often an ideal balance of sweetness for use at table, especially Kabinett wines
Trocken Dry, often good with food in the QbA and Spätlese categories, which have slightly more alcohol than Kabinett wines
Aus eigenem Lesegut From the producer's own estate
Weinkellerei Wine cellar or winery
Winzergenossenschaft Winegrowers' cooperative
Winzerverein The same

Southern & Eastern Europe and the Mediterranean

Switzerland

Switzerland is an intensely wine-conscious, insatiably wine-importing country as well as an important producer. She comes between France, the natural land of wine, and Germany, the land where wine is an extra, worth every bit of effort it demands. The Swiss are loyal to their own local wines, without pretending that better things do not happen in France. They are among the world's biggest importers of burgundy; Beaujolais is almost their national drink.

The Swiss wine industry is in evolution, as rising costs make it a problem to many growers whether or not to persevere. The inevitable result is that poor vineyards are abandoned as not paying their way. Studies are made as to how to run the remainder, the better ones, more profitably and with less labour – which often means a change to better varieties of vine and more modern ways of training them.

The Swiss are efficient, if sometimes unromantic, winemakers. By scrupulous care of their vines, using fertilizers and irrigation, they achieve yields twice as high as those in French appellation areas. They take sugaring for granted: there are no German-style indications of natural unsugared wine. By managing to produce such big quantities, assisted by sugar when necessary, they make grape growing pay in difficult terrain with a high standard of living.

At the same time the long near-monopoly of white wine in Switzerland has been broken. Red wine is in fashion, a development of the last 25 years. There has been an enormous increase in the planting of the Burgundian varieties of red grapes, Pinot Noir and Gamay, in the most important areas: Vaud, Valais and Geneva. The Ticino has concentrated on the Merlot, introduced from Bordeaux. The fashion has also saved the formerly dwindling vineyards of German Switzerland, which have long specialized in the Blauburgunder (Pinot Noir).

Almost every canton in Switzerland makes a little wine. Two areas apart from the Rhône valley and Lake Geneva have important industries: the Ticino and Neuchâtel.

Italian Switzerland, the Ticino, has not long been an exporter of wine. The local tradition is a peasant one, and only 50 or so years ago hardship was still sending emigrants to America. (The famous Italian Swiss Colony vineyards near Santa Rosa in California are one result.) The typical local red wine, called Nostrano, is no great matter. But the Merlot is growing well there, as it does in northeast Italy and northern Yugoslavia, making a strongish but rather soft wine. Better Ticino Merlots, attaining 12% alcohol, now use the name Viti to distinguish themselves from the rest.

Neuchâtel is equally famous for its red wine and its white – although the white is three-quarters of the crop. Without doubt the simplicity of the whole area calling its wine by the famous name of its capital has been a help. The north shore of the lake is temperate and well sheltered by the Jura. The Pinot Noir grows well on limestone here (there is no Gamay), giving a pale and light wine but with character and definition, often sold rosé, as *oeil de*

perdrix. The village of Cortaillod, south of Neuchâtel, is said to make the best.

White Neuchâtel is made from the Chasselas, like Fendant and Dorin wines from Valais and Vaud. It is lighter than either and encouraged to fizz faintly by being bottled *sur lie* – without being separated from its yeasty sediment. In some cases the process is carried further to making fully sparkling wines of real quality.

Lake Bienne (the Bielersee) just to the northeast has similar wines which fetch high prices, as 'Schafiser' or 'Twanner', in the cantonal capital of Bern.

The wines of other cantons do not travel much. The Bundner Herrschaft, a little district on the borders of Austria and Liechtenstein which has the distinction of being the first wine region of the infant Rhine, grows Blauburgunder (or 'Klevner') almost exclusively; the best are dear and can be excellent, benefiting from the warm autumn wind, the *foehn*. The Herrschaft also grows the otherwise-unknown Completer, which is

Swiss wines are known by regional names relating to grape varieties and qualities as well as to geographical origins. The following names occur on their labels:

Amigne: a local Valais white grape giving heavy, tasty, normally dry, wine.
Arvine or **Petite Arvine:** another similar; if anything, better.
Blauburgunder: Pinot Noir from a German-speaking canton.
Klevner: the same.
Dôle: red Valais wine of Pinot Noir or Gamay or both, of tested quality.
Dorin: white Vaud wine of Chasselas, the equivalent of Fendant from the Valais.
Ermitage: white Marsanne vines from the French Rhône grown in the Valais: rich, concentrated, heavy wine, usually dry.
Fendant: white Valais wine of Chasselas; Switzerland's most famous.
Gamay: the Beaujolais grape, largely grown around Geneva and in La Côte.
Goron: red Valais wine; Dôle that failed the test.
Humagne: rare red or white Valais wine of rustic character.
Johannisberg: Sylvaner from the Valais.

Malvoisie: heavy white Pinot Gris from the Valais; often made sweet from dried ('*flétri*') grapes.
Merlot: red Bordeaux grape grown for the best Ticino wine.
Nostrano: ordinary Ticino wine from a variety of French and Italian grapes.
Oeil de Perdrix: term used for light rosé from Pinot Noir, particularly in Neuchâtel and Geneva.
Perlan: white Geneva (or Mandement) wine from Chasselas.
Premier Cru: any wine from the maker's own domaine.
Rèze: rare grape traditionally used for 'glacier' wine.
Riesling-Sylvaner: Müller-Thurgau wine, common in eastern Switzerland.
Salvagnin: red Vaud wine of tested quality; the equivalent of Dôle from the Valais.
Schafiser or **Twanner:** the light but expensive wine of Lake Bienne in the canton of Bern, red or white.
Viti: red Merlot wine of a certain standard from Ticino.

Any Swiss wine which is not completely dry must by law carry the words '*légèrement doux*' or '*avec sucre residuel*'.

picked in November to give a sort of Beeren-auslese – although the early-ripening Müller-Thurgau is the commonest white grape in the German-speaking cantons.

Zürich, Schaffhausen, St Gallen, Basel, even Luzern maintain diminutive wine industries based predominantly on the Blauburgunder. All agree that their wine is expensive, and some that it has charm and delicacy. Certainly the evidence disappears promptly enough: none is available for export – even as far as Geneva.

Left: houses compete for space with the ramps and terraces of vines on the steep north shore of Lake Geneva. Reflected sunshine from the lake helps to ripen the golden Chasselas to make delicate but sometimes excellently lively wine.
Right: German- and Italian-speaking Switzerland rely for their red wines respectively on the Burgundian Pinot Noir and the Merlot of Bordeaux. The best Ticino Merlot carries the legend 'Viti'. Pinot Noir and Gamay (second row) are meanwhile increasingly being planted in the region of Geneva.

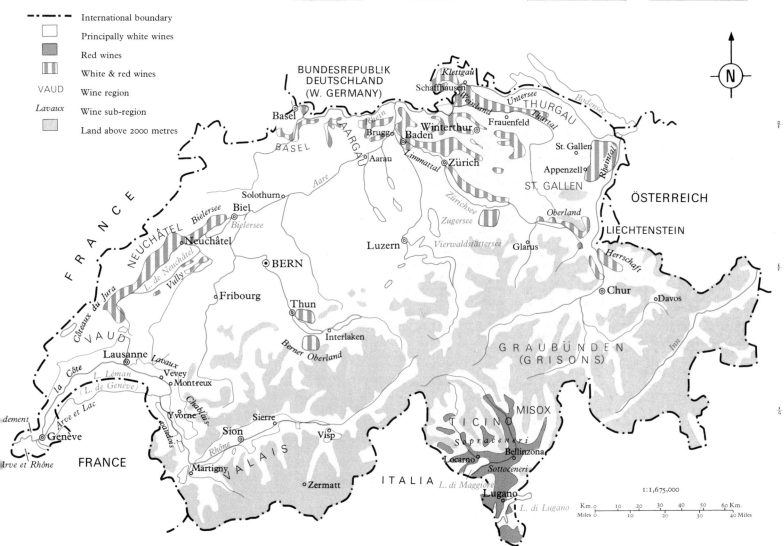

International boundary
Principally white wines
Red wines
White & red wines
VAUD   Wine region
Lavaux   Wine sub-region
Land above 2000 metres

BUNDESREPUBLIK DEUTSCHLAND (W. GERMANY)

Klettgau
Schaffhausen
Untersee
Bodensee
THURGAU
Rheintal
Thurtal
Basel
BASEL
Rhein
Weinland
Frauenfeld
St. Gallen
AARGAU
Brugg
Baden
Winterthur
Aarau
Limmattal
Zürich
Appenzell
ST. GALLEN
FRANCE
Aare
Solothurn
Zürichsee
ÖSTERREICH
Biel
Bielersee
Bielersee
Zugersee
Oberland
LIECHTENSTEIN
NEUCHÂTEL
Neuchâtel
L. de Neuchâtel
Vully
Luzern
Vierwaldstättersee
Glarus
Herrschaft
Côteaux du Jura
Fribourg
BERN
Chur
Davos
Thun
GRAUBÜNDEN (GRISONS)
VAUD
Interlaken
Berner Oberland
Inn
Lausanne
Lavaux
la Côte
Vevey
L. Léman (L. de Genève)
Montreux
MISOX
Yvorne
Chablais
Sierre
TICINO
Sion
Visp
Sopraceneri
dement
Arve et Lac
Genève
Rhône
VALAIS
Locarno
Bellinzona
Arve et Rhône
FRANCE
Martigny
Sottoceneri
Zermatt
ITALIA
L. di Maggiore
Lugano
L. di Lugano

1:1,675,000

Km. 0 10 20 30 40 50 60 Km.
Miles 0   10   20   30   40 Miles

N

Valais and Vaud

The steep sides of the valley which the young river Rhône has carved through the Alps are followed by gentler slopes where it broadens into Lake Geneva. An almost continuous band of vines hugs the river's sunny north bank all the way.

In the higher valley peculiarly Alpine conditions, dry and sunny, and by the lake the mildness brought about by a great body of water both favour the vine in different ways. The Valais and the Vaud, as the two regions are called, are Switzerland's biggest and best vineyards. Including the production of Geneva's vineyards, the Rhône valley gives more than three-quarters of the national total.

Four-fifths of this is white wine. The proportion used to be even higher, but Swiss growers have been planting the Pinot Noir on a large scale and the Gamay of Beaujolais on an even larger.

The great grape of both the Valais and the Vaud is the white Chasselas. In the Valais it is called Fendant, in the Vaud Dorin. It is not reckoned a fine-wine grape in France, but the best of it in Switzerland is extremely pleasant.

In the Valais the centre of Fendant-growing is Sion and the villages just to the west, Conthey, Vétroz and Ardon. There is little rain (Sierre is the driest place in Switzerland) and endless sun. If the vines escape spring frosts they make a powerful wine with as much as 13% alcohol. Irrigation, formerly done by wooden channels called *bisses* coming breakneck down the mountainside, is essential.

The 50-acre (20 ha) Domaine du Mont d'Or has the best site of all: a steep south-facing slope protected at the foot by an outlying hill. The Sylvaner ('Johannisberg') excels itself here, shrivelling on the vine to make splendid rich wines. Even Chasselas wine puts on flesh and stiffens its sinews. Notes on the vines of the Valais and their wines will be found in the Glossary on page 168.

The best red wine of the Valais is known as Dôle. In the Vaud, Dôle-type wine is called Salvagnin. Chablais, the district between Valais and Vaud, between Martigny and Montreux, although in the canton of Vaud, is transitional in character. Aigle and Yvorne and Bex are its best-known villages. Their white wine is strong, but drier and less full than Fendant. With each step westwards, the Chasselas makes more delicate wine.

The central part of the Vaud between Montreux and Lausanne is confusingly called Lavaux. Switzerland's most appealing Chasselas wines, dry, gentle and fruity, are grown in the villages of Lutry, Villette, Epesses, St-Saphorin, Chardonne and Vevey and sold as Dorin with the village name. Dézaley and Dézaley-Marsens are the exceptions; the best wines of the lake, lively and long, with their own appellations.

After Lausanne, La Côte has lighter and less distinguished wines; 40% of the Vaud total. The best is at Féchy. Nyon, the commercial centre, sees more and more light Gamay reds. The same is true of the Geneva vineyards: Gamay is the success. Mandement Chasselas, known as Perlan, tends to be dry and pallid: a far cry from the potent Fendant of Sion.

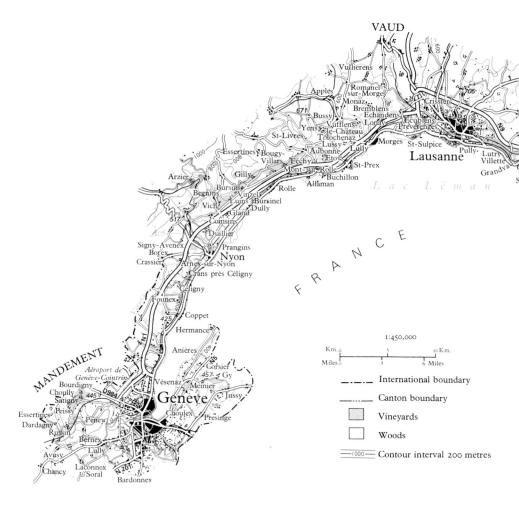

Below: the castle of Aigle stands out in the Rhône valley where it begins to broaden out to Lake Geneva. The centre and south-facing slopes of the valley are thickly planted with vines; where it faces north they are bare.

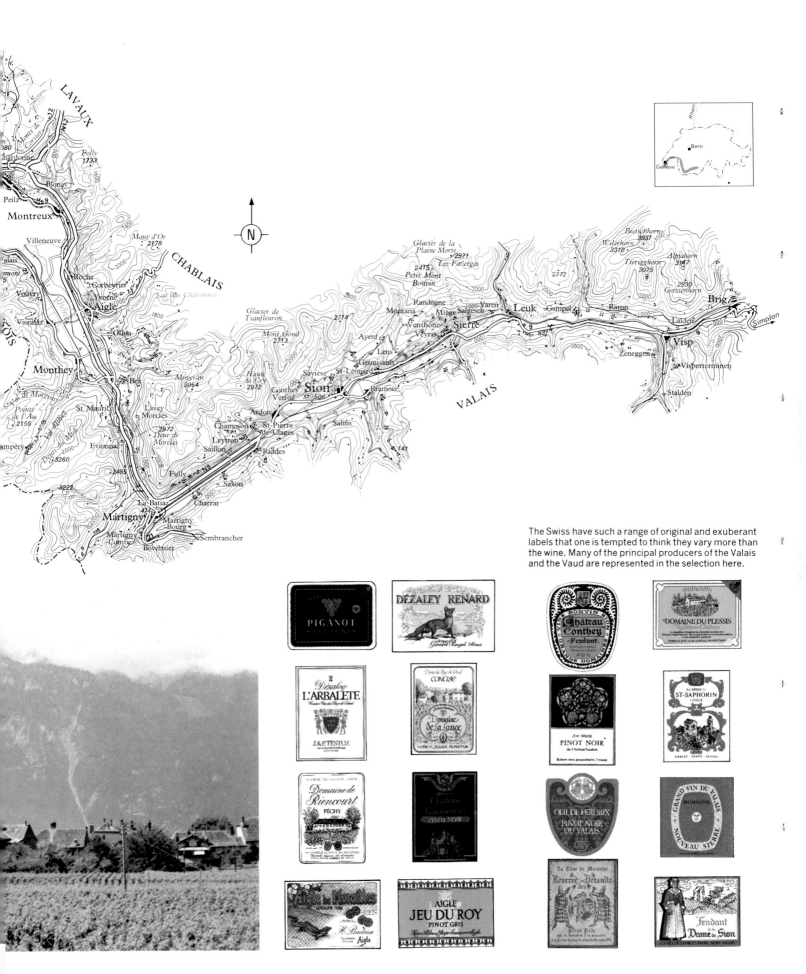

The Swiss have such a range of original and exuberant labels that one is tempted to think they vary more than the wine. Many of the principal producers of the Valais and the Vaud are represented in the selection here.

Austria

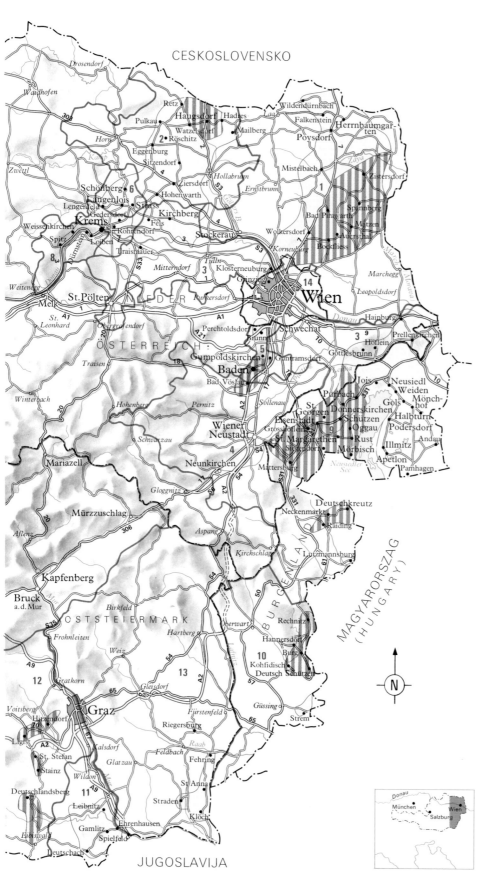

CESKOSLOVENSKO

JUGOSLAVIJA

International boundary

State boundary

Boundary of wine regions

St. Georgen — Commune with more than 300 hectares of vines

Principal white wine area

Principal red and white wine area

The wine regions of Austria

1 Falkenstein	8 Wachau
2 Retz	9 Rust-Neusiedler-See
3 Klosterneuberg	10 Eisenberg
4 Vöslau	11 Südsteiermark
5 Gumpoldskirchen	12 Weststeiermark
6 Langenlois	13 Klöch Oststeiermark
7 Krems	14 Wien

1:1,225,000

Km. 0   25   50 Km.

Miles 0   25 Miles

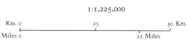

Above: Ruster Ausbruch (top right) is sweet wine from the Burgenland. The others come from Vienna, Gumpoldskirchen and Styria in the south.

Right: the vineyards of Nussdorf supply the Heurigen, or taverns, of Vienna and the Vienna woods.

Austria has such a famous and flourishing tradition of making light wine for local consumption that the world was long misled into thinking that that is all she does. Granted that her 'open' wines are as good as any on earth, they are not easy to bottle and export with their character intact. Fifteen years ago Austria had virtually no wine exports, and her small proportion of top-quality wines went ignored by the world along with the rest.

Now exports total some 450,000 hectolitres a year. New technology has revived old traditions all over Austria. Today she offers under still-unfamiliar names some of Europe's most exciting white wines.

New wine laws, passed in 1972, have been a big factor. Austria now has a system of Qualitätswein, Kabinetts and the rest parallel to the German. The chief difference is that all German quality wines are tested for their 'Prüfungsnummer', while in Austria only those with the 'Austrian Wine Seal' are officially approved – also that standards of ripeness, in this southern climate, are higher: an Austrian Spätlese has the (potential) alcohol of a German Auslese.

Red wine is only of local significance. All Austria's best wine, like Germany's, is white. Her central position among Europe's northern and eastern vineyards shows in the character of the wine she makes. There is something of the freshness of the Rhine in it – but more of the fieriness and high flavour of the Danube.

Only eastern Austria makes wine. The vineyards are concentrated north and east of Vienna. Styria (Steiermark) in the south, bordering on Yugoslavia's principal vineyard region, Slovenia, is of minor importance, although the Traminers of Klöch, grown on volcanic soil, are good. The regions that are flourishing, and of which we are likely to hear more, are the Wachau and Vienna with its Südbahn (both mapped in detail overleaf), Burgenland around the Neusiedler See southeast of the capital, and the Weinviertel (Falkenstein and Retz) in the northeast.

Burgenland (see the map below) lies on the Hungarian border – indeed the Hungarian wine district of Sopron is carved out of it. Like Hungary, it specializes in sweet wines. The country is flat and sandy around the lake (an extraordinary pool, more than 30 kilometres long and only a metre deep) and mists envelop it through its long warm autumns, making the noble rot a regular occurrence.

The most historically famous wine of Burgenland comes from Rust. Ruster Ausbruch (the local term for a wine between a Beeren- and a Trockenbeerenauslese) was formerly compared with Tokay. Today vineyards on both sides of the lake produce luscious wines of marvellous quality. The Esterhazy estate at Eisenstadt wins gold medals regularly, and Lenz Moser at Apetlon (among others) makes superb Ausleses.

The grapes include Riesling, Müller-Thurgau, Muskat-Ottonel (one of the many varieties of this ubiquitous grape), Weissburgunder, Ruländer and Traminer. Where the name Riesling is used alone it means the inferior Italian Riesling; real Riesling is always called Rheinriesling.

The red wines, made of Pinot Noir (Blauburgunder), Blaufränkisch, St-Laurent and Portugieser, are not up to the standard of the whites.

In contrast to those of Burgenland, the wines of the Weinviertel (the name means 'wine quarter') are in the main light and dry. The great grape here is Austria's favourite, the Grüner Veltliner, and the popular name Falkensteiner. Veltliner wine when it is well made and young is marvellously fresh and fruity, with plenty of acidity and an almost spicy flavour. To compare it with Rhine Riesling is like comparing a wild flower with a finely bred garden variety in which scent and colour and size and form have been studied and improved for many years.

There are times, when Grüner Veltliner wine is drawn straight from the barrel into a tumbler, frothing and gleaming a piercing greeny gold, when it seems like the quintessence of all that a wine should be. Drink it then, with a sandwich on the terrace. It will never taste like that under any other conditions.

In the past one reason for the disappointing quality of some Austrian wines shipped abroad was that they did not come from Austria at all. Austria used to be free and easy about labelling, both of her own and other countries' products. Unfortunately, the practice of using her name on wine from Eastern Europe and Italy helped to obscure the splendid quality of some of the wine she really makes.

·—·—·—	International boundary
—·—·—·	Provincial boundary
——————	Parish boundary
SONNENBERG	Grosslage
HOFÄCKER	Ried (Einzellage)

☐	Vineyards
☐	Woods
☐	Marsh
══250══	Contour interval 50 metres

Burgenland

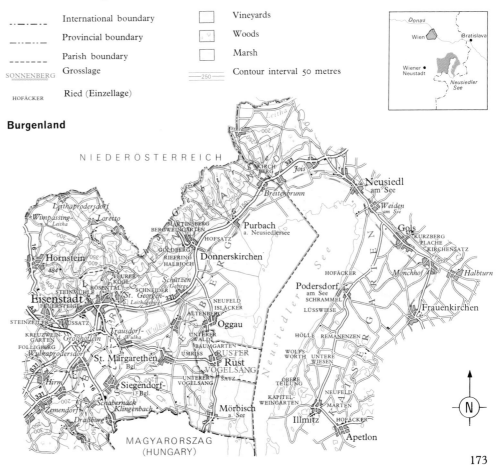

Vienna

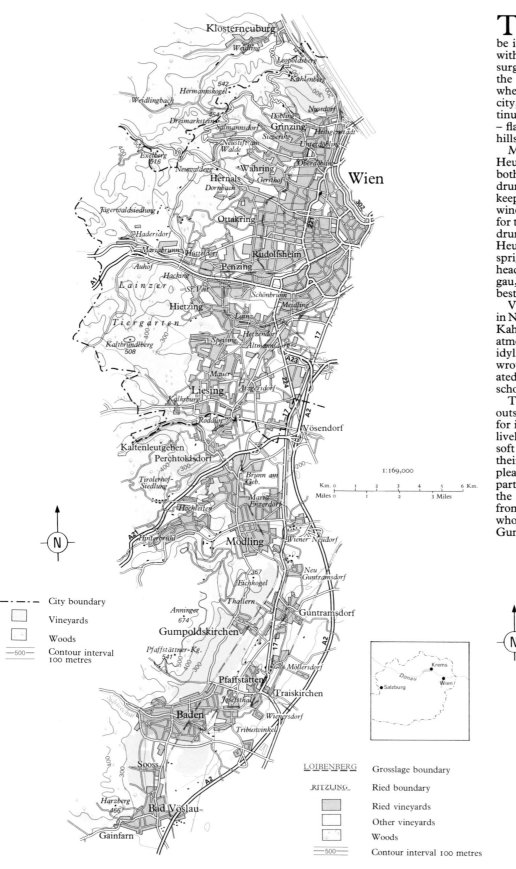

There is no capital city that is so identified with wine as Vienna. New wine seems to be its lifeblood. Vineyards hold their ground within the heart of the residential districts and surge up the side of the surrounding hills into the Vienna woods. North, east and south, where the line of hills circles and protects the city, there are vines. To the south they continue along the Südbahn – the southern railway – flanking the last crinkle of the Alpine foothills facing the Hungarian plain.

Most of their wine is drunk as Heurige, in Heurigen – for this untranslatable word means both the new wine and the tavern where it is drunk. Every vintner seems to be a tavern keeper as well, and chalks up on a board the wines he has and the (modest) prices he wants for them, by jug or litre bottle, label-less, to be drunk on the spot or carried away. When Heurige is good it is sensational; spirited, sprightly stuff which goes straight to your head. Most of it is Veltliner or Müller-Thurgau, some is Riesling, some is Traminer. The best of the new wines are not too dry.

Viennese connoisseurs know every grower in Neustift, Grinzing, Sievering, Nussdorf and Kahlenberg, the wine villages of Vienna. The atmosphere in their leafy taverns varies from idyllic to hilarious. In most of them Beethoven wrote at least a concerto. The region is dominated by the splendid monastic cellars and wine school at Klosterneuburg.

The Südbahn wines are better known to the outside world. Gumpoldskirchen, above all, for its fine late-gathered wines made from the lively Zierfändler, the heavier Rotgipfler or the soft Ruländer, and Baden and Bad Vöslau for their reds. The red wine is dark, dry and pleasant, appetizing and heady without having particular character. Some of the best wines of the area, including fine Rheinrieslings, come from the Heiligenstift monastery at Thallern, whose famous 'ried' of Wiege overlooks Gumpoldskirchen from the hill.

City boundary

Vineyards

Woods

Contour interval 100 metres

1:169,000

LOIBENBERG — Grosslage boundary

RITZLING — Ried boundary

Ried vineyards

Other vineyards

Woods

Contour interval 100 metres

174

The Wachau

The village of Dürnstein, with its castle and excellent hotel, is the spiritual heart of the Wachau. Richard Coeur de Lion was imprisoned here. Today the cooperative dominates the district.

The Wachau cooperative (top) is the biggest bottler, but individual growers and vineyards are becoming better known.

The Wachau is Austria's best-known wine area. It lies only 40 miles (65km) west of Vienna, at a point where the Danube broaches a range of 1,600-foot (490m) hills. For a short stretch the craggy north bank of the river, as steep as some of the Mosel slopes, is patchworked with vines on ledges and outcrops, along narrow paths up from the river to the crowning woods.

There are patches of deep soil and others where a mere scratching finds rock, patches with daylong sunlight and others that always seem to be in shade. There is no grand sweep of vines here; no big estates and no unique vine variety. The Wachau is a pattern of small growers with mixed vineyards – who make good wine.

The principal export from the Wachau is the Grüner Veltliner known as Schluck. Much of it also comes from the Kamp valley, an important vineyard area running south from Langenlois to Krems on strange soft 'loess', half soil, half rock. The real character of the region, though, is better seen in its individual vineyard Grüner Veltliners – often marvellously high-spirited and fiery, almost peppery, performances. Best of all, although rarer, is the Rheinriesling. In the long, dry autumns of the Wachau it can make great wine.

The dominant presence in the area is the efficient growers' cooperative. Nearly 3,000 growers belong to it. The cooperative is at Dürnstein, the scenic climax of the valley. A very good hotel by the river is named after Richard the Lionheart, who was imprisoned here. The baroque steeple, the ruined castle and the tilting vineyards of Dürnstein are irresistibly pretty and suggestive.

Near by, to the east of the Wachau, beyond Krems (and off the map), the hills slant away from the Danube to the northeast, are lower and become sandy. Just around this corner is the village of Rohrendorf, where Austria's most famous grower, Lenz Moser, has his cellars.

Lenz Moser is the originator of a method of training vines on wires at twice the usual height which has been adopted by many progressive growers all over the world. He achieves higher yields, better quality and lower labour costs, he says, with his 'high culture' system. Lenz Moser wines, made from the produce of his vineyards in several parts of Austria, are certainly an excellent advertisement for it.

THE LANGUAGE OF THE LABEL

Many of the words that used to appear on German labels before the 1971 German wine law are still seen on Austrian ones, including:

Naturwein Wine without added sugar
Reinsortig Only this particular type
Originalabfüllung Estate-bottled
Eigenbaugewächs From the maker's own vineyard
Weingarten, Weingut Wine estate
Ried Vineyard (as in French *clos*)

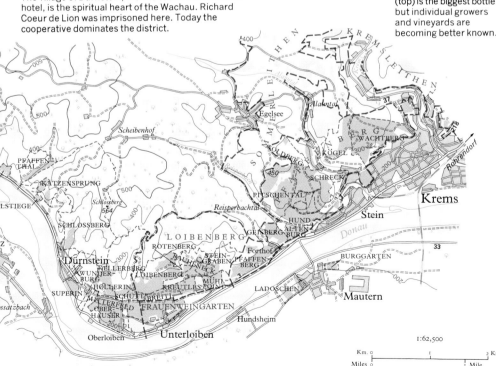

1:62,500

Km. 0   1   2 Km.
Miles 0   1 Mile

Italy

The Greeks called Italy Oenotria – the land of wine. The map reminds us that there is little of Italy that is not, at least marginally, wine country. Her annual production is now easily the biggest in the world.

The first edition of this Atlas described the Italian attitude to wine as amiably insouciant – chaotic enough, with its delights and disappointments, to drive a tidy-minded wine merchant to drink. Fourteen years have seen radical changes. The Italian is no longer insouciant – at least not about making and marketing wine. (Drinking it is another matter.) But there are still aspects of Italian wine that take patience and goodwill to understand.

In terms of geography, Italy cannot fail to produce good wine in great variety. If hill slopes, sunshine and a temperate climate are the essentials, Italy has more of them than any country in Europe. Her peculiar physique, that of a long spine of mountains reaching south from the sheltering Alps, almost to North Africa, means that there can hardly be a desirable combination of altitude with latitude and exposure that is absent. Many of her soils are volcanic; much is limestone or tufa; there is plenty of gravelly clay: Oenotria indeed.

To the consumer, however, Italy has a serious drawback: an impossible confusion of names. Because wine is omnipresent, so much a part of everyday life, made by so many proud and independent people, every conceivable sort of name is pressed into use to mark originality. Thus one bottle may carry on it not only the official (DOC) name, often the name of the grape, and the name of the producer, but the name of his property, of a part of his property, or of anything else that takes his fancy – and fantasy it very often is. It must be difficult sometimes for Italians to understand how bewildering a wine label can be, when a foreigner has no idea which name represents the maker, which the place, and which the liquid in the bottle. Matters are made much worse by the habit of omitting the name of the region. Often the name of an obscure town is the only geographical reference on a label.

Italy desperately needs a labelling system – not necessarily a new wine law – in which it is clear who made the wine, where, and how it should be referred to.

Over the past 22 years the Italian government has done a monumental job of tidying up the multiplicity of Italian wines into defined identities. The Italian DOC (Denominazione di Origine Controllata) system is described opposite – see Wine Law. At the same time, though, a serious drawback in the system has become clear. What it has effectively done is to fossilize the current practice of the majority of winemakers in each region, regardless of whether it led to the best results or not. Indeed, it actually penalizes the progressive winemaker who knows that certain changes of practice (whether, for example, of grape varieties, their treatment, or the ageing of the wine) could greatly improve his products.

On the maps that follow the lead is given by the official version. The boundary of almost every DOC created up to 1985 is shown. But many worthwhile 'unofficial' wines, those that

despite their splendid qualities may only use the humble grade of *vino da tavola*, are also marked with their names. (They have, of course, no boundaries to delineate.)

The Italian section of this Atlas is much extended in this edition, in response to the significant raising of quality standards in many regions. The map on this page is intended as a reminder of the disposition of the regions (e.g. Tuscany or Campania) and as a key to the subsequent more detailed maps. All the current DOCs appear on the four pages that carve up the country into northwest, northeast, centre and south, except those in the complex centres of quality winegrowing which are given

large-scale maps of their own. There are six more of these in this edition than in the last.

And the wine? Are all the best wines of Italy still red? Most, but by no means all. Italy conquered the art of modern white winemaking in the 1960s. In the 1980s she is adding back the character that was lost in the process. Her red wines have never been better. They range from the silky and fragile to the purple and potent. Above all their qualities, and the qualities of all Italian wine, must be seen in the context of the incredibly varied, simple, sensuous Italian table. The true genius of Italy lies in spreading a feast. In the great Italian feast, wine plays the chief supporting role.

The Italian wine law now recognizes five categories of wine:

Vino da Tavola The most basic and uncontrolled (but see below).

Vino da Tavola con Indicazione Geografica The same with its regional origin stated (and, by implication, subject to control) but without set standards. Wines that state their grape variety must also state their origin.

Vino Tipico A new category for wines of stated and proven origin not subject to the strict controls of DOC but officially approved as representing their area.

Denominazione di Origine Controllata (DOC) The principal category. A body of winegrowers may apply to have their wine registered as DOC. They must agree with Rome where it can be produced and the standards of quality it must reach (e.g. specific grapes, traditional methods, limited yields, proper ageing, adequate records). DOC wines are subject to test and must wear a DOC label in addition to their own.

Denominazione Controllata e Garantita (DOCG) The top rank, awarded only to tested and approved wines from top-quality zones. To be DOCG a wine must be bottled and sealed with a government seal by the producer or someone who takes full responsibility for it.

It has been assumed that eventually all the best wines in Italy would be DOCG. However, by 1985 only five had been declared: Barolo, Barbaresco, Chianti, Brunello di Montalcino and Vino Nobile di Montepulciano. It remains to be seen whether their quality will suddenly all become consistently high.

Meanwhile it has become abundantly clear that many independently minded and creative winemakers (those most likely, in fact, to make the best wine) dislike the shackles of the whole DOC system and prefer to accept that their more individual products can only be sold under the humblest title of all: that of *vino da tavola*. Ironically, the table-wine status reserved by the EEC for undemarcated wines has almost become a badge of nobility in Italy.

This Atlas maps the delimited areas of the 220-odd DOC wines declared by 1985. The fact of their acceptance does not prove their importance; there has been a bandwagon element with all sorts of minor productions climbing aboard. The maps also show, without delimited areas, a number of the *vini da tavola* with established reputations.

A north Italian grower returns to the primitive method of testing the ripeness of his grapes. A refractometer is more precise, but a mouthful can give a foretaste of the wine to come: its ripeness, acidity and aroma.

○ ITALY ○ FRANCE ○ OTHERS

Italy is the world's biggest wine producer: more than 77 million hectolitres a year to France's 71m. Total world production averages 345m.

FRANCE	33.6%
WEST GERMANY	26.4%
USA	15%
GREAT BRITAIN	5%
OTHER COUNTRIES	20%

Exports of Italian wine have generally risen steadily over the last decade, averaging more than 18 million hectolitres a year — one of the results of quality being raised by a revolution in Italian attitudes to winemaking. Exports now exceed imports by an average of 100 to 1. France and West Germany take (in bulk) more than half, followed by the USA (in bottle). Other large customers include Switzerland and the USSR.

Italy consumes 46 million hectolitres of wine a year: 91.4 litres per head of population — down from 104 litres in the mid-1970s and 115 litres in 1969.

THE LANGUAGE OF THE LABEL

Tenementi Holding or estate
Vendemmia Vintage
Denominazione di Origine Controllata e Garantita Similar to Appellation Contrôlée (see *Wine Law*)
Riserva Wine aged for a statutory period (usually three years)
Classico From the central and best area of its region
Imbottigliato (or **Messo in bottiglia**) **nel'origine** (or **del produttore all'origine**) Estate bottled
Imbottigliato nello stabilimento della ditta Bottled on the premises of the firm
Fiasco (pl. **fiaschi**) Flask (e.g. Chianti)
Infiascato alla fattoria Bottled in *fiaschi* at the winery
Vini da banco or **vino ordinario** (or **vino da tavola**) Non-DOC wine, ranging from the coarsest to the finest in the land
Bianco White
Rosso Red
Nero Very dark red
Chiaretto Very light red

Rosato Pink
Secco Dry
Amaro Bitter or very dry
Amabile or **Abboccato** Medium sweet
Dolce Very sweet
Spumante Sparkling
Frizzante Half-sparkling
Gradi (or **Gradi alcool** or **Grado alcoolico**) followed by a number: percentage of alcohol by volume
Casa vinicola Wine firm
Cantina Cellar, winery or bar
Cantina sociale (or **cooperativa**) Winegrowers' cooperative
Consorzio Local growers' association with legal standing
Vin or **Vino santo** Wine made from grapes dried indoors over winter
Passito Similar
Cotto Cooked (i.e. concentrated) wine, a speciality of a few regions
Stravecchio Very old, ripe, mellow
Vino liquoroso Fortified wine

Northwest Italy

Left: the presence of the Alps is felt everywhere in Piemonte. At Carema, on the road to the Valle d'Aosta, the houses already have the wide eaves of chalets.

Above: the neighbouring regions of Piemonte and Lombardy offer the widest range of high-quality wines in Italy, from pungent Nebbiolos to crisp sparkling wines.

Northwest Italy means Piemonte to any wine lover. In its bitter-sweet vermouths, its grapey spumantes, its pungent purple wines for dishes of game and cheese, it epitomizes the sensuality of gastronomic Italy. On the next two pages its heart is shown in detail.

But the Monferrato hills around Alba and Asti are not the only great vineyard of the northwest. The excellent grape that makes Barolo, the Nebbiolo, gives excellent, if different, results in several corners of the region. Surprisingly, though, nowhere else. There must be microclimates in the New World, and even farther south in Italy, that would bring out its character to perfection.

Two other northwestern centres of Nebbiolo growing are mapped on pages 182 and 183. (In each case the grape bears a different name.) North of Turin on the road up to the Valle d'Aosta and the Mont Blanc tunnel to France there are two more, of high reputation but low output, Carema and Donnaz. Carema is still in Piemonte (but nonetheless calls the Nebbiolo Picutener); Donnaz is over the provincial boundary in the Valle d'Aosta, Italy's smallest wine region. Alpine conditions

make these Nebbiolos less potent and deep-coloured but scarcely less fine than the best Barolos. They are rarities that can fetch a high premium.

Aosta's other notable red rarity is the Enfer d'Arvier, made of a grape known as the Petit Rouge which tastes not unlike the Mondeuse of Savoie: dark, fresh, berryish and bracing; altogether an excellent Alpine wine. The busy valley also has some recherché whites: the very light Blancs de la Salle and de Morgex, and some winter-weight Malvoisies.

Piemonte's 'other' wines, not mapped elsewhere, include a fresh and individual red and white from north of Turin: Rubino di Cantavenna and Erbaluce di Caluso. Rubino is Barbera-based, but light and lively, while the wine of Caluso is either light and dry or made into a full-bodied semi-sweet *passito*. One of the favourites of Turin itself is its local Freisa, a fizzy and frequently sweet red not unlike a more tart and less fruity form of Lambrusco. Confusingly enough, the Malvasia di Casorzo d'Asti is a similar red – just when you had thought that all Malvasias were white.

Central Piemonte, close as it is to the

Mediterranean, is sub-alpine and relatively extreme in climate. But south over the final curling tail of the Alps, known as the Ligurian Apennines, we are on the Mediterranean, with scarcely enough room between the mountains and the sea to grow grapes. Liguria's production is tiny, but highly individual and worth investigating. Of its grapes only Vermentino and Malvasia are widely grown elsewhere: the white Bosco, Pigato, Buzzetto and Albarola are as esoteric as they sound. Cinqueterre is the white-wine name you will hear, for the 'fish wine' of the steep coast near La Spezia. Its liquorous version is called Sciacchetrà. Other less-known coastal whites should be tasted on a visit to Genoa: you will not find them elsewhere.

Potentially the most memorable Ligurian wine, however, is the red Rossese, whether of Dolceacqua near the French border or Albenga, nearer Genoa. Unlike anything made west along the coast in the Alpes Maritimes, Rossese can be truly fresh, fruity in the soft-fruit or berry sense of Bordeaux, inviting to smell and refreshing to drink. Nor does it need any ageing.

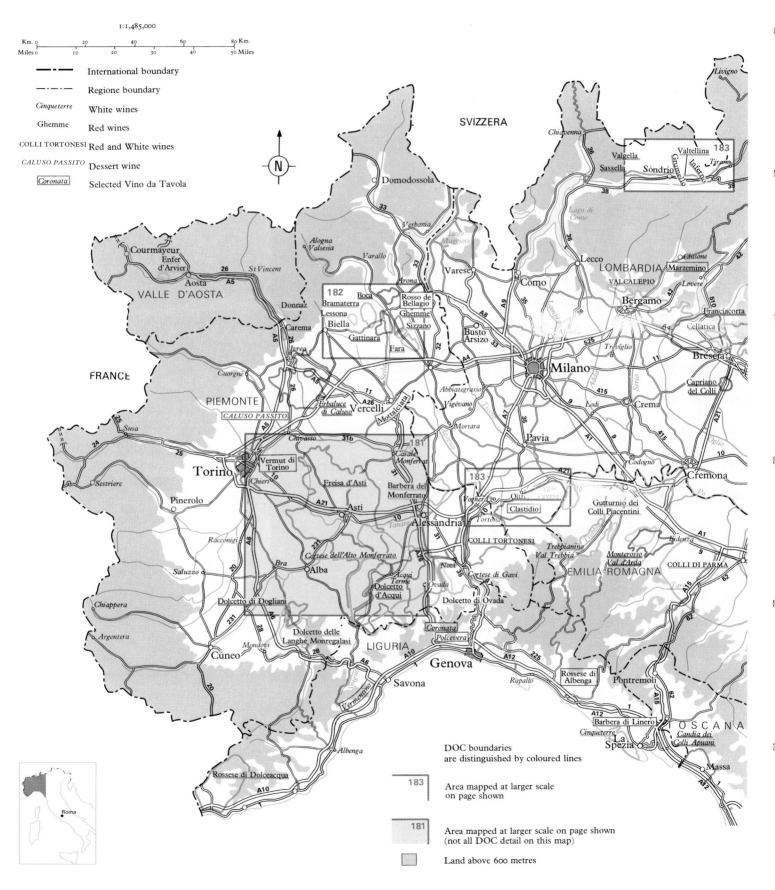

Km. 0   20   40   60   80 Km.
1:1,485,000

Miles 0   10   20   30   40   50 Miles

International boundary
Regione boundary

Cinqueterre   White wines
Ghemme   Red wines
COLLI TORTONESI   Red and White wines
CALUSO PASSITO   Dessert wine
Coronata   Selected Vino da Tavola

N

SVIZZERA

Livigno

Chiavenna

Valgella   Valtellina   **183**
Sassella   Sòndrio   Inferno   Tirano
Grumello

Domodossola

Lago di Como

Verbania

Lago Maggiore

Chisone

Alogna Valsesia

LOMBARDIA

Lecco

Marzemino

Varallo

VALCALEPIO

Lovere

Arona

Varese

Como

Bergamo

Franciacorta

FRANCE

Courmàyeur
Enfer d'Arvier
St Vincent

Aosta

Cellatica

VALLE D'AOSTA

182

Boca

Bramaterra

Rosso de Bellagio

Busto Arsizo

Treviglio

Brescia

Donnaz

Lessona

Ghemme

Capriano del Colli

Carema

Biella

Sizzano

Milano

Crema

Ivrea

Gattinara

Fara

PIEMONTE

Cuorgnè

Erbaluce di Caluso

CALUSO PASSITO

Vercelli

Mottalciata

Abbiategrasso

Vigèvano

Lodi

Codogno

Cremona

Susa

Chivasso

181

Casale Monferrato

Mortara

Pavia

Sestriere

Vermut di Torino

Torino

Chieri

Freisa d'Asti

Barbera del Monferrato

183

Voghera

Oltrepò Pavese

Clastidio

Gutturnio dei Colli Piacentini

Pinerolo

Asti

Alessandria

Tortona

COLLI TORTONESI

Ràcconigi

Novi

Trebbianino Val Trebbia

Fidenza

Bra

Cortese dell'Alto Monferrato

Alba

Cortese di Gavi

Monterosso Val d'Arda

COLLI DI PARMA

Saluzzo

Acqui Terme

Ovada

EMILIA-ROMAGNA

Chiappera

Dolcetto d'Acqui

Dolcetto di Ovada

Argentera

Dolcetto di Dogliani

Coronata

Cùneo

Mondovì

Dolcetto delle Langhe Monregalasi

LIGURIA

Polcevera

Genova

Rossese di Albenga

Pontremoli

Savona

Rapallo

Rossese di Dolceacqua

Barbera di Linero

TOSCANA

Albenga

Cinqueterre

Candia dei Colli Apuani

La Spezia

Massa

Roma

DOC boundaries
are distinguished by coloured lines

183   Area mapped at larger scale
on page shown

181   Area mapped at larger scale on page shown
(not all DOC detail on this map)

Land above 600 metres

Piemonte

Piemontese food and wine, like those of Burgundy, are inseparable. They are strong, rich, individual, mature, somehow autumnal. One feels it must be more than coincidence that this is the Italian province nearest to France.

Piemonte means at the foot of the mountains; the Alps. But it is on the substantial range of the Monferrato hills that the great Piemontese wines are grown. Nonetheless the Alps have their effect, encircling the region and giving it a climate of its own, with a very hot growing season and a misty autumn.

At vintage time in Barolo the hills are half hidden. Ramps of copper and gold vines, dotted with hazel and peach trees, lead down to the valley of the Tanaro, lost in the fog. It is a magical experience to visit Serralunga or La Morra and see the dark grapes coming in.

The two best red wines of Piemonte, Barolo and Barbaresco, take their names from villages. The rest have the names of their grapes – Barbera, Dolcetto, Grignolino, Freisa. If to the grape they add a district name (e.g. Barbera d'Asti) it means they come from a limited and theoretically superior area. The map shows the zones of central Piemonte – including that of the famous Moscato d'Asti spumante. The still, dry white Cortese di Gavi is grown south of Alessandria to the east. In recent years new techniques have been used to make Gavi one of Italy's most prestigious white wines; almost, in the right hands, the nation's white burgundy.

Barolo is a wine on the scale of Châteauneuf-du-Pape. Its minimum strength is 13%: going up to 15. It often throws a heavy sediment in its bottle, even after a minimum of three years in cask and often longer, so Barolo bottles are traditionally kept standing up, unlike all other red wines.

The flavour of Barolo, and above all its scent, are the most memorable of any Italian wine. The Nebbiolo grape gives it a suggestion of truffles, a touch of tar, a positive note of raspberry. The traditionalist school of thought still sometimes stores its best wines for as long as seven or eight years in huge tuns, giving

Left: Fontanafredda, under a ridge of Nebbiolo vines, is one of the finest estates of Barolo.
Below: dark red wines, full of character, and sweet sparkling white wines, delicate and grapey, are the specialities of Piemonte. Barolo and Barbaresco are the two noble wines. Soft dry Dolcetto and lively, cutting Barbera are the two favourites for everyday.

Torino · Chieri · Asti · Alessandria · Casale · Acqui · Bra · Alba

DOCG Barbaresco
DOC Barbera d'Alba
DOC Barbera d'Asti
DOC Barbera del Monferrato
DOCG Barolo
DOC Brachetto d'Acqui
DOC Cortese dell'Alto Monferrato
DOC Dolcetto di Acqui
DOC Dolcetto d'Alba
DOC Dolcetto d'Asti
DOC Dolcetto di Diano d'Alba
DOC Dolcetto di Dogliani
DOC Freisa d'Asti
DOC Freisa di Chieri
DOC Grignolino d'Asti
DOC Grignolino del Monferrato Casalese
DOC Malvasia di Casorzo d'Asti
DOC Malvasia di Castelnuovo don Bosco
DOC Moscato d'Asti
DOC Nebbiolo d'Alba
DOC Rubino di Cantavenna

Vineyards
Woods

1:365,000

Km. 0   10 Km.
Miles 0   10 Miles

Provincia boundary
—200— Contour interval 100 metres

them an astringency that can fatigue both the wine and the drinker. More modern makers bottle after three years, looking to the bottle to enchant the potent plummy wine into giving up its bouquet.

Barolos from the eastern hills of the little region, around Serralunga d'Alba and Monforte, tend to be the most masculine; those from Barolo itself and La Morra comparatively gentle, although still on a very big scale. Most favoured of all are the ridges of hill between the two, often indicated on the labels of proud growers by the term 'bricco' – the hilltop.

Barbaresco only differs from Barolo in coming from lower down, where fog affects the vineyard sooner, making a slightly milder, less

fully ripened wine. Barolo which fails to come up to strength, sold simply as Nebbiolo, although lighter, can still be excellent. To the north, around Novara (see map page 183), the same grape under the name Spanna makes equally remarkable wine.

Barbera is dark, tannic, often rather plummy and acidic; ideal wine with rich food. Freisa, the speciality of Chieri south of Turin, can be similar – or sweet and sparkling. Dolcetto is light, intriguingly balanced between dusty softness and a hard note of bitterness; not to be aged; the carafe wine of the region. The best Dolcetto comes from Diano d'Alba. Grignolino is also a lightweight but a finer, more piquant one; at its best extremely clean,

stimulating and happy. All these are to drink relatively young.

Other specialities of this prolific region, the spaghetti-junction of *denominaziones*, include another frothy sweet red wine, Brachetto d'Acqui, sweet pink or red Malvasia, the interesting yellow *passito* (made from semi-dried grapes) with the DOC Erbaluce or Caluso and the agreeable blend of Barbera and Grignolino sold as Rubino di Cantavenna (see page 179).

Traditions mean even more in this proud and wine-conscious region than in most of Italy. Yet here too winemakers are becoming inventive. One makes a delicious blend of Nebbiolo and Barbera. Nothing is sacred.

Piemonte and Lombardy

The country north of Novara (which lies on the autostrada between Turin and Milan) is a good 50 miles (80 kilometres) from Barolo, the spiritual home of the noble Nebbiolo. But its Alpine foothills, tilted towards Lake Maggiore to the east and the Po valley to the south, have the excellent drainage of glacial moraines and something of the same weather pattern as the Langhe hills: hot summer glazing over with autumn mists. The Nebbiolo flourishes here, too. Only here it is called by the local name of Spanna.

There are seven different DOCs in the Vercelli and Novara hills for wine of more or less the same identity: Spanna with a greater or lesser leavening of two or three less pungent local (and Lombardy) grapes, principally Bonarda (which has a variant called Croatina) and Vespolina. The more Nebbiolo they contain, the more exalted they are, or can be. Gattinara, in this sense, is the king, with Ghemme and Lessona as consorts. In approximate order of (potential) quality, the field consists of Boca, Bramaterra, Fara and Sizzano.

In practice, of course, all depends on the producer. Gattinara, as the best known, with a very limited zone, is the most often traduced. At best a near-Barolo (Monsecco is the classic example), the generality is a much-diluted version, most notable for its rich and far-reaching perfume. Ghemme is usually less expensive and as good or better. Lessona is different: a less brawny-textured wine, with something of the fluidity (although not the nose) of a good Bordeaux.

Bramaterra is a near neighbour to Gattinara, also limited in supply, more astringent and less ample. Boca is often admirable; Barolo's country cousin. Fara is smaller, easier, often pretty – but has an exceptional interpretation called Caramino. Sizzano is the most dilute. The term Spanna covers them all, and one conscientious producer, Antonio Vallana, has given it a dignity at least worthy of the official DOCs of the region.

Gattinara is the best-known name of the group of 'Spanna' (Nebbiolo) wines of northern Piemonte.

Lombardy, land of contrasts. There can hardly be a greater contrast in Italy than that between the plain of the Po and the deep trench cut by Lombardy's northernmost river, the Adda, on its way out of the Alps to join Lake Como.

The 30 miles (50 kilometres) where the Adda flows due west, under, as it were, the very walls of Switzerland, gives its valley a perfect sheltered southern slope, where vines can be tilted at the sun.

The vines in question are the Nebbiolo of Piemonte, growing on Lombardy soil under the *nom de terre* of Chiavennasca. All the best sloping sites are planted with Chiavennasca, and qualify for the DOC Valtellina Superiore. Four sub-zones have specific names: Sassella (considered the best), Valgella, Grumello and Inferno. It would, however, take long and careful study to find consistent differences. What they have in common is more important: the early bite, the developing texture, the emerging autumnal fragrances of the Nebbiolo, here always leaner and less sensuous than in the Langhe hills of Piemonte, but at best scarcely less fine.

Superiore is an essential qualification. The less-favoured sites of the valley give plain Valtellina, which is welcome enough in Switzerland (St Moritz is just over the hill), but bears little resemblance to a Nebbiolo. The other grapes that go into its constitution are Merlot, Pinot Noir, and lesser local fruit. The result is rarely more than clean and spare.

Half-dried grapes are used in the Valtellina to make Sfursat or Sforzato, an Alpine Recioto with the concentration to age for many years.

Gattinara

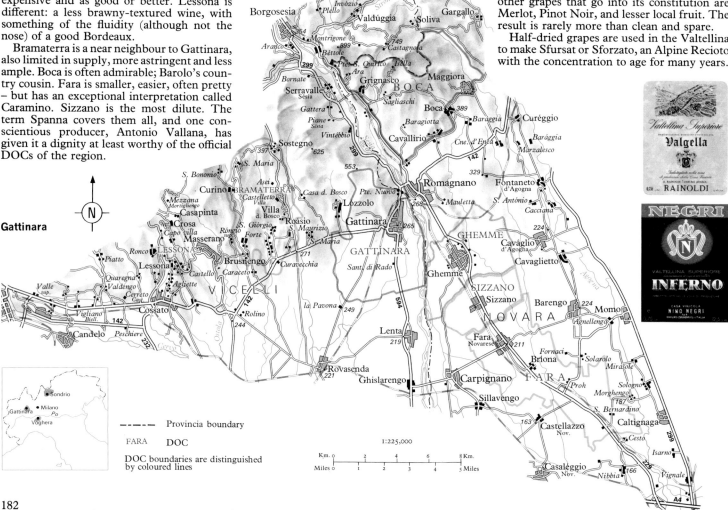

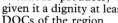

Provincia boundary

FARA   DOC

DOC boundaries are distinguished by coloured lines

1:225,000

Km. 0   2   4   6   8 Km.

Miles 0   1   2   3   4   5 Miles

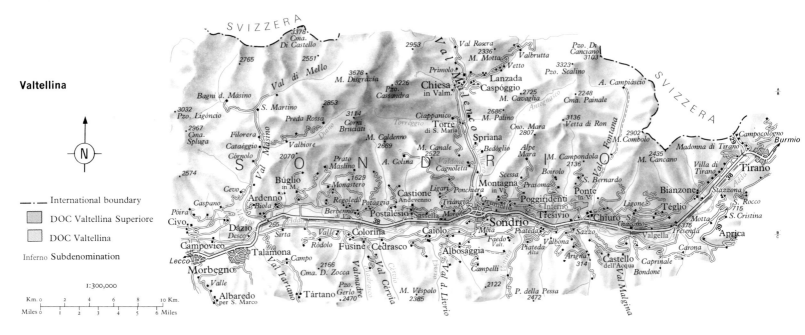

Valtellina

- ─·─ International boundary
- ▨ DOC Valtellina Superiore
- ▨ DOC Valtellina
- *Inferno* Subdenomination

1:300,000

Km. 0 2 4 6 8 10 Km.
Miles 0 1 2 3 4 5 6 Miles

It is hard to offer a translation as musical as the name of this fulcrum of Lombardic viticulture, mapped below. Oltrepò Pavese means the part of the province of Pavia that lies beyond the Po.

Far harder, though, is to convey in any orderly way the profusion of its wines, some blessed with a DOC, some not, and much even sold without its geographical origin at all. Much of Italy's best Pinot Blanc for the making of high-quality sparkling wines comes from here without mentioning the fact.

The best way to picture the region and its wines is as the dying ripples of the turbulence of hill and mountain in the northeast before the level Lombardy plain. The DOC Oltrepò Pavese Rosso is a guide to the usual blend of grapes that makes most (non-varietal) wines: it calls for two-thirds Barbera, fruity, rough and acidic, mollified with a variety of local grapes, of which Bonarda is the most prevalent. Bonarda balances sharp Barbera with heavier flavours and a touch of the bitterness in the finish that Italians love. Uva Rara and Ughetta are more esoteric minority seasonings. The best-known wine (and one of the best) to use the DOC is Frecciarossa, from Casteggio. Both Barbera and Bonarda are also sold straight, as varietal wines.

Oltrepò white wines include 'Pinot', which can be either Bianco or Nero (made white) or Grigio or all of these. Pinot Grigio is most common without bubbles: a dense and potentially delicious wine that suggests its relationship to a German Ruländer. One example, made of both Grigio and (white) Nero aged in oak, is a classic of the region: the Clastidium of the firm of Ballabio at Casteggio.

Riesling (usually the Italian kind) is also a success in the Oltrepò; Moscatos are excellent and even Müller-Thurgau makes respectable wines. In such conditions one can reasonably expect almost any grape to thrive. All that is lacking in this productive but scarcely celebrated area is a name to conjure with.

Above: Oltrepò Pavese is a portfolio DOC for many varieties, including Barbera. Frecciarossa is one of the best estate wines of the district.
Left: Valgella and Inferno are two of the subdivisions of Valtellina Superiore.

- ─·─ Regional boundary
- OLTREPO PAVESE DOC

DOC boundaries are distinguished by coloured lines

Oltrepò Pavese

1:240,000

Km. 0 2 4 6 8 Km.
Miles 0 1 2 3 4 5 Miles

Northeast Italy

Left: the vine luxuriates in fertile soil and gentle weather in the Veneto, the region of Venice. The traditional method is to train the plants high, allowing the air to circulate under the canopy of leaves to discourage rot, and making the grapes easier to pick.

Northeast Italy owes less to tradition and more to modern development than the rest of the country. Whether it is the realism of the Venetians, the pressure of Austrian influence, the moderate climate, or all these, more (bottled) wine is exported from the northeast than from elsewhere, more different grapes are grown and experimented with, and a more prosperous and professional air pervades the vineyards.

Verona and its wines – Valpolicella, Soave; Bardolino and the southern Lake Garda wines; the Alto Adige with its Lago di Caldaro and Santa Maddalena are mapped and discussed in detail on pages 186–187. The other biggest concentrations of winegrowing are due north of Venice around Conegliano, on the Yugoslav border in Friuli (mapped on pages 188–189) and in the Trentino, north of Lake Garda. The last red wines of Lombardy, the Valtellinas, are mapped on page 183.

Of the other Lombardy wines on this map, the Garda-side wines are very close to the Veronese Garda wines in character. There is little to choose between Chiaretto from the Riviera del Garda (of which the best part is south of Salo, particularly around Moniga del Garda) and Bardolino. Both are reds so light as to be rosé, or rosés so dark as to be red, with a gentle flavour, soft textured and faintly sweet, made all the more appetizing by a hint of bitterness, like almonds, in the taste which is common to all the best reds in this part of Italy. They should be drunk very young.

Red Botticino (a Barbera blend), Cellatica (a lighter one) and white Franciacorta (of Pinot Bianco) are the admirable wines of Brescia. Franciacorta also makes one of Italy's most excellent sparkling wines, Ca' del Bosco.

White Lugana, from the south end of Lake Garda, is a particularly appealing relation of Soave, with a hint of lusciousness in a perfectly dry wine.

Only one name from the flat Po valley is famous – the sparkling red Lambrusco from around Modena, above all from Sorbara. There is something decidedly appetizing about this vivid, grapey wine with its bizarre red foaming head. It cuts the richness of Bolognese food admirably.

The character of the wine changes in the Veneto and eastwards. Already in the Colli Euganei (and indeed south of that, at Legnago on the excellent Quarto Vecchio estate) the red grapes are the Cabernet and Merlot of Bordeaux, above all the Merlot, which plays an increasingly dominant role all the way from Yugoslavia to the valley of the Adige north of Lake Garda, and again in Italian Switzerland.

At their best both grapes succeed admirably here; some of the Merlots can seriously be compared with St-Emilions, and the best Cabernets have considerable character and staying power. Pinot Noir (Pinot Nero) also shows promise.

The white grapes are a mixture of the traditional – the Garganega of Soave, the Prosecco, the light, sharp Verdiso and the more solid Tocai (Pinot Gris) and Sylvaner, Riesling, Sauvignon Blanc and Pinot Bianco.

The DOCs of the region are a series of defined areas that give their names to whole groups of red and white wines. Those known simply as (for example) Colli Euganei Rosso are standard wines made of an approved mixture of grapes. The better wines use the 'varietal' name with the DOC name – although there are also DOCs, like Gambellara between Soave and the Colli Berici (Colli, incidentally, means hills), that are limited to a traditional grape, in this case the Garganega.

Breganze and Pramaggiore are known particularly from their Merlots and Cabernets. Farther east is traditionally white-wine country, mapped in detail on pages 188–189.

North of Lake Garda the valley of the Adige, running down from the Alps, produces its finest wine at its northern end (page 186). The middle part of the valley is the Trentino, famous above all for its full-blooded red Teroldego, from the grape of the same name grown on the cliff-hemmed, pergola-carpeted gravelly valley floor known as the Campo Rotaliano, between Mezzolombardo and Mezzocorona. (Mezzocorona appears on the map on page 186.) Teroldego Rotaliano is one of Italy's great characters, a dense purple wine of high extract and good ageing qualities, smooth and even soft in the mouth but marked, at least when young, with the penetrating bitterness that is the signal of the region. Wherever this (locally much appreciated) bitterness derives from, those who find it overwhelming can often eliminate it by early decanting. After 24 hours in a decanter a four-year-old Teroldego has plenty of life and fruit, without the Campari note.

The Schiava or Vernatsch, from the Tirol, is another red grape with some of the same bitterness, made here in the Trentino into two DOCs, the light Casteller and more substantial Sorni (which also contains Teroldego and the Lagrein of Bolzano). The best Schiava, however, is a *vino da tavola rosato* by the name of Faedo.

The general DOC Trento covers Cabernet and Merlot (both good here, reaching very high standards at the provincial research station at San Michele all'Adige), Pinot Noir, two Tirolese reds, the pale Lagrein and the dark Marzemino, and a range of whites including very tolerable Riesling and Chardonnay. Trento's most distinguished white wine, however, is the *méthode champenoise* of Ferrari, Cesarini Sforza, Equipe 5 and others, made principally of Pinot Bianco; perhaps Italy's best sparkling wine.

In complete contrast, the country south of Bologna and Ravenna produces the rich white wine of which Italy is apparently proudest (judging by the fact that it was the first to be recommended for the rank of 'DOCG'): the Albana di Romagna.

Albana, in fact, like so many Italian wines, can be all things to all men. If it was the *amabile* version that was originally famous, today it is more often made dry (and often very dull, too). You can also buy it *spumante*. To understand its reputation you must taste the work of the Fattoria Paradiso or one of its few rivals: lovely concentrated, faintly honeyed wine.

More reliable by far, if without claims to greatness, is Romagna's Sangiovese red: a big country boy whose company grows on you.

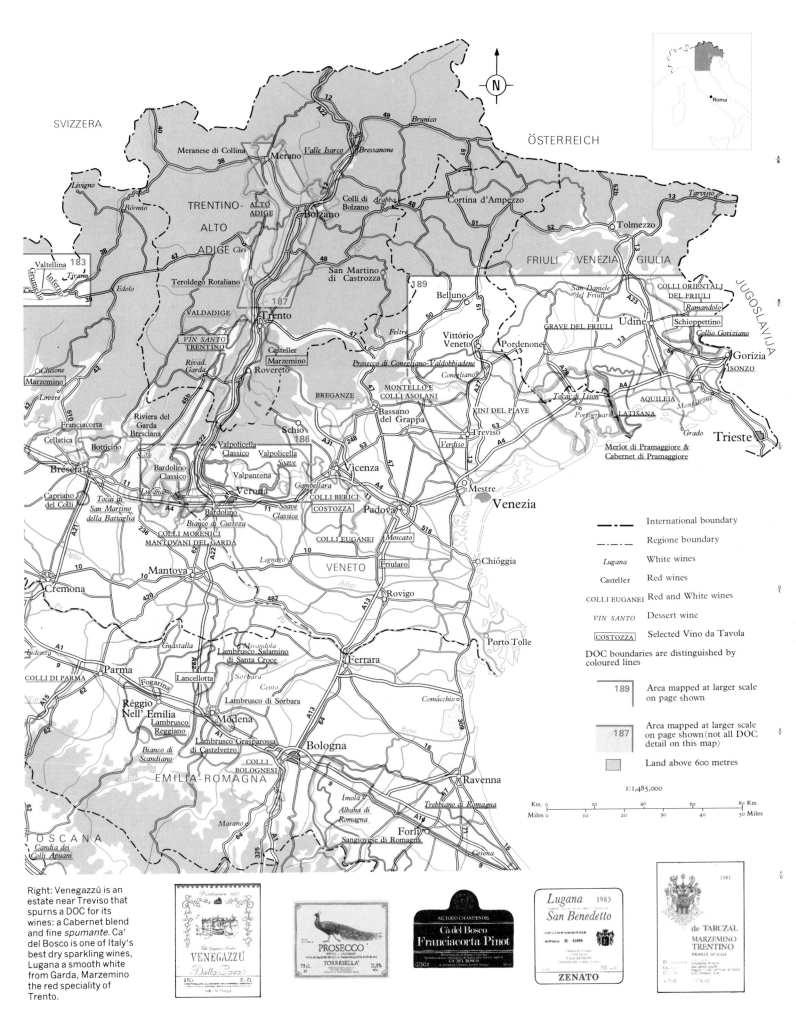

SVIZZERA

ÖSTERREICH

TRENTINO-ALTO ADIGE

12
A22
49 Brunico
Meranese di Collina
38 Merano *Valle Isarco* Bressanone
Livigno
40
Bórmio
Cles
ALTO
ADIGE
Colli di Bolzano
Arabba
48
Cortina d'Ampezzo
Tarvisio
13
51
52b
Tolmezzo
52
FRIULI VENEZIA GIULIA
13

Valtellina 183
Tirano
Inferno
38
42
San Martino di Castrozza
189
San Danele del Friuli
COLLI ORIENTALI DEL FRIULI
Grumello
39 Edolo
Teroldego Rotaliano
48
187
Belluno
51
GRAVE DEL FRIULI
Ramandolo
Schioppettino
VALDADIGE
Trento
50
Feltre
Udine
Collio Goriziano
56

Clusone
Marzemino
Lovere
VIN SANTO TRENTINO
Rivad. Garda
Casteller
Marzemino
Rovereto
47
Vittório Veneto
Pordenone
13
A23
A4
Gorízia
ISONZO

42
510
Riviera del Garda Bresciana
Prosecco di Conegliano-Valdobbiadene
Conegliano
Tocai di Lison
AQUILEIA
Montfalcone
LATISANA
Grado
Trieste

Franciacorta
Cellatica
Botticino
BREGANZE
MONTELLO E COLLI ASOLANI
Schio
186
A31
248
53
Bassano del Grappa
VINI DEL PIAVE
53
Treviso
A27
A4
Portogruaro
Merlot di Pramaggiore & Cabernet di Pramaggiore

Bréscia
11
Valpolicella Classico
Valpolicella Classico
Soave
Vicenza
47
A4
Verdiso
13
Mestre
Venezia

Capriano del Colli
Tocai di San Martino della Battaglia
Salò
Lugana
Bardolino Classico
Valpantena
Gambellara
A4
Verona
11
Soave Classico
COLLI BERICI
COSTOZZA
Padova
516

236
Bianco di Custoza
Bardolino
COLLI EUGANEI
Moscato
Chióggia

COLLI MORENICI MANTOVANI DEL GARDA
62
A22
Legnago
10
VENETO
Friularo
Rovigo

Cremona
Mantova
10
482
A13
Rovigo
Porto Tolle

420
Adige
516

Fidenza
A1
Guastalla
Mirandola
Lambrusco Salamino di Santa Croce
Sorbara
Cento
Ferrara
309

COLLI DI PARMA
Parma
Fogarina
Lancellotta
Lambrusco di Sórbara
Comácchio

Réggio Nell' Emília
Lambrusco Reggiano
Módena
64
A13
64
Ravenna

Bianco di Scandiano
Lambrusco Grasparossa di Castelvetro
Bologna
16
16
309

TOSCANA
EMILIA-ROMAGNA
COLLI BOLOGNESI
9
Ímola
Trebbiano di Romagna
67

Candia dei Colli Apuani
64
325
Marano
Albana di Romagna
A14
16
Forlì
Sangiovese di Romagna
Cesena
9

Legend:

— · — · — International boundary

— · · — · · Regione boundary

Lugana   White wines

Casteller   Red wines

COLLI EUGANEI   Red and White wines

VIN SANTO   Dessert wine

COSTOZZA   Selected Vino da Tavola

DOC boundaries are distinguished by coloured lines

189   Area mapped at larger scale on page shown

187   Area mapped at larger scale on page shown (not all DOC detail on this map)

Land above 600 metres

1:1,485,000

Km. 0   20   40   60   80 Km.
Miles 0   10   20   30   40   50 Miles

Roma

Right: Venegazzú is an estate near Treviso that spurns a DOC for its wines: a Cabernet blend and fine *spumante*. Ca' del Bosco is one of Italy's best dry sparkling wines, Lugana a smooth white from Garda, Marzemino the red speciality of Trento.

Verona

The lovingly gardened hills of Verona, stretching from Soave, east of the city, westwards to Lake Garda, are so fertile that vegetation is uncontrollable; the vine runs riot on terrace and pergola, among villas that are the image of Italian grace.

Their Soave is probably Italy's most famous white wine. The region is tiny, and largely controlled by its cantina sociale, one of the biggest in Europe. Considering the large-scale standardization involved, the wine is extremely good. It is relevant to wonder what the result would be if, say, all the wines of Pouilly-Fuissé were to be made together in one vat.

Soave (whether simple Soave or the slightly stronger and more expensive Classico) is a plain, dry, pale white wine. It is hard to characterize it in any more exciting way. And yet it has something – it may be a particularly soft texture – that singles it out and always makes it enjoyable. Its plainness also makes it very versatile. The thing to remember is to drink it young; even three-year-old Soave is no longer so fresh as it should be.

The same is true of the red wine of Valpolicella and its sub-district Valpantena. It has a beautiful cherry colour, a gentle sweet smell, a soft light flavour and a nice trace of bitterness as you swallow – when it is young. The best Valpolicellas (some are even kept in glass rather than wood from the start to stop them ageing) come from a few small producers in the Classico heart of the district – the prettiest imaginable hills. You may taste their wine with them, eating their bread and grilled sausage, and think you have never tasted better in the

Above: cypresses, pale stone and leggy vines in grass like a garden: Castelnuovo di Verona in Bardolino is typical of the gentle Veronese country.

world. They will insist you go on to taste their Recioto (sweet) or Amarone (strong and dry); dark and sometimes fizzy; made of grapes dried in racks in well-ventilated lofts until after Christmas.

Almost every part of Italy makes some of its wine from grapes dried either in this way or in the sun, and prizes it highly. Verona's Reciotos are some of the best.

Bardolino is a paler, more insubstantial wine than Valpolicella – almost a rosé; drinkable as soon as it is made. Chiaretto del Garda, from the opposite side of the lake, is similar.

Above: Verona and Garda wines are gentle, like the countryside that produces them; pale and smooth. White Soave and cherry-red Valpolicella are the best. Stronger Recioto is locally esteemed.

- –·–·– Provincia boundary
- Boundaries of DOC areas
- Boundaries of Classico areas
- Vineyards
- Woods
- —500— Contour interval 100 metres

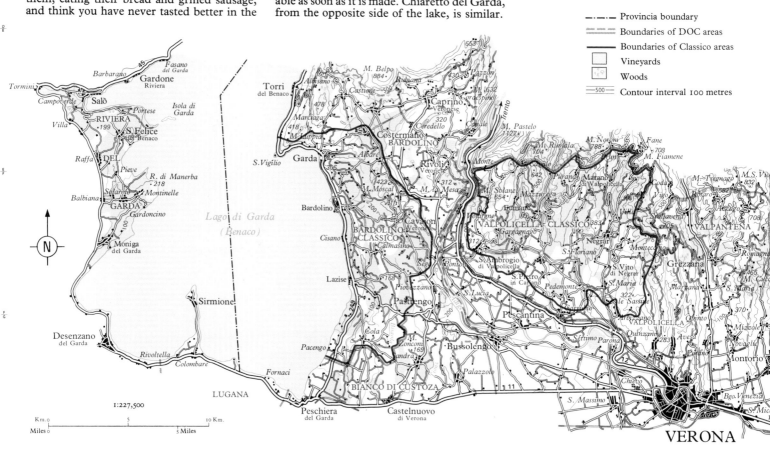

Alto Adige

The Alto Adige, the upper part of the Adige valley, around the city of Bolzano, is a vigorous and exciting region. Its connections with Austria are close and many of its people speak German – which partly explains why this small area supplies half Italy's wine exports, although it ranks only eleventh for production.

A wide range of both red and white wines are made, largely from local grapes, among which is the famous Traminer, native to the village of Tramin (Italian Termeno). The DOC Alto Adige plus the grape name applies to a large part of the region.

The red wines are soft and easy with a touch of bitterness. It is most noticeable in the excellent dark rosé made from the Lagrein grape and usually known by its Tirolean name, Lagrein-Kretzer. The Schiava, the most widespread local red grape, also has it; Lago di Caldaro (or Kalterer See) is the DOC of the large quantities of Schiava, often made mawkishly sweet for the German market, from the west side of the valley at Bolzano. The DOC Santa Maddalena on the hill above the city demands an extra degree of alcohol in better wine from the same grapes. Colli di Bolzano and Meranese di Collina are similar, but a shade lighter.

A little Pinot Noir and more Merlot are grown; both are extremely successful. Rare but potentially best of all is the Cabernet.

White wines are as good as red. Terlano, on the way north to Merano, has some of the best (and its own DOC). They include Riesling, Sylvaner, Traminer, Pinot Blanc (the classic Terlaner), Chardonnay and very good Sauvignon. On the steep hillsides all ripen well and make excellent fruity and lively wine. Valle Isarco is a less distinguished white-wine DOC higher in the hills.

Right: much of the wine from the Alto Adige is drunk north of the Alps; to Austria it is 'South Tirol'. The middle and bottom left labels are from Trentino to the south. Ferrari makes sparkling wine; Teroldego is red.

DOC

- – – – Meranese di Collina
- – – – Santa Maddalena
- ——— Kalterer See (Lago di Caldaro)
- ——— Teroldego Rotaliano
- ——— Trentino
- ——— Terlano
- – – – Colli di Bolzano
- ——— Sorni
- ▬ ▬ Provincia boundary

JOSEF BRIGL — Important cellars

▨ Vineyards

▢ Woods

——1000—— Contour interval 200 metres

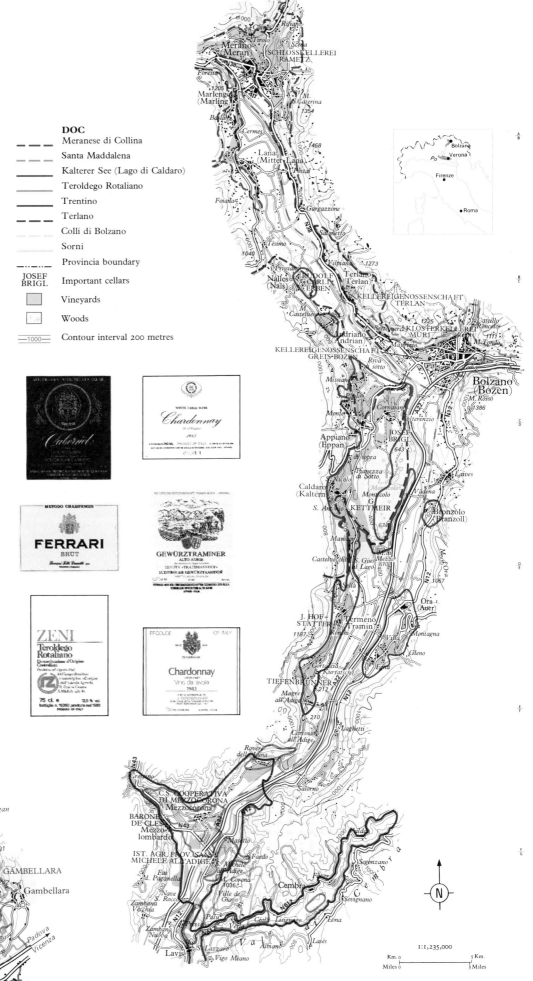

Veneto and Friuli-Venezia Giulia

Buyers are looking more and more to the northeast corner of Italy for wines, particularly white wines, of original character and notable quality. It is almost as new a development as their excitement about some of the regions of the New World. Not that Friuli and Venezia Giulia are viticultural virgins, but the potential excellence of their wines has only become apparent since winemakers started using modern methods. In their planting, too, they are slowly but steadily adding the international favourites to their traditional varieties. In their present state they offer a choice as bewildering as any in the great Italian lexicon.

The map embraces most of the easternmost region of the north, Friuli-Venezia Giulia, and a small part of its neighbour the Veneto. The Veneto has two great wine centres, Verona (page 186) and Conegliano, 40 miles (65km) north of Venice. Northern Veneto runs into the Dolomites, and the region of Conegliano-Valdobbiadene already has a faintly alpine feeling. Its local speciality, the white Prosecco grape, is rather charmless as a still wine, but very good base material for *spumante*.

Prosecco is thus the local fizz of Venice, and its *superiore* form, Cartizze from Valdobbiadene, one of Italy's best in the brisk, light-bodied manner. Nobody could accuse it of apeing champagne, but it goes down well in the famous Bellinis in Harry's Bar.

Conegliano has another fame in the wine world as Italy's principal viticultural research station. Every sort of grape is tried out, and the local restaurants in the pretty old town can serve you anything from a local Merlot to a Gewürztraminer. On the evidence, Prosecco or the small-scale white Verdiso are what the area does best.

Still within the Veneto, the wide plain of the Piave, heavily planted with vines, is a useful source of both fresh dry white Verduzzo (an important grape of the northeast), of a minor Tocai (much more important in Friuli) and of Cabernet and Merlot of fair to substantial quality. Eastwards from Venice is the only part of Italy where the great Bordeaux grapes make the running for red wine. At the Castello di Roncade, just south of Treviso, they have been married with other Bordeaux varieties into truly claret-like blends. But Cabernet (usually Cabernet Franc) pure or Merlot pure are the staples of the Piave DOC and five more to the east: Pramaggiore, Latisana, Aquileia and Isonzo, and above all Grave del Friuli.

On the whole the Cabernet is heartiest to the west of the region, especially in Pramaggiore (where the Merlot can be a little dry and heartless for the grape that makes Pomerol). Going east, Cabernet remains the better of the two but the Merlot, although still light, gains definition and character. In the huge DOC Grave del Friuli and in Isonzo, Merlot is dominant. Neither grape is as good in the coastal areas with their flat vineyards as in its more limited hillside plantations in the Colli Orientali del Friuli.

In the Piave an indigenous red grape, the Raboso, helps to define Venetian taste in red wine, which is definitely for the austere and

Prosecco grapes on the 'Strada del Vino Bianco' through the lovely Valdobbiadene near Conegliano. Their juice is the basis for the dry white sparkling wine that fuels Venice and its region. An 'ombra' is the local term for a glass of white wine sipped in a café, in Venice or the countryside, at any hour of day or night. The word means 'shade', perhaps because the wine gives relief to the sweltering.

dry. The Raboso is sometimes blended with Merlot, also grown in the Piave.

Two DOCs, the red Pramaggiore for Cabernet and Merlot, and the white Tocai di Lison, make the transition from Veneto to Friuli-Venezia Giulia. Tocai di Lison (which has a *classico* heartland around the town of Lison) begins to promise the silky satisfaction this grape will give farther east, in the Gorizian hills on the Yugoslav border.

Grave del Friuli is much the biggest DOC of Friuli-Venezia Giulia, covering all the (literally) gravelly lowlands in the centre of the region.

Half its harvest is Merlot, with some Cabernet and also the often underrated Refosco, the lively red known as Mondeuse in the French Alps. Grave white wines are chiefly the lean dry Verduzzo and the much more substantial Tocai, but a good quantity of Pinot Bianco (here often confused with Chardonnay) is also grown. Supplies of all these are plentiful, quality at least satisfactory and value assured. Certain producers' names stand out in the big and by no means homogeneous area: Duca Badoglio, Collavini and Plozner are among them – all in the province of Udine, towards the Colli Orientali del Friuli.

These hills, and those of Gorizia nearer the coast, form the natural boundary between Italy and Yugoslavia. Gorizia's hills have a mellow microclimate modified by the sea. They are the oldest-established and best vineyard of the region, often called, simply, 'Collio'. Wine called simply Collio is a dry white of Ribolla, Pinot and other grapes – which grow in confusing variety. Whites include Italian Riesling, Sauvignon, Traminer, Malvasia, Pinots Bianco and Grigio and the Tocai Friulano. Reds are Cabernet, Merlot and Pinot Noir.

Collio really rests its high reputation on the concentration and cleanness of its Tocai, supported by Pinot Bianco (sometimes Chardonnay) and Pinot Grigio. They combine high extract, a texture that caresses the tongue, with vivid and lively flavour and fragrance. If they are not Europe's showiest wines, they manage to convey a great feeling of class and sense of satisfaction almost unique in Italian whites.

The hills inland do the same, if not in quite the same degree. The Colli Orientali del Friuli feel less of the Adriatic, more of the Alps: a marginally more extreme climate. All the Collio grapes are grown, with the addition of Rhine Riesling, Refosco and Cabernet Sauvignon (as opposed to Franc). The Refosco is a character no visitor to these beautiful hills should miss. Whether that or the smooth and vibrant Tocai goes better with Italy's best prosciutto (that of San Daniele, near Udine) is a good debate. A great deal of local pride is tied up in Picolit, a strong white dessert wine like a Sauternes robbed of most of its aromas. Others describe it more extravagantly.

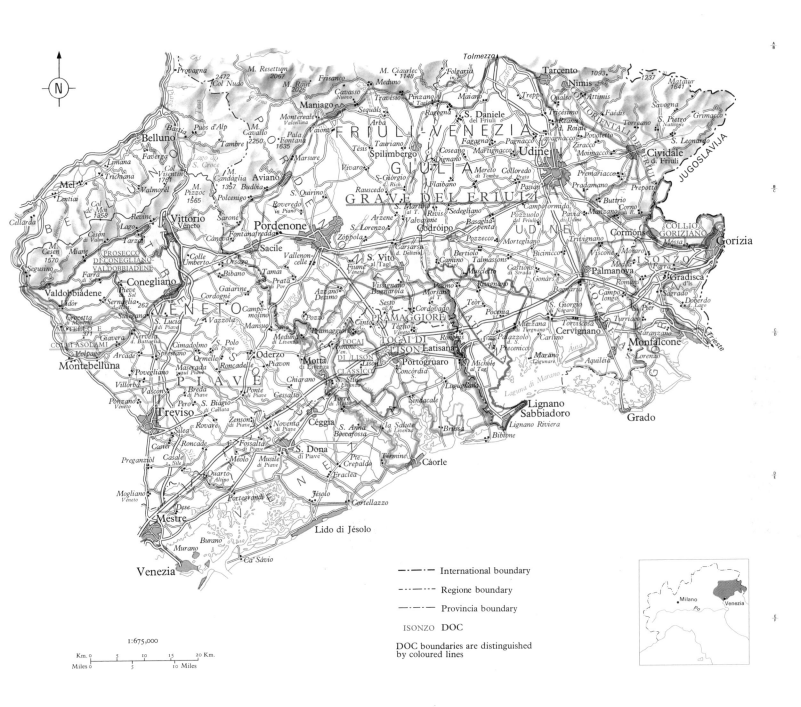

FRIULI-VENEZIA GIULIA

GRAVE DEL FRIULI

VENETO

PIAVE

—·—·— International boundary

—··—··— Regione boundary

—···—···— Provincia boundary

ISONZO **DOC**

DOC boundaries are distinguished
by coloured lines

1:675,000

Km. 0   5   10   15   20 Km.

Miles 0   5   10 Miles

Below: Cabernet and Merlot are the standard red
grapes of the coastal plains east of Venice. The
region's best wines are its whites, especially Tocai and
Pinot Blanc, of the surrounding hills.

Central Italy

The best-loved Italian wines, best known to travellers, most drunk in restaurants from Soho to Sydney, are encompassed by the map opposite. Above all Chianti, whose zone with its *classico* heart (see next page) occupies the better part of Tuscany.

Chianti and its blood-brothers (the blood being the juice of the red Sangiovese) are the dominant red wines of the northern part of the map. To the south they give way to the Cesanese of Latium and the Montepulciano of the Abruzzo. Going down the Adriatic coast the transition is in the Marche: Rosso Piceno is Sangiovese and Montepulciano mixed.

The white grapes that put their stamp on most central Italian wine are the Trebbiano of Tuscany and the Malvasia Bianco. Trebbiano is known as Procanico on the Tuscan coast and the island of Elba. The same grape is grown in the Midi as Ugni Blanc and in Cognac as St-Emilion, where its high acidity is as welcome as it is here in Italy. In the balance of central Italian white wines, whether Tuscan, Umbrian or Roman, Malvasia provides the body and Trebbiano the 'lift' – such as it is.

Neither, unfortunately, has any marked aromatic qualities. Hence a certain blandness and sameness only avoided by the best examples even of such famous names as Orvieto, Frascati, Est! Est!! Est!!! and the increasingly popular Bianco Vergine of southern Tuscany. Chianti has two DOCs for white wine, Bianco della Lega and Galestro (for a new low-strength thirst-quencher). Both are the same dull mixture.

Where other white grapes contribute it is all to the good. Montecarlo from near Lucca, often called the best Tuscan (DOC) white, contains Semillon, Sauvignon and the Pinot Bianco. Verdicchio, the standard fish wine of the Adriatic coast, relies on the contribution of the lively Verdicchio grape to the usual mix. Parrina from the Tuscan coast is seasoned with the more tasty Ansonica. Pitigliano can contain Grechetto, a minority grape with crispness and fragrance that also plays a large part in the very satisfying white of Torgiano near Perugia. Altogether more significantly, the new DOC Pomino, devised by the Frescobaldi family of Chianti, abandons the Tuscan varieties but manages to make an original Florentine wine of Sauvignon, Pinot Bianco and Chardonnay.

Character is not all a matter of grapes. Orvieto used to be much more distinctive than it is today. So did Frascati (see page 195). In the past Orvieto was kept fermenting slowly in huge casks for as much as two years, then usually sweetened with *passito*, the wine of dried grapes. It may not have been very stable by modern standards, but it had depth and delicacy. Antinori's Castello della Sala is the outstanding Orvieto today.

When Michelangelo wrote of Vernaccia di San Gimignano that it 'kisses, licks, bites, thrusts and stings', he was not talking of an educated modern wine but of a white wine made like a red, stiff with extract and flavour. It is largely the current dread of oxidation, of the wine going brown as it often used to, that robs it of identity.

Two famous red wines of the centre, Brunello and Vino Nobile, are discussed on page 194. The Adriatic coast is thick with DOCs for reds of more or less lively, but generally sturdy, character: Sangiovese di Romagna and dei Colli Pesaresi, full-bodied Rosso Cònero from Ancona, and the lighter Rosso Piceno from a wider area (it is worth looking for the *superiore* version), Montepulciano d'Abruzzo (which varies from fruity to flat) and its *rosato* version, Cerasuolo.

The Cesanese family over the border of Latium are remarkable chiefly for their unpredictability; they can be still or sparkling, sweet or dry. Aleaticos, from wherever you may find them, are a more intriguing proposition: red dessert wines with a strong suggestion of Moscato.

These multifarious local wines apart, however, there are independent spirits at large who in the long run will influence them all. One is Dr Giorgio Lungarotti of Torgiano, who was the first to 'design' his wine from the ground up, then claim for it and be granted a DOC. Rubesco di Torgiano is in essence a superior Chianti Riserva, made in a region that had no reputed red wines. (It now has several: look for Colli del Trasimeno and Colli Altotiberini.) Rubesco Riserva, known as Monticchio, stands beside the very best Tuscan reds. Like almost all modern Italian winemakers, the Lungarottis now have Cabernet and Chardonnay in their vineyards.

The other idiosyncratic planters were Tuscan noblemen who knew that whatever Sangiovese might be, Cabernet was better. Count Bonacossi of Carmignano, just west of Florence, was one. He established the practice of flavouring his Chianti with Cabernet many years ago. Carmignano is now a separate (and excellent) DOC. Another was the Marchesi Incisa della Rochetta, whose eccentricity in the 1960s was to plant Cabernet by the sea near Bolgheri. The Antinoris of Florence aided and abetted. The result, now famous as Sassicaia, may possibly be Italy's best red wine. Its repercussions are certainly shaking Chianti.

Left: a Tuscan press-house and its proprietor, unconcerned by the approach of the 21st century.
Below: Vernaccia is an ancient Tuscan white, Galestro a very modern one. Fiorano is one of the most renowned new 'table wines' of Italy.

Left: the view northwards from Montalcino in the morning light shows a more open, larger-scale landscape than the traditional Chianti pattern of vines and olives, villas and cypresses. The climate here is drier and warmer than farther north, the prospects for expansion considerable.

exceptional. Other growers, though, thought not only that the price demanded was over the top, but that the same could be said of the wine. It was a 19th-century insurance policy to make over-strength wines and keep them in oak until they were rigid with tannin. Modern manners are better suited by equally potent wine bottled earlier, while fruity flavours are still dominant.

Among the subscribers to this theory is the man who all seem to agree in calling Italy's greatest winemaker, Ezio Rivella. Rivella was invited by Villa Banfi, the biggest importer of Italian wine into the USA, to prospect for a vast model wine estate in central Italy. Rivella settled for Montalcino, not only (or primarily) for its Brunello, but for its soil and climate, and the fact that as much as 7,000 acres (some 3,000 hectares) were available, at Sant'Angelo Scalo, in huge uncluttered blocks. The Villa Banfi estate here is now by far the largest in Italy, possibly in the world, and its winery possibly the most modern.

Of the 1,750 acres (700 hectares) so far planted with vines, only 10% is Brunello. Fifty percent is another local grape, hitherto of modest fame, the pale Moscadello, to be made into a gently sweet sparkling Moscato, akin to Asti Spumante but quieter in style. The remaining 40% is boldly planted with Cabernet, Chardonnay, Sauvignon and Pinot Grigio, with the avowed intent of outshining the Napa Valley in 'the state of the art'.

What the neighbours will say, let alone the rest of Italy, remains to be heard. The neighbours to the east, across an intervening enclave of 'mere' Chianti, have ancient pretensions of their own embodied in their DOC, Vino Nobile di Montepulciano

Montepulciano is a hill town of great charm surrounded with Chianti-style vineyards, a mixture of their own Sangiovese, the Prugnolo, with the other normal Chianti ingredients. Depending on the producer, the wine tends to resemble either a poor Chianti or a very good one. Logic suggests that it should be a halfway house between Chianti and Brunello. In practice the hallmark of true Vino Nobile (as opposed to a Chianti from Montepulciano) is inky repulsiveness, a truly impenetrable youthful tannic hardness, giving ground only slowly to warmer and gentler flavour. (Two years in cask is the minimum legal age: three for a Riserva.)

To while away the waiting, the same producers will make a mild Chianti, and increasingly a very mild Bianco Vergine in the Val di Chiana to the north. Bianco Vergine can be a lovely light and lissome wine, although one without great flavour. Montepulciano's greatest triumph, to this observer at least, is its Vinsanto: orange coloured, smoky scented, extraordinarily sweet, intense and persistent, aged four years in tiny flat *carretelli* under the rooftiles of a Renaissance palazzo.

Castelli Romani
(Alban Hills)

For location map
see opposite page

—··—··— Provincia boundary

APRILIA DOC

——300—— Contour interval 100 metres

DOC boundaries are distinguished by coloured lines

1:350,000

Km. 0   2   4   6   8   10 Km.
Miles 0   2   4   6 Miles

The papal summer villa at Castel Gandolfo contains in its garden a long and lofty half-underground arcade: the very ambulatory in which the Emperor Domitian, whose summer house was on the same site, used to saunter in hot weather.

The villa commands views to the west over the Tyrrhenian Sea, and to the east over the round crater-lake of Albano. It perches, in fact, on the rim of an extinct volcano. That is what the Alban hills are. Reaching to 3,000 feet (900 metres) within 20 miles (30km) of Rome (and so near the sea) they provide today, as they did in ancient times, a wonderful retreat of green woodland and vineyard for summer weekends. Villas of every prosperous period of history rejoice in them. And the Romans rejoice, flocking into Frascati or Marino, Grottaferrata or Monteporzio Catone or Velletri to take their ease with a roast-pork sandwich and the thrilling local wine.

Frascati and its kin, found magical by Grand Tourists of the Augustan Age, must be the origin of the much-repeated truism that some wines 'didn't travel'. It is made of the two central Italian white grapes, Trebbiano and Malvasia, that are overprone to oxidation – to turning brown and tasting flat. The traditional method of making it, skins and all like a red wine, gave oxidation every chance. (The object, often splendidly achieved, was to give it an almost fatty richness of texture, as well as the perfume of Malvasia skins.)

Deep, cold cellars in the volcanic rock are enough to keep well-made Frascati fresh, even in barrel, until the summer visitors can drink it. Any other sort of handling, unfortunately, means changing its nature. It can be (and is) made by cold fermentation without skins today. The best producers make a good dense and aromatic wine. The interesting experiment is to compare a bottled Frascati with one straight from the barrel in an *osteria* on the hill.

Differences are commonly noted between the wines of Frascati and its neighbours in the Castelli Romani. Marino is the name most often mentioned as having a trifle more substance. Velletri also offers red wine.

Colli Lanuvini is an adjacent DOC to the south for white wines which could be confused with some of the better products of the Castelli Romani.

Southern Italy

There is always a faint air of unreality about any complete list of Italian wines. There are indeed that many names – but are there that many identities? Some proud local traditions, particularly here in the south, go straight into the blending vat every year to emerge as anything from Austrian wine to Beaujolais.

Those wines of southern Italy that do appear in public are gaining ground, however. They used to be mere poor relations, selling (if they sold at all) on the power of association – the vine-hung terraces of Amalfi – alone. The climate coupled with old methods usually produced flat wines, deficient in acidity. But modern methods improve them every year, and certainly point up differences.

Most famous of them are the ones tourists meet around Naples. Ischia was one of the first wines to claim a DOC, in 1966. It is easy enough for an island. Capri (not a DOC) has long been a sort of brand name for white wines; although those of the island itself are said to be much better than most 'Capri'. Lachryma Christi (not a DOC yet either) has the same status for normally inoffensive, sometimes good red and white wines from the area of Mount Vesuvius.

Ravello wines, particularly those made by the Caruso family, are well balanced; fresher than most of the south (the altitude of Ravello and its sea mists are said to help). And I cannot resist writing the name of Gran Furore Divina Costiera, awful though the wine is.

Less known than the wines of the coast are

Below and far right: some of the wines of southern Italy, Sicily, Sardinia and the smaller islands that have established reputations beyond their region. Not long ago Marsala was the only one with a famous name. Now such names as Mastroberardino, Sella & Mosca and Regaleali are respected internationally.

those of inland Campania, of which Taurasi is the majestic chief; broad, dark and deep as a southern wine should be. Its grape, the Aglianico (ellenico, i.e. from Greece, like civilization itself down here), makes another good, rather lighter, red, Aglianico del Vulture, in vineyards on the inland hills of Basilicata up to 2,500 feet (760 metres). The name of Greco di Tufo, a white wine of remarkably original flavour, dry, brisk and fragrant, from inland Campania, shares the credit between Greece and the tufa rock on which it grows.

In the same hilly province, Avellino, the master winemaker of the region, Mastroberardino, makes an even more remarkable and unexpected white called Fiano, a wine that combines lightness with firmness, lively length with deeply nutty flavour. Of Basilicata the only other well-known wine (not DOC) is Asprinio, which the Potenzans manage to make mercifully unpotent, pale and crisp.

Molise, north on the Adriatic, was formerly united with the Abruzzo. It has no real wine tradition, but at least one highly competent producer of its red Montepulciano and Ramitello: Majo di Norante.

Calabria has one strong red of reputation: Cirò (there is a white Cirò as well), but DOCs for several others, including Donnici, Savuto, Lamezia and Pollino. Calabria's most original wine is the sweetly perfumed Greco di Gerace from the south coast.

Puglia has registered a remarkable number of wines which have traditionally gone to market in bulk. Several are making their own reputations. The Primitivo from around Taranto is one; its full-bodied red is said to age very well, and in California the theory goes that it may be the origin of the estimable Zinfandel.

Negroamaro is the cautionary name of the principal red grape. It makes almost port-like roasted reds at Salento (as Salice Salentino), and under the DOCs Leverano, Copertino and Squinzano.

Both reds and whites in Puglia are being well made today, not over-strong but often rather neutral, the whites particularly, which makes them an ideal base for vermouth. Locorotondo and Martinafranca are typical of this school of strong bland white. Quite exceptional is the almost-Californian produce of an estate near Foggia, Favonio, which grows Pinot Bianco, Chardonnay and Cabernet. The only remote rival is the Torre Quarto estate in the same area. These apart, the rosés of Castel del Monte are perhaps the most attractive product of the region at present. There are good dessert wines, of Moscato and Aleatico, on all hands.

More than any of the wines of Puglia, it is Sicilian wine that has made a name for itself today. Its Marsala, like a distant cousin of sherry, has been famous since Nelson's day, when he fortified the Royal Navy with it. It is enjoying a great revival in quality, and should be tried. The best name is Samperi. The advent of Sicilian table wine, however, has been spectacular. Vast government grants have made the island Italy's biggest producer of inoffensive wines for blending, 75% of them white (and 80% made in cooperatives).

Brands rather than DOCs make the running.

The one important table-wine DOC is Etna, for wines from the immensely fertile volcanic soil of that spectacular mountain. The Barone Vilagrande's red and white are typical examples; lively, well-balanced wines.

Good brands that use grapes from other parts of the island are Regaleali and the very successful Corvo, made near Palermo at Casteldaccia. Alcamo is the table-wine DOC for vineyards in the northwest and Cerasuolo for light reds from Vittoria on the south coast. The rest of Sicily's DOCs are for her particular speciality: dessert wine. The Moscatos of Noto and the little island of Pantelleria and the Malvasia of Lipari are good examples of one of Italy's oldest vinous traditions.

Most of Sardinia's DOCs, too, are for sweet wines. On Sardinia the distinction between a table wine and a dessert wine is even more blurred than in other parts of Italy; traditionally all her reds (Cannonau, Monica, Girò and Oliena are the best known) were more or less sweet. Her best wines were Vernaccia, a strong dry white which has a distinct affinity with sherry, and Nuragus, a dry white without too much alcohol and (sometimes) with a firmness that makes it really appetizing. One firm in particular, however, has started making modern-style reds and whites in vast modern vineyards around Alghero in the northwest. Sella & Mosca wines are made and marketed by Piemontese and Milanese skills respectively. Attractive and reliable wines like this could come from almost anywhere in Italy.

Spain

The brown vastness of Spain's southern plains is cross-stitched with scores of thousands of acres of vines – almost always without posts and wires: low bushes conserve the scant water supply.

THE LANGUAGE OF THE LABEL

Con crianza Aged (**sin crianza**, unaged)
Cepa Wine or grape variety
Viña, viñedo Vineyard
Cosecha Crop, or vintage
Vendimia Vintage
Denominación de Origen Similar to Appellation Contrôlée
Consejo Regulador Organization for the defence, control and promotion of a denominación de origen
Reserva Mature quality wine (of red, usually 3 years old)
Gran reserva Aged at least 2 years in barrel and 3 in bottle
Fino Good (particularly meaning the driest sherry)
Vino de mesa (or **de pasto**) Table wine
Vino corriente Ordinary wine, not usually bottled
Vino de cosecha propria Wine made by the owner of the vineyard
Criado y embotellado por . . . Grown and bottled by . . .
Elaborado y añejado por . . . Made and aged by . . .
Embotellado or **Engarrafado de origen** Estate-bottled
Blanco White
Tinto Red
Rosado Rosé
Clarete Light red or dark rosé
Seco Dry
Dulce Sweet
Espumoso Sparkling
4° Año (or **4 Años**) Bottled in its 4th year
Bodega Cellar, anywhere where wine is kept or made or even drunk

Spain has the distinction of having more land under vines than any other country – even Italy. Curiously, however, she has only a third of Italy's production of wine. Much of Spain still crops wine at what others would think absurdly old-fashioned low levels. The national average, 20 hectolitres per hectare, is half that allowed for France's finest wines. It follows that concentration and higher strength are endemic.

The famous regions, Rioja, Penedés, the sherry country, produce bigger crops. But the great bulk of Spanish wine has until now either been drunk on the spot or exported for blending. Some five times as much table wine is exported in bulk (then to be blended) as in bottle. Vast quantities are sold to France, Germany, even the USSR. But the proportion has shifted significantly downwards, in favour of bottled wine, over the past 15 years. The world is beginning to buy Spanish wines for their character, and not just their strength.

Only 15 years ago zones, qualities and origins were casually defined in most of Spain. 1970 was the date of tightening up, with the founding of the Instituto Nacional de Denominaciónes de Origen.

The map opposite shows the regions that have so far been granted a 'DO' – a term, be it noted, much broader than an Appellation Contrôlée. What immediately emerges is the concentration of production on the plains of La Mancha. The town of Valdepeñas has traditionally given its name to a large part of this production; strong (about 13°) but pale red wine made largely of the white Airén grape, blended with the red Cencibel (or Tempranillo). The mixture is effective; at best Valdepeñas can be fruity and almost delicate, despite its strength. Methods are startlingly traditional: fermentation is still done in huge clay *tinajas* clearly descended from Roman amphoras.

This, though, is changing; a large modern winery at Manzanares, Vinícola de Castilla, has recently carried away prizes with wines made in the fruity modern manner.

The next highest production, although way behind La Mancha, is in Valencia and Utiel-Requena, and consists of heavier wines than those of the inland plain; in Valencia largely strong whites and in Utiel-Requena blackish reds for blending (and some racy rosé). Together with their neighbours Yecla and Jumilla in the province of Murcia, Almansa in Albacel, and Alicante, these eastern vineyards are known as the Levante. Alicante has some distinctive white and rosé wines and sweet moscatels. The mighty cooperative of Yecla is distinguished largely by its unforgettable name, La Purísima. Levante wine probably has an interesting future, but its present fate is primarily for blending.

Considerably more interest has been aroused recently by the introduction of modern standards in areas of smaller production in the north and west. Cariñena, the wine of Aragón, has long been a byword for biting potency. The new DO of Somontano shows promise of lighter wine here. Navarra has one estate of real distinction, the Señorio de Sarria, with wine as good as the best Rioja. Las Campanas, Cenalsa, Chivite, Monte Ory and Carricas are other bodegas with new ideas. In the Basque north a minority enjoy the sharp and pétillant Chacolí.

The basin of the river Duero in old Castile is mapped on page 208. Farther north and west the reds of Toro and León, particularly the latter, are adapting from traditional uncompromising strength and darkness to more civil manners. Farther still, into Galicia (famous for its cider), the vineyards feel the influence of the Atlantic. El Bierzo, still in León, is producing well-balanced, lighter reds. Valdeorras and Monterrey are similar. Ribeiro and Pontevedra specialize in 'green' wines like the Portuguese vinhos verdes, with some excellent Albariño white in Pontevedra.

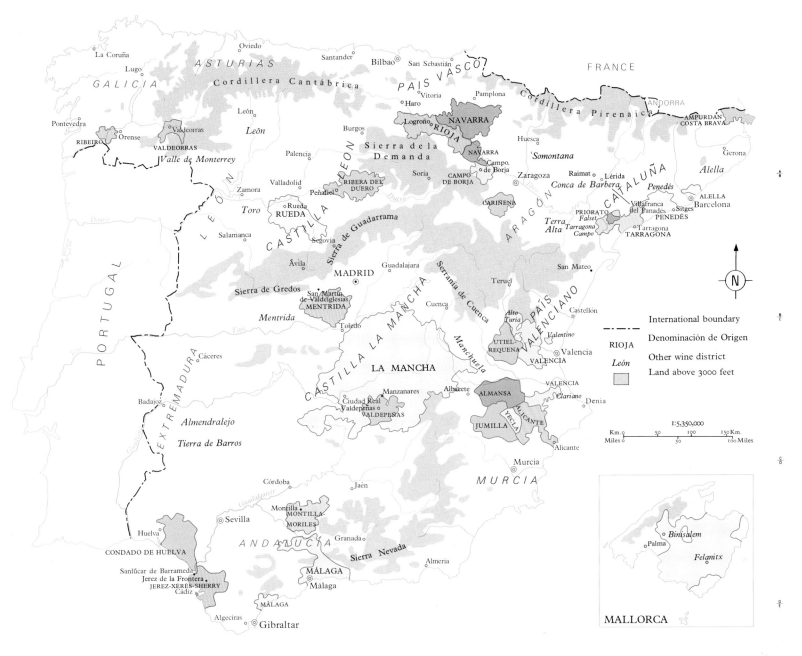

International boundary
Denominación de Origen
Other wine district
Land above 3000 feet

RIOJA

León

1:5,350,000

Km. 0   50   100   150 Km.
Miles 0   50   100 Miles

N

MALLORCA

The Señorio de Sarria estate has led Navarra in the north up to international standards. Valdepeñas and the plain of La Mancha still have a long way to go.

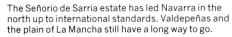

The distribution of Spain's vineyards

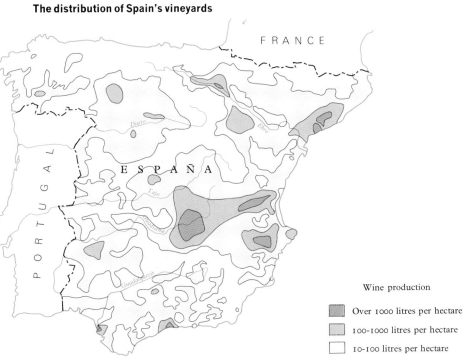

Wine production

Over 1000 litres per hectare

100–1000 litres per hectare

10–100 litres per hectare

The Sherry Country

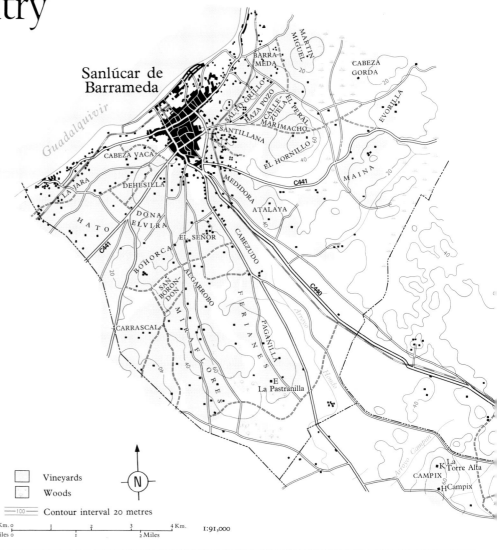

Sanlúcar de Barrameda

Vineyards
Woods
Contour interval 20 metres

Km. 0   1   2   3   4 Km.
Miles 0   1   2 Miles

1:91,000

Finesse – meaning fine-ness in its most literal sense, a combination of strength and delicacy – is not one of the qualities you normally find in scorched-earth wines. Where the sun fairly grills the ground, and the grapes ripen as warm as fruit in a pie, wine sometimes develops wonderful thews and sinews, power and depth. But finesse. . . .

This is sherry's great distinction. It is a question of chalk; of the breed of the Palomino grape; of huge investment and long-inherited skill. Not every bottle of sherry, by a very long way, has this quality. But a real fino, the rarely shipped unstrengthened produce of the bare white chalk dunes of Macharnudo or Sanlúcar de Barrameda, is an expression of wine and wood as vivid and beautiful as any in the world.

One does not think of sherry normally in direct comparison with the other great white wines of the world – but it is, strange to say, the cheapest of them, even bodega bottled and fully mature, ready to drink.

The sherry country, between the romantic-sounding cities of Cádiz and Seville, is almost a caricature of grandee Spain. Here are the bull ranches, the caballeros, the castles on the skyline, the patios, the guitars, the night-turned-into-day. Jerez de la Frontera, the town that gives its name to sherry, lives and breathes sherry as Beaune does burgundy and Epernay champagne.

The comparison between sherry and champagne can be carried a long way. Both are white wines with a distinction given them by chalk soil, both needing long traditional treatment to

Below and below right: there is a strange dazzling light reflected off the chalk in the sherry vineyards. Golden Palomino grapes almost cook in the heat; before they are pressed they are often laid out on esparto mats in the sun to sweeten even more, so that their high sugar content will give strong and stable wine. The miracle is that it is delicate as well.

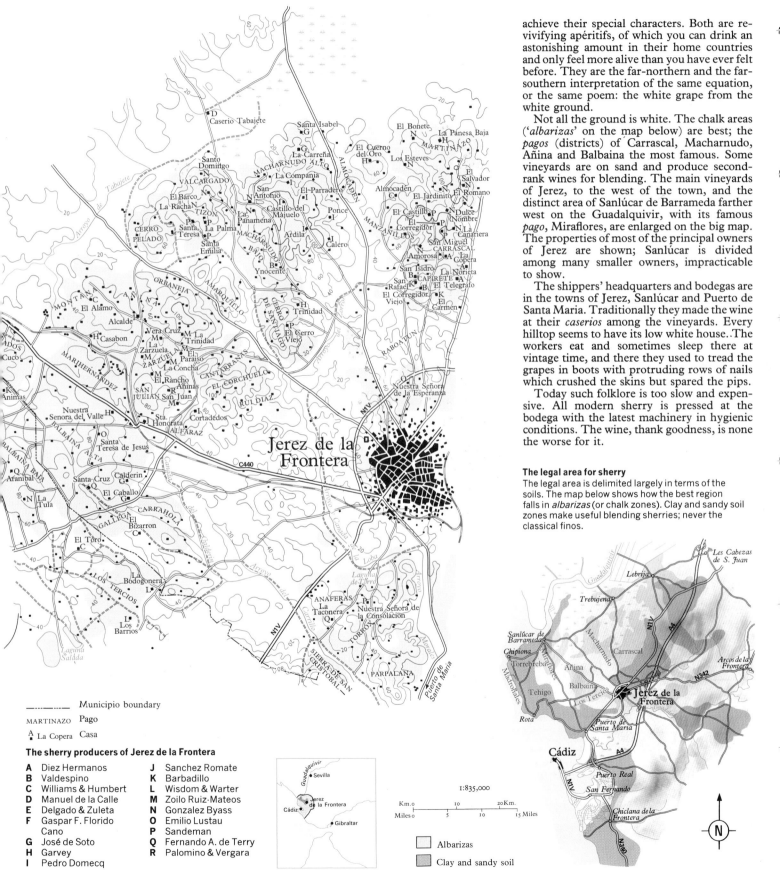

achieve their special characters. Both are re-vivifying apéritifs, of which you can drink an astonishing amount in their home countries and only feel more alive than you have ever felt before. They are the far-northern and the far-southern interpretation of the same equation, or the same poem: the white grape from the white ground.

Not all the ground is white. The chalk areas ('*albarizas*' on the map below) are best; the *pagos* (districts) of Carrascal, Macharnudo, Añina and Balbaina the most famous. Some vineyards are on sand and produce second-rank wines for blending. The main vineyards of Jerez, to the west of the town, and the distinct area of Sanlúcar de Barrameda farther west on the Guadalquivir, with its famous *pago*, Miraflores, are enlarged on the big map. The properties of most of the principal owners of Jerez are shown; Sanlúcar is divided among many smaller owners, impracticable to show.

The shippers' headquarters and bodegas are in the towns of Jerez, Sanlúcar and Puerto de Santa Maria. Traditionally they made the wine at their *caserios* among the vineyards. Every hilltop seems to have its low white house..The workers eat and sometimes sleep there at vintage time, and there they used to tread the grapes in boots with protruding rows of nails which crushed the skins but spared the pips.

Today such folklore is too slow and expensive. All modern sherry is pressed at the bodega with the latest machinery in hygienic conditions. The wine, thank goodness, is none the worse for it.

The legal area for sherry
The legal area is delimited largely in terms of the soils. The map below shows how the best region falls in *albarizas* (or chalk zones). Clay and sandy soil zones make useful blending sherries; never the classical finos.

Municipio boundary

MARTINAZO Pago

▲ La Copera Casa

The sherry producers of Jerez de la Frontera

A	Diez Hermanos	J	Sanchez Romate
B	Valdespino	K	Barbadillo
C	Williams & Humbert	L	Wisdom & Warter
D	Manuel de la Calle	M	Zoilo Ruiz-Mateos
E	Delgado & Zuleta	N	Gonzalez Byass
F	Gaspar F. Florido Cano	O	Emilio Lustau
		P	Sandeman
G	José de Soto	Q	Fernando A. de Terry
H	Garvey	R	Palomino & Vergara
I	Pedro Domecq		

1:835,000

Km.0   10   20 Km.

Miles 0   5   10   15 Miles

▢ Albarizas

▨ Clay and sandy soil

201

Jerez de la Frontera

There are little bars in Jerez where the tapas, the morsels of food without which no Jerezano puts glass to mouth, constitute a banquet. From olives and cheese to prawns, to raw ham, to peppery little sausages, to lobster claws, to miniature steaks streaked with amber onions, the path of temptation is broad and long.

Your little copita, a glass no more imposing than an opening tulip, fills and empties with a paler wine, a cooler wine, a more druggingly delicious wine than you have ever tasted. It seems at the same time dry as dust and just teasingly sweet, so that you have to sip again to trace the suggestion of grapes.

It comes in half-bottles, kept on ice. A half-bottle is reckoned a reasonable drink to spin out over an hour or two among the tapas. And in half-bottles it stays as fresh as it was when it left the bodega – for no bottle is left half full.

The most celebrated sights of Jerez are the bodegas of the shipping houses. Their towering whitewashed aisles, dim-roofed and crisscrossed with sunbeams, are irresistibly cathedral-like. In them, in ranks of butts sometimes five tiers high, the new wine is put to mature. It will not leave until it has gone through an elaborate blending process which is known as the solera system. Only the occasional wine of notable distinction is sold unblended as an 'almacenista'.

The first job when the new wine has got over its fermentation is to sort it into categories; better or worse, lighter or more full-bodied. Each wine is put into the *criadera*, or nursery, appropriate to its character. Each character, or category, of wine has a traditional name.

From these *criaderas* the shipper tops up a number of soleras, consisting of perhaps 20, perhaps several hundred butts; each wine again going into the solera nearest to its character. As new wine goes into butts at one end of the solera, mature wine for blending is drawn from the other. The solera system is simply a progressive topping up of older barrels from younger of the same style, so that wine is continuously being blended, and hence always emerges tasting the same.

The solera wines are the shipper's paintbox for the blending of his brands, or for brands ordered by other wine merchants for sale under their own names. Most sherry when it is sold is a blend of several, sweetened and strengthened to the public's taste. The few 'straight solera' sherries which are sold tend to be unsweetened and therefore wines for the connoisseur.

The categories into which all young sherry is classified begin with fino. Finos are the best sherries, delicate and distinctive wines which will need a minimum of blending and sweetening. They will age excellently, but they also have the qualities that make them perfect young. Their strong individuality comes from an unusual form of yeast, flor, which forms on their surface. Tasted from the butt, when the

The solera system utilizes the traditional 500-litre *botas*, or butts, for the storage of the maturing wine. Here they are being moved into the bodegas, where they are stacked often five high.

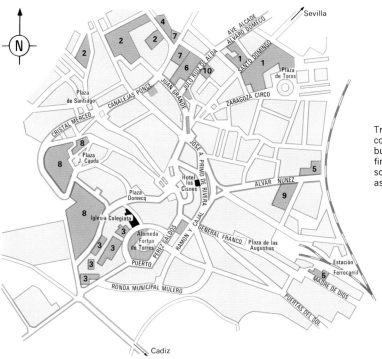

The sherry bodegas of Jerez de la Frontera map

Tres Palmas is the conventional sign on the butt for a superlative fino. La Riva bottles some very old sherries as well.

The most famous fino of all does not mention fino on the label. Extremely dry, fresh and young with real delicacy.

Excellent light fino from Valdespino's Ynocente vineyard in Macharnudo; the only sherry vineyard named on a label.

Carlos y Javier de Terry bodegas are in Puerto de Santa Maria, the second town of the Jerez area.

The Garvey family came to Jerez from Ireland, and call their best fino after Ireland's patron saint.

Varela is another of the shippers with bodegas in Puerto de Santa Maria. A typical popular, middle-ranking fino.

Dos Cortados signifies very dry oloroso with great distinction. Williams & Humbert's is one of the best sherries sold.

An old, unsweetened (al natural) wine from a good shipper. Amontillado character, although it does not say so.

The firm of Duff Gordon is owned by Bodegas Osborne. El Cid is their most popular wine. It is a medium-sweet amontillado.

A magnificent old dry oloroso from Macharnudo, one of the best wines from one of the biggest and best shippers.

Manzanilla is usually drunk as a brisk young fino. Don Zoilo produces a luxurious long-aged variety with deeper flavours.

Old oloroso is the basis for good sweet sherries; cream style is very sweet but should not mask the nuttiness of the base.

The most famous of all creams comes from a British firm in Bristol, made by them or to their requirements in Jerez.

The old English firm of Sandeman is famous for both port and sherry. Their fino, 'Apitiv', is also excellent.

capataz of the bodega thrusts his long cane-handled *venencia* through the flor into the pale wine to bring out a sample, they have a magical new-bread freshness and vitality; they are, beyond question, Spain's finest wine of all.

Amontillado – a softer, darker wine – comes next. The best amontillados are old finos, finos which did not quite have the right freshness to be drunk young, although the name is often used in commerce for middle-character blends of no real distinction. Great amontillado soleras (for only from the solera can you taste the real individuality of the wine) are dry and almost stingingly powerful of flavour, with a dark, fat, rich tang – but words fall short.

Oloroso is the third principal class. Wines which have great possibilities for ageing, but which seem a little heavy at first, go into this solera. They are the basis for the best sweet sherries – often known as milk or cream, which suggests their silky fatness.

Sweetening wines and colouring wines for blending are specially made from sun-dried grapes and kept in their own soleras. Lesser wines which go into cheaper blends are known as *rayas*, and a final rare character, something between fino and oloroso, as *palo cortado*.

In addition there are the wines of Sanlúcar de Barrameda, known as manzanillas. Manzanilla finos are some of the most delicate and lovely of all, always with a faintly salty tang which is held to come from the sea. A manzanilla amontillado is rare, but can be exquisite, salty and brown as burnt butter.

No blend, medium-sweet or sweet as most blends are, can compare with these astonishing natural sherries. They are as much collectors' pieces as great domaine-bottled burgundies.

The sherry bodegas of Jerez de la Frontera

1 Williams & Humbert
2 Zoilo Ruiz-Mateos
3 Gonzalez Byass
4 Sandeman
5 Diez Hermanos
6 Garvey
7 Valdespino
8 Pedro Domecq
9 La Riva
10 Agustin Blazquez

Right: a trade directory lists more than 600 brands of sherry. Many of them, including some famous ones, belong to wine merchants who have no establishment in Spain. They order wine to their own specifications, for sale under their own name, from one of the big shipping houses. Most of the best sherries, however, come from bodegas, large or small, who bottle their own style of wine themselves. All have a wide range from dry to sweet; these labels are a representative selection.

Rioja

Left: much of Rioja outside the river valley has a bare highland feeling emphasized by the Sierra de Cantabria in the distance, often snow-covered. Vineyards, crops and pasture alternate on the stony ground. The vines grow as low bushes without posts or wires.

For many years Rioja had a virtual monopoly of the wine lists of good restaurants in Spain. They offered local wines in carafes. But if you wanted bottled wine, especially red wine, Rioja was the Bordeaux and Burgundy of Spain. You were pointed towards Rioja.

It is partly a question of human geography, as well as the physical kind. Rioja is not far from the French frontier; not far from Bordeaux. When the phylloxera arrived in the 1870s many winegrowers took off for Spain. They found in Rioja rather different conditions, but an opportunity to make good wine all the same. Then the phylloxera caught up with them, and they went home. But they left French methods and ideas.

Rioja is distinctly mountainous in atmosphere. It lies in the shelter of the Sierra de Cantabria to the north, but its best vineyards are still 460 metres above sea level. They get plenty of rain and long springs and autumns, rather than endless parching summers. The wine is correspondingly less hearty and more interesting than other Spanish wine: well made and at the right age exceedingly delicate and fine, yet with a faintly toasted sweet warmth, which seems to proclaim it Spanish.

The area is divided into three by terrain and altitude. The areas farther up-river are cooler and wetter. Rioja Alta (the high Rioja) has the coolest climate and a mixture of clays, chalky and iron-rich, and silts that give its wine acidity, finesse and 'structure': it makes the longest-lived and potentially the best wines of the region. Rioja Alavesa has warmer, more alkaline slopes. Its Tempranillo is fragrant and pale, less sinewy, quicker to mature, but excellent in blends. Rioja Baja (the low Rioja) has a more Mediterranean climate with heavier soil, largely planted with Garnacha for the

strongest but coarsest wine of the three, the right booster for many blends but rarely becoming a Reserva in its own right. The three zones meet near the town of Logroño, one of the two main centres of the wine trade.

The chief wine centre is Haro. The rather insignificant town is dwarfed by its outskirts, which contain 13 large bodegas – almost a third of the total of Rioja. The country around is beautiful in an upland way: tall poplars and eucalyptus trees line the roads; orchards cover slopes along with tilting fields of vines. In the rocky valley bottom the infant river Ebro is joined by the little Rio Oja, whose shortened name the region has adopted.

There are few wine estates, large or small, in Rioja which grow, make and bottle their own wine. In many matters of technique the Bordelais left their mark, but châteaux (with the single exception of Castillo Ygay) are not among them. To qualify for a Rioja Certificate of Origin a bodega has to be big enough, and most bodegas operate as sherry houses do, or the wineries of California. They buy grapes from farmers to supplement those they grow themselves, and make a blend of wine of their own house style. Vineyard names appear frequently on Rioja bottles: Viña Tondonia, Zaco, Paceta, Pomal are all well known. They are not regulated as individual sites in, say, Burgundy are, but the style of the wines bottled with their names is generally very consistent – and high.

Red wine is far more important than white. It is made from a mixture of grapes, in which the Garnacha (the pale Grenache of the Rhône) is preponderant, but the Tempranillo, Spain's best red grape – said to be related to the Pinot Noir – is dominant in flavour. Bordeaux- and Burgundy-shaped bottles tend to be used

for, respectively, the lighter ('clarete') and fuller ('tinto') wines.

By and large these wines are still made rather as Bordeaux was 50 years ago, to be aged several years in barrels (two or three for standard, but far more than Bordeaux, up to five or ten, for Reservas), until their darkness and fruitiness has been tamed and replaced with the almost tawny colour and soft dry vanilla flavour that comes from oak. In Spain, where most red wine is inky, they are much appreciated light and smooth, as long ageing in wood makes them. The greatest change in Rioja in recent years has been the move to bottle earlier; to reduce the dominance of the oaky aroma and allow the grapey flavours to blossom. It is a marked improvement: only exceptional wines could stand up to the traditional Reserva treatment. A few, from such conservative bodegas as Lopez de Heredia and Muga, still do, with glorious results.

Even white Rioja wines were often given four or five years in barrel. When they had grown golden and rather thin, or flat with oxidation, they were reckoned at their prime, whereas earlier, sometimes marvellously stony and up to good Rhône standards, they were considered too young. Today many bodegas go to the other extreme, fermenting the aromatic must of the Viura grapes very cold in steel tanks, and bottling it while it still tastes more of fruit than of wine. Others hold to a middle course, ageing whites briefly in wood. The minority toe the classic line; theirs is the most memorable wine.

Map, bottom right: Rioja's finest vineyards surround the valley of the Ebro around Haro and downstream through Ollauri, Cenicero (see top map) and El Ciego.

Right: the big bodegas of Rioja keep a remarkably even and high standard for both their special and ordinary wines. Wines such as Imperial, Ygay and Lopez de Heredia are Rioja's finest. Heraldry and medals play a large part in label design.

Provincial boundary
Boundary of wine area
NAVARRETE Important wine-producing town

Vineyards - intensive cultivation
Vineyards - dispersed cultivation
Woods
450 Contour interval 150 metres

Haro

1:200,000
Km. 0   1   2   3   4   5 Km.
Miles 0   1   2   3 Miles

Provincial boundary
ELCIEGO Important wine-producing town
Vineyards
Woods
500 Contour interval 50 metres

Catalonia

On a coast whose traditional production was nearly all heavy and dark red wine for the world's blending vats, it is a surprise to come across the world's biggest cellars for sparkling wine. But Catalonia is different from the rest of Mediterranean Spain. The Catalans have more vitality, are more demanding, destructive, creative. They also have, on rising ranges of inland hills in the shelter of the eastern Pyrenees, with the ocean at their feet, a superbly temperate and reliable climate. In the past it has been the hottest areas near the sea, with their super-potent wine, that have been most in demand. Today it is the potential of the higher ground that is bringing recognition to a new sort of well-balanced table wine, combining the qualities of ripe Mediterranean grapes with the sort of finesse that is found in the best Riojas.

There are seven Denominaciónes de Origen in Catalonia today, but by far the most important is Penedés, running from just west of Barcelona 30 miles (50km) westward and northward up into the limestone hills. The heart of Penedés is the town of Villafranca, with several important bodegas, but its neighbour to the north, San Sadurní de Noya, is the most-visited wine centre, they say, in Spain: the city of sparkling wine, or *cava*.

Two vast concerns, Codorniú and Freixenet, control the industry. They use Catalonia's own white grape varieties, well adapted to produce acidic wines despite hot weather, to make fresh and well-balanced, if not very

aromatic, sparkling wines (the term *cava* is limited to the *méthode champenoise*). Parellada, Xarel-lo and Macabeo (alias, in Rioja, Viura) are the principal sorts.

Young, their creaming *cava* can be exquisitely fruity. Alas, in the typical Spanish manner, too much stress is laid on ageing. The premium put on older bottles would be better put on the top quality of gently pressed young wines while they are at their most delicate.

One name dominates the table wines of the region: that of the Torres family. Their bodegas at Villafranca, family owned for 300 years, have in the last 20 led a revolution of ideas and technology that has put Catalonian wine alongside Rioja as Spain's best reputed and best distributed.

Bodegas Torres have made the running by studying abroad, ignoring the rules, planting such non-traditional grapes as Cabernet and Pinot Noir, Chardonnay and Gewürztraminer, opening new vineyard areas at higher altitudes, using cold fermentation in stainless steel and ageing their wines more in bottle and less in cask. The traditional red grapes of the Penedés are not greatly different from Rioja's, with Garnacha and Tempranillo (known here as Ull de Lebre) preponderant. In the Torres standard brands, Tres Torres and Gran Sangre de Toro, a certain extra richness and ripeness is what distinguishes them from Riojas Reservas. Oak still plays an important part. The top Torres red, however, their Gran Coronas Black Label, is pure Cabernet and tastes

Left: glass *bombonas*, jars holding 30 litres, protected by plaited straw wrapping, used to be a common sight in Catalonia and northwards up the coast into the French eastern Pyrenees. They are used both for transporting everyday wine and for maturing strong sweet wines in contact with air, often actually in the open air, to acquire the taste known as *rancio*.
Above: a 17th-century cask in the Codorniú Museum at San Sadurní de Noya has each of its staves numbered with Roman numerals so that it can easily be dismantled and reassembled.

more like a complex, fruity, somehow faintly decadent red Bordeaux.

Torres, followed by several of their neighbours, have also reinterpreted the white wines of Penedés, adding the classic French and even German grapes. One of their neighbours, in fact, has taken the California view and planted nothing but Cabernet and Chardonnay.

The owners of Codorniú, meanwhile, had long intended to exploit the potential of inland Catalonia. In the 1930s, just before the Spanish Civil War, the Raventos family built an ambitious modern bodega at Raimat, on the high plateau near Lérida (off the map, 80km northwest of Tarragona) to make fine table wines. So far from the coast the climate is more continental, with minimal rainfall; irrigation is essential. After a 50-year delay, the Raimat estate has started to produce red and white wines of very promising quality, again from both native and French varieties. The Cabernet in particular is excellent.

The same family now owns the extravagant Masía Bach estate in Penedés, at Sant Esteve de Sesrovires. Extrísimo Bach, its best-known wine, is sweet and oak-aged, much in the style of the neighbouring Denominación of Alella, to the north of Barcelona.

Alella is a dwindling vineyard, interesting as its wines may have been. Farther north (off the map) the Costa Brava has its Denominación of Ampurdán, centred around Perelada in the Province of Gerona, producing sparkling wines (not up to Penedés standards) and (the bulk of production) *rosado*.

More important are the ancient vineyards of Tarragona and Priorato, to the south, and the recently created Denominaciónes of Conca de Barberà, extending Penedés-style wine farther up into cooler hills, and Terra Alta, a similar inland extension to the sprawling region of Tarragona.

Priorato is the true heart of Tarragona, a hot and rocky region of volcanic soil that produces red wines of formidable colour, strength and blackberryish flavour. Fermented dry, they are more used for blending than drinking. It takes a brave man. . . . With spirit added, as sweet dessert wine, aged many years to acquire dusty *rancio* flavours, Priorato Dulce can be superb.

Superlatives excluded, much the same can be said of the rest of Tarragona. Its wines, exploited and appreciated by the Romans (whose architecture is still much in evidence), are either strong dry reds for blending or passable substitutes for port. A very few are much better. But more could be, and Spain's entry into the European Common Market may encourage the quality producers.

Below: some of the best of Catalan wine (which includes good sparkling wine) is surprisingly dry and delicate. Tarragona and Priorato provide a complete contrast.

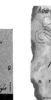

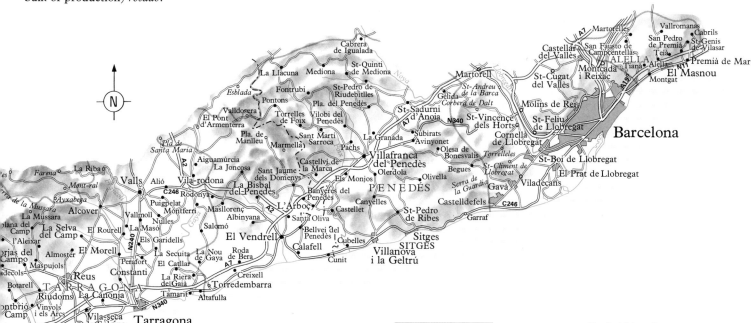

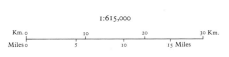

Provincial boundary

Denominación de Origen boundary

TARRAGONA Denominación de Origen

1:615,000

Rueda and the Duero

For many years before the late 1970s, Spain's most prestigious and expensive red wine appeared a complete maverick. Few had tasted Vega Sicilia, and fewer still knew where, in the vast dustbowl of central Spain, such a remarkable vineyard could be found.

The plain of Old Castile, stretching in tawny leagues north from Segovia and Avila to the old kingdom of León, is traversed by the adolescent Duero, the river that in Portugal becomes the Douro and the home of port. It is the shallow valleys of the Duero and its tributaries, around Valladolid, from Zamora upstream to Aranda de Duero, that have an ancient winemaking tradition – more, one would think, because they had a thirsty population (Valladolid was the capital of 17th-century Spain) than because the fierce climate favoured the vine. The wines were very alcoholic, the reds black and the whites like primitive sherry. On the credit side there were chalky clay soils that retained the sparse rainfall and gave the wine at least a suggestion of the quality associated with chalk. And at 2,000 feet (610 metres) the nights are remarkably cool.

Vega Sicilia, one perfectionist property at Valbuena on the Duero, proved that very fine red could be made. The estate was planted in imitation of Bordeaux in the 1860s, at the same time as the first such steps were being taken in Rioja. But here the Bordeaux grapes were used with only a minority of the native Garnacha and Tempranillo (known here as 'Tinto Fino'). Vega Sicilia, aged ten years in barrel, is a wine of astonishing, penetrating personality. For many people its younger brother, the five-year-old 'Valbuena' of the same estate, is an easier wine to understand.

The other wines of the region have not caught up, nor has Cabernet taken over. But since about 1970 the large cooperative at

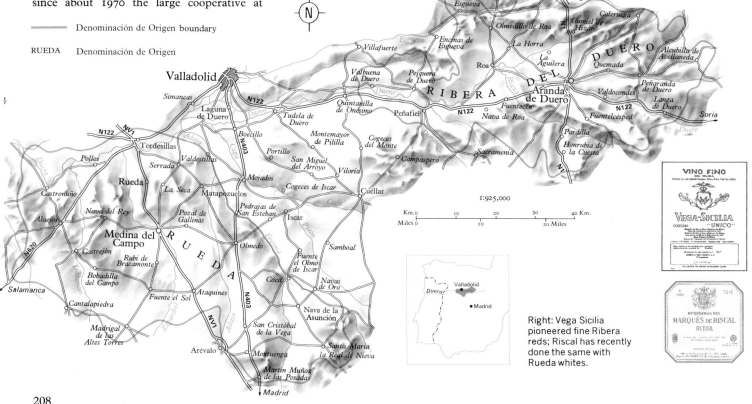

Left: in many minds the one-time 'first-growth' of Spain, the lovely bodega of Vega Sicilia at Valbuena de Duero is a centenarian precursor of a region that is now expanding its reputation. To the south, new investment is making white wines to the modern taste.

Peñafiel, just to the east, has greatly refined its winemaking, using the Tinto Fino and ageing its Reservas, notably the extremely tasty 'Protos', in oak. In 1982 the region (see the map) was defined as a Denominación de Origen under the name Ribera del Duero, along with the neighbouring Ribera de Burgos around Aranda in the Province of Burgos (whose wines tend to be paler and lighter than the hefty reds of Valladolid).

Meanwhile, south of Valladolid something more like a revolution was taking place. The old wine centres of Rueda and Nava del Rey, traditional producers of oxidized whites, came under the prospecting eye of the famous Rioja Bodega Marqués de Riscal, looking for a new source for white wines of fashionable fruity freshness. It was the local white grape, the Verdejo, that attracted Riscal's attention. Carefully vinified, it has good fruity acidity and the ability to age well in cask. In 1971, with the advice of Professor Peynaud from Bordeaux, Riscal built a modern 'inox' bodega. In 1980 Rueda was made a Denominación. At the same time, the local Sanz family's Bodegas de Crianza de Castilla la Vieja went into partnership with the Marqués de Griñon, who had already attracted attention by growing Cabernet at, of all places, Toledo. Griñon, like Riscal (and also with Peynaud advice) makes a Rueda Superior (which must be at least 60% Verdejo), but sells it unaged. It is remarkably crisp and aromatic, certainly one of Spain's best white wines.

- - - - - Denominación de Origen boundary

RUEDA   Denominación de Origen

1:925,000

Km.0   10   20   30   40 Km.

Miles 0   10   20 Miles

VINO FINO

VEGA-SICILIA
COSECHA "UNICO"

MARQUÉS DE RISCAL
RUEDA

Right: Vega Sicilia pioneered fine Ribera reds; Riscal has recently done the same with Rueda whites.

Montilla and Málaga

Andalucia is the province of *vinos generosos*, even more 'generous' than the strong wines of midland and Mediterranean Spain. Sherry, from where its low chalk hills meet the Atlantic, is much the most famous. But its mountainous eastern coast, the 'Costa del Sol', and the hot dry hills behind it also have their characteristic specialities, related to sherry but stylistically distinct. Sherry even takes the name of one of its principal styles, amontillado, from its resemblance to the soft strong wines of Montilla.

Montilla-Moriles, to give it its full name, lies just south of Córdoba, 100 miles (160km) inland, on 44,000 acres (18,000 hectares) of the very same chalk that gives rise to the marvellous finos and olorosos of Jerez.

Until 40 years ago its potent produce was blended at Jerez as though the two regions were one. But Montilla is different. Its special attraction lies in its very high natural strength, which allows it to be shipped without fortification, in contrast to sherry, which is nearly always strengthened slightly. It seems strange to speak of delicacy in a wine with a natural strength of 16% alcohol – but this is in fact the characteristic that distinguishes all finos, and in a really good Montilla it is easy to appreciate.

The Montilla grape is the Pedro Ximénez – the one that in Jerez is kept for the sweetest wine. The even hotter inland climate of Montilla gives it an even higher sugar content which ferments rapidly (fermentation is done in open earthenware jars). The flor yeast also comes quickly. Within a year or two the wine is ready, with all the finesse of a fino, but more softness than, for example, a manzanilla, which always has a characteristic bite. Montillas make deceptively perfect apéritifs, slipping down like table wines despite their high strength. People claim to find in them the scent of black olives (which are of course their perfect partners).

Although fine Montilla is probably at its best young, pale and dry, the bodegas use the same methods of solera ageing, and sweetening with concentrated must, as the bodegas of Jerez, to make a range running from apéritif to dessert.

It is ironic that the sherry shippers should have legally appropriated the term amontillado, along with fino and oloroso, so that Montilla may only be exported to Britain, its principal foreign market, as 'dry', 'medium' or 'cream'.

No great gulf, in fact no gulf at all, separates Montilla from Málaga. Málaga, once world famous for its dessert wines (also known as 'Mountain') is in reality a wide range of *vinos generosos* with one common factor: the bodegas must, by law, be in the city of the Costa del Sol. The vineyards are in two areas. The smaller is an enclave of some 4,000 acres (1,600 hectares) around Mollina to the north, adjacent to Montilla-Moriles, where the same grape, the Pedro Ximénez, is used largely to make dry amontillado-style wine sold as Málaga Blanco Seco. Much more important are 30,000 acres (12,000 hectares) along the coastal mountains east of the city: the region of Axarquia. Here the chief grape is the Moscatel, used to make sweet Málagas ranging from semi-dulce to the most

Left and below: different grapes and traditions produce similar *vinos generosos* in Málaga and Montilla.

Denominación de Origen boundary

1:1,000,000

unctuous 'Lagrima', the equivalent, in principle, of the 'essence' of Tokay; self-pressed from over-ripe grapes. Crops are very small (one-fifth as much per acre as Montilla) and the wines extremely concentrated and capable of indefinite ageing, the better qualities in soleras. *Arrope* – or boiled-down must, a technique used by the Romans – is used to concentrate the flavour further.

The market does not demand superlative Málagas today, but they have been, and still can be, made. Bodegas Scholtz is the name to look for.

Portugal

Portugal is the place for wine romantics. Even more than Italy it remains the country of groaning ox carts, of dappled sunlight through arbours of vines, of treading the purple must, of maidens bearing pitchers, of songs handed down for centuries. Some 15% of the population lives by making or selling wine, and this despite the fact that a good third of the country, south of the Tagus (the Tejo), is almost wineless. In some places it must be more like 50%.

The climate of Portugal is ideal for grapes. The winegrowing northern half of the country has ample rain, except in the high Douro beyond the mountains, and a long, bright rather than blazing, summer; Atlantic characteristics which make it rather like a more southerly Bordeaux. The general standard, even of *vinho de consumo*, is as high as any country's, and if the best wines (apart from port) cannot compete with those of France or even Italy, the run-of-the-mill produce is at least as good.

Portugal's greatest wine is port. It is treated in detail on pages 216–217. Besides the port area, the government distinguishes three major table-wine areas and a handful of minor ones in rather the same way as the French Appellations Contrôlées. Wines from these areas bottled in Portugal carry a government seal, *selo de origem*, as witness to their authenticity – a praiseworthy idea; but by no means all Portugal's best wines come from these areas, nor are all their wines very good.

The great export success among 'demarcated' wines is vinho verde, the 'green' wine of the northernmost province, the Minho, which accounts for a quarter of the whole country's wine harvest. Commercial carbonated rosés, inspired by the vinho verde idea but coming from undemarcated sources, have been the smash hit of Portuguese winemaking for 25 years. They may even have given the Portuguese the notion that such facile wine was all foreigners were interested in. Certainly for a long time the industry in *vinho maduro*, the term used for matured wine, remained remarkably conservative. With the exception of the Dão region (mapped overleaf) and three historic but scarcely significant Lisbon vineyards (opposite), the rest of Portugal's table wine was merged into an anonymity out of which skilful merchants produced their own favourite blends.

To a large extent this is still true. Two important changes have been the demarcation in 1979 of the Bairrada region (page 212) and the institution of a second tier of so-called 'determinate areas': distinct regions which we may assume, with Portugal's entry to the European Community, will eventually carry *selos de origem*.

Right: many of Portugal's best standard wines are merchants' brands which remain reticent about their origins. The word Garrafeira often distinguishes the best selected matured wine.

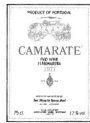

They are, from north to south, four sub-regions of the Douro (Alijó, Lamego, Sabrosa, Vila Real); two of the Beira Alta, north of Dão (Lafões, Meda); two of Estremadura, north of Lisbon (Palmela, Torres Vedras); one of Ribatejo (Cartaxo), up the River Tagus from Lisbon; and three across the Tagus, in the Alentejo (Borba, Reguengos, Vidigueira). In addition, one more southern region, the Algarve, has the dignity of demarcation – although for no very apparent reason – and just across the Tagus from Lisbon, Setúbal is demarcated for its very high-quality dessert Muscat.

Moscatel de Setúbal is one of the world's very best sweet Muscat wines. It is fortified, although much less than port, and the grape skins, which in Muscats contain much of the aromatic elements, are steeped in it to intensify the scent. Unlike the equivalent Muscats of the south of France, Setúbal improves with age – even with great age. Setúbal can be exquisite young or old.

In the past it has been the merchants' habit to draw their branded table wines from different parts of the country and blend them. The better wines would be aged as Reservas and the best, the pride of the house, as Garrafeira; which might be rendered as 'selected old wine'. Portugal's red grapes, processed in traditional fashion, give so much tannin that ten years is rarely excessive ageing and often not enough.

The rising trend among the leading merchants, however, is to become much more specific. Individual estates were almost unknown; today there are several, setting standards that others will have to follow. The first such wine, and still the best, was begun in the 1960s by the port house of Ferreira in, of all places, the high Douro. Their rare and sumptuous Barca Velha soon became for Portugal what Vega Sicilia is for Spain. Much more recently the house of Fonseca, makers of Setúbal, Lancers rosé and the admirable Periquita and Camarate reds, across the Tagus from Lisbon, have been marketing an estate Cabernet Sauvignon, Quinta de Bacalhoa, which far more closely resembles a modern Bordeaux than a traditional Portuguese red. While most Portuguese table wines remain what they were, robust and invigorating, tannic and a touch earthy, good value but not notably aromatic or complex, the number of exceptions is growing at an encouraging pace.

In keeping with Portugal's reputation as a maritime nation she brings vines as near as they ever get to the sea. At Colares, on the Atlantic coast, the vines grow on the beach in the sort of place where wind-beaten tamarisk and gorse are usually the only growing things.

The phylloxera cannot live in sand, so the vines are safe here. They creep low along the ground, their old limbs like driftwood, bearing small bunches of intensely blue grapes. Low stone walls or plaited cane fences for shelter wander among them; one old vine, straggling here and there, may fill a whole little pen of its own, for instead of pruning the growers go in for the old Roman method of layering their vines – making them reroot their long branches in the sand where they will.

The small, dark, thick-skinned Ramisco is the Colares grape. Its wine is correspondingly black and tannic and needs as long to mature as claret needed 100 years ago. It has always been esteemed Portugal's best red table wine, although little is made today, at least in the sandy soil where it is best, and even less is exported.

Carcavelos, another demarcated wine region, has been virtually swamped by Estoril. The remaining vineyards are in neighbouring villages. The wine they make is excellent, sweet and amber, but there are more profitable investments today around Lisbon than vineyards.

Of Lisbon's local wines the one in best shape is probably Bucelas (labels still use the old spelling 'Bucellas') – pleasant, fresh, white and dry, slightly oaky, but scarcely a memorable character. Much more important today are the vineyards of the Arrabida peninsula across the Tagus bridge, the home of Setúbal.

The village of Azenhas do Mar, north of Colares.

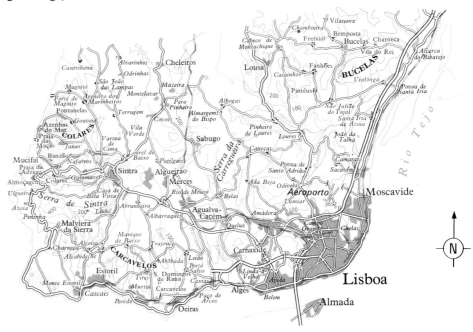

BUCELAS Demarcated region

Vineyards

Woods

—200— Contour interval 100 metres

1:353,000

Km. 0   5   10   15   20 Km.

Miles 0   5   10 Miles

Right: the pride of Lisbon used to be the local wines. Today much more wine is made across the Tagus bridge on the Arrabida peninsula, long famous for Setúbal Muscat.

Bairrada

The region of Bairrada is an important new (1979) recruit to the short list of Portugal's *selos de origem*. It is a rural district lying astride the dreadful 'highway' that links Lisbon and Oporto, filling most of the area between the granite hills of Dão and the Atlantic coast. Its low hills are of heavy lime-rich clay which gives body and typical Portuguese bite to its overwhelmingly (90%) red wine. A moderate climate, prone to sea mists, helps its balance and acidity.

Most of the credit for quality, though, must go to the local red grape, the Baga. Although on its own it is too tannic for non-Portuguese tastes, wines blended with a high proportion of Baga have deep fruitiness, splendid colour and vigour, and resist oxidation in ageing for years. An active research station and modern wineries are experimenting with the ideal blend of grapes, and recent vintages from such merchant-makers as Caves Aliança, São João, Barracão and Messias are heartily to be recommended.

What little white wine the region makes (of Maria Gomes, a fairly neutral grape, leavened and made aromatic by the obscure but excellent Bical) is now nearly all made sparkling, although old bottles of the still wine can have considerable quality.

The potential of the region for truly remarkable table wines has one eccentric and wonderful witness. Right on its southeast boundary, on the slopes of the hill of Buçaco, where Wellington first turned back Napoleon's Peninsular force in a famous battle, the Buçaco Palace Hotel makes and matures red and white wines in a wholly traditional way. The grapes are trodden in *lagars* and the wine aged for years in barrel in the Palace cellars. Both reds and whites on the hotel wine list go back for decades. The whites seem to be at their best at about 20 years and the reds, velvety but intense, at about 30.

Above: the magnificent Palace Hotel at Buçaco overlooks the Bairrada region from its wooded ridge to the east. Its cellars (right) age some of Portugal's very best and truly traditional wines. Both red and white are kept for years in barrel and live in bottle for decades.

Boundary of demarcated region

THE LANGUAGE OF THE LABEL

Vinha Vineyard
Quinta Farm, estate
Colheita Vintage
Região demarcada Demarcated legal area
Denominação de origem Similar to Appellation Contrôlée
Reserva Better-quality wine
Garrafeira 'Private cellar' – i.e. best quality
Vinho verde 'Green' or young wine
Vinho de mesa Table wine
Vinho de consumo Ordinary wine, not usually bottled
Maduro Old or matured
Engarrafado na origem Estate-bottled
Branco White
Tinto Red
Rosado Rosé
Clarete Light red or dark rosé
Séco Dry
Doce, Adamado Sweet
Espumante Sparkling
Adega Cellar (normally, a firm's cellars)
Aguardente Brandy

Top is the label of the Buçaco Palace Hotel. There are few producers in the region, but all are sound or better.

Minho and Dão

Portugal's most distinctive contribution in the way of table wines is the speciality of her northern counties: their vinho verde. The name green wine describes its fresh, slightly under-ripe style, not its colour, which is red (three-quarters of it) or almost water-white.

Partly as a result of land shortage in the Minho, this most densely populated part of the country, the vines are grown high up trees and on pergolas around the little fields. In late summer the sight of the grape-bearing garlands along every road gives almost pagan pleasure. High off the ground, the grapes stay cool and keep their fresh acidity.

The crop is picked early and fermented briefly – the object being wine with a low alcohol content and a decided tartness. Secondary fermentation is encouraged to convert the excess malic acid to lactic. The red wines tend to be cloudy, but both they and the whites (which foreigners prefer) have a scintillating little bubble about them which is marvellously refreshing. It is all too easy to gulp them like beer on a hot day.

They are best from the barrel in the spirited little taverns of Monção and Barcelos and Penafiel. Export versions tend, alas, to be sweetened and carbonated; still good, but less magically fresh and bracing.

A superior sort of vinho verde is made from the white Alvarinho grape around Monção. Alvarinho will keep several years in bottle, developing a freesia-like scent but losing its bubbles. It is almost certainly Portugal's best white wine.

Basto and Amarante are considered the next best areas of the Minho for wine, followed by the more productive Braga and Penafiel. Lima makes a slightly stronger and deeper-coloured red wine than the others. But officially it is all vinho verde, and wines from the different regions are often blended together.

Dão used to be almost the only Portuguese region regularly identified on bottles of *vinho maduro*. The name has long been associated with solid reds that are reliable rather than inspiring, and can improve considerably in bottle. Besides, the region, with its graceful provincial capital of Viseu, is one of the prettiest in Iberia.

Dão is granite hill country, where bare rocks show through the sandy soil. It is well inland, with a hotter and drier climate than down on the coast. Vineyards seem to have little part in the landscape, only cropping up here and there in clearings in the sweet-scented pine forests.

There are both red and white Dãos. While they are young the whites can be firm and fragrant, good value and attractive as everyday table wine. The red as it is usually sold – a blend from a big merchant perhaps four years old – is a clean, smooth and well-made wine, but hard and without attractive sweetness. Older red Dão Reservas – 15 years is not too old – gradually develop a sweet fragrance and lose their hardness, becoming gentle and interesting, if still faintly earthy.

Right: fizzy and tart vinho verde comes in infinite variety. Good Dãos, the complete contrast, smooth and solid, are made by relatively few producers.

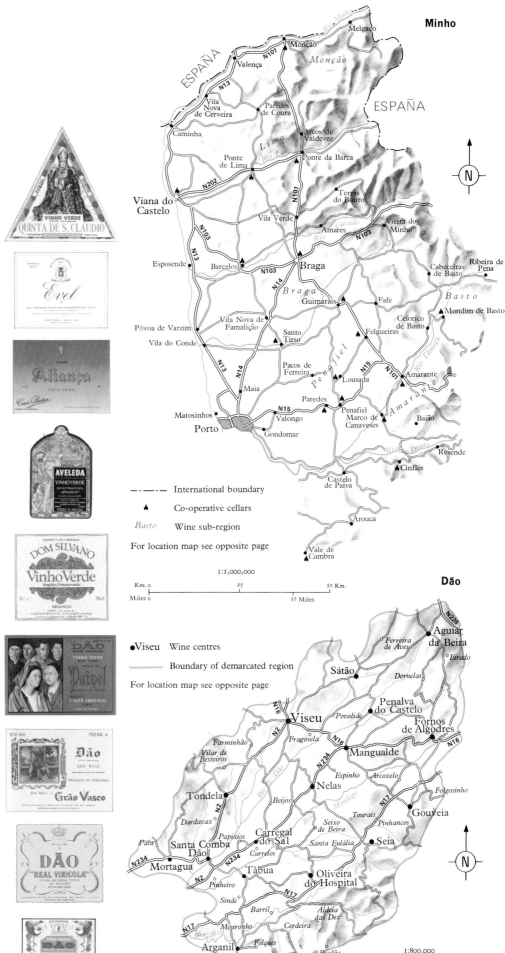

The Alto Douro

The Quinta do Noval, high in the hills to the north of Pinhão (see the map on this page), is the most famous of all the port-shippers' properties in the high Douro. A small patch of its parched upper terrace still grows ungrafted 'pre-phylloxera' vines. Their wine, sold as 'Nacional', has a concentration rarely found even in the greatest ports.

Of all the places where men have planted vineyards, the upper Douro is the most improbable. To begin with there was not even soil: only 60° slopes of slate and granite, flaking and unstable, baked in a 100° sun. It was a land of utter desolation.

The vine, however, is the one useful plant that is not quite deterred by these conditions. The Mediterranean-type climate of this region suits it. What was needed was simply the engineering feat of putting soil on the Douro slopes and keeping it there. Which meant building walls along the mountainsides, thousands of them, like contour lines, to hold up patches of ground (one could hardly call it soil) where vines could be planted.

Once the ground was stabilized and rainwater no longer ran straight off, it began to form soil, and plants began to add organic matter. Now olives, oranges, cork oaks and pines flourish. But before this could happen men had to blast and chip away at the slate, piling chunks of it into towering terrace walls.

Steps are the nightmare of workers in these vineyards. Every grape must be carried off the hill on the back of a man. New vineyards today are contoured with dynamite and bulldozers as far as possible to eliminate steps and walls.

The Douro reaches Portugal from Spain in a wilderness which is still inaccessible except by mule or canoe. It has carved a titanic canyon through the layered rock uplands. This is the port country. The 4,600-feet (1,400-metre) Serra do Marão to the west prevents the Atlantic rainclouds of summer from refreshing it. Often there is no summer rain at all.

Many of the original terraces dating from the 17th century survive in the mountains above Regua, in the original port-wine zone, given its first official limits (the first such limits ever given to any wine) in 1756. Today it remains the biggest producer, but the search for quality has led farther and farther upriver. The modern zone is 20 times the size it was in the 18th century, and all the best part is comparatively new. Below the tributary Corgo the wine is reckoned definitely inferior. The best vineyards of all today are those around and above Pinhão, including the tributary valleys of the Távora, Torto, Pinhão and Tua rivers.

–––––	District boundary
·····	Parish boundary
QTA. DA FOZ	Quinta
☐	Vineyards
☐	Woods
═500═	Contour interval 100 metres

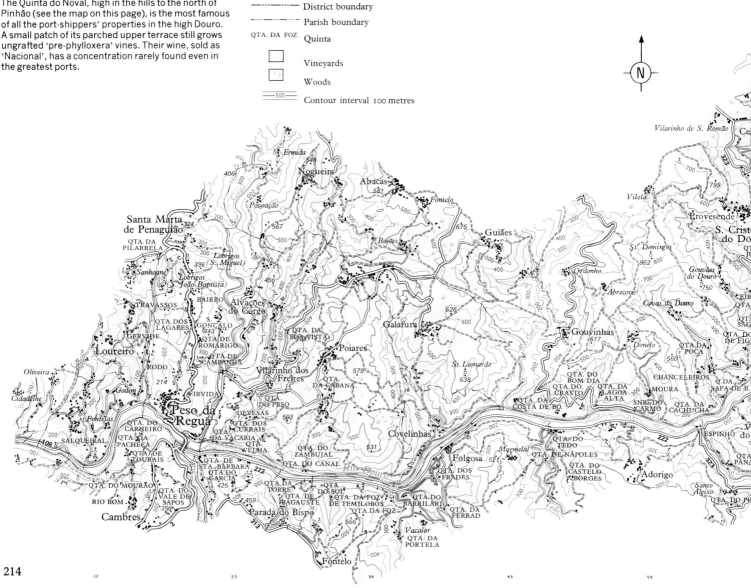

Vintage time anywhere is the climax of the year, but on the Douro, perhaps because of the hardship of life, it is almost Dionysiac. There is an antique frenzy about the ritual, the songs, the music of drum and pipe, the long nights of treading by the light of hurricane lamps while the women and girls dance together.

The famous shipping firms have their own quintas up in the hills, where they go to supervise the vintage. They are rambling white houses, vine-arboured, tile-floored and cool in a world of dust and glare. Most of the famous quintas are shown on the map on these pages. Quinta names, however, rarely appear as wine names. Only half a dozen of the whole valley, of which the most famous is Quinta do Noval above Pinhão, sell their wine unblended. The names of Taylor's Vargellas, Croft's Roeda and Graham's Malvedos are used for vintage wines in years not quite fine enough to be generally 'declared'. For the essence of port is blending, and the main source of grapes and wine is not big estates but a multitude of small farmers.

Cork oaks flourish up in the high Douro where the soil is deep enough. The cork is stripped from mature trees every 15 years, leaving a smooth glowing red trunk on which more cork will grow. Portugal is the world's biggest producer of this irreplaceable material. Most is grown in the Alentejo south of the river Tagus.

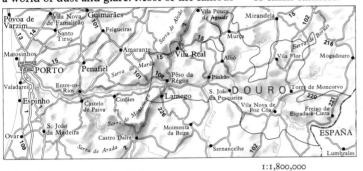

Coloured area mapped in detail below

1:1,800,000

1:122,500

PORT: THE QUALITY FACTOR

LOW YIELD	21%
ALTITUDE	21%
NATURE OF LAND	14%
LOCALITY	13%
TRAINING OF VINES	12%
GRAPE VARIETIES	6%
DEGREE OF SLOPE	4%
EXPOSURE	3%
SPACING OF VINES	2%
TYPE OF SOIL	2%
AGE OF VINES	1%
SHELTER	1%

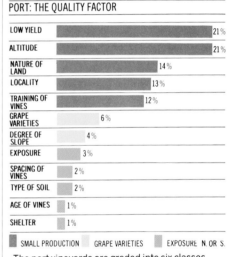

■ SMALL PRODUCTION □ GRAPE VARIETIES ▨ EXPOSURE N. OR S.

The port vineyards are graded into six classes. The quantity of wine they can sell as port is regulated by their standing. The factors by which they are judged are the same as in Burgundy, say, or Germany, but the emphasis is different. The diagram shows how for port small production – as little as 600 litres per 1,000 vines – and the altitude of the vineyard – it should be below 1,500 feet (300 metres) – are considered of primary importance in the marking.

215

The Port Lodges

Left: the old way of bringing new port wine down the River Douro on square-sailed boats came to an end in the 1960s when the river was dammed. The 'barcos rabelos', said to derive from ancient Phoenician vessels, shot frightening rapids with their cumbersome cargo. Today the river is dammed and the wine goes by truck. A great iron bridge by Eiffel (of the Tower) spans the Douro at Oporto, leading to Vila Nova de Gaia (above) on the southern bank, a suburb composed almost entirely of the simple barn-like buildings known as lodges where port is matured.

Port is made by running off the partially fermented red wine into a barrel a quarter full of brandy, while it still contains at least half of its grape sugar. The brandy stops the fermentation so that the resulting mixture is both strong and sweet.

The wine also needs the pigmentation of the grape skins to colour it, and their tannin to preserve it. In normal wines these are extracted during the course of fermentation. But since with port the fermentation is unnaturally short, pigmentation and tannin have to be procured some other way – which traditionally in the Douro means by treading.

Treading is a means of macerating the grape skins in their juice so as to extract all their essences. The naked foot is the perfect instrument for this, being warm and doing no damage to the pips, which would make the juice bitter if they were crushed. A dozen men for a dozen hours (they work in four-hour shifts), rhythmically stamping thigh-deep in the mixture of juice and skins in a broad stone trough (a *lagar*) is the traditional means of giving port its colour, its grapiness, and its ability to last and improve for many years, instead of being a pale and uninteresting liquid (see page 31).

A mechanical substitute for treading has now been introduced on a large scale. It consists of a closed fermenting vat in which the carbon dioxide pressure makes the juice circulate up a pipe from the bottom to the top, where it pours over the 'cap' of floating skins. In several days this continuous churning has the same effect as the more expensive man-hours in the *lagar*. The majority of port is now made in this modern way. But there are still shippers who feel that treading is best, and still many quintas where it goes on, particularly in the best area, above the Corgo (the area mapped on the previous pages).

Port that is kept up the Douro is rare. It is said to take on a character known as 'the Douro burn' – a faintly roasted flavour. Virtually all port is taken down the river soon after it is made, to complete its processing in the port suburb of Oporto, Vila Nova de Gaia.

The journey downriver used to be made in high-prowed sailing boats like Viking longships, which had to be controlled through the rapids by eight men working long sweeps in the bows. Now the port is taken by truck.

The shippers' warehouses in Vila Nova de Gaia are known as lodges. They have much in common with the sherry bodegas. In the lodges the port is kept in pipes, 522-litre barrels, for anything from two to 50 years.

Perhaps three years out of ten conditions are near perfect for port-making. The wine of these years needs no blending; nothing can be done to improve it except wait. It is bottled at two years just like claret, and labelled simply with its shipper's name and the date. This is vintage port, and there is never enough of it. Eventually, perhaps after 20 years, it will have a fatness and fragrance, richness and delicacy which is incomparable.

A great vintage port is incontestably among the world's very best wines. Other port, from near-vintage standard to merely moderate, goes through a blending process, to emerge as an unvarying branded wine of a given character. This wine, aged in wood, matures much faster than vintage port and loses some of its sugar in the process. A very old wood port is comparatively pale and dry, but particularly smooth. This sort of wine is called Tawny from its colour. Expensive tawnies cost as much as vintage port; many people prefer their mellowness and moderated sweetness to the full, fat and flowery flavour which a good vintage port keeps.

Run-of-the-mill wood ports are not kept for nearly so long, nor would such age find any great qualities in them to reveal. They taste best while they are still fruity with youth, and often fiery, too, with perhaps five years as the average age of a blend. France is the great market for these wines. They used to be the staple winter drink in British pubs, where they were kept in a barrel in the bar.

Vintage port has disadvantages. It needs keeping for a very long time. And it needs handling with great care. As the making of the wine does not reach its end until after bottling, the sediment forms a 'crust' on the side of the bottle; a thin, delicate, dirty-looking veil. If the bottle is moved, other than very gingerly, the crust will break and mix with the wine, so that it has to be filtered out again. In any case the wine must be decanted from its bottle before it is served. Which is enough to discourage many people from buying it.

As a compromise between vintage and 'wood' port, shippers now also offer Late-bottled Vintage wines – port from good years (although not always the very best) which is kept unblended but in barrel instead of being bottled at two years. After eight years or so it has rid itself of its crust and matured as far as it would in twice as long in bottle. In many ways it is the modern man's vintage port, being speeded up and cleaned up in this way. Yet there are those who argue that vintage port is not a modern man's drink, and that if you are going to indulge in an old-fashioned pastime you might as well do it properly. Certainly the old method makes the one port which truly deserves to be called great wine.

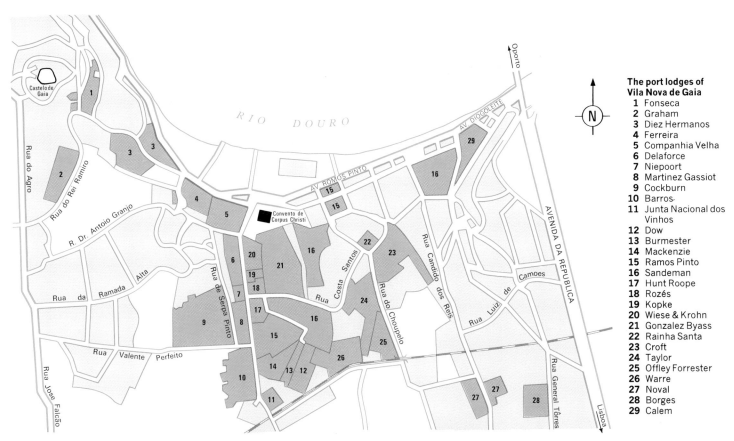

The port lodges of
Vila Nova de Gaia
1 Fonseca
2 Graham
3 Diez Hermanos
4 Ferreira
5 Companhia Velha
6 Delaforce
7 Niepoort
8 Martinez Gassiot
9 Cockburn
10 Barros
11 Junta Nacional dos
Vinhos
12 Dow
13 Burmester
14 Mackenzie
15 Ramos Pinto
16 Sandeman
17 Hunt Roope
18 Rozés
19 Kopke
20 Wiese & Krohn
21 Gonzalez Byass
22 Rainha Santa
23 Croft
24 Taylor
25 Offley Forrester
26 Warre
27 Noval
28 Borges
29 Calem

Left: the cooperage where barrels are made and repaired is a vital part of a port lodge; most port is kept in wood until it is ready to drink; from three to as many as 50 years. Good oak is the only material that allows its steady development.

Below: traditionally, vintage port bottles had no labels; a stencilled name in white paint, more durable than paper, is still used by one shipper, Quinta do Noval. Many of the best names in the port trade are British; a reminder that it was the British taste for sweet wine that built up the industry in the 18th century. Today France is the biggest customer.

THE LANGUAGE OF THE LABEL

Vintage The wine of a single exceptional year bottled early for laying down
Late-bottled vintage Similar wine bottled when mature, lighter than vintage
Crusted Good but not vintage port bottled early for laying down
Vintage character Similar to crusted
Tawny Port kept many years in wood until it fades to a tawny colour; smooth and lighter than any of the foregoing
Ruby Port aged in wood comparatively briefly; darker and rougher
White port From white grapes; often much drier than red and sold as an apéritif

Madeira

Above: the breakneck slopes of Madeira are terraced for vineyards from near sea level up to 3,250 feet (990 metres).

The map shows the western part of Madeira with place names including Ponta do Tristão, Porto do Moniz, Achadas da Cruz, Ponta do Pargo, Fajã da Ovelha, Paúl do Mar, Jardim do Mar, Prazeres, Estreito da Calheta, and Calheta.

Distribution of Vines

- Mostly Malmsey (Malvasia)
- Mostly Sercial
- Mostly Tinta Negra and Verdelho
- Mostly Tinta Negra and Bual
- Primarily American hybrids
- Woods

━━500━━ Contour interval 100 metres

The cluster of volcanic islands 400 miles (640km) off the coast of Morocco, which the ancients knew as the Enchanted Isles, are known to us as Madeira, Porto Santo and the Desertas. Madeira is the largest island of the little archipelago and one of the prettiest in the world, as steep as an iceberg and as green as a glade.

The story goes that when the Portuguese landed on the island (in 1420, at Machico in the east) they set fire to the dense woods that gave the island its name. The fire burned for years, leaving the already fertile soil enriched with the ashes of an entire forest.

Certainly it is fertile today. From the water's edge to more than halfway up the 6,000-foot (1,800-metre) peak it is steadily terraced to make room for patches of vines, patches of sugarcane, little flower gardens. As in northern Portugal the vines are grown above head height in arbours, making room for yet more cultivation beneath.

Wine has been the principal product of the island for 400 years. Madeira's natural wine, however, is not all that its beautiful vineyards seem to promise. It has a bite of acidity which makes it a taste not easy to acquire. Like port, it had to wait for a blender of genius to make it suitable for export, except as the ballast of sailing ships, to be drunk only in emergencies.

It was brandy (to stop the wine fermenting and keep it sweet) and travelling as ballast that made madeira. A long sea voyage, including a double crossing of the equator, would finish off any lesser wine, but it was found to hasten madeira's awkwardly long maturing process to a gallop. In the 18th century it became the favourite wine of the American colonies – a link that persists to this day.

Instead of long sea voyages, madeira today is subjected to ordeal by fire. A similar effect to the tropical heat is produced by warming the wine over a long period to a temperature of 120°F (49°C) or more. It stays in the hot stores (*estufas*) where this is done for four or five months. When it comes out it has the characteristic faintly caramel tang by which all madeiras can be recognized.

The shippers of Madeira use the solera system of Jerez to blend their wine into consistent brands. Very old soleras are common and their wine sometimes of very high quality. The

Above: most madeira is labelled with the name of the shipper and the grape variety: Sercial, Verdelho, Bual or Malmsey, in ascending order of richness and sweetness. A light Verdelho is sold under the name Rainwater.

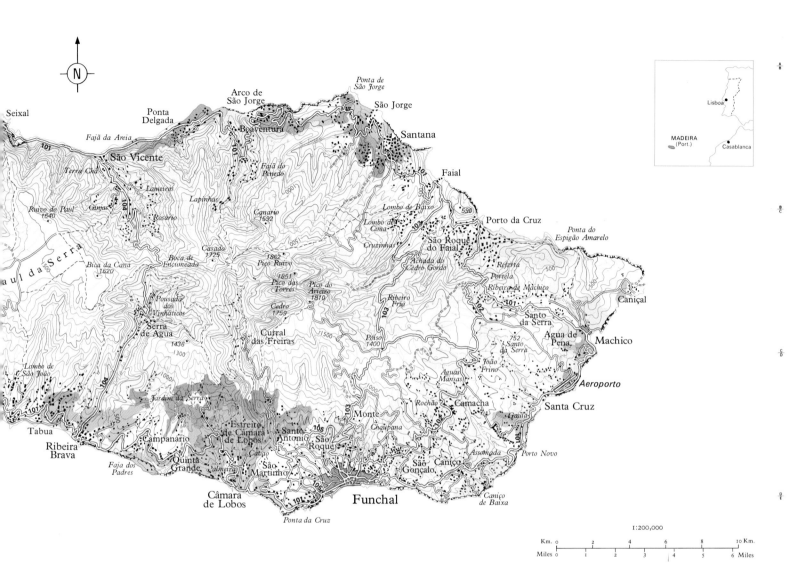

1:200,000

Km. 0   2   4   6   8   10 Km.
Miles 0   1   2   3   4   5   6 Miles

highest quality of madeira, as of port, has always been the reserve wine of a single vintage – and in the case of madeira, of a single grape variety.

The double disaster of oidium, or mildew, in the 1850s and phylloxera in the 1870s almost put an end to madeira, caused the closing or amalgamation of many merchant firms, and for a long while interrupted the flow of wine of top quality. Sadly, the vineyards were largely turned over to American hybrid vines, while the classical varieties became rarities.

Few bottles of the pre-phylloxera years still exist, none the worse for being more than 100 years old. Vintage madeira, in fact, is the one wine that age seems not to be able to exhaust or diminish. The older it is the better it is. Centenarian wines can combine intensity with freshness, depth with vivid pungency like no other product of the grape.

Today's madeira is known by the principal grape varieties used in its making. There are four, corresponding approximately to degrees of sweetness, although the sweetness is controlled not by the grape but by the amount of brandy and when it is added to the wine.

The sweetest of them all, and often the best, is Malmsey: dark brown wine, very fragrant

and rich, soft textured and almost fatty, but with the tang of sharpness that all madeiras have – the perfect wine to end a rich dinner on an uplifting note.

Bual madeira is lighter and slightly less sweet than Malmsey – but still distinctly a dessert wine. A smoky note sometimes steals in to modify its richness.

Verdelho is a shade less sweet than Bual; a peculiarly soft and sippable wine. The faint honey and distinct smoke of its flavour make it good either before or after meals.

Sercial, the driest wine of Madeira, is grown on the upper vineyards and harvested last. The grape is none other than the Riesling of the Rhine. Like the Riesling it is a late ripener, not a big cropper, and gives uncommonly good wine. Sercial wine is light, fragrant, slightly sharp – it has all these things in common with Riesling, but with the madeira tang. It is more substantial than a fino sherry, but still a perfect apéritif.

Each of the shippers of madeira sells all of these wines, as brands at various price levels. Cheaper qualities of madeira, and (we may assume) all the madeira used by chefs and housewives in France for 'sauce madère', are made not of the four noble grapes but of the

workhorse Tinta Negra Mole. Place names are very rarely mentioned on modern labels, and specific age not often.

Happily, in the last few years, however, some wines of stated age (e.g. ten-year-old) have re-emerged. Even more happily, there is once more a trickle of vintage wines of the 20th century, not 'declared', as port is, the year after the vintage, but after the passage of 30 years, 20 or so in cask and then a further period in glass demijohns before bottling. Some vintage wines of 1950, 1952 and 1954 are now available. Even now, though, they are far from being fully ready to enjoy.

Funchal is the headquarters of the trade, where the shippers' 'lodges' are, and used to be the principal vineyard area. Today Câmara de Lobos and Campanario (names that occasionally occur on fine old bottles) have most of the best vineyards.

Of the dozen or so merchants that carry on the business today more than half, including all the old British firms, have banded together to share facilities as the Madeira Wine Association. Together they are having gratifying success in re-establishing madeira as one of the noblest products of the vine – a wine no other country or region can parallel.

Hungary

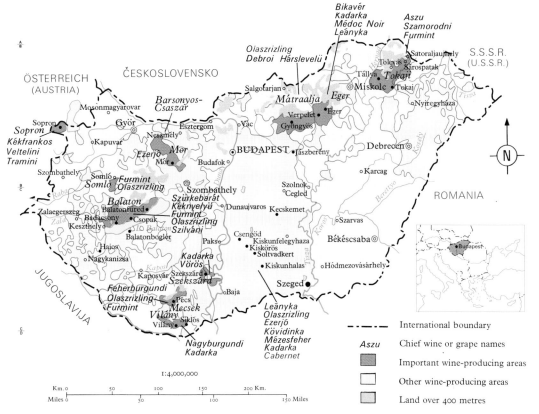

Bikavér
Kadarka
Médoc Noir
Leányka

Aszu
Szamorodni
Furmint

Olaszrizling
Debroi Hárslevelü

S.S.S.R.
(U.S.S.R.)

ÖSTERREICH
(AUSTRIA)

ČESKOSLOVENSKO

Satoraljaujhely
Tolcsva Sárospatak
Tállya *Tokaj*
Salgofarjan Miskolc Tokaj

Mátraalja *Eger*

Barsonyos-
Császár

Mosonmagyarovar
Nyíregyháza

Sopron
Kékfrankos
Veltelini
Tramini

Sopron Győr Kapuvar Neszmely Esztergom Vác Verpelét Eger
Gyöngyös

Ezerjó *Mór* Mór

BUDAPEST Jászberény Debrecen

Budafok

Szombathely

ROMANIA

Somló *Furmint*
Olaszrizling
Somló

Szolnok
Cegled

Kékfrankos *Balaton* Szombáthely
Balatonfüred Szürkebarát
Furmint
Zalaegerszeg Badacsony Csopák Kéknyelü
Keszthely Balatonbogler Furmint
Olaszrizling
Szilváni

Dunaujvaros Kecskemet
Pakse Csengöd Kiskunfelegyhaza
Kiskörös
Soltvadkert
Kiskunhalas

Karcag

Szarvas
Békéscsaba

Hajos Nagykanizsa

Kadarka *Vörös*

Kaposvár Szekszárd
Szekszárd Baja

Hódmezovásárhely

Szeged

Budapest

Feherburgundi
Olaszrizling
Furmint
Pécs Mecsek
Vilány

Vilány Siklós

Leányka
Olaszrizling
Ezerjó
Kövidinka
Mézesfeher
Kadarka
Cabernet

Nagyburgundi
Kadarka

1:4,000,000

Km. 0   50   100   150   200 Km.
Miles 0   50   100   150 Miles

— — — — International boundary

Aszu Chief wine or grape names

▨ Important wine-producing areas

☐ Other wine-producing areas

▨ Land over 400 metres

Around Lake Balaton (see page 222)

Hardly any country has a national character so pronounced in its traditional wine – and food – as Hungary. The characteristic Hungarian wine is white – or rather warmly gold. It smells more of a pâtisserie than a greengrocer, if one can so distinguish between ripe, yeasty smells and the green ones of fresh fruit. It tastes, if it is a good one, distinctly sweet, but full of fire and even a shade fierce. It is not dessert wine; far from it. It is wine for meals cooked with more spice and pepper and fat than a light wine could stand.

Like Germany, Hungary treasures her sweet wines most. Tokay (see facing page) is her pride and joy. But most of the country makes wine. The variety is rich in both traditional and international types.

On the map, the chief wine types are listed where they grow. They bear the names of their districts followed by those of their grapes.

More than half Hungary's vineyards are on the Great Plain of the Danube (Duna) in the southern centre of the country, on sandy soil which is little use for anything but vines. The vine, indeed, has been used for reclaiming sand dunes which used to shift in storms. Great Plain wine, about half of it red Kadarka, and much of it Italian (known as Olasz) Riesling, is the daily wine of Hungary.

The other half is scattered among the hills that cross the country from southwest to northeast, culminating in the Tokajhegyelja – Tokay hills. In the south the districts of Szekszárd, Vilány and Mecsek grow both red and white wines, but here the red are coming to the fore. Kadarka is the traditional grape; Pinot Noir and Cabernet the rising stars, making fruity, lightish wine of good quality. Cabernet from Hajos can be very fine.

Around Lake Balaton (see page 222) some of Hungary's best table wines are made. The small, isolated hill districts of Somló to the west, growing Furmint and Riesling, and Mór to the north, growing Ezerjó grapes, also have very distinct characters: Somló for gentler, Mór for drier and more highly flavoured wine. Both are among what Hungary calls its 'historical wine regions'.

Sopron, almost on the Austrian border, is a red-wine outpost, growing Kékfrankos, a lively wine but hardly a great one. Barsonyos-Császár to the east of Sopron makes dry white wine; unlike the other named 'historical' districts, it was formed by law in 1959.

Then along the south of the Mátra range to Eger comes the second biggest of Hungary's vineyards, formed by combining (again in 1959) the old districts of Gyöngyös-Visonta and Debrö. The sweet white Hárslevelü of Debrö (that is the villages of Aldebro, Feldebro and Verpelét) is its best-known wine, but Olasz Riesling and Kadarka, Hungary's commonest grapes, are also grown.

Best known, perhaps, of all Hungary's table wines is Eger's Bikavér, or Bull's Blood. The fine old town of Eger is one of Hungary's most important wine centres, with huge State cellars, magnificent caverns cut in the soft dark tufa of the hills. Hundreds of time-blackened oak casks, ten feet (three metres) in diameter and bound with bright red iron hoops, line their galleries.

Unfortunately, the recent production of Bull's Blood has been less than remarkable; a tendency in much of the Hungarian wine sold abroad. A visit to Hungary soon confirms, though, that the Hungarian flavour is there – both in the old varieties and in the new.

Traditional Hungarian labels use a simple combination of place-name and grape variety. The old Hungarian grapes are all distinct and worthwhile characters.

Tokay

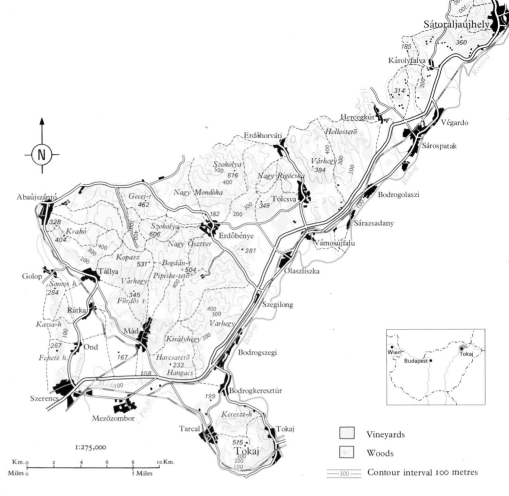

Painted yellow four-in-hand gigs overtake grey old wagons of barrels on the road into Tokay. The cobbles are covered in mud and straw. A mist steams up from the Bodrog river, wreathing the coppery vines on the hill. From the door of the Halászcsárda comes a great smell of pike and paprika and bacon and dumplings and sour cream and coffee.

Tokay is like one of the provincial towns in Russian novels which burn themselves into the memory by their very plainness. And indeed the USSR is only 40 miles (64km) away.

The Tokay hills are ancient volcanoes, lava covered with sandy loam – perfect soil for vines. From the plain to the south come warm summer winds and from the river moisture, while the hills themselves give shelter.

The same grapes as grow in other parts of Hungary, the Furmint, the classic grape of Tokay, and Hárslevelü ('lime-leaf'), ripen perfectly here. Better still, they undergo the same 'noble rot' as the grapes of Sauternes, concentrating their sugar and flavours into quintessential grapiness. They ferment slowly but give strong and intensely flavoured wine.

The Tokay method is to keep the most nobly rotten (or 'Aszú') grapes to one side and crush them into a pulp in tubs called *puttonyos*. A number of 30-litre *puttonyos* of pulp is added to 140-litre barrels (called Gönci) of one-year-old wine. Three *puttonyos* make it the rough equivalent of a German Auslese, four or five put it into the Beerenauslese class of sweetness and concentration. Three years in barrel is the minimum age for these 'Aszú' wines. If no *puttonyos* have been added the wine is 'Szamorodni' (literally 'as it comes') – rather heavy and harsh and either 'Száraz' (dry) or 'Édes' (fairly sweet). To many Hungarian connoisseurs four-*puttonyos* wine has the most balance and finesse.

In exceptional years the best vineyards produce the equivalent of a Trockenbeerenauslese; must so sweet that, even diluted with base wine in the Aszú manner, and using a selected strain of yeast, 'Tokaj 22', it takes years to ferment and remains intensely sweet. Ten years is the minimum age for this 'Aszú Essencia'. At 30 only the cream of old Sauternes can be compared with it.

The most luxurious Tokay of all is made only from the juice that Aszú berries naturally exude as they are waiting to be crushed. This 'essencia' is as much as 60% sugar and will hardly ferment at all. Formerly it was kept for the deathbeds of monarchs, where it was supposed to have miraculous powers. The State cellars at Tállya have only 60 barrels of essencia; none is bottled, but a persuasive visitor might be allowed a taste. Of all the essences of the grape it is the most velvety, peach-like and penetrating. Its flavour stays in the mouth for half an hour. What it is like at 200 years old (some of the great Polish cellars kept it that long) only the Tsars can tell.

Tokay is kept in narrow, pitch-black tunnels cut in the lava. With their single files of small barrels, their thickly moss-covered vaults and only the light from flickering candles, they are some of the world's most romantic cellars. The few bottles that survive of Tokay (Tokaji)

wines from the famous old private cellars of Erdöbénye, Sárospatak, Tállya and Tarcal suggest that the old wine was, at its best, even finer than today's. But even today an Aszú of four or five *puttonyos*, and even more an Aszú Essencia, has a silky texture, a haunting fragrance and flavour of mingled fruit and butter and caramel, and the breath of the Bodrog among October vines.

Below: the dark low-roofed tunnels of Tokay have held the vintages of centuries in their silent chill. The intensely sweet Aszú (the word means 'syrupy') wines ferment slowly in small barrels called 'gönci'. Tokay 'Essencia' hardly ferments at all.

The top left label is a dry apéritif Tokay, top right a tasty table wine, and left an Aszú wine, its sweetness measured in *puttonyos*.

Lake Balaton

L ake Balaton, besides being the biggest lake in Europe, has a special significance for Hungarians. In a country with few landmarks and no coast, it is the sea and the chief beauty spot. Its shores are thick with summer villas and holiday resorts, fragrant with admirable cooking. It has good weather and a happy social life. These things, rather than anything intrinsically unusual about the lake, are its attractions.

The north shore of Lake Balaton has all the advantages of good exposure and shelter, as well as the air-conditioning effect of a big body of water. It is inevitably a vineyard. In late summer the hot, moist air is said to make monster leaves on vines, which in turn hasten the ripening of the grapes.

Its special qualities come not only from the climate, but from the combination of a sandy soil and curious extinct volcano stumps, of which Mount Badacsony is the most famous, dotted around among otherwise flat land. The steep slopes of basalt-rich sand drain well and absorb and hold the heat. Grapevines are in their element.

At one time many of the noble families of the Austro-Hungarian Empire kept vineyards here. The Esterhazy farm, with a modest brick villa, stands in an ideal position halfway up the south side of Mount Badacsony, below that of

Top left and left: dark fertile volcanic soil gives the slopes of Mount Badacsony an extra advantage in ripening grapes on the already mild shores of Lake Balaton (just visible behind the hill). The standard wines of Balaton (two far-left labels) can be expected to have less concentration and character than Badacsony's wines – typically white Szürkebarát or Kéknyelü.

☐ Vineyards
☐ Woods
═250═ Contour interval 10 metres

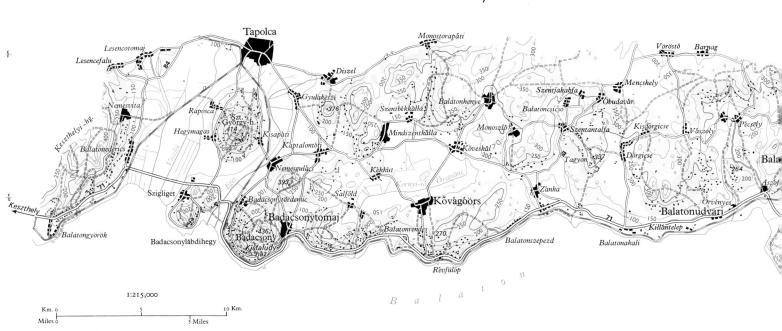

1:215,000

Km. 0   5   10 Km.
Miles 0   5 Miles

Czechoslovakia

the poet Kisfaludy, which is now a restaurant. In its plain cellars, the character of Hungarian wine is easy to grasp. It is strong and simple and fresh, and often has the beauty of things that are young and belong to the country.

Olasz (Italian) Riesling is the common white grape. Its wine is very good when it is only a year old; dry but fresh and clean and not too strong. The real specialities, however, are the grapes that make powerful, honey-scented wine: the Hungarian white varieties Furmint, Szürkebarát and Kéknyelü.

Even at a year old, tasted from the barrel, a Szürkebarát can still be as white as milk and prickly and fierce with fermentation. In two or three years these wines – of which the Kéknyelü is reckoned the 'stiffest' and best – have remarkable presence. They are aromatic and fiery; not exactly dessert wines but very much the wines for the sort of spiced and pungent food the Hungarians love.

The whole north shore of the lake produces them. Csopak, Balatonfüred and Badacsony are the main centres. Normally the ordinary district wine will carry the simple name Balatoni, with the name of the grape. The name Badacsonyi on a label implies a stronger, sweeter, and to the Hungarian way of thinking altogether better wine.

The singular flavour of Balaton is not limited to its native vines. More and more foreign grapes have been planted, and each picks up something of the dense and spicy style – Sauvignon and Chardonnay become honorary Hungarians. South of the lake, the big state wine farm of Balatonboglar is the centre for experiment with non-native varieties.

International Boundary – . – . –
District Boundary ....
Wine Area Towns •
Vineyards
Land above 1000 metres

Right: state cellars at Roudnice, near Prague, indicate the antiquity of Czech wine tradition. The central and southern states of Moravia and Slovakia are far more important wine producers today, with Moravia in particular making very sound wines in technically advanced conditions.

Lying along the northern borders of such incorrigibly vinous countries as Austria and Hungary, it would be strange if Czechoslovakia did not make good wine too. How good it is remains almost a secret, however, for so little reaches the West. Delegates to the regular international wine fair at Bratislava (where the Soviet Union wins more Golds than at the Olympic games) have reported very favourably for years. Recently some very well-made wines have begun to trickle onto the export market.

Of the three sections of Czechoslovakia, Slovakia is by far the biggest winemaker, with about two thirds of the acreage and production. Moravia makes most of the rest. Bohemia has only 400-odd hectares of vineyards along the right bank of the river Elbe north of Prague.

There are predictable parallels between the wines of the three regions and those of their neighbours in, respectively, Hungary, Austria and Germany. The southeastern corner of Slovakia is only just across the border from Tokay and includes a small part of the classic Tokay vineyard, growing the Tokay grapes,

the Furmint and others, and making very creditable wine in the same manner.

Slovakia's, and the whole country's, biggest vineyards lie north of Bratislava around Rača and Pezinok and scattered eastwards from there along the Hungarian border. They grow typical central European wine, mostly white, using much the same grapes as northern Hungary: Italian Riesling, Müller-Thurgau, Leányka, Muscat Ottonel, Ezerjó and Veltliner. Most of the wine is made in cooperatives and sold under brand names, not necessarily indicating the grape variety or the precise origin. Malokarpatské Zlato (Little Carpathian Gold) is an example. Rača's Frankovka is a remarkably hearty red.

Moravia's vineyards, south of Brno, are less extensive but seem to be making better wine. Velce Pavlovice, Mušov and Znojmo have considerable modern cellars whose Ruländer, Sauvignon, Traminer and Spätburgunder can be very pleasant. With luck a village cellar can provide a memorable experience. A peachy-ripe Sauvignon Blanc in Pavlovice would have won a medal in Bordeaux.

Yugoslavia

Yugoslavia has its feet in the Balkans, its head in the Alps, and leans towards Italy. The conundrum is not a bad way of visualizing Yugoslav wine. The range is exceptionally wide – from relatively northern, light and fruity white wine to profoundly southern, strong, soft red. She is the eleventh-biggest producer in the world, with a history of winemaking since ancient times. The six constituent republics and two autonomous regions all make wine, with small independent growers and state-owned farms each producing half the total crop.

The simplest way to think of the wine regions is as those of the north, Slovenia and parts of Croatia, which are the best; the coast from Rijeka south to Dubrovnik and beyond into Montenegro, which are the least predictable, and the eastern and inland areas – Vojvodina on the Great Plain, the Fruska Gora hills above the Danube (the Dunav), central Serbia, Kosovo and Macedonia, which are the most recent.

The map shows the main regions of production with the names of their most widely grown wines. EEC-style legal controls are now in force to define qualities and origins. Exports (20% of production) are generally reliable and good value. The inevitable tendency is for the 300-odd traditional grapes to give way to modern standards.

Slovenian white wines are the biggest export. The Riesling she grows is the Italian Riesling (also known as the Graševina) – not such a temperamental or distinguished plant as the Rhine Riesling, but performing at its best here under the combined influence of the Alps, the Adriatic and the central European plain. It gives well-balanced, full-bodied yet reasonably fresh wines lacking only the vitality of fruity acidity which German wine can achieve. Cold fermentation, widely used, has improved its balance and freshness. The best examples come from Ljutomer and Maribor in Slovenia; soft but stately Spätleses of real quality.

Croatia and Serbia, between them making three-quarters of the country's wine, are beginning to compete with Slovenia in quality. The Fruska Gora hills of Vojvodina have recently produced very attractive whites, Sauvignon Blanc and Traminer in particular.

Of the traditional varieties, Slovenia's most interesting whites are Šipon (Hungary's Furmint), Tocai, Malvasia and Ranina (Austria's Bouvier); her reds a strong Teran and a pale Cviček. Serbia and Croatia include in their repertoire such kinds as Hungarian Kadarka and Romanian Ottonel.

Recently, exports have included some less-familiar names; true local characters. Žilavka makes its best wine around the pretty old Turkish town of Mostar, north of Dubrovnik. Žilavka is dry and pungent and memorably fruity white wine – very often the best to be found in Yugoslav restaurants. Another is the red Prokupac, whose wine is the standard in southern Serbia and Macedonia. Between Smederevo and Svetozarevo, in Župa and Kruzevac and south into Macedonia it forms about 85% of the production. It makes good rosé, firm and with plenty of flavour, and a red

Above: hill-vineyards on the borders of Slovenia and Croatia produce Yugoslavia's staple export white wines of Laski (i.e. 'Italian') Riesling.
Right: labels vary from little-known native names to international names for the important export market.

wine varying from dark and bitter to pleasantly fruity and drinkable. Often it is blended with the milder Plovdina and given local names (e.g. in Župa, Župsko crno). But it is slowly being ousted by such imported vines as Cabernet and Gamay, planted by cooperatives with their eye on an international market.

The biggest contrast to the massive cooperatives of the north and east is on the Dalmatian coast. A number of wines of strong personality are made on the islands, often from little rocky patches under fig trees, pressed by an antique press and hoarded as a treasure which is none of the government's business. The dry brown Grk of Korčula, the pale and sometimes even perfumed Bogdanuša of Hvar and the similar Vugava of Vis, the thick sweetish Dingač and Postup of the Pelješac peninsula and the mighty Prošek, which can (occasionally) make a fair substitute for port, are all the specialities of small communities. Plavina, Plavac and Opol are their lighter reds, Maraština and Pošip their (none-too-light) whites. In Montenegro, Vranac is a red of remarkable character – and even, with three or four years' ageing, class.

With Dalmatian food – tiny oysters, raw ham, grilled fish, smoky and oniony kebabs and mounds of sweet grapes – the fire and flavour of such local wines can seem ambrosial.

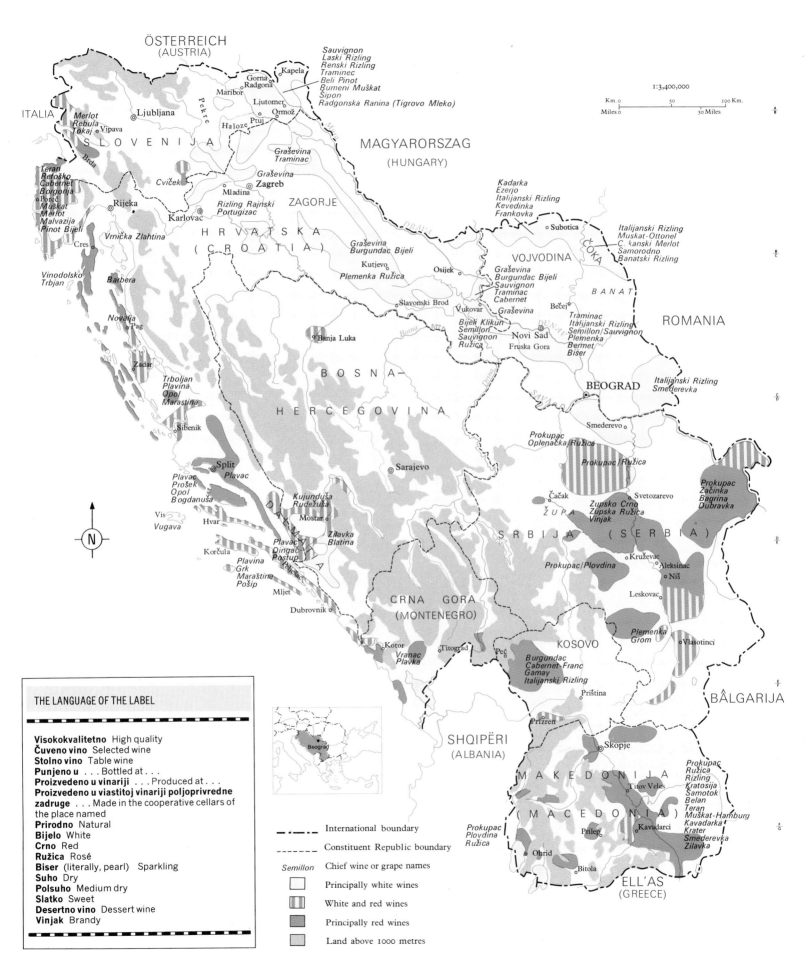

ÖSTERREICH
(AUSTRIA)

ITALIA

*Sauvignon
Laski Rizling
Renski Rizling
Traminec
Beli Pinot
Rumeni Muškat
Šipon
Radgonska Ranina (Tigrovo Mleko)*

Gorna
Radgona   Kapela

Maribor

Ljutomer

Ormož

Ptuj

*Merlot
Rebula
Tokaj*   Vipava

Ljubljana

Haloze

S L O V E N I J A

MAGYARORSZAG
(HUNGARY)

*Teran
Refošk o
Cabernet
Borgonja*
Poreč
*Muškat
Merlot
Malvazija
Pinot Bijeli*

Brda

Cres

Rijeka

Karlovac

*Graševina
Traminac*

Graševina

Zagreb

Mladina

ZAGORJE

H R V A T S K A

Cviček

*Rizling Rajnski
Portugizac*

(C R O A T I A)

*Graševina
Burgundac Bijeli*

Kutjevo

*Graševina
Plemenka Ružica*

Osijek

Subotica

VOJVODINA

*Kadarka
Ezerjo
Italijanski Rizling
Kevedinka
Frankovka*

*Italijanski Rizling
Muskat-Ottonel
C. kanski Merlot
Samorodno
Banatski Rizling*

Č O K A

B A N A T

ROMANIA

Vrnička Zlahtina

*Vinodolsko
Trbjan*

Barbera

Novalja
Pag

Zadar

Slavonski Brod

Vukovar

*Graševina
Burgundac Bijeli
Sauvignon
Traminac
Cabernet*

Graševina

*Bijeli Klikun
Semillon
Sauvignon
Ružica*

Novi Sad

Fruska Gora

*Traminac
Italijanski Rizling
Semillon/Sauvignon
Plemenka
Bermet
Biser*

BEOGRAD

*Italijanski Rizling
Smederevka*

*Trboljan
Plavina
Opol
Marastina*

Šibenik

Banja Luka

B O S N A -

H E R C E G O V I N A

Smederevo

*Prokupac
Oplenačka/Ružica*

*Plavac
Prošek
Opol
Bogdanuša*

Split
Plavac

*Kujunduša
Rudežuša*

Mostar

Sarajevo

Čačak

Prokupac/Ružica

Svetozarevo

Ž U P A

*Župsko Crno
Župska Ružica
Vinjak*

*Prokupac
Začinka
Bagrina
Dubravka*

Vis
Vugava

Hvar

D A L M A C I J A

*Žilavka
Blatina*

S R B I J A (S E R B I A)

Korčula

*Plavac
Dingač
Postup*

Pelješac

*Plavina
Grk
Maraština
Pošip*

Mljet

Dubrovnik

C R N A G O R A
(MONTENEGRO)

Prokupac/Plovdina

Kruševac

Aleksinac

Niš

Leskovac

*Plemenka
Grom*

Vlasotinci

Kotor

*Vranac
Plavka*

Titograd

Peč

*Burgundac
Cabernet-Franc
Gamay
Italijanski Rizling*

KOSOVO

Priština

BÂLGARIJA

Prizren

SHQIPËRI
(ALBANIA)

Skopje

*Prokupac
Ružica
Rizling
Kratosija
Samotok
Belan
Teran
Muškat-Hamburg
Kavadarka
Krater
Smederevka
Zilavka*

M A K E D O N I J A

Titov Veles

Kavadarci

(M A C E D O N I A)

*Prokupac
Plovdina
Ružica*

Prilep

Ohrid

Bitola

ELL'AS
(GREECE)

1:3,400,000

Km. 0   50   100 Km.
Miles 0   50 Miles

A/B

B/C

C/D

D/E

E/F

F/G

THE LANGUAGE OF THE LABEL

Visokokvalitetno High quality
Čuveno vino Selected wine
Stolno vino Table wine
Punjeno u . . . Bottled at . . .
Proizvedeno u vinariji . . . Produced at . . .
**Proizvedeno u viastitoj vinariji poljoprivredne
zadruge** . . . Made in the cooperative cellars of
the place named
Prirodno Natural
Bijelo White
Crno Red
Ružica Rosé
Biser (literally, pearl) Sparkling
Suho Dry
Polsuho Medium dry
Slatko Sweet
Desertno vino Dessert wine
Vinjak Brandy

Beograd

—·—·— International boundary
– – – – Constituent Republic boundary

Semillon Chief wine or grape names

☐ Principally white wines

▥ White and red wines

▨ Principally red wines

▨ Land above 1000 metres

225

1/2   2/3   3/4   4/5   5/6

Romania

Of the expanding wine country of the Black Sea and the Balkans, Romania might be thought to have the greatest potential for quality. It is not only a matter of situation – although Romania lies on the same latitude as France – but of temperament. There seems to be a natural affinity for the culture of France in Romania. Romanian wine literature shares the sort of hard-headed lyricism of much of French gastronomic writing. There is a great difference between the Atlantic influence which makes France moist and mild, and the continental influence which gives Romania blazing summers. But it is the more temperate conditions of the coast and the north of the country that give Romania's best wine.

The Carpathian mountains curl like a snail in the middle of Romania. They occupy almost half the country, rising from the surrounding plain to about 8,000 feet (2,400 metres) at their peaks, and enclosing the Transylvanian plateau, which is still about 2,000 feet (600 metres) above sea level. Across the south of the country the Danube (the Dunărea) flows through a sandy plain. Here, and in the southern and eastern foothills of the Carpathians, is Romania's biggest vineyard.

In Romania, as in the USSR, although not to the same extent, a great planting programme increased the national vineyard by 51% in 15 years, making her at present the sixth largest wine producer in Europe. They evidently overdid it. Since the mid-1970s a good part of the increase has been pulled up again.

Like Hungary, Romania has one wine whose name was once famous all over Europe. But Tokay, although shorn of its imperial glory, soldiers on in the wine lists of the world, whereas Cotnari, which used to appear in Paris restaurants as 'Perle de la Moldavie', has faded into obscurity. Cotnari is a natural white dessert wine like Tokay, only with rather more delicacy and less intensity. There is no doubt, in tasting it, that one is tasting something of unusual quality and character.

Cotnari comes from the part of Moldavia, in northeast Romania, that was left to the Romanians after the USSR had annexed a large slice of the country. The part the Russians took, anciently known as Bessarabia, contained a large proportion of Romania's vineyards. The great concentration of vineyards south of the Carpathians dates from since that time.

White wines are generally better than red. Both old-fashioned indigenous grape varieties, with such names as Fetească, Grasă and Tămîioasă, are used, and the international Rieslings and Pinots and Aligotés. The most widely planted sorts are the Italian Riesling and one called the Fetească regală.

Apart from Cotnari, two areas produce white wines of a quality worth exporting: Tîrnăve in Transylvania, which makes an adequate Riesling and a light, slightly sweet local speciality known as Perla, and Murfatlar near the coast on the plateau of Dobrogeia. Murfatlar's best-known wine is a sweet, pale golden-brown muscat, although Chardonnay and other French grapes are also successfully grown. It is possible that the muscat tradition here goes back to ancient times, for the Greeks are supposed to have taken the muscat grape as far north as the Crimea, and where the port of Constanța now stands stood the ancient city of Tomis.

The biggest wine region of modern Romania is Focsani, east of the Carpathians, including three wine towns with lilting names: Cotesti, Odobesti and Nicoresti. The terrain varies but much of it is sand, which has only recently been mastered, here as in the great plain of Hungary, for vines. The vines have to be planted in pockets dug deep enough for their roots to reach the subsoil, sometimes as much as ten feet (three metres) below the surface. It seems a desperate expedient, especially as it takes the vine some time to grow up to ground level and come into bearing. But in fact good light wines are being made where nothing would grow before, here and in places along the Danube.

The red Babească of Nicoresti is a good example of the character of the country; it is pleasantly acidic with a clove-like taste, fresh, original and enjoyable.

Following the curve of the Carpathians the next vineyard is Dealul Mare, where Romania's biggest state experimental vineyard, Valea Călugărească, lies in the foothills. The Cabernet is grown here with great pride, but with not always fortunate results. Like many Romanian red wines it can be sweet, heavy and without grace. Happily, exports to the West have corrected this fault; the Trakia Cabernet shipped to the USA is well made for Western palates, and very good value.

Farther west the vineyards continue with both red and white wines around Pitești and Drăgășani. From the south on the plain near the Danube, Segarcea Cabernet and Sadova rosé are exported. Both can suffer from the customary sweetness.

In the western corner of Romania the Hungarian influence makes itself felt; many of the red wines of Banat are made from the Kadarka (here spelt Cadarca) of the Hungarian plain.

Right: old-fashioned farmers' vineyards are still found in Romania (here near Murfatlar) as well as the long straight rows of state-organized viticulture.

THE LANGUAGE OF THE LABEL

Vie Vine
Viile Vineyard
Strugure Grape
Recolta Vintage
Vin superior Superior wine
Vin de masă Table wine
Vin ușor Light wine
GAS (Gospodariile Agricole de Stat) State agricultural enterprise
IAS (Intreprinderile Agricole de Stat) More up-to-date name for the same
Imbuteliat Bottled
Vin alb White wine
Vin roșu Red wine
Vin rose Rosé
Sec Dry
Dulce Sweet
Spumos Sparkling
Pivniță (pl. pivnițele) Cellar
Tuica Plum brandy
Vinexport The government exporting agency

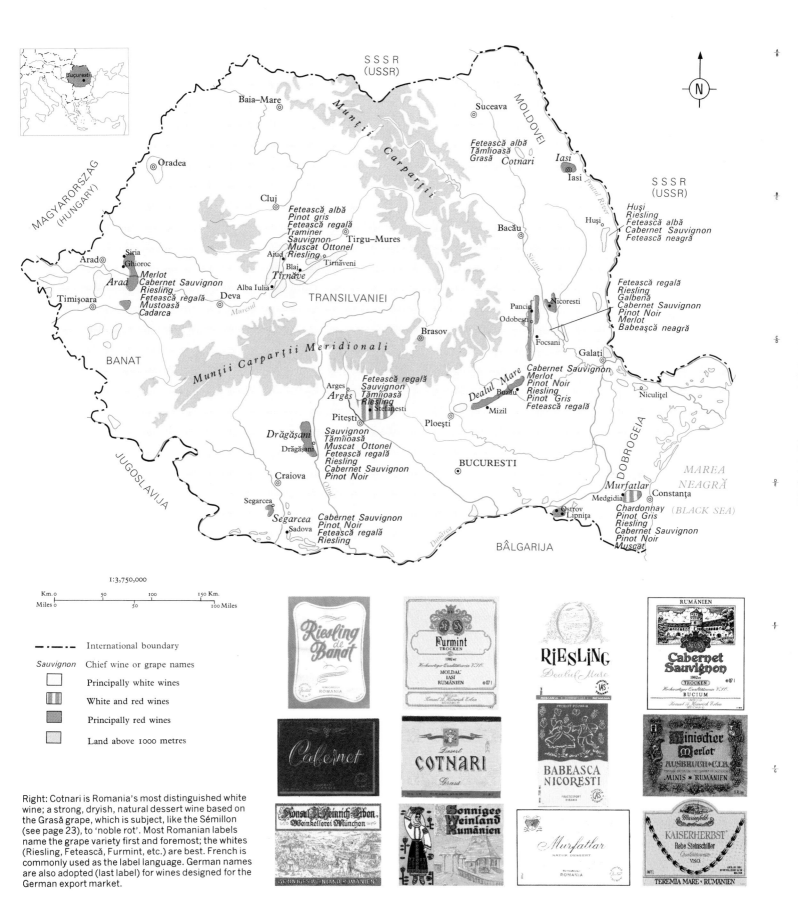

S S S R (USSR)

MOLDOVEI

Baia–Mare

Suceava

Oradea

MAGYARORSZAG (HUNGARY)

Cluj

Fetească albă
Tămîioasă
Grasă *Cotnari*

Iasi
Iasi

S S S R (USSR)

Fetească albă
Pinot gris
Fetească regală
Traminer
Sauvignon
Muscat Ottonel
Riesling

Tirgu–Mures

Bacău

Huşi

Huşi
Riesling
Fetească albă
Cabernet Sauvignon
Fetească neagră

Siria
Ghioroc

Ajud
Blaj
Tîrnave

Tirnăveni

Arad

Merlot
Cabernet Sauvignon
Riesling
Fetească regală
Mustoasă
Cadarca

Arad

Alba Iulia
Deva

TRANSILVANIEI

Nicoresti

Fetească regală
Riesling
Galbenă
Cabernet Sauvignon
Pinot Noir
Merlot
Babeaşcă neagră

Timişoara

Muresul

Panciu
Odobesti

Focsani

Galaţi

BANAT

Munţii Carparţii Meridionali

Brasov

Dealul Mare

Cabernet Sauvignon
Merlot
Pinot Noir
Riesling
Pinot Gris
Fetească regală

Buzău

Niculiţel

Arges

Fetească regală
Sauvignon
Tămîioasă
Riesling

Arges

Stefanesti

Mizil

DOBROGEIA

JUGOSLAVIJA

Pitești

Ploești

Drăgăşani

Sauvignon
Tămîioasă
Muscat Ottonel
Fetească regală
Riesling
Cabernet Sauvignon
Pinot Noir

Drăgăşani

BUCURESTI

MAREA NEAGRĂ

Craiova

Murfatlar

Medgidia

Constanţa

Segarcea

Cabernet Sauvignon
Pinot Noir
Fetească regală
Riesling

Segarcea

Sadova

Ostrov
Lipniţa

Chardonnay
Pinot Gris
Riesling
Cabernet Sauvignon
Pinot Noir
Muscat

(BLACK SEA)

Dunărea

BÂLGARIJA

1:3,750,000

Km. 0   50   100   150 Km.
Miles 0   50   100 Miles

—·—·— International boundary

Sauvignon Chief wine or grape names

☐ Principally white wines

▥ White and red wines

▨ Principally red wines

☐ Land above 1000 metres

Right: Cotnari is Romania's most distinguished white wine; a strong, dryish, natural dessert wine based on the Grasă grape, which is subject, like the Sémillon (see page 23), to 'noble rot'. Most Romanian labels name the grape variety first and foremost; the whites (Riesling, Fetească, Furmint, etc.) are best. French is commonly used as the label language. German names are also adopted (last label) for wines designed for the German export market.

227

Bulgaria

Bulgaria, of all the wine countries of Soviet-directed Eastern Europe, has been the most single-minded in directing its wine industry towards exports.

Once it had determined, in 1949, on complete State control, it forged ahead with modernization at a remarkable rate. By 1966 Bulgaria had become the sixth-largest wine exporter in the world. Today it comes fifth, after France, Italy, Spain and Portugal, exporting 85% of its entire crop. The wine industry, in fact, is looked on first and foremost as a hard-currency earner.

There is very little in the way of a peasant winemaking tradition. In ancient times, with Greek influence, wine was endemic, but Bulgaria's architecture, folk costumes and food all bear the marks of the Turkish domination, with its Islamic prohibition, which ended a bare century ago. Vineyards, as a result, are large, modern and efficient, cultivated entirely by machinery. Wine processing, in the last few years, has become extremely up to date. Quality control is first-class.

The wines that succeed beyond all expectation in Bulgaria are those made of French grapes for Western consumption – above all the Cabernet, the Chardonnay and the Merlot. The Cabernet in particular has fruit, vigour, balance – the robust qualities of red Bordeaux in a good vintage, if not quite its finesse.

Bulgaria, if its figures are to be believed, has four times as much Cabernet vineyard as California.

The national varieties are not neglected, nor are they without character. Of reds there is Gamza (or Gumza) – the lively Kadarka of Hungary; Pamid, which gives pale gulping wine, and Mavrud, which gives the opposite – Bulgaria's national pride. Among whites the dominant variety is Rcatziteli. Red Misket and Muscat Ottonel are both popular, but success success with Chardonnay, Riesling, Traminer and Aligoté will undoubtedly elbow most of the older varieties aside in due course.

In 1978 the Bulgarian government initiated what promises to be a useful system of geographical appellations, quite as strict, on paper, as French appellations contrôlées. It redivided the country from nine former regions to five, corresponding to natural physical zones. The northern region along the Danube grows largely red wines, its cooler climate giving particular quality to both the Cabernet and Gamza and a little Pinot Noir, Gamay and Muscat. It is separated from the southern region, which makes more full-bodied reds of Cabernet, Merlot and Mavrud, and light ones of Pamid, by the spine of the Balkan mountains, the Stara Planina (which specializes in Muscat – 'Hemus' is the brand – attar of roses, and, towards the east, Riesling).

The eastern region includes the whole coast and has one-third of the country's 420,000 acres (170,000 hectares) of vines, here principally white, concentrating on Chardonnay, Traminer and Riesling in the north, Muscats in the south

Against the Serbian border in the southwest is the fifth region, the home of Melnik, the most potent of Mavruds, and also of some powerful white wine.

The further refinement which is now coming into effect is the definition of wine centres which are 'Controliran', according to some documents, 'Reguliran' according to others, as producers of one particular wine. Thus the Chardonnay of Novi Pazar or the Cabernet/Merlot blend from Oryahovica (one of the biggest quality vineyards) should have a distinctive and consistent regional character. Five of the first 14 'Regulirans' are for Cabernets or Cabernet blends, three for Gamza, two each for Chardonnay and Red Misket, one each for Merlot, Riesling, Mavrud and Melnik. Six more are proposed, for Traminer, Merlot, Riesling and Aligoté.

First tastings of Cabernet and Chardonnay wines at this new higher level have been very promising. They are more expensive than we have become accustomed to paying for Bulgaria's produce, but it is satisfying to see a communist country trading up in this way.

Left: crop-dusting in the modern vineyards near Sukhindol. Intelligent planning to take advantage of the wide range of Bulgaria's natural conditions is paying dividends in distinct regional styles. Reds from the northern region are finer, from the south more full-bodied. The east concentrates on dry whites.

THE LANGUAGE OF THE LABEL

Лозова пръчка (Lozova prachka) Vine or variety of vine
Лозя (Lozia) Vineyards
Винопроизводител (Vinoproizvoditel) Wine-producer
Бутилирам (Butiliram) To bottle
Натурално (Naturalno) Natural
Бяло вино (Bjalo vino) White wine
Червено вино (Cherveno vino) Red wine
Сухо вино (Suho vino) Dry wine
С остатъчна захар (S ostatachna zakar) Semi-dry or medium wine
Сладко вино (Sladko vino) Sweet wine
Десертно (Desertno) Dessert or sweet wine
Искрящо вино (Iskriashto vino) Sparkling wine
Бренди (Brendi) Brandy
Vinimpex Bulgaria's 'State Commercial Enterprise for Export and Import of Wines and Spirits', a monopoly, controls the entire wine export trade

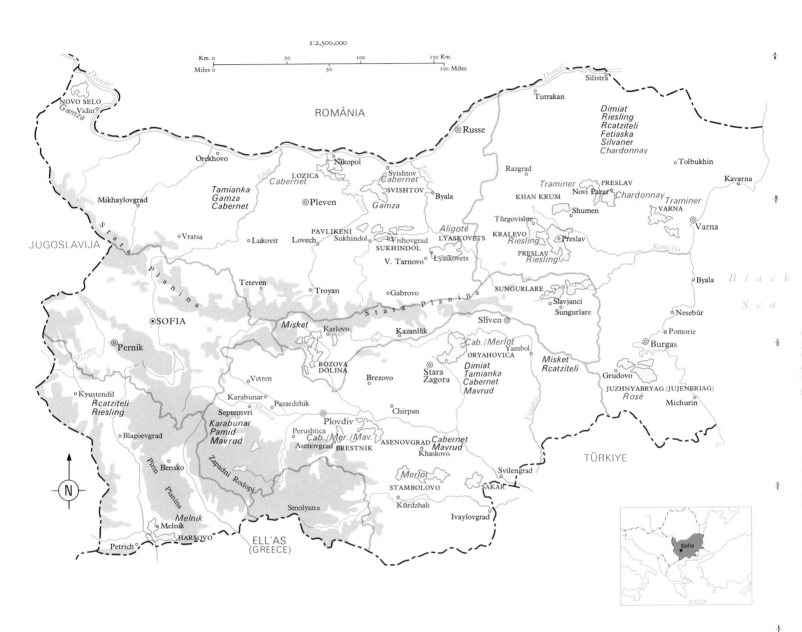

Map labels

1:2,500,000

Km. 0 · 50 · 100 · 150 Km.
Miles 0 · 50 · 100 Miles

ROMÂNIA

JUGOSLAVIJA

TÜRKIYE

ELL'AS (GREECE)

Black Sea

NOVO SELO · Vidin · *Gamza* · *Dunav*

Orekhovo · Nikopol · Svishtov · Russe · Tutrakan · Silistra

Mikhaylovgrad · LOZICA · *Cabernet* · Pleven · SVISHTOV · *Cabernet* · *Gamza* · Byala · Razgrad · Tolbukhin · Kavarna

Tamianka Gamza Cabernet

Vratsa · Lukovit · Lovech · Sukhindol · Vishovgrad · SUKHINDOL · V. Tarnovo · V. Tarnovo · PAVLIKENI · LYASKOVETS · *Aligoté* · Lyaskovets

Dimiat Riesling Rcatziteli Fetiaska Silvaner Chardonnay

KHAN KRUM · Novi Pazar · PRESLAV · *Chardonnay* · *Traminer* · Shumen · Türgovishte · KRALEVO · *Riesling* · Preslav · PRESLAV · *Riesling* · VARNA · Varna · *Traminer*

Teteven · Troyan · Gabrovo · *Stara planina*

Stara planina

SOFIA · Pernik · *Misket* · Karlovo · Kazanlŭk · Sliven · SUNGURLARE · Slavjanci · Sungurlare · Nesebŭr · Byala

Kyustendil · *Rcatziteli Riesling* · Vetren · ROZOVA DOLINA · Brezovo · Stara Zagora · *Cab./Merlot* · Yambol · ORYAHOVICA · *Dimiat Tamianka Cabernet Mavrud* · *Misket Rcatziteli* · Grudovo · Pomorie · Burgas

Blagoevgrad · Karabunar · Pazardzhik · *Karabunar Pamid Mavrud* · Septemvri · Chirpan · Plovdiv · JUZHNYABRYAG (JUJENBRIAG) *Rosé* · Michurin

Bensko · Pirin Planina · *Zapadni Rodopi* · Perushtica · *Cab./Mer./Mav.* · Asenovgrad · BRESTNIK · ASENOVGRAD · *Cabernet Mavrud* · Khaskovo

Melnik · *Melnik* · HARSOVO · Smolyan · *Merlot* · STAMBOLOVO · Kŭrdzhali · SAKAR · Svilengrad · Ivaylovgrad

Petrich

Struma · *Marica* · *Iskar* · *Vit* · *Osŭm* · *Jantra* · *Tundža* · *Kamcija*

Sofia

Legend

Wine labels

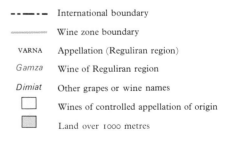

Left: a florid style (and Cyrillic script) is slowly giving way to more informative labelling as Bulgaria's recent appellation controls take effect. Gamza is the popular standard red, especially from the northwest. Misket is a good dry white to drink young (no relation to Muscat). But Cabernet, Merlot and Chardonnay are the wines of the future, already reaching high levels of quality.

The Soviet Union

The Soviet Union officially decided in favour of wine – at the expense of vodka – in the fifties. In 1950 she had some 400,000 hectares of vineyard. Today she has almost 1.4 million hectares, which makes her second only to Spain in the world-league table of area under vine, and third in production, behind Italy and France.

This is certainly the biggest and fastest extension of the world's winegrowing capacity ever seen. Yet even this is apparently not enough: the Union is an insatiable wine importer, buying in some 7 million hectolitres a year.

The industry that supplies these impressively thirsty throats has changed enormously in almost every way in recent years. A vast network of 'primary' and 'secondary' wine factories now covers the Union; the secondary plants finishing and bottling the wine in the consumer areas.

Wine qualities are defined in a way not unlike the EEC three-tier system, with a dash of the USA's approach to single-variety wines (which, in the USSR, must be 85% of the variety named).

The three tiers are 'ordinary' (unmatured and not regionally or locally named); 'named' (matured and declaring its origin); and 'kollektsionye' (from selected areas and varieties, with at least two years' bottle-age).

Western grape varieties have now infiltrated all areas, although they are much more frequent in the northern regions than in the conservative far south.

So much is simple. The complications begin with the names, which vary from the straightforward place + variety to the romantic/fantastic: 'Black Eyes' for Russian 'port'. The map groups the principal wine names over the approximate area where they are made.

The Soviet wine belt sweeps east around the north of the Black Sea from Moldavia – which was formerly in Romania – to Armenia on the border of Turkey. Two areas, the Crimean peninsula, and Georgia on the southern slopes of the Caucasus, have been famous since ancient times for good wine and remain the best today. The Russian taste is for sweet wine; the names of port, madeira and sherry are widely taken in vain. Many of the specialities named on the map are dessert wines of between 16% and 19% alcohol and more or less sweet.

The Moldavian vineyards grow the traditional Romanian varieties alongside the 'newcomers' like Cabernet and Aligoté. The Fetjaska makes fresh dry white; Negru de Purkar is the traditional dry but fruity red. Romanesti is made with a Bordeaux-like blend of Cabernet, Merlot and Malbec. But Chumai is Cabernet made into a dessert wine. Trifesti (Pinot – or Pineau–Gris) and Gratiesti (the local Rcatziteli) are white dessert wines.

Ukraine is the republic with the biggest vineyard area, including the Crimea. In the Crimea the name of the best-known estate, Massandra, the former property of Prince Woronzow, is widely used on dessert wines, which are the speciality of the south coast. Massandra muscat is full and brown, like Frontignan from the south of France. An official description of it suddenly bursts through the dull recitation of names and characteristics: 'rose and citron tones predominate in the bouquet, and the flavour is delicate with a pronounced oiliness. Plum, chocolate and balsam tones appear during maturation.' No one would be inspired like that by a routine sweet wine.

Of the others listed on the map, for the Crimea, Kokur Niznegorsky and Silvaner Feodosiisky are dry but full-bodied white

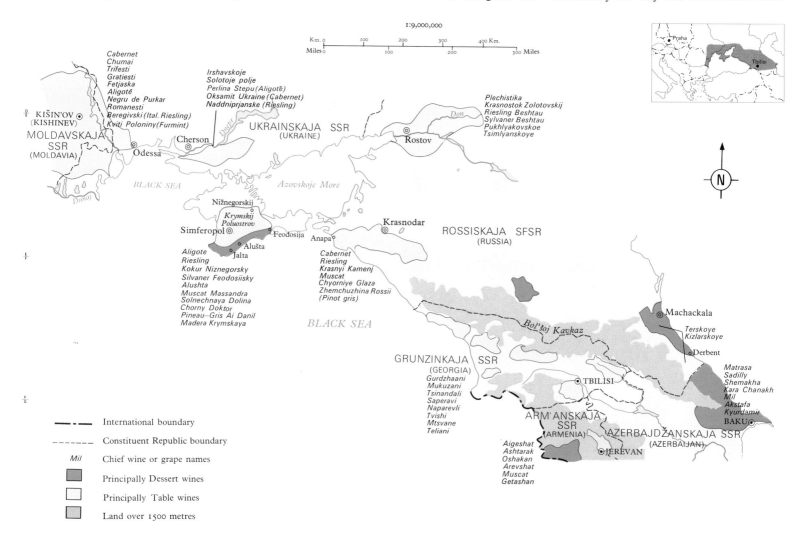

1:9,000,000

Km. 0   100   200   300   400 Km.
Miles 0   100   200   300 Miles

International boundary
Constituent Republic boundary
Mil   Chief wine or grape names
        Principally Dessert wines
        Principally Table wines
        Land over 1500 metres

wines. Alushta (from the valley behind the port) is reckoned the best red, Solnechnaya Dolina and Chorny Doktor are respectively white and red dessert wines and the Pinot Gris of Ai Danil is sweet, like Moldavian Trifesti.

The Don basin around Rostov specializes in sparkling wine. The red, sweet and sparkling Tsimlyanskoye is highly regarded. South of Krasnodar, the only Russian Riesling exported is grown at Anapa. Chyorniye Glaza ('Black Eyes') is the 'port' of the Russian republic.

Several of Georgia's traditional types have made a modest name for themselves in the world, as good dry everyday wines. In fact, Tsinandali and Gurdzhaani, which are white, the potent Mukuzani and lighter Saperavi and Naparevli reds are among the most historic of wines; powerful characters like their Georgian makers, and well worth investigating.

Armenia, Azerbaijan and the area along the Caspian up to Machackala are dessert-wine country. All the types listed are sweet and strong, red, brown or white, some cooked like madeira and one quaintly named 'Kaoursky' – presumably after the 'black' wine of Cahors. The Matrasa and Sadilly of Baku, red and white table wines, are the notable exceptions.

Right and below: newly planted vineyards in Moldavia are part of an integrated plan of agrarian reform, yet curiously the well-head is decorated like a traditional tea-mug – a sign of nostalgia, perhaps, for the old times so graphically pictured below. Russia has more than tripled her vineyard acreage in the last 30 years.

The labels of Georgian wines, the most interesting produce of the Soviet Union, are in both Georgian and Cyrillic script. Above, Gurdzhaani white; left, Tetra and Naparevli, one of the best of several good Georgian wines.

THE LANGUAGE OF THE LABEL

Винозавод (Vinozavod) Wine factory
Столовое вино (Stolovoe vino) Table wine
Белое вино (Beloe vino) White wine
Красное вино (Krasnoe vino) Red wine
Розовое вино (Rozovoe vino) Rosé
Сухое вино (Sukhoe vino) Dry wine
Дессертное вино (Desertnoe vino) Dessert wine
Шампанское (Shampanskoe) 'Champagne'
Грузинское вино (Gruzinskoe vino) Georgian wine

The Eastern Mediterranean

BLACK SEA

BÅLGARIJA
(BULGARIA)

ELL'AS
(GREECE)

III

Kirklareli

Uzunköprü

Tekirdağ

Istanbul

Erdek

Çanakkale

Bursa

Balikesir

AEGEAN
SEA

Akhisar

Bornova
Izmir

II

Tire

Söke

Denizlio

Burdur   Isparta

Antalya

Zonguldak

VII

Karabük

Izmit   Adapazari

Kütahya

Eskisehir

Uşak

Afyonkarahisar

Aksehir

Konya   IX

Karaman

Toros   Daglari

Bafrao

Samsun

Çorum   Amasya

Cubuk
Kalecik   Tokat

ANKARA

Keskin

TÜRKIYE   VIII   VI

Sivas

Kayseri

Ürgüp
Nevşehir

Nigde

Erežli

Malatya   Elåzig

Maraş

IV   V

Euphrates (Firat)

Adana
Mersin

Gaziantep
Kilis

Iskenderun

Antakya

Halab
(Aleppo)

KIPROS
(CYPRUS)

Al-Ladhiqiya
(Latakia)

AS-SOURIYA
(SYRIA)

Hamah

Tarābulus
(Tripoli)

Ghazir

BAYRUT
(BEIRUT)

AL-LUBNANIYA
(LEBANON)

MEDITERRANEAN

SEA

Hims
(Homs)

Ba'labakk
(Baalbek)

Ksara

DIMASHQ
(DAMASCUS)

Hefa
(Haifa)

Zichron-Jacob

YISRA'EL

Tel Aviv-Yafo
Richon-le-Zion

YERUSHALAYIM
(JERUSALEM)
Gazzah

Irbid

Ram
Allah

Bayt Lahm
(Bethlehem)

Az-Zarqa
(Zarqua)

AMMAN

AL-URDUNIYA
(JORDAN)

Be'er Sheva
(Beersheba)

Al-Iskandariya
(Alexandria)

Abú Hummus

Bür Sa'id
(Port Said)

Nile

Suez Canal

MISR AL-ARABIYA
(EGYPT)

International boundary

Limit of wine zones

Red and white wines

Principally white wines

Land over 1500 metres

1:6,400,000

Km. 0   100   200   300 Km.

Miles 0   100   200 Miles

Black Sea

Ankara

Mediterranean Sea

Al-Qahira

Above: Château Musar is Lebanon's First-Growth. Buzbağ and Dikmen are Turkish reds, Trakya and Köroğlu whites, Omar Khayyam Egypt's senior red.
Right: vineyards in the valley of Bekaa in the Lebanon.

It is a sobering thought that some spot on this map may be the very place where man first tasted wine. Whether it was in Turkey or Armenia that the first wine was made, there is no doubt that the Middle East is its home country. Noah, Naboth, Christ, St Paul, the great Roman temple at Baalbek are all evidence that the eastern Mediterranean was the France of the ancient world. And so it continued until the eighth century, until the advent of Islam.

The Prophet's followers forbade the use of wine. How effectively has often been discussed. Some winegrowing went on, but it was not until the end of the last century that wine began to come back to its homeland in earnest. As phylloxera destroyed Europe's vineyards, Asia stepped into the breach. In 1857 the Jesuits founded the cellars of Ksara in the Lebanon, still the biggest winery in the Middle East. In the 1880s a Rothschild established winegrowing once more in Israel. Turkey exported nearly 70 million litres in one year in the 1890s. In 1903 Nestor Gianaclis planted the first vines of a new Egyptian wine industry, near Alexandria, whose wine in Roman times was famous.

All gastronomic (as well as sympathetic) interest now centres around the Lebanon, where one remarkable man, Serge Hochar of Château Musar, continues to make outstanding wine in the manner of a Bordeaux in the heart of the notorious Bekaa. The evidence that Château Musar represents of the potential of the Levant for fine wine has fascinating implications. Did the Babylonians know?

Turkey is the biggest producer and exporter of the eastern Mediterranean. She has the fifth largest vineyard acreage in the world, but only 3% of her grapes are made into wine. The rest are eaten. The wine industry is held back by lack of a domestic market, for 99% of the population remains Muslim. Kemal Atatürk himself built a winery in 1925 in the hope of persuading Turks of the rightness of drinking wine, but progress is slow.

The country is divided into nine ecological zones. Zones II and III, the Aegean coast and Thrace/Marmara, are by far the biggest wine producers, making three-fifths of the total. They are followed by zone I, Ankara, and then, much smaller, IV and IX, southeast Anatolia and south-central Anatolia. The state monopoly has 21 wineries and accounts for most exports of Turkish wine. High-strength blending wine is most in demand, although the names of Trakya and Buzbağ, its lighter and darker red wines (from Thrace and southeast Anatolia, in that order) are familiar. Buzbağ is a noted bargain, a wine of powerful yet pleasing character from one of the nearest vineyards to Noah's. There is also a white Trakya, made of the Sémillon grape. Of the private firms, Doluca and Kavaklidere are probably the best, Doluca operating in Thrace (its Villa Doluca is reliable) and Kavaklidere in Ankara, with grapes from both Thrace and eastern Anatolia.

The considerable wineries at Richon-le-Zion and Zichron-Jacob were a gift to Israel from Baron Edmond de Rothschild. They make three-quarters of Israel's wine. Most of the 14,000 acres (570 hectares) of wine-grape vineyard is largely planted with the common French red grapes (41% is Carignan and 32% Alicante-Grenache); the white grapes are Muscat, Sémillon and Clairette, also familiar from the Languedoc. Despite the hot dry climate, modern equipment allows the making of a wide range, including a good sparkling wine, 'The President's'. Recently 'varietal' Cabernet Sauvignon, Sauvignon Blanc, Sémillon and Grenache rosé has been launched with considerable success. Most exports go to the USA. There is a substantial market for Kosher wine.

The Gianaclis vineyards still operate in Egypt, northwest of the Nile delta at Abu Hummus. Four times more white grapes than red are grown, but three-quarters of the white wine is distilled. The best-known whites are Cru des Ptolemées and Reine Cléopatre. One of the red wines, Omar Khayyam, is smooth and well made, with what seems an intriguing faint flavour of dates.

233

North Africa

Moroccan labels tend to be reticent. The second down is that of *vin gris*, the pale pink speciality of Boulaouane, south of Casablanca.

Northorth Africa's profile as a wine producer has sunk ever lower since its palmy days of a generation ago, when Algeria, Morocco and Tunisia between them accounted for no less than two-thirds of the entire international wine trade.

Almost all this vast quantity, 90% of their then colossal production, went to Europe as blending wine, appreciated for its strength, colour and concentration. Algeria was by far the biggest source. When it became independent from France in 1962 the decline was immediate: there was practically no domestic business. Algeria has continued to either pull up or neglect her vineyards. From 1966 to 1983 her crop has shrunk from 16 million hectolitres to less than two million – most of which is bought by the Soviet Union. Seventy percent of her vines are more than 40 years old and presumably will not be replaced.

This is not to say that all Algerian wine is, or need be, of poor quality. Light soils and hot sunshine make them strong, but certain wines of the hills were given VDQS status in French colonial days, and no doubt, if the French were still about, would have graduated, like most VDQS wines, to Appellations Contrôlées. There are certainly places in Algeria where Australians or Californians would make excellent wine. Moreover, it is the best hill vineyards that have been maintained, while the plains now grow cereals.

There are seven designated quality regions, all in the western provinces of Oran and Alger. The Coteaux de Tlemcen, nearest to Morocco, produces very adequate red, rosé and white; powerful and dry but not coarse, the white soft and rather pleasant. Wine from the Monts du Tessala seems not so good, but the Coteaux de

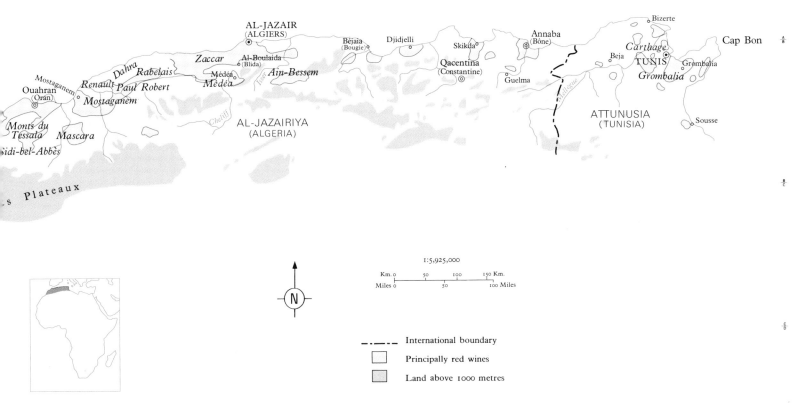

AL-JAZAIR (ALGIERS) · Béjaïa (Bougie) · Djidjelli · Skikda · Annaba (Bône) · Bizerte · Carthage · TUNIS · Grombalia · Cap Bon

Zaccar · Aïn-Bessem · Qacentina (Constantine) · Guelma · Beja · Grombalia

Mostaganem · Dahra · Rabelais · Al-Boulaïda (Blida) · Médéa · Médéa

Ouahran (Oran) · Renault · Paul Robert · Mostaganem

Monts du Tessala · Mascara

Sidi-bel-Abbès

les Plateaux

AL-JAZAIRIYA (ALGERIA)

ATTUNUSIA (TUNISIA)

Sousse

1:5,925,000

Km. 0   50   100   150 Km.
Miles 0   50   100 Miles

N

- · - · - International boundary

☐ Principally red wines

▨ Land above 1000 metres

Mascara has an old reputation and makes both rich reds and very respectable smooth and fruity white.

Taughrite, Aïn-Merane and Mazouna, the modern names of the Dahra crus formerly called Robert, Rabelais and Renault, make good strong, clean reds and very attractive lighter rosé. The Coteaux du Zaccar, farther from the sea, seems to produce less fruity flavours. To the east again the high Medea hills, with vineyards up to 4,000 feet (1,200 metres), and Aïn-Bessem Bouira make some of Algeria's best, most potent and most interesting wines. All in all it is the rosés that are most appealing. The top prestige wine, Cuvée du Président, is not necessarily as good as the best of the local offerings.

Commonsense would suggest that Morocco, benefiting from the influence of the Atlantic, should make North Africa's best wine. Although its vineyards, too, have shrunk (to about half their acreage in 1970), they have never been huge, and have aimed at quality rather than quantity. The Moroccan Appellation d'Origine Garantie is enforced by the central organization, SODEVI, that organizes all wine production.

The region of Fès/Meknès, at more than 1,500 feet (450 metres) in the middle Atlas foothills, is the most important, making the impressive reds exported as Tarik and Chantebled (respectively heavier and lighter, but both smooth and well made). Around Rabat on the coastal plain, satisfying soft reds are sold under

Left: Morocco's best wines are reds from the region of Fès and Meknès on the first foothills of the Middle Atlas mountains. Tarik and Chantebled – sold in Morocco as Les Trois Domaines – are good examples.

district names: Gharb, Chellah, Zemmour and Zaer. South of Casablanca *vin gris* is the speciality, white made of red grapes, which needs to be served ice-cold. The Gris de Boulaouane becomes a familiar friend to visitors in a land that seems to lack white wines made of white grapes.

Tunisia, like Morocco, is actively pursuing a policy of quality to generate exports. Muscat wines have always been her speciality – and probably were in Carthaginian times. Today she makes muscats both sweet and dry (the dry on Cap Bon), but some of her red and rosé wines may appeal more to conventional taste.

Private, State and cooperative wineries are all under the control of the Office du Vin, which was formed in 1970 and operates a system inspired by France's appellations.

The union of cooperatives is the biggest producer. Its standard lines are red Coteaux de Carthage from the hills around Tunis, Château Mornag rosé from hills farther east, dry Muscat de Kelibia from Cap Bon, and Magon, a richer red than the Coteaux de Carthage, from Tébourba in the Medjerdah valley to the west.

The State winery makes Château Thibar, a red from the northwest of Tunisia, and Sidi Selem, another red from Mornag. Two of the best independent producers, Lamblot and Château Feriani, make their notable reds north of Tunis, in the Coteaux d'Utique. Two others, Lavau and Tardi, are in the Tébourba region and the hills to the north.

Tunisia has plenty of sound and solid red wines, good sweet muscats, very attractive rosés (some of them, admittedly, muscat scented). So far there is a shortage of good white wine. Algeria, in this regard, still leads both her seemingly more ambitious neighbours.

Above: Tunisian wine harks back to the great days of Carthage. She makes good red *ordinaire* and muscats. Left-hand column: during the French regime a dozen Algerian wines were rated Vins Délimités de Qualité Supérieure. The technical problems of making good red wine in the African climate were largely overcome.

235

Greece

Ancient and modern Greece are divided by a gulf with few bridges. The taste for resinated wine, or retsina, is one; perhaps the only characteristic habit of Greece that goes straight back 3,000 years and beyond, to the time when gods walked on earth.

Traces of pine resin have been found in wine amphorae from earliest times. It is usually assumed that it was used to preserve the wine. But resinated wine does not age well. The real reason is surely that traditional Greek wine is much improved by the fresh, sappy, turpentine-like flavour which resin gives if added during fermentation. Half the wine made in Greece is so treated, and the result is one of the most individual and appetizing drinks of the world. Where peasant food is always oily (and often musty) it is also particularly effective in cancelling the flavour of a doubtful mouthful.

Attica, the region of Athens, is the home of retsina. Most of it is white, from the Savatiano grape, but some rosé or kokkineli is also made.

The other half of Greek wine consists of either such brand-named blends as Demestica, safe but not exciting products of the big wine companies of Athens and the Peloponnese (Patras, on the Gulf of Corinth, is the base of Achaia Clauss, the biggest firm) or of regional wines recently designated to fall in line with the EEC, of which Greece is now a member. There are 26 of these regional appellations.

The Peloponnese produces one-third of Greece's wine, from rather more than a half of her vineyards: wine of above-average concentration, therefore; at its best in the red wine of Nemea. The Nemean cooperative, the principal source, uses the name Hercules. (He slew the, presumably unpopular, Nemean lion.) Mantinia, the local white, and Rhoditis, the rosé, are not so good as the reds.

Mavrodaphne is the other celebrated red: a sweet dark wine made in the spirit of an Italian Recioto, similarly concentrated and intended for long ageing and solemn tasting. Other Peloponnese wines are fair: Patras red, Muscat and Muscat of Rion.

The north of Greece has less vineyards, but more apparent potential for good table wines. Macedonia's Naoussa and Amintaion are respectively heavier and lighter, but both have a cleaner, more refreshing finish than most Greek wine. Epirus surprisingly makes a Cabernet red at Metsovo and a plain, lighter white at Zitsa. Thessaly has one red-wine region, Rapsani, on Mount Olympus.

All attention recently has been focused on the central peninsula of the Khalkidiki trident, Sithonia, where great sums have been spent on yachting marinas and vineyards by the tycoon John Carras. So far his Château Carras is more correct than memorable, but much is promised.

Of the Greek islands, Crete is much the biggest wine producer, with four designated red-wine areas: all the reds are heavy and can be sweet; more suited, perhaps, for Minoan than modern man. Cephalonia and its Ionian neighbours comes next in importance, especially for fresh white Rombola (or Robola) and the Verdea of Zakinthos.

In the Aegean, many islands make sweet wines of Malvasia, and some of Muscat. Samos is the most famous of these and perhaps the only exporter. The wine of Rhodes is well known, particularly under the name of Lindos, but scarcely rises above the ordinary level. On the whole, island wines are for local drinking.

Left: grapes are brought home by donkey on the island of Crete – a scene that can hardly have changed in two thousand years.

THE LANGUAGE OF THE LABEL

Παλαιόν (Palaion) Old wine
Ένδίκως διατηρημένον (Endikos diatirimenon) Mature quality wine
Έπιτραπέζιο κρασί (Epitrapezio) Table wine
Οίνοπαραγωγάς (Oinoparagogas) Wine-producer
Οίνοποιείον (Oinopoieion) Wine factory
Παραγωγή καί Έμφιάλωσις (Paragogi ke emfialosis) Produced and bottled
Οίνος Λευκός (Oinos lefkos) White wine
Οίνος Έρυθρός or **Μαῦρος** (Oinos erythros) or (Mavros) Red wine
Ροζέ (Rosé) or **Κοκκινέλι** (Kokkineli) Rosé
Ρετσίνα (Retsina) Retsina
Ξηρός (Xiros) Dry
Άφρῶδες κρασί (Afrothes) Sparkling wine

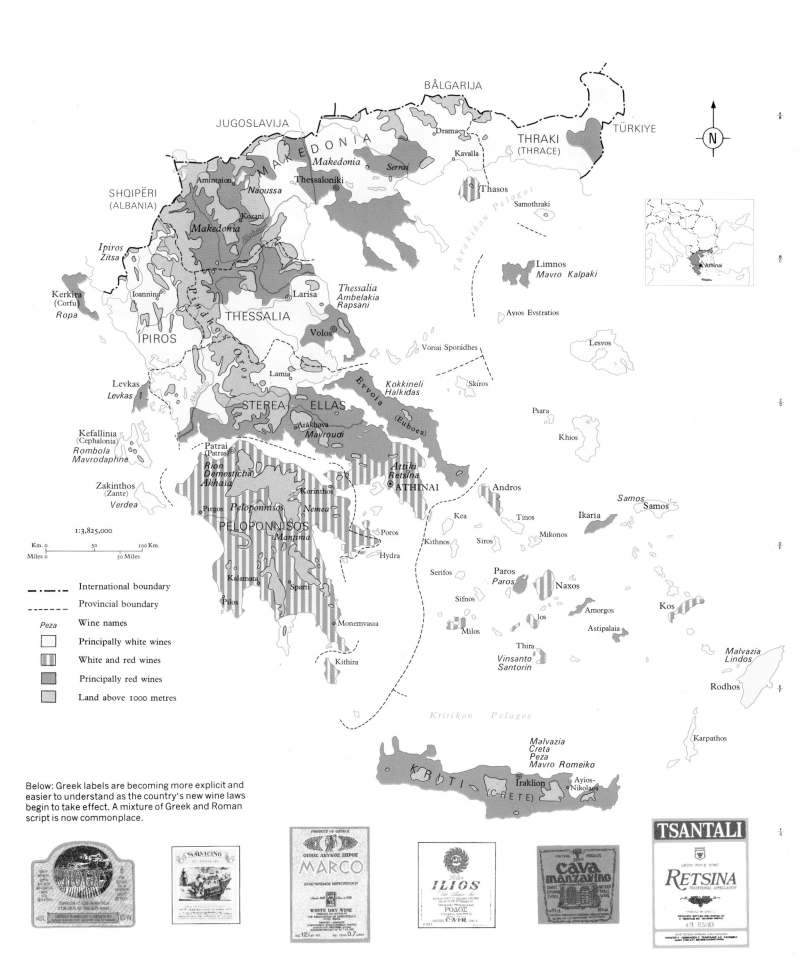

BÂLGARIJA

JUGOSLAVIJA

TÜRKIYE

THRAKI
(THRACE)

MAKEDONIA

Drama

Kavalla

Makedonia

Serrai

Amintaion

Thessaloniki

Naoussa

SHQIPËRI
(ALBANIA)

Thasos

Samothraki

Kozani

Thrakikon Pelagos

Makedonia

Ipiros
Zitsa

Limnos
Mavro Kalpaki

Aliakmon

Ioannina

Ayios Evstratios

Kerkira
(Corfu)
Ropa

*Thessalia
Ambelakia
Rapsani*

Larisa

Lesvos

THESSALIA

Pindhos

Volos

Voriai Sporádhes

IPIROS

Skíros

Psara

Levkas
Levkas

Lamia

*Kokkineli
Halkidas*

Khios

Akhelöos

STEREA   ELLAS

*Evvoia
(Euboea)*

Kefallinia
(Cephalonia)
*Rombola
Mavrodaphne*

Arákhova
Mavroudi

Patrai
(Patras)

Andros

*Rion
Demesticha
Akhaia*

*Attiki
Retsina*
ATHINAI

Kea

Tinos

Samos
Samos

Zakinthos
(Zante)
Verdea

Korinthos

Ikaria

Pirgos

Peloponnisos

Nemea

Kithnos

Siros

Mikonos

1:3,825,000

PELOPONNISOS

Mantinia

Poros

Serifos

Paros
Paros

Naxos

Km. 0   50   100 Km.

Hydra

Amorgos

Kos

Miles 0   50 Miles

Kalamata

Sifnos

Ios

Astipalaia

Sparti

Milos

International boundary

Pilos

Thira

*Malvazia
Lindos*

Provincial boundary

*Vinsanto
Santorin*

Rodhos

Peza   Wine names

Monemvasia

Principally white wines

Kithira

Kritikon   Pelagos

Karpathos

White and red wines

Principally red wines

Land above 1000 metres

Below: Greek labels are becoming more explicit and
easier to understand as the country's new wine laws
begin to take effect. A mixture of Greek and Roman
script is now commonplace.

*Malvazia
Creta
Peza
Mavro Romeiko*

KRITI
(CRETE)

Iraklion

Ayios-
Nikolaos

237

Cyprus

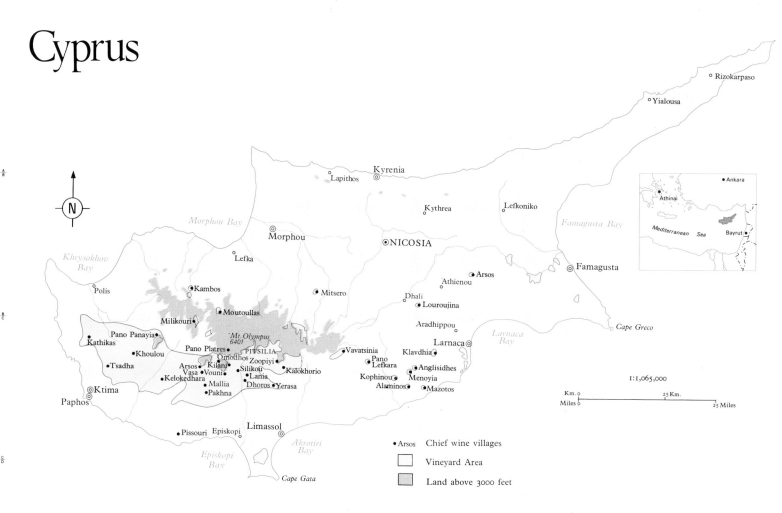

Cyprus not only has one of the oldest winegrowing traditions in the world, it is by far the most developed and successful of the wine countries of the eastern Mediterranean; the first (during her period of British rule, starting in 1878) to restore wine to a prime place in her economy, from which Islam had toppled it.

In the last 20 years an enlightened and enquiring approach to winemaking has opened a huge export market for Cyprus wine. Her 'sherry' has made the running so far, but her potential for high-quality table wines is no less. The Troodos mountains, attracting rain, make viticulture possible on what would otherwise be too dry an island. The vineyards lie where the rains fall, in idyllic green valleys, up to nearly 3,000 feet (900 metres) into the hills. The whole south-facing Troodos is possible wine country. Limassol, the port on the south coast, is the entrepôt and headquarters of the three big wine firms, Keo, Etko/Haggipavlu and Loel, and the cooperative Sodap.

The most individual of Cyprus wines is the almost liqueur-like Commandaria which is made of dried grapes, both red and white, in the villages of Kalokhorio, Zoopiyi, Yerasa and four or five others on the lower slopes of the Troodos. Commandaria has been made at least since the crusading Knights Templar established themselves in their Grande Commanderie on the island at the end of the 12th century. Its intense sweetness (it can have four times as much sugar as port) harks back in fact far further than records go; there are references in Greek literature to such wines, which were invariably drunk diluted with water (sometimes seawater). The sweetness is achieved by drying the grapes to raisins on sheets spread on the ground among the vines.

Commandaria is now made both as a straight commercial dessert wine of moderate age, popular for the Sacrament in churches, cheap and pleasant but without interest, and in very small quantities as the quite alarming concentrated wine of legend. The taste and texture of an old true Commandaria are more than treacly; they have a remarkable haunting fresh grapiness.

The range of grapes grown on Cyprus is much less eclectic than in most of the developing wine countries. The island has never had phylloxera, and rather than risk it by importing new stock, growers have until recently kept to the three traditional island grapes, the black Mavron, the white Xynisteri and the Muscat of Alexandria. There is also a traditional red grape, the Ophthalmo.

The last few years, though, have seen a substantial increase in vineyard acreage, and the introduction of new varieties. The Palomino of Jerez is used both for sherry and a very pleasant soft dry white wine. Carignan is used for lighter reds than the heavyweight Mavron normally produces (Domaine d'Ahera is one), and the first experiments with the noble grape varieties have encouraged further planting. Cabernet shows its character very well in the Troodos mountains.

In the near future we can expect to see new, more aromatic wines from this lovely island. For the moment, diners at the best Greek restaurants (all of which seem to be run by Cypriots) are very content with such plain but appealing reds as Othello and Semeli, Negro or Afames. They are best at three or four years old. The first choice for a refreshing white wine in the Cyprus sun is the lightly fizzy Bellapais made by Keo, and named after the abbey of Bellapais near Kyrenia.

The Far East: Japan

Suntory
Chateau
Lion
貴腐
Noble d'Or
1978

MANNS ESTATE
CHARDONNAY
1979
Japanese quality white wine
MANNS WINES

CHATEAU MERCIAN
1981
甲州
KOSHU
勝沼産
MIS EN BOUTEILLE AU CHATEAU

岩の原ワイン
IWANOHARA WINE

Three big firms control the quality-wine industry: Suntory (which also owns Iwanohara), Manns, and Sanraku (Chateau Mercian). Koshu is Japan's own white grape.

Japanese grape producing regions

Nature, in constructing Japan, had almost every form of pleasure and enterprise in view except wine.

Although the latitude of Honshu, the main island of the Japanese archipelago, coincides with that of the Mediterranean, its climate does not. Like the eastern United States (also in the same latitudes), it suffers from having a great continent to the west. Caught between Asia and the Pacific, the world's greatest land and sea masses, its predictably extreme climate is peculiar to itself. Winds from Siberia freeze its winters; monsoons from the Pacific and the Sea of Japan drench its springs and autumns. At the very moments when the vine needs sunshine, for flowering in early summer, and for ripening towards harvest, the rainy seasons, *baiyu* and *shurin*, come pat upon their cue. Between the two come the summer typhoons.

The land the typhoons lash is hard-boned and mountainous, almost two-thirds of it so steep that only the forests prevent the acid soil from being washed into the short, turbulent rivers. The plains have alluvial 'paddy' soils, washed from the hills, poor-draining and good for rice, not vines. The little gently sloping arable land there is consequently extremely valuable and demands a high return.

It is not surprising, perhaps, if Japan has hesitated about wine; hesitated, that is, for about 1,200 years. History is exact. Wine was grown in the 8th century AD at the court of Nara. Buddhist missionaries spread the grape vine around the country – although not necessarily with wine in mind. In 1186, near Mount Fuji, a seedling vine with thick-skinned grapes was selected and named Koshu: it remains the variety best suited to Japanese conditions, making decent white wine.

In the 15th century came Portuguese traders, and in the 16th St. Francis Xavier, preaching to the Yamaguchi court, introduced red 'tinta wine'. In 1569 a great warlord, Oda Nobunaga, held a famous wine-tasting party for his samurai generals. By the early 17th century the characteristic form of Japanese vineyard had been invented: a form of training the vine that counteracts, as far as possible, the tendency to rot brought on by summer rain. The 'tana-zukuri' system trains a vine vertically, as high as a man's reach, then fans out its branches horizontally on wire supports for ten metres or more in all directions. A Japanese vineyard is one vast pergola, with the advantages of taking up the minimum of valuable land, and allowing the maximum circulation of air around the hanging grapes.

The disadvantage of this system of vine-growing is that the spreading plant, its roots constantly watered, even in shallow soil, produces a huge crop of watery grapes. Sugar levels are so low that the law allows unlimited addition of sugar up to an amazing 260 grams per litre. 'Extract' is also low: the wine tastes at best mild, at worst downright watery.

A wine industry, in the modern sense, has nonetheless existed for 100 years. Japan's first outward-looking government, in the 1870s, sent researchers to Europe to study methods and to bring back vines. It soon became clear

that American vines did better than French or German. Nor were the Japanese averse to the 'foxy' flavour of eastern American grapes. The Delaware became the most planted variety, with the Muscat of Alexandria the only popular *vinifera* vine. The industry, from the start, was based in the hills around the Kofu basin, in Yamanashi Prefecture, within view of Mount Fuji and convenient for the capital. Table grapes still sell better than wine.

An important exception was the pioneer Zenbei Kawakami. His study of grapes and climate led him to the other side of the island, to the Niigata plain where the Sea of Japan moderates the summer heat and the central mountains catch some of the rain. Kawakami also produced his own hybrid grape, the red Muscat-Bailey A. The Iwanohara vineyard still uses it for its red table wine, rough and ready but full of character, not unlike many old-style Italian reds.

Up to the 1960s many small firms in Kofu made wine as sweet as possible for an unsophisticated market. Since 1970 a handful of big companies, able to distribute nationally, have taken over. Only one, Suntory, is a major grape grower. The others buy from farmers. But all now have at least small supplies of the best European grapes, which they process in gleaming new wineries. Their Cabernets and Chardonnays are correct, if a trifle faint. By far their most outstanding wine has been made from 'nobly rotten' Riesling and Sémillon: a truly memorable (and incredibly expensive) imitation of Sauternes.

For the rest, if 'tana-zukuri' cannot produce the flavour, nothing prevents the winemaker from blending in Australian or Chilean, Algerian or Romanian – or even French wine. Japanese law allows any such blend, and even allows it to be sold as Japanese wine from a specific Japanese region.

China

The human geography of wine poses some questions that must intrigue anyone who believes in wine as a blessing to mankind. The most imponderable concerns the East.

The vine travelled westwards with civilization from its earliest home in the region of the Caucasus. It also travelled east along the trade routes from Persia into China. An early Chinese word for grape, Putao, is not unlike the old Persian Budaw. The vine was known to second-century gardeners in China – who called one variety 'vegetable dragon pearls'. They knew how to make wine with it, and did so. Why did it not become part of their way of life, as it has in every Western country where it will grow successfully?

The late Edward Hyams, who made a study of the references to wine in oriental literature, concluded that it simply does not suit the Asiatic temperament. It clearly brings out the best in Western man, but for the Chinese wine from grapes, with its complexity of flavours and its soothing, inspiring effect, has never 'taken'. Perhaps the reason is even simpler. The Chinese eat strongly seasoned food hurriedly. They need something simply liquid to wash it down, plus a strong drink, a rice spirit, to toast each course with. To the Chinese, any alcohol should have fire in it.

This being said, there have been substantial vineyards in northern China at least during this century. The district of Tsingtao (now Qindao) in Shantung (Shandong) Province was under strong missionary influence early in the century; vineyards were planted and cellars built. Germans built the first Tsingtao winery. When they left, their barrels continued to be used – with deleterious effects on the wine. The taste of oxidation became familiar in the sherried condition of what little Tsingtao wine was seen in the West.

Recently, in China's new mood of enthusiasm for the West, several moves have been made to install a modern wine industry. It seems that soils are suitable. Climate is more problematical. Inland it suffers typical continental extremes, while the coast is subject to monsoons. Nothing wonderful has happened yet, but in the map you may be looking at an important wine region of the future.

The Shandong Peninsula (shown here) is the only region with any recent wine history. Yatai (formerly Cheefoo: the name still appears on labels) and Tsingtao had the first wineries. There are said to be some 35,000 acres (14,000 hectares) of vines in the province today (mainly of table grapes) producing about one million cases in five main wineries – the two mentioned plus Wei Fang, He Ze and Ji Nan. Little village operations add to the total. The old grape varieties seem to have been largely Russian.

One new initiative ('The East China Winery') has been undertaken by a Hong Kong Company as a joint venture with the Tsingtao winery and uses its well-established name for prototype Italian Riesling and Chardonnay. The earliest wines have been too bland, probably because of the high water table in the present vineyards. New vineyards are being planted on well-drained slopes facing south.

The Remy Martin Company was probably

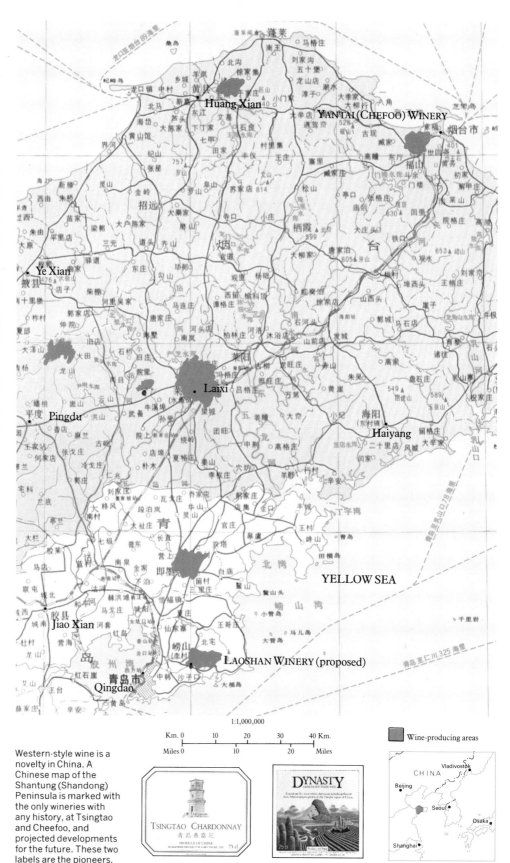

Western-style wine is a novelty in China. A Chinese map of the Shantung (Shandong) Peninsula is marked with the only wineries with any history, at Tsingtao and Cheefoo, and projected developments for the future. These two labels are the pioneers.

the first to collaborate with the Chinese in making a white wine of local grapes, flavoured with Muscat (the vines were brought from Bulgaria in 1958). They call it Dynasty. Its success in Chinese restaurants has encouraged them to plant classic varieties in Tianjin municipality, southeast of Beijing (and north of Shandong).

This much is perhaps not surprising, simply the thin end of a hopeful wedge. What is truly strange to learn is that the greatest concentration of vineyards in China is as far from

Western influence – and from the sea – as it is possible to get: in the extreme northwest, north of Tibet and close to Kazakhstan, in the Turpan Depression in the autonomous province of Xinjan Urgur. In the very heart of Asia, it lies on almost the perfect latitude for the vine: that of the south of France and north of Italy. There are 28,000 acres (11,000 hectares) of vines. Unfortunately, however, no wine. In the heart of the huge Asian landmass, summer is so fiercely and continuously hot that the grapes turn to raisins on the vine.

The New World

North America

'The goodliest soil under the cloak of heaven' was how one of Raleigh's men described the new-found Carolinas. One of their most impressive sights was their grapevines, whose luscious fruit festooned the forests. The grapes were sweet, if strange to taste. It was the obvious assumption that wine would be one of the good things of the New World.

Yet 300 years of American history are a saga of the shattered hopes of would-be winegrowers. First, of those who used the wild grapes they found. 'They be fatte, and the juyce thicke. Neither doth the taste so well please when they are made into wine,' wrote Captain John Smith in 1606. Then of those who imported European vines and planted them in the new colonies. They died.

The colonists did not give up easily. Having no notion what was killing their vines, they assumed it was their fault and tried different sorts and different methods. As late as the Revolution, Washington tried, and Jefferson, a great amateur of wine who toured France for the purpose, had a determined attempt. Nothing came of it. The American soil was full of the European vine's deadliest enemy, phylloxera. Aided by savagely cold winters and hot humid summers such as Europe never sees, which brought with them fungus diseases, America foiled everyone who tried to make European wine.

If American wines of American grapes were bad, some were worse than others. The ancestry of grapes is almost impossible to trace, but either a chance sport of an American vine, or else a natural hybrid between an American and a European vine which had lived long enough to flower, gave its grower hope of better things. More improvements came to diligent gardeners who planted pips and tried out the results. Some of these hybrids became famous. The Catawba was born thus, and in 1843 the Concord – one of the healthiest, most prolific, best looking and tastiest grapes ever introduced.

The peculiar quality of American grapes the colonists disliked only emerges fully when they are made into wine. The wine has a flavour known as 'foxy' – a distinct and easily recognized scented taste, which precludes any subtlety or complexity. There are many American species. Foxiness is most pronounced in *Vitis labrusca*. Unfortunately *V. labrusca* must have had its genes in Catawba and been one, if not both, of the parents of Concord. And it continued to be used by hybridizers who produced such other famous American grapes as the Delaware.

Since these were the best grapes Americans could grow, Americans grew them. Vineyards were started in New York, New Jersey, Virginia and, above all, Ohio. It was at Cincinnati, Ohio, that the first commercially successful American wine was born – Nicholas Longworth's famous Sparkling Catawba. Longworth hit on the fact that foxiness is least apparent and least objectionable in sparkling wine. By 1850 he had 1,200 acres of Catawba vineyards and was making a fortune.

It was short lived. Vine disease, the Civil War and finally Longworth's death in 1863

The Franciscan missionary Father Junípero Serra is said to have planted the first vines in California in 1769.

Thomas Jefferson, wine connoisseur and would-be winegrower, promoted wine as the best means of combating intemperance.

------- State boundary
● Austin State Capitals
◯ Pre-Prohibition vineyard area
· Active vineyards
· Wineries

ended Cincinnati's challenge to Reims. But the point was made. Longworth's champagne makers soon found new employers: the new Pleasant Valley Wine Co of Hammondsport on New York's Finger Lakes. This time American wine had found its permanent home.

The Finger Lakes region is described more fully on pages 264–265. Here we must trace the progress of America's other winemaking tradition, which came in under Spanish colours by the back door, while the Anglo-Saxons were struggling with the native vines at the front.

The earliest Spanish settlers in Mexico had established the vine there in the 16th century with tolerable success. Their primitive vine, known as the Mission (presumably a seedling, since it is not known in Europe) flourished in Baja California. But not for 200 years did the Franciscan fathers start missionary work northwards up the coast of California. In 1769 the Franciscan Junipero Serra, founding the San Diego Mission, is said to have planted California's first vineyard.

There were none of the problems of the

East Coast here. *Vitis vinifera* had found its Promised Land. The vine moved up the coast with the chain of mission stations, arriving at the northernmost, Sonoma, by 1805. There, although the missions declined, viticulture flourished. Jean-Louis Vignes brought better grapes than the Mission from Europe to Los Angeles. Came the Gold Rush and massive immigration. By the 1850s the redoubtable figure of Agoston Haraszthy had taken over, organizing, after a fashion, the new wine industry, and personally bringing 100,000 cuttings of innumerable varieties from Europe.

Thus by the mid-19th century America had two wine industries, poles apart. She still has – although the gap seems to be narrowing. Both limped through the disastrous Prohibition period making sacramental wine (even sparkling sacramental wine) and selling grape juice with the dire warning 'Caution – do not add yeast or the contents will ferment'. They took over a decade to find their feet again after Repeal, and Americans took more than a generation to take up regular wine drinking. But today the scene is a frenzy of activity and

The Hungarian Agoston Haraszthy galvanized the California industry by introducing scores of new vine varieties in the 1840s.

Frank Schoonmaker, writer and wine merchant, influenced California to make quality wine after Prohibition by promoting 'varietal' labelling.

Philip Wagner, writer and winemaker, introduced hybrid grapes to the eastern States; a historic move in the American wine history.

Eugene Hilgard, at the Agricultural Experiment Station, started in 1880 to lay the foundations of scientific viticulture in California.

James D. Zellerbach pioneered the use of French oak for ageing California wine. His Chardonnays of the '50s were a turning point.

Dr Konstantin Frank proved that good wine can be made from European grapes in New York's Finger Lakes district.

experiment, with vineyards being planted (in many cases replanted) not only in California and New York but (as the map shows) in most of the other states of the Union as well.

The South has a small wine industry of its own based on the native grape of its hot, moist woods: *Vitis rotundifolia*, the Scuppernong. The Scuppernong holds its big cherry-like grapes in clusters, not pressed together in bunches, and thus avoids the inevitable bunch-rot of normal grapes in the typical climate of Georgia and the Carolinas. Scuppernong wine is very sweet and uncompromisingly strange to *vinifera*-trained tongues.

Most of the other states with infant industries are planting either the well-proven American vines (of which Concord is far and away the most popular, poor though its wine is) or else the new French-American hybrids which were bred in France in the hope of solving the phylloxera problem, but are more appreciated in America as possible solutions to the riddle of the fox. The hybrids were first introduced by Philip Wagner of Boordy Vineyards in Maryland – perhaps a contribution

as significant as that of Jean-Louis Vignes.

On the other hand, most are now experimenting, gingerly to start, with the classic *vinifera* varieties that give them their one chance of entering the mainstream of wine.

The young vineyards of the mid-Atlantic States and the older ones of New York, Ohio and Michigan are mapped on pages 264–265. The most recent recruit to their number, recent at least for the making of quality table wine, is the Canadian province of Ontario, which benefits, like Ohio and Michigan, from the almost maritime influence of lakes the size of Lake Erie.

Meanwhile, on the West Coast the states of Washington, Oregon and Idaho are convinced of their potential for making wine at least as good as California's. Their enthusiasm has recently spilled over the Canadian border, too, into an infant wine industry in British Columbia. The new wine country of the Pacific Northwest is mapped on pages 262–263. Much more surprising is the current activity in southern and western states which appear complete strangers to the vine. West Texas is

doing things on the biggest scale, with considerable plantings near Lubbock, but New Mexico and Arizona also have vineyards that are going beyond the merely experimental stage. The secret here is a high enough altitude to provide cool growing conditions. Rainfall is too scant to be reliable; irrigation is essential.

In the Midwest, Missouri has a long history of growing American grapes, and more recently hybrids. Augusta made this point when in 1980 it became America's first designated viticultural area. Few people realize, though, that Swiss immigrants to Arkansas started planting *vinifera* grapes there more than 100 years ago, and are still working on it.

The question raised by all their enthusiasm is really an economic one. Given that it may be possible to make wines of adequate or better quality in almost all of the 50 states (Hawaii is included; alas, Alaska not), will it ultimately be worthwhile? California currently produces nearly 90% of American wine in near-ideal conditions. How long will it take for a market to develop in the minority offerings of aspiring new vineyards, however good?

California

Twenty years ago, in the mid-1960s, the ground rules of California wine were simple. A handful of traditional wineries, all grouped around San Francisco Bay but most of them in the Napa Valley, were making a few wines of superlative quality. Vast, technologically advanced wineries elsewhere in the State, using grapes drawn from both the Bay Area and the Central Valley, were making extremely sound and good-value everyday wines. Life was quiet in the vineyards: America did not appreciate her luck. You could buy a beautiful mature Beaulieu or Martini, Krug or Inglenook Cabernet for the price of a steak – but few people did.

The perceptive at the same time were aware of developments that were to start a revolution. It began with small-scale, almost 'hobby' wineries: Stony Hill in the Napa Valley making Chardonnay in a new style, firm yet delicate; Hanzell, over the hills in Sonoma, importing French oak barrels to bring burgundian flavours to Chardonnay and Pinot Noir; Heitz, in St Helena, buying wines and grapes and elaborating them with a boldness of touch that was almost shocking; the little Souverain cellars up the road making Riesling, Zinfandel and Cabernet in what seemed like a new key.

In 1966 Robert Mondavi left his old family firm of Charles Krug to build his own winery at Rutherford. The rest had been jostling at the gate: this was the gun. With Mondavi, wine became news; everything was in the open; not to know was to be behind the times. A trickle of new wineries grew rapidly to a spate. There were 25 Napa wineries in 1960. By 1972 the number was 44. In the ten years between 1972 and 1982, both the number of wineries and the vineyard acreage multiplied again by three. The figures for the whole of California are even more striking: three times as much wine-grape vineyard, and four times as many wineries.

Change has been almost as prodigious as growth. The accepted wisdom of California's wine geography has had a series of surprises. A glance at the map shows a broad and simple division into inland vineyards, those that run the length of the Central Valley behind the Coast Ranges, and more or less coastal grape-growing regions. An early study by the influential Department of Viticulture and Enology of the University of California divided the state into a series of zones, using the method known as heat summation (see the map opposite). Five zones were plotted, the coolest nearest to northern Europe in climate (or rather in average growing-season temperature), the hottest comparable to the south of Spain or North Africa.

The constant contention of the Department has been that the way ahead lies in planting the right grape variety in the right place. After a generation of following the Department's recommendations, growers have found that nothing is as simple as it seems. In France, growers are fond of saying that their soil changes with every step. In California, it is the climate that ducks and swerves. California's coastal soils are remarkably consistent, varying mainly in depth and porosity, and hence the speed of drainage they provide. But by the time

Hillside vineyards above the flat floor of the Napa Valley are on thin dry soil. Young vines need drip irrigation until they are established.

the exposure, elevation, heat summation, sun hours, frost risk and ten other factors have been counted, there is very little left on which to generalize besides certain obvious facts: above all, that the more mountains there are between you and the sea, the less chance of the sea air reaching you to moderate the climate.

So cold is the inshore water of the Pacific, all the way from Mendocino in the north down to Santa Maria (or Point Concepción) that it causes a perpetual fogbank all summer long just off the coast. Each day that the summer temperatures reach 90°F (32°C) inland, the rising hot air draws the fog inland to fill its space. The Golden Gate is its most famous pathway, but everywhere up and down the coast that the ridge of hills dips below about 2,000 feet (610 metres) the fog, or at any rate cold Pacific air, spills over and cools the land. Certain valleys that are end-on to the ocean act as funnels to allow sea air to invade 100 miles (160km) inland. San Francisco Bay even has an effect on the climate in the Sierra foothills nearly 200 miles (320km) to the east.

Previous editions of this Atlas have mapped the coastal regions immediately north and south of San Francisco Bay, from Sonoma's Russian River down to the Salinas Valley in

Monterey County (and also the Central Valley). This edition has two new dimensions. The first is the detailed mapping of recently planted areas much farther south down the coast where experiment has shown that conditions can be just as cool as in the north. These new maps cover the Central Coast as far south as Santa Barbara, and a stretch of Southern California in Riverside and San Diego counties. Farther north than ever, too, Mendocino County calls for detailed mapping for the first time as its wineries make their mark.

The second new dimension is the official concept of the 'viticultural area', instituted in 1980 as a form of appellation to help protect and to some extent guide the consumer. Compared with a French Appellation Contrôlée it is a toothless instrument. It is concerned only with geography, not with quality. The one demand it makes is that 75% of the grapes come from the area named and are of the variety (if any) specified.

Some of the viticultural areas are so small that they affect only one winery. Others are as large as several counties. Like Italian DOCs, they are requested by parties in the district in question and either granted, modified or rejected by a governmental authority – in this case the Bureau of Alcohol, Tobacco and Firearms.

There are excellent winemakers who ignore the whole appellation concept, preferring to use good grapes from wherever they can get them. Others are already totally specific about one vineyard and will presumably remain so. It seems likely, nonetheless, that California is moving on from the stage where it was the grape variety that counted first, then the brand name. The region and specific district have definitively entered the picture. It is a fair assumption that grapes and districts will eventually pair off with their most suitable partners, as they have in all the longest-established regions of the vine. Napa Cabernet, Alexander Valley Chardonnay, Carneros Pinot Noir and Santa Ynez Valley Sauvignon are some of the evidence to date.

CALIFORNIA WINE-GRAPE ACREAGE

Year	Acreage
1983	363.747 (147.200ha)
1979	332.681 (134.600ha)
1974	322.000 (130.300ha)
1970	147.000 (59.500ha)
1965	110.000 (44.500ha)

Above: wine-grape acreage in California has more than trebled since the mid-1960s, but is levelling off in the '80s.

Right: California exports almost three-quarters of her wine, mainly to markets within the US. Only some 2% of the total US wine production is exported to other countries. Canada takes nearly half, followed by the UK (15.5%).

PRODUCTION IN HECTOLITRES

1983		11.4m.
		1.3m.
		1.0m.
1974		6.7m.
		2.1m.
		0.5m.

TABLE WINE UNDER 14% ALCOHOL
DESSERT WINE OVER 14% ALCOHOL
SPARKLING WINE

In 1983 more than 70% of US wine consumption was home produced, with California accounting for 90% of the total US production. How the California harvest was divided, in 1974 and 1983, is shown above. Table-wine production forges ahead, dessert wines dwindle to a tiny proportion, while sparkling wines have doubled and may soon overtake dessert.

SHIPMENTS OF CALIFORNIA WINES

1983	3.9 m.hl.
	9.8 m.hl.
1974	2.6 m.hl.
	6.7 m.hl.

TO CALIFORNIA MARKETS
TO ALL OTHER MARKETS

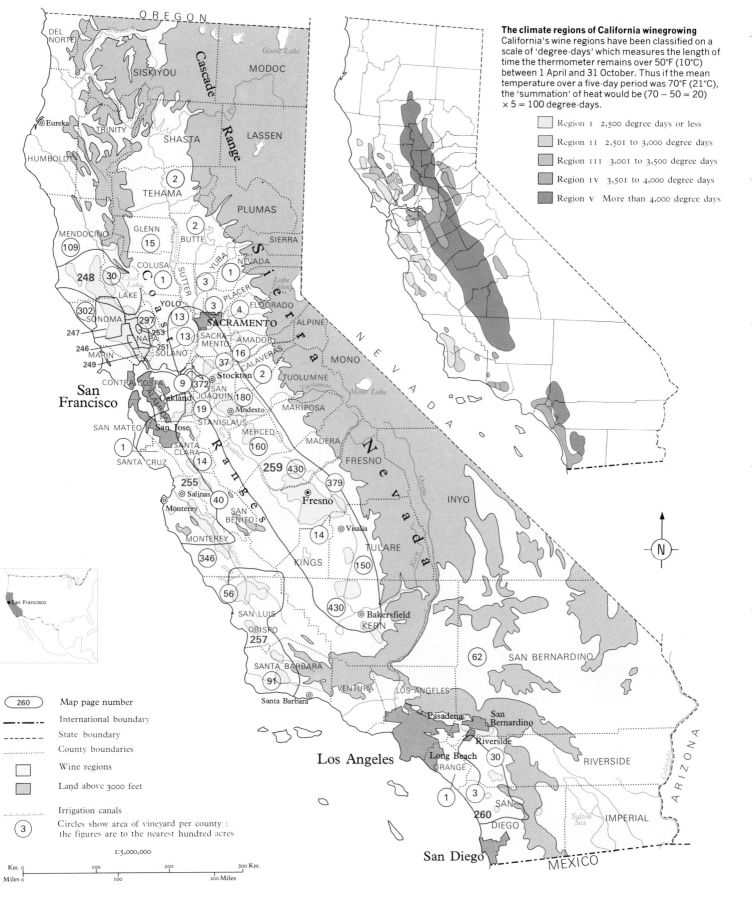

The climate regions of California winegrowing
California's wine regions have been classified on a scale of 'degree-days' which measures the length of time the thermometer remains over 50°F (10°C) between 1 April and 31 October. Thus if the mean temperature over a five-day period was 70°F (21°C), the 'summation' of heat would be $(70 - 50 = 20) \times 5 = 100$ degree-days.

Region I	2,500 degree days or less
Region II	2,501 to 3,000 degree days
Region III	3,001 to 3,500 degree days
Region IV	3,501 to 4,000 degree days
Region V	More than 4,000 degree days

O R E G O N

DEL NORTE
SISKIYOU
Cascade Range
MODOC
Eureka
TRINITY
SHASTA
LASSEN
HUMBOLDT
② TEHAMA
PLUMAS
MENDOCINO ⑩⑨
GLENN ⑮
BUTTE
SIERRA
248
⑳ COLUSA ① SUTTER YUBA NEVADA ①
LAKE
302 YOLO ③ PLACER
SONOMA ㉙⑦ ⑬ ④ ELDORADO
247 ㉕③ ⑬ SACRAMENTO ALPINE
NAPA ㉕①
246 MARIN SOLANO AMADOR ⑯ MONO
249 CALAVERAS
⑨ ㊳⑦② TUOLUMNE
CONTRA COSTA Stockton ②
San Francisco Oakland ⑨ SAN JOAQUIN ⑲ ⑱⓪ MARIPOSA
Modesto
SAN MATEO San Jose STANISLAUS
① SANTA CLARA MERCED ⑯⓪ MADERA FRESNO
SANTA CRUZ ⑭
255 259 ㊴⓪ INYO
Salinas ㊳⑨
⑳ ㊵ Fresno
Monterey SAN BENITO
MONTEREY ⑭ Visalia
㉞⑥ KINGS TULARE
⑤⑥ ①⓪
SAN LUIS ㊴⓪
OBISPO Bakersfield
257 KERN
SANTA BARBARA
⑨① VENTURA ⑥②
Santa Barbara LOS ANGELES SAN BERNARDINO
Los Angeles Pasadena San Bernardino
Long Beach Riverside
ORANGE ㉚ RIVERSIDE
① ③ SAN
260 DIEGO IMPERIAL
Salton Sea
San Diego
MEXICO
ARIZONA
NEVADA
Sierra Nevada
Coast Ranges

San Francisco

⟨260⟩	Map page number
—·—·—	International boundary
— — —	State boundary
··········	County boundaries
▢	Wine regions
▨	Land above 3000 feet
	Irrigation canals
③	Circles show area of vineyard per county : the figures are to the nearest hundred acres

1:5,000,000

Km. 0   100   200   300 Km.
Miles 0   100   200 Miles

245

Sonoma Valley

The California wine pilgrim should go first to Sonoma. The town has all the atmosphere of a little wine capital – in fact of the capital of a very little republic: the momentary Bear Flag republic of California. Sonoma's tree-shaded square, with its old mission buildings and barracks, its stone-built City Hall and ornate Sebastiani Theatre, is faintly Ruritanian in style, and thickly layered with history.

The hills overlooking the town were the site of Agoston Haraszthy's splendid estate of the 1850s and 60s. Part of his Buena Vista cellars still stands in the side-valley to the east. Another famous 19th-century winery, Gundlach-Bundschu, has been revived in recent years on the same southern slopes. Going out of town northwards, in Jack London's 'Valley of the Moon' on the road to Santa Rosa, Glen Ellen and Grand Cru wineries are both revivals of a centenarian heyday. This was where winemaking started in northern California. In modern times it represents only a small proportion even of the output of Sonoma County – most of the vineyards have migrated north to the Russian River Valley.

Yet there has been continual renewal of interest in what history has proved an excellent vineyard. In the 1940s Frank Bartholomew at Buena Vista became the first newcomer to revive a defunct winery. In the 1950s James D. Zellerbach built the tiny Hanzell, high on the hill above Sonoma, and installed the historic barrels that taught Chardonnay to taste like burgundy. In the 1970s Kenwood, from humble beginnings, and Chateau St. Jean from grander ones began to be short-listed among California's most interesting and original wineries.

Kenwood's name is largely for red wines, especially Cabernet with the Sonoma Valley appellation. Chateau St. Jean makes only whites, of good to excellent quality, and cites the precise vineyard ('Robert Young', in the Alexander Valley) for its best Chardonnays and truly remarkable late-harvest Rieslings, or 'McCrea' (above Kenwood in this valley) for Chardonnay. Most of the grapes for Chateau St. Jean's lively and delicate sparkling wines also come from other parts of the county.

Meanwhile the long-established Sebastiani, much the biggest winery in town, evolved from supplying colourful country wines (with Barbera as its speciality) to making some exceedingly suave products.

The appellation 'Sonoma Valley' runs from Los Carneros (see page 249) in the south up to (and just over) the watershed dividing the Sonoma and Russian River basins. 'Just over' because Matanzas Creek Winery, recent source of some exceptionally potent Chardonnays, lies a touch too far north for the simple rule to apply. Like the Napa Valley, but in a smaller compass, the Sonoma Valley shades from cool at Carneros to warmer at its northern end, excellently sheltered from the north all the way by the Mayacamas Mountains. It would be a brave taster who could claim to identify a Sonoma Valley character: so much depends on the winemaker. Sonoma Valley grapes have made some great wines. Perhaps Napa and Russian River have made greater.

Sonoma labels illustrate the variety of appellations available under the new system: Sonoma County, Sonoma Valley, Russian River, Alexander or Green Valley. Several name particular vineyards or 'ranches'.

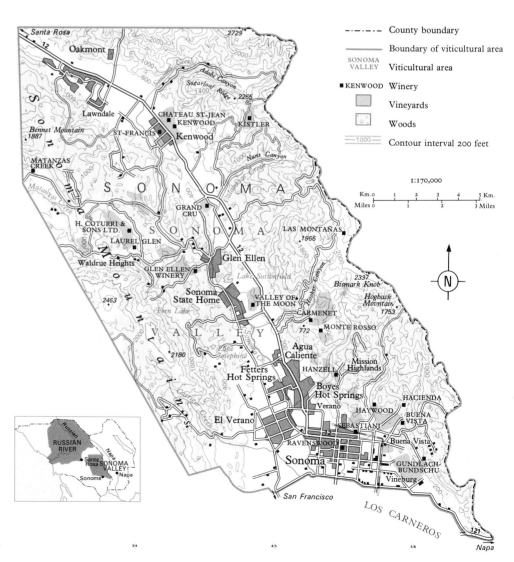

Russian River

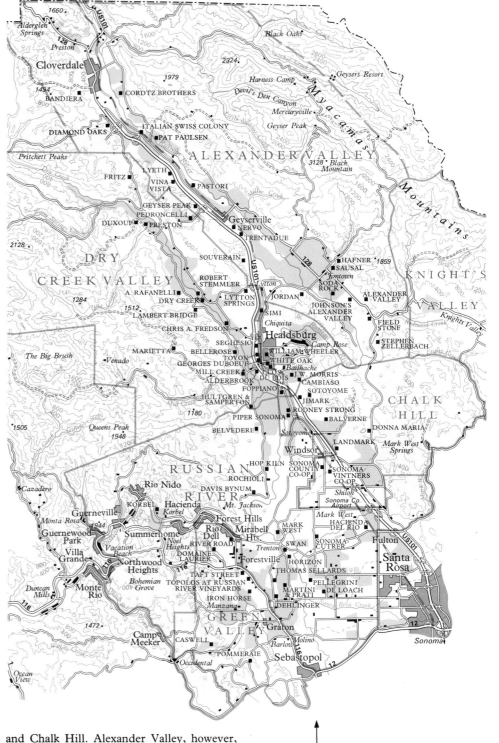

America's new appellation system of viticultural areas has imposed a pattern on the sprawl of vineyards over Sonoma County; for the moment the most complete and potentially helpful such demarcation of any region.

Sonoma County runs north up the coast from the head of San Francisco Bay, between the Napa Valley and the sea, its northern half drained by the Russian River (so-called from a former Russian trading post) and its tributary creeks. Most of its vineyards lie in this region, between Santa Rosa, 20 miles (32km) north of Sonoma city, and Cloverdale, 35 miles (56km) farther on. The original core of Sonoma planting lies around the old county capital – see the map opposite. A further, separate appellation, Carneros, links the southern end of the county with Napa (see page 249).

Traditionally the Russian River territory has been the source of good-quality 'bulk' wine, bought by the big firms of the Central Valley for blending. It is still a major source of the excellent Gallo standard wines. Wineries have flourished here (barring the Prohibition period) for a century, but in the main anonymously. The most famous exceptions were the Italian Swiss Colony, founded in 1881 at Asti, and Korbel, for long the source of California's best-quality sparkling wine.

The news of the last ten years is that the sense of purposeful excitement has spilled north from the Napa Valley and flooded the Russian River basin. Alexander Valley, whose first quality vines are a mere 15 years old, was the first appellation to command respect. The old stone-built Simi Winery woke to new life. A new Souverain was built in the expense-no-object style. The Pedroncelli family found recognition for what they had been quietly doing for years, and new wineries began to spring up like mushrooms after rain.

The Piper-Heidsieck company of Champagne was among the prospectors, joining forces with Sonoma Vineyards to outdo Korbel at what had been the region's best speciality. They have been joined by Iron Horse Vineyards in the Green Valley. Other sparkling-winemakers, some with French connections, are on the way. The Russian River grows the fruity-acid, not over-golden wines they need.

The coolest of these areas are those that have most direct access to Pacific air: Carneros by the Bay in the south, and the Russian River Valley (particularly at its seaward end, in the Green Valley appellation), where the river penetrates the 1,500-foot (460-metre) coastal hills. Progressively warmer conditions are found in the Chalk Hill area, then Dry Creek Valley, then Alexander Valley, with Knight's Valley, almost an extension of the head of the Napa Valley, warmer than Dry Creek but cooler (because higher) than Alexander Valley.

These, for the moment, appear to be the readings as they affect grape quality. New plantings are tending to follow their logic. Pinot Noir and Chardonnay, best with cooler conditions, are gravitating into the Russian River Valley and the cooler parts of Chalk Hill and Dry Creek. Cabernet and Sauvignon are dominant in the warmer parts of Dry Creek

and Chalk Hill. Alexander Valley, however, appears to break the rules by offering good conditions to a wide range of grapes.

The Alexander Valley boasts perhaps the most extravagant winery in the county, the neo-château of Jordan, built in the mid-1970s with the aim of becoming the Château Lafite of California. Higher in the hills, Alexander Valley Vineyards has made particularly good white wine for some years.

In the Dry Creek Valley, both Dry Creek Vineyards and Preston have stood out for excellent Sauvignon Blanc. Simi at Healdsburg (see pages 36–37) has a very strong range.

Farther south in the cooler Green Valley and east towards Santa Rosa, Iron Horse, Domaine Laurier, De Loach and Sonoma-Cutrer (a Chardonnay specialist) might be picked from a very close field, none with a long track record. Well-balanced and lively whites seem, so far, to be its outstanding contribution.

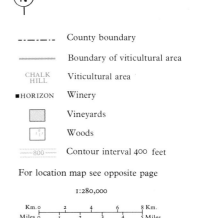

–·–·–·	County boundary
———	Boundary of viticultural area
CHALK HILL	Viticultural area
∎HORIZON	Winery
	Vineyards
	Woods
——800——	Contour interval 400 feet

For location map see opposite page

1:280,000

Km. 0   2   4   6   8 Km.
Miles 0   1   2   3   4   5 Miles

Mendocino and Los Carneros

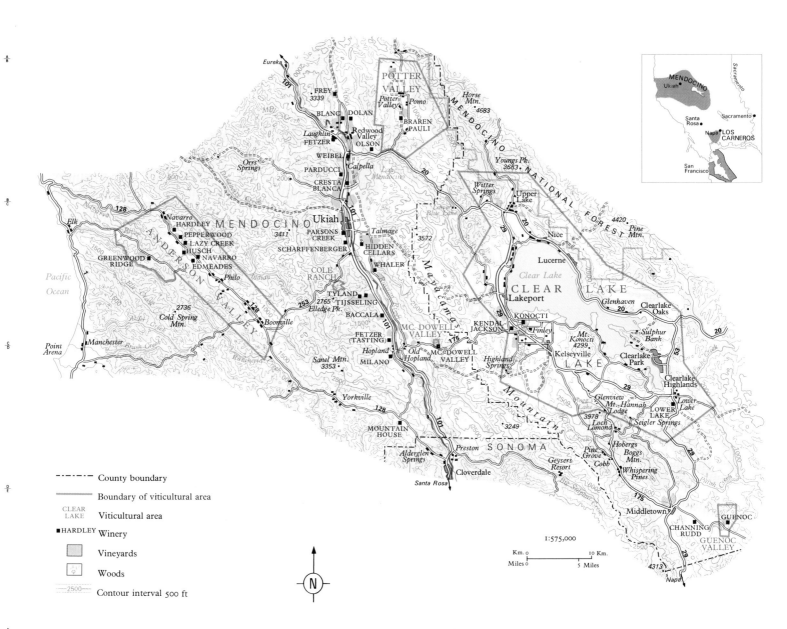

Mendocino County is the northernmost outpost of the vine in California. The instinct that tells you that it must be a cool-climate region is wrong. North of Cloverdale and the Sonoma county line the coastal hills rear up as more sudden and accentuated features, redwood country that stretches on up the coast it seems endlessly, misty and resin scented. But because the hills are higher, the valleys behind them are drier and warmer.

Most of the established vineyards of Mendocino are well tucked in behind a 2,000–3,000-foot (600–900-metre) range. The sea breezes do not reach Ukiah and the Redwood and Potter valleys – the latter one of the four viticultural areas of the county. They are warm enough to be rated Region III, or even IV in places, on the heat-summation scale. Their typical wines (from some deep alluvial soils) are full-bodied, often rather soft reds of Cabernet, Pinot Noir, Zinfandel or Petite Syrah.

The oldest and best-known winery in this region is Parducci (founded in 1931, a date that proclaims a visionary: Prohibition was still in force). Fetzer Winery was an important addition of the late 1960s. More recently Cresta Blanca, once a much-respected name in the Livermore Valley east of the Bay, has moved its operation to Ukiah to use the grapes grown here by members of the Guild cooperative. Weibel is another refugee from the urban sprawl of the East Bay. A dozen smaller wineries are too recent for any real consensus about their products, except that Ukiah can do well, with a wider range of grapes than you might expect from its summer temperatures.

At the same time Mendocino is building quite a different reputation for the one area where the hills part, and fogs find a limited access inland. The little Navarro River tumbles down the Anderson Valley through the forests. Anderson Valley has recently made a name for its super-cool, sometimes too-cool,

ripening season. Edmeades, Navarro and Husch are three of the small wineries that have made highly aromatic white wines from grapes that would ripen in Germany. The Champagne house of Roederer is also investing here.

The meeting place of the two extremes of Mendocino climate is McDowell Valley, a tiny appellation established by the highly competent owners of McDowell Valley Vineyards, on the winding Route 175 from Hopland to the out-of-the-way resort of Clear Lake.

Lake County is a warm region, too; comparable to the head of the Napa Valley not far to the south. Its tranquillity once attracted that troubled beauty Lily Langtry to settle here. She imported a Bordeaux vigneron and started an ambitious winery at Guenoc – unfortunately just before Prohibition. But Guenoc has revived and the new venture promises well. The few wineries of Lake County are not famous yet, but time can often seem foreshortened in the wine country of California.

Los Carneros, literally 'the sheep country', is a little district relatively new to the vine, but increasingly looked-to for the highest quality of grapes that require cool ripening conditions. It lies to the south of Napa city on the north shore of San Pablo Bay, the northern arm of San Francisco Bay: low rolling hills of variably claylike and coarse, rocky soil. Old farm buildings proclaim it until recently grazing land. But grapes grown by one of its farmers, Rene di Rosa, and sold to various wineries, made the reputation of his property, Winery Lake, and attracted others to buy and plant the sheep-walks.

Most renowned of the newcomers are Carneros Creek, which started making outstanding Pinot Noir here in the 1970s, and Acacia, which since 1979 has produced both Pinot Noir and Chardonnay of exciting quality, taking the unusual step of bottling wines from four separate plots of apparently similar land

separately. The results are consistently different: rich, velvety Pinot Noirs from the Madonna vineyard, for example, and firmer, more austere ones from St Clair.

The famous old name of Buena Vista, under new German owners, has moved down here from Agoston Haraszthy's original site in Sonoma. The evidence of their Carneros-grown Cabernet suggests that the region gives quite pointed acidity to this variety. Carneros-grown grapes are used, however, by many wineries outside the region, either alone or in blends, to leaven wines grown in warmer areas. Louis Martini, for example, blends Carneros Cabernet with rich wines from his Monte Rosso vineyard in the mountains, but uses Carneros Pinot Noir unblended.

Politically, Los Carneros straddles the Napa/Sonoma county line. As a viticultural area, therefore, it has three appellations: Carneros, Napa Valley or Sonoma Valley.

Above: Los Carneros still has the look of recently converted grazing country. Even in late spring the threat of frosts makes the cautious grower leave his oil stoves among the vines in case of emergency.

------- County boundary

——————— Boundary of viticultural area

NAPA VALLEY Viticultural area

■ ACACIA Winery

Vineyards

Woods

Contour intervals:
below 100 ft every 20 ft
above 100 ft every 100 ft

1:200,000

Km. 0   1 Km.
Miles 0   3 Miles

For location map see opposite page

Left: Parducci and Fetzer are pioneer Mendocino names. McDowell Valley Vineyards represent its new appellation; Kendall-Jackson is in Clear Lake. Even Simi from the Russian River is using Mendocino Chardonnay with excellent results. Buena Vista has moved house from Sonoma to Los Carneros.

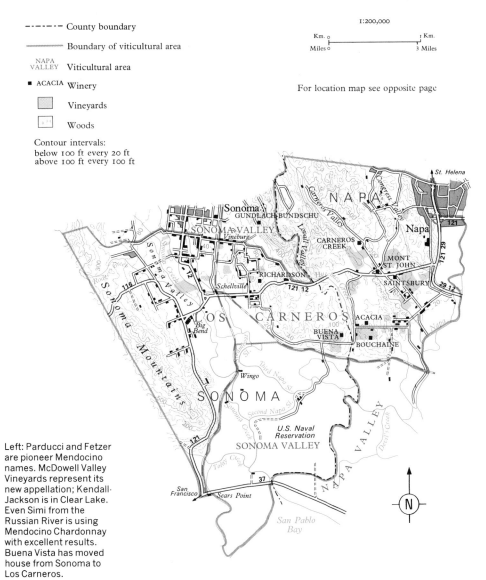

Napa Valley

Above: the Robert Mondavi Winery, built in 1966 in a style that recalls the adobe Mission buildings of old California, was the first great new winery in the Napa Valley since Prohibition, as revolutionary inside as it was nostalgic without. The fury of building since 1966 has filled the Valley with such wonderful eccentricities as Sterling's apparent Greek monastery (right) near Calistoga (figure 1 on the map).

The Napa Valley is the symbol as well as the centre of the top-quality wine industry in California. It does not have a monopoly, by any means. But in its wines, its winemakers and the idyllic Golden Age atmosphere which fills it from one green hillside to another, it captures the imagination and stays in the memory.

The valley runs in a shallow arc northwest from Napa city, most of its vineyards lying on its nearly flat floor, which is broken here and there by wooded knolls rising several hundred feet. The vineyards creep up the benchland on either side of the valley until (along the east side) the soil becomes too thin and rocky grassland takes over, dotted with dark oaks, or (on the west) the slope becomes too steep and forest of maple, madrone, laurel and redwood covers the ground, giving way, here and there, to bowls or ramps or amphitheatres of vineyard, even high up in the mountains.

The typical Napa Valley winery, large or small, is set beside the valley road in its vines, but has more vines scattered around on the flat and in the hills. Louis Martini, for example, has five vineyards, of which the most famous is Monte Rosso, high in the western Mayacamas Mountains overlooking the neighbouring Sonoma Valley. Other wineries, such as Schramsberg, Mayacamas, Chappellet or the new Newton Winery, have their vineyards around them in an elevated enclave of their own, remote from the bustle of the valley floor.

The valley falls into three climate zones. Its southern end, the separate district of Los Carneros (see page 249) and the valley proper from Napa north to Oakville, is Region I, the coolest. From Oakville to the northern end of St Helena is Region II. The head of the valley, around Calistoga, remotest from the influence of the Bay, is Region III – although a great deal depends on the altitude of the vineyard: Stony Hill and Chappellet are examples of hill vineyards whose wines have particular finesse. The Schramsberg that Robert Louis Stevenson loved is another: the top name in California sparkling wine. Moët & Chandon were so impressed with the potential of the Napa Valley that in 1973 they started their own winery, the Domaine Chandon, with highly successful results. The house of Mumm is now following suit.

There are two much-frequented routes for visiting the Napa Valley: the commercial artery, Highway 29, up the west side, or the more romantic Silverado Trail up the east. Infrequent and sometimes baffling cross-valley roads link them.

The first considerable winery going north on Highway 29 is on the first of the crossroads, Oak Knoll Avenue. Trefethen Vineyards is remarkable not only for its huge spread of immaculate vineyard (with labelled vines) and noble old wooden barn, but the well-judged elegance (the only word) of its wines, especially Chardonnay, Pinot Noir and Riesling. Follow Oak Knoll Avenue and turn north on the Silverado Trail to find two of the most distinguished cellars in the valley – again for the harmony and polish of their wines: Clos du Val and Stag's Leap.

The next essential visit on Route 29 is a few miles on: the Domaine Chandon, its sparkling-wine cellars and its admirable restaurant; next, beyond Oakville, the adobe Mission-style winery of Robert Mondavi, arguably the most influential in America, the winery that demonstrated how closely the flavour of white burgundy is related to its French oak barrels – and brought the taste of Meursault to California.

These places of pilgrimage are now a big tourist attraction. From here on up the valley the famous names clock up with increasing frequency: Inglenook, Beaulieu, Louis Martini – with a dense concentration around St Helena. Just north of the little town (which retains, despite the crowds, a potent charm) the Beringer Winery has extensive caves and excellent wines to show behind its 'Rhine House', a building almost ghoulishly faithful to Germanic tradition. Charles Krug is another of the great old names of the valley surviving from the 19th century. Freemark Abbey, by the road, founded in 1895 and refounded in 1967, has very high standards – but the same can be said for another dozen smaller wineries in this top section of the valley, from Smith-Madrone on Spring Mountain to the west to Joseph Heitz, or the spectacular Phelps and Chappellet wineries to the east.

The county here where the valley narrows becomes more and more beautiful. Oaks and pines, streams, darting birds, fruit trees, sunlit meadows stretch to the pretty little spa of Calistoga and beyond up into Knight's Valley over the Sonoma county line.

Before Calistoga is the last mandatory tourist stop: the astonishing vision of an apparent Greek monastery perching on a steep mid-valley knoll: Sterling, the flagship winery of the Seagram Corporation. Ascent is by canary-coloured cable car.

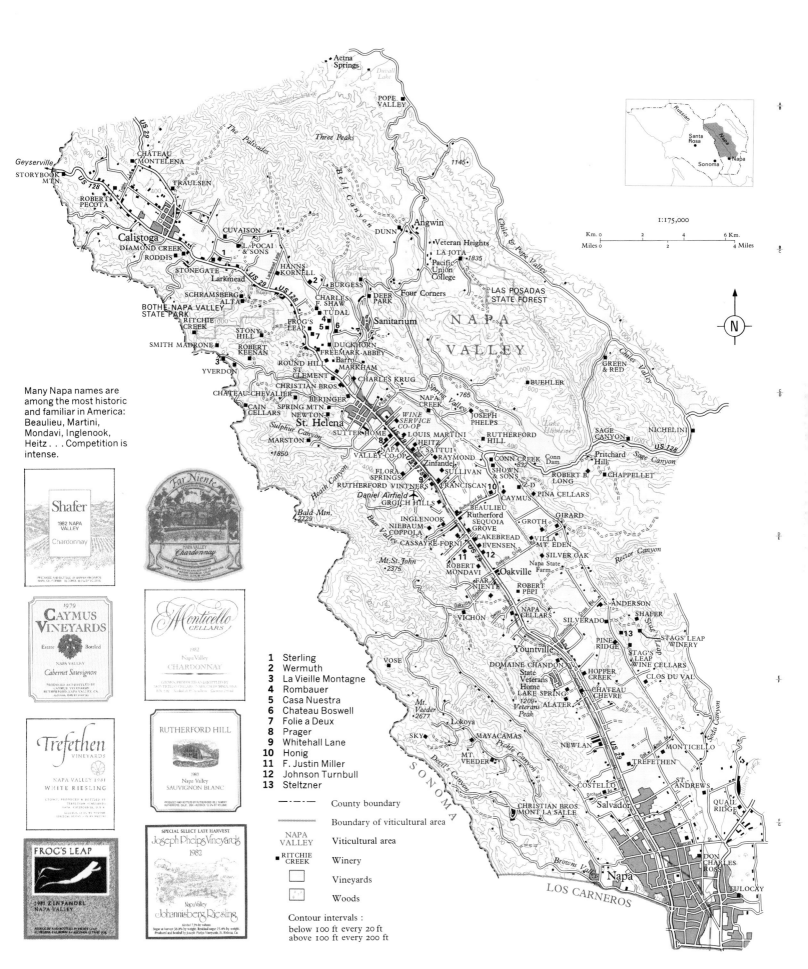

Napa: The Quality Factor

It used to be said that 'every year is a vintage year' in California. So far as the Central Valley is concerned it is true that grapes ripen regularly and the wine of one year is much like the wine of the next. But the coastal counties' vineyards have a more wayward climate, more varying microclimates and more differing soil structures than any broad generalizations can convey. As the wine industry matures it is learning to take advantage of local conditions to produce distinctive wines by planting precisely the right grape in the right place.

In Europe the experiments have taken centuries. California is moving faster. Individual sites have established reputations for growing particular grapes outstandingly well. The Cabernet Sauvignon of Martha's Vineyard, regularly bought and vinified by Joe Heitz of St. Helena, is perhaps the best-known example so far.

The maps on this page are a first step in plotting quality factors in detail for one small area, the northern Napa Valley. They were prepared for this Atlas by James Lider, for many years official agricultural adviser in the area, in collaboration with his brother Lloyd Lider of the University of California.

Three variables affect the grower's decision as to what vines to plant where. Soil is the first. There are two principal soil types in the area: 'upland soil', gravelly loam, quick-draining and warm, on the lower slopes of the surrounding hills, and the heavier clay of the valley floor. The former, as a general rule, gives finer quality.

The second is the average temperature, measured in California on the scale described on page 245. Even within this small area, 17 miles by five (27 by 8km), three different temperature zones are discernible. A larger-scale map (see opposite) shows innumerable local pockets of warmer or cooler conditions that in due course could create wines of particular character.

The third factor is the risk of destructive late spring frosts, worst on the valley floor where the cold air drains. Vines which come into leaf early are most at risk. After frost damage, vines are likely to replace the damaged flowers with a second flush, whose grapes will ripen later than those remaining from the first. Uneven ripeness makes high-quality wine unlikely.

In simple terms, therefore, the vineyards with the highest quality potential are those with upland soil and low frost risk (which usually go together) planted with the grapes indicated for that temperature zone. In practice, many more complex factors come into play. The timing and speed of the ripening process is perhaps the next most essential.

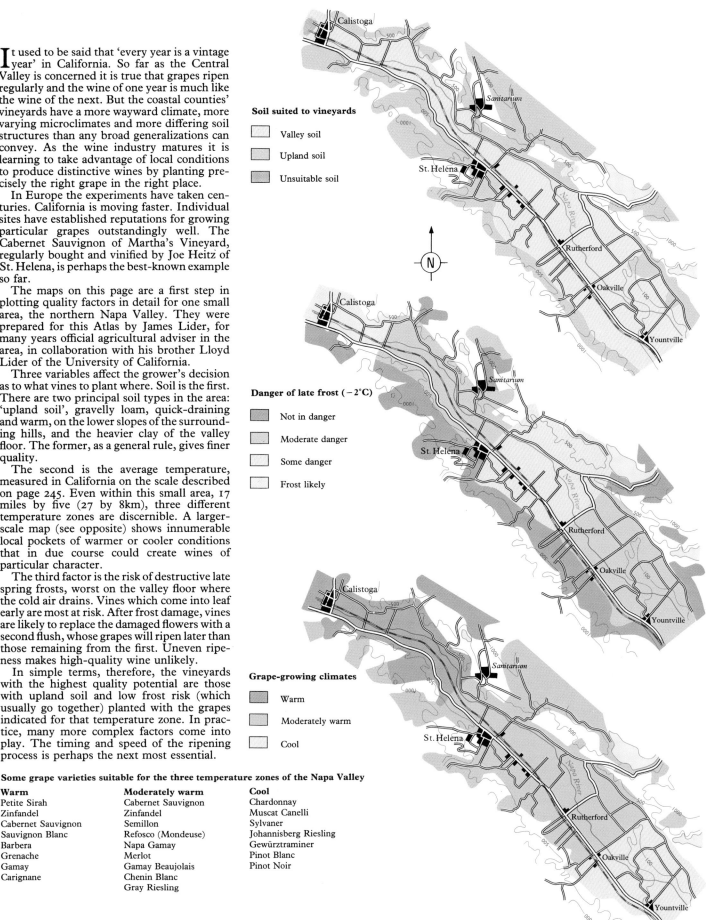

Soil suited to vineyards

- Valley soil
- Upland soil
- Unsuitable soil

Danger of late frost (− 2°C)

- Not in danger
- Moderate danger
- Some danger
- Frost likely

Grape-growing climates

- Warm
- Moderately warm
- Cool

Some grape varieties suitable for the three temperature zones of the Napa Valley

Warm	Moderately warm	Cool
Petite Sirah	Cabernet Sauvignon	Chardonnay
Zinfandel	Zinfandel	Muscat Canelli
Cabernet Sauvignon	Semillon	Sylvaner
Sauvignon Blanc	Refosco (Mondeuse)	Johannisberg Riesling
Barbera	Napa Gamay	Gewürztraminer
Grenache	Merlot	Pinot Blanc
Gamay	Gamay Beaujolais	Pinot Noir
Carignane	Chenin Blanc	
	Gray Riesling	

The Rutherford Bench

If there is a golden slope in California, one particular locality where wine of a recognizable type and often marvellous quality has been made since records start, it is the gentle foothill slope known as the Rutherford Bench, a length of gritty loam variously defined as starting just north of the village of Rutherford in the Napa Valley, and running south to just beyond Oakville, or going on farther south nearly to Yountville.

The 'Bench' is planted with a very high proportion of Cabernet Sauvignon, vines that have produced most of the long-term classics of Napa winemaking. The famous Inglenooks of John Daniel in the 1940s and 50s, the Georges de Latour Private Reserve of Beaulieu Vineyards in the 1940s, 50s and 60s, Heitz Martha's Vineyard from 1966 on and more recently his Bella Oaks, Cesare Mondavi Selection Cabernet from Charles Krug, Cabernet Bosche from Freemark Abbey, Robert Mondavi Reserve Cabernet from the late 1960s and, since 1979, his Opus One, produced in collaboration with Baron Philippe de Rothschild, all these famous wines were made of grapes grown in this stretch of dirt. Different as their styles of winemaking may have been, they have set a certain standard and evoked in those who have known them the pleasure of recognition. 'Rutherford dust' is one term sometimes used to try to pinpoint a characteristic taste they often share. Allspice is a more precise reference point.

Why this midpoint in the valley should be so ideal is a matter for debate. Efficient soil drainage is certainly a factor. Another is probably the generally northeastern exposure of the gentle slopes, which therefore catch the earliest morning sun in summer. Their soils warm up rapidly, then lose the direct rays of the sun in the afternoon when it is often hottest. As the shadow of the western hills falls over their vines, with soil and air both very warm, they enjoy a long, slow period of cooling. Grapes on an eastern slope ripen more slowly and later. Other things being equal, these are factors that enhance flavour and aromas in the fruit.

Just south of the Bench on Route 29 at Yountville the valley floor is considerably narrowed by two major outcropping eminences. It seems at least possible that these affect the flow of cool air northwards from the Bay. Tucked in under the south flank of one of them, the Yountville Hills, is a famous part of the old Inglenook property that now produces Dominus, the Napa creation of Christian Moueix, the director of Pétrus in Pomerol. Tucked behind the other, on the eastern side, is an area with the name of Stag's Leap (for the cliff edge above it). Stag's Leap Wine Cellars and the neighbouring Clos du Val are both famous for Cabernets in a more delicate style than those of the Rutherford Bench. Both have outstanding winemakers. Time will tell how much is the man, how much the vineyard.

The Napa Valley built its great modern reputation principally on the powerful Cabernet grown in its hillside and benchland soils. Examples here are from the Rutherford Bench and vineyards in the hills (e.g. Chappellet) around. Napa Chardonnays are usually impressively rich, dense, textured wines.

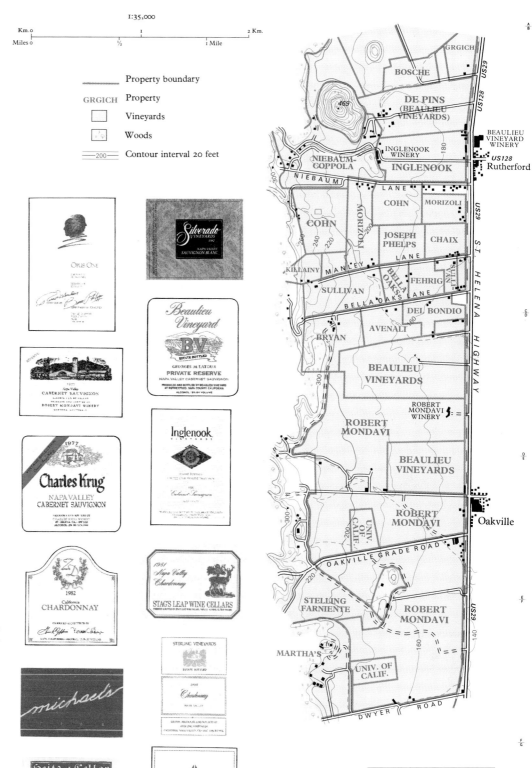

Land ownership in the 'Bench' is fragmented between a score of proprietors, several of them independent growers. On the map above, owners' names appear in red.

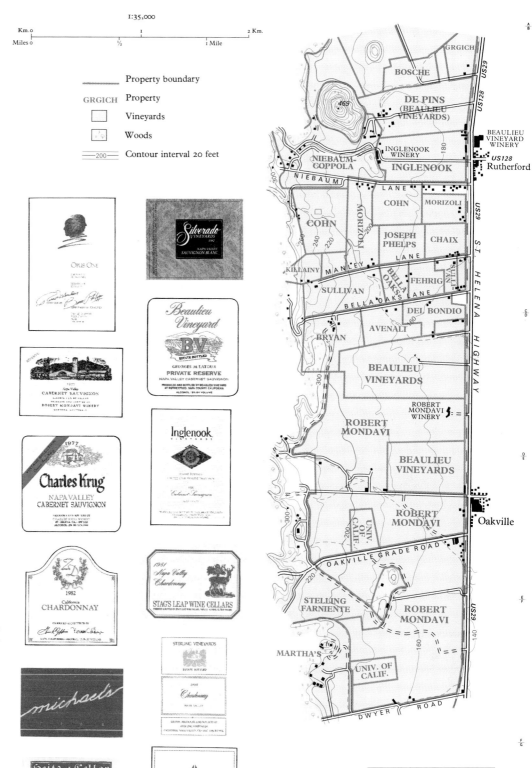

South of the Bay

The area just south and east of San Francisco Bay is wine country as old as the Napa Valley. Its wineries are fewer, but several of them are among California's most famous names. The dry, gravelly soil of the Livermore Valley has long been famous for white wine, especially Sauvignon, with perhaps the most individual style in the State. Paul Masson and Almaden were based until recently at Saratoga and Los Gatos.

In the 1960s the exploding conurbation of the Bay Area drove them to look for new vineyards. Encouraged by climate studies from the University of California, they moved south.

Almaden was the first company to make a move on a big scale – planting 2,000 acres (810 hectares) of Cabernet and Chardonnay at an elevation of 1,000 feet (300 metres) at Paicines in San Benito County. Farther south still, said the University. Paul Masson from Saratoga, Mirassou from San Jose and Wente Bros from Livermore all planted in what promised to be a wonderfully cool-climate zone: the gently sloping sides of the Salinas Valley, its mouth open to the ocean just north of Monterey; a

Mechanical harvesters have revolutionized vintage time in the massive new vineyards of California. The grapes are shaken from the vine by rods that beat their wires, then conveyed by belt up a chute into a truck travelling in the row alongside. Machines can pick all night while the grapes are cool, gathering them at the precise moment of ripeness.

highly efficient funnel for a regular afternoon visitation of cold sea air.

The valley has a history of growing excellent salads and vegetables. It was enthusiastically turned over to vines in a planting spree that covered more than 30,000 acres (12,000 hectares), largely between Gonzales and King City. Unfortunately, the funnel proved all too efficient. On a hot day inland, clammy coastal air comes rushing up the valley with such force that it actually tears off vine shoots. Some remarkable wines were made. A Zinfandel, for example, that did not ripen until December. 'Green' flavours in Salinas wines were fancifully attributed to the lettuces that had grown there before.

In reality, the search for coolness had gone too far, and much of the huge planting of the early 1970s has now been removed. The planters have emigrated still farther south. On the present evidence Arroyo Seco is as close to the sea as top-class wine can be made. The Jekel Winery there has produced Cabernets and Chardonnays of splendid quality. But now the concentration is on planting south of King City, on down towards the county line of San Luis Obispo.

Wineries have not proliferated among the new vineyards. Much the biggest complex is the Monterey Vineyard at Gonzales and its neighbours and colleagues Taylor California Cellars and Paul Masson. The former produced distinctive Salinas-style wines at

first, but now uses grapes from many different areas. Taylor and Paul Masson set good standards in their different price ranges. There are far more wineries in the Santa Cruz Mountains which, in comparison, have scarcely any vineyards at all. The Hecker Pass has a cluster of long-established family affairs, but it is the isolated vineyards in the hills that have nationwide reputations for their diminutive output.

Martin Ray was the first winemaker to bring renown to this beautiful forested mountain area. His touch (or at least the grapes he used) has now passed to the little Mount Eden Vineyards company. Ridge Vineyards, high on a ridge overlooking the ocean one way and the Bay the other, is the leader today, with Cabernet from the highest patch, Montebello, often as fine and long-lived a red wine as any in California. (Ridge also makes a splendid Napa Cabernet under the name York Creek.) Above Santa Cruz, Felton-Empire, in contrast, has built its reputation on beautiful late-harvested sweet white wines. Not far off, Ahlgren is another name to watch. Roudon-Smith near Scotts Valley is another.

Most individual of all the scattered producers of this wide and variable area is the isolated Chalone Vineyard, remote on a 2,000-foot (600-metre) limestone hilltop on the road up from Soledad to the Pinnacles National Monument. Chalone makes Chardonnay and Pinot Noir with the conviction that Burgundy's Corton has somehow migrated west.

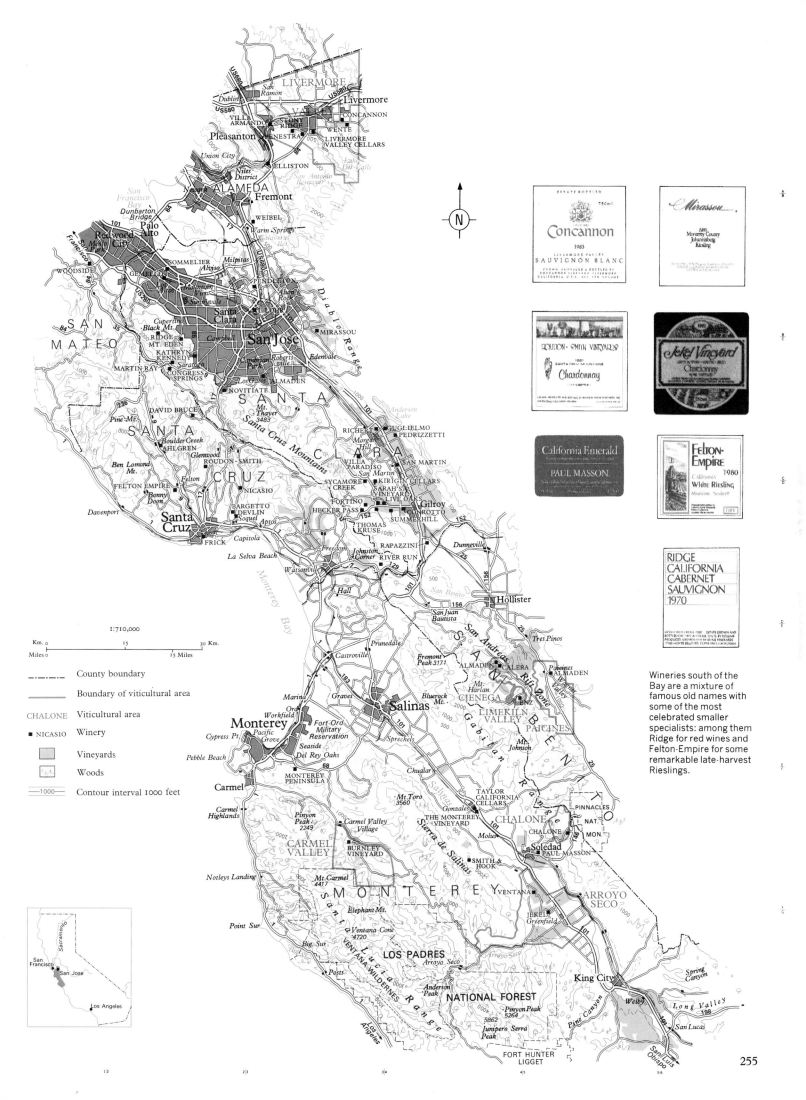

Wineries south of the Bay are a mixture of famous old names with some of the most celebrated smaller specialists: among them Ridge for red wines and Felton·Empire for some remarkable late-harvest Rieslings.

South Central Coast

The pattern is familiar by now: a river-worn gap in the Coast Ranges, access to a fertile valley for the cold, foggy sea air, and grapes taking over from cattle, or apples, or whatever farmers raised before the vine began its colonizing progress down the coast.

The logic that filled the Salinas Valley in Monterey County with grapevines in the early 1970s scarcely paused to take stock, but applied the same principle to the next two counties southwards: San Luis Obispo and Santa Barbara. By 1980, both had enough vines in enough locations to begin serious investigations into their relative qualities.

Already they have been divided into five recognized viticultural areas. There may well be more to come. But the variety of coastal conditions is well enough evidenced by these five.

To the north, the appellation Paso Robles covers a wide stretch of country, varying from wooded hill terrain west of Highway 101 to rolling grassland east of the road. The fame of Paso Robles, such as it is, comes largely from potent Zinfandels, with Templeton as their favoured centre. It rates as Region II or warmer, with no direct access for cooling ocean breezes. Its best vineyards, for this

The lookout tower on the Estrella River Winery commands a panoramic view of the Paso Robles area. After early success with Zinfandel, Sauvignon Blanc and Cabernet are proving their worth here.

reason, are probably those that are cooled by their altitude.

The pioneer new-generation winery of the district is HMR, started in 1964 as Hoffmann Mountain Ranch, which used Pinot Noir, Riesling and Chardonnay grown locally, but also bought white grapes in cooler regions. A little farther north, Caparone is one of the few in America to take Italian vines seriously; the Nebbiolo of Piemonte in particular. Martin Brothers is another that stands out for intelligent use of the local fruit, while Estrella River stands out for its hilltop site, a vantage point dominating the increasingly viticultural landscape to the southeast. Present evidence suggests that Sauvignon and Cabernet are the varieties best suited to Paso Robles.

Edna Valley, over the Cuesta Pass to the south, could hardly be more distinct. If sea air hardly touches Paso Robles, it swirls in from Morro Bay and cools the valley above San Luis Obispo to a Region I climate. Chardonnay appears so far to be the prime grape for the area, Edna Valley Vineyards (related to the celebrated Chalone) its prime local user, although several wineries elsewhere (including HMR) buy grapes. The Champagne firm of Deutz has built a sparkling-wine cellar at Arroyo Grande.

The Santa Maria Valley provides conditions that are, if anything, cooler still. Some of its vineyard land is so low-lying that sea fog moves

in at midday and the fruit can be under-ripe and over-acid. Almost all is owned by farmers rather than wineries (with Los Viñeros and the little Rancho Sisquoc the only ones in the district). The best grapes, Chardonnay in the main, are grown on the south slope high enough – 600 feet plus (180 metres) – above the valley floor to be on the fringe of the fog belt. The 1,400-acre (566-hectare) Tepusquet Vineyard is the major pioneer.

Over the Solomon Hills to the south conditions are warmer and more stable. The Santa Ynez Valley viticultural area is no obvious physical feature, but a sprawl of vineyards around and to the north of Solvang, a town as peculiarly Danish as its name. The grape that seems best suited to the area is the Sauvignon Blanc; most of the local wineries have done well with it: Santa Ynez Valley, Zaca Mesa, Firestone and Brander particularly so. The region is warm enough to develop flavours deeper and more interesting than the sometimes facile 'fumé' character of the variety.

Firestone is the principal winery, and a landmark for reliability and value. Chardonnay, Gewürztraminer, Pinot Noir, Cabernet and (especially) Merlot are all successes. Brander and Zaca Mesa are perhaps the bellwethers for quality. Sanford alone has edged west towards the ocean and its fog, searching for an ideal site for California's Holy Grail, the temperamental Pinot Noir.

The four main viticultural
areas of the South
Central Coast each has
different specialities.
Edna Valley is wedded to
Chardonnay, Sanford's
Pinot Noir comes from
Santa Maria, Martin
Brothers uses the
Zinfandel of Paso
Robles, while Firestone
conjures a remarkable
range from the Santa
Ynez Valley.

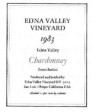

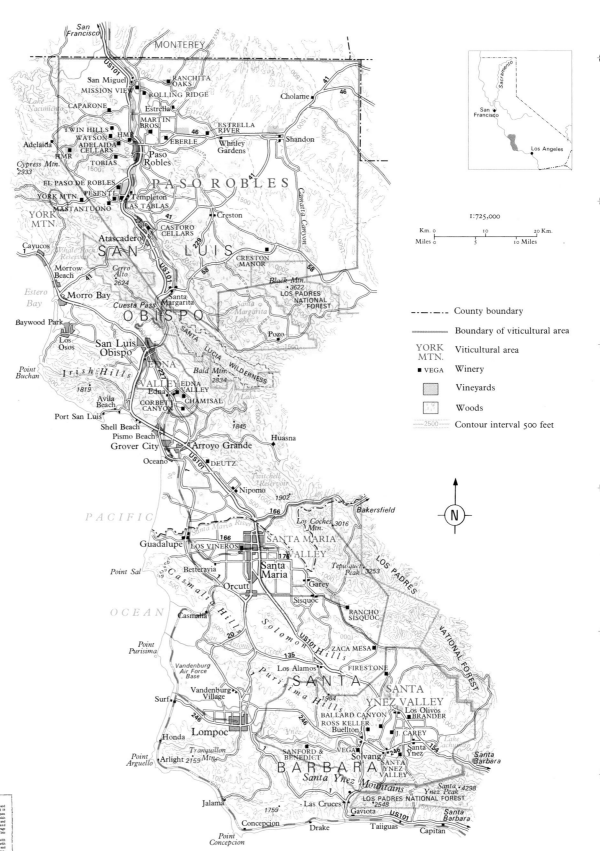

The Central Valley

The San Joaquin Valley, alias the Central Valley, produces four bottles out of five of California wine. To put it another way, if all America's wine filled one bottle, all but one-and-a-bit glasses of it would come from this giant vineyard.

Conditions are totally different here from those among the coastal hills. The soil is rich, fertile and flat for 400 miles (645km) north-south and up to 100 miles (150km) across. Vines take their place with orchards, and among the vines table and raisin grapes with wine grapes. Many are of adaptable varieties that will do for either at a pinch.

The climate is reliably, steadily, often stupefyingly hot. For most of the length of the Valley the Coast Ranges seal it off from any Pacific influence. On the University of California scale most of it is Region V. The natural produce of such a climate is grapes with high sugar content and virtually no acidity. In practice, high cropping levels caused by generous fertilizing and irrigation tend to make watery wine – the equivalent of the notorious 11° Midi wine of France. Strong sweet dessert wines were the best the Valley could do, until technology came to its rescue.

Twenty years ago Americans drank 70% high-strength wine, 30% light table wine. Today the proportions are reversed. The Valley adapted to the new demand with creditable speed and success – indeed helped to shape the pattern of American winedrinking by designing new kinds of light wine, making them reliably and selling them reasonably.

The University of California provided the means, in the form of new grape varieties, new ways of growing them and new winemaking techniques – not to mention new winemakers. Some of their new varieties, such as Emerald Riesling and Ruby Cabernet, are now established as California standards. Others such as Carmine, Centurion and Carnelian (see page 24) have turned out even better. New varieties apart, elimination of unsuitable old ones has been an important part of the improvements.

New ways of growing them have consisted mainly of high trellising with various devices to give the maximum curtain of leaves over the grapes, of mist sprays to cool the vineyard in hot weather, and of provisions for mechanical harvesting – now standard practice in these industrialized vineyards.

In the cellar the great developments have been stainless steel and other neutral tanks, protecting the grapes, the must and wine from oxygen, various forms of presses, pumps and filters – but above all temperature control. Refrigeration, more than any single factor, has made good light wine possible in the Central Valley.

The lead in these developments was taken and is firmly held by the brothers Ernest and Julio Gallo, whose family-owned business at Modesto is the biggest single wine operation on earth. Its statistics are startling: a capacity of 795 million litres; the biggest glass factory west of the Mississippi at the start of the bottling line; a 25-acre (10-hectare) warehouse holding only four weeks' stock.

The figures would be impressive if it were beer they were dispensing, or even soda water.

What makes them awe-inspiring is that the product is wine: on the whole very good wine. The Gallos have been a major influence on America's taste for wine – it could hardly be otherwise, as they make every third or fourth bottle (the figures are not available). They take the responsibility seriously, providing as it were a beginners' course from apple and other 'pop wines' by easy degrees of sweetness and fruitiness to some of the best standard 'burgundy' and 'chablis' in the business and beyond to fully dry, well-matured varietals.

They do not, and nor do the other good Valley winemakers, necessarily limit themselves to Valley grapes. Gallo is one of the biggest buyers in the North Coast counties, including the Napa Valley. But the progress of Valley viticulture means they will have to rely less on the coast in future.

The Gallos have two big colleagues in the San Joaquin valley – big enough for their wineries to remind you more of oil refineries than of any agricultural operation.

Guild, based at Lodi, is a growers' cooperative whose Italian-style (i.e. sweet) Tavola-brand wines are immensely popular. Winemasters' Guild is their premium brand.

ISC of California is a conglomerate company whose brands include Colony, Italian Swiss Colony, Petri, Lejon and Jacques Bonet. The smaller, but still huge, Franzia Winery identifies all its wines as 'made and bottled in Ripon'.

Besides the Valley-based wineries, other well-known companies with their bases elsewhere grow or buy much of their wine there:

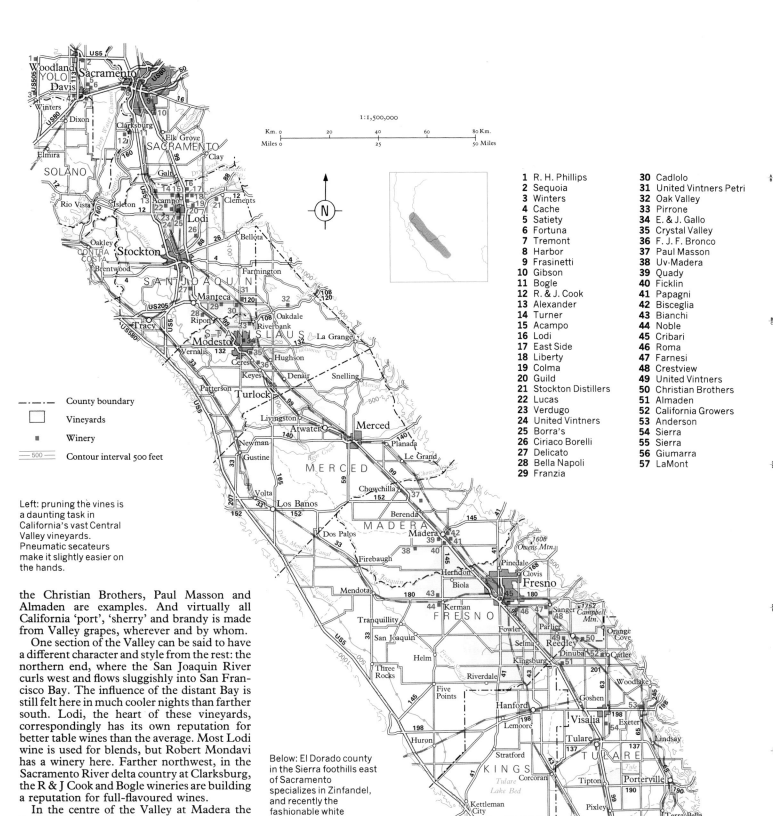

1:1,500,000

Km. 0   20   40   60   80 Km.
Miles 0   25   50 Miles

N

1	R. H. Phillips	30	Cadlolo
2	Sequoia	31	United Vintners Petri
3	Winters	32	Oak Valley
4	Cache	33	Pirrone
5	Satiety	34	E. & J. Gallo
6	Fortuna	35	Crystal Valley
7	Tremont	36	F. J. F. Bronco
8	Harbor	37	Paul Masson
9	Frasinetti	38	Uv-Madera
10	Gibson	39	Quady
11	Bogle	40	Ficklin
12	R. & J. Cook	41	Papagni
13	Alexander	42	Bisceglia
14	Turner	43	Bianchi
15	Acampo	44	Noble
16	Lodi	45	Cribari
17	East Side	46	Roma
18	Liberty	47	Farnesi
19	Colma	48	Crestview
20	Guild	49	United Vintners
21	Stockton Distillers	50	Christian Brothers
22	Lucas	51	Almaden
23	Verdugo	52	California Growers
24	United Vintners	53	Anderson
25	Borra's	54	Sierra
26	Ciriaco Borelli	55	Sierra
27	Delicato	56	Giumarra
28	Bella Napoli	57	LaMont
29	Franzia		

- - - - - County boundary

☐ Vineyards

■ Winery

═ 500 ═ Contour interval 500 feet

Left: pruning the vines is a daunting task in California's vast Central Valley vineyards. Pneumatic secateurs make it slightly easier on the hands.

the Christian Brothers, Paul Masson and Almaden are examples. And virtually all California 'port', 'sherry' and brandy is made from Valley grapes, wherever and by whom.

One section of the Valley can be said to have a different character and style from the rest: the northern end, where the San Joaquin River curls west and flows sluggishly into San Francisco Bay. The influence of the distant Bay is still felt here in much cooler nights than farther south. Lodi, the heart of these vineyards, correspondingly has its own reputation for better table wines than the average. Most Lodi wine is used for blends, but Robert Mondavi has a winery here. Farther northwest, in the Sacramento River delta country at Clarksburg, the R & J Cook and Bogle wineries are building a reputation for full-flavoured wines.

In the centre of the Valley at Madera the little Ficklin winery has an almost legendary name for its 'port'. Quady is another more recent 'port' specialist who also makes an intense orange Muscat dessert wine by the name of Essensia. But far more surprising is the quality of Chardonnay produced in this hot region by Angelo Papagni; perhaps a signal that careful growing and perfectly timed picking could transform Valley standards – if the demand was there.

Right in the south near Bakersfield the firms of Giumarra and M. LaMont break the rules by making table wines of character in some of the hottest conditions in the State. The grapes ripen so early here that they can be picked before they feel the full effect of the summer heat.

Below: El Dorado county in the Sierra foothills east of Sacramento specializes in Zinfandel, and recently the fashionable white Zinfandel.

ERNEST & JULIO GALLO

CRIBARI
CALIFORNIA
CHENIN BLANC

1982 WHITE-ZINFANDEL
SIERRA VISTA

Southern California

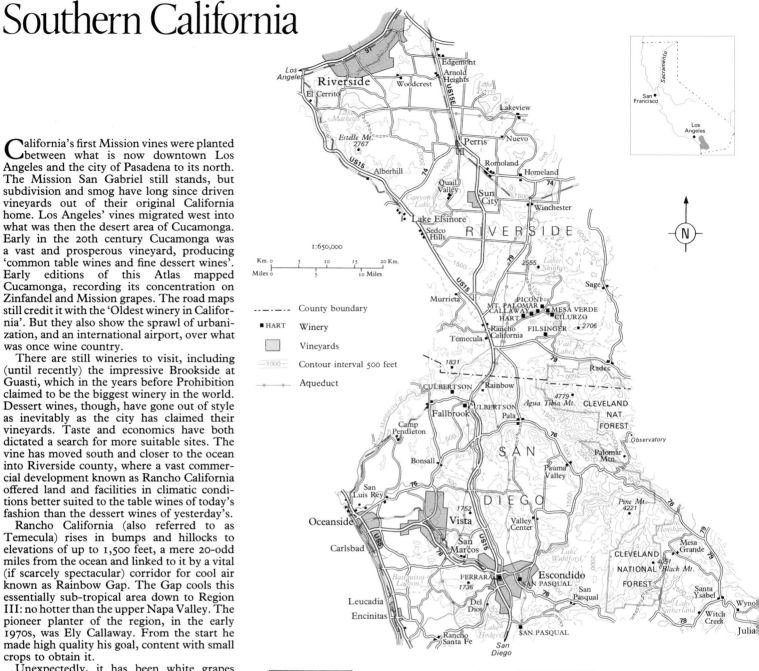

California's first Mission vines were planted between what is now downtown Los Angeles and the city of Pasadena to its north. The Mission San Gabriel still stands, but subdivision and smog have long since driven vineyards out of their original California home. Los Angeles' vines migrated west into what was then the desert area of Cucamonga. Early in the 20th century Cucamonga was a vast and prosperous vineyard, producing 'common table wines and fine dessert wines'. Early editions of this Atlas mapped Cucamonga, recording its concentration on Zinfandel and Mission grapes. The road maps still credit it with the 'Oldest winery in California'. But they also show the sprawl of urbanization, and an international airport, over what was once wine country.

There are still wineries to visit, including (until recently) the impressive Brookside at Guasti, which in the years before Prohibition claimed to be the biggest winery in the world. Dessert wines, though, have gone out of style as inevitably as the city has claimed their vineyards. Taste and economics have both dictated a search for more suitable sites. The vine has moved south and closer to the ocean into Riverside county, where a vast commercial development known as Rancho California offered land and facilities in climatic conditions better suited to the table wines of today's fashion than the dessert wines of yesterday's.

Rancho California (also referred to as Temecula) rises in bumps and hillocks to elevations of up to 1,500 feet, a mere 20-odd miles from the ocean and linked to it by a vital (if scarcely spectacular) corridor for cool air known as Rainbow Gap. The Gap cools this essentially sub-tropical area down to Region III: no hotter than the upper Napa Valley. The pioneer planter of the region, in the early 1970s, was Ely Callaway. From the start he made high quality his goal, content with small crops to obtain it.

Unexpectedly, it has been white grapes rather than red that have benefited most from the long growing season and relatively cool late summer of the region. After ten years of experience, Callaway has become an all-white winery, with fog in fall even provoking noble rot and allowing the making of luscious 'botrytized' wines. A number of small estate-wineries have followed similar patterns, though without abandoning the red varieties. But the quality of the white grapes of Temecula is such that an avocado-grower from Fallbrook, over the county line in San Diego county, has made a reputation from a minute output of sparkling wine (the name is Culbertson) made of Temecula-grown Pinot Blanc, Chardonnay and Chenin Blanc.

Southernmost of all, in the mini-mountains between the ocean and the Cleveland National Forest, grapes are a traditional part of the rich mixed farming of Escondido, just north of San Diego. Two old wineries make dessert wines and one new one, San Pasqual, specializes in estate-grown white wines. We are four hundred miles south of Mendocino county, in avocado and orange country. But California can always find you a cool corner.

Above: Southern California used to be thought of as dessert-wine country. Even here, though, sites have been found that suit Cabernet, Chardonnay and even Riesling.

Left: the Callaway winery at Temecula led the way with high-quality wine in Southern California. Its white wines have turned out to be more successful than its reds.

Seventeen of the best varieties are described here, with the climate regions (see page 245) for which they are recommended by the University of California, and the normal yield per acre. One ton of grapes gives about 160 US gallons (606 litres) of wine. So 5 tons an acre = 3,030 litres = 350 cases an acre, or approximately 73 hectolitres per hectare. Lower yields usually give higher quality. The 1983 acreage figures for the leading counties for each grape are given, followed by the State total for the variety in 1983 (1975 figure in brackets).

Barbera (regions III–IV; 5–8 tons) Dark red wine with good balance of acidity even when grown in very hot conditions. Italian style. Fresno 4,798; Madera 3,789; Kern 3,291. Total 17,346 (15,242).

Cabernet Sauvignon (regions I–II; 4–6 tons) The best red wine: perfumed, fruity, dry, long-lasting. Needs ageing at least four years. Napa 5,283; Sonoma 4,355; Monterey 3,322; Lake 1,071. Total 20,457 (12,700).

Carignane (regions III–V; 6–12 tons) The bulk-wine grape of the south of France, used principally for jug-wine blends in California, but in decreasing amounts. San Joaquin 6,408; Madera 4,528; Mendocino 1,744. Total 21,103 (28,209).

Chardonnay (regions I–II; 4–6 tons) The best white wine: dry but full and sappy; perfumed; grape flavour; improved by short time in oak. Lasts well. Sonoma 3,981; Napa 3,726; Monterey 3,307. Total 15,615 (4,900).

Chenin Blanc (sometimes wrongly called White Pinot; is not Pinot Blanc) (region I; 6–10 tons) In hills sometimes makes well-balanced, rich but tar† wine. Often not very distinctive. Kern 4,934; Madera 3,325; Fresno 3,149; Merced 3,131. Tota. 29,554 (14,776).

French Colombard (regions III–IV; 6–10 tons) Rather neutral dry white used for blending; in cooler areas fresh and pleasant unblended. Fresno 7,374; Madera 6,799; Kern 5,104; San Joaquin 4,492. Total 38,478 (23,814).

Gamay (also known as Napa Gamay) (regions I–II; 6–9 tons) In fact the true French Gamay, but only good for pink wine. Napa 1,002; Monterey 923; Sonoma 433; Lake 280. Total 4,140 (2,617).

Gewürztraminer (region I; 4–6 tons) Gentle, often slightly sweet, distinctively spicy white wine. Monterey 987; Sonoma 965; Napa 452. Total 3,305 (1,183).

Merlot (regions I–II; 4–6 tons) The deep red grape of Pomerol, increasingly used both for blending with Cabernet and as a 'varietal' on its own. Napa 660; Sonoma 468; Santa Barbara 191. Total 2,052 (1,129).

Petite Sirah (region II; 4–8 tons) Dark red, strong, tannic and long-lasting. Monterey 1,958; San Joaquin 1,409; Napa 810; Sonoma 784. Total 8,245 (7,831).

Pinot Noir (region I; 3–4 tons) Good lightish red with distinctive grape aroma; rarely absolutely first-rank in California. Sonoma 2,649; Napa 2,205; Monterey 1,741; Santa Barbara 623. Total 8,660 (5,580).

Sauvignon Blanc (regions II–III; 4–7 tons) Good to very good earthy/grapey dry white. Napa 1,528; Monterey 1,147; Sonoma 689. Total 6,532 (1,760).

White Riesling (also called Johannisberg Riesling) (regions I–II; 4–6 tons) Scented, fruity, ideally tart, but often soft, first-class white. Monterey 2,773; Santa Barbara 1,300; Napa 1,271; Sonoma 1,255. Total 8,742 (3,535).

Zinfandel (region I; 4–6 tons) 'California's Beaujolais'; raspberryish, spicy and good; also used for blending. San Joaquin 10,487; Sonoma 4,114; Monterey 2,225; Napa 1,966; San Bernardino 1,806. Total 26,548 (22,519).

Mexico

Hernando Cortes founded the Mexican wine industry in 1524. For 450 years it almost marked time. In the past ten years it has moved further than in its whole history.

Change started with the planting of noble grape varieties to replace the ignoble Mission. At first in the Guadalupe Valley near Ensenada in Baja California, then later in Querétaro Province, just north of Mexico City – but at an altitude of 6,700 feet (2,040 metres). The pioneers were Bodegas Santa Tomas at Ensenada, who have made good wines of Barbera as well as Cabernet and the other great French grapes. Bodegas Pinson with their Don Eugenio brand, and Cetto, with successful Cabernet and Sauvignon Blanc, developed the reputation of Baja California. But it was Pedro Domecq from Spain, investing with remarkable confidence, that really set Mexican wine on a new course. About half the 6,500 acres (2,600 hectares) in the Guadalupe Valley are theirs, producing both their very satisfactory standard Los Reyes and premium Cabernet, Zinfandel and others.

In Querétaro, Cavas de San Juan at San Juan del Rio were the pioneers, with respectable Cabernet and Pinot Noir. Domecq has joined them up in the Querétaro Mountains, while Pinson has planted farther north at Zacatecas.

The irony is that Mexican taste lags far behind the potential of Mexico's modern vineyards and wineries. All bodegas lean heavily for their profits on low-quality sweet wines, and above all brandy, to mix with Mexico's national drink, Coca Cola.

- PARRAS   Town with winery

- - -   International boundary

   Land above 2000 metres

The Pacific Northwest

Mendocino County is as far north as California's vineyards go. It is not just the redwoods that stop them, but the configuration of the coastal hills. No longer a persistent ridge, admitting fog through occasional niches, they rise and fall in disorder, beset by the perpetual drizzle the redwoods love. Not until the Oregon border does the Coast Range line up again as a sheltering sea wall. But here the ocean is different, too, with the warm North Pacific current bringing rain and modifying what might otherwise be more severe temperatures. Portland, Oregon is, after all, farther north than Portland, Maine.

Conditions, in a word, become much more European. The valleys of Oregon suffer the same sort of irregular and perplexing weather as Bordeaux or Burgundy. It seems odd that there is no history of winegrowing here. But it is barely 20 years since the pioneers began – both here and in the equally promising, but utterly different, eastern Washington.

Now the northwest has two thriving wine industries. Western Oregon rapidly found that its gentle climate produced a style of wine that California, at that juncture, was lacking: wines of moderate alcohol, good acidity and balance, flavoury but not overemphatic. Pinot Noir, at that time California's despair, showed the fresh juiciness of some of the lighter burgundies. Chardonnay made delicate wines and Riesling racy ones. There was a catch, though: rain, especially at vintage time.

Eastern Washington (and eastern Oregon) is another world. Rain at any time is improbable. The vineyards are two mountain ranges inland, the towering Cascades fending off all but a bare ten inches (25cm) a year. In this semi-desert, irrigation is essential. But the Columbia River provides endless water, and the clear skies give long, hot days contrasting sharply with the low temperatures at night.

Grapes in this northern continental climate taste quite different from either the low-key subtlety of Oregon or the frank fruitiness of California. They ripen reliably but slowly, the night-time temperatures keeping their acidity remarkably high for all their ripeness, with consequent intensity and length of flavour.

Just as distinct as their grapes are the sizes and styles of the two industries. Oregon has only 2,500 acres (1,000 hectares) and no big wineries (Knudsen Erath at Dundee making 12,000 cases a year is the biggest). Out of the total of 40, perhaps 12 regularly make wine of exciting quality. Eyrie Vineyards is the pioneer of Pinot Noir, and still normally makes the best. Amity, Knudsen Erath, Sokol Blosser, Oak Knoll, Ponzi, Elk Cove, Adelsheim, Henry, Hillcrest, Shafer, Siskiyou, Valley View and Tualatin all have established track records, with Amity, Ponzi and Elk Cove most notable for their Rieslings, Sokol Blosser for Chardonnay (and Eyrie also for Pinot Blanc and Pinot Gris).

The State strictly regulates four winegrowing regions. The Willamette Valley is the principal one. Fifty miles (80km) farther south, the Umpqua Valley is a shade warmer. Hillcrest here grows Cabernet, little seen in the Willamette Valley. Another 50 miles south the

Above: the Willamette Valley between Portland and McMinnville is the cradle of Oregon winegrowing. The northwestern feeling is strong here in the cleared woods, the timber buildings and the often grey skies. Wines are correspondingly delicate, less emphatic in flavour than wines from farther east.

Rogue River region is warmer still; its Valley View Vineyard has made good Cabernet.

There is a new, fourth, Oregon region, though, that will upset all preconceptions. It lies 200 miles (60km) to the east, just across the Columbia River from Washington's latest plantings. The landscape is bizarre here: the vineyards vast discs of green, half a mile (805 metres) in diameter, clustered like pieces on a checkerboard in a tawny waste of undulating scrub. The hub of each disc is a mighty hydrant, pumping water from the Columbia along a quarter-mile (400-metre) irrigation boom rotating on tracks among the vines.

The leader of the Washington winemaking community is Chateau Sainte Michelle, based near Seattle, away from the vineyards, but now operating a spectacular underground winery in the strange circular vineyards at Paterson.

The company owns at least half of the 10,000-odd acres (4,000 hectares) of *vinifera* grapes in the State, both on the Columbia and in the Yakima Valley around the great river bend. It makes as consistent a range of wines as any in America, including excellent Cabernet and Merlot (the best Cabernet coming from Cold Creek Vineyard), very tasty Riesling and Chardonnay, extremely clean and dry Pinot Noir sparkling wine and notable Semillon. Semillon is also a staple of Columbia Winery, the Washington pioneer in the 1960s (under the name of Associated Vintners). The real value of this splendid dry white begins to emerge after three or four years in bottle. Otis Vineyard Cabernet, Gewürztraminer, Chardonnay and dry Riesling are all very good.

The more than 50 wineries in Washington have very little track record. F. W. Langguth

(alias Saddle Mountain Winery) is a large-scale German creation. Arbor Crest at Spokane has made good Chardonnay, Riesling and Merlot from other farmers' grapes, and has now planted its own near Mattawa. Preston has made prizewinning Riesling; Quail Run, Hoodsport, Haviland and Salishan are new names to toy with.

British Columbia is a very recent arrival on the scene. The centre of the infant wine industry is the Okanagan Valley, 200 miles (320km) east of Vancouver, where a long, narrow lake runs north–south. Hybrids have been grown here for 40 years, but only in the last ten have trials with *vinifera* been encouraging. Gewürztraminer, Riesling (not to be confused with the inferior 'Okanagan Riesling') and Chardonnay have all made satisfactory light wines. Calona was the first winery in the province. Now Canada's two biggest, Andres and Brights, have establishments. Jordan Ste. Michelle (no relation to either California's Jordan or Washington's Chateau Ste. Michelle) is another large-scale operation. The best wines seem at present to be coming from smaller companies: Sumac Ridge, Claremont and Mission Hill.

Altogether in another direction, far off this map to the east, is perhaps the most surprising high-quality vineyard in North America today: in the Snake River Valley of Idaho. The Symms family pioneered the region, on the latitude of Oregon's Umpqua Valley but 400 miles (640km) from the Pacific. Like eastern Washington's, the climate is continental, made more extreme by being farther south, but also considerably higher, at 2,700 feet (820 metres). The Yakima Valley is about 900 feet.

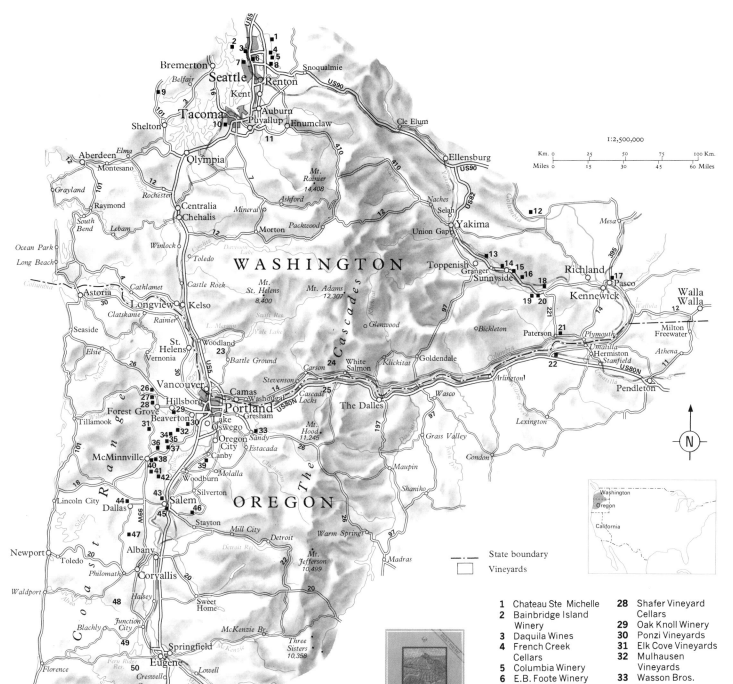

I:2,500,000

Km. 0   25   50   75   100 Km.

Miles 0   15   30   45   60 Miles

The Symms' Ste. Chapelle Winery is now the second largest in the northwest, using mainly Washington-grown grapes. But it is becoming clear that their top-quality Chardonnay and Riesling are from the 'Symms Vineyard', some 600 acres (240 hectares) near Caldwell, Idaho. The Chardonnay combines intensity with silky richness to a level that challenges the best in California. With such success, they were not alone for long: Idaho now has seven wineries.

Chateau Ste Michelle dominates the northwestern wine industry. Ste Chapelle is Idaho's very successful winery, off the map here to the southeast.

State boundary

Vineyards

1 Chateau Ste Michelle	28 Shafer Vineyard Cellars
2 Bainbridge Island Winery	29 Oak Knoll Winery
3 Daquila Wines	30 Ponzi Vineyards
4 French Creek Cellars	31 Elk Cove Vineyards
5 Columbia Winery	32 Mulhausen Vineyards
6 E.B. Foote Winery	33 Wasson Bros. Winery
7 Vernier Wines	34 Adelsheim Vineyard
8 Paul Thomas	35 Knudsen Erath Winery
9 Hoodsport Winery	36 Chateau Benoit
10 Cascade cellars	37 Sokol Blosser Winery
11 Manfred Vierthaler Vineyard	38 The Eyrie Vineyards
12 F.W. Langguth Winery	39 St-Josef's Weinkeller
13 Quail Run Vintners	40 Arterberry Winery
14 Stewart Vineyards	41 Amity Vineyards
15 Tucker Cellars	42 Hidden Springs Winery
16 Grandview (Ch. Ste Michelle)	43 Glen Creek Vineyards and Winery
17 Preston Cellars	44 Ellendale Vineyards
18 Hinzerling Vineyards	45 Honeywood Winery
19 Yakima River Winery	46 Silver Falls Winery
20 The Hogue Cellars	47 Serendipity Cellars
21 River Ridge (Ch. Ste Michelle)	48 Alpine Vineyards
22 La Casa de Vin	49 Forgeron Vineyard
23 Salishan Vineyards	50 Hinman Vineyards
24 Mont Elise Vineyards	51 Henry Winery
25 Hood River Vineyards	52 Hillcrest Vineyard
26 Cote des Colombes Vineyards	53 Bjelland Vineyards
27 Tualatin Vineyard	54 Girardet Cellars
	55 Jonicole Vineyards

263

New York, the Eastern States and Ontario

The wine tradition of the eastern states has its base long-established in upper New York State, in the area around the series of deep glacial trenches known as the Finger Lakes, just south of the great inland sea of Lake Ontario.

The sight of fields of vines comes as a shock in these distinctly northern, New England-style surroundings, with low hills covered with birch and oak around the long blue lakes, and frame houses painted cream and blue and green like any quiet corner of the northeast.

Despite the fact that the Finger Lakes and Lake Ontario help to moderate the climate, it is tough and continental: there is a short growing season and a long, bitterly cold winter.

Winegrowing started here in the 1850s and 60s, while the native American vines were the only vines that could be grown in the east (see pages 242–243). The taste of the wine they make, while it is strange to anyone reared on European wine, is a long-established part of American tradition. Furthermore, American vines are still the easiest and most productive to grow. Sparkling wines have been the speciality of the Finger Lakes from the start, and today about a quarter of the production is 'New York State Champagne'. Most of it is too fruity and sweet for educated tastes, but this is by design, not necessity: the best dry wines are excellent.

The inescapable discussion about New York wines is over the future of the traditional American varieties. The bigger wineries are all broadly based on this market, yet almost all feel that it needs modifying in the light of new knowledge – first of the French-American hybrids introduced by Philip Wagner, and more recently of European varieties: the universally demanded Chardonnay and its peers, which have led a perceptible drift towards less-foxy and even non-foxy wine, suggesting that the industry will eventually move into the mainstream of winemaking.

The central figure in the progress towards European grapes is Dr Konstantin Frank, a Russian-born German whose company, pointedly called Vinifera Wines, has had startling successes with Riesling, Chardonnay and Pinot Noir. His Finger Lakes Riesling Trockenbeerenauslese caused a sensation when it appeared in 1961.

Frank's contention, which is now well proven, is that *vinifera* vines grafted on the right rootstocks and earthed-up for protection in winter are just as hardy as American or hybrid ones. They also ripen just as well. A considerable body of conservative opinion, however, still regards them as a risky proposition – not least because California can make *vinifera* wine so cheaply and well that a different product makes commercial sense.

Until the late 1970s the Finger Lakes wineries were few but big. Then a 1976 change in State law opened the way for small 'farm wineries' – and to just the sort of open-minded experiment and competition the industry needed.

Hammondsport, at the southern end of Lake Keuka, is the centre of the industry; Taylor's is the biggest firm, making mainly traditional 'generic' wines under such names as sherry, burgundy and sauternes, but also under an 'appellation' of its own coinage: Lake Country. Taylor's was the company that led the way with French-American hybrids.

Taylor's sister company is Pleasant Valley, whose brand name is Great Western. Great Western 'champagne' is their best-known product, but the company also makes a range of 'varietals' from such hybrids as Baco Noir, Chelois and Aurora; pleasant table wines which compromise between American and European flavours.

The Gold Seal Company, although as firmly American in its traditions as Taylor's, was the first to produce a *vinifera* wine in New York. It was Gold Seal's Charles Fournier (one of the company's long line of French champagne makers) who employed Dr Frank and encouraged him to experiment with European vines. Dr Frank left to start his own company in the early 1960s.

Gold Seal now have more than 100 acres (40 hectares) of Chardonnay and Riesling at Valois on Seneca Lake. Their best champagne carries Fournier's name; popular lines are called Henri Marchant.

The third famous old name, Widmers, has held firm with American vines – was, in fact, the pioneer in selling Delaware, Isabella, Vergennes, Niagara, Elvira and the rest under their own names.

Among smaller companies, Bully Hill was started in 1970 by one of the Taylor family, Walter, to make both American and hybrid wines: both now reckoned among the best of their sort. It was probably the last to cleave to the old way of thinking. Since then, Heron Hill at Hammondsport has started as a Chardonnay and Riesling specialist, and two wineries, Glenora and Wiemer, have found that Dundee on Lake Seneca benefits from the great depth of this lake functioning as a heat storage and mollifying the climate. Both started with Riesling but have added Chardonnay and Gewürztraminer.

Meanwhile, a long tradition of grape growing along the Hudson River Valley has had a revival, with at least eight new wineries in this area, convenient for New York City, since the 1976 farm-winery law. The leader in both age and quality is Benmarl at Marlboro, the creation of the illustrator Mark Miller since the 1950s. Benmarl has both French-American hybrids and Chardonnay. Chablis would not be ashamed of some of his crisp Chardonnays after five years in bottle.

Still more encouraging is the creation of a new vineyard area on the North Fork of the eastern end of Long Island, taking advantage of an almost sea-surrounded site with its consequently relatively mild winters. The growing season is 45 days longer than in the Finger Lakes, and the soil deep, easily worked,

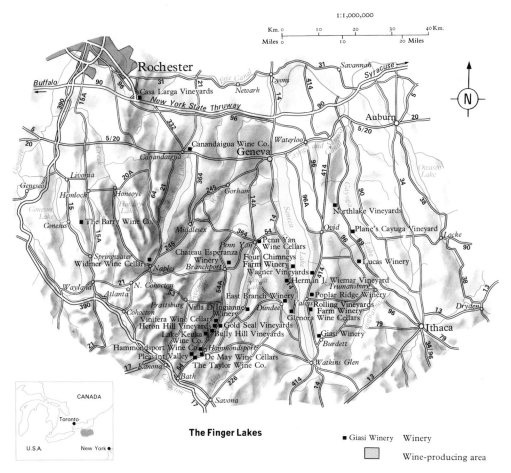

The Finger Lakes

■ Giasi Winery Winery

　　Wine-producing area

sandy loam. The Hargrave Vineyard was the pioneer here in 1973, making Chardonnay, Sauvignon Blancs, Cabernet and Pinot Noir that seemed to have closer relations in the Pacific Northwest than across Long Island Sound. At least a dozen other Long Islanders have since followed their example.

The 'fury of planting' in the east is not limited to New York. Ohio has a long history of winemaking along the south shore of Lake Erie in the Chautauqua area. Even here, hybrids are ousting American grapes, and experiments with European vines are encouraging. The low-lying islands along the south lakeshore near Sandusky seem to offer the best potential.

Michigan has a surprising number of wineries, taking advantage of Lake Michigan's huge body of deep water. (It rarely freezes.) Several, from Tabor Hill near the Indiana border in the south, to Chateau Grand Travers on a lake-girt peninsula more than 200 miles (320km) farther north, have succeeded in growing very creditable Chardonnay and Riesling, and even Merlot and Gamay – in addition to the hardier hybrid vines.

Across the state of Michigan, near Detroit, Canada reaches its southernmost point at Pelee Island in Lake Erie. Southern Ontario, along the north Lake Erie shore and particularly where the Niagara Peninsula is air-conditioned by lakes both north and south, is Canada's principal wine region. One quarter of all

Above: wine in the heart of America. Wineries were founded on the Missouri, upstream from St Louis, in the 1840s.

Canadian wine is grown between Niagara Falls and Hamilton. Bright's is the biggest winery, followed by Jordan Ste. Michelle, then Chateau Gai and Andres, with Chateau des Charmes, Hillebrand and Inniskillin (Canada's first 'estate' winery) as smaller, premium producers. Until the late 1970s, those who knew Canadian wine found it hard to take seriously the sickly sherries and pop wines that were its principal products. They still are, but in the last few years have been eclipsed in interest by a small proportion of well-made hybrid and *vinifera* table wines. Ontario Chardonnay, Riesling, Gewürztraminer are more than palatable. It has been a dramatic change, and bodes well for the future.

In the north, winter cold and the short growing season are the problems. Now the mid-Atlantic states have joined in earnest planting they face the diseases and summer humidity that frustrated Jefferson and so many would-be winegrowers in the past. Virginia has the biggest acreage, including a major Italian investment in European vines. Most of the native planters of both Virginia and neighbouring Maryland and Pennsylvania are hedging their bets, planting more of the resistant hybrids than European vines. There is little evidence yet that the public will pay the inevitably higher prices for regional *vinifera* wines, when so much good wine is available at lower prices from both California and Europe.

Above: New York's labels represent widely different traditions of winemaking.

- - - - - - International boundary

- - - - - - State boundary

▨ Wine-producing areas

1:9,500,000

Km. 0   50   100   150   200   250 Km.
Miles 0   50   100   150 Miles

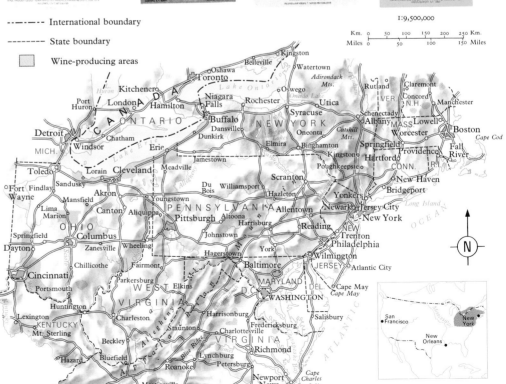

GRAPE GUIDE

Aurora See Seibel.
Baco Noir (Baco No. 1) Red hybrid from *Vitis riparia*. Great acidity but good clean dark wine.
Catawba Early development from *V. labrusca* and still one of the best. A pale red grape, makes white, red or rosé wine. Not too acid.
Chelois A Seibel hybrid. Dry red, slightly foxy.
Concord The dark red, small *V. labrusca* which is most widely planted. Needs sugaring and makes strongly foxy wine.
De Chaunac A good red French-American hybrid; dark colour; rich, heavy wine.
Delaware A pink grape, only slightly foxy; ripens well and hardly needs sugaring.
Duchess White wine; rather neutral.
Elvira White wine; now not much planted.
Isabella Sweetish dark red grape; very foxy.
Moore's Diamond Dry white; fairly neutral.
Niagara For sweet white wine; very foxy.
Seibel French-American hybrid, several varieties, including the popular Aurora.
Seyve-Villard Several varieties of white grape. Good but rather neutral.

Australia

Of all the wine countries of the colonized world, Australia took to the grape most readily and has developed its industry most consistently and to the best effect. Today she produces (admittedly as a tiny proportion of her total harvest) red and white table wines, and certain dessert wines, comparable to the best in the world.

If she played wine Test matches, it would have to be with California. Each would win the 'home' games, for the judges of each have palates tuned to their national products. A British-trained judge, I fancy, would tend to favour the wines Australia is making today. If the match were limited to white wines, there would be less of a contest. Australia now not only makes Chardonnay as well as California, in as wide a range of styles; she has made herself complete mistress of the Riesling. Australian 'Rhine' Riesling is very different from German, perhaps a little closer to Alsace, but in reality is one of the world's great originals, worth long ageing and potentially sublime. In addition, Australia long ago developed the Semillon, a second-line grape almost everywhere else, into a noble variety.

For red wines, the Shiraz or Syrah (also called Hermitage from its home on the Rhône) long held pride of place. Old Australian Hermitage was usually heavy, often soft with an appetizing salty flavour, but also often tangy with what may have been unrestrained tannins, but could taste just like iron. In careful and creative hands it can be barrel-aged and judiciously blended to make superb red wine – perhaps better than its makers themselves realize. Penfolds' Grange Hermitage is the one first-growth of the southern hemisphere.

Excellent and original as Shiraz can be, in the market place recently it has been almost swamped by the universal appeal of Cabernet Sauvignon. Cabernet pure, or blended with

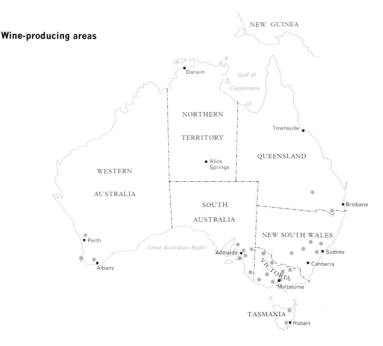

Shiraz, or blended with Malbec, or occasionally Merlot, hogs most of the limelight in Australia today. New, cooler vineyards have been opened up that suit it to perfection. Now there is evidence that Pinot Noir can probably be equally well accommodated.

Winegrowing got off to a flying start in Australia, even in Anglo-Saxon hands. The First Fleet of 1788, bringing the first permanent settlers, brought vines among its cargo; the first Governor made wine; the first number

Left: the master-blender of Australia's most luxurious speciality: 'Mick' Morris of Rutherglen in northeast Victoria uses a 'thief' to take a sample of velvety brown liqueur muscat from its ancient barrel.

of the *Sydney Gazette*, in 1803, carried an article (translated from the French) called 'Method of Preparing a Piece of Land for the Purpose of Forming a Vineyard'. By the 1820s the first of the present-day vineyards of New South Wales was making wine.

One reason that the immigrants, whether seamen, doctors, labourers or brewers, put their faith in winemaking was that natural conditions were hostile to many crops, but at least possible and sometimes excellent for the deep-rooting vine.

Almost all the early Australian colonies (unlike the American) have the Mediterranean-type climate in which the vine luxuriates. Melbourne is near the 38th parallel of latitude, the same as Córdoba in Spain (and Sicily and San Francisco). Sydney is near the 34th, the same as Rabat, the capital of Morocco. Strong wines full of sugar but lacking acidity are what you would expect – and what Australia, for more than a century, was happy to produce. Certain areas were quickly identified as having soils and microclimates with special qualities. What is strange (as Max Lake, Hunter Valley winegrower and author, points out) is how adept the settlers were at choosing their sites. They sniffed out patches of potentially good vineyard miles from anywhere. To a great extent, it is those early sites that produce the best wine today.

As to 'style' (Australia's favourite wine word), everything began to change in about 1960. Controlled fermentation (first under pressure, then by refrigeration) revolutionized the making of white wines. Where they had been made, like red, by fast fermentation to total dryness (and great strength) in open vats, losing in the process all the fragrance of their fruit, control allowed the winemaker to

Wine-producing areas

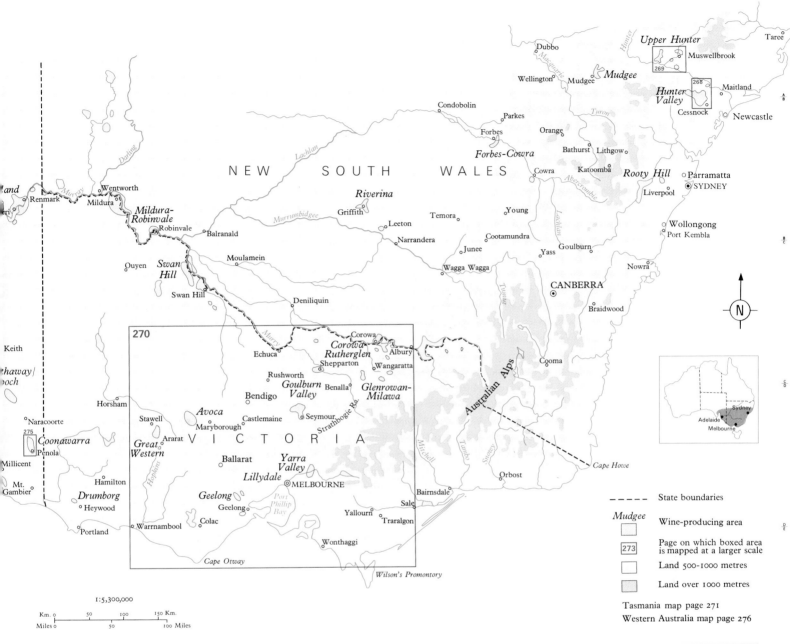

1:5,300,000

Km. 0   50   100   150 Km.
Miles 0   50   100 Miles

Upper Hunter
Taree
Dubbo
Muswellbrook
Wellington · Mudgee · Mudgee
Maitland
Hunter Valley
Cessnock · Newcastle
Condobolin
Parkes
Forbes
Orange
Bathurst · Lithgow
Forbes-Cowra
Cowra · Katoomba
Rooty Hill · Parramatta
Liverpool · SYDNEY

N E W   S O U T H   W A L E S

Riverina
Griffith
Temora · Young
Leeton
Narrandera
Junee · Cootamundra
Wagga Wagga · Yass · Goulburn
Wollongong · Port Kembla
Nowra

CANBERRA
Braidwood

Renmark · Wentworth
Mildura
Mildura-Robinvale
Robinvale · Balranald
Swan Hill · Moulamein
Ouyen
Swan Hill · Deniliquin

Cooma

270
Echuca · Corowa · Corowa-Rutherglen · Albury
Shepparton · Wangaratta
Rushworth · Benalla · Glenrowan-Milawa
Goulburn Valley
Bendigo · Seymour
Keith
Avoca · Castlemaine · Strathbogie Ra.
Maryborough
Stawell · Ararat
Naracoorte
Coonawarra
Penola
Great Western · V I C T O R I A
Millicent
Ballarat · Yarra Valley
Mt. Gambier
Drumborg · Lillydale
Hamilton · MELBOURNE
Heywood · Geelong
Warrnambool · Geelong · Port Phillip Bay
Colac
Portland
Bairnsdale
Sale
Yallourn
Traralgon
Yass
Wonthaggi
Cape Otway
Wilson's Promontory

Australian Alps
Mitchell
Tambo
Snowy
Orbost
Cape Howe

Australian Alps

- - - - - State boundaries

Mudgee   Wine-producing area

273   Page on which boxed area is mapped at a larger scale

Land 500-1000 metres

Land over 1000 metres

Tasmania map page 271
Western Australia map page 276

produce aromatic, partly sweet wines that were more like a cross between wine and grape juice. The Australian term for them is Moselle. For a while this is what many did – and some still do. The effect on consumption was revolutionary. For wine to be a refreshing drink was quite new. Dessert wines dwindled; red was rapidly overtaken by white. Even beer suffered.

Australia, in one generation, became a true wine-drinking nation, with a consumption per capita more than twice that of Britain or the United States. The great majority (about 70%) of this is so-called 'cask' wine – everyday quality in a plastic bag inside a box. The minority, meanwhile, has been refined by technological wizardry and constant open competition at Shows. Australia's wine judges deserve the credit for her standards today. The wine can be no better than they are. In a country that still has no attempt at a system of appellations, where labels can say as much or as little as they like with no central direction, the direct influence of experienced tasters is the crux of the whole business.

○ SOUTH AUSTRALIA
○ NEW SOUTH WALES
○ OTHER STATES

Above: South Australia, with 2.35 million hectolitres, and New South Wales with 850,000, account for more than 80% of Australia's total wine production of 3.85 million hectolitres a year (average figures). Two-thirds of Australian wine grapes are white varieties.

Right: table-wine production grows steadily while fortified wines, traditional for Australia, are dwindling as a proportion of the total wine production. In the mid-1970s almost half the annual crop was distilled: for brandy, for fortifying wine, or (most of it) as industrial alcohol. In 1984 only 12% was distilled for brandy and fortified spirit combined, and the total amount of distilled wine has fallen as a percentage of all wine.

Below right: Great Britain, traditionally Australia's best customer, now buys much less of her wine than the New World markets. Japan is the fastest-growing export market, with New Zealand also taking an increasing share (1984 figures).

	TABLE WINES	DESSERT WINES
1984	3.3m. hl	212.790 hl
1983	2.4m. hl	335.410 hl
1982	2.5m. hl	519.070 hl
1981	2.4m. hl	456.590 hl
1980	2.6m. hl	547.460 hl
1979	2.1m. hl	580.410 hl
1978	1.8m. hl	426.720 hl
1977	1.9m. hl	624.710 hl
1976	1.6m. hl	681.370 hl
1975	1.6m. hl	684.840 hl

JAPAN	14.3%
NEW ZEALAND	12.1%
CANADA	11.1%
USA	9.1%
GREAT BRITAIN	6.3%

New South Wales

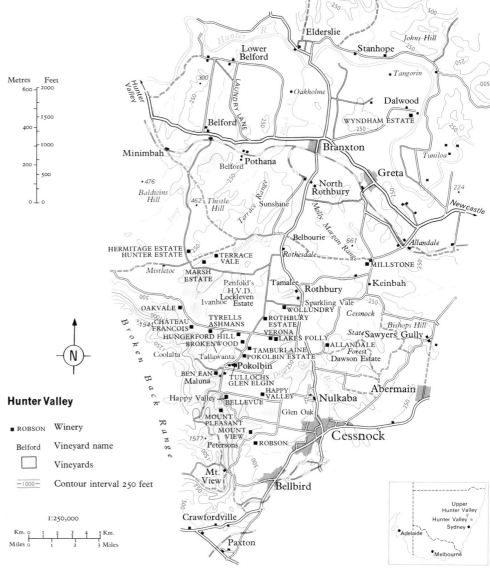

Hunter Valley

- ▪ ROBSON   Winery

Belford   Vineyard name

☐   Vineyards

—1000—   Contour interval 250 feet

1:250,000

Km. 0 1 2 3 4 5 Km.
Miles 0 1 2 3 Miles

New South Wales, the cradle of Australian winegrowing, has long since been overtaken by South Australia as the nucleus of the industry. But there remains one district 100 miles (160 kilometres) north of Sydney as famous as any in the country: the Hunter River Valley around Branxton and the mining town of Cessnock.

Exceptionally, being so far north, the Hunter area is one of the few in Australia that concentrates entirely on table wines. Its production is small. Vines were planted here (at Dalwood, near the river just east of Branxton) as early as 1828, but the soil that gave the Hunter Valley its reputation is found to the south in the foothills of the Broken Back range. Around the east side of the hills there is a strip of weathered basalt, the sign of ancient volcanic activity.

The famous old wineries of the Valley, reinforced by a later generation that includes Rothbury Estate, Hungerford Hill and Lake's Folly, lie on the lower slopes and the first flat land under the hills. The Hunter Valley is the farthest north of Australia's first-class vineyards, almost subtropical, in fact; the summer is very hot and the autumn often vexingly wet. To counter the extreme heat and northern sunshine, on the other hand, the summer skies are often cloud-covered and the direct sun diffused. The ripening process is thus lengthened and delayed, giving grape aromas time to develop.

Hermitage (or Shiraz) is the classic red grape of the Hunter, and Semillon the traditional white. Rather soft and earthy but long and spicy, Hunter Hermitage lasts well and grows complex with time. Pinot Noir is successful, too. Many think a blend of Pinot Noir and Hermitage has given some of the Hunter Valley's best wine.

Cabernet is less important here than in other areas, despite the brilliant wines made since 1966 by Max Lake at Lake's Folly.

Old-style white Hunter wines were broad and golden, soft and deceptively light in flavour when young. Such mild wines are normally a bad risk for ageing – but not the 'honey Hunters', as their friends call them. Age only intensifies and deepens their flavours and rounds out their texture. Modern technique has made them crisper and more aromatic when young, but the true virtue of 'Hunter Riesling', as the Semillon is wryly called, still lies at the end of a four- or five-year wait – at least.

The vogue grape in the Hunter, as almost everywhere in Australia, is the Chardonnay. For years it lurked in a Penfolds' blend with Semillon known as Pinot Riesling. Then in the 1970s Murray Tyrrell did what Max Lake had done with Cabernet: put down a marker no winemaker could ignore. Chardonnay now makes wines of surprising delicacy under Hunter skies, with each vintage and almost every winery adding to the accumulating experience of how long it can be kept with advantage in barrel, how long in bottle.

Three big wine companies used to dominate the Hunter Valley. Lindeman's (although established all over Australia) have a powerful

presence with their Hunter 'Riesling' and 'Chablis', 'Burgundy' (red and white) and sweet 'Porphyry' grown in the Ben Ean and Sunshine vineyards near Pokolbin. McWilliams is untypical in being the only big-scale, long-established winery to (almost) confine its operations to one state, New South Wales. The bulk of its production is in the Riverina irrigation district farther south (whose wines are much tastier than you would expect). But McWilliams' banner is at Mount Pleasant near Pokolbin, using grapes from its neighbouring vineyards, Rosehill and Lovedale.

Long-established names also include Drayton's Bellevue, Tulloch and the Tyrrell family at Ashman's who, after 120 years of a quiet life, became ringleaders of the rejuvenated region. New blood began with Max Lake, rapidly followed by a syndicate that built the spectacular Rothbury Estate, and Hungerford Hill, a company divided between the Hunter Valley and Coonawarra in South Australia, often blending the products of the two. Such practices, long common in Australia, have made clear ideas about regional characters difficult. A third large-scale newcomer was Saxonvale, which has built a reputation for outstanding white wines from vineyards at

Pokolbin, Fordwich and St. Leonards. At the same time Penfolds' old 'Dalwood Estate' became independent again, using an old name, Wyndham, for well-made, big-scale commercial 'lines', and several much smaller companies introduced new ideas and high ideals. Brokenwood and Robson have so far been the most remarkable.

Meanwhile, activity was moving farther to the northwest onto higher ground in the Upper Hunter Valley, around Wybong and Muswellbrook. After some hesitant starts, several substantial wineries now operate wholly or in part of this new region.

Rainfall is much lower here and irrigation, unknown in the Hunter Valley proper, is essential. Nonetheless, Rosemount produces very high-quality wines, particularly magnificent Chardonnays, and Arrowfield is not very far behind. 'Hollydene' is a property belonging to the rejuvenated Wyndham Estate.

Even farther west, above 1,500 feet (450 metres) up on the western slopes of the Great Dividing Range, the little district of Mudgee has also sprung to life in the last ten years. Its origins are almost as old as the Hunter Valley's, but Mudgee dwelt in obscurity until the hunt began for cooler districts to make wines of

Above: the heart of the Hunter Valley: Tyrrell's 'Ashman's' estate with the Broken Back Range to the west. Tyrrell's was the Hunter pioneer in the late 1970s with Chardonnay of international class. Five years later the Upper Hunter was in high fashion, with Rosemount Estate (label, left) winning the prizes: evidence that both districts have the highest potential.

Upper Hunter Valley

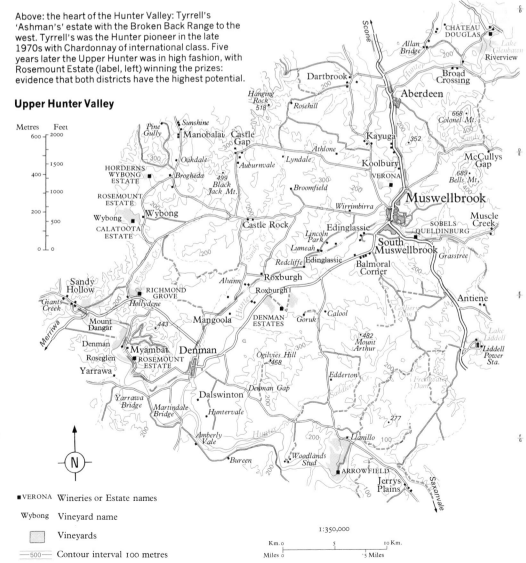

■ VERONA Wineries or Estate names

Wybong Vineyard name

☐ Vineyards

═500═ Contour interval 100 metres

1:350,000

Km. 0   5   10 Km.

Miles 0   5 Miles

more pronounced grape flavours. Intense Chardonnay is a speciality; Cabernet is doing well and Merlot is promising. The admirable Huntington, Botobolar (Australia's highest winery), Craigmoor (the oldest here) and Montrose are all small-scale concerns.

No map is needed for the Riverina irrigation district 300 miles (480km) southwest near Griffith, where canalized water from the Murrumbidgee River turns bush into orchard and vineyard. After a long career making poor-quality wines, mostly fortified, the Riverina was reborn in the era of refrigeration. McWilliams were the pioneers in making light wines of startling freshness and quality on irrigated land at Hanwood.

Other scattered vineyards in New South Wales belong some to the past, some to the future. Minchinbury is retained as the name of a Penfolds' sparkling wine made at Rooty Hill, 30 miles (50km) south of Sydney. Cowra, 50 miles (80km) west, is an exciting new development: a still-small vineyard at 1,800 feet (550 metres) whose first Chardonnays, made by Brown Brothers in Victoria and Petaluma in South Australia, fluttered dovecotes all over this intensely wine-conscious country. Even the nation's capital, Canberra, now has several small but interesting new vineyards.

269

Victoria and Tasmania

At the end of the last century, Victoria had as many vineyards as New South Wales and South Australia together: 1,200, scattered over the entire state. But phylloxera, which never reached South Australia, was fatally destructive here. Combined with agricultural expansion, it reduced the Victorian vineyards to a scattered rearguard. Significantly, they remained among the producers of Australia's most famous and individual wines.

The most important survivor was the region in the northeast, straddling the infant Murray River and the border with New South Wales at Rutherglen and Corowa. Together with Wangaratta and Milawa a little farther south they continued to specialize in dessert wines, among them Australia's finest: a 'liqueur' muscat of astonishing silky richness which may be a

descendant of the once-famous Constantia of the Cape. Morris's have perhaps made the most velvety of all these wines, but the names of Baileys, Chambers, Campbells, Stanton & Killeen and Brown Brothers all set the knowledgeable salivating. The world has no greater treat for the sweet tooth.

The traditional table wines of northeast Victoria are best summed up by the majestic Bundarra Hermitage of Bailey's, described by a French visitor as 'a three-course meal and a good cigar'. Addicts of Bundarra will either drink it young, when the effect is almost like dry vintage port, or keep it 30 years, when it will have become the epitome of 'Australian burgundy'.

Brown Brothers of Milawa have taken the opposite tack, looking outside the district for

high-altitude sites – as high as 2,500 feet (760 metres) at Whitelands, above the King River Valley – to provide cool growing conditions. The all-family team has been prodigiously successful in widening their range, scoring successes with delicate dry whites (Semillon, Chardonnay, Riesling, even pale muscat) that were previously unheard of in inland Victoria.

Of the other older vineyards that survive, the biggest are westwards along the Murray River, irrigated areas formerly used only for dessert wines and brandy. Mildura and Renmark (which is over the border in South Australia) are the most important centres of what is commonly called the Riverland (see maps on pages 266–267). At Mildura the firm of Mildara [sic] has long made some of Australia's best 'sherries'. (They are also very active with

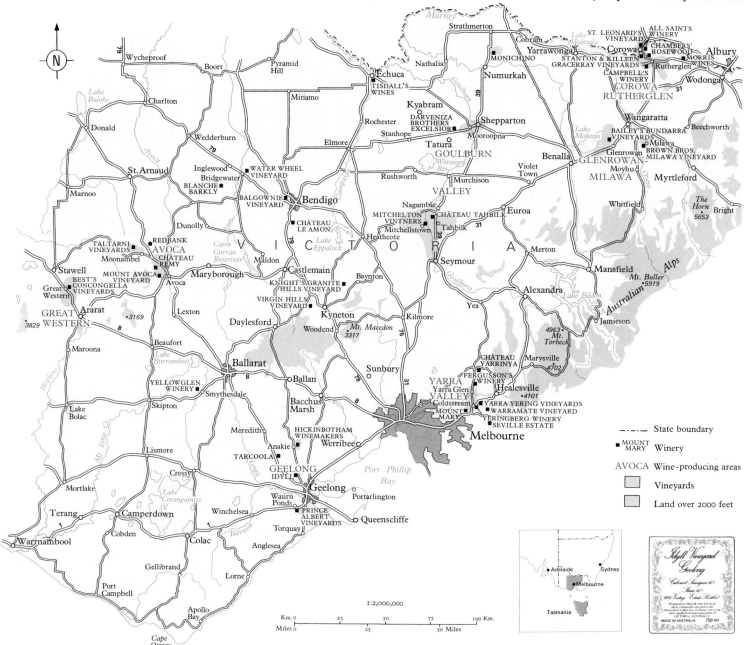

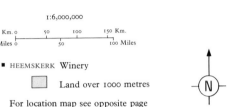

Left: dawn breaks over the stainless-steel insulated fermenting vats at Brown Brothers winery in Milawa, NE Victoria. Browns are among growers in this warm area who are finding new quality by planting high in the foothills of the Australian Alps.

1:6,000,000

Km. 0   50   100   150 Km.

Miles 0   50   100 Miles

■ HEEMSKERK Winery

☐ Land over 1000 metres

N

For location map see opposite page

table wines in Coonawarra.) The Riverland, largely cooperative country (Berri and Renmano have the best known), is following fashion by turning to table wine, and doing it surprisingly well.

Great Western, the district made famous by Seppelt's excellent 'champagne', never gave up. It lies 140 miles (225km) northwest of Melbourne, 1,100 feet (335 metres) up at the westernmost end of the Great Dividing Range, on soil that is rich in lime but otherwise infertile, like that of some of Europe's best vineyards. Seppelt and Best's, a miniature by comparison, have a long record of producing good-quality still wines as well as sparkling at Great Western. Seppelts indeed can prove, with examples, that their best vintage of Shiraz and Malbec, and even the white Ondenc at Great Western, can mature superbly.

One other district that never disappeared, although it dwindled to one estate, was on the Goulburn River 80 miles (130km) north of Melbourne. Chateau Tahbilk at Tabilk [sic], the estate, garden, stables and winery, remains like a film-set of Victorian Victoria. Tahbilk Cabernet should be drunk at about 15 years and even the staunchly conservative Rhine Riesling at eight or nine. The estate's other speciality is a lightish but also long-lived white from the Marsanne grape of the Rhône valley. Since 1969 Tahbilk has had a new neighbour, the ambitious Mitchelton Winery at Nagambie, which uses both Goulburn grapes and fruit from Coonawarra to make a wide range of very good wines (Marsanne among them).

What has happened since about 1970 in Victoria is the systematic search for good vineyard land in cooler regions. Some of the new plantations have a pre-phylloxera history, others are completely new; but the general move has been either southwards towards the sea, or up into hilly areas. That is as far as a pattern goes. Individuals have planted where the fancy took them.

The dozen-odd in the centre (that is, more or less in the gold-rush country between Bendigo, Ballarat and Avoca) show both promise and variety. This is not a notably cool region and its showpiece wines are very ripe, big-scale Cabernets from such as Balgownie at Bendigo (which also makes splendid Chardonnay and Pinot Noir), Mount Avoca, Virgin Hills at Kyneton and Taltarni at Moonambel (not far from Great Western). At the same time, Yellowglen near Ballarat and Chateau Remy (related to Rémy Martin and Krug) near Avoca are set up to make delicate sparkling wines, and show signs of real promise.

Two much cooler districts, however, have started to demonstrate another dimension, a really new taste in Australia, with Cabernet of no more than Médoc, one might even say Margaux, weight, and such a canopy of soft-fruit fragrance that their future must be brilliant. The Tisdall Winery at Echuca uses grapes from Mount Helen in the Strathbogie Ranges to make very vivid Chardonnay and Riesling, too. The Yarra Valley, almost in the outskirts of Melbourne to the north, is old wine country which used to win European prizes a century ago. Its sheep paddocks are rapidly going back under vine as people taste the vivid flavours of its fruit. Its wineries are small, but Mount Mary, Seville Estate, Yarra Yering and their neighbours are certainly among Australia's most exciting recent developments.

Across Port Philip Bay at Geelong, equally fresh and marvellously seductive wines are being made by Idyll and Hickinbotham vineyards. A 1980 Idyll Cabernet had less than 11° of alcohol, yet at five years the bloom was still on its mouth-watering fruit.

The search for a cool climate in Australia logically leads to its southernmost, and sea-girt, state: Tasmania. As Andrew Pirie, one of its pioneers, says, it is a land where the grass stays green all summer, as it does in northern Europe.

What has been seen of Tasmanian wines so far has been highly encouraging. There is a tiny fistful of players at present; the longest-established at Hobart on the South Coast. The evidence is that this is a very cool place to grow red grapes, particularly Cabernet, but that Riesling, Chardonnay and other whites, and maybe Pinot Noir, can produce exceptionally lively and delicate aromas. South Australian dry Rhine Riesling has little or nothing to do with Germany; Tasmanian Riesling could be growing on the Rhine.

The Hobart estate is called Moorilla. The climate here tests Cabernet like a medium year in the Médoc: you can find finesse and stringiness in the same glass. Riesling is much more at home. Piper's Brook and Heemskerk huddle together on a hill at the north tip of the island. The only condition that seems less than ideal in this vineyard carved out of Tasmania's rich and floriferous bush is the sea wind. Screens are necessary to preserve the vineleaves on the seaward slope. But ripening is as slow and sure as any vintner could hope for, and flavour correspondingly intense. Tasmania's future vintages are a certain pleasure in store.

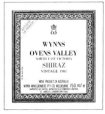

Left: Victoria's wines, traditionally strong reds and sweet muscats, are finding new, more delicate characters in new locations. Geelong (far left) is making very fine Cabernet. Yellowglen is a leader in sparkling wines.

Adelaide, the capital of South Australia, and hence of Australian winegrowing, is fittingly hemmed about with vineyards. A few still exist in the suburbs of the city. They stretch south through the Southern Vales and across the Mount Lofty Ranges to Langhorne Creek, 80 miles (130km) north up into the hills from Watervale to Clare, but most of all northeast to fill the Barossa Valley, only 35 miles (55km) from the city, a settlement that was originally largely German, and keeps certain German characteristics to this day.

With its 17,500 acres (7,100 hectares), Barossa is Australia's biggest quality-wine district. It follows the Para River for about 20 miles (30km), and spreads eastwards into the next valley, from the 750 feet (230 metres) of Lyndoch to 1,800 feet (550 metres) in the Barossa Range, where vineyards are scattered among rocky hills.

Almost every major Australian wine concern has a presence here, from Gramp's, who planted the first vines (in 1847, at Jacob's Creek), to Lindeman's from New South Wales, who today own Leo Buring's, one of the best Barossa Riesling specialists. Penfolds own at least 1,000 acres (400 hectares), including the Kalimna estate (source of at least some of their celebrated 'Grange Hermitage') and the former Kaiserstuhl Cooperative, besides having their huge blending cellars at Nuriootpa. Seppelt's began in the 1850s at Seppeltsfield, Smith's at about the same time at Yalumba, over the hill at Angaston. Salter, Hardy, Henschke and Tolley are all respected old names in the area, while more recent times have brought Hamilton's and Wynn's to the Eden Valley, and the colourful figure of Wolf Blass to Bilyara.

The Barossa industry was founded on some of Australia's best dessert wines. The stocks of mature, sometimes ancient, 'ports' and 'sherries' at such wineries as Seppeltsfield and Yalumba are extremely impressive. When modern times called for table wines, it was the Rhine Riesling, strangely enough, that Barossa did best. Growers found that the higher they went into the hills the finer and more crisply fruity the wine became. Gramp's planted a patch of schistous hilltop that a sheep would scarcely pause on, called it their 'Steingarten', and gave Australian Riesling a new dimension. Most Riesling is now grown up in the eastern hills at Eden Valley, Pewsey Vale and Springton, while the main valley grows Shiraz, Grenache and Cabernet both for table wines and 'port'.

Many Barossa reds in the past have been rather dull and dry wines. Today's winemakers have learned what earlier picking, blending with grapes from other areas, and perhaps above all ageing in small casks can do. The region that produces 'Grange Hermitage' must have potential for other great wines. Recently such companies as Smith's (with their Hill-Smith Estate), Tollana, Henschke and, most spectacularly, Wolf Blass (scarcely visible for gold medals) have justified the Barossa Valley's reputation with reds on a sturdy scale as well made as any in Australia.

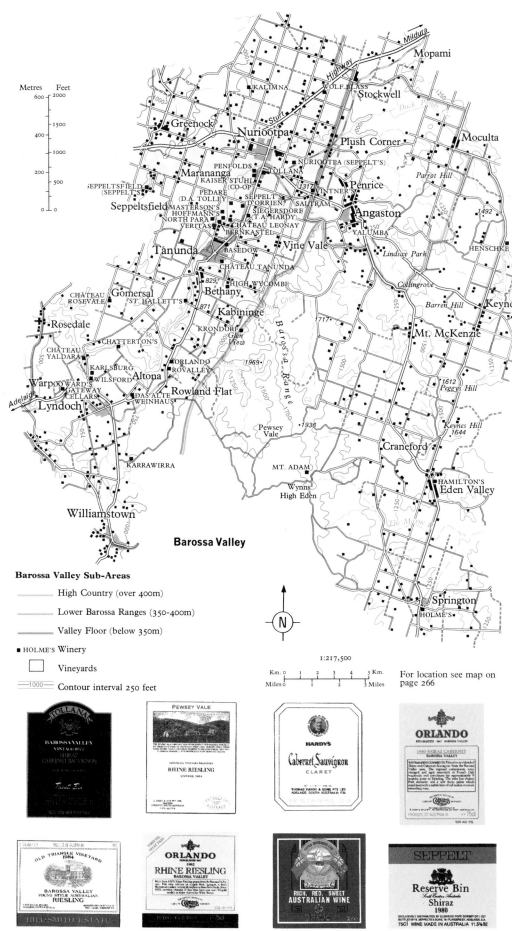

Barossa Valley

Barossa Valley Sub-Areas

High Country (over 400m)

Lower Barossa Ranges (350-400m)

Valley Floor (below 350m)

■ HOLME'S Winery

☐ Vineyards

Contour interval 250 feet

1:217,500

Km. 0 1 2 3 4 5 Km.
Miles 0 1 2 3 Miles

For location see map on page 266

The district of Clare is a mere quarter of the size of Barossa, but with almost as long a history and a singular quality of wine that attracts some of Australia's most skilful makers and blenders. Its oldest brand name, Sobel's Quelltaler, for a soft, dry white wine classified as 'hock', was for many years one of the best-known Australian wines abroad. (The firm now belongs to France's Rémy Martin.)

Limestone soil and a warmer (or at least more extreme) climate than Barossa made the Clare style sturdy yet 'structured'. The red wines are no more juicy or delicate than those of Barossa, but they can seem to have more definition; more 'backbone'. The Stanley Wine Company's 'Leasingham' reds are good examples.

Rhine Riesling from Clare has recently been used by, among others, Petaluma and Lindeman's local wineries, Enterprise, Stanley (Leasingham), Mitchell and, of course, Quelltaler to make wines with both dash and delicacy: admirable examples of Australia's best white 'style'.

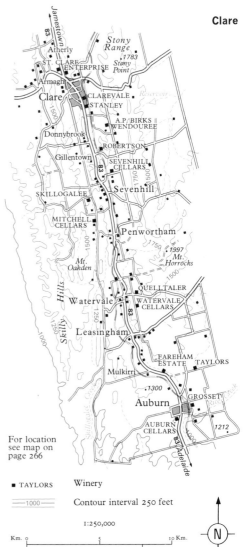

Clare

Above: the Steingarten ('garden of stones') is an apt name for one of Barossa's best vineyards. Gramp's Orlando planted Rhine Riesling on a parched hilltop overlooking the valley. The resulting wine is intensely perfumed and long-lived.
Right: the Petaluma winery near Adelaide is among those using Rhine Riesling grapes from Clare, choosing them in preference to Barossa or Coonawarra Riesling.
Left: Shiraz reds and Rhine Riesling whites are still the staples of the Barossa Valley.

For location see map on page 266

■ TAYLORS   Winery

——1000——   Contour interval 250 feet

1:250,000

Km. 0   5   10 Km.
Miles 0   5 Miles

273

South Australia 2

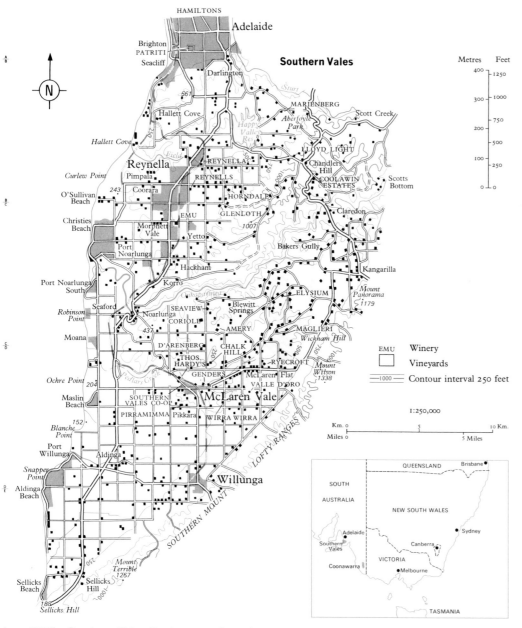

The Southern Vales district starts almost in the southern outskirts of Adelaide. It is South Australia's oldest: the John Reynell who gave his name to Reynella planted his vines in 1838.

For most of the intervening century and a half 'Chateau Reynella' claret and 'port' have been respected names, and the original underground cellar Reynell built one of the historic spots of Australian wine. Today it is the headquarters of the almost equally ancient firm of Thomas Hardy & Sons. Young Tom Hardy went to work for John Reynell in 1850 before buying the Tintara property down the road. Talking to one of the flourishing Hardy family can make it seem like yesterday.

Natural conditions for the vine could hardly be better than in this coastal zone, a narrow band between the sheltering Mount Lofty Ranges and the temperate sea. There is usually adequate rainfall, a warm but not torrid summer, good air drainage to prevent frosts but a reasonably cool vintage season. Some of the earliest vineyards were actually in Adelaide and the foothills of Mount Lofty to the east. Much the most famous is Penfolds' 'Grange', from which at least a small part of their fabulous Hermitage still comes (much of the historic hill site has been sold as building land). The Piccadilly Valley in the same area has been staked out by the celebrated little Petaluma winery as a very cool microclimate for Chardonnay and Pinot Noir.

Vineyards near the city were soon followed by others across the Onkaparinga River in McLaren Vale. Here, and increasingly in the cooler foothills of the encircling range, is where most of the vineyards are today. They seem equally capable of producing sonorous 'ports', macho Shiraz (the true speciality of the area) and very characteristic and lively Chardonnay, Riesling and Sauvignon Blanc.

The battle of the takeovers has made many changes among the respected old names in the area. Seaview Cabernet is one that has kept its identity; D'Arenberg marches on with husky red wines, Pirramimma with more subtle ones. Coriole, Clarendon, Marienberg, Haselmere, Wirra Wirra and Thomas Fernhill are newer names whose early vintages have promised well in widely different veins.

Meanwhile, a few kilometres to the east, one of Australia's smallest but most historic little wine regions continues to produce its own idiosyncratic wines. Langhorne Creek is a bed of deep alluvium irrigated by (deliberate) flooding from the Bremer River. Bleasdale is the name of the vineyard that Frank Potts planted in the 1860s. He also cut down the titanic red gums thriving on the deep soil, sawing and working them with his own hands into (among other things) his winepress, yachts and a piano.

Langhorne Creek wines (the other little estate here is called Metala) have a distinctive salty (some say sweaty) flavour that you will either love or hate. Some of Australia's best blenders (Wolf Blass among them) find them the perfect seasoning.

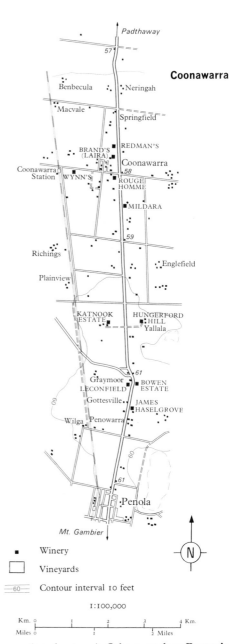

Coonawarra

- ■ Winery
- ▢ Vineyards
- ═60═ Contour interval 10 feet

1:100,000

Km. 0   1   2   3   4 Km.
Miles 0   1   2 Miles

Above: Wynn's handsome winery building on the edge of Coonawarra's famous red earth is familiar from the labels of its Cabernet and Riesling (left).

Farther left are labels from Adelaide's Southern Vales and Langhorne Creek (off the map to the east). Chateau Reynella is now the headquarters of the house of Hardy.

Two hundred and fifty miles (400km) to the south of the Adelaide region and its essentially Mediterranean climate, early settlers as far back as the 1860s became aware of a very odd patch of ground. Just north and east of the village of Penola, a long, narrow rectangle, only nine miles by less than one (14 by 1.5km) of completely level soil was distinctively red in colour and crumbly to touch. A mere 18 inches (45cm) down the red soil changed to pure limestone, and a mere five feet (1.5 metres) to a constant table of pure water.

No land could be better designed for fruit growing. The entrepreneur John Riddoch started the Penola Fruit Colony and by 1900 the area, under the name of Coonawarra, was producing large quantities of a quite unfamiliar kind of wine, largely Shiraz, low in alcohol but brisk and fruity: in fact, not at all unlike Bordeaux.

The soil was not the only reason. Coonawarra was considerably farther south, and hence cooler, than any other South Australian

vineyard, and only 50 miles (80km) from an exposed coast, washed by the Antarctic current and fanned by westerlies all summer. Frost is a problem in spring and rain at vintage time – enough to make a Frenchman quite nostalgic.

This great resource, an Australian vineyard producing wines with a quite different structure from the majority, was for a long time appreciated by very few. It has only been since the wine boom began in the 1960s that its potential has been fully realized, and the big names of the wine industry have moved in.

A substantial part of the strictly limited vineyard area belongs to growers who sell their grapes – to such as Petaluma at Adelaide, for example, who blend the wine with something a little more powerful, from Clare. Wynn's is much the biggest winemaking landowner, with 1,700 acres (690 hectares). Mildara has 600 acres (250 hectares), Lindemans 500 acres (200 hectares), Hungerford Hill (from the Hunter Valley) 350 acres (140 hectares). Penfolds also own land. Katnook is a big estate with 500

acres (200 hectares). Others, such as Bowen's, Brand's Laira, Redman and Leconfield, are far smaller – more on the scale of a little St-Emilion château.

Shiraz was the original Coonawarra speciality. In the late 1960s, however, Mildara demonstrated that the conditions were just as near to ideal for Cabernet, and added Riesling with some success. Now, with Chardonnay in high demand, Riesling is giving ground to the vogue grape.

Coonawarra, strictly limited by the extent of its eccentric soil, has not been able to satisfy the demand for its type of cool-climate wines. Diligent research in country farther north and nearer the sea produced an alternative in the Padthaway and Keppoch area. Since the late 1970s several companies, led by Lindemans, Seppelts and Hardys, have been very happy with this new source of grapes. Padthaway in particular gives extremely tasty fruit. Australians are inveterate blenders between districts. Perhaps others have something to learn.

Western Australia

The first colonists of Western Australia were almost as quick to start winemaking as those of New South Wales. The Swan River Valley, just upstream from the capital, Perth, saw its first vintage in 1834. From the searing heat of the summer, with dry winds from the interior keeping temperatures close to 100°F (38°C) for weeks, the early vintners realized that their forte was going to be dessert wines.

It still is, yet curiously it was an experimental lot of dry white wine, made of Chenin Blanc in 1937, that put Western Australia on the nation's wine map. Houghton's 'White Burgundy' became a staple even in the east, recognized as a consistent bargain. Originally it was a huge golden wine of intense flavour. It has been tamed today to be soft yet lively, dry yet faintly honeyed in character.

It is hard to imagine old-fashioned techniques producing a better white wine from so hot a region. Perhaps this is why it took Western Australia another 30 years to realize what potential lay elsewhere in this vast, almost-empty state.

Perth has a blistering summer, but 200 miles (320km) down the coast the influence of the Antarctic current and on-shore westerlies is felt in much more temperate conditions. The southwestern corner of the Australian continent shares these conditions with the south coast of Victoria and South Australia. When the move to cool-climate areas began in the late 1960s, Western Australia produced two, with quite different conditions.

The first was the Margaret River region, enclosed within the coastal bulge of Cape Mentelle 160 miles (270km) south of Perth. 'The Margaret' has Mediterranean conditions, with plenty of winter rain but dry, warm summers tempered by on-shore winds. Australia has few landscapes as green, or forests as splendid as the soaring karri and jarrah woods of this area.

The second was Mount Barker and the Frankland River region, just inland from the port of Albany. Average temperatures are much lower here, particularly in autumn, giving a long, cool ripening season. Rainfall is lower, too, but tends to occur in summer.

The two areas produced their first wines in the early 1970s. Vasse Felix was the first Margaret River label, followed by Moss Wood – both the enterprises of doctors. Judges immediately recognized a quite remarkable concentration of flavour in both red wines (Cabernet, Shiraz, Pinot Noir, Merlot and a little Zinfandel) and white (Riesling, Chardonnay, Semillon and Sauvignon). Sandalford, Houghton's neighbour and rival in the Swan Valley, rapidly moved in with a large plantation. Robert Mondavi from California became enthused and gave his backing to the ambitious 220-acre (90-hectare) Leeuwin Estate. Chardonnay from this estate made headlines. Now there are well over 1,200 acres (400 hectares) of vineyard and a score of wineries in the area. The current show-stopper with Cabernet is the Cape Mentelle Winery.

If Mount Barker has grown less dramatically, it shows no less promise. The pioneers were Forest Hill (which started as a government

research project) and Plantagenet Vineyards.

Grapes show their distinctive aromas equally forcefully here, but the red wines have less body and 'fat'. Time will tell how well they mature. Whites, especially Riesling, promise to be extremely aromatic and well balanced. Houghton's (who have also moved north of Perth, to a relatively cool coastal area called Moondah Brook) have so far decided for Mount Barker rather than the Margaret River.

It may be that in due course each will specialize: the former in white wines, the latter in reds. But meanwhile their very tasty fruit is adding a new dimension to the wines of the two big old Swan River wineries. One of the most interesting developments is the Verdelho of Madeira, originally planted for dessert wine but now used to make a totally original white, with aromas and longevity that are a reminder of Madeira, but the full, soft, tasty style known to Australians as 'white burgundy'. Houghton and Sandalford both make excellent examples, from Moondah Brook and 'The Margaret' respectively.

The potential of the west coast is by no means realized yet. South of Perth a peculiar dusty grey soil formation known as Tuart Sands is adding another dimension. Light-bodied Chardonnay and Cabernet from Capel Vale, and Chenin from Peel Estate, are likely to encourage even more experiments.

Right: wines from the west have added a new dimension to the flavour of Australia: aromatic, clearly defined, balanced and refreshing.

The Southwest

Bunbury
THOMAS
LESCHENAULT
CAPE VALE
Boyanup
Capel
Busselton
Donnybrook
HAPPS WINES
MOSS WOOD
CULLENS
WRIGHTS
Metricup
VASSE FELIX
Jarrahwood
Ballingup
Margaret River
.369
Nannup
Bridgetown
CAPE MENTELLE
LEEUWIN ESTATE
Witchcliffe
Blackwood
Donnelly River
Karridale
Glenoran
Augusta
Manjimup
Frankland
Cranbrook
ALKOOMI
FRANKLAND RIVER
Pemberton
Kendenup
Rocky Gully
PERILLUP
CHÂTEAU BARKER
FOREST HILL
PLANTAGENET WINES
Shannon
Northcliffe
Denbarker
Mount Barker
NARANG
Porongurup
411
NARRIKUP
654
Windy Harbour
TINGLEWOOD
REDMOND
King River
Walpole
Kenton
GOUNDREY
Denmark
Espera
Peaceful Bay
Wilson Inlet
Torbay
Albany

1:2,250,000
Km. 0 25 50 75 Km.
Miles 0 25 50 Miles
■ Winery
Contour interval 200 metres

1:250,000
Km. 0 2 4 6 8 Km.
Miles 0 1 2 3 4 5 Miles
■ PETERS Winery
100 Contour interval 100 metres

WESTERN AUSTRALIA
Perth
Albany

Metres Feet
300 1000
750
200 500
100 250
0 0

Upper Swan
Geraldton
Mt. Mambup
224
SWANVILLE
EVANS & TATE
WESTFIELD
BASKERVILLE
TWIN HILLS
VISNICA
Millendon
HENLEY PARK
LAMONTS
PETERS
Pioneer 230
GLENALWYN
Herne Hill
Mt. Oakover 240
REVELRY
VINDARA
ADRIATIC
HIGHWAY
West Swan
HOUGHTON
Middle Swan
VIGNACOURT
WALDECK
SANDALFORD
Wexcombe Swan View
Caversham
Midvale
Lockridge
VIVEASH
VALENCIA
Eden Hill
Bassendean
Bellevue
ELLENDALE (SVETA MARI)
Guildford
Perth
South Guildford
RIVERSIDE
OLIVE FARM
Kalgoorlie
Redcliffe
Helena
Swan
Darling

Chardonnay LEEUWIN ESTATE Margaret River 1988

1983 Jane Brook Estate Chenin Blanc Vignacourt Wine Cellars

CHENIN BLANC 1984 MOONDAH BROOK ESTATE

1982 VASSE FELIX Cabernet Sauvignon

HOUGHTON CABERNET SAUVIGNON 1982

MOUNT BARKER Cabernet Sauvignon 1981

SANDALFORD MARGARET RIVER ESTATE 1984 AUSLESE RHINE RIESLING

1981 EVANS & TATE GNANGARA SHIRAZ

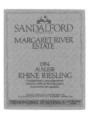

New Zealand

Such wine industry as New Zealand had before the 1970s was a matter of purely local interest. Interested locals knew that good, even very good, red and white wines could be made, both near Auckland and along the east coast of North Island. The nation's cultural attitudes needed to change, however, before a serious wine industry could begin. When the time was ripe it took off faster than anyone expected, to reach standards few can have dreamed of. In 1960 the country had less than 1,000 acres (400 hectares) of vines, mainly north of Auckland. By 1980 there were 14,000 acres (5,600 hectares), 2,000 of them on South Island in a totally new area producing some of the best wines of all.

Winegrowing New Zealand lies between the 35th and 44th parallels of latitude – in European terms, between Morocco and the Rhône valley. The effects of latitude are countered, though, by the surrounding ocean, by the strong prevailing westerlies, by the effects of the mountains on their rainclouds: factors that give the two islands a wide range of growing conditions.

It is only unfortunate that in enthusiasm for the relative coolness (compared with Australia) of the New Zealand climate, many planters took Germany as their model and planted Müller-Thurgau. New Zealand should not be judged by the produce of a second-rate grape. Almost everything it has planted since is making more exciting wine.

Auckland's vineyards, mainly in the Huapai Valley just north of the city, were established early in this century for the usual (and the best) reason: the locals, settlers from Dalmatia, wanted wine where they were working, which was in the kauri-gum forests around the capital. They persisted despite a rainy and subtropical climate; several of the families in what is now a surprisingly successful red-wine area have Dalmatian names. As in the Hunter Valley in New South Wales, cloud cover moderates what could be over-much sunshine and gives steady ripening conditions. But vintage-time rain and rot are problems.

Some wine had been made at Hawkes Bay, on the central east coast of North Island, for more than a century. Conditions here could hardly be better, with Ruapehu and the other high central peaks of the island to windward catching the rain, and a variety of deep glacial and alluvial soils. Some Cabernets made by McWilliams (of New South Wales) here in the 1960s indicate the long-term promise of the area.

To the north of Hawkes Bay, Poverty Bay, with its city of Gisborne, provides a similar environment with less of a mountain backdrop, hence more cloud and rain, particularly in autumn. Phylloxera is also a problem here. Gisborne has made a name recently specifically for white wines, Gewürztraminer and Chardonnay being particularly successful.

The innovation that may well promise most of all is the move to South Island. The (Yugoslav-founded) Montana Wines led the way. The narrow plain between mountains and sea at Marlborough, near the north tip, offered a very sunny but relatively cool climate and deep soil, practically no rain (irrigation is essential); only rather too much wind for comfort. Already its grapes are making notably aromatic wines. Will the quality be even better farther south? Planting near Christchurch may provide an answer soon.

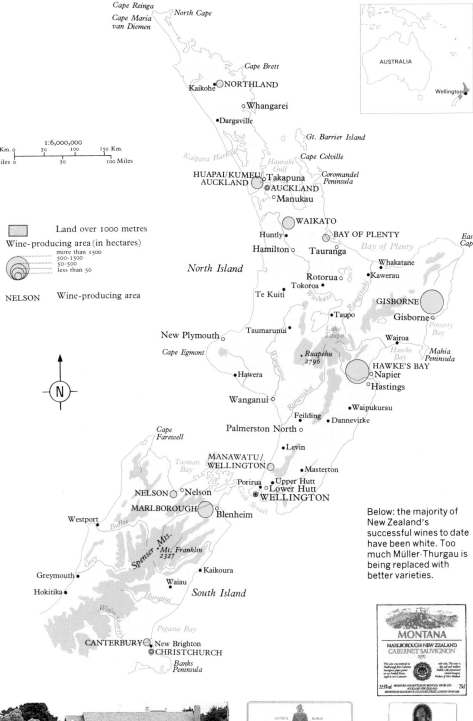

Land over 1000 metres

Wine-producing area (in hectares)
- more than 1500
- 500-1500
- 50-500
- less than 50

NELSON — Wine-producing area

Below: the majority of New Zealand's successful wines to date have been white. Too much Müller-Thurgau is being replaced with better varieties.

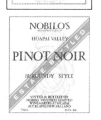

Above: Nobilo's vineyards at Huapai, north of Auckland, are at the heart of New Zealand's original wine industry. Growing conditions here are warm but humid. Newer vineyards are in cooler and drier areas.

South Africa

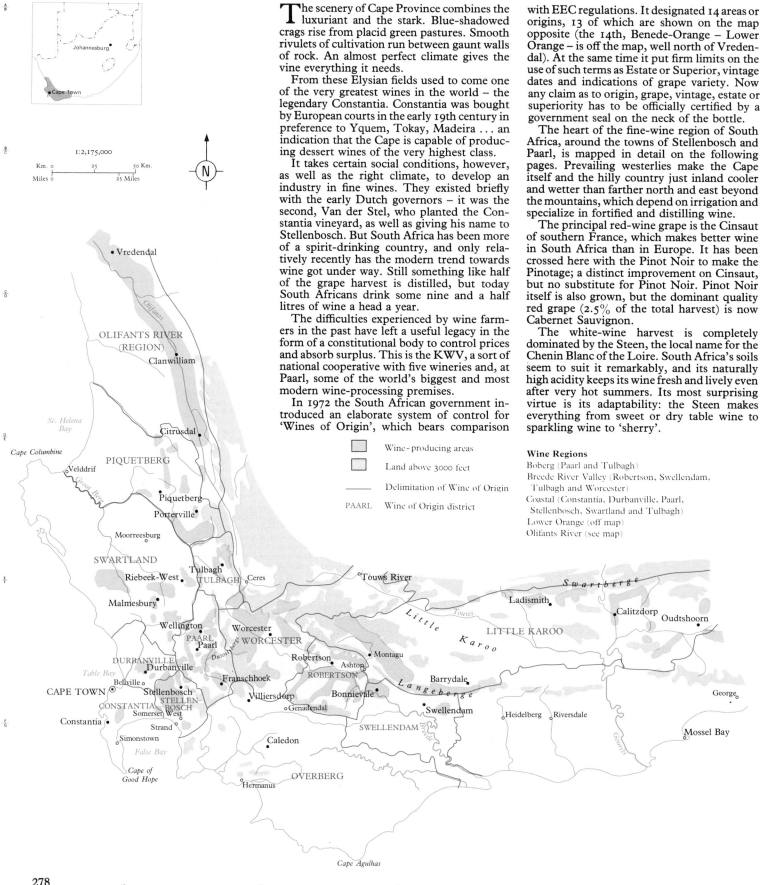

The scenery of Cape Province combines the luxuriant and the stark. Blue-shadowed crags rise from placid green pastures. Smooth rivulets of cultivation run between gaunt walls of rock. An almost perfect climate gives the vine everything it needs.

From these Elysian fields used to come one of the very greatest wines in the world – the legendary Constantia. Constantia was bought by European courts in the early 19th century in preference to Yquem, Tokay, Madeira ... an indication that the Cape is capable of producing dessert wines of the very highest class.

It takes certain social conditions, however, as well as the right climate, to develop an industry in fine wines. They existed briefly with the early Dutch governors – it was the second, Van der Stel, who planted the Constantia vineyard, as well as giving his name to Stellenbosch. But South Africa has been more of a spirit-drinking country, and only relatively recently has the modern trend towards wine got under way. Still something like half of the grape harvest is distilled, but today South Africans drink some nine and a half litres of wine a head a year.

The difficulties experienced by wine farmers in the past have left a useful legacy in the form of a constitutional body to control prices and absorb surplus. This is the KWV, a sort of national cooperative with five wineries and, at Paarl, some of the world's biggest and most modern wine-processing premises.

In 1972 the South African government introduced an elaborate system of control for 'Wines of Origin', which bears comparison with EEC regulations. It designated 14 areas or origins, 13 of which are shown on the map opposite (the 14th, Benede-Orange – Lower Orange – is off the map, well north of Vredendal). At the same time it put firm limits on the use of such terms as Estate or Superior, vintage dates and indications of grape variety. Now any claim as to origin, grape, vintage, estate or superiority has to be officially certified by a government seal on the neck of the bottle.

The heart of the fine-wine region of South Africa, around the towns of Stellenbosch and Paarl, is mapped in detail on the following pages. Prevailing westerlies make the Cape itself and the hilly country just inland cooler and wetter than farther north and east beyond the mountains, which depend on irrigation and specialize in fortified and distilling wine.

The principal red-wine grape is the Cinsaut of southern France, which makes better wine in South Africa than in Europe. It has been crossed here with the Pinot Noir to make the Pinotage; a distinct improvement on Cinsaut, but no substitute for Pinot Noir. Pinot Noir itself is also grown, but the dominant quality red grape (2.5% of the total harvest) is now Cabernet Sauvignon.

The white-wine harvest is completely dominated by the Steen, the local name for the Chenin Blanc of the Loire. South Africa's soils seem to suit it remarkably, and its naturally high acidity keeps its wine fresh and lively even after very hot summers. Its most surprising virtue is its adaptability: the Steen makes everything from sweet or dry table wine to sparkling wine to 'sherry'.

Wine Regions
Boberg (Paarl and Tulbagh)
Breede River Valley (Robertson, Swellendam, Tulbagh and Worcester)
Coastal (Constantia, Durbanville, Paarl, Stellenbosch, Swartland and Tulbagh)
Lower Orange (off map)
Olifants River (see map)

Wine-producing areas
Land above 3000 feet
——— Delimitation of Wine of Origin
PAARL Wine of Origin district

Semillon (or 'Green Grape') and a so-called Riesling have long been grown with mixed success, and Palomino for sherry, but other traditional white grapes have been of second-rate quality. The Rhine Riesling is a recent introduction. Government policy actually excluded Chardonnay and Sauvignon until very recently, and there is still not enough to give substantial evidence. For sweet wines, farmers inland grow red Muscadel and Muscat of Alexandria (which they call Hanepoot).

The famous Groot Constantia estate at the Cape (illustrated on page 280) is now a state winery of 250 acres (100 hectares) specializing in red wines. Going north up the coast the Malmesbury and Piquetberg areas, lacking hills to catch the rainclouds, are not ideal wine country, but make port-style reds and some dry whites. Farther north still, Olifantsrivier is even drier and irrigation is essential. Table-winemaking is relatively new here; the tradition is for distilling wine and sweet grape juice.

Among the mountains in Tulbagh the conditions are better and some of the best white wines, both light Steens and Rieslings and strong wines for sherry making, are grown. The Montpellier, Twee Jonge Gezellen and Theuniskraal estates are all well known. Tulbagh is included with Paarl in the demarcated origin Boberg, which is reserved for 'ports' and 'sherries'.

Worcester, Robertson, Swellendam and the Klein Karoo are specialists in dessert and distilling wines, although here too (at Robertson in particular) the move towards table wines is perceptible.

Right: trends in planting of the top grape varieties since 1960 shows the rise to dominance of Chenin Blanc (KWV Survey 1984). Below: the relative importance in production of the eight wine districts into which the Cape is divided for statistical purposes. Wine is classified as 'good' unless it is destined for distilling. Production is increasing, but the proportion of good wine has fallen in recent years to below 50%, after being in the majority in the early 1970s. Most of the wine from the biggest producers is distilled. Worcester also makes good fortified wine and brandy.

WORCESTER	23.6%
PAARL	15.2%
ROBERTSON	15%
STELLENBOSCH	13%
OLIFANTS RIVER	13%
ORANGE RIVER	8.7%
MALMESBURY	7.1%
MONTAGU	4.4%

Below: South Africa's exports are nearly all made by the KWV, the state cooperative. Canada has overtaken Great Britain as the biggest customer: in the mid-1970s Britain took 54% of exports, Canada 26%. Continental Europe, taking 10%, includes Scandinavia. (1984 figures.)

CANADA	42%
GREAT BRITAIN	23%
CONT. EUROPE	10%
USA	9%

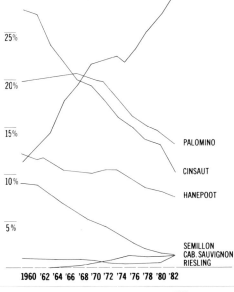

30% OF TOTAL VINES — CHENIN BLANC
25%
20%
15% — PALOMINO
CINSAUT
10% — HANEPOOT
5%
SEMILLON
CAB. SAUVIGNON
RIESLING
1960 '62 '64 '66 '68 '70 '72 '74 '76 '78 '80 '82

Above: Cape labels carry estate or maker's names plus grape name.
Left: calm white Cape Dutch farms are the châteaux of the Cape, set among soaring crags.

Above: South Africa's Seal of Origin. A blue band certifies origin; red the vintage. A green band guarantees that 80% of the wine is of the grape variety named. The word Estate is limited to some 70 properties that bottle only the wine they grow. A 'Superior' wine must be 100% of the variety named. Centre are identification numbers.

Paarl and Stellenbosch

Stellenbosch is the centre of estate wine-making in South Africa and the seat of the country's biggest wine company, the Stellenbosch Farmers' Winery. Paarl is the capital of the sherry and dessert-wine industry and the headquarters of the state cooperative KWV (Kooperative Wijnbouwers Vereniging).

The winemakers of Paarl do not let you forget that their vineyards lie on almost the equivalent latitude to Jerez. The sherry they make, using Spanish methods, including both the solera system and flor yeast, has been their fortune since they started it in the 1930s. They do make the best imitation of Spanish sherry in the world – to most people virtually indistinguishable from the original. The chalky soil of Jerez, which gives the wine its ultimate finesse, is all they lack.

Paarl is also the centre of the industry in Tawny, Ruby and Vintage port-style wines – which again, at their best, are truly remarkable.

Today's demand for table wines has been met with concerted efforts to convert from the old burly, coarse style of reds to cleaner, grapier flavours, and estates are emerging that are well placed to do this. With the adaptable Steen, good white wine is scarcely a problem. The soils of Stellenbosch vary from light and sandy in the west, which is largely planted with Steen grapes, to decomposed granite at the foot of the Simonsberg and Stellenbosch mountains in the east, where the tradition is good solid reds of Cinsaut, Pinotage and Cabernet. Each vintage sees more skill and new successes, both in the individual estates and in the cooperatives that still make a large proportion of the crop.

The finer wines seem on the whole to be coming from estates that are either in the southern sector, near Stellenbosch, open to the ocean at False Bay, or high enough in the hills for altitude and cooling winds to be a factor. As everywhere, there are exceptions where a notably intelligent and dedicated grower turns received ideas on their head. One example is De Wetshof, a property at Robertson, formerly considered too hot for table wines, now producing some of the Cape's freshest new-style whites.

Left: Groot Constantia near Cape Town once made one of the world's great wines. It is a museum today.
Above: the floor of the Hex River Valley looking west towards Buffelshoekkloof and the peaks of Hexrivierberge.

Below: labels from estate wines – Meerlust and Zandvliet among them – and from the giant wine concerns such as the KWV, the state cooperative. Nederburg, which is not technically an estate, makes a wide range of wines including the notable intensely sweet dessert wine Edelkeur.

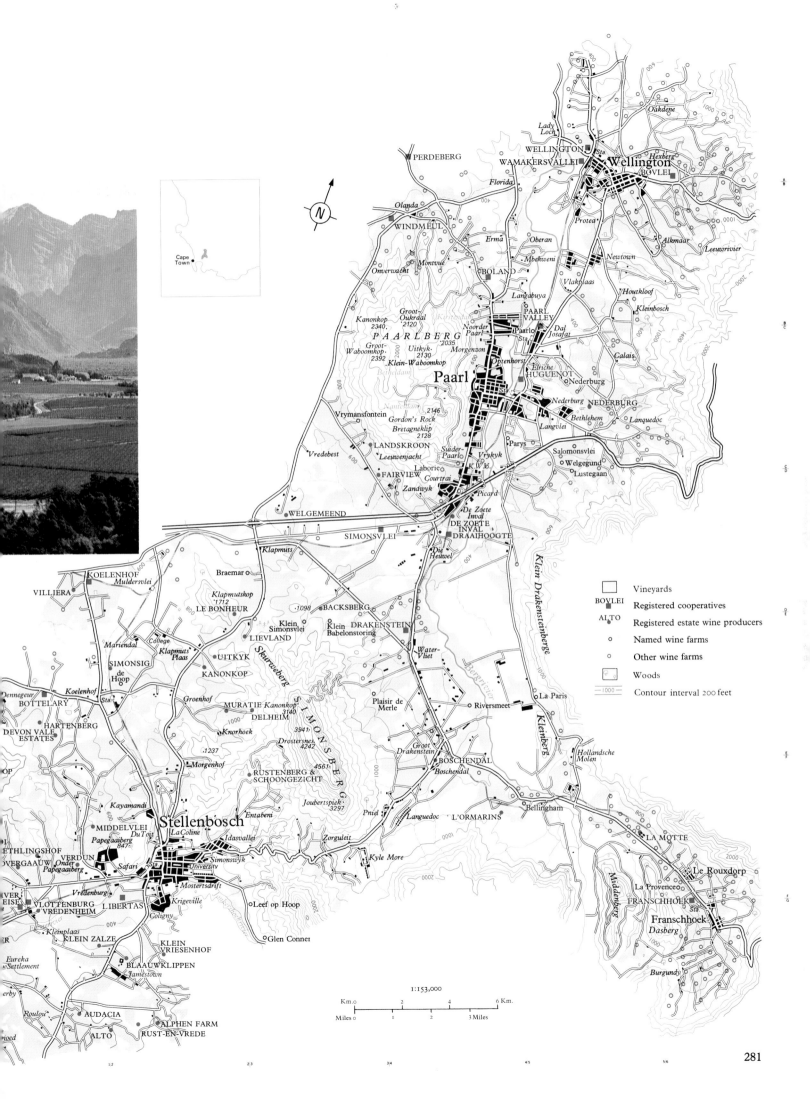

South America

Above: the vineyards of Chile and Argentina share a spectacular skyline: the 20,000-foot (6,000-metre) ridge of the Andes. To both it means the vital guarantee of unfailing water supplies for irrigation. Without the melting snow most of Chile's vineyards, and all of Argentina's, would be barren scrub.

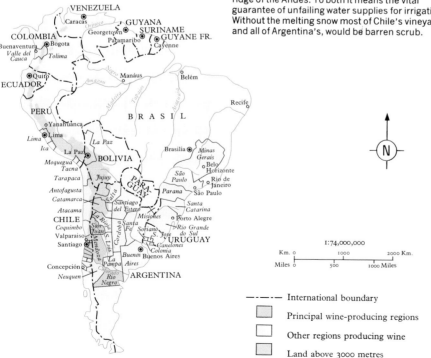

1:74,000,000

Km. 0   1000   2000 Km.
Miles 0   500   1000 Miles

- - - - - International boundary

☐ Principal wine-producing regions

☐ Other regions producing wine

☐ Land above 3000 metres

South America makes one bottle in seven of the world's wine. Argentina is number five in the world's production table. Yet the world hears little more of Argentine wine than it does of Russian, and for the same reason: the domestic market is apparently insatiable; Argentinians use wine like the French and Italians. We can expect to hear more, however, for two reasons: Argentina needs exports, and her wine has reached a level of quality the world cannot ignore.

The industry is organized on a mass-production basis. There are few wines of individual interest. No Napa Valley. Instead, an endless stream of sound, satisfying and enjoyable standard wines from plump, ripe, healthy grapes growing under ideal conditions.

Seventy percent of the vineyards of Argentina (or more than half those of South America) are in the state of Mendoza, under the Andes and on the same latitude as Morocco. San Juan to the north has the second-biggest acreage. The climate is arid and the massive flat vineyards are irrigated from the Andes by canals. Two-thirds of the volume of the USSR is produced here on one-third of the acreage. With little disease in the dry air, on ungrafted roots and with abundant water, the yields are enormous. Equipment is modern and technology sophisticated. One new winery, San Telmo, has produced 'varietal' wines that would do credit to California. Peñaflor, the biggest, also reaches very creditable standards.

Apart from the traditional Criolla, now dwindling, the most widely planted grape is the Malbec, one of the less important varieties of Bordeaux. Its best wine is rich and vigorous. Plantings of Cabernet and Pinot Noir are on the increase, and the good Cabernets can take their place with those from Chile as wines of serious merit. Red wines are generally much better than white, which either tend towards the oxidized condition of sherry (the Spanish Pedro Ximénez is the main grape, and the name Jerez is freely used) or are just strong and dry, without the aromas of fruit. Strangely, one of the best of the country is a sparkling wine made by a subsidiary of Moët & Chandon and sold without a blush as Champagne.

Argentina's red 'jug' wines are appetizing and good, inclining to sweetness in the Italian style. Those of Chile, by contrast, are drier and more French in feeling.

The centre of Chilean winegrowing lies only 150 miles (240km) due west of Mendoza. But in those 150 miles the Andes climb to 17,000 feet (5,200 metres). The highest peak in the Andes, Aconcagua, reaches 23,000 feet (7,000 metres) just to the north. There is a radical change of climate here, with the arid zone which reaches into northern Chile from the Bolivian plateau crossing the Andes into Argentina. Arica in northern Chile gets one millimetre of rain a year. Santiago gets 370. Concepción, only 250 miles (400km) farther south, gets 1,320. Mendoza gets 200.

Santiago's rainfall is still scarcely enough to grow grapes without irrigation; an astonishing network of canals and streams originated by the Incas supplies most of the vineyards with water. But the oceanic climate seems to suit

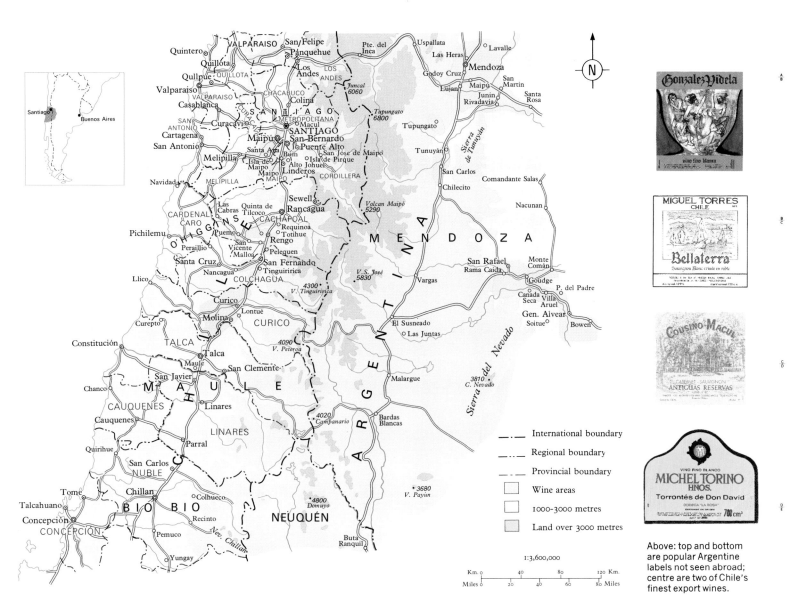

International boundary
Regional boundary
Provincial boundary
Wine areas
1000-3000 metres
Land over 3000 metres

1:3,600,000

Km. 0   40   80   120 Km.
Miles 0   20   40   60   80 Miles

Bordeaux's grapes perfectly. The valleys of the Aconcagua, Maipo, Cachapoal and Maule rivers, cooled by the sea to the west and the Andes soaring in the east, are planted with Cabernet, Merlot, Sauvignon and Sémillon, Bordeaux fashion. And much of their wine could be worthy of Bordeaux, given better cellar conditions.

The Cabernet is fruity, tannic, balanced and long-lived. Treated like claret, bottled after two years and kept for another four or five, it can develop into very fine wine. Too often, however, it is kept in old barrels of 'rauli', the indigenous beech, which are evidently difficult to keep properly clean. Stainless steel and new oak are commodities beyond the reach, alas, of most Chilean bodegas.

As for Chilean white wine, conservative local taste looks for age and oxidation, while a new vogue, promoted by Miguel Torres from Catalonia, demands it cold-fermented, young and fruity. The grapes are excellent for either: Riesling, Sauvignon, Sémillon and Chardonnay are all available.

With light but fertile soil and complete control of the water supply, grape growing looks absurdly easy. Phylloxera has never reached Chile. Vines can grow on their natural roots without grafting. So a new vineyard is made by simply sticking canes of the desired vines in the ground at two-metre intervals. Within a year they are growing happily as new vines and within three years are bearing their first grapes.

The best-known bodegas lie in and around Santiago: Santa Carolina right in the city, Cousiño at Macul in the eastern suburbs, Undurraga to the west, Concha y Toro southeast at Pirque, Santa Rita south in the Maipo valley. Some fine lighter Cabernets come from farther south in Talca province, from Viña San Pedro and Torres at Lontué, and the excellent Los Vascos estate in Colchagua. Heavier ones come from farther north, notably Viña Errazuriz at Panquehue. Chile's most modern big bodega, José Canepa, uses grapes from both Maipo and the cooler Lontué in Talca. The best wines of any of these bodegas are excellent in any company.

Brazil and Uruguay both have flourishing wine industries for the home market. The centre of Brazilian viticulture, the province of Rio Grande do Sul, lies on the same latitude as Mendoza and Santiago, just north of Buenos Aires. Rainfall here is high and the climate mild and humid. *Vinifera* grapes have suffered in the past, and American vines have been grown. Nonetheless the University of California has encouraged new planting and such enterprises as National Distillers, Cinzano, Pedro Domecq and Moët & Chandon have taken an interest in a local supply for the growing Brazilian market. Cinzano has a vineyard near Recife only ten degrees from the equator which produces two grape crops a year. The area is dry and the vines are forced to go dormant and make new buds by taking off the irrigation.

The newest surprise in this roll call of regions is wine of quite startling quality from Peru. The Tacama vineyards in Ica province benefit from the cold Pacific alongside in much the same way as those of the Central California coast. Their Cabernet, Sauvignon Blanc and a *méthode champenoise*, made with the advice of Professor Peynaud from Bordeaux, are another revelation of what the least expected quarters of the globe are learning to do.

England and Wales

The past few years have seen the dawn of confidence in English wine. It used to be thought that England lies too far north for the grape to ripen – and besides that there is too much rain.

The fact remains, however, that in the early Middle Ages the monastic vineyards of England were extensive and by all accounts successful. Had it not been for England's acquisition (by the marriage of Henry II to Eleanor of Aquitaine in 1152) of Bordeaux they would probably have continued to this day. But they faded away in the later Middle Ages, and since then only spasmodic attempts at winegrowing in England and Wales were made until recently.

Now England and Wales have some 1,000 acres (400 hectares) of vineyard – including the many small, non-commercial but enthusiastic growers – almost all in white grapes. Most are in the south of England. The map shows the sites of the main vineyards today in comparison with known medieval vineyards.

Müller-Thurgau and Seyval Blanc (a French hybrid) are the two most popular vines at present, being early ripeners and disease resistant. Various German crosses, including the new Reichensteiner, show signs of promise. The wine normally needs the help of sugar, as it does in Germany and often in Burgundy. But the quality has improved from a tentative start to steady and confident progress. England now has experienced winemakers who can make good white wines almost every year. Imports can be cheaper, but there is a brisk market (abroad, too) for the sort of aromatic and original wine England and Wales are making now.

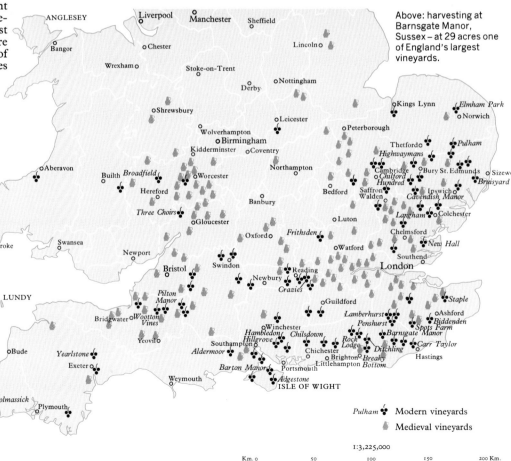

Above: harvesting at Barnsgate Manor, Sussex – at 29 acres one of England's largest vineyards.

Left: almost all modern English wine is white. There is already an elegant country-house style of label design: the Hambledon motif comes from the first cricket club, which was at Hambledon.

Pulham ● Modern vineyards

Medieval vineyards

1:3,225,000

Spirits

The World of Spirits

The wine countries are limited to the temperate zone, and to places where Mediterranean civilization has set the pattern of life. Spirits have no such climatic or cultural limits. They can be made wherever they are wanted. Distilling is not agriculture, with its roots directly in the ground, but industry. Where water runs and a truck can go, you can make whisky, brandy, gin, rum or any other spirit.

But there is an élite among spirits – and for very much the same reasons as there is an élite among wines. Occasionally a complex set of natural conditions adds up to a style and quality of drink that can be imitated but never reproduced. These are the spirits that bear their geographical origins like a coat of arms, and whose production, like winemaking, is partly science, mostly hard work, but also partly a creative art. International trade in spirits consists almost entirely of these superior products.

Spirits can be distilled from anything that can be induced to ferment; anything containing sugar which can be turned into alcohol. Mankind has shown real ingenuity in finding fermentable and distillable supplies in the most unlikely places.

Listed here are some of his resources, from wine, fruit and berries to milk, hogweed, potatoes and cactus. The figures below and on the facing page show his capacity for drinking (or at least for paying for) spirits, and the remarkable way it has fluctuated over the last decade and a half.

Apples
Applejack: New Jersey, USA; Batzi: Switzerland; Calvados: France; Eau de vie de cidre: Northern France; Trebern: Austria

Apricots
Barack pálinka: Hungary

Cactus
Cocui: Venezuela; Pulque: Mexico

Cherries
Kirsch: Austria, Germany, Switzerland; Kirsebaelikoer: Denmark

Coconut-palm juice
Arak, Arrack: East Indies

Dates
Arak, Arrack: Middle East, North Africa; Zibib: Egypt, Middle East

Fruits
Alcools blancs, ... Geist, ... Wasser: France, Germany, Switzerland; Aliziergeist: Alsace; Baie de Houx: France; Prunelle: Alsace, Loire

Gentian
Enzian, Gentiane: Germany, Switzerland

Grain
Akvaviitti, Akvavit: Denmark, Finland, Norway, Sweden; Bourbon whiskey: USA; Genever: Netherlands; Gin: England, North America; Korn, Schnapps: Germany; Vodka: Poland, USSR; Whiskey: Ireland, North America; Whisky: Scotland

Grape skins
Aguardiente: Portugal, Spain; Bagaceira: Portugal; Grappa: California, Italy, Uruguay; Komovica: Yugoslavia; Marc: France; Tresterschnapps: Germany

Hogweed
Bartzch: Northern Asia

Milk
Awein, Koumiss: Tartar Russia; Skhou: Caucasus

Molasses
Arak, Raki: Indonesia; Basi: Philippines; Rum: Central and S. America, Java, Madagascar, New England, Philippines, West Indies

Pears
Birngeist: Germany; Császarkorte: Hungary; Poire Williams, Williamine: France, Switzerland

Plums
Mirabelle, Quetsch: France, Germany, Switzerland; Sljivovica, Slivovitz, Szilva, etc: Austria, Bulgaria, Hungary, Romania, Yugoslavia

Potatoes
Akvaviitti, Akvavit, Aquavit: Denmark, Finland, Norway, Sweden; Schnapps: Germany; Vodka: Finland, Sweden

Rice
Arak, Arrack: Far East; Ragi: Java; Shochu: Japan

Sugar cane
Aguardiente: Chile, Colombia, Ecuador; Cana: Paraguay, Uruguay; Cane spirit: South Africa; Ron: Colombia; Rum: West Indies

Watermelons
Kislav: USSR

Wine
Arak, Arrack, etc (or dates, rice, coconut palm): Africa, Far East, Middle East; Armagnac: France; Brandy: Australia, California, Germany, Greece, Italy, South Africa, Spain; Cognac: France; Coñac, Kanjak, Konjak, etc: Chile, Eastern Europe, Greece, Portugal, Spain, Turkey, USSR; Mastika: Balkans, Cyprus, Greece; Ouzo: Greece, Middle East; Pisco: Chile, Bolivia, Peru; Rajika, Raki, etc: Balkans, Middle East, Turkey; Vinjak: Yugoslavia

WORLD CONSUMPTION OF SPIRITS

The consumption of spirits by nations over the last decade and a half is shown in litres, at an average strength of 50% alcohol, per head of the population. Asterisks indicate estimated consumption when official figures are not available. The figures for Luxembourg reflect the large border traffic in alcoholic drinks – the actual per-head-of-population consumption is considerably lower.

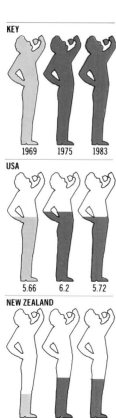

KEY

1969	1975	1983

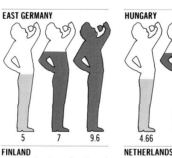

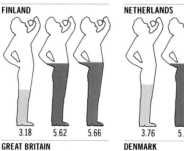

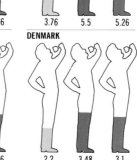

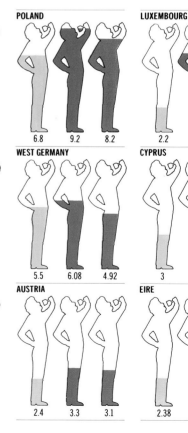

Country	1969	1975	1983
EAST GERMANY	5	7	9.6
HUNGARY	4.66	7	9.6*
POLAND	6.8	9.2	8.2
LUXEMBOURG	2.2	7	8*
USA	5.66	6.2	5.72
FINLAND	3.18	5.62	5.66
NETHERLANDS	3.76	5.5	5.26
WEST GERMANY	5.5	6.08	4.92
CYPRUS	3	3.2	4.6
NEW ZEALAND	2.04	3.54	3.38
GREAT BRITAIN	1.6	2.94	3.26
DENMARK	2.2	3.48	3.1
AUSTRIA	2.4	3.3	3.1
EIRE	2.38	4.06	2.8

PRINCIPAL NATIONAL PRODUCTS

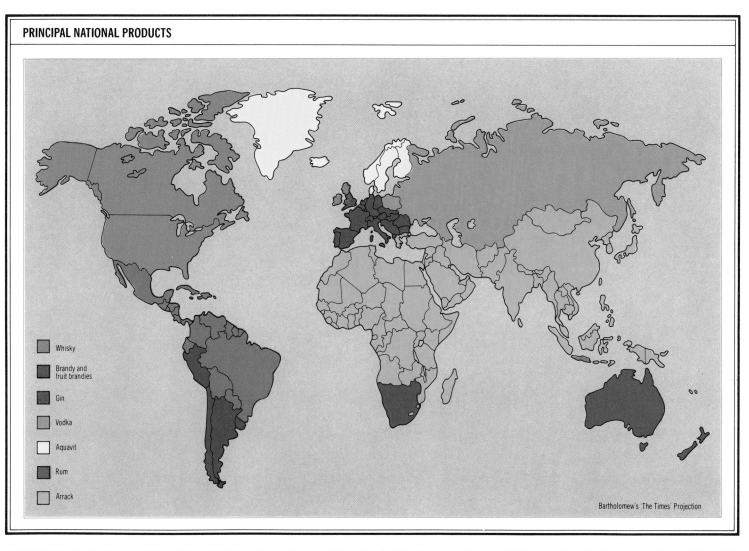

Whisky

Brandy and
fruit brandies

Gin

Vodka

Aquavit

Rum

Arrack

Bartholomew's 'The Times' Projection

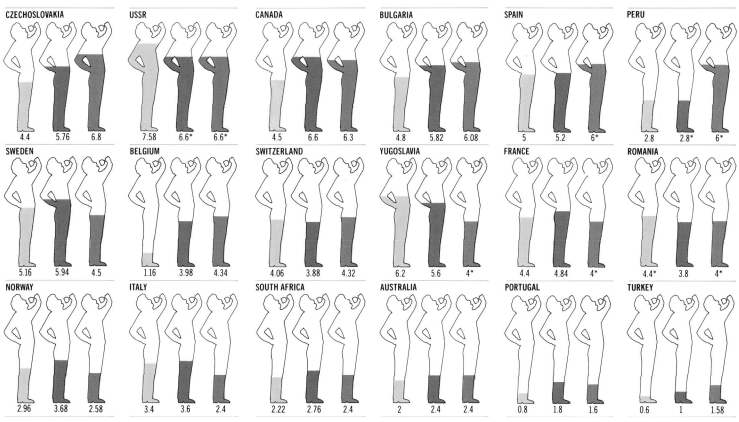

CZECHOSLOVAKIA
4.4 5.76 6.8

USSR
7.58 6.6* 6.6*

CANADA
4.5 6.6 6.3

BULGARIA
4.8 5.82 6.08

SPAIN
5 5.2 6*

PERU
2.8 2.8* 6*

SWEDEN
5.16 5.94 4.5

BELGIUM
1.16 3.98 4.34

SWITZERLAND
4.06 3.88 4.32

YUGOSLAVIA
6.2 5.6 4*

FRANCE
4.4 4.84 4*

ROMANIA
4.4* 3.8 4*

NORWAY
2.96 3.68 2.58

ITALY
3.4 3.6 2.4

SOUTH AFRICA
2.22 2.76 2.4

AUSTRALIA
2 2.4 2.4

PORTUGAL
0.8 1.8 1.6

TURKEY
0.6 1 1.58

287

How Spirits are Made

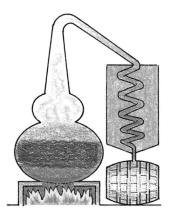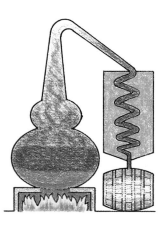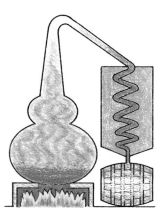

Above: the pot still or alembic; the original design and still the best. A kettle holding 1,200 litres of white wine (in the case of cognac) sits on a fire. Highly volatile elements vaporize first. These are condensed in the copper coil (which is immersed in cold water)

and collected in a barrel. They are known as headings (for whisky, foreshots). As it heats further the alcohol vaporizes and is in turn condensed and collected in another barrel. This is 'brouilli' (or in whisky 'low wines'). The less volatile part goes into a third barrel; these

tailings (for whisky, feints) and the headings are added to the next kettle of wine to be distilled. Then the process is repeated, using the brouilli, or 'low wines', in place of wine. This time the middle third is brandy (or whisky).

Above: brandy flows from the condenser of a pot still in Cognac. The clear white spirit is running into a brass tray with a funnel into the oak barrel below.
Below: one of the few big distilleries of Cognac has six identical pot stills built over brick furnaces. In the smaller vase-like tanks on top (right) the wine is warmed by the vapour before it goes into the alembic.

Put at its simplest, distilling is a way of concentrating the strength and flavour of any alcoholic drink by removing most of the water. It relies on the fact that alcohol is more volatile than water – which is to say that it boils at a lower temperature. If you boil wine in a saucepan it will lose all its alcohol and most of its aromatic elements into the air long before the pan is dry. So if you collect the steam and condense it you will have the alcohol and very little of the water; you will have, in fact, brandy.

This fact has been known in the East for thousands of years. It entered the Western World in the 14th century, via the Arabs, whose words *al embic* (meaning a still) and *al cohol* we still use.

The original form of still, the pot still (illustrated left), is simply a kettle on a fire, with a long spout, usually curled into a worm, in which the vapour condenses. Even now this is the best design and is used for all the highest-quality spirits. Its great advantage is that it gives total control. The distiller can choose precisely what part of the vapour he wants to

Above: the art of distilling arrived in Europe late in the Middle Ages. This engraving of 1519 from Strasbourg is one of the earliest illustrations of a still.

keep, as containing the desirable proportion of alcohol and flavour. He can eliminate undesirable elements which vaporize sooner than alcohol and 'pass over' first or which are less volatile and 'pass over' later. The pot still's disadvantage is that it is slow, it needs a craftsman to operate it, and it needs to be cleaned out and filled up after every operation.

Most modern distilling is done in the patent continuous still, which was invented by an Irish exciseman called Coffey. The illustration on the right shows how it uses steam to vaporize the alcohol, letting the waste run away continuously, which makes it faster in operation than the pot still and much cheaper to run. The only drawback is that you must distil at very high strength in order to get a clean enough spirit to drink; you cannot choose precisely which 'fraction' of the vapour you will keep. Continuous-still spirits therefore normally have less of the congenerics, as the flavouring elements which 'pass over' with the alcohol are called. They have less of the original taste and smell of the raw material; they also need less time in wood to mature.

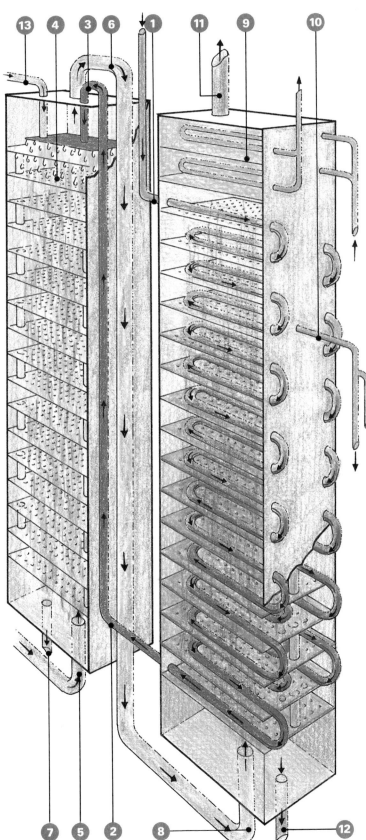

Left: most spirits are made in the continuous still. It takes in a steady stream of 'wash' (which can be wine, beer, or fermented molasses) at one end and emits a stream of spirit at the other: a more efficient and time-saving process than the pot still on the opposite page. The continuous still consists of two columns as much as 80 feet (25 metres) high. Cold 'wash' goes into the 'rectifier' column at **1** and passing down twisting pipes is heated by mounting hot vapour. At **2** it emerges very hot from the rectifier and is taken to the top of the 'analyser' **3** where it flows into an open trough. The trough overflows, letting the hot wash fall on to perforated plates **4**. Meanwhile very hot steam enters at **5**, rises and meets it, causing the volatile elements to boil away immediately. They pass as vapour out of the analyser at **6**. Most of the water in the wash continues to fall down the column and is drained away at **7**. At **8** the spirit vapour (from **6**) re-enters the rectifier. As it rises in this column, being cooled by the incoming wash pipes, less volatile elements ('feints') condense first and fall back to **12**. From there they are pumped to join the fresh wash in the analyser at **13** and go through the process again. The spirit alone reaches the top. A cold-water radiator **9** finally condenses it and it flows out of the column at **10**. Only the most volatile elements (the equivalent of the foreshots of a pot still) remain as vapour and emerge at **11**. While this method is much less laborious than the old one, there is not the nicety of control; the distiller does not choose an exact moment to separate spirits from foreshots and feints. To be safe he must treat a smaller and stronger fraction of the total as drinkable spirit and reject or redistil the rest. Hence the use of the pot still for the fine spirits (e.g. cognac and malt whisky) which need to retain more of the congenerics which give flavour.

Cognac

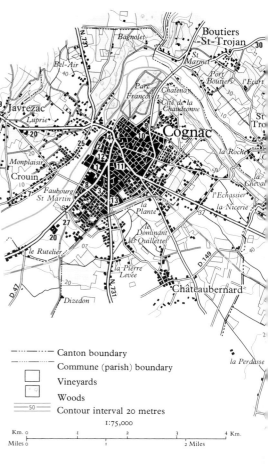

The cognac houses

⚭ 1 Martell		▲ 17 Croizet-Eymard
⚭ 2 Hennessy		▲ 18 Dist. de Segonzac (Martell)
⚭ 3 Rémy Martin		▲ 19 Dist. de Galienne (Martell)
⚭ 4 Otard-Dupuy		▲ 20 Dist. de St-Martin (Martell)
⚭ 5 Courvoisier		▲ 21 Moulineuf (Martell)
▲ 6 Ricard-Bisquit Dubouché		⚭ 22 Hennessy
▲ 7 Hardy		▲ 23 Viticulteurs Réunis
⚭ 8 J. G. Monnet		⚭ 24 Coop. de Cognac et
⚭ 9 Camus		Vins Charentais
⚭ 10 Salignac		⚭ 25 Hennessy
⚭ 11 Prince de Polignac		⚭ 26 Hennessy
⚭ 12 Castillon		⚭ 27 Martell
⚭ 13 Larsen		▲ 28 Hennessy
⚭ 14 Hine		▲ 29 Hennessy
▲ 15 Tiffon		▲ 30 Hennessy
⚭ 16 Frapin		⚭ 31 Delamain

▲ Distillery   ⚭ Warehouse

Above: tasting ancient cognac from the barrel.
Below: fume-blackened warehouse roofs in Cognac.
Bottom: cognac matures at least three years in cask.

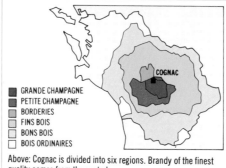

GRANDE CHAMPAGNE
PETITE CHAMPAGNE
BORDERIES
FINS BOIS
BONS BOIS
BOIS ORDINAIRES

Above: Cognac is divided into six regions. Brandy of the finest
quality comes from the central zones.
Below: since the mid-1970s the USA has overtaken France as
the chief buyer of cognac, and Japan and Hong Kong have
become major consumers.

		1975 / 1983
FRANCE	10.6%	24%
GREAT BRITAIN	12.7%	17%
HONG KONG	7.1%	
JAPAN	8%	
USA	8%	20.8%
WEST GERMANY	8% / 7.7%	**1975** / **1983**

There is an uncanny fresh-grape sweetness
about good cognac, as though the soul of
the vine has been etherealized and condensed.
It makes you think not just of wine but of great
wine – it has the same elusive complexity; the
same raciness and excitement.

And yet the wine it comes from is not great at
all. The Charente vineyards, now given over
exclusively to cognac, were originally the poor
pedlars of very inferior stuff to seamen from
Britain and the Low Countries coming to buy
salt. It was only in the 17th century that some
of these immigrants began 'burning' the wine.
But once the experiment had been made the
word got around. A Mr Martell came from
the Channel Islands, a Mr Hennessy from
Ireland and a Mr Hine from Dorset. Cognac
had found its métier.

The Appellation Contrôlée Cognac covers
almost two whole *départements* just north of the
Gironde estuary, the whole sparsely contoured
basin of the River Charente, and even the small
islands off-shore in the Bay of Biscay.

Some 37,500 farmers in this area grow white
grapes, and as many as one in ten have a still of
their own for distilling the wine. The variety
they grow – today mainly Ugni Blanc, known
locally as St-Emilion – gives wine without

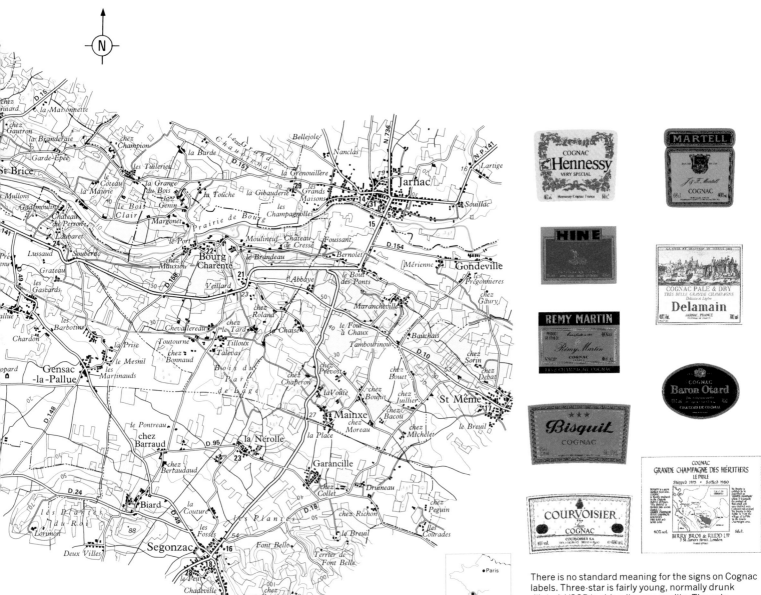

many other possibilities; only about $7\frac{1}{2}$% alcohol and with as much as 10 grammes per litre of acidity. Indeed, they tend to pick before the grapes are fully ripe to be sure of this acidity, which makes it the perfect wine for distillation.

The quality of the resulting brandy depends almost entirely on the soil. At its best, in the heart of the Charente (small map, page 290) it it is as chalky as in Champagne. Hence the similarity of names between the two unrelated regions. Concentric circles of progressively less chalky and (for this purpose at least) inferior soils surround it. From a topsoil of 35% chalk, with 80–90% chalk only 20cm down, to 25%, to 15% is the progression from Grande Champagne to Petite Champagne to Borderies. The corresponding progression in the cognac is from maximum finesse to a more full-bodied and high-flavoured spirit – still excellent in its way. Beyond the small and central Borderies, however, the three Bois – Fins, Bons and Ordinaires – have yellower, richer soil which results in less delicate cognac with a distinct *goût de terroir* or earthiness.

Cognac is distilled in the winter months as soon as possible after the wine has stopped fermenting. The pot still used is shown on page 288. The wine is warmed in a tank beforehand and then boiled away by a steady gas fire. Two distillations are needed to get the fraction with exactly the right amount of alcohol and congenerics: it runs from the still for the second time, white and clear, at about 70% alcohol: one barrel of brandy for every ten of wine which went in.

New cognac is harsh, overstrong, incomplete. Ageing in oak is as much part of the process as distillation. The forest of the Limousin or Tronçais, to the northeast, supplies the perfect material: oak with a high porosity and rather low tannin content. Three years in a Limousin barrel is the legal minimum for any cognac; most good ones in practice have three and VSOPs (Very Special Old Pale) have five or more. The airy *chais* where the barrels lie are scattered throughout the region, their roofs blackened with a fungus which lives on the fumes, for the rate of evaporation is daunting: as much cognac is lost into the air every year as is drunk in the whole of France.

Seven years is now the maximum age which the law allows a firm to claim on the label for its cognac, however old it may really be. The former practice of keeping unblended vintages has been outlawed as being impossible to control. One kind of certified older cognac, however, is still available: cognac that has been 'early-landed' in a foreign port in barrel and kept in the customs cellar while it matures. The London docks have long been famous for the gentle and exquisite, faintly sweet and faintly watery-tasting, very pale old cognac which has passed 20 or 30 years gradually losing alcohol and gaining finesse in their particularly damp cellars.

Normal commercial cognac is diluted to 40% alcohol with distilled water, and its sweetness and colour are adjusted with sugar and caramel. Each shipper has his house style, which he keeps constant from year to year.

The large map shows the heart of Cognac: the country between Cognac, the prosperous little capital, Jarnac and Segonzac. The area south of the Charente is in Grande Champagne, north is mainly Fins Bois and northwest, facing Cognac, is Borderies. The principal distilleries and warehouses are marked. In the well-tended but rather dull countryside the characteristic building is the *logis*: the old fortified farmhouse, high-walled and gated. Many have stills: the greater part of cognac is made by farmers and sold by them to be matured by shippers.

Armagnac

The world has only one other brandy which can be compared with cognac – and it too comes from western France, from an area which at its closest point is only 80 miles (130 kilometres) from the Charente. But armagnac shares only its subtlety and its very high standards with cognac, for the two brandies are poles apart in style and in the techniques used to make them.

Armagnac is a remote country region, hilly in the south, known as Haut-Armagnac, and almost a plain in the north – Ténarèze and Bas-Armagnac, the areas that give the best-quality brandy. Bas-Armagnac might be called the Grande Champagne of the region, except that in place of chalk it has sandy soil.

Apart from the soil and Armagnac's generally warmer climate, the big differences between armagnac and cognac come from the type of still and the local wood. The armagnac still is something between a pot still and a continuous still, a sort of double boiler in which the wine is distilled once, at a much lower strength than most spirits: 53% as against cognac's 70% – although recently high-strength distillation has been allowed.

The lower the strength of the distillation the more flavouring elements are left besides the alcohol in the brandy. Thus armagnac starts with a stronger flavour and scent than cognac. To this the local 'black' oak, sappy (so sappy in fact it should be hewn with an adze rather than sawn) and itself full of flavour, adds its character. In black oak brandy ages much faster than in white Limousin oak in Cognac. At eight years it is well-aged; at 12 fully mature.

Until 1905 Armagnac had no real identity. It sold all its good brandy to shippers in the Charente; a large part of the cognac of those days was really armagnac, for the deep blackish colour and seeming extreme age of armagnac helped young cognacs to appear older.

Comparisons of the flavours of armagnac and cognac always class armagnac as 'rustic', with the implication that it is a coarser spirit. It has been compared with hand-woven tweed in contrast with worsted. But tweed is a rough cloth, and it is armagnac's special distinction to be marvellously velvety smooth. At the same time it is dry; sugar is not normally added, as it is to cognac. Armagnac has a great pungent smell, which stays in your mouth or even in an empty glass for a long while. Its spirity, fiery quality is very similar to cognac's. The only great quality of the best cognacs it does not have is the brilliant, champagne-like finesse.

There are no great shippers like Martell and Hennessy in Armagnac. The labels here are those of some of the best of the many small houses; some of which also make liqueurs – the lower-quality brandy of Haut-Armagnac lends itself to this kind of processing. The main centres of the industry are the market towns of Auch, Condom and Eauze. As in most of the wine areas of France, a good deal of private buying goes on direct from farmers.

Top left: the Armagnac pattern of still is quite different from those of Cognac and produces lower-strength spirit with more flavour-giving congenerics.
Left: the rolling green countryside of Bas-Armagnac (here near Eauze) produces the best brandy.

Two small Appellation Contrôlée areas for wine adjoin Armagnac's best area in the south. Madiran is a strong red (which must legally stay three years in cask); Pacherenc du Vic-Bilh is a sweet white.

Limits of Appellation Contrôlée Madiran

— · — · — Département boundary

☐ Haut-Armagnac

☐ Ténarèze

☐ Bas-Armagnac

● Panjas
● Mont   Production centres

1:720,000

Km.0   10   20   30   40 Km.
Miles 0   10   20 Miles

Below: a large number of small producers make Armagnac an interesting subject to explore. Armagnac ages more rapidly than cognac, and at ten years has a dark colour and enormously attractive scent. The traditional bottle is round and squat; labels usually conform to this shape.

Scotch Whisky

Any whisky that is made in Scotland, whether in the Highlands or the Lowlands, whether of barley or corn, whether in a pot still or a continuous patent still, is Scotch. The vast majority of the Scotch that is sold, in fact, is a mixture of all these different kinds of whisky, adding up to a standard drink with a pronounced but not too highly distinctive flavour. There are more than 2,000 such blends. Anybody could devise a new one tomorrow. But of the individual whiskies that go into them there are only about 100, from the same number of distilleries. About 90 of the 100 are also sold 'single', unblended, under their own names.

Very loosely speaking, whisky is distilled beer; beer unflavoured with hops. The distiller's first job is the same as the brewer's: to make malt from barley, to dissolve it in water and to ferment the resulting 'wash'. The brewer would add hops to the resulting 'worts'; the whisky maker distils it, twice over. The first and last of the liquid that runs from the condenser the second time goes back to be distilled again. The middle part is raw, unmatured whisky.

What sort of whisky it is is determined by where it is done and with what equipment and materials. Five kinds of Scotch are recognized.

The first is grain whisky, distilled from barley and maize in continuous stills – a comparative newcomer but now the bigger part of the industry. Grain whisky has relatively little flavour. Practically none of it is ever drunk unblended. But it is the vehicle for the flavours of all blended Scotch in a proportion ranging from about 30% to 70%. Being milder and lighter it needs less maturing than the more highly flavoured kinds.

One straight grain whisky, from Cameronbridge distillery, is sold, under the name 'Old Cameron Brig'. It is rare, but for the curious an interesting experience: a smooth, pleasant and mild-flavoured whisky.

All the other kinds of Scotch whisky are known as malts – being made from malted barley. There are four, because four areas of Scotland make them; and each has its own particular character.

Best and most famous of all are the malts from the district of the river Spey. They are mapped and described on the following two pages. The malts of northern Scotland come nearest to them. Some are equally fine; often with rather stronger flavours. Of the northern malts Clynelish, Dalmore, Glenmorangie and Balblair are all bottled 'single'. One particularly fragrant and full-flavoured malt from the island of Orkney, Highland Park, is considered in the top rank.

Most distinctive of all are the malts from the western islands Islay and Skye. They are known by the strong peaty smell and flavour which gives them a slightly medicinal character. One theory is that the island peat consists of ancient deposits of seaweed which contain iodine. Certainly they are the easiest malts to recognize; those who like them will drink nothing else. A little goes a long way in a blend. Laphroaig is the most famous of the island malts. Another Islay distillery, Lagavulin, sells a little in bottle and is highly thought of. Talisker on Skye also has a following.

Just south of the islands on the promontory of Kintyre are two remaining distilleries from what was once a thriving centre: Campbeltown. Its Springbank and Glen Scotia are both very fine.

The rest of the malt distilleries are classed as Lowland and are reckoned to produce rather gentler, less high-flavoured Scotch. All except three, Bladnoch in the southwest and Rosebank and Littlemill in the centre, sell their entire production for blending.

Of the hundreds of blends of Scotch, perhaps the most famous are the six classics produced by the giant Distillers Co: John Haig, Johnnie Walker, Black & White, Dewar's White Label, White Horse and Vat 69. All are irreproachable and wholly consistent. Many knowledgeable people think Haig the best of them; Johnnie Walker is the best seller; White Horse is the maltiest. The Distillers Co owns almost half the malt distilleries in Scotland and accounts for half the exports of Scotch . . . and about 85% of the total is exported.

Their principal rivals include two favourites in America, Cutty Sark and J & B Rare, which are light in colour and flavour, and such brands as Grant's Standfast, Teacher's, Bell's, Long John, Ballantine's, Whyte & Mackay's and The Famous Grouse.

Then there are some excellent smaller concerns with such blends as Catto's, Usher's, McCallum's, Queen Anne and Spey Royal.

And finally there are a number of de luxe blends, among them Dimple Haig, Johnnie Walker Black Label, Islay Mist and Chivas Regal, which contain more and older malts and are correspondingly more expensive.

Above: such handsome distilleries as Coleburn, between Elgin and Rothes, add with their purposeful presence to the tranquillity of the Highlands.
Left: Scotch whisky starts on the broad floors of the maltings, where barley grain is patiently turned by hand while it germinates. Cooking then transforms it to malt: malt fermented is to Scotch what the thin white Charentais' wine is to Cognac.

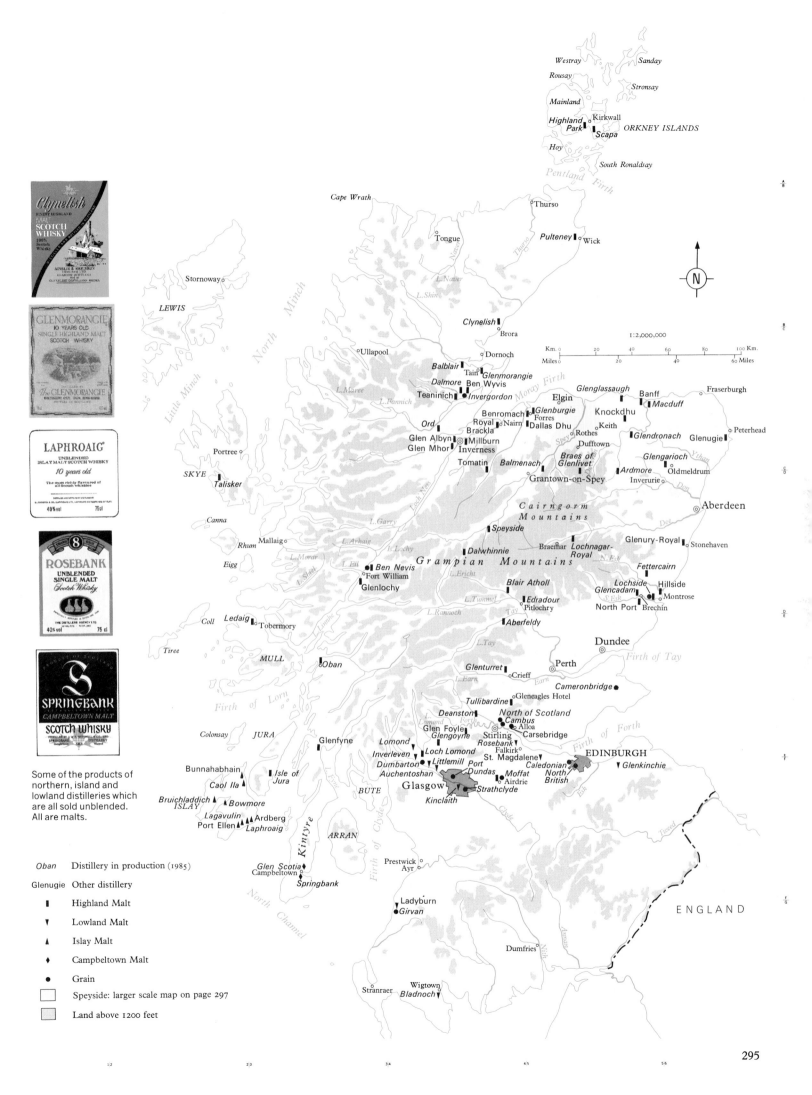

Westray
Rousay
Sanday
Stronsay
Mainland
Highland Park ■ Kirkwall
Scapa ■ ORKNEY ISLANDS
Hoy
South Ronaldsay

Pentland Firth

Cape Wrath
■ Thurso
■ Tongue
Pulteney ■ Wick

Clynelish ■
Brora

Stornoway ○

LEWIS

Ullapool ○
■ Dornoch
Balblair ■ Tain
Glenmorangie
Dalmore ■ Ben Wyvis
Teaninich ■ ● Invergordon
Elgin
Glenglassaugh ■ ■ Banff
Macduff
Fraserburgh
Benromach ■ Forres
Royal ■ Dallas Dhu   Knockdhu ■
Ord ■ Brackla   Nairn   Keith
Glen Albyn ● Millburn   Rothes   *Glendronach* ■   Glenugie ■ Peterhead
Glen Mhor Inverness   Dufftown
Tomatin ■ *Balmenach*   *Braes of*   *Glengarioch* ■
Glenlivet Oldmeldrum
Grantown-on-Spey   Ardmore ■ Inverurie

Portree ○

SKYE
Talisker ■

Canna

Cairngorm Mountains
Aberdeen ◎

Speyside ■

Rhum
Eigg

Mallaig
Grampian Mountains
Dalwhinnie ■ Braemar   *Lochnagar-Royal* ■
Glenury-Royal ■
Stonehaven ○
■ Ben Nevis *Fettercairn* ■
Fort William
Glenlochy *Blair Atholl* ■ Lochside ■ Hillside
Glencadam ■ ● Montrose
North Port Brechin

Edradour ■
Pitlochry
Coll   *Ledaig* ■
Tobermory ○
Aberfeldy ■

Tiree
Dundee ◎

MULL
Firth of Tay

○ Oban
Glenturret ■
Perth ◎
Crieff ○
Cameronbridge ●

Tullibardine ■
Gleneagles Hotel ○
Deanston ■ *North of Scotland*
Cambus ●
Firth of Lorn Glen Foyle ■ Alloa
Glengoyne ■ Stirling ◎ Carsebridge ●
Colonsay
JURA   *Lomond* ▼ *Rosebank* ▼
Glenfyne ■   Inverleven ▼ Falkirk
Loch Lomond ▼ St. Magdalene ▼
Dumbarton ● Littlemill ▼ Port Caledonian ● EDINBURGH
Auchentoshan ▼   Dundas ● North *Glenkinchie* ▼
Bunnahabhain ▲ *Isle of Jura* ▲   Moffat ● British ●
Caol Ila ▲   BUTE   Glasgow Airdrie
Bruichladdich ▲ *Strathclyde* ●
ISLAY
Lagavulin ▲ ▲ Ardberg   ARRAN Kinclaith ●
Port Ellen *Laphroaig* ▲

Glen Scotia ◆
Campbeltown
Springbank ◆

Prestwick ○
Ayr ○

Ladyburn ●
Girvan ●

Dumfries ○

Stranraer ○
Wigtown ○
Bladnoch ▼

ENGLAND

Some of the products of northern, island and lowland distilleries which are all sold unblended. All are malts.

Oban   Distillery in production (1985)

Glenugie   Other distillery

■   Highland Malt

▼   Lowland Malt

▲   Islay Malt

◆   Campbeltown Malt

●   Grain

☐   Speyside: larger scale map on page 297

▨   Land above 1200 feet

1:2,000,000
Km. 0   20   40   60   80   100 Km.
Miles 0   20   40   60 Miles

Scotland: The Highland Malts

Above: the fire and water of the Highlands; peat for drying the malt and the silver thread of the river Spey. Below: some of their classic products. Many of the malt distilleries mapped opposite sell their whisky unblended; these are among the most famous.

The 'single', or unblended, malt whiskies of the Highlands around the river Spey are to Scotch what château-bottled classed growths are to Bordeaux. The highest quality is combined in them with the maximum individuality and distinction. Each of them is superb, recognizable, consistent, and exactly like no other whisky on earth.

Most malt whisky is used to give character to the famous blends which sell all over the world. Only a little is sold 'single'. It has much more body, fragrance, texture and usually sweetness than blended whisky – but no two are alike.

On the previous pages the products of the whole of Scotland are mapped. On the facing page is singled out the very heart of the whisky world: the extraordinary concentration of an industry that is also an art, miles from anywhere in barren and beautiful hills beside the Moray Firth in northeastern Scotland.

A typical Speyside distillery is a quiet place. It seems to have the pace of farm life rather than industry. On a bright cool summer morning or in the almost permanent darkness of a Scottish winter the same simple processes are repeated by quiet men.

One long building covers the malting floor. Painted iron pillars punctuate a sea of barley, knee-deep, raked patiently this way and that while it germinates by men who do not speak.

The pointed building with the little hat contains the drying kiln, where peat from Pitsligo to the south smoulders on the red coke under a smoking hill of the germinated malt.

The next big stone barn is full of tanks and pipes and copper covers and the soothing smell of a brewery. And the next with the strange massive heads of stills, monster kettles squatting on bright points of fire, rumbling like old men who have lost touch with the world.

In this last is the first sight of whisky: a smooth little burn running a short course in a brass-bound glass case. Padlocked. And silent.

There is endless debate about the sources of quality and character in Scotch. The water

is one favourite topic. There is general agreement that it should be soft, since soft water is a better solvent than hard, and extracts more proteins from the malted barley. Traditionally the best water is said to come through peat over red granite – as the burns do which flow down from the hills of the treeless deer forests past the distillery doors.

Another factor is the barley. Highland barley is not 'fat', but full of protein, which means more flavour. Another is the peat for the fire on which the barley is dried. Its smoke contributes to the taste. Another is the shape of the still; any alteration will alter its product. Another is the oak barrels in which it is matured – old sherry casks are best.

And most important is the age. Three years is the legal minimum, but at ten years or more a malt reaches its peak. Beyond 15 years or so in oak it is said to go 'slimy'.

The most famous of all the distilleries is the Glenlivet, standing on a bare slope overlooking the little river Livet where it runs down from Glenlivet forest to join the Avon, a tributary of the Spey. It was the first distillery to conform to the licensing laws which in 1823 made the hundreds of small stills of the Highlands illegal. Its fame today rests on its gently sweet, slightly smoky, marvellously delicate whisky.

No fewer than 23 other firms all over Speyside have annexed Glenlivet's name to their own at some time, among them Glen Grant, Macallan, Longmorn, Dufftown and Glenfarclas – all superb in their own right, all sold unblended. Glenfiddich is the only other name as widely known.

The last decade has seen a sharp increase in interest in the 'single' malts as individuals: for softer or smokier, drier or sweeter, or richer in tasty 'congenerics'. Most of the musical, savage names on the map can now be found on bottles, at least in bars or pubs with a specialized interest. No spirit tastes so vividly of its origin as this essence of the Highlands, bottled by the burn.

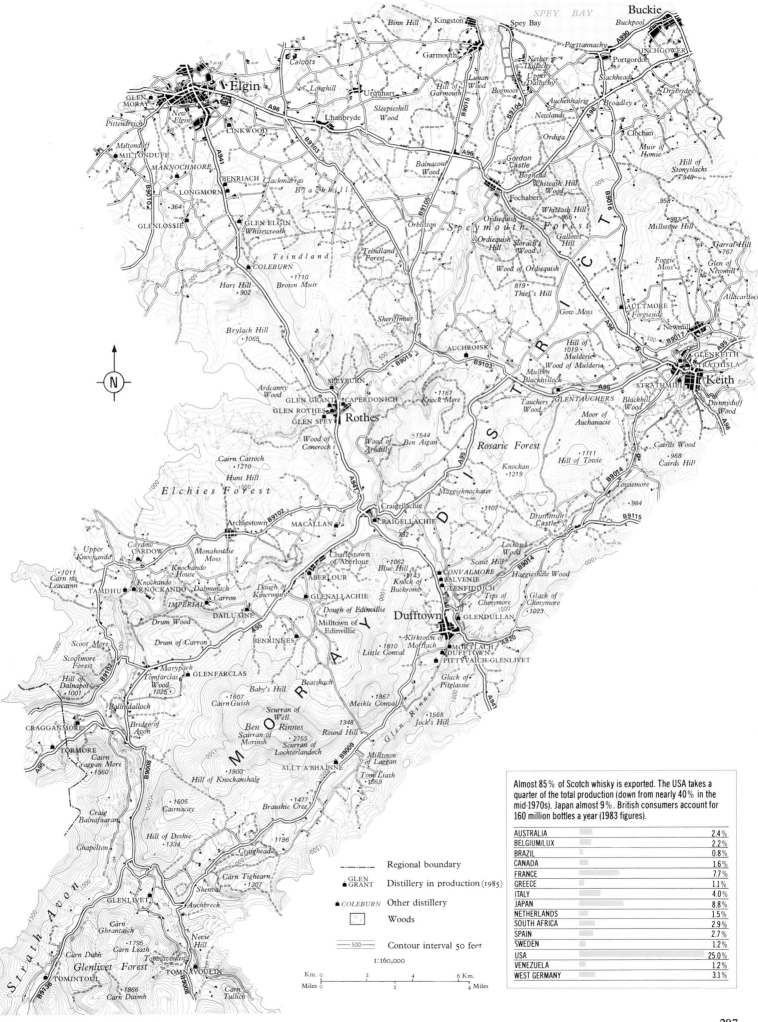

Almost 85 % of Scotch whisky is exported. The USA takes a quarter of the total production (down from nearly 40 % in the mid-1970s), Japan almost 9 %. British consumers account for 160 million bottles a year (1983 figures).

Country		Percentage
AUSTRALIA		2.4 %
BELGIUM/LUX		2.2 %
BRAZIL		0.8 %
CANADA		1.6 %
FRANCE		7.7 %
GREECE		1.1 %
ITALY		4.0 %
JAPAN		8.8 %
NETHERLANDS		1.5 %
SOUTH AFRICA		2.9 %
SPAIN		2.7 %
SWEDEN		1.2 %
USA		25.0 %
VENEZUELA		1.2 %
WEST GERMANY		3.1 %

Regional boundary

GLEN GRANT Distillery in production (1985)

COLEBURN Other distillery

Woods

500 Contour interval 50 feet

1:160,000

Km. 0   2   4   6 Km.

Miles 0   2   4 Miles

Rum

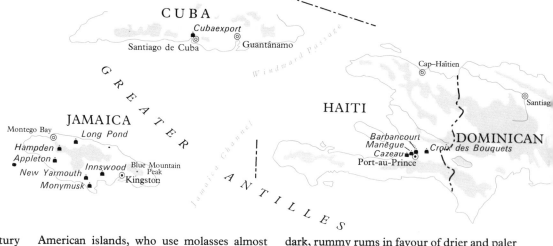

Ever since the Spaniards in the 16th century took sugar cane, which had come to Europe from China, to their colony of Santo Domingo, its pungent distilled essence has been the drink of the chain of Caribbean islands which curves like a cutlass from Cuba to Venezuela.

All these islands make at least a little rum. Sometimes it is only in a palm-thatched shelter in the cane gardens, with a decrepit old copper pot still. In Guyana such moonshine is known as 'Bushie'; in St Kitts 'Hammond'; in St Lucia 'L'Esprit d'Amour'.

The modern rum industry, however, has little to do with such folklore. Its big distilleries grow bigger and fewer year by year as rum gets in line as a polite social drink.

Rum is made of either cane juice, crushed out of fresh cane by roller mills, or molasses, the residue after the juice has been boiled to make sugar. Distillers on the British and American islands, who use molasses almost exclusively, call it by the intimidating name of blackstrap. The French contrast their cane-juice rum by calling it 'agricole'.

Either material is first fermented. Then it can be distilled in either of the two kinds of still: pot or continuous. Just as with whisky, the continuous still makes a more neutral but cheaper spirit; the pot still, operated with skill, can give the perfect fraction, without too much or too little of the flavouring properties. Commercially the same answer has been found for rum as for whisky: most rums on the market are a blend of the two.

Different methods and tastes give different styles to the rums of various islands. Distillers also give credit for the individuality of their products to the yeasts they use, their water, their local variety of cane, the soil it grows on (in about that order). Particular attention is paid to yeasts. The modern trend is for laboratory-developed pure yeast cultures which give a quick clean fermentation, in place of the chance natural yeasts of the cane gardens. But for what in Jamaica is known as Plummer or Wedderburn rum or in Martinique as Grand Arôme, the residue from previous distillations is stored in 'dunder pits' where it ferments slowly and continuously, a black and astonishingly pungent concentration of everything that gives rum its taste and smell. Dunder is used to start the fermentation of fresh batches, just as 'sour mash' is used in Kentucky. The result is a sort of ancestral character continuing from batch to batch.

Rum does not need nearly so much ageing as brandy. Six months in oak is enough for good light rum. Five years would be enough for any.

Fashion today is abandoning the sweet, dark, rummy rums in favour of drier and paler sorts which impose their character less forcefully on mixed drinks. France and Germany (where it accounts for 12% of all spirits sold) still like the taste of rum, but the United States is in two minds about it. In fact the best rums manage to keep the familiar happy pungency but in a lighter and more elegant vehicle.

Cuba, the original home of Bacardi, exports little now, but Cuban rum is apparently excellent and light.

Jamaica is by tradition the home of the heaviest rum. Some (Hampden) is still made hyper-flavoured for mixing with neutral spirit to make the German 'Rum Verschnitt', but most are of medium richness today.

Haiti: fully flavoured rum, but being double pot-distilled the best have real finesse. Barbancourt is the most famous.

Puerto Rico, the world's biggest producer; all

Left from top: Bacardi moved from Cuba to Puerto Rico and is now also made in the Bahamas, Mexico and even Spain; Lemon Hart is a Jamaican blend; the three famous French rums are from Martinique; Mount Gay is from Barbados, Caroni from Trinidad and Lamb's from Guyana.
Right and below: cane gardens and a farm in Guadeloupe.

BLIC

to Domingo

Puerto Rico
Distillers Bacardi ● ▲ San Juan
● Cárioca ● ▲ Fernandez
Ponce ● Serrallez ⊙

PUERTO RICO

VIRGIN
ISLANDS Cane Garden
(U.S.)(U.K.) ▲ Bay
● TORTOLA
ST. THOMAS
West Indies
Distilleries Ltd.

▲ ST. CROIX
Virgin Island
Rum Distilleries Ltd.

ANGUILLA
(U.K.)

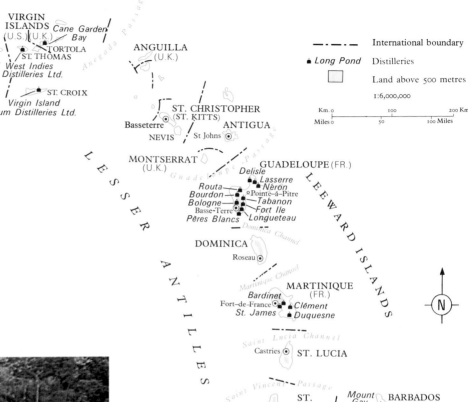

International boundary
▲ Long Pond Distilleries
Land above 500 metres
1:6,000,000

Km. 0   100   200 Km.
Miles 0   50   100 Miles

ST. CHRISTOPHER
(ST. KITTS)
Basseterre ● ANTIGUA
NEVIS St Johns ⊙

MONTSERRAT
(U.K.)
GUADELOUPE (FR.)
Delisle
Lasserre
Routa Néron
Bourdon ○ Pointe-à-Pitre
Bologne Tabanon
Basse-Terre Fort Ile
Pères Blancs Longueteau

DOMINICA
Roseau ⊙

L E S S E R   A N T I L L E S

MARTINIQUE
(FR.)
Bardinet
Fort-de-France ● ▲ Clément
St. James ▲ Duquesne

Castries ⊙ ST. LUCIA

ST. Mount
VINCENT Gay BARBADOS
Kingstown ⊙ ● ▲ Bridgetown
West Indian
Rum Refinery

W I N D W A R D   I S L A N D S

St. George's ⊙ GRENADA

L E E W A R D   I S L A N D S

N

continuous still, the classic rums are Bacardi Carta Blanca and Carta Oro, respectively white and dry and pale gold and a little richer.

Martinique and Guadeloupe tend to make fine and richly flavoured rums. Martinique in particular makes some of the best: St James is Jamaica-style, dark and fruity. Clément is very highly regarded.

Barbados uses both kinds of stills to make good-quality medium-light rum. Mount Gay is considered one of the best.

Trinidad: continuous-still rum of good quality rather than great character.

Guyana: rum and sugar from Guyana are better known as Demarara. They are not the fruitiest rums, but they have quite a dark colour as well as considerable character. One-third of the production is pot distilled. 'Fruit-cured' – which means fruit- and spice-flavoured – rum is the celebrated local drink.

TOBAGO

Siegert's
Port of ● ▲ Fernandez
Spain ▲ Caroni
TRINIDAD

Delta
del
Orinoco

VENEZUELA

GUYANA

Versailles
Uitvlugt ▲ ⊙
Georgetown
Diamond ▲ Enmore

Kentucky's Bourbon

Bourbon whisky, or whiskey, is defined in terms of what it is made of and how, rather than where it comes from. Kentucky has no monopoly of its production. Yet history and sentiment identify bourbon with the state where it was first made (in Bourbon County), and even today more than half of America's bourbon distilleries are in Kentucky.

United States regulations lay down that bourbon must be made from not less than 51% corn grain; be distilled at not more than 160 US proof (or 80% alcohol); be reduced with water to not more than 125 proof before maturing; be matured for two years or more in new barrels of white oak, charred on the inside, and be bottled at not less than 80° proof (40% alcohol).

In more sensual terms, bourbon is a light brown, fruity-flavoured, often rather sweet whiskey, with a penetrating and unforgettable taste composed of charred oak and caramel. In practice it is made of a mixture of corn (maize), rye and barley malt fermented together with the distiller's own strain of yeast and often a little 'sour' or matured mash for continuity.

Distillers who use a higher proportion of corn get a lighter whiskey. By increasing the proportion of rye they make one with more body and flavour which needs longer ageing.

Bourbon has been traced back to the still of Elijah Craig, a Baptist preacher in Georgetown, just north of Lexington. He is reputed to have made the first bourbon in 1789, the year George Washington became first president. His innovation was using a mixture of grains for his mash.

The spirit that emerged differed from the modern whiskey chiefly in being made in a copper pot still, whereas today gigantic continuous stills are used. Hence the regulation setting a maximum strength: a continuous still could remove all the flavouring elements and leave pure alcohol.

Bourbon is normally sold 'straight' – either just the produce of one distillery or as 'a blend of straights', the produce of several. If it is mixed with neutral spirit, as in some of the cheaper blends, it is no longer called bourbon but simply 'blended whiskey'. If labelled Bottled in Bond it is stronger (50% alcohol as against the normal 43), older (at least four years) and probably fuller-flavoured.

Geography is not totally irrelevant to bourbon-making. What first made Kentucky a distilling centre was partly the good supply of corn, and the difficulty of moving it to market – a keg of whiskey being easier to transport than 11 bushels of grain – and partly the ample supply of limestone spring water for making the mash and cooling the condenser.

Most of the bourbon distilleries outside Kentucky lie in states on the same limestone belt: Virginia makes excellent bourbon; Pennsylvania and Maryland (traditionally the centre for rye whiskey) also have bourbon distilleries. And Tennessee makes, in the 'sour mash' Jack Daniels and George Dickel, bourbon of a particular style, produced by 'leaching' the raw whiskey through powdered maple charcoal, which is certainly some of the best in America.

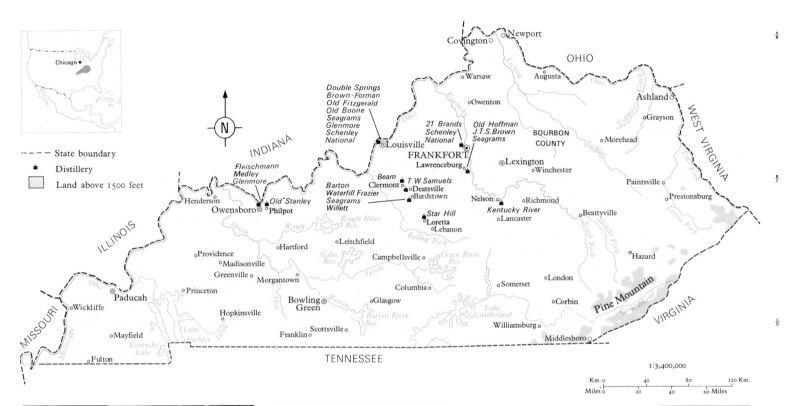

State boundary
Distillery
Land above 1500 feet

1:3,400,000

Km. 0   40   80   120 Km.
Miles 0   20   40   60 Miles

Charcoal is a key ingredient in the making of Kentucky bourbon and its Tennessee rivals. For bourbon, the new white oak barrels are charred inside before filling; for Tennessee 'sour mash' whiskey the raw spirit is filtered through powdered charcoal of the local maple wood, which gives it a characteristic smoothness and flavour.
Top left: the 'rick yard' at the Jack Daniels' distillery in Tennessee.
Left: in the same yard, the smouldering charcoal is hosed down to put out the fire.
Above: new barrels (charred inside) are filled in Kentucky.

Right: the flamboyant labels of some of Kentucky's best bourbons, with one (Bourbon Supreme) from neighbouring Illinois. The map shows the location of Kentucky's major distilling companies.

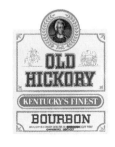

The Kirsch Family

Every fruit that grows in the orchards of Switzerland, the Vosges mountains and the Black Forest is distilled to make high-strength clear white spirit of great fragrance. Right: some of the scores of producers.

Distilling nowadays is nearly all big business. There are bootleggers still – probably more than most people suppose – but in most countries the old cottage industry has been taxed out of existence. Only where the results are exceptional does it still flourish. That place, above all, is the stretch of Europe east and south of the Vosges; the Black Forest and the northern half of Switzerland.

The local eau-de-vie is distilled in pot stills from every edible fruit, and several which are not eaten. Kirsch, made of cherries, is the most common and widespread of these 'alcools blancs' – so-called because they are aged in glass or pottery rather than wood, and thus have no colour. But pears, apricots, blue plums, and more extravagantly raspberries, wild strawberries, and even holly berries (which give a fantastically pungent – and expensive – spirit, baie de houx) are distilled. The soft fruits and small berries are needed in huge quantities; prices for the genuine article are thus very high.

There are comparatively few big firms in the business: names such as Schladerer, Jacobert, Etter are well known, and Alsace wine shippers sell alcools, whether they make them or buy them, under their own names. Some of the finest of all come from farmhouses in the Black Forest or the Vosges, with the still in a little room off the kitchen and a vat house no bigger than a one-car garage, lined with little tanks of the essences of the local orchards.

The French tend to distil lightly for maximum flavour; the Swiss distil further and get a more neutral spirit. The Germans distinguish between a 'Wasser', which is a spirit obtained by direct distillation of the fermented fruit, and a 'Geist', which is partly a Wasser, but partly also made by infusing the fruit in alcohol – the method used with soft fruit.

The best fruit brandies are made of pears (called in France Poire William, in Germany Birngeist), raspberries (framboise, Himbeergeist), cherries (Kirsch), apricots (abricot, Aprikosengeist), blue plums (quetsch, Zwetschgenwasser), gentian (gentiane, Enzian) and, principally in France, yellow plums (mirabelle), wild strawberries (fraise des bois) and bilberries (myrtille).

302

Calvados

Calvados du Pays d'Auge is the Appellation Contrôlée for the best Calvados, fiery and with a strong scent of apples when it is newly distilled, then matured in big oak casks (right) until it grows nearer to brandy.

An Armada galleon, *El Calvador*, wrecked on the Normandy coast as it ran from the guns of Drake's flotilla, is supposed to have given its name to the *département* of Calvados, and hence to the world's most famous apple brandy. Cider is the local wine of this grapeless part of France. And the local brandy is cider 'burnt' in a still. There are records of cider distilling going back to the 16th century on the Cotentin peninsula, west of Calvados. Now 11 regions, shown on the map above, use the name, followed by their own.

In 1946 one limited area and one method of distilling cider was given an Appellation Contrôlée: Calvados du Pays d'Auge. It must be made of cider from fruit crushed in the traditional fashion and fermented for at least six weeks (although in a whole month it only reaches about 4.5% alcohol). It must be distilled twice in a pot still, in exactly the same way as cognac, and at about the same strength (72% alcohol). It must be sold at between 40% and 45% and must have been aged for at least two years.

Well-made Calvados is quite drinkable, although very fiery, when new, but in practice the best is aged for several years in big oak casks. It is not normally sweetened, so it remains a very dry spirit. In its degree of scent and flavour it is very like brandy. But good Calvados recaptures in an uncanny way the evocative smell of apples. It plays an important part in Norman cooking: terrines, tripes, creamy dishes of chicken or sole are perfumed with it, and often called Pays d'Auge. There is a famous local custom of drinking a glass of Calvados between two courses of a long meal, to make a hole, a 'trou Normand', to fill with yet more delectable dishes.

The other regions that make Calvados are not obliged to use the pot still, but if they use a continuous still it must have devices for extracting undesirable essences from the column. This less refined Calvados is only Appellation Contrôlée Calvados, not Pays d'Auge.

Cheaper apple brandy is permitted to be made in an ordinary continuous still, but is not allowed the name Calvados. It can call itself eau de vie de cidre (or poire, from pears) de Normandie, Bretagne or Maine.

Acknowledgments

In addition to the hundreds of wine lovers whose help has been invaluable in making this Atlas, the author and the publishers particularly acknowledge the contributions in information, time and advice of the following:

France
Bureau Interprofessionnel de l'Armagnac, Eauze; Comité Interprofessionnel des Vins des Côtes de Provence, Les Arcs-sur-Argens; Comité Interprofessionnel des Vins des Côtes du Rhône, Avignon; Comité Interprofessionnel des Vins Doux Naturels et Vins de Liqueur à Appellations Contrôlées, Perpignan; Comité Interprofessionnel du Vin d'Alsace, Colmar; Conseil Interprofessionnel des Vins Appellation Contrôlée de Touraine, Tours; Conseil Interprofessionnel des Vins de la Région de Bergerac, Bergerac; Conseil Interprofessionnel du Vin de Bordeaux; M Jean-Henri Dubernet, Narbonne; M Thévenet, Comité Interprofessionnel des Vins de Touraine, Touraine; André Enders, Conseil Interprofessionnel du Vin de Champagne, Epernay; M Yves Fourault of Eschenauer, Bordeaux; Fédération Nationale des Vins Délimités de Qualité Supérieure, Paris; Fédération Régionale des Vins de Savoie, Bugey, Dauphine, Chambéry; M Francis Gardère, Pauillac; Groupement Interprofessionnel des Vins de l'Ile de Corse; M Davesne, Office National Interprofessionnel des Vins de Table; Mme Claudie Gomme; M Pierre Goutier, Paris; M Jean Latour, Hospices de Beaune, Beaune; M Jean Hugel of F.E. Hugel & Fils, Riquewihr; Institut National des Appellations d'Origine; M Jacques Legrand; Mr T. Marshall, Nuits-St-Georges; Martell & Co, Cognac; Mr Stephen Moss of Michael Druitt Wines; M Christian Moueix; M J. C. Berrouet of J-P Moueix & Co, Libourne; M Bruno Prats; M Philippe Roudié, Bordeaux; Mr Peter Sichel, Château d'Angludet, Cantenac; Syndicat du Cru Corbières, Lézignan; Union des Grands Crus de Bordeaux; Union Interprofessionnel de la Côte d'Or et de l'Yonne pour les Vins de Vins de Bourgogne, Beaune; Union Interprofessionnel des Vins du Beaujolais; Union Viticole Sancerroise, Sancerre; Mr Peter Vinding-Diers; Food & Wine from France, London.

Germany
Dr Hans Ambrosi, Verwaltung der Staatsweingüter im Rheingau, Eltville am Rhein; Dr H. Becker, Geisenheim; Dr H. Breider, Bayerische Landesanstalt für Wein-, Obst- und Gartenbau; Erwein, Graf Matuschka-Greiffenclau; The late Dr G. Horney, Deutsche Wetterdienst, Geisenheim; Mr Ian Jamieson of Deinhard, London; Dr F.W. Michel, Stabilisierungsfonds für Wein, Mainz; Dr H.G. Woschek, Deutsche Wein-Information, Mainz; Ministerium für Landwirtschaft, Weinbau und Forsten, Mainz; Staatsdomänen of Hessen und Mosel-Saar-Ruwer; Dr Aichele, Deutscher Wetterdienst, Trier; Professor Heinrich Zakosek, Hessisches Landesamt für Bodenforschung, Wiesbaden; Hessische Lehr- und Handelskammer, Stuttgart; Dr Goedecke, Staatliche Weinbaudomänen Niederhausen-Schlossböckelheim; Herr Manfred Volpel of Deinhard, Koblenz; Verwaltung der Bischöflichen Weingüter, Trier; Herr A. von Schubert, Maximin Grünhaus, Trier; Herr Rolf Temming; Herr Karl-Felix Wegeler, Oestrich; Olr. F. Rath, Weinbauschule, Bad Kreuznach; Georg Westermann Verlag, Braunschweig.

Algeria
Office de Commercialisation des Produits Viti-Vinicoles, Alger.

Argentina
Mr Derek Foster, Buenos Aires; Mrs Sheila Roland Holst; Vinos Argentinos Exportadora, Buenos Aires.

Australia
Mr Michael Hill-Smith, Barossa Valley; Mr James Halliday; Hamilton Ewell Vineyard Prop., Adelaide;
Thomas Hardy & Sons, Mile End, South Australia; Hazel Murphy, Australian High Commission, Manchester; Mr John Parkinson; Mr Michael Rayment, Rosemount Estates, London; The South Australian Department of Agriculture, Adelaide.

Austria
Prince Metternich-Sandor; Herr Lorenz Moser, Rohrendorf bei Krems; Österreichisches Weininstitut; Dr Johann Traxler, Weinwirtschaftsfonds; Winzergenossenschaft Wachau, Dürnstein.

Bulgaria
Mr Tim Bleach; Mr Todorov, Bulgarian Vintners Co. Ltd; Vinimpex, Sofia.

Canada
The Canadian High Commission, London.

Chile
Mr Pablo Dias; Asociación Nacional de Viticultores, Santiago; Emmanuel de Kadt, Valdeca; Mr Rodrigo Moore; Miss Olga Kliwadenko, Chilean Embassy, London.

China
Mr Michael Parry, Hong Kong.

Cyprus
Keo, Limassol; Vine Products Commission SAP, Limassol.

Czechoslovakia
Dr Erich Minarik, Bratislava.

England
The English Vineyards Association.

Greece
Ministry of Agriculture, Athens.

Hungary
Hungarovin, Budapest; Mr John Lipitch, London; Mr Istvan Pusztai, Budapest.

Israel
Israel Wine Institute, Rehovot.

Italy
Mr Burton Anderson, Tuscany; Cynthia Bacon; Comitato Nazionale per la Tutela delle Denominazione di Origine dei Vini; Consorzi di Vini di Asti, di Verona, di Alto Adige; Italian Institute for Foreign Trade, London; Arnoldo Mondadori Editore; Mr Ezis Rivella; Rivista di Viticoltura e di Enologia, Conegliano, Treviso; Dr Bruno Roncarati, London; Mr Carmel Tintle, Villa Banfi; Unione Italiana Vini, Milan.

Japan
John Victor Gano; Suntory Wine Company.

Lebanon
Caves de Ksara, Ksara; Serge Hochar of Château Musar.

Luxembourg
Fédération des Associations Viticoles de Luxembourg, Grevenmacher; Station Viticole, Remich.

Madeira
Mr Noel Cossart, Cossart Gordon; Mr A. Jardim of Henriques & Henriques; Mr David Pamment.

Morocco
Comité National de Géographie du Maroc, Rabat.

New Zealand
New Zealand Trade Commission, London; Viticultural Advisory Committee, Department of Agriculture, Wellington.

Portugal
Casa do Douro, Régua; Comissão de Viticultura da Região dos Vinhos Verdes, Porto; Instituto do Vinho do Porto, Porto; Miss Flavia Torreo, Portuguese Government Trade Office; Mr Jan Read; Mr Alistair Robertson of Taylor, Fladgate & Yeatman, Vila Nova de Gaia.

Romania
Institutul de Cercetari Pentru Viticultura si Vinificatie Romagricola, Bucharest.

Scotland
Distillers Co. Ltd, London; Miss Josephine Clark, William Grant & Sons Ltd.

South Africa
KWV, Paarl; Mr Nick Clarke MW of Henry C. Collinson & Sons Ltd; Mr Henry Damant of SAWFA London; Mr Peter Finlayson, Groot Drakenstein; Mr Graham Knox.

Spain
Mr Brian Buckingham, London; Consejo Regulador de Denominación de Origin Jerez; Mr John Lockwood of Sandeman Bros, Jerez; Mr Derrick Palengat of Williams & Humbert, London; Don Manuel Raventos; Mr Jan Read; Sindicato Nacional de la Vid, Madrid; Don Miguel Torres; Vinos de España; Mr Zarraluqui, Croft & Co. Ltd, Jerez.

Switzerland
M Philippe Orsat, Martigny; Mr Michael Rothwell; Société des Exportateurs de Vins Suisses, Lausanne; Société Suisse des Liquoristes, Berne.

Tunisia
Union Centrale des Coopératives Viticoles, Tunis.

Turkey
Turkish State Monopolies, Istanbul.

USA
The Bourbon Institute, New York; Brother Timothy, The Christian Brothers, California; Professor Maynard A. Amerine, California; Mr Leon Adams, Sausalito; Professor H.W. Berg, Davis; Mr Bob Betz, Chateau Ste Michelle; Mr Fred Delkin of Oregon Wines Advisory Board; Dr Mark Kliewer, Davis; Mr Matt Kramer, Portland, Oregon; Mr James Lider, St Helena; Ms Zelma Long, Sonoma; Mr Robert Mondavi, Oakville; National Distillers' Products, New York; Dr Harold Olmo, Davis; Mr Brian St Pierre, Wine Institute, San Francisco; Mr Mark Savage of Windrush Wines, England; Miss Catherine Scott, London; Mr Robert Sievers, The Distilled Spirits Council of the United States, Washington DC; Mr Robert Thompson, St Helena; Mr John Walter of The Wine Studio, London; The Wine Institute, San Francisco.

USSR
Ministry of Food Production, Moscow; Sojuzplodoimport, Moscow.

West Indies
Mr Ben Cross de Chavannes of Booker Brothers McConnell, London; Mr Robert Engelhard, Comité Français du Rhum; United Rum Merchants, London; West Indies Rum Committee, Barbados.

Yugoslavia
Mr E.C. Burgess, Teltscher Brothers, London.

General
Mr Gerald Asher; Mr Michael Broadbent MW of Christies, London; Mr Geoffrey Francom; Dr Peter Hallgarten of S. F. & O. Hallgarten, London; Institut Technique du Vin, Paris; Mr Tony Laithwaite; Mr George Bull and Mr James Long of International Distillers & Vintners, London; Mr Anthony Goldthorpe of O. W. Loeb, London; Office International de la Vigne et du Vin, Paris; Mr David Peppercorn MW, London; Mr Richard Perse of Eldridge, Pope and Co. Ltd; Miss Isabel Plevin of Caxton Tower Wines Ltd; Mr Peter Reynier of J. B. Reynier, London; Miss Phillipa Richardson; Mr Geoffrey Roberts; Dr James Rose, Birkbeck College, London; The late André L. Simon; Miss Serena Sutcliffe MW, London; Mr Robin Yapp, Mere; The regional Comités Interprofessionnels in France, Weinbauämter in Germany, Consorzi in Italy, Consejos Reguladores in Spain, the Commercial Counsellors of London Embassies of all winegrowing countries; University Departments, and scores of growers, shippers and wine lovers all over the world.

General Index

Alphabetization is word by word ignoring de, du, etc. Asterisks indicate the main entry on the subject. All château names appear under *Châteaux* in the Gazetteer.

Gazetteer

This 10,000-entry gazetteer includes place-name references of vineyards, châteaux, general wine areas and other information appearing on the maps in the Atlas, with the exception of minor place names which appear as background information in italic type. All châteaux are listed under C (e.g. Châteaux Palmer) in the gazetteer; where a page number appears in italic it refers to text, figures in roman type are the map pages and grid references. All place names, vineyards, etc., beginning with le, la or les (e.g. la Perrière) are indexed under L. Names of wine or spirit producers appearing on the maps are also listed.

310

Château
Dudon 101 B4
du Gaby 106 C6
du Gazin 106 C5
du Glana *91;* 91 C5
du Grand Soussans 93 F5
Duhart-Milon-Rothschild *88;* 87 G4, 89 A4
du Mayne, Barsac 101 B4
du Mayne, Preignac 101 D4
du Monthil 85 B2
du Nozet *119;* 123 F4
du Paradis 107 G4
du Pick 101 D4
Duplessis-Fabre 93 G3
du Pont de Langon 99 D5
du Puy 107 D5
du Raux 93 C5
du Rayas 127 B5
Durfort Vivens *94;* 95 B3
du Rozay 125 C2
du Tailhas 103 E4, 105 B1
du Tertre *94;* 95 D2
Dutruch-Poujeaux *92*
Dutruch-Grand Poujeaux 93 F3
d'Yquem 101 F4
Eyquem *108;* 108 F2
Falfas *108;* 108 F3
Fatin 87 E5
Faurie-de-Soutard 105 C5
Fayau *96*
Ferrand 103 E4
Ferrière *94;* 95 B2
Feytit-Clinet *102;* 103 C4
Figeac *104;* 105 B2
Filhot *100*
Fombrauge *106;* 107 E5
Fonbadet 89 E5
Fonpiqueyre 89 C2
Fonplegade 105 D4
Fonréaud *92;* 93 G1
Fonroque 105 C4
Fontpetite 87 F5
Fort-de-Vauban 93 D4
Fortia *127;* 127 C4
Fougas 108 F4
Fourcas-Dupré *92;* 93 E1
Fourcas-Hosten *92;* 93 F1
Fourney 107 F5
Franc Maillet 103 C6
Franc-Mayne 105 C4
François 268 C4
Gaillard 75 G2
Garaud 107 C3
Gaudin 89 E5
Gazin, Léognan 99 F2
Gazin, Plassac 108 D2
Gilet Bayard 107 C5
Gilette *100;* 101 C5
Gironville 95 D5
Giscours *94;* 95 D4
Gloria *90, 91;* 91 C5
Gombaude-Guillot 103 C4
Gontet 107 D6
Gontier 108 D1
Gorce *17*
Goujon 107 B3
Grand Barrail-Lamarzelle-Figeac 105 B2
Grand Bigaroux 107 E3
Grand Corbin Despagne 105 A3
Grandes-Murailles 105 D5
Grandis 87 C4
Grand-Jour 108 G5
Grand-Mayne 105 C3
Grand Moulinet 103 B3
Grand Ormeau 107 C2
Grand Pontet 105 C4
Grand Poujeaux *92;* 93 E4
Grand-Puy-Ducasse 89 D6
Grand-Puy-Lacoste 89 D4
Grate-Cap 103 D4
Graulet *108;* 108 D2
Gravas 101 B4
Gravet 107 E3
Gressier-Grand-Poujeaux *92;* 93 F4
Greysac *84;* 85 B4
Grillet *17, 125;* 124 B5, 125 C2
Grillon 101 C4
Gros-Moulin 108 G4
Gruaud-Larose *90, 91;* 91 D4, 93 A3
Guadet St-Julien 105 C5
Guerit 108 F4
Gueyrosse 107 E2
Guibeau 107 C6
Guillemot 107 E4
Guillotin 107 D5
Guillou 107 D3
Guionne 108 F4
Guiraud *100;* 101 F4
Guitard 107 C4
Guiteronde 101 C3
Guitignan 93 F3
Hallet 101 B4
Hanteillan *86;* 87 F3
Haut-Bages-Averous 89 D5
Haut-Bages-Libéral 89 D5
Haut-Bages-Monpelou 89 D4
Haut-Bailly *98;* 99 F4
Haut-Ballet 107 C3
Haut-Batailley 89 F4, 91 B3
Haut-Bergey 99 F2
Haut-Bernon 107 C5
Haut-Bommes 101 F3
Haut-Breton-Larigaudière 93 G6, 95 A1
Haut-Brignon *96*
Haut-Brion *98;* 99 A2
Haute-Canteloup 85 E4
Haute-Faucherie 107 C4
Hauterive 85 G4
Haut-Madère 99 C4
Haut-Madrac 89 E2
Haut Maillet 103 C6

Château
Haut-Marbuzet *86;* 87 F5
Haut-Peyraguey *100*
Haut-Piquat 107 C5
Haut-Sarpe *106;* 105 C5, 107 E4
Hortevie *91*
Houissant *86;* 87 F5
Hourbanon 85 F2
Hourtin-Ducasse 89 D2
Hourtou 108 F4
Jacques-Blanc 107 F5
Jappe-Loup 107 E5
Jean-Blanc 107 F5
Jean-Faure 105 B3
Junayme 106 D6
Kirwan *94;* 95 C3
Labarde *108;* 108 F4
la Bastienne 107 C4
l'Abbaye Gorsse de Gorsse 95 B2
l'Abbaye-Skinner 85 E1
la Bécade 93 E2
Labégorce 95 A2
Labégorce-Zédé *94;* 95 A2
Laborde 107 B2
Labrède 108 E4
Labrousse 108 C1
la Cabanne 103 C4
la Cardonne *84;* 85 E3
la Carelle 108 C2
la Carte et le Chatelet 105 D4
la Chaise 77 G2
la Chapelle Lescours 107 E2
la Chesnaye 93 B4
la Clare *84;* 85 C3
la Closerie-Grand-Poujeaux *92;* 93 F4
la Clotte 105 D5
la Clotte-Blanche 108 F3
la Commanderie, Libourne 103 E3
la Commanderie, St-Estèphe 87 F4
la Conseillante *102;* 103 D5, 105 A2
la Côte-Haut-Brion 99 A2
la Couronne 89 E4, 91 B3
la Couspaude 105 D5
la Croix, Chevrol 107 C3
la Croix, Pomerol 103 D4
la Croix, Saillans 106 C6
la Croix-de-Gay *102;* 103 C5
la Croix-du-Casse 103 E3
la Croix Landon 85 C3
la Croix-Millorit *108*
la Croix-St-Georges 103 D4
la Croix Taillefer 103 E4
la Dominique *104;* 103 D6, 105 A3
Ladouys 87 F4
Lafaurie-Peyraguey *100;* 101 E4
la Ferrade 99 B4
Laffitte-Carcasset 87 E5
Lafite *16, 17;* prices *40, 82, 88, 126*
Lafite-Canteloup 95 G5
Lafite-Rothschild 87 G5, 89 A4
Lafleur *102;* 103 C5
Lafleur-Gazin *102;* 103 C6
Lafleur du Roy 103 D4
la Fleur-Milon 89 B5
la Fleur-Pétrus *102;* 103 C5
Lafon 93 E3
Lafon-Rochet *86;* 87 G4, 89 A4
la France 85 E3
la Gaffelière *104;* 105 E4
la Garde *98;* 108 C2
la Garelle 107 F4
la Grande Gardiole 127 A5
Lagrange, Pomerol 103 C5
Lagrange, St-Julien *91;* 91 D3
Lagrange-de-Lescure 107 F3
la Graulet 108 E2
la Grave 104 F4
la Grave Trigant de Boisset *102;* 103 B4
Lagüe 106 C6
la Gurgue 95 B2
la Haye 87 F4
la Lagune *94;* 95 F5
Lalande *86*
Lalande Borie *91*
Lalibarde 108 F3
la Louvière *98;* 99 E4
la Maréchaude 107 C2
la Marzelle 105 C2
la Mission-Haut-Brion *98;* 99 A3
Lamothe, Lansac 108 F4
Lamothe, Sauternes 101 G3
Lamothe-Bouscaut 99 E5
Lamothe-Cissac 87 G2
Lamothe-de-Bergeron 93 C5
la Mouleyre 107 E5
Lamourette 101 E3
Landon 85 D3
Lanessan *92;* 91 D4, 93 B3
l'Angélus 105 D3
Langlade 107 D5, 125 C9
Langoa *90, 91;* 91 C5
la Papeterie 107 C3
la Pelleterie 105 D6
Lapelletrie 107 E4
la Perrière 107 C5
la Pointe *102;* 103 D3
La Providence 103 C5
la Rame *96*
Larmande 105 C5
la Rose-Pauillac 89 C5
Larcis-Ducasse *106;* 105 E5, 107 E3
Larose-Balguerie *17*
Larose-Trintaudon *91;* 91 B3
Laroze 105 C3
Larrivaux *86;* 87 G3
Larrivet-Haut-Brion *98;* 99 F4
l'Arrosée 105 E4
Lartique 87 F5
la Salle 108 B1
Lascombes *17, 94;* 95 B2
la Serre 105 D5

Château
Lassègue 107 E4
Latour *17, 41, 82, 86, 88;* 89 F6, 91 B5
Latour-à-Pomerol *102,* 103 B4
la Tour Blanche, Bas Médoc 85 D5
la Tour-Blanche, Sauternes 101 F3
la Tour-Carnet *91;* 91 D2
La Tour de By *84;* 85 B4
la Tour-de-Grenet 107 B5
la Tour-de-Marbuzet 87 F5
la Tour-de-Mons *92, 94;* 93 G6
La Tour de Pez 87 E3
la Tour de Ségur 107 B5
La Tour des Termes 87 D4
la Tour-du-Haut-Moulin 93 D4
la Tour-du-Mirail 87 G2
la Tour du Pin Figeac 103 D5, 105 B2
la Tour Figeac *104;* 103 E5, 105 B2
la Tour-Gayet 108 B2
la Tour-Haut-Brion *98;* 99 B2
la Tour-Haut-Caussan 85 E3
la Tour-Léognan 99 E4
la Tour-Martillac *98;* 99 G6
la Tour Pibran 89 C5
la Tour-Prignac 85 E2
la Tour St-Bonnet *84;* 85 C4
la Tour-St-Joseph 87 G2
la Tour Seran 85 C4
la Tuilière 108 E2
l'Aubépin 101 F3
Laujac *84;* 85 C1
Launay *108;* 108 E3
Laurensanne *108;* 108 F3
Laurétan *96*
la Valade 106 C6
la Ville-Haut-Brion *96;* 99 A2
Lavinot-la-Chapelle 107 C3
la Violette 103 C4
Le Amon 270 E3
le Basque 107 C5
le Bedou 108 C2
le Boscq *86;* 85 C5, 87 D4
le Bourdieu *86;* 87 F2
le Breuil 87 G3
le Caillou 103 D4, 108 F4
le Castelot 107 E3
le Cauze 107 E4
le Chay 107 D5
le Crock *86;* 87 F5
le Cros 107 D5
le Désert 99 E4
le Fournas 89 D2
le Gay *102;* 103 C5
le Gazin *102;* 103 C6
l'Eglise-Clinet *102;* 103 C4
le Grand-Mazerolle 108 C2
le Guiraud 108 E2
le Hannetot 99 E4
le Here 101 F3
le Landat 87 F2
le Mausse 106 C6
le Mayne 107 D5
le Menaudat *108;* 108 B1
le Meynieu *86;* 87 E3
le Moulin-Rompu 108 F3
l'Enclos *102;* 103 B3
Léonay 272 B4
Léoville *17, 90*
Léoville-Barton 91 C5
Léoville-Lascases *84, 90, 91;* 91 B5
Léoville-Poyferre *91;* 91 B5
le Pape 99 F4
le Peillan 107 F4
le Pont 125 B3
les Alberts 108 B2
Lescadre 108 D2
les Carmes Haut Brion *98*
les Chaumes 108 B2
les Cônes-Sebizeaux 108 C1
Lescours 107 E2
les Cruzelles 107 C2
les Eyquems 108 F5
les Fines Roches 123 C5
les Heaumes 108 E2
les Jouans 107 F3
Les-Ormes-de-Pez *86;* 87 E4
les Ormes-Sorbet *84;* 85 D4
les Petits-Arnauds 108 C2
les Plantes 101 A5
les Prés 77 D4
les Remparts 101 D4
les Richards 108 E4
Lestage, Listrac-Médoc *92;* 93 F2
Lestage, Parsac 107 D5
Lestage, St-Seurin 87 B4
le Teyssier 107 C5
L'Evangile *102;* 103 D5, 105 A2
Lieujean 89 D2
Ligondras 95 D2
Liot 101 C4
Liversan *84, 87;* 89 B2
Livran 85 G3
Longueville *90*
Louberis *96*
Loudenne *84, 86;* 85 E6, 87 A4
Loumède 108 D3
Loupiac *96*
Lousteau-Vieil *96*
Lucas 107 C5
Ludeman la Côte *96*
Ludon-Pommiés-Agassac 95 G6
Lussac 107 C5
Lynch-Bages *34–35, 86;* 89 D5
Lynch-Moussas 89 D3
Lyonnat 107 B6
Macau 108 F5
MacCarthy Moula 87 F5
Magdelaine *104;* 105 D4
Magence *96*
Maison Blanche 107 C3
Malartic-Lagravière *98;* 99 F3

Château
Malengin 107 D5
Malescasse *92;* 93 E5
Malescot-St-Exupéry *94;* 95 B3
Malleprat 99 F6
Marchand 107 C5
Margaux *17, 94;* 95 B3
Marquis-d'Alesme-Becker *94;* 95 A3
Marquis de Terme *94;* 95 B2
Marsac-Séguineau 95 A2
Martinens 95 C2
Martinet 107 D1
Marzy 103 D3
Matras 105 D4
Maucaillou *92;* 93 E4
Maucamps 95 E5
Maucoil 127 A3
Mauras 101 E3
Maurens 107 E5
Mauvezin *92;* 105 C5
Mayne-Blanc 107 B5
Mazeris 106 C6
Mazeyres 103 C2
Mendoce 108 E2
Menota 97 B4
Meyney *86;* 87 E5
Mille Secousses 108 G4
Minière 121 B4
Monbazillac *109*
Monbousquet 107 F3
Monbrison 95 E8
Moncets 107 C3
Monconseil 108 E2
Mondou 107 E3
Montaiguillon 107 D3
Montbrun 95 B3
Montelena 251 B2
Monthil *84*
Montlabert 105 B3
Montrose *86;* 87 F5
Morin 87 D4
Moulin-à-Vent, Listrac-Médoc *98;* 93 G1
Moulin-à-Vent, St-Emilion 107 C2
Moulin-Blanc 107 C3, C5
Moulin de la Rose *91;* 93 A4
Moulin des Laurets 107 D6
Moulinet *102;* 103 B3
Moulin-Pey-Labrie 106 C6
Moulin-Riche 91 B4
Moulin-Rose 93 E5
Moulin Rouge *92;* 93 B4
Moulin St-Georges 105 D5
Moulins-de-Calon 107 C4
Moulis 93 G2
Mouton-Baron-Philippe *88;* 89 B4
Mouton-Rothschild *88;* 89 B4
Musar *233*
Musset 107 B2, D5
Myrat 101 B4
Nairac *100;* 101 A4
Negrit 107 C4
Nenin *102;* 103 D3
Nodaz 108 F5
Nodot 108 F3
Notton-Baury 95 D3
Olivier *98;* 99 F3
Pabeau 85 F5
Pailhas 107 F4
Palmer *92, 117;* 95 B3
Paloumery 95 F4
Panigon 85 D2
Pape-Clément *94;* 99 A1
Pardaillan *108;* 108 D2
Parsac 107 D5
Partarieu 101 F6
Patache d'Aux 85 C3
Paveil-de-Luze *92;* 93 G5
Pavie *104;* 105 E5
Pavie-Decesse 105 E5
Pavie-Macquin 105 E5
Pedesclaux *89;* 89 C6
Peillon-Claverie 101 G5
Perenne 108 C2
Pernaud 101 C4
Perron 107 C2
Perruchon 107 B5
Petit Bigaroux 107 F3
Petit Faurie de Souchard 105 C5
Petit-Gravet 107 E3
Petit Village *102;* 103 D5
Pétrus *102;* 103 C5
Peychaud 108 E4
Peyrabon 89 C2
Peyredoulle 108 D3
Peyron 101 G6
Peyroutas 107 F3
Phélan-Ségur *86;* 87 E5
Piada 101 B4
Pibran 89 C5
Picard 87 E5
Pichon-Longueville Baron *88;* 89 E5, 91 B4
Pichon-Longueville-Lalande *88;* 89 E6, 91 B4
Pierre-Bibian 93 F2
Pinet 108 D2
Piot 101 C4
Pipeau 107 F4
Plaisance 107 D3
Plantier Rose 87 E4
Pleytegeat 101 D5
Plince 103 D3
Pomys 87 F4
Pontac-Lynch 95 B3
Pontac-Monplaisir *98*
Pont-de-Pierre 107 B4
Pontet-Canet *88;* 89 C4
Pontet-Clauzure 105 C4
Pontoise-Cabarrus 87 C4
Pontus 106 C6
Potensac *84;* 85 F4
Pouget *94;* 95 C4

Château
Poujeaux 93 E4
Poujeaux-Theil *92*
Poumey 99 D2
Preuillac 85 F3
Priban 93 E6
Prieuré-Lichine *94;* 95 C3
Prost 101 A5
Puy-Blanquet *106;* 107 E5
Puy-Castéra 87 G3
Queyrats *96*
Queyron 107 F3
Quinault 107 D1
Rabaud-Promis 101 E4
Rahoul *96*
Ramage la Batisse 89 B2
Rasclet 107 F4
Rausan-Ségla *94;* 95 C2
Rauzan *17*
Rauzan-Gassies 95 B3
Rayas *127*
Raymond-Lafon *100;* 101 E4
Rayne-Vigneau 101 E3
Respide *96*
Rêve-d'Or 103 B3
Reynon *96*
Reysson *86;* 87 E2
Richelieu 106 D6
Rieussec 101 F5
Rigaillou 99 D4
Rigaud 107 D5
Ripeau 105 B3
Riverdeau 104 E4
Rivereau 108 E4
Robin 107 D4
Roc de Puisseguin 107 D6
Roc du Boissac 107 C5
Rochemorin 99 F5
Rocher-Corbin 107 C4
Rocheyron 107 E4
Rolland 87 G5, 89 A5, 101 B5
Romer 101 E5
Rosevale 272 C3
Roudier 107 D4
Rouet 106 C5
Rouget *102;* 103 B5
Roumieu 101 C4
Rousselle 108 E2
Rousset *108;* 108 F3
Rozier 107 E4
Ruat Petit Poujeaux 93 G3
St-Amand 101 B5
St-André 107 C4
St-André Corbin 107 D4
St-Bonnet 85 C5
St-Christoly *84*
St-Estèphe 87 E4
St-Georges *106;* 107 D4
St-Georges Côte Pavie 105 E5
St-Georges-Macquin 107 D3
St-Germain 108 D2
St-Jean 246 E4
St-Paul 87 C4
St-Pierre 93 A4
St-Pierre-Bontemps-et-Sevaistre *91;* 91 C4
St-Pierre-de-Pomerol 103 C4
St-Saturnin 85 C3
Sansonnet 105 D5
Saransot-Dupré 93 E2
Segonzac 108 C1
Sémeillan 93 F1
Siaurac *106;* 107 C3
Sigalas-Rabaud 101 E3
Sigognac 85 D5
Simon 101 B4
Simone *131*
Sipian 85 B2
Siran *94;* 95 C5
Smith-Haut-Lafitte *98;* 99 E5
Sociando-Mallet *86;* 87 C4
Soucarde 108 F3
Soudars 87 B4
Soutard 105 C5
Suau 101 B5
Suduiraut *100;* 101 E4
Tahbilk *270;* 270 D4
Taillefer 103 E4
Talbot *90, 91;* 91 C4
Tanunda 272 B4
Tayac, Bourg *108;* 108 F3
Tayac, Soussans 93 G5
Terrefort 95 D5
Terrey-Gros-Cailloux *91;* 91 C4
Tertre-Daugay 105 E3
Teyssier 107 F4
Thivin 77 G3
Touilla 101 E5
Toumalin 106 C6
Toumilon *96*
Tourans 107 E5
Tour du Haut-Moulin *92*
Tour du Roc 93 F5
Tournefeuille *106;* 107 C3
Tourteran 89 C2
Tramont 93 F4
Trapaud 107 E5
Trimoulet 105 B5
Trois Moulins 105 C4
Tronquoy-Lalande *86;* 87 E5
Troplong-Mondot 105 D5
Trotanoy *102;* 103 C4
Trotte-Vieille 105 D5
Vaisinerie 107 D6
Valoux 99 E5
Verdet 107 E2
Verdignan *86;* 87 B4
Vernous 85 F2
Veyrac 107 E5
Victoria *86;* 87 F3
Videlot 107 E1
Vieux Château Cloquet 103 B3
Vieux Château Certan 103 C5
Vieux Chevrol 107 C2

Château
Villegeorge *92;* 93 G5
Villemaurine 105 D5
Vincent 95 B3, 106 C6
Vrai-Canon-Bouché 106 D5
Vrai-Canon-Boyer 106 D5
Vray-Croix-de-Gay *102;* 103 C5
Yaldara 272 C3
Yon 107 D4
Yon-Figeac 105 C3
Yquem *41, 100, 140*
Châteaubernard 290 B6
Châteaumeillant 59 D2
Châteauneuf-du-Pape 127 C4, 129 D4
Châteaurenard 129 E4
Châteauroux 59 D2
Châteauthébaud 118 F2
Châteauvert 132 B3
Chatenay 77 C3
Chatham 265 F4
Chatillon-en-Diois 59 E5
Chatterton's 272 C3
Chaudefonds-sur-Layon 120 D2
Chaume 120 D3
Chaumont 59 C4
Chavanay 125 D2
Chaves 210 A5
Chavignol 123 F2
Cheffes 118 A5
Chehalis 263 B2
Cheilly 61 D5
Cheleiros 211 E4
Chemillé 118 C4
Chénas 61 F5, 77 B4, B5
Cherbaudes 72 F6
Cherson 230 E2
Chevagny-les-Chevrières 75 E4
Chevalier-Montrachet 66 F3
Cheverny 59 D2, 119 B3
Chevigné 75 E3
Chevrette 121 B2
Chevrol 107 C3
Chexbres 171 B1
Chez Barraud 291 D2
Chezenas 125 F2
Chianciano 194 F5, 194 F4, G2
Chianciano Terme 194 F5
Chianti 191 A3, 193
Chianti Classico 191 B3, 193
Chichée 79 E5
Chieri 181 B2
Chignin 131 D1
Chigny-les-Roses 111 B4
Chihuahua 261 B4
Chile (Chili) 282 F1, F2, 283 B2, C2, D2
Chilecito 283 B4
Chilford Hundred 284 E5
Chille 133 G4
Chillicothe 265 G3
Chilsdown 284 G5
Chindrieux 133 C1
Chinon 118 C6, 121 E4
Chioggia 185 E4
Chiquet 99 B2
Chiroubles 61 F5, 77 C3, 77 D3
Chirpan 229 D4
Chiuro 183 B5
Cholame 257 B4
Cholet 118 C4
Chouilly 111 E3
Choulex 170 D4
Choully 170 C3
Chouzé-sur-Loire 121 C1
Chowchilla 259 D4
Christchurch 277 E4
Christian Bros., Fresno 235 G1
Christian Bros., Napa 251 C3, F5
Christies Beach 274 C1
Christine Woods 248 C2
Chur 169 F5
Chusclan 129 D4
Ciampino 195 B4
Ciclopi 197 F3
Cienega 255 E4
Cilurzo 260 E5
Cincinnati 265 G3
Cinfâis 213 D6, 215 C2
Cinqueterre 179 E5
Ciro 197 D5
Cissac-Médoc 87 G2
Cisterna di Latina 195 D6
Citrusdal 278 E2
Ciudad México 261 C4
Ciudad Real 199 C3
Civo 183 B2
Civrac-en Médoc 85 D3
Clairette de Bellegarde 129 E3
Clairette de Die 124 E6
Clairette du Languedoc 131 B1
Clairvaux 59 F3
Clanwilliam 278 D2
Claremont 265 E6
Clarendon 274 C3
Clarevale 273 D5
Clare/Watervale 266
Clarksburg 259 A2
Clastidio 179 D5
Clavaillon 66 G4
Clavoillons 66 G4
Clay 259 A2
Clear Lake 248 C4
Cle Elum 263 E4
Cle. d. Mandria 195 C5
Clément 299 C5
Clements 259 B2
Cle. Nuovo di Bresciano 195 C5
Clermont 301 C4
Clermont-Ferrand 59 E3
Clermont-l'Hérault 131 B1
Clessé 75 D5
Cleveland 265 F4
Clisson 118 C3, F3

Clochan 297 A5
Clos Arlot 70 F4
Clos Baulet 72 F4
Clos-Blanches 67 F6, 68 F1
Clos de Avaux 68 F3
Clos de Bèze 72 F6
Clos de la Combe 103 B4
Clos de la Commaraine 67 F6, 68 E1
Clos de la Legume 68 E4
Clos de la Maréchale 70 E3
Clos de la Perrière 7 F6
Clos de la Roche 72 F5
Clos de l'Echo 121 E3
Clos de Mosny 122 E5
Clos de Perrières, Meursault 66 F5
Clos de Réas 71 F4
Clos des Barraults 74 C4
Clos des Chênes 66 F3, F4
Clos des Ducs 67 E5
Clos des Grandes Vignes, Prémeaux 70 F4
Clos des Grandes Vignes, Preignac 101 C6
Clos des Meix 66 G4
Clos des Montaigus 74 D3
Clos des Ormes 72 F5
Clos des Papes 127 C4
Clos de St-Jacques 73 E1
Clos de Tart 72 F4
Clos de Tavannes 65 G4, 66 G2
Clos de Verger 67 F6, 68 E1
Clos de Vougeot 71 F5, 72 F1
Clos du Château 67 F6, 68 F1
Clos du Chêne Marchand 123 F2
Clos du Jolivet 121 B3
Clos du Pape 101 F5
Clos du Parc 121 E3
Clos du Roi 68 F6
Clos du Val 251 E5
Clos du Vigneau 121 B1
Clos Faubard 65 F4
Clos Fontmurée 107 C4
Clos Fourtet 105 D4
Clos Grand Faurie 105 B5
Clos Haut Peyraguey 101 F3
Clos l'Église 103 C4
Clos l'Évêque 74 C4
Clos Mazeyres 103 C2
Clos Micot 67 F5
Clos Mouches 65 F4
Clos Pitois 65 F5
Clos Prieur-Haut 73 F1
Clos Quéron 121 E5
Clos René 99 B2
Clos St-Denis 71 F5, 72 F4
Clos St-Jean 66 F2
Clos Salomon 74 E4
Clos Sorbés 72 F4
Cloverdale 247 A3
Clovis 259 D5
Cluj 227 C3
Clusone 179 B6, 185 D1
Clynelish 295 B4
Clyre 252 F4
Coastal 278
Cochem 141 B2
Codevilla 183 F3
Codroipo 189 C4
Cognac 290 A6
Cogolin 132 C5
Cohn 253 C5
Coimbra 210 C4
Coin 209 E4
Coinsins 170 B4
Coka 255 C5
Colac 267 D2, 270 G2
Colares 210 D3, 211 E3
Coleburne 297 B3
Cole Ranch 248 C3
Colldejou 206 F6
Colli Albani 191 F3, 195 B4
Colli Aretini 191 B4
Colli Altotiberini 191 C5
Colli Berici 185 E3
Colli Bolognesi 185 G3, 189 B3
Colli del Trasimeno 191 C4
Colli di Bolzano 185 C3, 187
Colli di Parma 179 D6
Colli di Val d'Elsa 193 F2
Colli Euganei 185 E3
Colli Fiorentini 191 B3, 193 B3
Colli Lanuvini 191 F3, 195 C5
Colli Morenici Mantovani del Garda 185 E2
Colline Lucchesi 191 A3
Colli Orientali del Friuli 185 D6, 189 B5
Colline Pisane 191 A2
Collio Goriziano 185 D6, 189 C5
Collioure 130 F3
Colli Perugini 191 C4
Colli Senesi 191 B3, 193 F2
Colli Tortonesi 179 D4, 183 G2
Colmar 59 B5, 114 E5, 117 C1, 141 F2, 302 D3
Colognaola ai Colli 181 G1
Colombier, Dordogne 109 F5
Colombier, Neuchâtel 302 F3
Colonia 282 G2
Colonna 195 A5
Colorina 183 B3
Columbia 301 C4
Columbu 265 F3
Combe-au-Moine 73 E2
Como 176 A4, 179 B5
Comps 108 F3
Conca 197 C2
Concannon 255 A3
Concepción 257 G4, 283 E1
Conchez de Béarn 293 D3
Concord 265 E6
Condobolin 267 A4
Condom 135 E3, 293 C5
Condorcet 127 D5

Condrieu 124 B5, 125 C3, D1, D2
Conegliano 189 C2
Conesus Lake 264 F3
Congress Springs 255 C2
Conn Creek 251 D4
Conrotto 255 D4
Consorzio Agrario Provinciale di Siena 193 E2
Constanta 227 E5
Constanti 207 F2
Constantia 278 G1
Constantine 235 B4
Conthey 171 D3
Conti Serristori 193 C3
Contres 119 B3
Convalmore 297 D4
Converso 197 B7
Coolalta 268 C4
Coolawin Estates 274 B3
Cooma 266 C5
Coonawarra 267 D1, 275 B5
Coop de Cognac et Vins Charentais 291 B1
Coorara 274 B2
Cootamundra 267 B4
Copertino 197 C6
Coppet 170 C4
Coquimbo 282 F2
Corbera d'Ebre 206 G5
Corbères-Abères 135 F4
Corbett Canyon 257 D3
Corbeyrier 171 C1
Corbières 59 G3, 130 C3
Corbin 301 C5
Corbonod 133 B1
Corcelles-en-Beaujolais 77 E5
Corcolle 195 A5
Corcoran 259 F5
Cordes 135 D6
Córdoba, Argentina 282 G2
Córdoba, Spain 199 D3, 209 B4
Corfu (Kerkira) 237 C1
Cori 191 F3, 195 C6, 197 B1
Corinth (Korinthos) 237 D3
Coriole 274 C2
Cormons 189 C5
Cormontreuil 111 A4
Cornas 124 D5
Cornellá de Llobregat 207 E5
Cornudella de Montsant 206 F6
Coronata 179 E4
Corowa 267 C3, 270 C3
Corowa-Rutherglen 267 C3, 270 D5
Corrèze 59 E3
Corsier 170 C4
Cortadedos 201 D2
Corte 138 E4
Cortes dell'Alto Monferrato 179 D4, 181 D5
Cortese di Gavi 179 D4
Cortina d'Ampezzo 185 C4
Cortz Brothers 247 A4
Coruche 210 D4
Corvino S. Quirico 183 F4
Corvo 197 F2
Cosne-sur-Loire 119 B6
Cossato 182 F2
Costalunga 187 G2
Costermano 186 E3
Costières du Gard 59 G4, 129 E3
Costozza 185 E3
Cotas 215 E2
Côte d'Or 61 C5
Coteaux d'Aix-en-Provence 59 F5, 132 B2
Coteaux d'Ancenis 59 D1, 118 B3
Coteaux de la Loire 118 B3, B4
Coteaux de l'Aubance 118 B5, 120 C4, E6
Coteaux de Pierrevert 59 F5
Coteaux de St-Christol 59 F4
Coteaux de Saumur 118 C6
Coteaux des Baux de Provence 59 F5, 129 F4
Coteaux de Vérargues 59 G1
Coteaux du Jura 169 F1
Coteaux du Languedoc 59 G4
Coteaux du Layon 118 B5, C5
Coteaux du Loir 119 A1
Coteaux du Tricastin 124 F5, 59 G5
Coteaux du Vendômois 59 C2, 119 A2
Coteaux Varois 59 G5, 132 B3
Côte Blonde 125 B3
Côte Brune 125 B3
Côte de Brouilly 77 F3
Côte de Fontenay 79 C4
Côte de Léchet 79 D2
Côte Roannaise 59 E4
Côte-Rôtie, Chiroubles 77 D3
Côte-Rôtie, Côtes du Rhône 124 B5, 125 B2, B3
Côte-Rôtie, Morey-St-Denis 72 E4
Côtes d'Auvergne 59 E3
Côtes de Bordeaux-Saint-Macaire 80 F6
Côtes de Castillon 80 E5
Côtes de Canon Fronsac 80 E4, 106 C6
Côtes de la Malepère 59 G3
Côtes de Néac 80 E4
Côtes de Provence 132
Côtes de St-Mont 59 G2
Côtes de Toul 59 B4
Côtes du Brulhois 59 F2
Côtes du Forez 59 E4
Côtes du Frontannais 59 G2
Côtes du Lubéron 59 F5, 129 E5
Côtes du Marmandais 59 F2
Côtes-du-Nord 58 C6
Côtes-du-Rhône 59 E4, F4, 124
Côtes-du-Roussillon 130 E3
Côtes du Ventoux 59 F5
Côtes du Vivarais 59 F4, 129 C3
Coturri, H., & Sons 246 E3
Coueron 118 C2
Coulée de Serrant 120 B3
Cour-Cheverny 59 C2, 119 B3
Courgis 79 F2
Courmayeur 179 B2
Courvoisier 291 B3
Coutras 80 D5
Covelinhas 214 G4
Covilhã 210 C5
Covington 301 B4
Cowra 267 B5
Cragganmore 297 E1
Craigellachie 297 D4
Craiova 227 D3
Cramant 111 F3
Craneford 272 D5
Crans-près-Celigny 170 C4
Crasssier 170 C4
Cravant-les-Coteaux 121 E5
Crawfordville 268 E4
Cray 122 D6
Crazies 284 F5
Creixell 207 F2
Crema 179 C5
Cremona 176 A4, 179 D6, 185 E1
Crémone (Cremona) 176 A4, 179 D6, 185 E1
Créon 96 D5
Cresta Blanca 248 B3
Creston 257 C4
Creston Manor 257 C4
Crete (Kriti) 215 F4
Creux de la Net 69 D3
Creysse 109 F6
Crézancy-en-Sancerre 123 F2
Crieff 295 E4
Crissier 170 A6
Crna Gora (Montenegro) 225 F4
Crouin 290 B5
Croix des Bouquets 298 A5
Croizet-Eymard 291 C4
Crosa 182 F2
Crotone 197 E5
Crozes-Hermitage 124 D6, 126 B4
Cru Barjuneau 101 G3
Cru Caplane 101 F4
Cru Commarque 101 G3
Cru de Bergeron 101 D3
Cruet 133 D1
Cru la Clotte 101 B5
Cru Lanère 101 G3
Cru Thibaut 101 G5
Cruzille 75 B5
Csengöd 220 C2
Csopak 220 C2, 223 F1
Cuba 298 A4
Cubaexport 298 A4
Cubelles 207 F3
Cuéllar 208 F3
Cuenca 199 B4
Cuers 132 C3
Cuis 111 E3
Cullens 276 C3
Cully 170 B6
Cumières 111 D2
Cunèges 109 F5
Cuneo 176 B3, 179 E2
Cunit 207 F3
Cureggio 182 E5
Curicó 283 C2
Curino 182 E3
Cussac 91 E5, 93 C4
Cutler 259 E5
Cuvaison 251 B2
Cygnet 271 C6

D

Dachsberg 156 F3
Dahra 235 B2
Daignac 96 D6
Dailuaine 297 E3
Dallas 263 D2
Dallas Dhu 295 C5
Dalmatia 225 E3
Dalmore 295 C4
Dalswinton 269 F4
Dalwhinnie 295 D4
Dalwood 268 B5
Damascus (Dimashq) 232 F5
Damazan 138 D2
Dambach-la-Ville 114 D5
Damery 111 D2
Dansville 265 F4, G4
Dão 210 B4, 213
Dar bel Amri 234 C5
Darbonnay 133 F4
Dardagny 170 D3
D'Arenberg 274 C2
Darlington 274 B2
Darmstadt 141 B4
Dartbrook 269 D5
Das Alte Weinhaus 272 D3
Daubhaus 160 G5
Daubos 89 E5, 91 A4
Davayé 75 F4
David Springs 255 C2
Davis 259 A1
Davis Bynum 247 D4
Davos 169 F5
Dawson Estate 268 C5
Dax 134 F6
Daytesford 270 E3
Dayton 265 F3
Dazio 183 B3
Deanston 295 E4
Deatsville 301 C4
Debrecen 220 B4
Debroi Hárslevelü 220 B3
Deer Park 251 C3
Dehesilla 200 B4
Dehlinger 247 E5
de Hoop 281 E2
Deidesheim 141 C4, 159 B2, F5
Delamain 291 B3
Delano 259 F5
Delgado and Zuleta 200 C5
Delheim, Carneros 249 E2
Delheim, S. Africa 281 E2
Delisle 295 C5
Dellchen 152 F6
Del Norte 245 B1
De Loach 247 E5
De May Wine Cellars 264 G4
Denair 259 C3
Denheim 141 B4
Denia 199 C5
Deniliquin 267 C3
Denman 269 F3, F4
Denman Estate 269, F5
Denwortham 273 E5
De Pins 293 F3
Derbent 230 F5
Derrière-la-Grange 72 F3
Derrière chez Edouard 66 D2
Derrière la Tour 66 E3
Derrière le Four 71 F4
Desenzano del Garda 186 G1
Detroit 265 F3
Deutelsberg 157 F1
Deutschherrenberg 150 C5
Deutschkreutz 172 E3
Deutschlandsberg 172 G1
Deutschschutzen 172 F3
Deutz 257 D4
Deux Sèvres 59 D1
Deva 227 C2
Devesas 214 G2
Devlin 255 D2
Devonport 271 B5
Devon Vale Estates 281 E1
Dezize 61 D5
De Zoete Inval 281 D4
Dhali 238 B4
Dhron 149 D1
Diamond 297 G6
Diamond Creek 251 C2
Diamond Oaks 247 A3
Diedesfeld 159 C2
Dienheim 141 B4, 160 G5
Dieulefit 129 C5
Di Giorgio 259 G6
Digne 59 F5
Dijon 59 C4, 61 C6
Dimashq 232 F5
Dimcha 229 C3
Dimiát 229 B5, D4
Dinuba 259 E5
Dirmstein 159 A2
Ditchling 284 G5
Dittelsheim 161 F3
Dixon 259 A1
Dizy-Magenta 111 D3
Djidjelli 235 A4
Döbling 174 B3
Dobrogeia 227 D6
Doctor 151 F2
Doganello 195 D6
Doktorberg 147 F6
Dolan 248 B3
Dolceacqua Rossese 179 F3
Dolcetto d'Alba 181 E3
Dolcetto d'Asti 179 D4, 181 E4
Dolcetto delle Langhe Monregalasi 179 E3
Dolcetto di Acqui 179 F3, 181 E5
Dolcetto di Diano d'Alba 179 D3, 181 E3
Dolcetto di Dogliano 179 E3, 181 E2
Dolcetto d'Ovada 179 D4
Domaine Chandon 251 E5
Domaine d'Arche Pugneau 101 E4
Domaine de Becamil 193 B5
Domaine de Chevalier 99 G2
Domaine de Hannetot-Grandmaison 99 E4
Domaine de la Combe 103 B4
Domaine de la Garde 99 G6
Domaine de l'Eglise 103 C5
Domaine de l'Ile de Margaux 94 A4
Domaine de Plagnac 85 D3
Domaine de Sarry 123 G2
Domaine la Solitude 99 G5
Domaine Laurier 247 D4
Domane 145 D3
Domblans 133 F4
Dombleck 161 G3
Domherr, Piesport 149 C2
Domherr, Rheinhessen 161 E3
Domherrenberg 147 D2, E3
Dominica 299 C4
Dominican Republic 298 A6
Domodossola 179 B3
Domprobst 150 E1
Doña Elvira 200 B4
Don Charles Ross 251 G5
Donna Maria 247 D5
Donnaz 179 B3
Donnerskirchen 172 D3, 173 F4
Donnici 197 D4
Donnybrook 273 D5
Doosberg 156 F5
Dordogne 59 E2, 80 D6
Dornach 302 E3
Dorney 284 F5
Dornoch 295 C4
Dos Palos 259 D3
Double Springs 301 B3
Doubs 59 C5
Douby 77 D4
Doué-la-Fontaine 118 C5
Douro (Duero) 210 A5
Douro-Littoral 210 A4
Douvaine 133 A2
Douville 109 E6
Drachenstein 155 F3
Drăgăsani 227 D3
Draguignan 59 B4
Drake 257 G4
Drakenstein (Coop) 281 E3
Drama 237 B4
Driesprong 281 E3
Drôme 129 C4
Drumborg 267 D1
Dry Creek 247 C4
Dry Creek Valley 247
Dubbo 267 A5
Duboeuf, Georges 248 C4
Dubois, France 122 C4
Du Bois, USA 247 C5
Dubrovnik 225 E3
Duckhorn 251 C3
Ducor 259 F6
Düdingen 302 F3
Dufftown 295 C5, 297 E4
Duillier 170 B4
Dulce Nombre 201 C4
Dully 170 B4
Dumbarton 295 F4
Dumfries 295 G5
Dunajska Streda 223 C5
Dunaujvaros 220 C2
Dundee 295 E5
Dunkirk 265 F4
Dunn 251 B4
Duquesne 299 C5
Duras 97 E3, 109 G4, 135 C2
Durbach 163 D2
Durbanville 278 F2
Dürnstein 172 C1, 175 G1
Durtal 118 A5
Duxoup 247 B4

E

Earlimart 259 F5
East Branch Winery 264 F4
Eauze 135 E2, 293 C4
Eberbach 141 C5
Eberle 257 B3
Ebersberg 160 E3
Ebersweier 302 C4
Echaillé 66 D2
Echandens 170 A5
Echézeaux de Dessus 71 F5
Echuca 267 C5, 270 C3
Eckelsheim 161 F2
Eclubens 170 A5
Ecueil 111 B3
Edelberg 151 B4
Edelmann 156 F4
Edenkoben 159 C2
Eden Valley 272 D6
Edmeades 248 C2
Edinburgh 295 E5
Edinglassie 269 E5
Edison 259 G6
Edna 257 D3
Edna Valley 257 D3
Edradour 295 D5
Egelsee 175 F3
Eger 220 B3
Eggenburg 172 B2
Eglise-Neuve d'Issac 109 E5
Eguisheim 114 E5, 116 C5
Egypt 232 G3
Ehrenberg 147 G6
Ehrenhausen 172 G2
Ehrenstetten 163 F1
Eibelstadt 164 F3
Eibingen 155 F4
Eichberg, Alsace 116 C5
Eichberg, Eltville 157 E1
Eichoffen 114 C5
Einzellagenfreie Flächen 145 C4
Eisenstadt 172 D3, 173 F3
Eitelsbach 147 D4
El Alamo 201 C1
Elba 176 C4, 191 B1
El Barco 201 C2
El Bizarron 201 E2
El Bonete 201 B4
El Caballo 201 E2
El Carmen 201 C4
El Castillo 201 C4
El Catllar 207 F2
El Cerro Viejo 201 D3
El Ciego 204 B6, 205 G4
El Corchuelo 201 D2
El Corregidor 201 C4
El Corregidor Viejo 201 C4
El Cuco 201 D1
El Cuerno del Oro 20 B3
Elderslie 268 A5
Elgin 295 C5, 297 A2
El Hornillo 200 B5
Elisenberg 150 G6
Elizabeth 266 C6
El Jardinito 201 C4
Ellendale (Sveta Maria) 276 C5
Ellensburg 263 B4
Ellergrub 151 C4
Elliston 255 A3
Elk Grove 259 A2
Elkins 265 G4
El Masnou 207 E6
El Masroig 206 F6
Elmham Park 284 E6
Elmira, Australia 269 F5
Elmira, California 259 A1
El Molar 206 F6
El Morell 207 F2
Elne 130 E3
El Paraiso 201 D2
El Parradero 201 C3
El Paso de Robles 257 B3
El Peral 200 A5
El Pinell de Brai 206 G5
El Pollero 200 D6
El Pont d'Armenterra 207 E2
El Prat de Llobregat 207 F5
El Rancho 201 D2
El Romano 201 C4
El Rourell 207 F2
El Salvador 201 C4
El Señor 200 B4
Els Garidells 207 F2
Els Guiamets 206 F6
Els Monjos 207 F3
Elster 159 E5
El Telegrafo 201 C4
El Toro 201 E1
Eltville 141 B4
Eltville-am-Rhein 157 G3
Elvas 210 D5
El Vendrell 207 F3
El Verano 246 G5
Elysium 274 C3
Emeringes 77 B4
Emilia-Romagna 176 B4, 179 D5, 185 G2, 191 A4
Emme 302 F4
Emmendingen 302 D4
Emporia 265 G5
Emu 274 C2
en Cailleret, Chassagne Montrachet 65 F6, 66 G1
en Cailleret, Meursault 67 F4
en Caradeux 69 D4
en Champans 67 F4
en Charlemagne 69 E4
en Chevret 67 F3
en Creot 66 D3
Endingen 163 E1
Enfer d'Arvier 179 B2
Engadin 169 G5
Engelgrube 149 F2
Engelsberg 160 B5
Engelmanns Berg 156 G6
en Genêt 68 E6
En Guinelay 77 B5
Enkirch 151 B4
en la Chapelle 72 F6
en la Perrière-Noblet 71 F3
en la Rancha 66 D3
en Làrgillière 68 F2
en l'Orme 66 E6
en l'Ormeau 67 F4
en Montceau 66 E3
Enmore 299 G6
Enna 197 F3
en Orveaux 71 E5
Ensenada 261 B3
Entrayques 59 F3
Entre-Deux-Mers 80 F4
Entre-os-Rios 215 C1
Enumclaw 263 A3
en Verseuil 67 F4
Enzan 239 B5
Epernay 111 E3
Epesses 170 B6
Epinal 59 B5
Epiré 120 B3
Episkopi 238 C2
Erback 157 F2
Erbaluce di Caluso 179 C3
Erben, R.C. 187, C5
Erdek 232 B2
Erden 150 C5
Ereğli 232 D4
Erie 265 F4
Erlenbach 163 C4
Erntebringer 156 E2
Ervedosa do Douro 215 F2
Eschbach 159 D1
Escherndorf 164 E4
Escondido 260 G4
Escurès 293 E3
Eskisehir 232 C3
España 175
Esperanza Winery 264 F4
Espinho 214 G6, 215 C1
Esposende 213 B4
Essaouira 234 D3
Essertines 170 B4 D3
Essonne 59 B2
Estagel 130 D2
Estaing 59 F3
Est Est Est di Montefiascone 191 D3
Estoril 211 F4
Estrella 257 B3
Estrella River 257 B4
Estremadura 210 C4
Estremoz 210 D5
Esvres 119 B1
Etna 197 F3
Etournelles 73 E1
Etoy 170 B5
Etroyes 74 C4
Euboea (Evvoia) 237 D4
Euchariusberg 145 A3, A6
Eugene 263 B2
Euphrates (Firat) 232 D5
Eure 59 B2
Eure-et-Loir 59 B2
Eureka 245 B1
Euroa 270 D4
Euskirchen 141 A2
Evans & Tate 276 A5
Evensun 251 E4
Evionnaz 171 D2
Evora 210 E4
Evorilla 200 A6
Evreux 59 B2
Evvoia 237 C3
Ewig Leben 164 E3
Exeter 259 E5
Eymet 109 G5
Eyrans 108 B2
Eysines 80 E3, 96 C3
ez Crets 66 G2
ez Crottes 65 G5
ez Folatières 66 F4

F

Fabriano 191 C5
Fafe 213 C5
Fahrwangen 302 C5
Fairmont 265 G4
Fairview 281 D3
Falcognana 195 B4
Falerio 191 C5
Falerno 197 B2
Falklay 151 A4
Falkenberg 149 C2
Falkenstein 172 B2
Falkirk 295 E4
Falset 206 F6
Famagusta 238 B5
Famoso 259 G5
Fanhões 211 E5
Fara 179 C4, 182 G5
Fareham Estate 273 F6
Fargues 101 F6
Farmington 259 B3
Far Niente 251 E4
Faro, Italia 197 E4
Faro, Portugal 210 F4
Fattoria S. Altomena 193 B5
Faugères 59 G3, 130 B6
Favaios 215 D2
Faye-d'Anjou 120 D5
Fayssac 135 D6
Féchy 170 B5
Fehrig 253 C6
Fehring 172 G2
Feld 145 B2
Felgueiras 213 C5, 215 C2
Fels 172 C2
Felslay 147 E4
Felsenberg 152 G4
Felseneck 153 F2
Felsenkopf 149 G1
Felsensteyer 152 F5
Felton Empire 255 D2
Fenestra 255 A3
Feodosija 230 E2
Fergusson's Winery 270 E4
Ferianes 200 C5
Fernandez 299 B2, E5
Fernando A. de Terry 201 E1, F3
Fernán Núñez 209 B4
Ferrais-les-Corbières 130 C3
Ferrara, Italy 176 B4, 185 F3
Ferrara, California 260 G4
Ferres 149 C1
Fès 234 C5
Fetiaska 229 B5
Fettercairn 295 D5
Fetters Hot Springs 246 F4
Fetzer 248 B3, C3
Feuerberg (Bad Dürkheim) 159 B2, B5
Feuersteige 173 F3
Feurer Kogl 173 F4
Feydieu 95 F4
Fiano di Avellino 197 C3
Fiefs Vendéens 59 D1
Field Stone 247 C5
Fiesole 193 A4
Figari 138 G4
Figline 193 D5
Filhot 101 G3
Filsinger 260 E5
Filzen 145 B3, 149 B4
Findlay 265 F3
Findling 160 D4
Finistère 58 C5
Finocchio 195 A5
Fiorano 191 E3
Firat (Euphrates) 232 D5
Firebaugh 259 D3
Firenze 176 B4, 191 A4, 193 B3
Firestone 257 F5
Firvida 214 F2
Fitou 130 D4
Fiuggi 191 F4
Five Points 259 E4
Fixin 61 C6, 73 E4
Flagey-Echézeaux 71 G5
Flaugeac 109 F5
Flaujagues 109 F3
Flein 163 C4
Fleischmann 301 C3
Fleurance 135 E3, 293 C6
Fleurie 61 F5, 77 C4
Fleury-les-Aubrais 119 A4
Fleys 79 D6
Flohhaxn 175 F1
Floirac 80 E3, 96 D4
Flora Springs 251 D4
Florence (Firenze) 176 B4, 191 A4, 193 B3
Fochabers 297 B5
Focsani 227 D5
Fogarina 185 F2
Foggia 176 C6, 197 B4
Foix 59 G3
Folgosa 214 G4
Foligno 191 D4
Folligberg 173 G3
Fonroque 109 G5
Fontalioux 125 F2
Fontana di Papa 195 C4
Fontanelas 211 E3
Fontanelle 191 D6
Fontaneto d'Ayognay 182 E5
Fontelo 214 G3
Fonteny 73 E1
Fonterntoli 193 F4
Fontès 130 B6
Fontevrault d-l'Abbaye 118 C6
Fontrubi 207 E3
Foppiano 247 C5
Forbes 267 B4
Forbes-Cowra 267 B4
Forcine 121 B1
Forest Grove 263 C2
Forest Hill 276 D6
Forest Hills 247 D4
Forestville 247 D4
Forez 125 F2
Forli 176 B5, 185 G4, 191 A5
Fornos de Algodres 213 F6
Forres 295 C5
Forst 153 C1, 159 B2
Forst a. d. Weinstrasse 159 E5
Forsterlay 151 C1
Fort-de-France 299 C5
Forte Ile 299 C4
Forthof 175 G3
Fortino 255 D3
Fortunago 183 G4
Fort Wayne 265 F3
Fort William 295 D3
Fossignano 195 C4
Fos-sur-Mer 129 G4
Fougueyrolles 109 F9
Foujouin 122 B4
Founex 170 C4
Four Chimneys Farm Winery 264 F5
Four Corners 251 C4
Fourques 130 E2
Fours 108 B2
Fowler 259 E5
Fraisse 109 E4
Francemont 65 F5
Francesco Bertoli 193 F3
Franciacorta 185 D1
Franciscan 251 D4
Frangy 133 B1
Franken 141 B6
Frankenthal 155 E1
Frankfort, Kentucky 301 B4
Frankfurt 141 B4
Frankland River 276 C5
Franklin 301 D3
Franschhoek 278 F2, 281 G6
Frapin 291 D2
Frascati 191 F3, 195 B5
Fraserburgh 295 C6
Fratenilli 193 E2
Frauenfeld 169 D4
Frauengarten 174 F6
Frauenkirchen 173 G6
Frauenweingarten 175 G2
Fredericksburg 265 G5
Fredson, Chris A. 247 C4
Freemark Abbey 251 C3
Freiburg 141 F3, 163 F2, 302 D4
Freinsheim 159 B2
Freisa d'Asti 179 D3, 181 C3, C4
Freisa di Chieri 179 C3, 181 B1, B2
Freixial 211 D5
Freixo de Espada-a-Cinta 215 C3
Frelmersheim 159 C2
Frémiets 67 F5
Fremont 255 B3
Fresno 245 E3, 259 D4
Fréterive 133 C2
Freudenstadt 141 E4
Freundstück 159 E5
Frey 248 B3
Fribourg 169 F2, 302 F3
Frick 255 D2
Frickenhausen 164 F4
Frithsden 284 F5
Fritz 247 B4
Friularo 185 E4
Friuli-Venezia 189 B3, B4
Friuli Venezia Giulia 176 A5, 185 C5
Frog's Leap 251 C3
Frohnhof 159 C5
Fronsac 80 E4, 106 D6
Frontignan 131 D7
Fronton 59 F2, 135 E5
Frosinone 191 F4, 197 B2
Fruska Gora 225 D4
Fuchs 145 E3
Fuchsberg 155 F5
Fuchsmantel 159 C4
Fuenmayor 205 B6
Fuissé 75 G4
Fuji-San 239 C5
Fuji-Yoshida 239 C5
Fully 171 D2
Fulton, California 247 D5
Fulton, Kentucky 301 D1
Fumane 186 F4
Funchal 219 E3
Furmint 220 A4, C2, B2
Furore Divina Costiera 197 C3
Fürsteneck 163 D2
Fürstentum 117 C3
Fusine 183 C3
Fyé 79 C5

G

Gabarret 135 F2
Gabbiano 193 D3
Gabilan Range 255 E4
Gabrovo 229 C4
Gaeta 197 B2
Gageac-et-Rouillac 109 F5
Gaillac 59 F3, 135 D6
Gainfarn 174 G2
Gaisböhl 159 F5, G5
Gaispfad 151 C4
Galafura 214 F4
Galati 227 D5
Galbenă 227 E5
Gallega 201 E1
Gallicano nel Lazio 195 A6
Gallipoli 197 C5
Galt 259 A2
Gamay 66 E3
Gambellara 185 E3, 187 G3
Gamlitz 172 G2
Gampel 171 C5
Gamza 229 B2
Gan 135 G1

S

Photographs and Pictures

6 MARY EVANS PICTURE LIBRARY. 9 Colin Maher/FOTOBANK. 12 t Werner Forman, b Michael Holford. 13 t BPC Library, b Reading Museum. 14 tl Bodleian Library, tr John Rylands, c, b Michael Holford. 15 r GIRAUDON. 16 t Louvre/Réunion des Musées Nationaux. 18 Pierre Mackiewicz. 26/ELIZABETH PHOTO LIBRARY, r COLORIFIC. 31 M. Rosenfeld/MAURITIUS. 32 tB. Lehn/MAURITIUS, b Musée des Arts et Traditions Populaires, Paris. 38/GIRAUDON. 39 r Historisches Museum der Pfalz. 43 Denis Hughes Gilbey. 47 Hugh Johnson. 48 ROBERT HARDING PICTURE LIBRARY. 50 Kim Sayer. 57 H. Gruyaert/MAGNUM. 58 P. Bardou. 60 Jean Michot. 64 t Jean-Daniel Sudres/SCOPE, b Guy Gravett. 66 t, bl, br Hugh Johnson, bc Chapman/TOPHAM. 69 Hugh Johnson. 70 Guy Gravett. 71 Hugh Johnson. 73 Bernard Beaujard. 74 Guy Gravett. 76/PICTUREPOINT, r Alain Vivier/SCOPE. 78 Guy Gravett. 81 Adam Woolfitt/SUSAN GRIGGS. 84 Michel Guillard/SCOPE. 86 t Bernard Beaujard, b International Distillers & Vintners. 88 Adam Woolfitt/SUSAN GRIGGS. 90 Colin Maher/FOTOBANK. 92 Editions des Deux Coqs d'Or. 97 TONY STONE WORLDWIDE. 98 Adam Woolfitt/SUSAN GRIGGS. 100 Hugh Johnson. 102 Guy Gravett. 104 t Marc Riboud, b Guy Gravett. 106 Guy Gravett. 109 t Colin Maher/FOTOBANK, b Jean-Daniel Sudres/SCOPE. 110 Claude Huyghens. 112 l, tr Colin Maher/FOTOBANK, br Denis Hughes-Gilbey. 114 TONY STONE WORLDWIDE. 119 Guy Gravett. 120 Michel Guillard/SCOPE. 123 Patrick Eagar. 124 Holt Studios. 126 Patrick Eagar. 127 Suzanne Schapowalow. 128 ROBERT HARDING PICTURE LIBRARY. 131 Michael Boys. 132 T. Grundelwein/MAURITIUS. 134 ZEFA. 138 ZEFA. 139 MAURITIUS. 144 Jon Wyand/FOTOBANK. 146 BAVARIA-Verlag. 148/Hugh Johnson, r Adam Woolfitt. 149 Toni Schneiders. 150 Deinhard & Co. 151 Deinhard & Co. 152 Jon Wyand/FOTOBANK. 154 t Peter Hallgarten, bl, br Editions des Deux Coqs d'Or. 155 Peter Hallgarten. 158 t Editions des Deux Coqs d'Or, bl, br Urbanus-Fotopress. 160 Adam Woolfitt. 161 t ZEFA, b Colin Maher. 162 Rudolf Holtappel/BAVARIA-Verlag. 164 Rodney Todd-White. 165 t Bayerische Verwaltung der Staatlichen Schlösser, Gärten u. Seen, b Bayerische Landesanstalt für Weinbau u. Gartenbau Wurzburg/Veitshochheim/Bildarchiv Kurt Furtner. 167 Anthony Blake. 168 Monique Jacot/SUSAN GRIGGS. 170 CAMERA PRESS. 172 ZEFA. 175 MAURITIUS. 177 Michael Boys. 178 Jon Wyand/FOTOBANK. 180 Guy Gravett. 184 Marcella Pedone/BAVARIA-Verlag. 186 Camera Press. 188 Guglielmo Mairani/Grazia Neri. 190 Bohnacker/Prenzel. 192 Jan Traylen/Patrick Eagar. 194 Michael Boys. 198 MAURITIUS. 200/Guy Gravett. 202 Adam Woolfitt/SUSAN GRIGGS. 204 PICTUREPOINT. 206/Vinos de España, t, br Antony Denney. 208 Vinos de España. 211 Hugh Johnson. 212 Hugh Johnson. 214 Hugh Johnson. 215 Hugh Johnson. 216/ROBERT HARDING PICTURE LIBRARY, r Melanie Freud/CHL. 217 Guy Gravett. 218 PICTUREPOINT. 221 Bo Bojesen. 222 ZEFA. 224 F.H.C. Birch/SONIA HALLIDAY. 226 ZEFA. 228 BAVARIA-Verlag. 231 NOVOSTI. 233 M. E. ARCHIVES. 234 ZEFA. 236 TONY STONE WORLDWIDE. 241 Michael Freeman. 242/243 Crown Zellerbach Corp., D. J. Flanagan/Buffalo, Philip Wagner, Konstantin Frank. 244 Harolyn Thompson. 249 Harolyn Thompson. 250 Harolyn Thompson. 254 Dick Rowan/SUSAN GRIGGS. 256 Harolyn Thompson. 258, 260 Harolyn Thompson. 262 Robert V. Eckart jr./IMAGE BANK. 265 David Hiser/IMAGE BANK. 266 Patrick Eagar. 269 J.-P Ferrero/FOTOBANK. 271 Patrick Eagar. 273 J.-P Ferrero/FOTOBANK. 274 Patrick Eagar. 277 Patrick Eagar. 279 Brian Lewis/ASPECT. 280 KWV. 282 W. Hasenberg/ZEFA. 284 S. & O. Mathews. 285 Brian Seed/JOHN HILLELSON AGENCY. 290 Cognac Information Centre. 292 t J.-P Ferrero/EXPLORER, b F. Gohier/EXPLORER. 294/IMAGE BANK, r BTA. 298 Yves Alexandre. 300 t, b Michael Freeman/BRUCE COLEMAN LTD. 301/IMAGE BANK. 302 Swiss National Tourist Office. 303 Guy Gravett.

Picture researcher: Diana Korchien

Illustrations

Revisions and new illustrations and diagrams for this edition:

2/3 Bill Sanderson; 10/11 Grundy and Northedge; 16/17 Grundy and Northedge; 20/1 Sue Sharples; 22 Lesli Sternberg; 24 Grundy and Northedge; hydrometer: Sue Sharples; 26/7 Grundy and Northedge; 28/9 Emma Crosby; 31 Grundy and Northedge; 32/3 colour tinting: Trevor Lawrence; 34/5 Stephen Biesty; 36/7 Stephen Biesty; 40/1 Grundy and Northedge; 44 colour tinting: Trevor Lawrence; 48 line drawings: Sue Sharples; 49 line drawings: Sue Sharples; colour tinting: Trevor Lawrence; 52 Grundy and Northedge; watercolours: Sue Sharples; 58 Grundy and Northedge; 60 Grundy and Northedge; 63 Grundy and Northedge; 82 Mulkern Rutherford; 83 Grundy and Northedge; 140 Grundy and Northedge; 142 Grundy and Northedge; airbrushing: Mulkern Rutherford; 177 Grundy and Northedge; 215 Grundy and Northedge; 244 Grundy and Northedge; 267 Grundy and Northedge; 279 Grundy and Northedge; 286/7 Grundy and Northedge; 288/9 Sue Sharples; 290 Grundy and Northedge; 297 Grundy and Northedge.

Original illustrations:

Norman Barber, Roger Bristow, Marilyn Bruce, Ray Burrows, David Cook, Diagram, Chris Forsey, David Fryer, Gilchrist Studios, Patrick Leeson, Michael McGuinness, Vernon Mills, Peter Morter, Shirley Parfitt, Charles Pickard, Quad, Colin Rose, Rodney Shackell, Alan Suttie, Peter Wrigley.